英文详解

汉语新词语词典

A DICTIONARY OF NEW TERMS AND PHRASES OF CONTEMPORARY CHINA

李振杰　凌志韫　编著

新世界出版社
NEW WORLD PRESS

First Edition 2000
Compiled by Li Zhenjie and Vivian Ling
Edited by Li Shujuan and Ren Lingjuan
Cover and Book Design by He Yuting

Copyright by **New World Press**, Beijing, China
All rights reserved. No part of this book may be reproduced in any form or by any means without permission in writing from the publisher.

ISBN 7-80005-566-3

Published by
New World Press
24 Baiwanzhuang Road, Beijing 100037, China

Distributed by
New World Press
24 Baiwanzhuang Road, Beijing 100037, China
Tel: 0086-10-68994118
Fax: 0086-10-68326679
E-mail: nwpcn@public.bta.net.cn

Printed in the People's Republic of China

说　明

一、本词典选收中国自 1949 年至 1999 年半个世纪汉语中出现并有一定影响的词语，重点放在 1978 年改革开放以后这一历史阶段；同时选收少量重新复活或具有新义和新用法的旧词语，以及产生较早但原来仅限于特定的地区、行业、社团和政党使用而今天已进入普通话的词语。全书共选收词语 7400 多条。

二、为帮助读者更好地理解和掌握词语，全部词条都标有拼音和英文解释。多数词语附有词、词组或句子作为例证。全书例证共 2800 多条。

三、所收词语皆出自中国大陆公开出版的书报、杂志，涉及到政治、经济、文化、军事、科技等各个方面；词语类型有词、词组、简称以及惯用语、流行语等。

四、条目领头字不以笔画顺序排列，而是按领头字的汉语拼音字母次序排列，同音节的字按阴平、阳平、上声、去声的顺序排列，领头字相同的按第二个字的拼音字母次序排列，第二个字相同的按第三个字的拼音字母顺序排列，以下类推。

五、条目用汉语拼音方案注音，凡词和联系紧密的结构皆连写，简称词语的各单位之间用横号"－"隔开，如：环保 huan－bao。专名的第一个字母大写。声调不注变调，轻声字注音不标调号。含有外文字母的词语，外文字母不注音。

六、不便对译的词语，先直译再解释词义；对具有文化内涵的词语，介绍该词产生的时代背景和使用范围。

七、本词典的主要对象为学习和使用汉语的外国人以及中国的英语教师和翻译工作者。

编者
2000 年 8 月

Introduction

This dictionary consists of 7400 new terms that have appeared in China between 1949 and 1999. Most of them originated after 1978. Some are previously established terms with new meanings or first came into use only in special regions, trades, sections of society or the party and have become popular in recent years.

To help readers understand and learn them, they are also written in the Chinese phonetic alphabet (pinyin), together with explanations in English. Most entries are provided with phrases, and altogether 2800 examples are given for most.

The entries selected for this dictionary are drawn from a wide range of books, newspapers and magazines published in China. They include terms used in political affairs, economics, cultural and military affairs, science and technology, and other areas. The entries themselves can be words, phrases, abbreviations, colloquial expressions, and popular terms.

All entries are arranged according to the Chinese phonetic alphabet and the four tones of the word. A hyphen is used between words of a short term. Special terms are capitalized. If a term does not have an appropriate English equivalent, a literal translation is given, followed by a detailed explanation. If a term has many connotations, further clarification of its background and sphere of usage are given in English.

This dictionary is compiled mainly for people who are interested in learning new Chinese terms. Readers who find it particularly helpful will be English speaking students of contemporary Chinese, translators and interpreters working in China and abroad, Chinese teachers and students of English, and other inquisitive souls.

Editors
August, 2000

目 录

词目表   1
Stroke Index

词典正文   1
Dictionary

音序索引   583
Alphabetical Index

词 目 表
Stroke Index

一画

一刀切	512
一竿子插到底	512
一大二公	511
一小撮	516
一个中心， 两个基本点	512
一专多能	517
一五	516
一五计划	516
一不怕苦， 二不怕死	511
一手硬，一手软	515
一片红	515
一长制	517
一化三改	513
一分为二	512
一月风暴	517
一风吹	512
一斗二批三改	512
一打三反	511
一平二调	515
一用二批 三改四创	517
一头沉	516
一边倒	511
一对红	512
一次性	511
一批二用	515
一批二看	514
一批二养	514
一批两打	515
一把手	511
一体化	516
一汽	515
一穷二白	515
一拉平	514
一国两制	513
一府两院	512
一线	516
一要吃饭， 二要建设	516
一厘钱精神	514
一点论	512
一哄而上	513
一哄而起	513
一哄而散	513
一看二帮	513
一胎化	516
一胎率	516
一班人	511
一碗水端平	516
一元化领导	517
一阵风	517
一颗红心， 两种准备	513
一贯制	512
一锅煮	513
一言堂	516
一锅端	512
一课三会	514
一野	516
一盘棋	514
一揽子计划	514
一揽子会议	514
一揽子交易	514
一揽子学校	514
一慢二看 三通过	514
乙肝	518
乙型肝炎	518
乙脑	518

二画

二五普法	113
二手	113
二手车	113
二手烟	113
二月逆流	113
二月提纲	114
二地主	112
二百方针	112
二传手	112
二级市场	113
二进宫	113
二把手	112
二汽	113
二线	113
二炮	113
二为	113
二哥大	112
二为方向	113
二锅饭	113
二遍苦	112
二茬罪	112
二部制	112
二野	113
二等公民	112
二等残废	112
二道贩子	112
二道贩子	112
十一大	396
十二大	396

十七年	396	人口素质	352	人造棉	355
十三大	396	人口高峰	352	人造器官	355
十大	396	人口普查	352	人委	355
十六条	396	人卫	355	人际	351
十年内乱	396	人平	354	人类工程学	352
十年浩劫	396	人代会	351	人才库	350
十佳	399	人头粮	354	人才学	350
丁克族	100	人民大会堂	352	人才流动	350
厂风	45	人民内部矛盾	353	人海战术	351
厂史	46	人民公社	352	人流	352
厂礼拜	46	人民代表大会	352	人梯	354
厂休	46	人民民主专政	352	人蛇	354
厂社挂钩	46	人民团体	353	人售	354
厂点	45	人民英雄纪念碑	353	人气	354
厂校挂钩	46	人民性	353	人情方	354
厂矿企业	46	人民战争	353	人情味	354
厂家	45	人民币	352	人潮	350
厂情	45	人民委员会	353	入主	358
厂商	46	人民调解委员会	353	入托	358
七千人大会	329	人民陪审员	353	入团	358
七五	330	人居	351	入关	358
七五计划	330	人机对话	351	入库	358
七·一	329	人行横道	355	入档	358
七·二一大学	329	人产	350	入党	357
儿童片	111	人字呢	355	入党申请书	357
儿童剧	111	人防	351	入党志愿书	357
人工生态	351	人防工程	351	入伍	358
人工合成胰岛素	351	人均	351	入世	358
人工流产	351	人武	355	入场券	357
人工智能	351	人武部	355	入脑	358
人工湖	351	人事处	354	入藏	358
人工器官	351	人事制度	354	八一厂	8
人大	350	人事科	354	八一建军节	8
人大会堂	351	人事调动	354	八一面	8
人大常委会	351	人治	355	八五	7
人口自然增长率	352	人造小平原	355	八五计划	8
人口质量	352	人造卫星	355	八互	7
人口学	352	人造地球卫星	355	八字方针	8
人口经济学	352	人造纤维	355	八字宪法	8
		人造革	355	八级工资制	7
		人造胰岛素	355	八宝山	7

八项经济技术指标	8	三个市场	369	三级体制	370
九一三事件	231	三个好转	368	三讲	370
九二米	231	三个面向	368	三麦	373
九三	231	三个面向，五到现场	368	三来一补	372
九大	231	三个梯队	369	三连冠	372
力争上游	264	三门干部	373	三忠于四无限	377
力克	264	三开人物	371	三乱	372
力作	264	三不主义	364	三转一响	378
力度	264	三不政策	364	三轮汽车	372
力挫	264	三支两军	376	三轮摩托车	372
又红又专	532	三气	374	三明治	373
		三化	370	三和一少	369
三画		三反	366	三定	366
		三反分子	367	三居室	371
三七开	373	三反运动	367	三项建设	376
三八红旗手	362	三风五气	367	三线	375
三八红旗集体	362	三户两场	369	三荒	370
三八作风	362	三无企业	375	三要三不要	376
三八线	362	三五普法	375	三面红旗	373
三八式干部	362	三北地区	363	三点式	366
三三制	374	三史	374	三种人	377
三大平衡	365	三包	363	三秋	374
三大民主	365	三包一奖	363	三保	363
三大件	365	三边工程	363	三保三压	363
三大任务	365	三老四严	372	三保田	363
三大纪律，八项注意	364	三机一扇	370	三总部	378
三大运动	366	三过思想	369	三突出	375
三大作风	366	三西地区	375	三降一灭	376
三大改造	364	三同	375	三结合	371
三大法宝	364	三年困难时期	373	三班制	363
三大实践	366	三优	376	三班倒	363
三大革命运动	364	三优一学	376	三热爱	374
三大革命实践	364	三自一包	378	三夏	375
三大战役	366	三会一课	370	三铁	374
三大差别	364	三名三高	373	三缺户	374
三大球	365	三多一少	366	三废	367
三大领主	365	三论	372	三S	374
三个不变	367	三农	373	三材	364
三个世界	368	三好学生	369	三灶	376
		三级过渡	370	三就方针	371
				三朋四友	373

三番两次	366	工号工程师	146	土地证	448
三兼顾	371	工代会	146	土改	448
三高	367	工仔面	148	土法上马	448
三高政策	367	工纠队	147	土建	449
三座大山	378	工休	148	土政策	449
三资企业	378	工休日	148	土洋并举	449
三料	372	工行	146	土洋结合	449
三家村	370	工交	146	土高炉	448
三宽	372	工交口	146	土暖气	449
三陪	373	工交战线	146	下三烂	481
三通	374	工农干部	147	下马	481
三通四流	374	工农子弟	147	下马观花	481
三基	370	工农子弟兵	147	下乡知识青年	481
三野	376	工农中学	147	下乡镀金论	481
三脱离	375	工农讲师团	147	下中农	481
三联单	372	工农兵学员	147	下毛毛雨	481
三跑田	373	工农速成中学	147	下连当兵	481
三搞一篡	367	工运	148	下岗	480
三靠队	371	工均	147	下拨	480
三靠社	372	工作队	148	下放	480
干休所	137	工作组	149	下馆子	480
干扰素	135	工作面	148	下海	480
干货	135	工作室	149	下调	481
干革命	136	工作烟	149	下游产品	481
干洗	135	工作餐	148	下游企业	481
干校	137	工间操	146	万马奔腾	458
干龄	136	工青妇	148	万金油干部	458
干部下放	136	工转干	148	万元户	458
干部责任制	136	工贸	147	大三线	78
干部服	136	工宣队	148	大干快上	73
干部路线	136	工属	148	大上大下	78
干预生活	135	工矿企业	147	大专	79
干群关系	136	工读生	146	大飞	73
干鲜果品	135	工读学校	146	大比武	72
干警	136	工商联营	148	大手术	78
亏损包干	250	工程语言学	146	大气候	77
工人工程师	148	工薪阶层	148	大公共	73
工分	146	寸头	67	大方向	73
工分挂帅	146	土风舞	448	大户	74
工业工程	148	土老帽	449	大巴	72
工业券	148	土地入股	448	大节	74

大田	78	大轰大嗡	73	上纲上线	383
大包干	72	大是大非	78	上环	383
大包大统	72	大轿车	74	上挂下联	383
大包大揽	72	大而全	73	上钢	383
大立柜	75	大辩论	72	上馆子	383
大礼拜	75	大撒把	78	上、管、改	383
大民主	76	大寨县	79	上浮	382
大老粗	75	大锅饭	73	上浮企业	384
大考	74	大龄青年	75	上调	382
大团结	78	大庆式企业	77	上调	384
大吃大喝	72	大庆红旗	77	上影	384
大杂烩	79	大庆精神	77	小儿科	488
大休	78	大部头	72	小人物	490
大会战	74	大案要案	72	小三线	490
大字报	79	大展	79	小土地出租者	490
大农业	76	大球	78	小土群	490
大农学	76	大排档	76	小小说	491
大红伞	74	大跃进	79	小山头	490
大进大出	74	大款	74	小广播	488
大运会	79	大帽子	76	小天地	490
大批判	76	大集体	74	小五金	491
大批判专栏	77	大腕儿	78	小不拉子	487
大批促大干	76	大道理	73	小太阳	490
大男大女	76	大路	75	小区	489
大串联	73	大路货	75	小水电	490
大陆	75	大路菜	75	小水泥	490
大陆桥	76	大粮食观点	75	小气候	489
大陆妹	75	大赛	78	小化肥	488
大呼隆	74	大操大办	72	小巴士	487
大鸣大放	76	上大课	382	小打小闹	487
大参考	72	上山下乡	383	小节无害论	488
大帮轰	72	上市公司	383	小业主	491
大毒草	73	上市股票	383	小兄弟	491
大秋作物	78	上台阶	384	小百货	487
大洋古	78	上扬	384	小团体主义	491
大起大落	77	上机	383	小字报	491
大破大立	77	上网	384	小字辈	491
大钱	77	上传下达	382	小米加步枪	489
大倒	73	上访	382	小红书	488
大梁	75	上岗	383	小报告	487
大哥大	73	上纲	383	小呼隆	488

小爬虫	489	夕阳产业	479	卫星厂	464
小金库	489	个人电脑	144	卫星云图	464
小炒	487	个人迷信	144	卫星田	464
小春作物	487	个人崇拜	144	卫星国	464
小春耕	487	个体户	144	卫星城	464
小秋收	489	个体农户	144	卫校	464
小皇帝	488	个体劳动	144	卫冕	463
小将	488	个体经济	144	子公司	573
小费	488	个体经营户	144	子弹列车	573
小钱柜	489	个体所有制	144	飞人	125
小鞋	491	个体商贩	144	飞过海	125
小辫子	487	个股	144	飞迁	125
小脚女人	488	个案	144	飞行物	125
小段包工	487	个展	144	飞行药检	125
小而全	487	义卖	521	飞行集会	125
小媳妇	491	义录	521	飞行器	125
小资	491	义诊	522	飞碟	125
小流域	489	义展	522	飞鸽牌	125
小家庭	488	义演	521	马大哈	284
小圈子	490	义赛	521	马王堆汉墓	284
小商品	490	凡是派	177	马太效应	284
小商品经济	490	广开	162	马列	284
小康水平	489	广交会	162	马约	284
小款	489	广告人	162	马钢宪法	284
小集团主义	488	广告躲避	162	马屁精	284
小集体	488	广种薄收	162	马路新闻	284
小道消息	487	广而告之	162	马蜂窝	284
小道理	487	广播讲话	161	马鞍形	284
小意思	491	广播体操	161	女双	311
口	247	门店	289	女团	311
口子	247	门将	289	女足	311
口头革命派	247	门前三包	289	女单	310
山头主义	380	门镜	289	女将	310
山地车	380	门球	289	女垒	311
山姆大叔	380	尸检	396	女能人	311
山海经	380	卫士	464	女排	311
千里马	332	卫生纸	464	女童	311
千年虫	332	卫生院	464	女强人	311
千禧婴儿	332	卫生所	463	女篮	310
夕阳工业	479	卫生员	464	乡土文学	485
夕阳工程	479	卫星	464	乡土教材	485

三画 – 四画 词目表

乡企	484	天安门事件	435	艺校	520
乡社合一	485	天南海北	436	艺术片	520
乡规民约	484	天然气	436	艺德	520
乡镇企业	485	天然公园	436	扎根农村	542
		天才论	435	扎根串连	542
四画		天量	436	扎堆	542
【一】		无产阶级		扎啤	542
		国际主义	468	五七干校	474
王子	458	无底洞	469	五七指示	474
木卡姆	298	无限上纲	469	五七战士	474
丰产田	128	无核	469	五七道路	474
开小灶	239	无核区	469	五小	475
开口子	238	无核化	469	五小工业	475
开门办学	238	无党派人士	469	五小竞赛	475
开门红	239	无笔画	468	五个一	471
开门整风	239	无序	469	五反运动	471
开门整党	239	无绳电话	469	五分制	471
开司米	239	无烟工业	469	五风	471
开发区	237	井喷	230	五四三	474
开发性生产	237	井灌	230	五年计划	473
开发性承包	237	厄尔尼诺现象	111	五多	471
开考	238	专区	569	五讲四美三热爱	473
开机	238	专业户	569	五好文明家庭	472
开后门	238	专业村	569	五好企业	472
开关	238	专业承包	569	五好战士	472
开村	237	专列	569	五好竞赛	472
开拓型	239	专访	568	五好家庭	471
开拍	239	专柜	568	五好职工	472
开取	239	专政工具	569	五定	470
开顶风船	237	专政对象	569	五定一奖	470
开放大学	237	专政机关	570	五毒	470
开放政策	237	专署	569	五荒	473
开卷考试	238	专属渔区	569	五荒一小	473
开院	239	专家至上	568	五星红旗	475
开架	238	专家路线	568	五星级	475
开镜	238	专案组	568	五种人	476
开具	238	专控	568	五保	470
开绿灯	238	专控商品	568	五保户	470
云图	537	专著	570	五匠	473
天天读	436	专营	569	五类分子	473
天价	436	艺坛	520	五一六	475

五一六兵团	475	支左	552	少年庭	385
五一六通知	475	支边	551	少年宫	385
五爱	470	支农	551	少先队	385
五通一平	474	支持产业	551	少慢差费	384
五湖四海	472	支前	552	少而精	384
不力	34	支派	552	少管	384
不正之风	34	支委	552	少管所	385
不可比产品	34	支柱产业	552	中子弹	563
不发达国家	34	支部书记	551	中专	562
不抓辫子	34	支教	551	中长纤维	560
不明飞行物	34	巨无霸	232	中心小学	562
不承认主义	33	车位	50	中巴	560
不结盟运动	34	车况	50	中办	560
不起眼	34	车间主任	50	中央文革	562
不戴帽子	34	车组	50	中央政治局	562
历史反革命	262	车匪路霸	50	中生代	561
友协	531	车提	50	中考	561
友谊第一， 比赛第二	531	区位	342	中西医结合	562
尤里卡	530	区间	341	中成药	560
太平官	427	区间车	341	中行	561
太阳房	427	区委	341	中师	561
太阳炉	427	区段	341	中产阶级	560
太阳灶	428	区域自治	342	中农	561
太阳镜	427	区域经济	342	中导	560
太阳能	427	区域旅行	342	中导条约	560
太阳能电池	428	匹料	321	中观	560
太阳能热水器	428	互市	185	中纪委	561
太阳帽	427	互联网	185	中技术	561
太空人	427	互访	185	中间人物	561
太空垃圾	427	互助组	185	中间地带	561
太空服	427	互补	185	中间产品	561
太空城	427	互教互学	185	中层干部	560
太空食品	427	比例失调	25	中直	562
太空笔	427	比学赶帮超	25	中转	563
太空病	427	比萨	25	中国通	560
太空站	427	比较文学	25	中试	561
太空棉	427	比基尼	25	中组部	563
支工	551			中指委	562
支书	552	【丨】		中科院	561
支节产业	551	少工委	384	中宣部	562
		少代会	384	中档	560

四画　词目表

中顾委	560	水分	410	牛郎织女	305
中委	562	水文站	411	牛鬼蛇神	305
中梗阻	560	水电	410	牛棚	305
中航	561	水电费	410	片儿警	322
中资	563	水针疗法	411	片约	322
中联部	561	水利化	410	片面观点	322
中程导弹	560	水疗	411	片面性	322
中游思想	562	水货	410	片商	322
日托	356	水泥船	411	气区	332
日光灯	356	水荒	410	气功疗法	331
日光浴	356	水浇地	410	气田	332
日杂	356	水源林	411	气垫船	331
日均	356	水俣病	411	气粗	331
见马克思	209	水景	410	气管炎	331
见习工程师	209	水暖工	411	长龙	44
见缝插针	208	水警	410	长考	44
内斗	301			长余产品	45
内功	301	**【丿】**		长征干部	45
内伤	303	手工业合作社	403	长治久安	45
内向型	303	手扶拖拉机	403	长官意志	544
内企	303	手机	403	长话	44
内招	303	手读	403	长线	45
内画	302	手提电脑	403	长线产品	45
内定	301	手球	403	长项	45
内参	301	毛片	287	长途	45
内查外调	301	毛选	287	长效	45
内贸	303	毛孩	287	长假	44
内退	303	毛泽东思想	287	长期共存	45
内耗	302	毛泽东思想体系	287	化工	187
内核	302	毛泽东思想		化公为私	187
内紧外松	302	宣传队	287	化纤	187
内留私分	302	毛哔叽	287	化疗	187
内资	303	毛著	287	化肥	187
内控	302	升级过渡	394	化解	187
内联	302	升级换代	394	反左防右	120
内联外挤	302	升温	394	反右	119
内联单位	302	升溢	394	反右防左	119
内销	303	牛气	305	反右派斗争	119
内需	303	牛仔裤	305	反右倾	120
内装修	303	牛市	305	反对党	118
水门事件	411	牛鼻子	305	反动学术权威	118

反导弹体系	118	分散主义	127	公照	152
反攻倒算	118	分裂主义	126	月月红	537
反批评	119	分税制	127	月均	537
反社会主义分子	119	分数线	127	风景线	129
反贪	119	分数挂帅	127	风头主义	129
反革命分子	118	分餐	126	风纪扣	129
反革命两面派	118	父子党	133	风派	129
反面人物	119	公车	150	风派人物	129
反面教材	119	公文旅行	151	风衣	129
反面教员	119	公方	150	风味小吃	129
反冒进	118	公办	149	风雨衣	129
反思	119	公平尺	150	风能	129
反修	119	公平秤	150	风险投资	129
反差	117	公用月票	152	风幕	129
反党	117	公务员	151	欠产	333
反党集团	117	公共食堂	150	欠佳	333
反特	119	公共积累	150	欠税	333
反馈	118	公共课	150	乌拉圭回合	468
反殖	120	公休	151	乌金	468
反馈	118	公决	150	乌兰牧骑	468
反帝	118	公交	150	仓容	39
反骄破满	118	公关	150	仓储式	39
反弹	119	公安部门	149		
反腐蚀	118	公安部队	149	【、】	
反潮流	117	公私合营	151	文山	466
反霸	117	公社	150	文山会海	466
从众行为	66	公社化	151	文艺会演	467
从群众中来，		公社史	151	文艺轻骑队	467
到群众中去	65	公养	151	文艺调演	466
分子生物学	128	公派	150	文艺黑线专政论	467
分片包干	127	公费医疗	150	文友	467
分权	127	公积金	150	文化大革命	465
分成	126	公厕	150	文化专制主义	466
分导	126	公益广告	151	文化户	465
分食	127	公厕广告	150	文化市场	466
分配式	126	公式化	151	文化产品	465
分贝	126	公益劳动	152	文化垃圾	466
分秒必争	126	公益金	151	文化宫	465
分灶吃饭	127	公烟	151	文化馆	465
分类排队	126	公检法	150	文化衫	466
分流	126	公勤人员	150	文化站	466

四画 词目表

文化圈	466	斗批会	104	引种	524
文化街	466	斗批改	103	引黄灌区	524
文斗	465	斗私批修	104	引智	524
文电	465	斗妍	104	办学	14
文代会	465	斗艳	104	办复	13
文攻武卫	465	计划生育	201	办结	14
文坛	466	计划外用工	201	办案	13
文体活动	466	计划单列	201	丑星	57
文改	465	计划调拨	201	丑闻	57
文明公约	466	计时工资	201	孔塔多拉集团	247
文明村	466	计委	201	双万户	409
文革	465	计经委	201	双千田	409
文保	465	计算机	201	双反运动	408
文秘	466	计算机病毒	201	双巴	407
文牍主义	465	计算器	201	双文明	409
文联	466	认同	356	双卡	409
文摘	467	认指	356	双包	407
六个优先	277	认养	356	双包户	407
六五计划	279	认捐	356	双百方针	407
六好企业	278	户均	185	双轨制	408
六好职工	278	户造户管	185	双先	409
六条政治标准	278	户营	185	双休日	409
六害	277	户售	185	双向	409
冗余	357	心头肉	495	双扶	408
方队	121	心有余悸	495	双扶户	408
方城	121	心战	495	双抢	409
方便面	121	心态	495	双声道	409
方便食品	121			双证	410
忆苦	521	【一】		双补	408
忆苦会	521			双拥运动	410
忆苦饭	521	邓选	88	双佳活动	408
忆苦思甜	521	书市	406	双学位	410
忆苦教育	521	书荒	406	双学士	410
火	193	书展	406	双面卡	409
火电	193	巴金森氏病	8	双科学	409
火线入党	193	巴统	9	双重国籍	408
火药味	193	巴士	9	双重领导	408
火箭干部	193	巴解	8	双保	407
火炬计划	193	引火烧身	524	双突	409
斗争会	104	引发	524	双突干部	409
斗争哲学	104	引产	524	双语	410
		引种	524		

词目表 四画－五画

双紧	408	示范村	398	扒窃	313
双肩挑	408	玉雕	534	石化	396
双肩背	408	未来学	463	石煤	396
双铧犁	408	未委会	463	古为今用	154
双职工	410	末班车	297	功夫片	149
双基	408	刊大	239	功能结构主	
双赢	410	刊授大学	239	义语言学	149
劝退	345	击剑衫	195	去伪存真	342
队友	107	正儿八百	547	去粗取精	342
【ㄣ】		正研	548	龙头	279
		正面人物	548	司乘人员	415
以人划线	520	正面经验	548	司售人员	415
以干带学	519	正面教育	547	甘居中游	136
以工代干	519	正餐	547	本本主义	24
以工补农	519	世行	399	本位主义	25
以太网	520	世界村	399	可口可乐	244
以丰补歉	518	世界环境日	399	可比产品	243
以古非今	519	世界贸易组织	399	可比经济指标	243
以权谋私	520	打斗	70	可比能耗	244
以论代史	519	打击面	70	可乐	244
以农代干	519	打卡	70	可行性研究	244
以阶级斗争为纲	519	打头炮	71	可的松	244
以进养出	519	打老虎	70	可持续发展	244
以点带面	518	打压	71	可视电传	244
以钢为纲	519	打死老虎	71	可视电话	244
以派划线	520	打私	71	可读性	244
以党代政	518	打非	70	可控硅	244
以虚带实	520	打的	70	艾滋病	1
以畜促农	520	打点滴	70	节支	218
以我为中心	520	打前站	71	节水	218
以副养农	518	打派仗	71	节电	218
以偏概全	520	打砸抢	71	节育	218
以假乱真	519	打砸抢分子	71	节育环	218
以税代利	520	打屁股	71	节资	218
以粮为纲	519	打预防针	71	节流	218
		打假	70	节能	218
五画		打假办	70	节能灶	218
【一】		打着红旗反红旗	72	节假日	218
		打棍子	70	节煤	218
示范户	398	打游击	71	右派分子	531
示范田	398	打翻身仗	70	布设	35

五画　词目表

布点	34	归侨	162	电话传真	96
布展	35	归档	162	电话会议	96
布票	35	目无组织	298	电话银行	96
布控	34	目标管理	298	电话磁卡	96
平均主义	324	甲肝	205	电视大学	97
平板三轮	324	甲型肝炎	205	电视片	97
平战结合	325	申办	389	电视文化	97
平叛	324	申领	389	电视机	97
平抑	324	史无前例	398	电视柜	97
平绒	324	央行	507	电视传输	97
平调	324	电大	95	电视病	96
平销	324	电子计算机	98	电视剧	97
平暴	324	电子计算器	98	电视塔	97
平衡生产	324	电子台灯	98	电视墙	97
灭虫宁	292	电子地图	97	电热褥	96
灭资兴无	292	电子自由		电热炉	96
东风压倒西风	103	职业经济	98	电衡门	97
东西对话	103	电子报刊	97	电褥子	96
东盟	103	电子邮件	98	电脑	96
		电子邮局	98	电脑犯罪	96
【｜】		电子玩具	98	电脑病毒	96
北约	23	电子表	97	电瓶车	96
北京话	23	电子货币	97	电烤箱	96
卡巴迪	237	电子货币工程	98	电教	96
卡拉OK	237	电子显微镜	98	电教片	96
卡介苗	237	电子信箱	98	电猫	96
占用	544	电子音乐	98	电影周	97
占线	544	电子秤	97	电灌	96
业大	510	电子琴	98	电霸	95
业务专长	510	电子银行	98	田协	437
业务尖子	510	电子游戏	98	田坛	437
业务挂帅	510	电子商务	98	田联	437
业务班子	510	电子数据		号型	170
业务第一	510	交换业务	98	兄弟民族	499
业余华侨	510	电老虎	96	兄弟单位	498
业余学校	510	电光源	96	兄弟院校	499
业余爱好	510	电传	95	兄弟党	498
业余教育	510	电针疗法	97	另行	276
旧社会	231	电针麻醉	97	另起炉灶	276
旧框框	231	电饭煲	96	叫花子主义	214
归口	162	电饭锅	95	叫卖语言	214

词目表 五画

词目	页码	词目	页码	词目	页码
叫响	214	四新	421	生搬硬套	391
四二一综合症	417			失足青年	396
四人帮	419	【丿】		失信于民	396
四大	416	生化	392	失调	395
四大件	417	生产大队	391	失控	395
四大自由	417	生产队	391	失落感	395
四小龙	421	生产建设兵团	391	失衡	395
四个一样	418	生产线	392	斥资	55
四个现代化	418	生产经营型	392	瓜菜代	155
四个伟大	417	生产要素	392	冬奥会	103
四个第一	417	生产型	392	用材林	529
四个落实	417	生产教养院	391	甩手掌柜	407
四个窗口	417	生产管理委员会	391	甩站	407
四马分肥	419	生防	392	代购	80
四无限	420	生拉硬扯	393	代耕	80
四专一包	422	生物工程	394	代沟	80
四不清干部	416	生物节律	394	代际	80
四化	418	生物电	394	代码	80
四旧	419	生物防治	394	代培	80
四务缠身	420	生物物理学	394	代培生	81
四边地	416	生物钟	394	代职	81
四有	421	生物能	394	代营食堂	81
四有三讲两不怕	422	生物圈	394	代销	81
四当年工程	417	生命节律	393	仔猪	539
四自一联	422	生育龄	394	白马王子	10
四自精神	422	生活关	393	白专	11
四好	418	生活作风	393	白专道路	11
四好家长	418	生活补助	392	白手起家	10
四环素	418	生活福利	392	白色污染	10
四项政治保证	421	生态	393	白色农业	10
四项基本原则	421	生源	394	白色革命	10
四荒	419	生态工程	393	白条	10
四旁	419	生态平衡	393	白纸	11
四害	418	生态农业	393	白亮污染	10
四类分子	419	生态系统	393	白度	10
四属户	420	生态学	394	白洞	9
四·五运动	420	生态经济学	393	白衣战士	11
四通一平	420	生态屏障	393	白衣教练	11
四野	421	生态效益	393	白骨精	10
四清	419	生态爆炸	393	白领工人	10
四提倡、四反对	420	生猛	393	白领阶层	10

五画 词目表

白领犯罪	10	外调	455	主题词	565
白牌	10	外商	456	市风	400
白旗	10	务实	476	市花	400
句型	233	务虚	477	市政工程	400
句型教学	233	包干到户	16	市府	400
处理品	60	包干到劳	16	市况	400
外专局	457	包干到组	16	市委	400
外片	456	包车	15	市树	400
外化	455	包户小组	17	市场经济	399
外办	455	包户扶贫	17	市场信息	400
外汇存底	456	包户制	17	市盈率	400
外汇券	456	包机	17	市场调节	399
外引	457	包交提留	17	市场预测	400
外引内联	457	包产田	15	市容	400
外因论	457	包产到户	15	市管人员	400
外伤	456	包产到组	15	市徽	400
外向型	457	包护小组	16	立交工程	263
外企	456	包购包销	16	立交桥	263
外运	457	包房	16	立足点	264
外事	457	包换	17	立体电影	263
外事口	457	包乘	15	立体农业	263
外事组	457	包装	17	立体声	263
外劳	456	印发	524	立体种植	264
外卖	456	印件	524	立党为公	263
外轮	456	印制	525	立党为私	263
外购	455	印售	525	立等可取	263
外货	456	乐坛	537	写字楼	492
外空	456	乐迷	537	穴头	502
外经	456			永久牌	528
外挤内联	456	【、】		闪光灯	380
外贸	456			帅气	407
外战	457	主刀	565	半工半读	13
外星人	457	主干家庭	565	半无产阶级	13
外派	456	主页	566	半边天	13
外借	456	主观能动性	565	半机械化	13
外需	457	主体工程	565	半导体收音机	13
外籍华人	456	主体错误	565	半劳动力	13
外航	455	主治医生	566	半官方	13
外资	457	主线	566	半脱产	13
外烟	457	主战场	566	半截子革命	13
外流单干	456	主流	565	头头儿	446
		主教练	565		

词目表　五画

词目	页码	词目	页码	词目	页码
头头脑脑	446	民主生活	295	边贸	27
头针疗法	446	民主生活会	295	边缘科学	27
头道贩子	446	民主改革	295	边际效益	27
汇价	191	民主党派	294	边销茶	27
汇报思想	191	民主集中制	295	圣火	395
汇款单	191	民主管理	295	对口	107
汇路	191	民企	294	对口支援	108
汇演	191	民进	293	对口词	107
汉字信息处理	169	民运会	294	对不上号	107
汉语拼音方案	169	民兵工作三落实	293	对立面	108
汉堡包	169	民兵师	293	对立统一规律	108
宁左勿右	305	民建	293	对台九条	108
让步政策	348	民政	294	对讲机	107
让利	348	民革	293	对抗性矛盾	107
让贤	348	民品	293	对话	107
让渡	348	民庭	294	对调	107
议价	522	民倒	293	对接	107
议价油	522	民柬	293	对着干	109
议价粮	522	民盟	293	对象	108
议会迷	522	民委	294	矛头向上	287
议会道路	522	民调	294	矛盾上交	287
议购	522	民营	294	皮包公司	321
议政	522	民族大家庭	296	皮包商	321
议案	522	民族区域自治	296	皮试	321
议销	522	民族学院	296	皮草	321
记工本	201	民族隔阂	296		
记工员	201	民意测验	294	【丶】	
记协	201	民警	293	母老虎	298
记实小说	201	加工订货	204	母夜叉	298
礼宾司	262	加班	204	出工	58
必然王国	26	加班加点	204	出土文物	59
		加班费	204	出口买方信贷	58
【一】		加速器	205	出口转内销	58
尼龙	304	加盟	204	出山	59
民工潮	293	加密	205	出气筒	59
民办	292	加塞儿	205	出头鸟	59
民办教师	292	加温	205	出台	59
民用三表	294	加餐	204	出血	59
民代国储	293	边卡	27	出纳员	59
民主人士	295	边民	27	出炉	58
民主办社	294	边茶	27	出线	59

出乘	58	邦联	14	考务	242
出槽	58	刑警	497	考评	242
出栏	58	动手术	103	考研	242
出资	60	动迁	103	考点	241
出赛	59	动迁户	103	考级	241
奶山羊	299	动态	103	考纪	241
奴隶主义	310	老八路	258	考照	242
奴才哲学	310	老三届	259	地下人行道	92
发达国家	115	老三篇	259	地下工厂	92
发运	115	老黄牛	259	地下工作	92
发乳	115	老干部	258	地下刊物	92
发屋	115	老大难	258	地下包工队	92
发债	115	老子党	260	地下组织	92
发型	116	老五篇	260	地下活动	92
发廊	115	老区	259	地下党	92
发烧友	115	老少边穷（地区）	259	地下党员	92
发案	115	老中青	260	地区霸权主义	91
发展中国家	115	老中青三结合	260	地方民族主义	90
发寄	115	老化	259	地方国营企业	90
台件	426	老外	260	地主	92
台阶	427	老帅	260	地主婆	92
台独	426	老年型国家	259	地对地导弹	90
台胞	426	老字辈	260	地对空导弹	90
台笔	426	老红军	258	地尽其力	91
台属	427	老革命	258	地板革	90
台盟	427	老冒	259	地空导弹	91
台扇	427	老保	258	地热	91
台资	427	老框框	259	地热田	91
台商	427	老虎	258	地铁	91
台联	427	老龄	259	地矿	91
台港	426	老龄化	259	地委	91
丝绸之路	415	老鼠会	259	地膜	91
幼师	532	老龄问题	259	地宫	90
幼教	532	老虎屁股	258	地效飞机	92
纠风	231	老弱病残	259	地税	91
纠风办	231	老黄牛	259	地缘	92
		考本	241	地缘外交	92
六画		考博	241	地籍	91
【一】		考区	242	地掷球	92
		考风	241	地膜覆盖	91
吉祥物	198	考量	241	地球日	91

词目表 六画

地球村	91	亚太	505	机播	196
地滚球	91	亚文化	505	机器人	197
地漏	91	亚行	505	机器手	197
地震棚	92	亚运会	505	机灌	197
地霸	90	亚运村	505	过电影	165
场馆	46	亚非拉	504	过失犯罪	166
托儿	452	亚银	505	过头粮	166
托门子	453	耳针疗法	111	过关思想	165
托幼	453	共同纲领	153	过热	166
托老所	453	共产风	152	过伐	165
托收	453	共产主义		过"长江"	165
托卖	453	劳动大学	152	过渡时期总路线	165
托派	453	共产主义青年团	152	过得硬	165
托裱	452	共产主义道德	152	过街天桥	166
托哥	453	共运	153	过滤嘴	166
托姐	453	共识	153	再教育	539
托福	452	共青团	153	协议离婚	492
扣子	248	共建	152	协作区	492
扣球	247	权位	343	西化	478
扣帽子	247	权股	343	西风	478
扩大内需	250	权欲	343	西北风	478
扩大企业自主权	250	机工	197	西兰花	478
扩印	251	机井	197	西欧共同体	478
扩权	251	机电	196	西单墙	478
扩招	251	机务	197	西部大开发	478
扩股	251	机务人员	197	西装鸡	478
扩建	251	机动车	197	压力锅	504
扩种	251	机顶盒	196	压车	504
扩音机	251	机帆船	197	压级	504
扩容	251	机关党委	197	压级压价	504
扩展	251	机库	197	压库	504
扫尾工作	379	机制	197	压货	504
扫盲运动	379	机组	197	压轴戏	504
扫毒	379	机修	197	压船	504
扫描	379	机耕	197	压逼	504
扫黄	379	机载卫星电话	197	压港	504
执导	555	机恤	197	压缩空气	504
执政党	556	机具	197	百分点	11
执委会	555	机械人	197	百色齐全	11
执教	555	机械臂	197	百花齐放，	
扬长避短	507	机插	196	百家争鸣	11

百褶裙	11	死教材	416	光脑	161
灰色收入	189	死硬派	416	光缆	161
灰色经济	189	死缓	416	光通讯	161
灰色消费	189	成人节	52	光盘	161
灰领工人	189	成人教育	52	光彩事业	161
在业	539	成龙配套	52	劣生	274
在岗	539	成名成家	52	劣质	274
在建	539	成药	52	劣质低价	274
在野党	539	成品粮	52	劣品	274
在编人员	539	成活率	51	当权派	83
有成分论	531	成型玻璃	52	当家	83
有戏	531	夹生饭	202	同一性	442
有限战争	531	夹克	205	同工同酬	442
有线电视	531	夹缝	202	同比	442
有破有立	531	轨道站	162	同声传译	442
有序	531	划成分	186	同步	442
有偿服务	531	划拨	186	同步辐射	442
有偿新闻	531	划线	186	同龄	442
存车处	67	划线排队	186	团支部	450
存休	67	划圈	186	团团转	450
存活	67	匡算	250	团伙	449
存档	67			团组织	450
存栏数	67	【丨】		团总支	450
存储	67			团结-批评-	
夸克	248	师专	395	团结	450
夸海口	248	师资	395	团场	449
夺杯	110	师德	395	团员	450
夺标	110	尘封	51	团委会	450
夺冠	110	尘埃落定	50	团票	450
夺魁	110	尖刀班	206	回乡知识青年	190
达标	69	尖子	207	回乡知青	190
列支	274	尖子班	207	回忆录	190
列车长	274	尖端	206	回归	190
列车员	274	尖端科学	206	回收	190
死不改悔	415	光电技术	161	回顾展	190
死分活评	416	光电话	161	回炉	190
死老虎	416	光导纤维	161	回潮	190
死光武器	416	光纤	161		
死面	416	光杆儿司令	161	因特网	523
死亡婚姻	416	光荣院	161	早市	540
死教条	416	光荣榜	161	早班车	540
		光亮派	161	肉牛	357

肉羊	357	网络文学	459	传真	62
肉鸡	357	网络电话	459	传阅	62
肉兔	357	网络电视	459	传家宝	62
肉鸭	351	网络银行	459	传销	62
肉票	357	网民	459	传媒	62
肉鸽	357	网校	459	传感器	62
曲协	342	网页	459	传播媒介	61
曲坛	342	网友	459	休市	499
曲库	342	网站	459	休养所	499
吊运	99	网址	459	休班	499
吁请	534	网路	459	优才生	529
吐故纳新	449			优化	529
吐疏纳亲	449	【丿】		优化经济结构	529
吃大户	53			优生	529
吃大锅饭	53	竹雕	565	优先股	529
吃小灶	54	竹筒倒豆子	565	优先认股权	529
吃老本	54	竹幕	565	优价	529
吃劳保	54	年历工资	304	优抚	529
吃闲饭	54	年报	304	优质优价	530
吃皇粮	54	年均	304	优质名牌	530
吃透	54	年轻化	304	优质高产	530
吃透两头	54	年龄结构	304	优育	530
吃准	55	年资	304	优胜劣汰	529
吃请	54	年检	304	优胜红旗	529
吃偏饭	54	迁建	332	优选	529
吃偏食	54	迁装	332	优选法	530
吃喝风	53	先导市场	482	优养	530
吸存	478	先进工作者	482	优教	529
吸尘器	478	先进集体	482	优等生	529
吸纳	478	先锋派	482	件次	209
吸顶灯	478	乒坛	324	伪劣	463
吸毒	478	乒联	324	伪证	463
帆板运动	116	伟哥	463	伪冒	463
网上大学	459	传达报告	61	任务观点	355
网大	458	传声筒	62	任教	355
网主	459	传译	62	任聘	355
网虫	458	传呼电话	62	伤残	381
网吧	458	传经送宝	62	伤残人	381
网坛	459	传帮带	61	伤痕文学	381
网点	458	传统观念	62	价改	205
网络	459	传统剧目	62	价位	205
		传统教育	62		

价差	205	血防	502	全球定位系统	344
价格补贴	205	血亲	502	全勤	344
价值工程	205	血统论	502	全塑汽车	344
份儿饭	128	血脂	502	会风	190
华人	185	向阳院	485	会考	191
华文	185	向前看	485	会来事	191
华约	186	向钱看	485	会荒	191
华语	122	后现代	184	会战	191
仿生学	122	后现代主义	184	会倒	190
仿冒	122	后市	184	会堂	191
仿真	122	后门	184	会诊	191
自办	573	后处理	183	会海	191
自发户	574	后发性	183	会道门	190
自动柜员机	574	后进	183	会签	191
自负盈亏	574	后进队	184	会演	191
自考	574	后备干部	183	合二为一	174
自报公议	573	行政手段	498	合议庭	174
自护	574	行政公署	497	合成师	173
自来红	574	行政拘留	498	合成军	173
自助	575	行为科学	497	合成纤维	174
自助银行	576	全天候飞机	344	合成革	173
自助邮局	576	全景电影	344	合同工	174
自助餐	575	全方位	343	合同医院	174
自画衫	574	全方位外交	343	合同制	174
自学考试	575	全民文艺	344	合同制工人	174
自选市场	575	全民皆兵	344	物质财富	174
自费生	574	全托	344	合伙企业	174
自律	575	全优	345	合作化	175
自由王国	575	全优工号竞赛	345	合作医疗	175
自由化	575	全优工程	345	合作社	175
自由市场	575	全会	343	合作商店	175
自我设计	575	全运会	345	合拍	174
自然保护区	575	全劳力	344	合法斗争	174
自留山	575	全国一盘棋	343	合资	174
自留地	574	全国粮票	343	合资企业	175
自留畜	574	全面开花	344	合资经营	174
自娱	575	全面专政	344	合理化建议	174
自控	574	全息	344	企划	330
自营	575	全员	345	企业下放	331
自销	575	全脂奶粉	345	企业文化	331
自筹	574	全能运动	344	企业电视	331

词条	页码	词条	页码	词条	页码
企业法	331	危途	461	交际舞	212
企业承包		色拉子	379	交流学者	212
经营责任制	330	色狼	379	交售	212
企业素质	331	色酒	380	交警	212
企业党组织	331	争分夺秒	547	产业结构升级	44
企业家	331			产业结构重组	44
企业集团	331	【、】		产成品	43
杀手	380			产品结构	43
杀关管	379	充电	55	产前产后	44
创三好	64	次文化	65	产羔率	43
创业精神	64	冲刺	55	产假	43
创汇	64	冲剂	55	产销	44
创记录	64	冲浪运动	55	产销平衡	44
创优	64	冲销帐目	55	忙音	286
创导者	64	冰坛	30	闭卷	26
创收	64	冰场	30	闭路电视	26
创利	64	冰毒	30	问事处	468
创编	64	冰崩	30	问卷	468
创新	64	冰雕	30	问鼎	467
创意	64	冰灯	30	问题小说	468
名优	296	冰袋	30	闯关	63
名声大振	296	冰砖	30	闯红灯	63
名特	296	冰舞	30	闯劲	63
名模	296	决心书	233	闯将	63
多极性	110	决策机构	233	关门办学	157
多发	109	壮行	571	关门主义	157
多发病	109	庄家	571	关门读书	157
多吃多占	109	亦工亦农	520	关门整风	157
多劳多得	110	齐飞	330	关系方	158
多极化	109	交工	212	关系户	158
多快好省	110	交心	212	关系网	158
多国公司	109	交电	212	关系学	158
多面手	110	交代历史	212	关爱	157
多种经营	110	交代问题	212	关停并转	157
多速	110	交白卷	211	羊毛衫	507
多媒体	110	交学费	212	羊绒衫	507
多管齐下	109	交待政策	212	并存	30
负面	133	交班	211	并轨	30
危房	461	交叉科学	211	并网	30
危重	461	交谊舞	212	并网发电	30

兴无灭资	497	讲桌	211	农区	308
守摊子	404	讲排场	210	农中	310
宇宙人	533	论资排辈	282	农办	306
宇宙飞船	533	访贫问苦	122	农业八字宪法	308
宇宙服	533	访视	122	农业工程	308
宇宙线	533	访谈	122	农业区划	309
宇宙语	533	设籍	389	农业中学	309
宇宙站	533	军工	234	农业队	308
宇航服	533	军民一致	235	农业生产合作社	309
宇航员	533	军民共建	235	农业生产责任制	309
安办	3	军地两用人才	234	农业老四化	308
安乐死	4	军列	235	农业合作化	308
安乐窝	4	军运	236	农业社	309
安民告示	4	军兵种	234	农业信用合作社	309
安全网	5	军体	236	农业集体化	308
安全月	5	军事民主	236	农电	306
安全电压	4	军转	236	农代会	306
安全生产	5	军政训练	236	农民工	307
安全带	4	军威	236	农民意识	308
安全岛	4	军品	235	农机	306
安全部	4	军贸	235	农机户	306
安全套	5	军宣队	236	农行	306
安全哨	5	军垦农场	235	农运会	310
安全帽	5	军委	236	农技	306
安老院	4	军企	235	农林牧副渔	307
安钉子	3	军嫂	235	农转非	310
安定团结	3	军令状	235	农轻重	308
安居工程	4	军容	235	农贷	306
安居房	4	军控	235	农科户	306
安家立业	4	军售	236	农科示范户	307
安家费	4	军婚	235	农科所	307
安家落户	4	军博	234	农科院	307
安理会	4	军管	234	农贸	307
安营扎寨	5	军管会	235	农贸市场	307
安检	4	农工	306	农垦	307
安检站	4	农工党	306	农膜	308
字根	576	农工商联合企业	306	农委	308
讲用	211	农大	306	农资	310
讲用会	211	农口	307	农家肥	306
讲师团	210	农门	307	农展馆	310
讲评	210	农艺师	310	农副产品	306

米袋子	290	防风林	122	收效	403
		防护林带	122	收案	402
【一】		防沙林	122	收理	402
尽如人意	222	防盲	122	收盘	402
导入	87	防治	122	阴暗面	523
导向	87	防特	122	阴谋文艺	523
导买	87	防雹	121	妇代会	134
导医	87	防寒服	122	妇幼保健站	134
导购	87	弘扬	179	妇产医院	134
导购员	87	那达慕	299	妇男	134
导游	87	羽坛	534	妇联	134
导播	87	羽绒	534	好人主义	170
寻呼	502	羽绒服	534	好八连	170
寻呼台	502	羽球	534	好处费	170
寻呼机	502	观瞻服	159	妈妈桑	284
寻根	502	观摩演出	159	红小兵	182
阳光产业	508	观照	159	红小鬼	182
阳光农业	508	观潮派	159	红卫兵	182
阳刚	508	戏说	480	红专	182
阳谋	508	欢宴	187	红专大学	182
阶级分析	216	买方市场	285	红五月	182
阶级分化	216	买单	285	红五类	182
阶级斗争熄灭论	216	买家	285	红心	182
阶级队伍	216			红包	179
阶级兄弟	217	【丨】		红头文件	182
阶级立场	217	收托	402	红会	180
阶级矛盾	217	收存	402	红色政权	181
阶级成分	215	收杆	402	红色种子	181
阶级异己分子	217	收尾工作	403	红色保险箱	181
阶级观点	216	收拍	402	红条子	182
阶级报复	215	收贮	403	红宝书	179
阶级苦	216	收治	403	红线	182
阶级性	217	收审	402	红茶菌	179
阶级敌人	216	收视	402	红热线	181
阶级觉悟	216	收录机	402	红透专深	182
阶级烙印	216	收看	402	红灯	180
阶级阵线	217	收养人	403	红灯区	180
阶级调和论	217	收养子女	403	红道	180
阶级教育	216	收活	402	红帽子	180
阶级路线	217	收紧	402	红哨兵	181
防暴	122	收枰	402	红海洋	180

红娘	180	形象思维	497	扶贫	130
红眼病	182	进尺	222	扶贫小组	130
红领人	180	进宫	222	扶标	130
红领章	180	进贡	222	扶志	130
红领巾	180	进销	222	技工	200
红牌	181	违价	461	技改	200
红筹股	180	违约	461	技校	201
红管家	180	违纪	461	技术入股	201
红旗	181	违规	461	技术市场	201
红旗手	181	违例	461	技术服务专业户	200
红旗单位	181	违宪	461	技术经济学	200
红旗竞赛	181	违章	461	技术职称	201
红潮	179	违控	461	技术第一	200
纤维板	482	运力	537	技术密集型	200
约见	536	运动员	537	抠机	247
约请	536	运价	537	扰民	348
约谈	536	运作	538	扮演	13
纪委	202	运载火箭	538	抛荒	316
纪念邮票	202	运能	537	批文	321
纪念封	202	运营	538	批斗	320
纪念币	202	运量	537	批件	320
纪检	202	运销	537	批次	320
巡回医疗	503	运筹学	537	批条	320
巡回学校	503	远导	536	批判会	320
巡回演出	503	远南	536	批判现实主义	320
巡诊	503	远程教育	536	批林批孔	320
巡航导弹	503	远销	536	批转	321
巡展	503	韧劲儿	355	批购户	320
		韧性	355	批修整风	321
七画		攻关	149	批捕	320
【一】		攻博	149	批调	320
		赤脚医生	55	批售	320
寿险	405	赤脚兽医	55	批量	320
麦当劳	285	赤潮	55	批销	321
麦饭石	285	豆制品	104	找米下锅	545
麦乳精	285	豆腐老虎	104	扯皮	50
戒毒	220	豆腐帐	104	抄收	49
戒毒所	220	豆腐渣工程	104	抄拿	49
形左实右	497	扶正祛邪	130	折返线	545
形式主义	497	扶本	130	折股	545
形象工程	497	扶优限劣	130	折叠床	545

折叠伞	545	抗税	241	块块	249
折叠椅	545	护田林	184	声像	391
抓生产	568	护苗	184	声讯	391
抓两头,带中间	568	护林员	184	声讨书	391
抓纲治国	567	护航	184	声讨会	391
抓拍	568	护嫂	184	声情并茂	391
抓苗头	568	扭亏为盈	305	声控	391
抓典型	567	扭亏增盈	305	花岗岩脑袋	185
抓革命,促生产	567	扭曲	306	花架子	185
抓点带面	566	扭送	306	劳务	257
抓思想	568	把关	9	劳务市场	257
抓捕	566	把脉	9	劳务出口	257
抓根本	567	报支	22	劳务合作	257
抓获	567	报价	21	劳务费	257
抓辫子	566	报批	22	劳务旅行	257
抢手	335	报告会	21	劳动人事部门	256
抢手货	335	报修	22	劳动力市场	256
抢收	335	报矿	22	劳动日	256
抢红灯	334	报捕	21	劳动化	255
抢拍	334	报检	21	劳动合同制	255
抢建	334	报领	22	劳动观点	255
抢点	334	报禁	21	劳动改造	255
抢种	335	劫机	218	劳动英雄	256
抢险	335	走穴	578	劳动服务公司	255
投入产出	446	走过场	578	劳动定额	254
投工	446	走后门	578	劳动组合	256
投价	446	走访	577	劳动组合制	256
投向	446	走红	578	劳动保护	254
投诉	446	走低	577	劳动保险	254
投拍	446	走村串户	577	劳动致富户	256
投保	446	走钢丝	578	劳动镀金论	255
投降主义	446	走俏	578	劳动教养	255
投档	446	走势	578	劳动密度	256
投售	446	走资派	578	劳动密集型	256
投递员	446	走街串巷	578	劳动密集型行业	256
抗上	241	走跌	577	劳动模范	256
抗大	240	坑骗	245	劳均	257
抗生菌	241	坛坛罐罐	429	劳改	257
抗灾	241	坏分子	187	劳改犯	257
抗美援朝	241	坏头头	187	劳保	254
抗洪	241	均衡裁军	234	劳保所	254

劳损	257	两分法	268	连轴转	266
劳逸结合	257	两忆三查	271	连续片	266
劳资处	257	两户	269	连续剧	266
劳资科	258	两户一体	270	连锁店	266
劳教	257	两平一稳	270	远导	536
劳教所	257	两田制	271	远南	536
劳模	257	两用人才	272	远销	536
苏区	423	两用衫	272	医风	517
克星	244	两头在外	271	医务室	518
克格勃	244	两权分离	270	医务所	518
克隆	244	两会	270	医护	517
杠杠	138	两论起家	270	医疗队	517
村干	67	两报一刊	267	医改	517
村史	67	两劳人员	270	医龄	517
村民	67	两极分化	270	医德	517
村民委员会	67	两条腿走路	271		
村委会	198	两条道路	271	【丨】	
极左	198	两条路线	271	步调	35
极左思潮	198	两快一慢	270	步道桥	35
极右	198	两定一奖	268	坚挺	206
极端分子	198	两参一改三结合	268	旱冰	168
极端民主化	198	两点论	268	旱冰馆	168
求实精神	341	两种生产	273	旱冰鞋	168
求职	341	两种市场	273	旱冰场	168
更年期	145	两种劳动制度	272	旱涝保收	168
更新换代	146	两种责任制	273	时代感	397
严办	505	两种资源	273	时代精神混合论	397
严打	505	两种教育制度	272	时程	397
严处	505	两种基数，		时弊	397
严肃音乐	505	三种价格	272	助工	566
严控	505	两保一挂	267	助导	566
严管	505	两类矛盾	270	助学	566
两山	271	两张皮	272	助研	566
两个凡是	268	两弹	268	助残	566
两个文明	269	两弹一星	268	助耕队	566
两个估计	269	来件装配	253	助耕包产	566
两个积极性	269	来样加工	253	助编	566
两个离不开	269	来料加工	253	县委	484
两个基本点	269	连队	266	困退	250
两不变	267	连体	266	园区	536
两手抓	271	连冠	266	园丁	536

词目表 七画

围斗	461	串味	63	私枭	415
围观	461	串灯	62	私售	415
围垦	461	串联	63	谷地	154
围堵	461	串联会	63	谷底	154
吨公里	109	财办	36	含金量	168
吨粮田	109	财会	36	余权	532
吨粮县	109	财政包干	36	余毒	532
吧女	7	财贸	36	余热	532
吹风会	64	财税	36	余粮	532
吹冷风	64	财路	36	延安精神	505
吹奏乐	65	岗位责任制	137	延安整风运动	506
吹喇叭	64			延展	506
呐喊助威	299	【丿】		估价师	153
足协	578	针刺疗法	545	估产	153
足坛	578	针刺麻醉	546	体力劳动	435
邮市	530	针麻	546	体工队	435
邮发	530	钉子户	100	体外受精	435
邮坛	530	钉子精神	100	体外循环	435
邮政编码	530	告吹	144	体坛	435
邮品	530	告败	144	体疗	435
邮展	530	利民活动	263	体改	435
邮售	530	利多	262	体改委	435
邮商	530	利好	262	体院	435
邮程	530	利改税	262	体校	435
邮编	530	利空	262	体委	435
男子气	300	利润挂帅	263	体能	435
男子汉	300	利润留成	263	体检	435
男士	300	利税	263	伸手派	389
男女同酬	300	兵工企业	29	作业面	581
男女作风	300	兵马俑	29	作业班	580
男双	300	兵团农场	30	作协	580
男团	300	兵运	30	低产	89
男单	300	私有化	415	低谷	89
男科	300	私企	415	低质优价	89
男保姆	300	私字当头	415	低俗	89
男朋友	300	私房	415	低耗	89
男排	300	私养	415	低档	89
男童	300	私活	415	低龄	89
男篮	300	私倒	415	低龄化	89
忠字舞	563	私校	415	低调	89
串讲	63	私了	415	低聘	89

位次	463	冷柜	261	快餐	249
伯乐	32	冷板凳	261	闲言碎语	482
住读	566	冷背	261	闲散资金	482
伴音	13	冷点	261	闷棍	289
身份证	389	冷销	261	泛光灯	121
返销	120	沉淀	51	泛读	121
返销粮	120	没戏	288	判读	315
坐机关	581	泡吧	316	宏观经济	179
坐直升飞机	581	兑换券	107	宏观管理	179
坐班	581	辛苦费	492	宏富	179
坐喷气式	581	亩产	298	穷过渡	340
希望工程	479	亩均	298	穷棒子社	340
肝功	136	床头柜	63	穷棒子精神	340
角色	233	床罩	63	良性循环	267
角刺人物	212	库区	248	证交所	551
角逐	233	库容	248	证券交易所	551
条子工程	438	疗养院	274	证监会	551
条形码	438	疗效	274	评工记分	325
条块	437	疗效食品	274	评工摆好	325
条块分割	437	疗程	273	评比	325
条条	437	应用科学	527	评介	325
条条专政	437	应市	527	评传	326
条条块快	437	应标	527	评优	326
条条框框	437	应试教育	527	评级	325
条码	437	应战书	527	评估	325
饭票	120	应选	527	评考	325
饮品	524	应聘	527	评卷	325
饮誉	524	忘本	459	评法批儒	325
系列	479	忧思录	530	评审	326
系列片	480	快人快语	249	评选	326
系列化	479	快中子	249	评委	326
系统工程	480	快件	249	评委会	326
系统论	480	快克	249	评教评学	325
		快克婴儿	249	评职	326
【丶】		快译通	249	评聘	326
冻雨	103	快货	249	评模	326
冷门货	261	快相	249	评薪	326
冷吧	261	快班	249	词典学	65
冷处理	261	快捷	249	识大体	398
冷饮	261	快递	249	识字班	398
冷库	261	快硬水泥	249	译制	522

词目	页码	词目	页码	词目	页码
译码	522	社会关系	386	改制	135
补亏	33	社会青年	386	驱赶	342
补台	33	社会语言学	386		
补休	33	社会渣滓	386	【丨】	
补血	33	社会集团	386		
补助票证	33	社交	388	姊妹城	573
补贴工分	33	社来社去	388	纵向	577
补选	33	社科	388	纲要	137
补差	32	社科院	388	纳米	299
补偿贸易	32	社员	389	纳新	299
补课	33	社庆	388	纸老虎	557
补假	32	社教	388		
补液	33	社教运动	388	八画	
社区	388	社圈	389	【一】	
社长	389	社情	388	玩车族	457
社办企业	385	社群	389	玩伴	457
社队	385	初级产品	58	环卫	188
社队企业	385	初级社	58	环卫工人	188
社务会	389	初评	58	环发	188
社会工作	386			环保	187
社会工程	386	【丿】		环保工业	187
社会主义所有制	387			环保部门	187
社会主义 人道主义	387	尾工	463	环委会	188
社会主义大院	386	尾气	463	环幕电影	188
社会主义异化论	388	尾巴	463	现反	483
社会主义 初期阶段	386	尾巴工程	463	现丑	483
社会主义改造	386	尾巴主义	463	现代戏	483
社会主义 现实主义	388	尾市	463	现代迷信	483
社会主义学院	388	尾牌	463	现市	483
社会主义 建设总路线	387	层面	41	现汇	483
社会主义革命	387	层高	41	现行反革命分子	483
社会主义 教育运动	387	局麻	232	现场办公	483
		劲射	223	现场会议	483
		劲舞	223	现案	482
		阿盟	1	现职	483
		陇兰经济带	279	到位	87
		附中	133	武卫	469
		附加工资	133	武斗	469
		附捐邮票	133	武打片	469
社会主义 精神文明	387	改产	135	武坛	469
				武英	470

武林	469	垃圾学	252	拥军优属	528
武星	469	顶门杠	100	拥政爱民	528
武校	469	顶尖	101	拉力赛	252
武检	469	顶冒	100	拉下马	253
武警	469	顶岗	100	拉下水	253
规模经营	162	顶换	100	拉山头	253
规模效益	162	顶班	100	拉开帷幕	252
青工	337	顶峰论	100	拉尼娜	252
青运会	337	顶替工	100	拉出去,打进来	252
青贮饲料	337	顶级	101	拉关系	252
青饲料	337	拐卖	157	拉练	252
青春偶像	337	拐棍	157	拉帮结派	252
青霉素	337	拓宽	454	拉锯战	252
青料	337	拓展	454	拦洪	253
青联	337	拔白旗	9	招干	545
责权利	540	拔钉子	9	招工	545
责任山	541	拔高	9	招办	544
责任田	541	担纲	83	招行	545
责任事故	541	拖拉机手	452	招贤榜	545
责任制	541	拖拉机站	452	招股	545
责任状	541	抽肥补瘦	56	招商	545
责编	540	抽试	56	择优	541
表决器	29	抽奖	56	拨乱反正	31
表报	29	抽测	56	拨付	31
表现力	29	抽样	56	抬轿子	426
表面文章	29	抽样调查	57	取向	342
表面性	29	抽紧	56	取证	342
表态	29	抽调	56	取经	342
表演赛	29	抽验	56	取信于民	342
幸运儿	498	抽球	56	取消主义	342
幸福院	498	抽检	56	苦大仇深	248
妻管严	329	抱大腿	21	苦果	248
直观教学	555	拍马	313	苗子	292
直挂	555	拍让	313	苗木	292
直面	555	拍板	313	苗床	292
直选	555	拆迁	43	苗情	292
直航	555	拆迁户	43	苗期	292
直落	555	拆封	43	苗禽	292
直销	555	拆借	43	英烈	525
直播	555	拆装	43	英模	525
坦诚	429	押车	504	范读	120

苔肥	426	奋飞	128	软科学	359
杯赛	23	奋进	128	软班子	358
柜员	162	转干	570	软卧	360
柜员机	162	转口贸易	570	软雕塑	359
林片	275	转正	571	软席	360
林业专业户	275	转业	570	软座	360
林权证	275	转业军人	571	软商品	360
林网	275	转包	570	软着陆	360
林带	275	转发	570	软懒散	359
林科户	275	转产	570	欧元	312
板儿爷	12	转轨	570	欧共体	312
板报	12	转轨经济	570	欧安会	312
板材	12	转岗	570	欧佩克	312
松口鞋	423	转录	570	欧洲共同体	312
松松垮垮	423	转型	570	欧币	312
松脆	423	转氨酶	570	欧盟	312
松绑	423	转基因	570		
松垮	423	转销	570	【丨】	
枪击	333	轮休	282	非书资料	124
构想	153	轮次	282	非对抗性矛盾	124
枕头风	546	轮作	282	非农化	124
画坛	186	轮换工	282	非欧佩克	124
画展	186	轮训	282	非官方	124
画圈圈	186	轮伐期	282	非组织观点	124
事务主义	399	轮岗	282	非组织活动	124
事务性工作	399	轮滑	282	非贸易外汇收入	124
事权	399	软工厂	359	非党人士	124
事典	399	软广告	359	非党群众	124
刺刀见红	65	软开业	359	非斯计划	124
卖大户	285	软生产	360	非婚性行为	124
卖大号	285	软包装	358	肯德鸡	245
卖方市场	285	软件	359	呼拉圈	184
卖招纸	285	软任务	360	呼姐	184
卖家	285	软设备	360	咖啡伴侣	237
奇缺	330	软赤字	358	岩画	505
奇效	330	软技术	359	岸吊	5
奇谈怪论	330	软投入	360	岸炮	5
矿管	250	软饮料	360	旺销	459
矿泉壶	250	软环境	359	贤内助	482
矿泉水	250	软指标	360	易拉罐	520
矿务局	250	软贷款	359	昆交会	250

八画　词目表

词目	页码	词目	页码	词目	页码
昂奋	6	固体水库	155	知难而进	552
明白人	296	固体饮料	155	牧工商联合企业	298
明补	296	固定工	155	物业	476
明贴	296	图文并茂	448	物质刺激	476
果茶	165	迪厅	89	物质鼓励	476
果农	165	迪斯尼	89	物耗	476
果珍	165	迪斯科	89	物流	476
鸣放	296	典型示范	95	物探	476
国土规划	164	典型试验	95	狗崽子	153
国土经济学	164	贩私	120	垂直领导	65
国啤	164	败因	12	刮风	155
国手	164	贬值	27	和风细雨	172
国计民生	163	购物中心	153	和平队	172
国办	163	购货本	153	和平共处	172
国务委员	163	购销联社	153	和平共处	
国民经济		购粮本	153	五项原则	172
恢复时期	164	贮运	566	和平过渡	172
国优	165			和平攻势	172
国合企业	163	【丿】		和平改造	172
国企	164	钓鱼工程	99	和平解放	172
国防科委	163	制导系统	557	和平竞赛	172
国库券	164	制衡	557	和平演变	172
国威	164	制冷	557	和美	172
国格	163	制种	557	和稀泥	193
国资局	165	制式	557	季节工	201
国脚	163	制售	557	委培	463
国际大循环	163	知本	552	迫降	327
国际共运	163	知本家	552	伊妹儿	518
国际回信券	163	知本主义	552	供不应求	149
国际社会	163	知名度	552	供气	149
国际笔会	163	知产阶级	552	供应学派	149
国宾馆	163	知识化	553	供给制	149
国家队	163	知识产业	553	供热	149
国家公园	163	知识产权	553	供销社	149
国营企业	164	知识库	553	供暖	149
国营农场	164	知识青年	553	例会	263
国营经济	164	知识经济	553	例假	263
国奥队	163	知识流动	553	侧记	40
国税	164	知识管理	553	使领馆	398
国道	163	知青	553	佳绩	202
国嘴	165	知青商店	553	侃	240

词目	页码	词目	页码	词目	页码
侃大山	240	爬行主义	313	乳制品	357
侃价	240	爬行哲学	313	版协	12
侃爷	240	爬格子	313	肤色	130
侦办	546	爬坡	313	肥力	125
侦破	546	刹车	380	肥水	125
侦察卫星	546	金三角	221	肥猪粉	126
侨乡	336	金卡工程	221	肥皂粉	125
侨办	335	金边债券	221	肥皂剧	126
侨汇	335	金农	221	服务行业	131
侨汇券	335	金珠玛米	221	服务费	130
侨胞	335	金霉素	221	服务员	131
侨委	336	金领工人	221	服务态度	131
侨属	336	金牌	221	服软	130
侨眷	335	金融工程	221	肢残人	553
侨资	336	命令主义	297	肢障	553
侨领	336	贪大求全	428	股市	155
侨商	336	贪大求洋	428	股权	155
侨联	335	贪占行为	428	股灾	155
依循	518	贫下中农	323	股盲	154
货仓式商店	194	贫下中农协会	323	股民	155
货的	194	贫下中农讲师团	323	股指	155
货机	194	贫下中牧	323	股份合作制	154
货运	194	贫下中渔	323	股份制	154
货柜	194	贫协	323	股潮	154
货币主义学派	194	贫牧	323	周边	564
货流	194	贫宣队	323	周转粮	564
的士	90	贫渔	323	周界	564
的卡	89	鱼水情	532	备荒	24
的哥	89	鱼品	532	备战	24
的姐	89	受冲击	405	备选	24
的站	90	受惠	405	备耕	24
的确良	90	受阅	405	备料	24
征迁	547	受聘	405	备课	24
征购	546	采区	37	备勤	24
征订	546	采写	37	饰演	399
征婚	546	采购团	37	饲养员	423
征管	546	采购员	37		
往返票	459	采购站	37	【、】	
质检员	559	采样	37	变天复辟	28
质量月活动	559	采编	37	变天帐	28
质量经济学	559	采暖	37	变节分子	28

变色龙	28	性状	498	炒买炒卖	50
变色镜	28	性别比	498	炒更	49
变相涨价	28	性骚扰	498	炒作	50
变修	28	性解放	498	炒冷饭	49
变型金刚	28	性感	498	炒卖	50
变数	28	怕字当头	313	炒股	49
京郊	223	怪圈	157	炒鱿鱼	50
京官	223	闹工资	301	炒家	49
京剧革命	223	闹革命	301	炊拨儿	65
店风	98	闹独立性	301	炊事员	65
店堂	98	闹待遇	301	炕肥	241
庙堂	292	闹情绪	301	净化	231
底价	90	闹翻身	301	净空	231
底肥	90	卷扬机	233	净菜	231
夜大	511	单一经济	83	法盲	115
夜生活	511	单一种植	83	法塔赫	115
夜市	511	单人宿舍	82	河网	175
郊县	212	单干风	82	河肥	175
放下包袱	123	单干户	82	油老虎	531
放下架子	123	单卡	82	油品	531
放卫星	123	单列	82	油耗	530
放飞	122	单向	83	油耗子	530
放开	122	单产	82	油票	531
放权	123	单兵教练	81	泡巴	316
放羊	123	单兵装备	82	泡汤	316
放足鞋	123	单极世界	82	泡沫灭火器	316
放疗	123	单身贵族	83	泡沫经济	316
放空	123	单亲	82	泡沫塑料	316
放空炮	123	单速	83	泡病号	316
放音机	123	单缸	82	泳坛	528
放养	123	单纯业务观点	82	泳装	528
放活	122	单纯任务观点	82	注资	566
放宽政策	123	单元楼	83	沼气池	545
放眼	123	单剧本	82	泥足巨人	304
盲打	286	单晶体	82	泥饭碗	304
盲校	286	单晶炉	82	沸腾炉	126
盲流	286	炎黄子孙	506	治厂	559
育龄	534	炒	49	治穷	560
育秧	534	炒风	49	治穷致富	560
刻瓷	244	炒汇	49	治国安邦	560
性自由	498	炒买	49	治贫	560

治保	559	审计	390	空间技术	245
泊位	32	审批	390	空间垃圾	245
学工	501	审听	390	空间科学	245
学分	501	审评	390	空间渡船	245
学分制	501	审视	390	空间站	246
学生官	501	审看	390	空政	246
学军	501	审结	390	空嫂	246
学农	501	审阅	391	空姐	246
学运	502	审验	390	空域	246
学位制	502	官工作风	158	空调	246
学前班	501	官办	158	空调器	246
学前教育	501	官本位	158	空难	246
学习班	502	官兵一致	158	空港	245
学部	501	官倒爷	158	空勤	245
学联	501	官暮骄娇四气	159	空播	245
学僧	501	官商	159	房老虎	121
宝钢	21	官商作风	159	房市	121
宗派主义	576	官瘾	159	房贷	121
定心骨	103	宠物	56	房改	121
定向	102	实力政策	398	房改房	121
定向广播	102	实干家	398	房管	121
定向分配	102	实干精神	398	房管所	121
定向招生	102	实体	398	试飞	401
定向培养	102	实事	398	试办	401
定向销售	102	实诚	398	试刊	401
定产	101	实况转播	398	试产	401
定岗	101	实绩	398	试点	401
定位	102	空天飞机	246	试点班	401
定评	102	空中大学	246	试种	401
定购	102	空中小姐	246	试映	401
定点	101	空中公共汽车	246	试读	401
定息	102	空中走廊	246	试验区	401
定势	103	空中客车	246	试验田	401
定员	103	空中预警飞机	246	试销	401
定调子	101	空中教育	246	试管婴儿	401
定销	103	空气质量和排放标准	246	试播	401
定编	101	空气浴	246	话务员	187
定额计酬	101	空头政治	246	话亭	187
定额包工	101	空对空	245	话筒	187
定额记分	101	空防	245	话路	187
审干	390				

详备	485	限产压库	484	组建	579
询访	502	限产产品	484	组织生活	579
询查	502	限收	484	组织关系	579
视听	400	限购	484	组织疗法	579
视众	401	承包	52	组织建设	579
视窗	400	承包山	53	组雕	578
视频	400	承包田	53	组阁	579
视盘	400	承包经营责任制	53	组稿	579
		承包商	53	组装	579
【一】		承购	53	组编	578
驾校	206	承建	53	组歌	579
驾照	206	承销	53	细菜	480
建行	209	函大	168	织补	553
建设公债	209	函索	168	终身制	563
建设周期	209	函授大学	168	终身教育	563
建军节	209	函调	168	终审	563
建构	209	孟泰精神	290	终端	563
建党学说	209			经互会	225
建材	209	【丶】		经风雨,见世面	225
建委	209	参评	39	经办	225
建材工业	209	参股	38	经贸	229
建销	209	参试	39	经委	229
肃反	424	参试人员	39	经警	229
肃反扩大化	424	参选	39	经济一体化	228
肃贪	424	参政	39	经济人	227
录入员	280	参展	39	经济开发区	226
录制	280	参赛	39	经济支柱	228
录放机	280	姓公	498	经济区划	226
录音本	280	姓私	498	经济手段	227
录像	280	姓社	498	经济计量学	225
录像机	280	姓资	498	经济立法	226
录像带	280	始发站	398	经济民主	226
居民大院	232	线民	484	经济动物	225
居民身份证	232	线报	484	经济协作区	228
居民委员会	232	练摊	266	经济师	227
居室	232	组办	578	经济合同	225
居委会	232	组台	579	经济杠杆	225
居留证	232	组团	579	经济体制	227
屈居	342	组合机床	579	经济作物	228
限价	484	组合柜	579	经济责任制	228
		组合家具	579	经济林木	226

经济实体	227	毒枭	105	政治嗅觉	550
经济结构	226	封山育林	129	政治帐	551
经济核算	225	封冻	128	政治觉悟	550
经济特区	227	封顶	128	政治委员	550
经济员	228	封镜	128	政治庸人	551
经济帐	228	封杀	129	政治资本	551
经济渗透	227	封资修	129	政治部	549
经济效益	228	封盘	128	政治辅导员	549
经济基础	225	城乡分割	51	政治骗子	550
经济圈	227	城市规划	51	政治路线	550
经济联合体	226	城市经济学	51	政审	549
经济适用房	227	城运会	51	政经	548
经济增长点	229	城郊	51	政委	549
经营方向	229	城建	51	政策性亏损	548
经营作风	229	城标	51	挂历	156
经营层次	229	城雕	51	挂拍	156
经营责任制	229	城际	51	挂线疗法	156
经营性亏损	229	城管	51	挂起来	156
经营承包制	229	政工	548	挂鞋	156
经营思想	229	政工组	548	挂靴	156
经援	230	政历	548	挂钩	155
经销专业户	229	政风	548	挂钩会	155
		政务院	549	挂职	157
九画		政协	549	挂牌	156
【一】		政企合一	548	挂牌售货	156
		政纪	548	挂靠	156
玻璃小鞋	31	政坛	549	挂靠户	156
玻璃钢	31	政社分开	548	持平	55
珍稀	545	政社合一	548	持币抢购	55
帮伙	14	政制	549	持币待购	55
帮伙体系	14	政治扒手	550	持币选购	55
帮扶	14	政治立场	550	挺升	441
帮派	14	政治台风	550	拾遗补缺	397
帮派体系	14	政治协商会议	550	挑大梁	439
帮倒忙	14	政治局	549	挑战书	439
帮教	14	政治夜校	550	指认	556
帮厨	14	政治学习	550	指压疗法	556
春交会	65	政治挂帅	549	指导性计划	556
春秋衫	65	政治指导员	551	指导员	556
春游	65	政治面目	550	指挥棒	556
毒草	105	政治素质	550	指战员	556

指令长	556	带电作业	79	标号	29
指令性	556	带头羊	79	标灯	29
指令性计划	556	带钢	79	标志服	29
指控	556	带原	80	标准像	29
挤占	200	带职回乡	80	查处	42
挤牙膏	200	荒诞派	189	查体	42
挤提	200	荣民	356	查证	42
拼死拼活	323	荣退	356	查补	42
拼杀	323	荣退军人	356	查苗	42
拼抢	322	荣获	356	查实	42
拼音字母	323	荧屏	525	查核	42
拼搏	322	荧幕	525	查获	42
拼搏精神	322	草木经	40	耍态度	407
拼装	323	草业	40	要素市场	510
挖、革、改	455	草库伦	40	要害部门	510
挖墙角	455	草根工业	40	要案	510
挖潜	455	草编	40	歪风	455
按质论价	5	草签	40	歪嘴和尚	455
按资排辈	5	茶吧	42	研议	505
按揭	5	茶话会	42	研制	505
挪占	311	药工	509	研修	505
革命人道主义	143	药枕	509	研修生	505
革命气概	142	药政	510	研习	505
革命化	142	药茶	509	研讨会	505
革命文物	143	药点	509	研读	505
革命乐观主义	142	药具	509	研商	505
革命圣地	143	药膳	509	泵房	25
革命发展阶段论	142	药检	509	泵排量	25
革命传统	141	药检所	509	砂洗	379
革命闯将	142	胡子	184	砍	240
革命现实主义	143	胡子工程	184	砍大山	240
革命英雄主义	143	胡子牌	184	厚古薄今	183
革命前辈	142	胡吃海塞	184	厚今薄古	183
革命派	142	南水北调	300	厚爱	183
革命热情	143	南北对话	299	面世	291
革命样板戏	143	南北合作	299	面包车	291
革命熔炉	143	南泥湾精神	300	面市	291
革命浪漫主义	142	南南对话	299	面对面	291
革命委员会	143	南南合作	300	面向	291
革命接班人	142	南南关系	299	面向农村	291
革委会	144	南粮北调	299	面向群众	291

词目表 九画

面的	291	省际	394	思想疙瘩	412
面试	291	省府	394	思想觉悟	413
面面观	291	省委	395	思想僵化	413
面值	292	省道	394	思想烙印	414
面授	291	显效	482	思想波动	412
面料	291	冒失鬼	288	思想摸底	414
牵头	332	冒尖儿	287	思想禁区	413
牵线搭桥	332	冒尖儿户	287	思想路线	414
残次	39	冒尖儿队	287	思想意识	414
残疾人	39	冒领	288	思想境界	413
残疾院	39	冒富	287	思想懒汉	414
残联	39	冒富大叔	287	品位	323
轻机产品	337	冒傻气	288	品种花样	324
轻轨交通	337	星火计划	496	品味	323
轻纺	337	星级	496	品牌	323
轻重缓急	338	星城	496	骂娘	284
轻音乐	338	星战	497	哄动效应	179
轻骑	337	星际	497	哄抢	179
轻骑兵	337	星球大战计划	497	哄抬	179
轻装上阵	338	星探	497	哄闹	179
		罚没	115	哈达	167
【丨】		趴窝	313	响当当	485
背包袱	23	蚂蚁啃骨头	284	贴标签	440
背篓商店	23	界定	220	贴面	440
背黑锅	23	思想工作	412	贴息贷款	440
背销	24	思想见面	413	骨干	154
背靠背	24	思想方法	412		
战和	544	思想包袱	412	【丿】	
战备导弹		思想过硬	413	钞票挂帅	49
防御系统	544	思想交锋	413	钡餐	24
临门	275	思想问题	414	钢城	137
临时工	275	思想体系	414	钢领工人	137
临战	275	思想作风	415	贷学金	81
览胜	254	思想库	413	牲畜肥	394
点子公司	95	思想改造	412	香风	484
点面结合	95	思想武装	414	香格里拉	484
点钞机	95	思想性	414	香波	484
省优	395	思想建设	413	种子公司	563
省报	394	思想政治工作	415	种子队	563
省直	395	思想革命化	412	种子选手	564
省油灯	395	思想修养	414	种子站	564

九画　词目表

种子基金	564	复关	132	保健组织	19
种子球员	564	复转军人	132	保健按摩	18
种苗	563	复制	132	保健食品	19
种畜	563	复贫	132	保健费	19
种猪	563	复录	132	保健员	19
种蛋	563	复种	132	保健所	19
种禽	563	复垦	132	保健站	19
秋杂	340	复退军人	132	保健箱	19
秋后算帐派	340	复述	132	保健操	19
秋游	340	复式住宅	132	保墒	20
科考	243	复读	132	保洁	19
科协	243	复读生	132	保龄球	19
科技	242	复读班	132	保理	19
科技户	242	复课	132	保教	19
科技示范户	242	顺产	412	保职停薪	21
科坛	243	顺价	412	保税区	20
科盲	243	俗众	423	保温杯	20
科学学	243	修旧利废	499	保鲜	20
科学城	243	修宪	499	保管员	18
科学种田	243	修理地球	499	促进派	66
科研	243	保本	18	促退派	66
科贸	243	保四争五	20	促销	66
科室	243	保幼人员	20	便民	28
科委	243	保守疗法	20	便民措施	28
科幻小说	242	保守派	20	便当	28
科教片	242	保安服务公司	18	便利店	28
科普	243	保护主义	18	便携式	28
科普读物	243	保护地	18	俏色	336
科影厂	243	保护价	18	俏货	336
看好	240	保护伞	18	信用卡	496
看涨	240	保苗	20	信用社	496
看跌	240	保质	21	信访	495
重头	564	保底	18	信访部门	495
重组	56	保函	18	信息工业	495
重点户	564	保皇派	18	信息工作者	495
重点学校	564	保送生	20	信息中心	496
重奖	564	保费	18	信息处理	495
皇粮	189	保险箱	20	信息网	496
复旧	132	保真	20	信息社会	496
复印机	132	保值	21	信息服务	495
复壮	132	保健网	19	信息经济	496

信息革命	495	选聘	501	音箱	523
信息点	495	选题	501	奖优罚劣	210
信息高速公路	495	适体	399	奖金挂帅	210
信息爆炸	495	适销	399	奖学金	210
信仰危机	496	适销对路	399	奖励工资	210
侵权	336	追加	571	奖售	210
独生子女	105	追肥	571	奖牌	210
独生子女证	105	追星	571	奖勤罚懒	210
独立王国	105	追星族	571	奖旗	210
独立自主	105	追授	571	将军肚	210
独立国家联合体	105	追烈	571	亲系	336
独立性	105	逃汇	430	亲等	336
独资	105	逃夜	430	逆反	304
独联体	105	逃单	429	逆反心理	304
待业	81	逃亡地主	430	逆向	304
待岗	81	逃票	430	逆序词典	304
衍传	506	逃跑主义	430	迷你	290
盆花儿	319	贸发会议	288	迷你裙	290
盆栽	319	贸易货栈	288	迷思	290
食协	398	贸易战	288	迷彩	290
食疗	397	贸易保护主义	288	迷彩服	290
食品街	397	贸促会	288	送审	423
食俗	397			送养人	423
食雕	397	【、】		美化	288
食宿	397	亮丑	273	美发	288
食街	397	亮红灯	273	美发厅	288
饼肥	30	亮证经营	273	美食	288
胞波	15	亮底牌	273	美食家	288
胜券	395	亮相	273	美食街	288
胜券在握	395	亮丽	273	美院	288
胜面	395	亮点	273	美容	288
胎教	426	亮短	273	美展	288
选民证	501	亮牌子	273	美编	288
选育	501	度假村	106	美联储	288
选点	500	庭院经济	441	美餐	288
选美	501	音乐茶座	523	差生	42
选配	501	音协	523	差价	41
选读	500	音带	523	差劲	42
选调	500	音碟	523	差旅费	42
选编	500	音像制品	523	差额招生	41
		音像带	523	差额选举	41

九画　词目表

养老金	508	测试	41	洋框框	507
养成教育	508	测控	40	洋倒	507
养殖	508	测算	41	洋为中用	507
养殖业	508	洗手间	479	洋教条	507
叛国	316	洗头膏	479	洋跃进	508
叛逃	316	洗发剂	479	洋插队	507
叛党	315	洗钱	479	洋啤	507
叛徒哲学	316	洗碗机	479	洲际导弹	564
前卫	333	洗衣机	479	举报	232
前科	333	洗衣粉	479	举坛	232
前沿科学	333	洗脑筋	479	举借	232
前瞻性	333	洗涤剂	479	举旗抓纲	232
首日	404	洗煤	479	宣传车	500
首日封	404	活化石	192	宣传队	500
首发	403	活靶子	192	宣传机器	500
首发式	403	活命哲学	192	宣教	500
首创精神	403	活学活用	193	客户	244
首汽	404	活标本	192	客队	244
首季	404	活思想	193	客饭	244
首战	404	活神仙	193	客房	244
首钢	404	活样板	193	客源	245
首映	404	活教材	192	客里空	244
首映式	404	活愚公	193	客流	245
首航	404	派	314	客隆	245
首演	404	派出机构	314	窃密	336
总工	576	派饭	314	突击入党	447
总工会	576	派购	314	突击手	447
总支	577	派性	315	突击队	447
总后	577	派送	315	突击提干	447
总体规划	577	派活	315	突出政治	447
总参	576	派仗	315	突发	447
总政	577	派驻	315	突发性	447
总路线	577	派售	315	突破口	447
剃光头	435	洽购	332	突显	448
炮打	316	洽谈	332	突增	448
炮轰	316	洽谈会	332	穿小鞋	61
烂摊子	254	洋八股	507	穿针引线	61
洪峰	179	洋大全	507	穿帮	61
浇注	212	洋奴思想	507	穿梆	61
浇灌	212	洋奴哲学	507	穿梭外交	61
测评	40	洋冒进	507	穿新鞋,走老路	61

词目	页码	词目	页码	词目	页码
穿鞋戴帽	61	屏幕	326	统购包销	444
穿靴戴帽	61	除四害	60	统购统销	444
语录	533	除尘器	60	统建	444
语录歌	534	除草剂	60	统战	445
语录操	533	除害灭病	60	统战部	445
语种	534	险工	482	统保	443
语音信箱	534	险区	482	统配	445
语委	534	险胜	482	统配物资	445
语态	534	险段	482	统配煤矿	445
语料	533	降下帷幕	211	统配煤	445
语流	533	降解	211	统调统配	444
语感	533	降幅	211	统揽	445
语境	533	降温	211	统销	445
诱购	532	院风	536	统编	443
误工	477	院校	536	统筹安排	443
误区	477	院部	536	统筹医疗	443
误导	477	架构	206	统筹法	443
误班	477	架空	206	统筹学	443
误诊	477			统筹兼顾	443
误餐	477	【丶】		统算	445
说服教育	412	结扎手术	219	统管	444
神化	390	结汇	218		
神仙会	390	结对子	218	十画	
神经兮兮	390	结构工资制	218	【一】	
		结构主义语言学	218		
【→】		结转	219	耕读小学	145
贺卡	175	结党营私	218	耕读学校	145
贺岁片	175	绘制	191	耗电	170
垦区	245	给出路	145	耗能	170
退生	451	绝对平均主义	234	素肉	423
退团	452	绝对权威	234	秦俑	336
退休	452	绝育	234	索要	425
退运	452	绝活	234	索赔	425
退役	452	绝情	234	索贿	425
退役军人	452	绞肉机	213	班干	12
退居	451	统一口径	445	班车	12
退耕还林	451	统包统配	443	班会	12
退党	451	统考	444	班级	12
退赃	452	统存统贷	443	班组	12
退赔	451	统观	443	班费	12
退场	451	统收统支	445	珠峰	564

珠影	565	热点	348	核威慑	172
赶超	136	热核武器	349	核威胁	172
起飞	330	热钱	349	核战争	172
起居室	330	热岛效应	348	核保护伞	171
起获	330	热启动	349	核讹诈	171
载誉	539	热得快	348	核恐怖	171
埋头业务	285	热销	350	核牙齿	172
埋线疗法	285	晋职	222	核废料	171
捧杯	319	恶补	111	核垄断	171
捕杀	32	恶性差错	111	核资	172
捞油水	254	恶性循环	111	核谈判	172
捞稻草	254	恶性案件	111	核能	171
捞资本	254	恶战	111	核基地	171
捂盖子	476	恩格尔系数	111	核裁军	171
损公肥私	425	贾桂思想	205	核装置	172
捐资	233	框架	250	核骗局	171
挨斗	1	框框	250	核算单位	171
挨批	1	档次	86	核糖核酸	172
挨棍子	1	株式会社	565	核霸王	171
挨整	1	核力量	171	核霸权	171
捅马蜂窝	442	核大国	171	根子正	145
换工	188	核反应堆	171	根红苗壮	145
换马	188	核心人物	172	根雕	145
换汇	188	核心小组	172	根植	145
换休	188	核心家庭	172	校外辅导员	492
换血	188	核电	171	校纪	492
换届	188	核电厂	171	校际	491
换脑筋	188	核电站	171	样片	509
热	348	核冬天	171	样书	509
热土	349	核发	171	样机	509
热门货	349	核动力	171	样板	508
热门股票	349	核扩散	171	样板田	509
热门话题	349	核优势	172	样板戏	509
热区	349	核冲突	171	速生丰产林	424
热水器	349	核军备	171	速成识字法	423
热气球	349	核导弹	171	速成材	423
热身	349	核武库	172	速冻	423
热身赛	349	核武器	172	速溶	424
热狗	349	核备战	171	速效	424
热线	349	核试验	171	速递	423
热战	350	核查	171	速滑	424

词目表 十画

配电	318	套话	430	党纪	84
配发	318	套种	431	党报	83
配购	318	套换	430	党规	84
配送	318	套裁	430	党性	85
配送中心	318	套装	431	党法	83
配股	318	套裙	430	党建	84
配种站	318	套餐	430	党组	86
配给制	318	顾大局	155	党政工团	86
配歌	318	致气	557	党政分开	85
配演	318	致公党	557	党政机关	86
配额	318	致富	557	党总支	86
配餐	318			党费	83
夏收	482	【丨】		党校	85
夏时制	482	监听	206	党委	85
夏种	482	监事	206	党龄	84
夏播	481	监审	206	党章	85
破中有立	327	监测	206	党委制	85
破旧立新	327	监理	206	党课	84
破四旧,立四新	327	监控	206	党票	84
破字当头,		监督电话	206	党群	84
立在其中	327	监管	206	党群关系	84
破私立公	327	紧迫感	221	圆珠笔	535
破译	327	紧俏	221		
破罐破摔	326	紧俏商品	221	【丿】	
殉葬品	503	紧缺	221	钻劲	579
殊荣	405	紧张	221	铁人	440
获选	193	紧跟	221	铁人精神	441
荷兰豆	170	罢驶	9	铁牛	440
原子笔	535	逍遥派	486	铁交椅	440
原子能发电站	536	党八股	83	铁杆儿	440
原声带	535	党支部	86	铁饭碗	440
原珠笔	535	党中央	86	铁板凳	440
原装	535	党日	85	铁画	440
套书	431	党内生活	84	铁哥们	440
套用	431	党内和平论	84	铁娘子	440
套汇	430	党风	84	铁幕	440
套红	430	党刊	84	缺门	346
套改	430	党代会	83	缺档	346
套利	430	党外人士	85	缺斤少两	346
套购	430	党团	85	缺斤短两	346
套服	430	党团关系	85	缺编	346

十画 词目表

狼孩	254	造神运动	540	健美操	209
氧吧	508	造势	540	倾斜	338
特工	431	乘务员	52	候补委员	183
特艺	433	乘警	52	候诊室	183
特区	432	敌对分子	90	息影	479
特权阶层	432	敌百虫	90	臭老九	57
特优	433	敌敌畏	90	臭美	58
特优生	433	敌我矛盾	90	胶子	211
特异功能	433	敌情观念	90	胶球	211
特许经营	433	积代会	198	脑库	301
特级战斗英雄	431	积极分子	198	脑体倒挂	301
特级教师	431	积非成是	198	脑瘫	301
特批	432	积淀	198	脏话	539
特护	431	积案	198	胸卡	499
特医	433	笑星	492	胸花	499
特困	432	笔会	25	胸针	499
特困户	432	笔杆子	25	胸章	499
特困生	432	笔墨官司	26	射门	385
特体	432	借东风	220	航天	169
特快	432	借考	220	航天飞机	170
特招	433	借鸡下蛋	220	航天服	170
特供	431	借读	220	航天站	170
特版	431	借调	220	航天器	170
特殊化	432	值周生	556	航拍	169
特殊教育	432	倒儿爷	86	航空港	169
特诊	433	倒三七	87	航空器	169
特需	432	倒汇	86	航母	169
特辑	431	倒休	86	航保	169
特味	432	倒买倒卖	86	航测	169
特稿	431	倒卖	86	航摄	169
特邀代表	433	倒春寒	87	航模	169
特型演员	432	倒挂	87	爱厂如家	2
特首	432	倒错	87	爱人	2
特教	432	倡议书	46	爱卫会	2
特等劳模	431	倍加	24	爱心	2
特集	431	倍棒	24	爱民公约	2
特嫌	432	倍感	24	爱民月活动	2
特警	432	倍增	24	爱社如家	2
透明度	447	健身	209	爱国卫生运动	2
造反派	540	健身球	209	爱国公约	2
造血	540	健美	209	爱校如家	2

爱牙日	2	高举	139	资不抵债	572
爱委会	2	高架路	139	资本主义尾巴	572
爱资病	3	高架公路	139	资产阶级反动	
爱滋病	3	高校	140	学术权威	572
拿牌	299	高速公路	140	资产阶级	
鸳鸯楼	535	高速铁路	140	反动路线	572
颂古非今	423	高峰	138	资产阶级	
脂肪肝	553	高峰会议	139	司令部	572
留成	276	高新技术	140	资产阶级右派	573
留后手	276	高姿态	140	资产阶级权利	572
留后路	276	高效节能	140	资产阶级	
留余地	276	高消费	140	自由化	573
留党察看	276	高难	139	资产阶级	
留言簿	276	高能物理学	140	自发势力	572
留职停薪	277	高能燃料	140	资产阶级法权	572
		高聘	140	资产重组	572

【 丶 】

		高精尖	139	资信	573
高干	139	高薪	140	资费	573
高工	139	高薪阶层	140	资敌罪	573
高大全	138	恋人	266	资讯	573
高分低能	138	恋情	266	资深	573
高发	138	席梦思	479	资深院士	573
高考	139	唐人街	429	准工业化	572
高压手段	140	座果率	581	准妈妈	572
高压锅	140	病休	30	竞投	231
高师	140	病残	30	竞赛	231
高价	139	病退	30	站风	544
高企	140	病虫害	30	剖腹产	327
高产田	138	效益工资	492	部优	35
高产稳产	138	离土不离乡	261	部件	35
高级社	139	离休	262	部际	35
高级知识分子	139	离任	261	部委	35
高技术	139	离经叛道	261	阅批	537
高危	140	离职	262	阅报栏	537
高低柜	138	旅行车	280	阅卷	537
高层	138	旅行剪	280	瓶颈	325
高知	140	旅游	280	瓶插	325
高法	138	旅游车	280	拳头产品	345
高空作业	139	旅游图	280	粉尘	128
高指标	140	旅游经济学	280	粉碎机	128
高研	140	旅游鞋	280	粉领工人	128

十画 词目表

粉领族	128	流动电影队	277	容留	357
料子服	274	流动红旗	277	案证	6
料理	274	流动服务	277	案例	6
烤箱	242	流动站	277	案底	6
烧香	384	流动售货	277	案值	6
烧烤	384	流向	277	案犯	6
烟民	505	流行色	277	宰	539
涉外单位	385	流食	277	宰客	539
涉外婚姻	385	流氓团伙	277	请吃	339
涉外税收	385	流脑	277	请战	339
消化	486	流通领域	277	请调	339
消极因素	486	冤假错案	535	诸侯经济	565
消协	486	家长制	204	诸葛亮会	565
消纳	486	家史	202	读书无用论	105
消纳场	486	家电	202	读书班	105
消纳站	486	家访	202	读卡机	105
消费合作社	486	家肥	202	课间操	245
消费基金	486	家居	202	课间餐	245
消费税	486	家庭工业	203	调干生	99
消肿	486	家庭出身	203	调干生助学金	99
海外关系	167	家庭妇女	203	调干学员	99
海协会	167	家庭劳动服务		调节器	438
海政	168	介绍所	203	调休	439
海南	167	家庭学	204	调价	438
海洋经济学	168	家庭经济	203	调级	438
海监	167	家庭病床	203	调运	100
海峡	167	家庭副业	203	调改	438
海绵田	167	家庭联产承包		调拨	99
海瑞罢官	167	责任制	203	调和主义	438
海瑞精神	167	家庭影院	204	调房	438
海难	167	家属工厂	202	调试	439
海基会	167	家委会	204	调度员	99
海滋	168	家属宿舍	202	调派	99
涨幅	544	家属委员会	203	调档	99
浮动工资	131	家教	202	调幅	438
浮夸风	131	家装	204	调频	439
浴罩	534	宽松	249	调解组织	439
浴帽	534	宽带通信	249	调峰措施	438
涤纶	90	宽限期	249	调解委员会	439
涤棉	90	宽展期	249	调高	438
流生	277	宽银幕	249	调离	99

词目表 十画－十一画

调资	439	弱质	361	预警	535
调阅	100	弱视	360	桑拿按摩	379
调控	439	弱项	360	桑拿浴	379
调减	438	弱势	360	桑塔纳	379
调演	100	弱能	360		
调赛	99	弱智	361	【乚】	
谈心活动	429	陶艺	430	娘家	304
谈资	429	陶雕	430	娱乐片	533
被动吸烟	24	陪风	317	能上能下	303
被罩	24	陪斗	317	能级	303
被管制分子	24	陪护	317	能官能民	303
		陪住	317	能耗	303
【一】		陪床	317	能源	303
恳谈	245	陪夜	317	能源结构	303
恳谈会	245	陪审员	317	继往开来	201
展区	544	陪练	317	继续教育	201
展台	544	陪宴	317		
展团	544	陪酒女	317	十一画	
展评	543	陪读	317		
展延	544	陪餐	317	【一】	
展柜	543	通天	441	球王	341
展卖	543	通气	441	球手	341
展览业	543	通用月票	442	球风	340
展映	544	通汇	441	球坛	341
展馆	543	通关	441	球星	341
展厅	544	通信卫星	442	球籍	340
展销	544	通透	442	球员	341
展播	543	通胀	442	球龄	341
剧协	233	通勤	441	球幕电影	341
剧运	233	通勤车	441	理论界	262
剧坛	233	通膨	441	理论至上	262
剧评	233	难产	301	理疗	262
剧组	233	预考	535	理念	262
剧展	233	预制板	535	理顺	262
剧减	233	预制构件	535	理赔	262
剧增	233	预备党员	534	培干	317
验收团	506	预备期	534	域名	535
验收组	506	预选	535	教工	213
验钞机	506	预委会	535	教代会	213
验资	506	预展	535	教务长	213
弱化	360	预售	535	教务处	213

教师节	213	控产压库	247	基本核算单位	195
教条主义	213	控诉会	247	基本路线	195
教改	213	控购	247	基本群众	196
教改组	213	控股	247	基因	196
教育附加费	214	控股公司	247	基因工程	196
教育面	214	控编	247	基层政权	196
教学大纲	214	探风	429	基建	196
教学医院	214	探明	429	基础工业	196
教参	213	探空气球	429	基础科学	196
教研组	214	探视	429	黄牛	189
教研室	214	探查	429	黄条	189
教龄	213	探亲假	429	黄金	189
教委	213	探察	429	黄皮书	189
教职工	214	探摸	429	黄金海岸	189
教职员工	214	探家	429	黄带	189
排头兵	314	掺杂使假	43	黄昏恋	189
排污	314	掺沙子	43	黄牌	189
排坛	314	职工代表大会	554	黄潮	189
排忧解难	314	职大	553	著作权	566
排放	314	职中	555	果珍	165
排险	314	职介	554	菜牛	38
排档	313	职介所	554	菜农	38
排序	314	职业中学	555	菜畜	38
排涝	314	职业病	554	菜场	38
排难解优	314	职业道德	555	菜鸽	38
排灌	314	职代会	554	菜蓝子	38
排灌站	314	职务工资	554	菜蓝子工程	38
推入	451	职级	554	营业员	525
推出	450	职改	554	营运	525
推介	451	职改办	554	营养学	525
推拒	451	职校	554	营养食堂	525
推陈出新	450	职高	554	营养钵	525
推展	451	职等	554	营养灶	525
推理小说	451	基干民兵	196	营员	525
推普	451	基本工资	195	营销	525
掠影	282	基本口粮	195	营销学	525
接轨	215	基本功	195	雪坛	502
接访	215	基本矛盾	196	雪柜	502
接待日	215	基本劳动日	195	雪雕	502
接班人	215	基本建设		雪顿节	502
控办	247	经济学	195	检修	207

词目表 十一画

检测	207	晚汇报	458	第一世界	94
检举箱	207	晚生代	458	第一产业	94
检索	207	晚育	458	第一把手	94
检疫	207	晚点	457	第一线	94
检察院	207	晚恋	458	第一夫人	94
梯队	434	晚婚	458	第一类物资	94
梯次	434	喇叭裤	253	第一流	94
梳辫子	405	啤酒肚	321	第一梯队	94
副标题	131	唱主角	46	第二文化	93
副研	131	唱盘	46	第二世界	93
副食本	131	唯上	462	第二产业	92
副食关系	131	唯书	462	第二线	93
副食商店	131	唯生产力论	462	第二类物资	93
票证	322	唯成份论	461	第二课堂	93
票贩子	322	唯条件论	462	第二职业	93
票房价值	322	唯武器论	462	第二梯队	93
票提	322	唯实	462	第三世界	93
票霸	322	唯我独左	462	第三产业	93
聋童	279	唯我独革	462	第三线	94
硅谷	162	唯意志论	462	第三者	94
硕导	412	蛇头	385	第三类物资	93
辅导员	131	跃居	537	第三梯队	93
辅料	131	圈批	343	第四产业	94
【丨】		圈护	343	移动电话	518
		圈定	343	移动通讯	518
常见病	44	圈阅	343	袋装	81
常设	44	崭露头角	543	停机	441
常规武器	44	崇洋非中	55	停产	441
常规战争	44	崇洋哲学	56	停建	441
常规能源	44	崇洋媚外	56	停薪留职	441
常委	44	【丿】		售汇	404
常委会	44			售后服务	404
常智	44	银团	524	售武	404
野人	510	银色浪潮	523	售缺	404
野战军	510	银坛	523	售票员	404
眼库	506	银屏	523	做秀	580
眼量	506	银弹	523	做爱	580
悬疑	500	银弹外交	523	偷逃	445
晨运	51	银牌	523	偷渡	445
晨练	51	甜蜜事业	437	偏远地区	321
晨跑	51	笨鸟先飞	25	偏饭	321

偏科	321	领导班子	275	商社	382
偏食	321	领导核心	276	商函	381
偏题	321	领导骨干	275	商城	381
假大空	205	船难	62	商战	382
假劣	205	船检	62	商品化	381
假条	205	脱口秀	453	商品房	381
假性近视	205	脱产	453	商品经济	382
假冒	205	脱岗	453	商品畜	381
偶像明星	312	脱困	453	商品棉	382
铜牌	442	脱贫	454	商品粮	382
得主	88	脱盲	453	商贸	381
猜奖	36	脱毒	453	商亭	382
猴市	183	脱敏	453	商厦	382
猎头公司	274	脱钩	453	商海	381
猎装	275	脱氧核糖核酸	454	商流	381
猫儿腻	286	脱脂	454	商调	381
猫耳洞	286	脱期	454	商展	382
猛增	290	脱帽加冕	453	商检	381
够意思	153	脱销断档	454	商嫂	382
盘活	315	脱瘾	454	商摊	382
盘档	315			商潮	381
盘菜	315	【、】		康帕斯	240
盘整	315			康体	240
盒饭	175	减亏	208	康复车	240
盒式录音机	175	减负	208	康复国际	240
盒式磁带	175	减并	208	望子成龙	459
鸽派	141	减灾	208	谋职	298
彩车	37	减肥	208	谜团	290
彩电	37	减幅	208	着装	572
彩印	38	减员	208	粗肥	66
彩扩	37	减税	208	粗放经营	66
彩色片	38	减缓	208	粗放型	66
彩色电视	38	盗版	88	粗养	66
彩纸	38	盗录	88	粗菜	66
彩卷儿	37	盗伐	88	断线	107
彩灯	37	情人节	339	断指再植	107
彩球	38	情商	339	断档	106
彩照	38	情治	339	断想	107
彩管	37	情结	339	剪刀差	208
彩旗	38	惯骗	160	递减	95
领办	275	商业街	382	递增	95
		商机	381		

婆婆	326	盖浇饭	135	维和	462
婆婆嘴	326	盖了	135	维纶	462
清仓挖潜	338	盖洛普	135	维棉	462
清仓查库	338	盖帽儿	135	综合大学	576
清队	338	寄销	201	综合平衡	576
清污	339	密报	290	综合劳动服务	576
清产核资	338	密码箱	290	综合治理	576
清运	339	密商	290	综指	576
清组织	339	密植	290	绿化工程规划	280
清经济	338	密集劳动	290	绿卡	281
清查	338			绿色产品	281
清思想	338	【一】		绿色长城	281
清退	339	隆乳	279	绿色证书	281
清场	338	随行就市	425	绿色革命	281
清障	339	随军	424	绿色食品	281
清洁工	338	随份子	424	绿色GNP	281
清资	339	随身听	425	绿色照明	281
清理阶级队伍	338	隐形	524	绿色塑料	281
添加剂	436	隐形人	524	绿条	281
添砖加瓦	436	隐形眼镜	524	绿证	281
渎职罪	105	隐性	524	绿党	280
混双	192	隐性就业	524	绿茵	281
混关	192	弹力衫	428	绿茵场	281
混级抬价	192	弹拨乐	428	绿委会	281
混纺	192	弹钢琴	428	绿衣使者	281
混凝剂	192	弹劾	428	续建	500
深化	389	骑警	330	续展	500
深加工	389	蛋鸡	83		
深指	390			**十二画**	
深挖洞,广积粮,不称霸	389	【丶】		【一】	
渔工商联合企业	533	婚外恋	192	款爷	250
渔区	533	婚补	191	超支户	49
渔政	533	婚育期	192	超生	48
涵盖	168	婚恋	192	超生游击队	48
淡化	83	婚检	192	超市	48
液化气	511	婚假	192	超负荷	47
液化气罐	511	绩优股	198	超产	47
液压技术	511	绯闻	125	超产粮	47
盖	135	维生素	462	超导	47
盖饭	135	维尼纶	462	超收	48
		维权	462		

超级大国	48	提干	434	联产到劳	264
超级市场	48	提价	434	联产承包	264
超级城市	48	提级	434	联产承包责任制	264
超声波	48	提速	434	联体	265
超纲要	47	提租补贴	434	联机检索	265
超英赶美	48	提掖	434	联社	265
超购加价	47	提纯复壮	434	联购联销	265
超购粮	47	提留	434	联姻	266
超标	47	提职	434	联谊	265
超前	48	握手言欢	468	联谊会	265
超前消费	48	握手言和	468	联展	266
超前精神	48	揭丑	214	联营	266
超耗	47	揭老底	215	联营户	266
超龄团员	48	揭批	215	联检	265
超容	48	揭秘	215	联销	265
超常	47	揭盖子	214	联赛	265
超甜玉米	48	揭牌	215	联播	264
超越遏制	49	援建	536	厨艺	60
超短波	47	援借	536	雁过拔毛	506
超短裙	47	援藏	536	斑马线	12
超储	47	插队落户	41	期市	329
超编	46	插红旗	42	期房	329
趋同	341	插杠子	41	期望值	329
趋同化	341	插足	42	欺行霸市	329
趋利避害	341	插秧机	42	散手	378
朝阳工业	544	插播	41	散记	378
博导	32	揪斗	231	散件	378
博士后	32	搀水股票	43	散货	378
博爱工程	32	搀杂兑假	43	散客	378
塔吊	426	替身演员	435	敬业	231
塔式	426	替补	435	敬老院	230
塔楼	426	替补队员	435	落下帷幕	283
搭车	69	联手	265	落马	283
搭卖	69	联户	265	落地灯	282
搭班子	69	联办	264	落地扇	283
搭载	69	联动	265	落实	283
搭桥	69	联网	265	落标	282
搭桥牵线	69	联合体	265	落聘	283
搭售	69	联产计酬	265	落幕	283
揽胜	254	联产到人	265	森林公园	379
揽储	254	联产到户	264	森警	379

棋圣	330	【丨】		黑白机	176
棋坛	330			黑字	178
棒协	15	敞开思想	46	黑客	177
棒杀	14	最佳	580	黑匣子	178
棒针	15	最佳精神	580	黑条子	177
棒针衫	15	最高指示	580	黑社会	177
植物人	555	量化	273	黑货	176
植保	555	量刑	273	黑金政治	177
植被	555	暑运	406	黑线	178
棍子	163	景区	230	黑线人物	178
棚户	319	景观	230	黑线专政	178
棉白糖	291	景点	230	黑经济	177
棉华达呢	291	晶体管	223	黑箱作业	178
棉农	291	喷云吐雾	319	黑帮	176
棉花糖	291	喷气式	319	黑样板	178
棉府绸	291	喷浆	318	黑孩	176
棉茧绸	291	喷灌	318	黑洞	176
逼和	25	喝西北风	170	黑牌	177
逼供信	25	喝墨水	170	黑道	176
硬功夫	527	跑火	316	黑潮	176
硬件	528	跑面	316		
硬任务	528	跑冒滴漏	316	【丿】	
硬设备	528	跌幅	100	销区	486
硬赤字	527	跌势	100	销价	485
硬技术	527	遗传工程学	518	销脏	486
硬投入	528	遗传密码	518	销量	486
硬环境	527	跆拳道	427	锈蚀	497
硬指标	528	蛤蟆夯	167	铺路	327
硬科学	528	蛙人	455	铺路石	327
硬笔	527	赎买政策	406	馊主意	423
硬卧	528	赌风	106	毽球	209
硬席	528	黑七类	177	短平快	106
硬座	528	黑八论	175	短导	106
硬通货	528	黑马	177	短线	106
确保	346	黑五类	178	短线专业	106
裂变	274	黑车	176	短线产品	106
雄风	499	黑手	177	短池	106
雄踞	499	黑手党	177	短尺少秤	106
雅皮士	504	黑六论	177	短训班	106
雅钱	504	黑户口	176	短斤缺两	106
翘尾巴	336	黑白电视	176	短效	106

词目	页码	词目	页码	词目	页码
短期行为	106	集市贸易	199	象形食品	485
短程	106	集成电路	199	【、】	
智力工程	557	集成板	199		
智力开发	557	集约化经营	199	装卸工人	571
智力支边	558	集约经营	200	痦气	321
智力引进	558	集体化	199	裙裤	346
智力投资	557	集体户	199	裤袜	248
智力库	557	集体主义	199	普九	328
智力测验	557	集体英雄主义	199	普六	328
智产阶级	557	集体经济	199	普法	327
智育第一	558	集体宿舍	199	普治	328
智残	557	集体所有制	199	普建	328
智龄	558	集贸市场	199	普测	327
智障	559	集资	200	普校	328
智囊团	558	集装运输	200	普惠制	328
智能	558	集装箱	200	普高	328
智能化产品	558	集餐	199	普调	328
智能卡	558	焦裕禄精神	211	普通话	328
智能建筑	558	傍大款	15	普教	328
智能服装	558	储运	60	善待	381
智能型	558	储备粮	60	尊师	580
智商	558	储源	60	尊师重教	580
智密区	558	储币待购	60	尊师爱生	580
程控	52	牌号	314	道德法庭	88
稀植	479	奥班	6	港人	137
税负	411	奥校	6	港台	138
税利	411	奥委会	6	港事	137
税政	411	街景	215	港星	138
税基	411	街道工厂	215	港府	137
税款	411	街道办事处	215	港衫	137
等外品	88	街道企业	215	港式	137
等价交换	88	街道服务站	215	港属	138
等身	88	惩办主义	52	港商	137
等量劳动	88	惩处	52	港澳	137
等额选举	88	惩罚价格	52	湖吃海喝	184
筒子楼	443	惩前毖后，		温室效应	464
筒裤	442	治病救人	52	温馨	464
筒裙	443	腈纶	225	温饱工程	464
答卷	70	腕	458	滋扰	573
答疑	70	禽苗	337	滞压	559
筛选	380	禽场	337	滞后	559

滞背	559	【一】		编钟	27
滞洪	559				
滞胀	559	强人	334	**十三画**	
滞容	559	强手	334		
滞缓	559	强化	333	【一】	
溅落	209	强化食品	334	鼓足干劲	154
滑水	186	强加于人	334	鼓劲	154
滑草	186	强买强卖	334	摸底	297
滑坡	186	强劳	334	摸老虎屁股	297
滑雪衫	186	强身	334	摸透	297
游山玩水	531	强制机关	334	摸论	297
游斗	531	强制劳动	334	摸着石头过河	297
游击习气	531	强项	334	摄制	385
游乐园	531	强势	334	摄录	385
游乐场	531	骗买骗卖	322	摄录机	385
游戏机	531	骗赔	322	摄像机	385
游资	531	骗销	322	摆功评好	11
童贩	442	登山服	88	摆件	12
童星	442	疏运	406	摆花架子	12
童商	442	疏解	405	摆放	11
童装	442	疏离	406	摆桌	12
割尾巴	141	疏理	406	搬迁	12
割资本主义尾巴	141	疏港	405	搬迁户	12
富民	133	隔离审查	144	搬运工人	12
富民政策	133	隔离带	144	辐照	130
富农	133			摇摆乐	509
富国	133	【ㄴ】		摇摆舞	509
富裕中农	133			摇滚乐	509
寓教于乐	534	媒体	288	搞小圈子	141
窝工	468	媚俗	289	搞卫生	141
窝气	468	缉毒	198	搞对象	141
窝电	468	缓行	188	搞活	141
窝边草	468	缓建	188	搞通思想	141
窝囊气	468	缓解	188	摊车	428
窝里斗	468	编队	27	摊书	428
窝脏	468	编外	27	摊主	428
窗口	63	编发	27	摊市	428
窗口行业	63	编列	27	摊位	428
窜升	67	编导	27	摊贩	428
雇佣观点	155	编报	27	摊点	428
雇佣思想	155	编采	27	摊档	428
		编委	27		

十三画　词目表

词目	页码	词目	页码	词目	页码
摊商	428	楼堂馆所	279	遣俘	333
摊棚	428	楼群	279	鉴证	208
摊群	428	概念化	135	暗处理	5
填平补齐	436	概念车	135	暗补	5
填鸭式教学法	436	输血	405	暗贴	5
瑜珈	532	输面	405	暗箱作业	5
聘用	324	输家	405	暖身	311
聘任	324	感冒	136	照主	545
聘约	324	碰头会	319	照排	545
聘选	324	碰克	319	蜕化变质分子	451
聘职	324	碰软	319	蜂王浆	129
聘期	324	碰硬	319	蜂窝煤	129
酬宾	57	碰碰车	319	睡袋	411
勤工助学	336	碰碰船	319	督导	205
勤杂工	337	碑廊	23	督政	205
勤政	337	雷区	260	督学	205
勤俭办社	336	雷打不动	260	督查	104
勤俭建国	336	雷射	260		
蒸气熨斗	546	雷锋精神	260	【丿】	
蒸气浴	546	零部件	275	错位	68
墓群	298	零料	275	错案	28
幕墙	298			错漏	28
蓝色农业	253	【丨】		锦标主义	222
蓝领工人	253	愚人节	532	锦纶	222
蓝帽子	253	愚公精神	532	筹交	57
蓝筹股	253	歇班	492	筹拍	57
蓄水保墒	500	歇菜	439	筹建	57
蓄洪工程	500	跳槽	492	筹组	57
蓄洪区	500	跳蚤市场	439	筹委会	57
蒙古大夫	290	跨世纪	248	筹资	57
蒙在鼓里	289	跨纲要	248	签约	333
蒙混过关	289	跨国公司	248	签批	332
献艺	483	跨黄河	248	简历	208
献血	483	路风	279	简化汉字	207
献映	484	路考	280	简写	208
献演	483	路线斗争	280	简并	207
禁区	222	路障	280	简报	207
禁运	222	路肩	280	简易房	208
禁毒	222	路警	280	简明新闻	208
禁赛	222	跻身	195	简政放权	208
楼宇	279	跟班劳动	145	简介	208

傻大黑粗	380	腾退	433	新殖民主义	494
傻瓜相机	380	触电	60	新领工人	493
傻冒	380	触角	61	新新人类	494
傻蛋	380	触及	61	新意	494
催动	69	解教	219	新影厂	494
催产素	69	解押	220	新潮	493
躲让	110	解禁	219	意见簿	521
微车	460	解困	220	意见箱	521
微电子技术	460	解困房	220	意气风发	521
微电脑	460	解危	220	意向书	521
微机	460	解释学	220	意识流	521
微机病毒	460	解冻	219	廉政	266
微观世界	460	解放干部	219	粮油关系	267
微观经济	460	解放区	219	粮油补贴	267
微货	460	解放军	219	粮状元	267
微软	460	解放战争	219	粮票	267
微客	460	解放思想	219	粮管所	266
微刻	460	解剖麻雀	220	数字化	407
微科学	460	解读	219	数字地球	406
微笑服务	460	【、】		数字电视	407
微轿	460			数字服装	407
微脑	460	新人类	493	数字激光视盘	407
微雕	460	新人口论	493	数据库	406
微型	460	新中农	494	数控	406
微型小说	461	新长征	493	数管齐下	406
微型机	461	新长征突击手	493	塑料贴面	424
微型技术	461	新生力量	493	塑料袋	424
微波炉	460	新生代	493	塑料鞋	424
微波能	460	新生事物	493	塑料壁纸	424
微调	460	新西兰	494	煤气罐	288
微缩	460	新产业革命	492	煤老虎	288
遥测	509	新兴力量	494	煤质	288
遥想	509	新医疗法	494	煤倒	288
遥诊	509	新秀	494	煤砖	288
遥控	509	新招	494	满天飞	286
遥感	509	新苗	493	满负荷工作	285
遛早儿	279	新高	493	满产满报	285
腰牌	509	新贫族	493	满园春色	286
腾飞	433	新岸	492	满点	285
腾让	433	新星	494	满员	286
腾出	433	新闻片	494	满堂红	286

十三画-十四画 词目表

满堂灌	286	墙布	333	管教	160
满勤	286	摺挑子	274	管教所	160
滥发	254	摘取	543	豪华型	170
溢价	522	摘除	543	豪的	170
滚打	162	摘帽	543	腐化变质分子	131
滚雪球	163	摘帽右派	543	瘟神	464
溺弃	304	摘播	543	旗帜鲜明	330
滤嘴香烟	280	榻榻米	426	敲定	335
溜门撬锁	276	模糊语言	297	煽情	380
溜拍	276	歌王	141	慢件	286
溜派	276	歌后	141	慢班	286
溜撬	276	歌坛	141	慢镜头	286
福利院	131	歌星	141	精讲多练	223
福祉	131	歌迷	141	精兵简政	223
裸戏	282	酷	248	精英	225
裸露土地	282	酸奶	424	精制	225
		酸豆乳	424	精饲料	224
【一】		酸雨	424	精品	223
殿堂	98	遭灾	540	精选	224
群防群治	346	磁化杯	65	精养	225
群体	346	磁卡	65	精神万能	224
群英会	346	磁卡电话	65	精神支柱	224
群雕	346	磁疗法	65	精神公害	224
群众工作	347	磁带	65	精神文明	224
群众专政	347	磁带录音机	65	精神污染	224
群众团体	347	磁碟	65	精神产品	224
群众关系	347	磁浮列车	65	精神武器	224
群众观点	347	磁浮铁道	65	精神贵族	224
群众性	347	磁悬浮列车	65	精神食粮	224
群众组织	347	稳产高产	467	精神原子弹	224
群言堂	346	稳准狠	467	精神鸦片	224
群众路线	347	稳拿	467	精神枷锁	224
		稳操胜券	467	精瘦	224
十四画		鲜活	482	精料	223
		管片	160	精读	223
静止轨道	230	管卡压	160	精简机构	223
熬年头	6	管件	159	精煤	223
截瘫病人	217	管护	159	滴滴涕	89
截留	217	管制劳动	160	滴灌	89
截流	217	管线	160	演职人员	506
境外	230	管界	160	演练	506

演播	506	增幅	541	影剧院	526
漏斗户	279	增值税	542	影票	526
漏划地主	279	增资	542	影圈	526
漏判	279	增量	541	影楼	526
赛区	362	增销	542	影赛	526
赛风	362	鞍钢	3	题外话	434
赛事	362	鞍钢宪法	3	题写	435
赛制	362	横扫	178	题库	434
赛艇	362	横向	178	题海战术	434
赛势	362	横向联合	178	踢皮球	434
赛场	362	震派	546	踩点	37
赛程	362	震情	546	踏足	426
缩印	425	弊政	26	镇反运动	546
缩微	425	暴力工具	22	靠边儿	242
熊市	499	暴力机器	22	靠边站	242
		暴丑	22	舞坛	476
十五画		暴发户	22	舞星	476
		暴走族	22	舞迷	476
撮一顿	67	暴露思想	22	德才兼备	88
播出	31	暴跌	22	褒誉	18
播发	31	暴富	22	褒恤	18
播讲	31	瞎指挥	480	遵纪守法	580
播报	31	瞎信	480	额度	111
播放	31	瞒报	285	潜亏	333
播映	31	影子股	526	潜水器	333
播唱	31	影业	526	潜地导弹	333
播散	31	影协	526	潜返	333
撞车	571	影后	526	潜质	333
撤并	50	影坛	526	潜科学	333
撤军	51	影视	526	潜能	333
撂荒	274	影城	526	潮汐电站	49
增亏	541	影带	526	澳抗	6
增产节约	541	影星	526	澳属	6
增设	542	影界	526	嬉皮士	478
增收	542	影碟	526	慰安妇	463
增收增支	542	影碟机	526		
增选	542	影帝	526	**十六画**	
增容	541	影射史学	526		
增容费	541	影调	526	操办	40
增值	542	影展	526	融物	356
增殖	542	影剧	526	融资	357

融通	356	壁纸	26	镭射唱片	261
飙升	29	壁饰	26	镭射影碟	261
薪炭林	492	壁挂	26	翻车	116
薄利多销	32	壁球	26	翻斗车	116
薄膜	32	避风港	26	翻老帐	116
整风	547	避孕环	26	翻身	116
整团	547	避孕药具	26	翻身斗争	116
整合	547	避孕套	26	翻身户	117
整社	547	避孕栓	26	翻身奴隶	117
整改	547	避税	26	翻身农民	117
整复	547	避震	26	翻身农奴	117
整党	547			翻改	116
整党建党	547	**十七画**		翻建	116
橡皮图章	485			翻录	116
餐位	38	戴帽小学	79	翻番	116
餐饮	38	擦边球	36	翻船	116
餐鸽	38	擦屁股	36	翻牌公司	116
餐盒	38	藏书票	40	鹰派	525
嘴烟	580	藏医	540		
噪光	540	藏学	539	**十九画**	
噪声监控	540	藏品	40		
赞助	539	藏胞	539	警力	230
篮坛	253	繁体字	117	警车	230
篡军	66	徽记	190	警民	230
篡国	66	徽标	190	警阶	230
篡政	67	朦胧诗	290	警政	230
篡党	66	癌变	1	警亭	230
篡党夺权	66	癌痛	1	警督	230
儒法斗争	357	癌魔	1	警嫂	230
儒商	357	赢面	525	警务	230
膨化	319	赢球	526	警衔	230
膨化食品	319			警容	230
磨合	297	**十八画**		警徽	230
瘾君子	524			蘑菇云	297
燎原计划	274	覆盖率	132	攀比	315
燃爆	348	鞭打快牛	27	攀升	315
懒汉鞋	254	蹦极	25	蹲点	109
糖衣炮弹	429	蹦迪	25	蹲点跑面	109
糖弹	429	蹦蹦车	25	蹼泳	328
激光	198	镭射电影	261	曝光	22
激光视盘	198				

爆冷门	22	魔球	297	字根	576
爆响	22	魔棍	297	B超	7
爆炸性消息	22	灌区	160	BB机	7
爆棚	22	灌制	160	BP机	7
爆满	22	灌录	160	CD机	36
爆燃	22	灌装	160	T恤	426
		霹雳舞	320	863计划	7

二十画以上

		霸气	9	211工程	112
		霸权主义	9	571工程纪要	473
魔方	297	罐装	160		

A

a

阿盟 Ā - Méng
the League of Arab States
Abbreviation for 阿拉伯国家联盟 the League of Arab States.

ai

挨斗 ái - dòu
to suffer criticism and be struggled against
E.g. 他在"文革"中经常挨斗。*He was often struggled against during the Cultural Revolution.* / 他永远忘不了挨斗的滋味。*He will never forget the taste of being struggled against.*

挨棍子 ái gùnzi
to be hit with a stick
A metaphor for being subjected to criticism and attack.
E.g. 他在政治运动中挨了不少棍子。*He was subjected to a great deal of criticism and attack during the political movement.* / 挨棍子他不怕。*He is not even afraid of being criticized and attacked.*

挨批 ái - pī
to be subjected to criticism
E.g. 他之所以挨批,是因为工作没有做好。*The reason why he was subjected to criticism is that he did not perform well in his work.* / 他挨批后工作比以前认真了。*After he was criti-*

cized, he became more earnest in his work than before.

挨整 ái - zhěng
to be subjected to punishment; to suffer bitterness
E.g. 不能等着挨整。*One cannot just sit and wait to be punished.* / 他怕得罪人,挨整。*He is afraid of offending others and suffering punishment (for it).*

癌变 áibiàn
transformation of normal cells to cancerous cells; transformation of a benign ailment to cancer
E.g. 最近他因患胃溃疡癌变动了手术。*Due to the transformation of his ulcer into cancer, he was operated on recently.* / 萎缩性胃炎往往是癌变的前兆。*Atrophic gastritis is often the precursor of cancer.*

癌魔 áimó
"cancer demon," metaphor for cancer
E.g. 癌魔夺去了他的生命。*The "cancer demon" has snatched his life away.*

癌痛 áitòng
pain caused by cancer

艾滋病 àizībìng
AIDS; Aids
Short for 后天免疫缺乏综合症 Acquired Immune Deficiency Syndrome.
E.g. 艾滋病患者日益增多。*Aids patients are increasing in number each*

day.

爱厂如家 ài chǎng rú jiā
to love the factory as family
To cherish the factory as much as one's own family.

爱国公约 àiguó gōngyuē
patriotic pledge
Pledges formulated voluntarily in the early 1950s by residents of China's cities and countryside, as well as by grass-roots units, for ardently loving the motherland and abiding by laws and regulations.

爱国卫生运动 àiguó wèishēng yùndòng
patriotic health campaign
A mass health campaign conducted nationwide from 1952 on. Central to the campaign are eradicating the four pests (flies, rats, bedbugs and mosquitoes), emphasizing hygiene, and eradicating diseases.

爱民公约 àimín gōngyuē
a pledge to love the people
A set of regulations, adopted by the Chinese People's Liberation Army, People's Police Units and their personnel, to be concerned with and protective of the masses, and to serve the people with one's heart and mind.

爱民月活动 àimínyuè huódòng
love-the-people monthly activities
Activities conducted by China's public security personnel every year around New Year or Spring Festival to highlight policies, observance of discipline, love for the people, and its close relationship with the masses. These activities take on the following main forms: conducting police-citizen seminars, making reports on their work to the masses, listening to people's opinions and criticisms, examining the observance of discipline and the enforcement of policies. The goal is to do well by the people and to serve them even better.

爱人 àirén
spouse; husband or wife

爱社如家 ài shè rú jiā
to love the commune as family
To cherish the people's commune as one's own family.

爱委会 ài-wěi-huì
patriotic committee
Abbreviation for 爱国卫生运动委员会 the Patriotic Public Health Campaign Committee. Taking prevention as its guiding principle, the committee is responsible for: integrating routine and extraordinary measures; running health campaigns to eliminate scourges and diseases; lowering the rate of infectious diseases; improving urban and rural sanitary conditions; raising the level of people's health. Also called 爱卫会 Patriotic Health Committee.

爱卫会 ài-wèi-huì
Patriotic Health Committee
Abbreviation for 爱国卫生运动委员会 Patriotic Public Health Campaign Committee. Also called 爱委会.

爱校如家 ài xiào rú jiā
to love school as family
To cherish one's school as much as one's own family.

爱心 àixīn
loving heart
The mentality of being kind and tender toward others.

爱牙日 àiyárì

Love Teeth Day

A special day set aside for activities promoting oral hygiene and dental care; September 20 of each year has been designated Love Teeth Day.

爱资病 àizībìng
"love-capitalism sickness"

The Eulogizing of capitalism, and the pursuit of a bourgeois life style.
E.g. 有些人得了爱资病。*Some people have contracted the "love-capitalism sickness," i.e., have embraced capitalism.*

爱滋病 àizībìng
AIDS; Aids
Same as 艾滋病:

an

鞍钢 Ān-Gāng
Anshan Iron and Steel Company
Abbreviation for 鞍山钢铁公司 Anshan Iron and Steel Company.

鞍钢宪法 Ān-Gāng Xiànfǎ
Charter of the Anshan Iron and Steel Company

毛泽东1960年提出的管理社会主义企业的根本原则。基本内容是：坚持政治挂帅，加强党的领导，大搞群众运动，实行两参（干部参加劳动，工人参加企业管理）、一改（改革不合理的规章制度）、三结合（工人、干部和技术人员三结合），开展技术革新和技术革命。
The basic principles expounded by Mao Zedong in 1960 for the management of socialist enterprises. The content of the principles are: uphold the command of politics; strengthen the Party's leadership; promote mass campaigns; implement the two participations (cadres participating in labor; workers participating in management), the one reform (reform unreasonable rules and regulations), and the unity of three elements (the unity of workers, cadres, and technicians); launch technical innovations and revolutions.

安办 ān-bàn
re-settlement office
Abbreviation for 安置办公室 re-settlement office. 1) Offices set up in the relevant government departments to re-settle ex-servicemen who are demobilized or changing careers. 2) Offices that were set up at one time in relevant government departments to re-settle educated youths returning from the countryside to the city.

安钉子 ān dīngzi
to install a "nail"
Metaphor for implanting someone of one's own camp in the midst of the opposing camp; To plant one's own trusted followers in a certain organization in order to harm the opponent.
E.g. 四人帮的爪牙，专门搞打砸抢，还搞特务活动，"安钉子"。*The lackeys of the Gang of Four specialized in attacks, vandalism, plundering, intelligence activities, and installing "nails" (planting their trusted followers in a rival group).*

安定团结 āndìng tuánjié
stability and solidarity
A stable political situation in society and solidarity among all the national ethnic groups. This was proposed by Mao Zedong in 1974 to counter the

chaotic situation of the Cultural Revolution.

安家费 ānjiāfèi
fixed sums of money given by the state to relevant personnel for household settlement

安家立业 ānjiālìyè
to establish a family and to build a career

安家落户 ānjiā luòhù
to settle one's home; make one's home in a new place
1) Urban residents and educated youths moving to rural villages to live and participate in labor. 2) Intellectuals taking residence for a term in factories and rural villages in order to understand the life, work, thoughts and feelings of workers and peasants.

安检 ān-jiǎn
safety inspection
Short for 安全检查 safety inspection.

安检站 ān-jiǎn-zhàn
safety inspection station
Short for 安全检查站 safety inspection station.

安居房 ānjūfáng
live in a peace house
Refers to non-profitable houses built by local governments with the state loans and funds raised independently by the local governments for middle and low income families.

安居工程 ānjū gōngchéng
"tranquil-housing" construction project
The Chinese government's construction plan designed to solve China's housing problem. Starting from 1994, in addition to the existing construction targets, 150,000,000 square meters of low cost housing will be built in order to solve the housing problem.
E.g. 我们要确保安居工程的顺利进行。 *We'll guarantee the smooth realization of the residential housing project.*

安老院 ānlǎoyuàn
senior citizens' home; old people's home

安乐死 ānlèsǐ
euthanasia

安乐窝 ānlèwō
an environment or location conducive to a tranquil comfortable life
E.g. 他在为自己经营一个安乐窝。 *He is managing a comfortable nest for himself.* / 整天躺在安乐窝里,工作怎么能做好。 *How can someone who lies in his comfortable nest all day long carry out his work well?*

安理会 ānlǐhuì
Security Council
Abbreviation for 安全理事会 Security Council (of the United Nations).

安民告示 ānmín gàoshì
a notice to reassure the public
1) Originally a notice issued by the government or officials to reassure the public. 2) Usually the term means giving advance notice to concerned individuals about the issue to be discussed or the business at hand.

安全部 ānquánbù
Ministry of Security

安全带 ānquándài
1) safety belt; 2) safety zone

安全岛 ānquándǎo
safety island (traffic)

安全电压 ānquán diànyā
safe voltage

Safe voltage, any voltage below 36 volts, which is low enough not to cause electrical shock or be a serious danger to humans.

安全帽 ānquánmào
safety helmet

安全哨 ānquánshào
safety sentry
Personnel in industrial and mining enterprises responsible for the inspection and supervision of safety and accident prevention.

安全生产 ānquán shēngchǎn
safety in production
A series of measures and activities to create a good and orderly work environment so as prevent accidents.

安全套 ānquántào
condom

安全网 ānquánwǎng
safety net

安全月 ānquányuè
safety month
A month in which industrial and mining enterprises, and public transportation departments launch propaganda and inspection campaigns aimed at production and vehicular safety, and the prevention of accidents. Since 1980, China has designated the month of May as Safety Month. During Safety Month awareness of safe and civilized production is strengthened and earnest efforts are made to solve the practical problems of safety and sanitation.

安营扎寨 ānyíng zhāzhài
(originally) referred to military units setting up tents and railings for encampment; (currently) refers to the construction of temporary lodgings (often done by relatively large-scale construction teams)

按揭 ànjiē
mortgage loan
Mortgage loan given by a bank or financial institution to a home buyer.
E.g. 按揭客户 *mortgage loan client/* 按揭率 *mortgage rate/* 按揭契约 *mortgage contract*

按质论价 àn zhì lùn jià
to base price on quality
To fix the price of a product according to its quality.

按资排辈 àn zī pái bèi
to assign priority according to seniority
Same as 论资排辈.

暗补 àn-bǔ
covert or indirect subsidy
E.g. 通过价格体系改革,把暗补改为明补。*Through reforming the pricing system, a covert subsidy has been changed to an overt subsidy.*

暗处理 àn chǔlǐ
covert operation; to proceed with a matter clandestinely
E.g. 事情不要暗处理,要公开。*Matters should be dealt with openly rather than clandestinely.*

暗贴 àntiē
covert or indirect subsidy
Same as 暗补.

暗箱作业 ànxiāng zuòyè
black case work
To work in secret and let nobody know. Also called 黑箱作业 black case work.

岸吊 àndiào
cranes set up along a harbor

岸炮 ànpào
cannons set up along the coast

案底 àndǐ
criminal record of a certain person kept at a public security organization
E.g. 此人因偷窃而留有案底。 *This person has a criminal record as a result of having committed theft in the past.*

案犯 ànfàn
case criminal
The culprits in a criminal case.
E.g. 案犯全部抓获。*The criminals in the case have all been captured.* / 两个案犯交代了自己的问题。 *The two criminals in the case have confessed to the crime.*

案例 ànlì
documentation
Documents used in analyzing and proving a certain conclusion.
E.g. 典型案例 *classic documentation* / 其他案例正在查处。 *The other documents are being examined and dealt with.*

案证 ànzhèng
criminal evidence

案值 ànzhí
the material value or amount of currency involved in a case
E.g. 这是一起走私大案, 案值800万元人民币。 *This is a big smuggling case involving 8,000,000 yuan.*

ang

昂奋 ángfèn
high spirited; full of vim and vigor
E.g. 昂奋心情 *high spirited* / 他听到这个消息, 精神就昂奋起来。 *When he heard this piece of news, he became high spirited.*

ao

熬年头 áoniántóu
to get by with a mediocre unambitious performance, seeking only to work more years and to make more money
E.g. 评定职称要看业务水平, 不能靠熬年头。 *A professional title should be determined by the level of one's duties, and not by the number of years one has put in.*

奥班 ào-bān
Olympic class
Abbreviation for 奥林匹克班 Olympic class, special classes set up to discover and cultivate talents for the international academic Olympic competitions, or to raise the level of scientific knowledge of especially talented students.

奥委会 Ào-Wěi-Huì
Olympic Committee
Abbreviation for 奥林匹克委员会 Olympic Committee.

奥校 ào-xiào
Olympic school
Abbreviation for 奥林匹克学校 Olympic school, special schools set up to discover and cultivate talents for the international academic Olympic competitions, or to raise the level of scientific knowledge of especially talented students.

澳抗 àokàng
Australian antigen
Type B hepatitis antigen (H B Ag). Formerly called 澳大利亚抗原 Australian antigen or 肝炎相关抗原 hepatitis-associated antigen.

澳属 àoshǔ
Relatives of Macao people living in China's mainland

B

b

B超 B-chāo
type-B ultrasonic
Abbreviation for B型超声波, an X-ray method.
E.g. 明天他去医院做B超。*Tomorrow he is going to the hospital to have a ultrasonic type B X-ray.* / B超检查 *to have ultrasonic type B X-ray exam*

BB机 BB-jī
beeping mechanism
Abbreviated term for a beeping mechanism used in signaling or summoning selected parties

BP机 BP-jī
beeper
Popular term for little device called "beeper" in English. Also called BB机. (cf. 寻呼机)

ba

吧女 bānǚ
bar girl

863计划 bā-liù-sān jìhuà
the 863 Plan
Outline Plan for Advanced Technological Research and Development, proposal made by four scientists in March, 1986. "863" refers to 1986, March.

八宝山 Bābǎoshān
Eight Treasure Mountain
Ba Bao Shan (Eight Treasure Mountain) Revolutionary Public Cemetery in Beijing. People of Beijing now refer to dying as "going to or entering Ba Bao shan".

八互 bāhù
eight mutuals
指周恩来、邓颖超夫妇根据共产主义道德和彼此相处的实践所提出的夫妻关系中应当遵循的八项原则，即：互敬、互爱、互信、互勉、互助、互让、互谅、互慰。
The eight principles that married couples should adhere to, as proposed by Zhou Enlai and his wife Deng Yingchao. The eight principles, based on communist morality and Zhou and Deng's experience in their relationship, are: mutual respect, mutual love, mutual trust, mutual encouragement, mutual help, mutual compromise, mutual forgiveness, and mutual consolation.

八级工资制 bājí gōngzīzhì
eight-grade wage system
One type of wage system currently in existence in China. The wages of workers are classified into eight ranks according to the complexity of the work and the degree of technical proficiency. The eighth rank is the highest. Highly technical kinds of work can have a maximum of only fourth or fifth rank.

八五 bāwǔ

the Eighth Five-Year Plan
Abbreviation for 八五计划.

八五计划 bāwǔ jìhuà
the Eighth Five-Year Plan
Abbreviation for 中华人民共和国国民经济和社会发展第八个五年计划 the Eighth Five-Year (1991-1995) Plan for the National Economic and Social Development of the People's Republic of China. Also called 八五.

八项经济技术指标 bāxiàng jīngjì jìshù zhǐbiāo
the eight economic and technical indicators
全面考核企业生产经营情况的指标，即产量、品种、质量、消耗、劳动生产率、成本、利润、流动资金占有等八项。

Indicators that give a complete assessment of the production management situation of an enterprise. The eight indicators are: production output, product types, quality, expenditure, the ratio of labor to output, production cost, profit, and the amount of circulating funds.

八一厂 Bā-Yī chǎng
August First Film Studio
Abbreviation for 中国人民解放军八一电影制片厂 August First Film Studio of the Chinese People's Liberation Army.

八一建军节 Bā-Yī Jiànjūnjié
August First Army Day
The founding day of the Chinese People's Liberation Army. On August 1, 1927, the Chinese Communist Party led the Nanchang Uprising, thereby firing the first shot of the armed revolt against the Kuomintang reactionaries. This was the beginning of the Chinese Communist Party's independent leadership of the armed revolution and the founding of the revolutionary army. On July 1, 1933, the Central Workers' and Peasants' Democratic Government passed a resolution designating August 1 as Army Day.

八一面 bāyīmiàn
eighty-one flour
"eighty-one flour", another name for wheat, derived from the fact that eighty-one catties of flour can be ground from one hundred catties of wheat.

八字方针 bā zì fāngzhēn
the Eight-Character Principle
1) 中国在50年代初采取的"调整、巩固、充实、提高"的调整和发展国民经济的方针。2) 70年代末提出的"调整、改革、整顿、提高"的方针。

1) The policy of revamping, consolidating, strengthening, and upgrading that China adopted in the early 1950s as a means of developing. 2) The policy of revamping, reforming, rectifying, and upgrading proposed in the late 1970s.

八字宪法 bā zì xiànfǎ
the Eight-Point Charter
即农业八字宪法。
The Eight-Point Charter for Agriculture. (cf. 农业八字宪法)

巴解 Bā-Jiě
the Palestinian Liberation Organization
Abbreviation for 巴勒斯坦解放组织. Also called 巴解组织.

巴金森氏病 bājīnsēnshìbìng
Parkinson's disease
Parkinson's disease (paralysis agitans), named after the English doctor who first took note of it and described it.

巴士 bāshì
bus

巴统 Bātǒng
Paris Plan Committee

巴黎统筹委员会的简称。主要西方国家对社会主义国家实行封锁禁运的国际组织。1949年11月成立，总部设在巴黎。

Abbreviation for 巴黎统筹委员会, the Chinese name for the Coordinating Committee for Export Control (COCOM), an international organization founded in November, 1949 to impose embargoes on socialist nations (its headquarters are in Paris).

拔白旗 bá báiqí
uprooting negative examples

Referring mainly to the criticism and handling of negative models in a political movement.

E.g. 拔白旗运动 *Movement to eradicate negative examples* / 1958年拔白旗时，他被当做典型受到批判。 *During the 1958 movement to eradicate negative examples, he was criticized as an archetype.*

拔钉子 bá dīngzi
to pull out nails

A metaphor for eliminating obstacles or persons impeding progress.

拔高 bágāo
to deliberately elevate (the rank or status of a person, issue, or thing)

E.g. 评选先进时要实事求是，不要人为地拔高。*We should stick to reality in nominating those who are meritorious, and not artificially elevate people.*

把关 bǎguān
guard a pass

A metaphor for conducting strict inspections according to set standards and for closing loopholes and preventing errors.

E.g. 把好质量关 *guard well the quality*

把脉 bǎmài
hold the pulse

A metaphor for seeking a way to solve a problem through investigation and study.

霸气 bàqì
style or habit of being high handed and unreasonable

E.g. 有的工作人员霸气十足。*Some workers are really domineering.* / 那个人法制观念淡薄，而且有点霸气。*That person has little concept of legality, and is also a bit tyrannical.*

霸权主义 bàquán zhǔyì
hegemonism

罢驶 bàshǐ
drivers' strike

E.g. 昨天有部分香港司机罢驶。*Yesterday there was a strike by some drivers in Hong Kong.*

---

bai

白洞 báidòng
white hole

White hole – the hypothetical antithesis of the black hole – which was proposed by the American astronomer Gamow. It is believed that matter in the universe never vanishes. It is gradually sucked into the black hole, and channeled into a counter-universe. The exit of this channel is the white hole. Thus, indestructible matter is sucked into the black hole and expelled out of the white hole.

白度 báidù
degree of whiteness

白骨精 báigǔjīng
White Bone Demon

A mythical character in the classical Chinese novel *Journey to the West* (also known as Monkey in translations) who was a creature in human form created from a withered bone. She was a highly changeable creature who caught and ate strangers. The name is now a metaphor for devious cunning females.

白亮污染 báiliàng wūrǎn
white light pollution

The negative effect on human vision resulting from excessive light.

白领犯罪 báilǐng fànzuì
white-collar crime

Crimes committed using intelligence and special knowledge. White collar refers to the white-collar class.

白领工人 báilǐng gōngrén
white-collar worker

The opposite of 蓝领工人 blue-collar worker.

白领阶层 báilǐng jiēcéng
white-collar class

白马王子 báimǎ wángzǐ
prince on a white horse; Prince Charming

白牌 báipái
white card

A metaphor for people who belong to no political organization (jocular)

E.g. 我不在组织,是个白牌。 *I am not in the organization, so I am a white card.*

白旗 báiqí
white flag

1) A flag used in battle to signal surrender. 2) A flag used in battle when the opposing sides want to make contact. 3) Backward units that do poor work and are plagued by problems, and individuals with backward or reactionary political ideas. The opposite of a red flag.

E.g. 拔白旗 *to uproot a white flag*

白色革命 báisè gémìng
White Revolution

The promulgation of the technique of using plastic field covering to raise agricultural production. The term is derived from the fact that the covering is white.

E.g. 白色革命使粮食产量提高了。 *The White Revolution has raised grain production.*

白色农业 báisè nóngyè
white agriculture

Also called "white engineering agriculture." It refers to microbiological agriculture and biological cell agriculture. This type of new agricultural production is carried out in super clean controlled indoor environments, where workers all wear white work clothes, hence the term "white agriculture".

白色污染 báisè wūrǎn
white pollution

The environmental pollution caused by discarding plastic field coverings.

白手起家 báishǒu qǐjiā
to raise a house with empty hands; to pull oneself up by one's own bootstraps

Also called 白手成家.

白条 báitiáo
white slip

An informal note without an official seal

affixed, an unofficial memo, etc.

白衣教练 báiyī jiàoliàn
colloquial term for personnel in physical education research

白衣战士 báiyī zhànshì
warriors in white
Namely medical personnel. They save the dying, tend to the wounded, battle diseases, and because they wear a white gown they have been eulogized as white warriors.

白纸 báizhǐ
white paper; clean slate
A metaphor for something that is untainted or devoid of prior bias.
E.g. 中国在科技上从一张白纸到能发射同步卫星,是了不起的飞跃。*In technology, China made an amazing leap in developing from a white paper (i.e., a blank) to a country with the ability to launch synchronized satellites.*

白专 báizhuān
merely-expert
An expression of Leftist ideology in the late 1950s. At that time students and intellectuals were wrongly labeled as peolpe who neglected politics, going the merely-expert path. This term is no longer used.

白专道路 báizhuān dàolù
white and expert path (in the political sense) (cf. 白专)
E.g. 在五十年代,一个刻苦钻研业务的人,往往被斥之为走白专道路。*In the 1950s, a person dedicated to (scientific) research was often denounced as following the white and expert path.*

百分点 bǎifēndiǎn
percentage point (for example, an increase from 3% to 5% is called a rise of 2 percentage points)
E.g. 工业增长率为百分之十,比去年增加二个百分点。*Industrial growth is 10%, up two percentage points from last year.*

百花齐放,百家争鸣
bǎihuā qífàng, bǎijiā zhēngmíng
let a hundred flowers bloom and a hundred schools of thought contend
The policy set forth by the Chinese Communist Party in 1955 for the promotion of the development of the arts and sciences, and of a flourishing socialist culture. Under the premise of strengthening the leadership of the Party and the development of the socialist cause, different forms and different scientific schools could freely engage in rival debate. The abbreviated name of the policy is 双百方针 double hundred policy or 二百方针 two-hundred policy.

百色齐全 bǎisè qíquán
a complete range of colors
A wide selection in the color and style of commodities that satisfies the varied needs of customers.

百褶裙 bǎizhěqún
multi-pleated skirt

摆放 bǎifàng
to settle something in a fixed position
E.g. 摆放位置要合理。*The placement of things should be rational.* / 街道两旁摆放很多花盆。*Many flower pots are placed along both sides of the street.*

摆功评好 bǎigōng pínghǎo
i.e. 评功摆好 (cf. 评功摆好)

摆花架子 bǎi huājiàzi
a metaphor for presenting an attractive facade but in reality lacking substance
E.g. 要防止摆花架子。*We must prevent the practice of hollow attractive facades.*

摆件 bǎijiàn
handicrafts and art objects used for interior decoration
E.g. 各种首饰摆件 *various jewelry and decorative objects*

摆桌 bǎizhuō
to put on a banquet
E.g. 这对青年结婚时不摆桌，不收礼。*This young couple did not put on a banquet or accept gifts at their wedding.* / 订货会不靠礼品、摆桌吸引顾客。*The commodities-ordering conference does not rely on gifts and banquets to attract clients.*

败因 bàiyīn
cause of failure

ban

斑马线 bānmǎxiàn
zebra stripes, painted stripes indicating pedestrian crossings on streets

班车 bānchē
regular bus service; shuttle bus
Usually a vehicle dispatched by an office or organization at fixed times along a fixed route to transport employees to and from work.

班费 bānfèi
activities fee (for school classes, usually paid by the students)

班干 bān-gàn
class cadre
A student who serves as a cadre in class, such as a class monitor.

班会 bānhuì
class meeting (in schools)

班级 bānjí
classes and year levels (in schools)

班组 bānzǔ
teams and groups
A general term for small groups organized in enterprises and institutions for the purpose of work, study, etc.

搬迁 bānqiān
to relocate
E.g. 从东城搬迁到西城 *to relocate from the eastern part of the city to the western part*

搬迁户 bānqiānhù
a relocated unit or household
E.g. 政府拨专款安排搬迁户。*The government allocated special funds to settle the relocated units.* / 对所有搬迁户都做了妥善的安置。*Proper arrangements have been made to settle all the relocated units.*

搬运工人 bānyùn gōngrén
transport worker

板报 bǎnbào
blackboard news
E.g. 每月出两期板报。*News is posted on the board twice monthly.*

板材 bǎncái
board material, boards formed through an industrial process using wood or other materials

板儿爷 bǎnryé
(colloquial) those employed in pedaling flatbed tricycles

版协 bǎn-xié
the Association of Workers in Pub-

lishing
Abbreviated name for 出版工作者协会 the Association of Workers in Publishing.

扮演 bànyǎn
originally, the make-up and role-playing of an actor; now the term refers to the role played by an individual in life or in an event (carries negative connotation)
E.g. 他在这件事中扮演了极不光彩的角色。 *He played an extremely inglorious role in this affair.*

伴音 bànyīn
musical accompaniment (in films and TV programs)

半边天 bànbiāntiān
half the sky
1) A section of the sky. 2) A metaphor for the tremendous role played by new China's women in the socialist revolution and construction. 3) A general term for women of new China.

半导体收音机 bàndǎotǐ shōuyīnjī
semi-conductor radio
Also called 晶体管收音机 transistor radio.

半工半读 bàngōng bàndú
part-time work and study
To work half the day and attend school for the other half, or to work for a period of time and attend school for a period of time. Usually income from one's work pays for tuition and living expenses.

半官方 bànguānfāng
semi-official

半机械化 bànjīxièhuà
semi-mechanization

半截子革命 bànjiézi gémìng
half-way revolutionary
A revolutionary who gives up the cause of revolution halfway, his will fails and he is unable to follow through on the revolution or to maintain the integrity of the revolution to the end.

半劳动力 bànláodònglì
semi-able-bodied worker
A person in a rural village who is physically weak and is only able to do light manual labor. Also called 半劳力 half labor.

半脱产 bàntuōchǎn
A partial sabbatical from work
To use a portion of work time for study or other kinds of work, but to continue normal work for the rest of the work-time. For example, the practice of having workers or cadres work half a day and study half a day is called 半脱产学习 semi-sabbatical study.

半无产阶级 bànwúchǎn jiējí
semi-proletarian
People who have very few means of production and have to sell some of their labor to make ends meet. This includes most of the semi-tenant farmers, small artisans, shop assistants, and peddlers in old China.

办案 bàn'àn
to handle a case
E.g. 充实办案力量 *to strengthen the ability of handling cases* / 严格依法办案 *to rigorously follow the law in handling cases*

办复 bànfù
to handle (a matter) and reply (pertaining to a proposal or draft resolution)
E.g. 办复率 *the rate of response* / 办复工作 *the work of responding to proposals* / 办复提案 1000 多件 *to have*

responded to over one thousand proposals

办结 bànjié
to handle and conclude (a case)
E.g. 所有大案都及时办结。 *All the major cases were concluded in time.*

办学 bànxué
to found an educational institution
E.g. 依靠社会力量办学 *to rely on societal resources in founding a school*

bang

邦联 bānglián
commonwealth
A joint entity formed by several mutually independent nations.
E.g. 邦联方案 *commonwealth plan*

帮厨 bāngchú
kitchen help
Non-cooks who help the cook in the kitchen.

帮倒忙 bāngdàománg
trying to help but causing more trouble in the process
E.g. 宣传不当就会给改革帮倒忙。 *Improper publicity would result in more trouble than help for the reform process.*

帮扶 bāngfú
to help and to support
E.g. 他看见一位老大娘走路很困难，急忙走上去帮扶她。 *As soon as he saw an old lady walking with difficulty, he rushed over to support her.* / 经过领导帮扶，他当了先进典型。 *Through the help and support of the leadership, he became an example to others.*

帮伙 bānghuǒ
cliques formed for the sake of certain common private benefits
E.g. 结成帮伙 *to form a clique* / 盗窃帮伙 *a clique of thieves*

帮伙体系 bānghuǒ tǐxì
gang network
People in society who form gangs and engage in fighting, mugging, robbery, and other crimes.

帮教 bāngjiào
help and teaching
Patient help and teaching administered to juvenile delinquents.

帮派 bāngpài
cliques or factions formed for the sake of certain common private benefits
E.g. 帮派思想 *cliquish mentality* / 帮派活动 *factious activity* / 帮派小集团 *factious clique* / 帮派团伙 *factious clique*

帮派体系 bāngpài tǐxì
factional organization
The counter-revolutionary organization formed during the Cultural Revolution by the counter-revolutionary conspirators Lin Biao, Jiang Qing, and the three types of people who tagged along behind them (those who made their way by rebelling, hard-core factionalists, and ruffians). This clique destroyed the organizational principles and discipline of the proletarian party, incited bourgeois factionalism, created factional divisions, practiced nepotism, suppressed dissent, used the clique for personal gain, usurped a portion of the authority of the Party, the nation, and the military, and created a tremendous loss for the Party and the nation.

棒杀 bàngshā
to attack publicly so as to lead to

defeat

棒协 bàng-xié
the Baseball Association
Abbreviation for 棒球协会 the Baseball Association.

棒针 bàngzhēn
a kind of thick knitting needle suitable for knitting heavy yarn

棒针衫 bàngzhēnshān
heavy-yarn sweaters knitted with thick knitting needles

傍大款 bàngdàkuǎn
to attach to money bags; to accompany a rich man; to rely on someone with a lot of money
The word 大款 means rich man, or money bag.

bao

胞波 bāobō
a term of Burmese origin meaning compatriots and relatives
The Burmese are accustomed to calling the Chinese people 胞波 as a way of expressing endearment.

包产到户 bāochǎn dào hù
production contracted to the household
One form of the agricultural responsibility system. Under the unchanging premise of collective ownership of the basic means of production, the production team ministers unified planning, accounting, and allocation. All or most of the tillable land is contracted out to households on a per-capita equalization basis. Quotas, work points, and investments are determined. The contracting household keeps any surpluses but has to make up any shortfalls. This form closely links material rewards with the peasants' labor, and motivates production.

包产到组 bāochǎn dào zǔ
production contracted to the team
One form of the agricultural responsibility system. Under the premise of unified planning, accounting and allocation by the production team, the labor force is divided into several large field production work teams according to production needs, special labor characteristics, and the residency situation. Moreover, the land, draft animals, medium and large scale farm implements are proportionately allocated to the work teams. Contracts for production, labor and investment outlays are implemented. The work teams can keep any surpluses but must make up for any shortfalls. The work teams bear responsibility for the entire work process of the large fields they contracted and their remuneration is based on the output.

包产田 bāochǎntián
contracted fields
Fields that are contracted from the production team by peasant work teams according to the production responsibility system. (cf. 包产到户 and 包产到组)

包车 bāochē
to charter a vehicle (bus, train car, etc.); a chartered vehicle
E.g. 会议包车太多, 引起旅客的不满。 *The conference has too many chartered buses, which caused the travelers to complain.*

包乘 bāochéng

a group of train or boat attendants who take responsibility for being on duty and for maintenance in a designated area; to charter and ride a vehicle

E.g. 包乘组 *maintenance committee (on a train or boat)* / 这是代表团包乘的飞机。*This is a plane chartered by the delegation.* / 一位外国人长期包乘他的汽车。*A foreigner has leased his car (with chauffeur) for long term.*

包房 bāofáng
to reserve rooms in a hotel or guest house for exclusive use

E.g. 他住在旅馆的包房里。*He is living in a reserved room in a hotel.*

包干到户 bāogān dào hù
work contracted to the household

One form of the agricultural responsibility system, also known as 大包干 big contract work or 家庭承包责任制 family contracted responsibility system. It works as follows: under the premise of maintaining the production team system and the collective ownership of the basic means of production, the production team classifies the tillable land and sets quotas for grain yields. The team then averages out the amount of land per person and contracts the land to households, then signs an agreement with each contracting household. The household pays an agricultural tax and sells a fixed amount of agricultural products to the state according to the terms of the contract. Moreover, the household pays its share of the collective accumulation fund, public welfare fund, and other kinds of assessments. The remaining products are the contractor's to do with as he wishes.

包干到劳 bāogān dào láo
work contracted to the laborer

One form of the agricultural responsibility system whereby land is contracted out to people with labor power. This works the same way as work contracted to the household. (cf. 包干到户)

包干到组 bāogān dào zǔ
labor contracted to the group

One form of the agricultural responsibility system. It works as follows: under the premise of maintaining the production team system and the collective ownership of the basic means of production, the production team classifies the tillable land and determines fixed quotas for grain yields. The team averages out the amount of land per peasant and contracts out the land to voluntarily production groups, then signs an agreement with each contracting group. The group pays an agriculture tax and sells a fixed amount of agricultural products to the state according to the terms of the contract. Moreover the group pays its share of the collective accumulation fund, public welfare fund, and other kinds of assessments. The remaining products are for the contracting group to do with as it sees fit.

包购包销 bāogòu bāoxiāo
exclusive right to purchase and sell

A government commercial department contracts with a production unit to purchase its total production output and assumes responsibility for marketing the goods.

包护小组 bāohù xiǎozǔ
small care teams

Mass social service organizations formed

by urban street agencies with cadres and employees of service agencies to provide a door-to-door service for the elderly, infirm, and handicapped, and to attend to their everyday household needs.

包户扶贫 bāohù fúpín

responsibility to households and aid to the poor

Small groups formed by leaders of the county, communes, and production teams, Communist Party and Youth League members, as well as prosperous peasant families, to divide up and take responsibility for tasks to aid poor peasant families. For example, they teach peasant families that are suffering hardship technical skills and help them to open up diversified businesses. Their aim is to make these families prosper.

包户小组 bāohù xiǎozǔ

small teams with responsibility to households

Mass social service organizations in many cities and villages that are formed voluntarily by the Communist Youth League and other youths to help households in hardship and "five-guarantee households" (cf. 五保户) to overcome difficulties in production and everyday life.

包户制 bāohùzhì

system of responsibility to households

Also known as 包户责任制. The system whereby county, township, and village cadres, together with members of support-households-in-hardship groups, follow their defined responsibilities in helping poor peasant households to develop agricultural production and open up diversified enterprises, so that the poor peasant families may prosper.

包换 bāohuàn

to guarantee to accept the return or exchange (of products that do not meet standards)

E.g. 商品不合格包换。 Exchange or return is guaranteed if the commodity does not meet the standards.

包机 bāojī

to charter a plane; a chartered plane

E.g. 包机服务已开办。 A chartered plane service has begun. / 中国旅游包机公司 China Travel Chartered Plane Company / 定期直航包机航线 scheduled direct flight on a chartered plane

包交提留 bāojiāo tíliú

responsibility for submitting products and paying assessments

After the implementation of the agricultural responsibility system, the producer pays an agricultural tax and sells a fixed amount of agricultural products to the state (包交 responsibility for submitting). The producer also pays his share of the public accumulation fund, public welfare fund and other expenses to the collective (提留 assessments). This is abbreviated as 包交提留.

包装 bāozhuāng

to package

Originally, to wrap or package commodities in paper, boxes, bottles, etc. Now it is a metaphor for the huge publicity given to singers, movie stars, literary works, magazines, etc., in order to generate fame and expand influence. E.g. 包装歌星 to "package" a singer / 包装刊物 to package a magazine

褒恤 bāoxù
compensation for personnel injured or killed in the line of duty

褒誉 bāoyù
to praise and commend

E.g. 他受到大家的褒誉。 *He is praised and commended by everyone.*

保安服务公司 bǎo'ān fúwù gōngsī
security service company (commercial)

保本 bǎoběn
to keep one's capital investment secure, not to lose money

E.g. 保本薄利出售商品住房。 *To sell commodity housing with a guaranteed small return on capital.* / 出版社为了保本，征订数量少的书一般都不出。 *In order to guarantee capital, publishing companies generally do not publish books with low pre-publication orders.*

保底 bǎodǐ
to maintain a floor

To maintain a lowest limit.

E.g. 上不封顶，下不保底。 *To set no ceiling on top, and maintain no floor at the bottom.*

保管员 bǎoguǎnyuán
warehouse attendant; storekeeper

保费 bǎofèi
insurance fee

保函 bǎohán
letter of guarantee

Also called certificate of guarantee, a written document issued by a guarantor (a bank, an enterprise, or an individual) certifying the benefactor's trustworthiness.

保护地 bǎohùdì
protected land, agricultural land protected by facilities that control temperature, prevent high winds, etc.

E.g. 保护地生产投资大。 *The production investment for protected land is high.* / 保护地面积扩大了。 *The acreage of protected land has expanded.*

保护价 bǎohùjià
protected price, the artificially-set price (which can be below the market value) paid by the state when purchasing a certain commodity in order to protect the producers

保护伞 bǎohùsǎn
protective umbrella

1) The use of military power – especially through the intimidating effect of nuclear weapons – by superpowers to protect countries that adhere to them politically and militarily.

E.g. 核保护伞 *nuclear umbrella*

2) A metaphor for using one's power to shield evil people and things.

E.g. 保护伞作用 *the protective umbrella function*

保护主义 bǎohù zhǔyì
protectionism

保皇派 bǎohuángpài
royalists

People who, in the early stage of the Cultural Revolution, supported cadre leaders and Communist Party organizations at all levels. They were opposed to the kicking aside of the Party Committee to make revolution. At the time, these people were derisively called 保皇派 royalists.

保健按摩 bǎojiàn ànmó

therapeutic massage

Pushing, pressing, kneading and rubbing a person's body by hand in order to promote blood circulation, build up skin resistance, and regulate the nerve functions, with the goal of maintaining good health.

保健操 bǎojiàncāo
health exercises

Exercises that synthesize Chinese medical techniques, such as massage and acupressure, in order to prevent illness and improve health. Eye exercises are an example.

保健费 bǎojiànfèi
health fee

1) An item of expense set up by the state specifically to protect the health of workers in state enterprises and institutions. 2) An expense set up specifically to protect the health of workers engaged in extraordinary kinds of work (work that is harmful to health). 3) A nutrition subsidy paid by the state to single children as a way of encouraging fewer births.

保健食品 bǎojiàn shípǐn
health foods

保健所 bǎojiànsuǒ
clinic

A simply equipped medical facility set up by units at the grass-roots level to protect the health of their workers.

保健网 bǎojiànwǎng
health care network

Various levels of organizations for medical treatment and disease prevention set up to protect the people's health.

保健箱 bǎojiànxiāng
health valise; medical kit

A medical valise, containing commonly used drugs and medical instruments, carried by medical workers as they make their rounds.

保健员 bǎojiànyuán
basic level health care workers

保健站 bǎojiànzhàn
health stations

Grass-roots health organization set up in urban neighborhoods, in rural village's production teams, and in enterprises and institutional units. They are responsible, in their respective localities or unit, for carrying out the Patriotic Public Health Campaign which has as its central mission the elimination of scourges and diseases, the administration of medical first-aid, and the management of health propaganda, etc.

保健组织 bǎojiàn zǔzhī
health organizations

保教 bǎo-jiào
child care and education

Contraction of 保育 child care and 教养 education.

E.g. 幼儿园的保教人员 *child care and teaching personnel in kindergartens*

保洁 bǎojié
sanitation

E.g. 保洁工 *sanitation worker* / 保洁工作 *sanitation work*

保理 bǎolǐ
guaranteed management

A method of payment used in international trade whereby financing, accounting, money management, and credit guarantee are rolled into one.

保龄球 bǎolíngqiú
bowling

Also called 地滚球 floor-rolling ball.

保苗 bǎomiáo
to protect seedlings

To ensure that sufficient seedlings are planted in the ground and to promote their healthy growth. This is an important measure in ensuring bountiful harvests.

保墒 bǎoshāng
preserving soil moisture

To preserve the moisture content of the soil in the fields through raking, intertilling, increased ground cover, and other methods, as a means of enhancing sprouting and the growth of crops.

保守疗法 bǎoshǒu liáofǎ
conservative treatment

The use of non-surgical methods for the treatment of complaints usually treated by surgery. These methods can cure illness or improve the general condition of patients as well as the functioning of affected organs. The treatment can also serve as a preparation for surgery. Also known as 非手术疗法 non-surgical treatment.

保守派 bǎoshǒupài
conservatives

保税区 bǎoshuìqū
tax-protected zone

Zones under the jurisdiction of special customs regulations, whereby special customs duty policies and management measures apply. Tax-protected zones have the combined function of manufacturing export commodities and foreign trade. The tax-protection system is comprehensively implemented within such a zone, i.e., imports may enter the zone without customs duties, domestic products entering such a zone are treated as exports, commodities within the zone can be shipped abroad freely.

保四争五 bǎo sì zhēng wǔ
maintain four, strive for five

指在中国国民经济和社会发展第六个五年计划期间(1981－1985)，工农业总产值，在提高经济效益的前提下，保证每年平均增百分之四，在执行中努力争取达到百分之五。

During the period of the Sixth Five-Year Plan (1981-1985) for National Economic and Social Development, under the premise of raising economic benefits, it was proposed that an annual growth rate of 4% should be ensured for the total economic and agricultural output but in practice a rate 5% should be striven for.

保送生 bǎosòngshēng
guaranteed acceptance students, students with excellent characters and academic standards who are accepted into high school without examination

保温杯 bǎowēnbēi
thermo cup

保鲜 bǎoxiān
to retain freshness

To retain the freshness of vegetables, fruit, and other foods, and to prevent shriveling and rotting.

保险箱 bǎoxiǎnxiāng
security box (for prevention of fire or theft), safe; metaphor for a safe and secure environment or place

保幼人员 bǎoyòu rényuán
daycare workers

保真 bǎozhēn
to retain the original true state

E.g. 激光电唱机具有保真度高的优点。 *CD players have superior sound fidelity.*

保职停薪 bǎo zhí tíng xīn

to retain the job but suspend the salary

指在职人员经单位同意后保留原职,停发工资,不定期地离开原来单位。也称"留职停薪"或"停薪留职"。

After the Third Plenary Session of the Eleventh Central Committee of the Chinese Communist Party, some workers with special skills wished to go voluntarily to rural villages to engage in sideline production and to open up wild, undeveloped areas in order to develop the rural economy. The state supported their wishes and granted them leave. Their original positions were retained for them but their salaries were suspended. After several years, they could return to work in their original units, where their years of service would be calculated as usual and salary adjustments would not be adversely affected. The term also applies to personnel on government salaries who study abroad on non-government funds. According to regulations, these people retain their positions but their salaries are suspended. This is also called 留职停薪 retain job, stop salary or 停薪留职 stop salary, retain job.

保值 bǎozhí

(banking) to guarantee value; to guarantee stability of interest rates, and not allow money held to be affected by currency depreciation

E.g. 保值储蓄贴补率 *Subsidy rate for guaranteed-value savings* / 华侨定期储蓄也可以享受保值。*The scheduled savings of overseas Chinese can also enjoy guarantee value.*

保质 bǎozhì

to guarantee quality

E.g. 食品保质 *the guaranteed quality of foods* / 保质期三年。*The period of guaranteed quality is three years.*

宝钢 Bǎo-Gāng

Baoshan Iron and Steel Plant

Reputed to be the largest Chinese iron and steel plant to date, built in the late 1970s and the early 1980s in Baoshan County of Greater Metropolitan Shanghai.

抱大腿 bào dàtuǐ

to embrace the thighs

A metaphor for toadying up to someone with power and authority.

E.g. 此人善于抱领导的大腿往上爬。*This person is adept at climbing by toadying up to the leadership.*

报捕 bàobǔ

report to arrest; apply for permission to arrest someone

Public security units apply to higher authorities for permission to arrest suspects.

报告会 bàogàohuì

report meeting; public lecture

报价 bàojià

published price

E.g. 产品报价 *the published price of products* / 每吨纸报价 5000 元。*The published price of paper is 5,000 yuan per ton.*

报检 bàojiǎn

to voluntarily report articles for customs inspections

报禁 bàojìn

restrictions placed on the free publication of newspapers

E.g. 开放报禁。*Censorship on news-*

papers has been lifted.

报矿 bàokuàng

to report the discovery of minerals or mineral reserves（to relevant agencies）

E.g. 向有关部门报矿 to report mineral discoveries to the relevant sectors

报领 bàolǐng

to apply for and obtain

E.g. 报领劳动用品 to submit a request for supplies to be used in one's work

报批 bàopī

to report and seek comments

To report on a matter or give an opinion in written form to one's superior and request instructions or comments from him.

报修 bàoxiū

to report to the relevant office and request the repair of something

E.g. 住房漏雨打电话到房管所报修。The roof of the house is leaking, so a request for repairs was made by telephone to the housing management office.

报支 bàozhī

to file a request for reimbursement of expenses

E.g. 他这次出差报支2000多元。He filed a reimbursal request for more than 2,000 yuan for this business trip.

暴丑 bào chǒu

to reveal or expose one's shortcomings, errors, or problems

E.g. 不怕暴丑。Don't be afraid to reveal (your) shortcomings, errors, or problems.

暴跌 bàodiē

sudden drastic fall（usually referring to price）

E.g. 股市暴跌 drastic fall on the stock market / 油价暴跌 drastic drop in oil prices / 美元暴跌 drastic fall in the foreign exchange rate of U.S. dollars

暴发户 bàofāhù

persons or households who suddenly became rich through unscrupulous means or unexpected opportunities

E.g. 政治暴发户 a new star who surged into the political arena.

暴富 bàofù

suddenly rich; to become rich overnight

暴力工具 bàolì gōngjù

violent tools

It mainly refers to state organs authorized to use violent methods（eg. police）.

暴力机器 bàolì jīqì

violent machinery

Synonymous with 暴力工具.

暴露思想 bàolù sīxiǎng

to expose thoughts

An individual laying bare his true thoughts and knowledge concerning certain matters or issues to his organization or comrades. In general, these are ideas difficult for individuals to express.

暴走族 bàozǒuzú

(Taiwan) youths who ride motorcycles wildly

爆冷门 bàolěngmén

unexpected results that suddenly occurred（often referring to the realm of sports）

E.g. 世界杯足球赛爆冷门，尼日利亚队夺得冠军。Totally by surprise, the Nigerian team won the World Cup in soccer. / 科研中也会爆冷门，一些不

知名的小人物在某些学科中有了突破性的进展。Surprises can also occur in science, as some breakthroughs in some fields are made by hitherto unknown researchers.

爆满 bàomǎn
full house; filled to capacity
E.g. 演出场场爆满。The show had a full house at every performance.

爆棚 bàopéng
1) **popular songs or music, transliteration of the English word "pop"**
E.g. 爆棚唱片 pop phonograph record
2) **filled beyond capacity**

爆燃 bàorán
(of flammables) to ignite and explode
E.g. 大量液化气外漏,引起重大爆燃事故。A big leak of liquefied gas ignited and exploded.

爆响 bàoxiǎng
to explode with tremendous noise; to suddenly emit a huge noise; to attain a meteoritic rise in reputation
E.g. 1954年中国第一颗原子弹爆响了。In 1954, China's first atomic bomb exploded onto the scene. / 大厅里喝彩声爆响。A burst of cheering exploded in the hall. / 电视连续剧《渴望》在全国爆响。The television series "Yearning" made a splash throughout the country.

爆炸性消息 bàozhàxìng xiāoxi
explosive news; shocking news

曝光 bào guāng
to be exposed to light (as in photography)
(Figurative) a secretive affair being exposed to the public (also called 暴光).
E.g. 让非法交易曝光。to expose illegal trade

bei

杯赛 bēisài
cup competitions, athletic competitions named after certain cups
E.g. 新秀将在这次杯赛上亮相。The new stars are about to make a showing in the upcoming World Cup.

碑廊 bēiláng
corridors in which carved tablets are exhibited

背包袱 bēi bāofu
to carry a bundle on one's back
A metaphor for an ideological burden that affects one's work, study and progress.

背黑锅 bēi hēiguō
to bear a black pot
A metaphor for suffering for the faults of others or being unjustly wronged.

背篓商店 bēilǒu shāngdiàn
back-basket store
A merchant who carries his merchandise in a basket on his back and peddles his wares in distant and almost inaccessible mountain villages.

北京话 běijīnghuà
Beijing patois; modern standard Chinese or speech representing the central government's spirit (as a result of Beijing being the nation's capital and the Beijing pronunciation being taken to be the standard)

北约 Běi-Yuē
NATO
An abbreviation for 北大西洋公约组织 the North Atlantic Treaty Organiza-

tion. Also called 北约组织.

背靠背 bèikàobèi
back facing back, metaphor for carrying out an activity behind the relevant person's back
E.g. 进行背靠背评议 to raise objections behind one's back / 背靠背地提意见 to make suggestions behind one's back

背销 bèixiāo
sluggish sale
E.g. 这种商品已趋向背销。 This kind of commodity is already tending toward sluggish sales.

钡餐 bèicān
barium meal, a method of examining the digestive tract

倍棒 bèibàng
(Beijing colloquialism) doubly good

倍感 bèigǎn
to feel doubly...
E.g. 他的和蔼态度使人倍感亲切。 His congenial attitude makes others feel doubly friendly toward him.

倍加 bèijiā
to increase two fold; extraordinarily; extremely
E.g. 对刚栽下的小树, 我们要倍加爱护。 We will have to redouble our loving care of the saplings that have just been planted.

倍增 bèizēng
to increase many times; to grow by multiples
E.g. 收入倍增 the income has multiplied

备耕 bèigēng
to prepare for plowing
To make preparations for plowing by repairing farm implements, digging irrigation ditches, collecting manure, etc.

备荒 bèihuāng
famine prevention
To guard against famine by stockpiling rations and fodder, etc.

备课 bèikè
lesson preparation (of a teacher)

备料 bèiliào
preparation of materials
E.g. 备料车间 materials preparation workshop

备勤 bèiqín
preparing to go on duty
E.g. 值班备勤 to prepare to go on a shift / 备勤期间严禁饮酒。 During the preparation period, drinking is strictly forbidden.

备选 bèixuǎn
to nominate a candidate

备战 bèizhàn
preparation for war

被动吸烟 bèidòng xīyān
passive smoking (inhaling the smoke generated by others)

被管制分子 bèiguǎnzhì fènzǐ
elements under surveillance
Persons who have been stripped of their political rights and are controlled by a state institution and supervised by the masses.

被罩 bèizhào
quilt cover (which quilts can slip in and out of)

ben

本本主义 běnběn zhǔyì
bookism
A style of handling matters that departs

from practicality and relies blindly on books, documents, or on the instructions of superiors.

本位主义 běnwèi zhǔyì
selfish departmentalism
Also known as 小团体主义 narrow groupism. To be only concerned with the gains and convenience of one's own unit, department or region, ignoring the collective good and lacking a broader point of view. This is a manifestation of individualism.

笨鸟先飞 bèn niǎo xiān fēi
stupid bird flies first
A metaphor for a person of low ability, who, out of fear of falling behind, always begins a task before others.

beng

蹦蹦车 bèngbèngchē
colloquial term for small motorized three-wheel transport vehicles

蹦迪 bèngdí
disco dancing
E.g. 蹦迪已成为一种需要。 *Disco dancing has already become a fad.*

蹦极 bèngjí
bungee jumping

泵房 bèngfáng
pump house

泵排量 bèngpáiliàng
pumpage
The amount of fluid that a pump discharges in a fixed period of time.

bi

逼供信 bī-gòng-xìn
to force a confession and give credence to it
To force a defendant to confess by threats and torture, and then to use this confession to convict him.

逼和 bīhé
to force a tie (usually referring to a ball game)
E.g. 在首场比赛中，红队以二比二逼和蓝队。 *In the first round of competition, the red team forced a tie with the blue team with a score of 2 all.*

比基尼 bǐjīní
bikini

比较文学 bǐjiào wénxué
comparative literature

比例失调 bǐlì shītiáo
to be out of proportion

比萨 bǐsà
pizza
Also called 比萨饼.

比学赶帮超
bǐ-xué-gǎn-bāng-chāo
emulate, learn, catch up, help, surpass
Labor competition activities launched by factories and enterprises to emulate, learn from, catch up to, and surpass the advanced, and to help those who are backward.

笔杆子 bǐgǎnzi
pen shaft
A metaphor for someone good at writing. E.g. 他是这个单位的笔杆子，总结报告都由他写。 *He is the pen shaft of his unit, so all the summary reports are written by him.* / 用枪杆子对付笔杆子 *to counter the power of the pen with the power of the gun*

笔会 bǐhuì
Pen Association

International Pen Association; an international organization of writers and scholars, which was founded by C.A. Dowson Scott – an Englishwoman and writer, in 1921. It is a very influential contemporary organization of writers from all over the world. Some countries have set up corresponding national writers associations. China's Pen Association Center was formally set up in Beijing, in April, 1981.

笔墨官司 bǐmò guānsi
pen and ink lawsuit, a debate or suit carried out in writing
E.g. 打笔墨官司 *to conduct a lawsuit through writing* / 笔墨官司打上了法庭。*The lawsuit being conducted in written form has reached the court.*

闭卷 bìjuàn
closed-book exam
E.g. 闭卷考试 *closed-book exam* / 实行闭卷、开卷相结合的办法（*in exams*）*to carry out a combination of the open-book and closed-book methods*

闭路电视 bìlù diànshì
closed-circuit television
Also called 工业电视 industrial television or 水下电视 underwater television when used for underwater observation.

弊政 bìzhèng
bad policies

必然王国 bìrán wángguó
realm of necessity

壁挂 bìguà
wall hangings (decorative textile work)

壁球 bìqiú
squash
A racket sport that originated in England and grew out of tennis. The rubber ball is hit against the wall, then hit by the other player after it has bounced on the floor. 壁球 also refers to the ball used in this sport.

壁饰 bìshì
wall decorations

壁纸 bìzhǐ
wallpaper

避风港 bìfēnggǎng
harbor
1) Originally, a harbor where boats could be protected from the wind and waves. 2) Now used as a metaphor for a place or work unit untouched by political movements.

避税 bìshuì
evade tax
E.g. 跨国公司避税已成为国际上普遍存在的问题。*Tax evasion on the part of transnational companies has already become a common international problem.*

避孕环 bìyùnhuán
contraceptive ring, diaphragm (a female contraceptive)

避孕栓 bìyùnshuān
contraceptive suppository

避孕套 bìyùntào
condom

避孕药具 bìyùn yàojù
contraceptive medicines and devices

避震 bìzhèn
to avoid earthquake damage
E.g. 出城避震的人已陆续回来了。*Those who left the city to escape the earthquake have gradually returned.*

bian

鞭打快牛 biāndǎ kuàiniú
to whip a fast ox
A metaphor for harshly driving efficient units or hard workers (and treating the lackadaisical ones in a laissez-faire manner).

边茶 biānchá
border region tea (cf. 边销茶)

边际效益 biānjì xiàoyì
marginal benefit
A term used in production management to refer to the additional benefit derived from one additional unit of production.

边卡 biānqiǎ
border post
A sentry or outpost on the border.

边贸 biānmào
foreign trade in border areas

边民 biānmín
people living in border areas

边销茶 biānxiāochá
border region tea
Species of tea leaves – such as 茯砖 and 青砖 – earmarked for use by national minorities in border regions. Also called 边茶.

边缘科学 biānyuán kēxué
borderline science

编报 biān–bào
to draft a budget plan and submit it to one's supervising unit

编采 biāncǎi
(of a reporter) to compile and gather material
E.g. 报社的编采人员都出去了。 *All the reporters of the newspaper have gone out (to gather information).*

编导 biāndǎo
to write a script and to direct (a film, a play, etc.); script-writer and director

编队 biānduì
to organize a team
To organize air planes, ships, personnel, etc., so that they can carry out a task together.
E.g. 中国赴南极考察编队。 *China organized a South Pole exploration team.*

编发 biānfā
edit and send (a manuscript)
Contraction of 编辑 to edit and 发稿 to send a manuscript (to a publisher).

编列 biānliè
to formulate a budget and to list items of expenditure
E.g. 编列预算 *an itemized budget* / 编列的教育经费 *the educational expenses listed in the budget*

编外 biānwài
outside of the official plan or authorized quota
E.g. 编外人员 *personnel outside the authorized quota* / 编外机构 *organizations outside the authorized quota* / 编外干部 *cadres outside the authorized quota*

编委 biān–wěi
editorial member

编钟 biānzhōng
a set of bells; chimes
A percussion instrument consisting of a set of bells with different tones. To play the bells with a wooden hammer.

贬值 biǎnzhí
devaluation of a currency (paper currency against coins, domestic

currency against foreign currencies, etc.); now often used in referring to the decreased value of something (other than currency)

E.g. 知识贬值 *depreciation of knowledge* / 武打小说贬值。 *Kungfu fiction has declined in value.*

便当 biàndāng
fast food in box

便利店 biànlìdiàn
chain store

便民 biànmín
to make (something) convenient for the people

E.g. 便民商店 *convenient store*

便民措施 biànmín cuòshī
to make things convenient for people

Systems and measures formulated by the police or the industrial and transportation service professions to make things more convenient for people.

便携式 biànxiéshì
portable; easy to carry

E.g. 便携式电话越来越普遍。 *Portable phones are more and more popular.*

变节分子 biànjié fènzǐ
turncoat

变色镜 biànsèjìng
spectacles made of lenses that take on different colors or shades in response to changes in external lighting

变色龙 biànsèlóng
chameleon

1) A vertebrate animal that is able to change color at any time for self-protection. 2) A metaphor for an opportunist who is facile at seeing which way the wind is blowing and at changing his attitude accordingly.

变数 biànshù
variable; changeable factors

原指表示变量的数；又指事物中可变的因素。

变天复辟 biàntiān fùbì
weather-change restoration

An overthrown reactionary class returning to power and restoring the old order.

变天帐 biàntiānzhàng
weather-change accounts

Title deeds of former real estate holdings, property accounts, and other counter-revolutionary documents hidden away by members of the overthrown exploitative class. They saved these, hoping in vain for a comeback, when they would retaliate against the masses and snatch back everything they had lost.

变相涨价 biànxiàng zhǎngjià
disguised inflation

Underweighing, passing off inferior merchandise as good, and other tricks that violate state pricing regulations and cause customers to suffer economic loss.

变形金刚 biànxíng jīngāng
transformable Buddha's warrior attendant (called "Transformer" in the U.S.), a toy made up of segments that can be twisted into the shape of different things

变修 biàn-xiū
to change in one's revolutionary nature and to become revisionist

E.g. 有一种谬论说："穷则革命，富则变修"。 *There is a fallacy that poverty leads to revolution, wealth leads to revisionism.*

辩护士 biànhùshì
defender (of a person or an issue,

often carries negative connotation)
辩论会 biànlùnhuì
debate meeting

biao

标灯 biāodēng
signal lights such as those used in navigation

标号 biāohào
grade
Numbers used to indicate the products (mostly used for physical properties). For example, using No. 200, No. 300, etc., to denote compression-resistance of cement.

标志服 biāozhìfú
uniforms with distinct characteristics worn by employees in certain professions
E.g. 投递员上班要穿标志服。*Mail delivery personnel must wear uniforms at work.*

标准像 biāozhǔnxiàng
standard photograph (frontal, hatless, from top of head to chest) (often referring to photos of national or other high-level leaders)

飙升 biāoshēng
to rocket; to rise quickly
E.g. 资产价格大幅飙升。*The price of assets is rocketing.*

表报 biǎobào
to report with charts
To use statistical tables to report to the authorities on work progress, production, revenue, expenditure, etc.

表决器 biǎojuéqì
electronic equipment for tabulating votes at large meetings; it may also be used for recording attendance and making statements

表面文章 biǎomiàn wénzhāng
surface formality; lip service
To do something perfunctorily simply to cope with superiors or public opinion.

表面性 biǎomiànxìng
surface appearance
To look only at surface phenomena or external connections and not understand the inner essence of things. As a result, problems cannot be properly understood or dealt with. This is also a subjective way of doing things.

表态 biǎotài
to declare one's stance
To express one's opinion and attitude on a question or matter.

表现力 biǎoxiànlì
power of expression
The ability of literary and artistic works to reflect life and express things objectively.

表演赛 biǎoyǎnsài
exhibition match

bing

兵工企业 bīnggōng qǐyè
arms enterprise; arsenal

兵马俑 bīngmǎyǒng
soldier and horse figures; terra-cotta figures
Statues of soldiers and horses buried with the dead in ancient China.
E.g. 秦始皇兵马俑 *the soldier and horse statues buried with Emperor Qin Shihuang, the first emperor of the Qin Dynasty*

兵团农场 bīngtuán nóngchǎng
army farms
Farms run by the People's Liberation Army Production and Construction Corps.
E.g. 新疆生产建设兵团先后建立了150多个农场。*The Xinjiang Production and Construction Corps successively established over 150 farms.*

兵运 bīng-yùn
troop movements

冰崩 bīngbēng
ice blocks crashing down from mountains

冰场 bīngchǎng
skating rink

冰袋 bīngdài
ice bag; ice pack

冰灯 bīngdēng
lighted ice sculptures
E.g. 冰灯游园会 *ice sculpture festival (at a park)* / 冰灯展览 *ice sculpture exhibition*

冰雕 bīngdiāo
ice sculpture

冰毒 bīngdú
synthetic drug amphetamine

冰坛 bīngtán
the world of ice-skating

冰舞 bīngwǔ
dancing on ice

冰砖 bīngzhuān
ice-cream block
A frozen block-shaped confection made of such things as cream, fruit juice, and sugar.

饼肥 bǐngféi
cake fertilizer
The general term for fertilizers like bean cake, and peanut cake.

病残 bìngcán
disease and disability; sick or handicapped persons
E.g. 老弱病残 *the old, the weak, the sick, and the handicapped* / 照顾病残人 *to care for the sick and handicapped* / 扶助病残 *to assist the sick and handicapped*

病虫害 bìngchónghài
crop diseases and insect pests

病退 bìngtuì
withdrawal due to illness
1) Employees retiring due to illness. 2) Educated youths in the "go up to the mountains and down to the countryside" program (cf. 上山下乡) returning to their original cities due to illness.

病休 bìngxiū
sick leave
E.g. 他已离开工作,病休在家。*He has already left his job and is at home on sick leave.*

并存 bìngcún
coexistence

并轨 bìngguǐ
combination of two methods
A metaphor for joining two systems into one.
E.g. 施行汇率并轨 *to implement the unification of currency exchange rates*

并网 bìngwǎng
merging single electrical lines into a network
E.g. 并网运行 *to move in a network* / 并网使用 *to use a network*

并网发电 bìngwǎng fādiàn
combined to the grid
Merging two or more large electrical grid systems in order to regulate electricity

玻播拨 bō

generation capacity.

bo

玻璃钢 bōligāng
glass steel; glass fiber reinforced plastic

玻璃小鞋 bōli xiǎoxié
little glass shoes
It's the expansion of 穿小鞋 wearing tight shoes. A metaphor for the odious practice of some cadres using rather covert means to retaliate against subordinates holding different views, and to embarrass them in work and life.

播报 bōbào
to disseminate a report
E.g. 电视报纸每天都播报股市行情。 Television broadcasts and newspapers have daily reports on the stock market.

播唱 bōchàng
broadcasting singing
E.g. 电台播唱了新编的唱段。 The station broadcasted a newly composed aria.

播出 bōchū
to broadcast (radio or television)
E.g. 今天晚上电台将播出美国电视连续剧。 This evening the television station will broadcast an American television series.

播发 bōfā
to deliver through broadcasting
E.g. 电视台播发了国家领导人讲话的全文。 The TV station transmitted the entire text of the speech by the national leader.

播放 bōfàng
to broadcast a program on radio or television
E.g. 播放影片 to broadcast a film / 播放音乐 to broadcast music / 播放大会实况 to broadcast the proceedings of the conference / 播放录像 to broadcast a videotape / 录像播放了十次。 The videotape was broadcasted ten times.

播讲 bōjiǎng
to make a speech or deliver a lecture over the radio or on television
E.g. 播讲人 broadcaster / 播讲小说 to broadcast a novel / 播讲电视节目 to broadcast the list of television programs / 播讲技巧 broadcasting skills

播散 bōsàn
to disseminate; to diffuse
E.g. 现代经营的新思想已播散到中国。 New ideas on modern management have been disseminated in China.

播映 bōyìng
film broadcast
A television station broadcasting a regular feature film or a television film; to broadcast a film or television movie.
E.g. 播映电影片 to broadcast a film / 播映新闻 to broadcast news

拨付 bōfù
to appropriate
E.g. 拨付经费 to allocate and issue funds

拨乱反正 bōluàn fǎnzhèng
bring order out of chaos
Originally, the term meant bringing stable rule to a chaotic world and restoring normalcy. Now it specifically refers to bringing order to the destructive chaos created by Lin Biao and the Gang of Four during the Cultural Revolution, correcting the mistakes of Mao Zedong in his later years, restoring the correct

path of Mao's thought and re-establishing the practical and realistic ideological line of Marxism-Leninism.

薄利多销 bó lì duō xiāo
small profit, large sale volume

To increase the sale volume by using a small profit margin, thereby accelerating the circulation of capital and attaining greater economic efficiency.

E.g. 这个工厂坚持薄利多销,企业越搞越活,生产发展很快。 *This factory upholds small profit and large sale volume, therefore its business has flourished and production has developed rapidly.*

薄膜 bómó
thin film-like material such as plastic food wrapping material

E.g. 塑料薄膜 *plastic film* / 食用薄膜 *film-like food-wrapping material* / 薄膜食品 *foodstuff wrapped in film-like wrapping*

博爱工程 bó'ài gōngchéng
universal love project

A philanthropic project to develop health care in areas of poverty.

博导 bó-dǎo
tutor of a Ph.D. student

Abbreviation for 博士生导师.

博士后 bóshìhòu
post-doctoral

伯乐 bólè
a name of a legendary person in the state of Qin during the Spring and Autumn Period who excelled in evaluating horses

A metaphor for someone who excels in discovering, training, and utilizing talent.

泊位 bówèi
berth (of a ship); parking lot

Originally it referred to the berth of a ship. Now it also refers to a parking lot.

E.g. 停车泊位证明 *parking lot certificate*

bu

捕杀 bǔshā
to capture and kill

E.g. 严禁捕杀珍贵稀有动物。 *Capturing and slaughtering rare (endangered) animals is strictly forbidden.*

补差 bǔchā
to make up for the amount short of the quota, or for a shortfall in funds, also refers specifically to a retired worker rejoining the work force in order to receive a certain additional income to make up for the difference between his pension and his pre-retirement salary.

E.g. 他每月拿40元的补差。 *Each month he receives a subsidy of 40 yuan.*

补偿贸易 bǔcháng màoyì
compensatory trade

A form of international trade commonly used in China. Foreign machines, equipment, and technology are bought on credit and then goods are subsequently produced and other commodities are used to pay the bill. This is an effective way of using foreign capital and of increasing exports.

补假 bǔjià
1) make-up vacation, i.e., a vacation taken to make up for one that was missed; 2) make-up leave re-

quest, i.e., a request for leave submitted after the leave was taken because it was not possible to request the leave in advance

补课 bǔkè

to make up school work

A metaphor for redoing an unfinished or unsatisfactory job.

E.g. 老师在假期里要给学生补课。 *The teacher wants to make up classes for the students over the holidays.* / 凡违章司机都要参加学习班，接受补课。 *All drivers who have committed traffic violations must attend a class and receive supplementary education for drivers.*

补亏 bǔkuī

the state subsidizing deficit enterprises

E.g. 凡属经营性亏损的，国家不再补亏。 *All losses arising from management will no longer be subsidized by the state.*

补台 bǔtái

to repair a platform

A metaphor for supporting leaders and colleagues in their work by seeking to repair the deleterious effects or damage created through their faulty work.

补贴工分 bǔtiē gōngfēn

work point subsidies

When rural communes were implementing the system of work points, production team cadres and other commune members who were engaged in public work and were thereby held up in their farm labor were given a subsidy of work points by the production team.

补休 bǔxiū

make-up vacation

Make-up vacation days for people who keep working during holidays and official days of rest.

补选 bǔxuǎn

to select or elect new members to fill vacancies

E.g. 依法补选人大代表 *to follow the law representatives are elected to fill vacancies in the National People's Congress*

补血 bǔxuè

to replenish or supplement blood

A metaphor for supplementing with new components or new members.

补液 bǔyè

fluids injected intravenously; any fluids containing nutrients

E.g. 护士正在给病人补液。 *The nurse is giving the patient an intravenous injection.*

补助票证 bǔzhù piàozhèng

subsidy coupons

Coupons enabling people in special circumstances – such as at times of births, marriages, funerals, or those participatig in special work – to buy extra rations of state monopoly items or scarce goods.

E.g. 补助油票 *subsidized oil ration coupons*

不承认主义 bùchéngrèn zhǔyì

policy of nonrecognition

1) Stimsonism. The preposterous proposition made by the American Secretary of State Henry Lewis Stimson (served as Secretary of State 1929-1933) after the incident of September 18, 1931 (Japanese seizure of Shenyang, China) whereby Manchuria (northeast China provinces)

would be sacrificed in exchange for Japanese recognition of American interests in China. 2) An attitude of not acknowledging objective realities.

不戴帽子 bùdài màozi
not putting on caps （cf. 三不主义）

不发达国家 bùfādá guójiā
economically undeveloped nations

不结盟运动 bùjiéméng yùndòng
non-aligned movement
A political force which appeared on the world scene in the early 1950s. Twenty-five nations participated in the first conference of non-allied nations convened in the Yugoslav capital, Belgrade, in September 1951. The conference promulgated the non-aligned movement's aims and policies of independence, self-determination, and opposition to the formation of blocs. Today over eighty nations are members of the non-aligned movement. They have become a powerful force in guarding national sovereignty, developing national economies and cultures, opposing imperialism, colonialism, and all forms of foreign domination, establishing a new international economic order, and preserving world peace.

不可比产品 bùkěbǐ chǎnpǐn
products which have been produced for the first time on a normal, non-experimental, basis in any given year （in contrast to 可比产品）

不力 bùlì
no effort
Not applying one's full strength, not efficient.
E.g. 办事不力 *to make no effort in one's work*

不明飞行物 bùmíng fēixíngwù
unidentified flying object – UFO
（cf. 飞碟）

不起眼 bùqǐyǎn
not attention-grabbing, not noteworthy
E.g. 植树在当时虽然不起眼，但却大大地改善了今天的环境。*Although planting trees was not noteworthy at the time they have greatly improved the environment today.*

不正之风 bù zhèng zhī fēng
unhealthy tendencies
Unhealthy tendencies that violate Party discipline, national laws, the norms of socialist political life, and the moral standards of socialism. These tendencies include liberalism, sectarianism, selfish departmentalism, suppression of democracy, extreme democratism, nepotism, special treatment, using unauthorized methods to achieve or acquire something, etc.

不抓辫子 bùzhuā biànzi
not to pull the pigtail
A metaphor for refraining from mentioning a person's mistakes, faults or weak points. （cf. 三不主义）

布点 bùdiǎn
layout; location distribution
To centrally map out the distribution of relevant organs in the process of setting them up.
E.g. 要避免重复建设，盲目布点，各搞一套的弊病。*We must avoid repetitious construction, blind distribution and malpractice that each does in one's own way.*

布控 bùkòng

arrange to control

To take measures to keep a watch on and control suspects or certain areas.

E.g. 公安局将他列为嫌疑犯,并布控起来。 *The Public Security Bureau listed him as a suspect and arranged to put him under surveillance.*

布票 bùpiào

clothing ration coupons

Ration coupons used at one time in China to buy cotton cloth and cotton textile products.

布设 bùshè

to disperse and set up

E.g. 广泛布设示范区,推广先进科技成果。 *Widely set up model districts, so as to aid the spread of advanced technology.*

布展 bùzhǎn

to set up an exhibition

E.g. 布展水平 *caliber of the exhibition* / 书展的布展方式很有特色。 *The set-up of the book exhibition is very distinctive.*

步道桥 bùdàoqiáo

pedestrian overpass

步调 bùdiào

pace

A metaphor for the style, steps, and speed of carrying out certain activities.

E.g. 统一步调 *to synchronize pace*

部际 bùjì

inter-departmental

E.g. 加强部际合作 *to strengthen inter-departmental cooperation*

部件 bùjiàn

component

部委 bù-wěi

ministries and commissions

A general term for all ministries and commissions under the State Council.

部优 bùyōu

(pertaining to products) the ranking of "excellent" at the national ministry level

E.g. 部优产品 *products rated as "excellent" by the national agency* / 产品获得部优称号。*The product attained a rating of excellent at the national level.*

C

c

CD机 CD jī
CD player

ca

擦边球 cābiānqiú
scrape-edge balls; to hit a ball on the edge of a table (ping-pong)
A metaphor for squeaking by on the fringe of legality.

擦屁股 cāpìgu
to wipe one's bottom
A metaphor for taking over others' unfinished business.
E.g. 厂长调走了，但留下很多问题没有解决，别人得给他擦屁股。 *The factory manager was transferred, but many unresolved problems remain. Others must clean up his unfinished business.*

cai

猜奖 cāijiǎng
guessing games with prizes; guessing game prizes
E.g. 举办猜奖活动 *to set up guessing games (with prizes)*

财办 cáibàn
treasurer's or controller's office
Abbreviation for 财政办公室.

财会 cáikuài
merged term for financial affairs and accounting
E.g. 财会干部 *fiscal and accounting cadres* / 财会队伍 *the ranks of fiscal and accounting personnel* / 财会部门 *fiscal and accounting departments* / 财会专业人员 *fiscal and accounting specialists*

财路 cáilù
a way to produce wealth
E.g. 开辟财路 *to open up paths to generate wealth*

财贸 cáimào
finance and trade
Contraction of 财政 finance and 贸易 trade.

财税 cáishuì
finance and taxation
Fiscal management and collection of taxes.
E.g. 财税部门 *(re government) organs of finance and taxation*

财政包干 cáizhèng bāogān
fiscal responsibility system
A method of fiscal management instituted in China in 1971. After the annual budgeted income and expenditure targets for each province, municipality, and autonomous region were examined and approved by the central government, it was the responsibility of each area to follow through. Unless the central government assigned new responsibilities to

the area, the budget remained fixed. Each locality managed its expenditure as a whole and made adjustments as necessary. Any surplus income or savings in expenditure was disposed of by the locality as it saw fit. The locality must also balance any shortage of income or excessive expenditure. If there was trouble in balancing the budget due to unforeseen difficulties, appropriate adjustments could be made after a report was made to the State Council and permission had been granted.

踩点 cǎidiǎn
(in parachuting) to land on the stipulated spot
E.g. 在集体定点跳伞中，女队连续三次踩点。 *In the group target parachuting exercise, the women's team hit the mark three times in a row.*

采编 cǎibiān
(of a reporter) to gather material and compile
E.g. 采编人员 *reporters (of a newspaper or magazine)* / 这个报社的采编人员很强。 *This newspaper has a strong reporting staff.*

采购团 cǎigòutuán
purchasing delegation
Large-scale delegations that go abroad to negotiate the purchase of commodities; most are organized by the government.

采购员 cǎigòuyuán
purchasing agent of an organization or enterprise

采购站 cǎigòuzhàn
purchasing station
An organization that selects and purchases raw materials and commodities for government agencies or enterprises.

采暖 cǎinuǎn
to attain a comfortable indoor temperature
E.g. 冬季采暖 *heating in the winter* / 采暖期 *indoor-heating season*

采区 cǎiqū
mining area
1) A certain mining area delineated in the process of mining. 2) An administrative organization of a certain standing in the mining enterprise.

采写 cǎixiě
(of a reporter) to gather material and write it up
E.g. 采写真人真事 *to interview and write stories about real people and real events* / 采写通讯 *to write up interviews and investigations for a news dispatch.*

采样 cǎiyàng
to collect samples
E.g. 食品采样检查 *to examine food samples*

彩车 cǎichē
decorated vehicles; floats (in a parade)
Vehicles decorated with colorful ribbons, flowers, etc. They are used at weddings and other festive occasions.

彩灯 cǎidēng
color or multi-color lights

彩电 cǎidiàn
color TV
Abbreviation for 彩色电视机.

彩管 cǎiguǎn
color kinescope
Abbreviation for 彩色显像管.

彩卷儿 cǎijuǎnr
color film
Abbreviation for 彩色胶卷儿.

彩扩 cǎikuò

enlargement of color photos
E.g. 彩扩快件一小时可取。*Enlarged color photos urgently needed can be ready in one hour.*

彩旗 cǎiqí
colorful banners
E.g. 彩旗迎风飘扬。*Colorful banners flutter in the breeze.*

彩球 cǎiqiú
colored balloons or balls

彩色电视 cǎisè diànshì
color television

彩色片 cǎisèpiān
color film
Also called 天然色感光片 natural color-sensitive film or plate; this term also refers to colored movie film.

彩印 cǎiyìn
color printing
Abbreviation for color printing.
E.g. 彩印材料 *color-printing material* / 彩印公司 *color-printing company* / 彩印厂 *color-printing factory* / 彩印效果 *result (quality) of color-printing*

彩照 cǎizhào
color photographs
Contraction of 彩色照片.

彩纸 cǎizhǐ
paper for color photos

菜场 càichǎng
vegetable and food market

菜畜 càichù
animals raised specifically for food (beef, poultry, pork, etc.)

菜鸽 càigē
pigeons raised for food
Also called 肉鸽 and 餐鸽.

菜篮子 càilánzi
food-shopping basket
A metaphor for the profession of producing and supplying food.
E.g. 要稳定菜篮子。*Food supply must be stabilized.* / 要丰富市民的菜篮子。*We must enrich the food supply for urban residents.*

菜篮子工程 càilánzi gōngchéng
the building of the infrastructure for producing groceries and supplying them to urban areas

菜牛 càiniú
beef cattle
Also called 肉牛.

菜农 càinóng
vegetable farmers

can

餐鸽 cāngē
pigeons raised for food (cf. 菜鸽)

餐盒 cānhé
dining box; dinner pail
E.g. 一次性餐盒 *disposable food box*

餐位 cānwèi
seating in a restaurant or dining hall
E.g. 餐馆增加了30多个餐位。*The restaurant increased its seating capacity by over thirty.*

餐饮 cānyǐn
food and drinks
E.g. 餐饮价格 *cost of food and drinks* / 餐饮质量 *quality of food and drinks*

参股 cāngǔ
to engage in stock management
E.g. 参股是一种投机行为。*To engage in stock management is a type of opportunistic behavior.* / 欢迎港台同胞来大陆参股和竞买。*To welcome Hong Kong and Taiwan compatriots to come to the mainland to compete and*

invest in joint-stock enterprises. / 企业之间可以互相参股。 Enterprises may invest in each other's joint-stock ventures.

参评 cānpíng

to participate in evaluation and selection (for prizes, etc.)

E.g. 参评作品要突出创新。 Works submitted for the competition must be distinctive and break new ground. / 录像片不在参评之列。 Video films are not included in the competition.

参赛 cānsài

to participate in a competition

E.g. 参赛学生 students who participate in a competition / 运动员参赛 athletes participate in a competition

参试 cānshì

to participate in an examination; to engage in (scientific) research and development

E.g. 专业合格证书考试去年开始举行, 很多中学教师报名参试。 Examinations for speciality certification started last year; many high school teachers registered to take the exams.

参试人员 cānshì rényuán

test personnel

Personnel who participate in experiments and trial production runs (of new technologies, products, etc.).

参选 cānxuǎn

participate in an election

参展 cānzhǎn

to participate in an exhibition

E.g. 中国食品在东京参展。 Chinese food products participated in an exhibition in Tokyo. / 参展单位 participating (in an exhibition) units / 参展产品 participating (in an exhibition) products / 参展影片 participating (in an exhibition of) films

参政 cānzhèng

to participate in political activity or to join a political organization

E.g. 政协委员参政议政意识强烈。 Members of the Chinese People's Political Consultative Conference participated and discussed state affairs.

残次 cáncì

(of products) inferior; defective

E.g. 残次品 defective items / 残次零部件 defective components

残疾人 cánjírén

disabled persons

E.g. 大力发展残疾人福利事业 to make a major effort to develop welfare services for the disabled

残疾院 cánjíyuàn

an institution which provides living quarters and treatment for disabled people

残联 cán-lián

the Association of Disabled People

Abbreviation for 残疾人联合会.

cang

仓储式 cāngchǔshì

stockroom-style

A type of marketing whereby the shopping area or store is of a simple construction, the goods are shipped directly from the manufacturers, and the prices are lower than ordinary stores.

仓容 cāngróng

the capacity of a warehouse or storehouse

E.g. 仓容不足。 The storage capacity is insufficient. / 腾出仓容, 解决秋粮

入库的问题。*Clear out warehouse space, in order to solve the problem of storing the autumn harvest.*

藏品 cángpǐn
precious objects in a museum or private collection

藏书票 cángshūpiào
book labels identifying a collector or collection, some are specially printed and some are hand-drawn.

cao

操办 cāobàn
to arrange and manage
E.g. 帮助青年操办婚事 *to help young people arrange their weddings* / 儿子的婚事已操办出眉目来。*Arrangements for the son's wedding are taking shape.*

草编 cǎobiān
straw weavings
Handicraft items or articles for everyday use woven from the stems or leaves of grasses and other plants.

草根工业 cǎogēn gōngyè
grass root industry
Refers to village and township enterprises which take root among farmers and grow like wild grass.

草库伦 cǎokùlún (Mongolian phrase) fenced-in pasture

草木经 cǎomùjīng
botany
1) A body of knowledge pertaining to plant growth (usually agricultural and forest plants). 2) Governmental policies, methods and ways adopted in the arid northwest region to adapt measures to local conditions, to plant grass and trees, and thereby promote economic growth of the region.

草签 cǎoqiān
the signing of a draft treaty or agreement by representatives of the signatory sides
E.g. 举行协议草签仪式 *to conduct a ceremony for signing a draft treaty* / 上海与其他省草签了很多项经济合作项目合同。*Shanghai has signed many agreements with other provinces for cooperation on economic and technological projects.*

草业 cǎoyè
the enterprise of developing and cultivating pasture

ce

侧记 cèjì
sidelights
E.g. 奥运会女排比赛侧记。*Sidelights on the women's Olympic volleyball competition.*

测控 cèkòng
to observe and control
E.g. 测控任务 *observation and control duty* / 测控工作 *observation and control work* / 中国航天测控技术进入先进行列。*The technology of air traffic control in China has been listed as advanced.*

测评 cèpíng
to observe and evaluate
E.g. 人员测评工程 *personnel evaluation project* / 人员功能测评法 *method of evaluating functions of personnel* / 有些学校实行德育测评。*Some schools are carrying out an evaluation of moral education.*

测试 cèshì
to test

Originally, testing the functions and accuracy of machines, instruments, and electrical appliances; now it refers broadly to all kinds of tests as well as academic examinations.

E.g. 测试中心 *testing center* / 测试是检查学生学习情况的主要手段。 *Tests are the primary measure for examining how well students have learned.*

测算 cèsuàn
to survey or to calculate

E.g. 据抽样测算,全市有20%的科技人员专业不对口。 *According to a sample survey, twenty percent of the city's sci-tech personnel are professionally mismatched.* / 据有关单位测算,国家每年实际用于房租补贴约50亿元。 *According to a survey by a relevant agency, the actual annual national expenditure for housing subsidies is about 5 billion yuan.*

ceng

层高 cénggāo
the number of stories and the height of a building

层面 céngmiàn
levels and aspects; the parameters of various levels

cha

差额选举 chā'é xuǎnjǔ
the kind of election where there are more candidates than positions to be filled

差额招生 chā'é zhāoshēng
a method of recruiting students that involves elimination through competition: if the number of admitted students exceeds the target number, then each year substandard students are eliminated, with the result that the number at graduation equals the original target

差价 chājià
price differential caused by differences in time and place, between wholesale and retail, between the state-subsidized price and the free-market price, etc.

E.g. 该公司将平价商品转议销,获差价收入10万多元。 *When this company changed their commodities from state prices to free market prices, it gained an income differential of more than 100,000 yuan.*

插播 chābō
to interrupt a regular, scheduled program (on radio or television) to broadcast a special program

E.g. 电台在第二套节目中经常插播重要新闻。 *In broadcasting its second set of programs, this station often interrupts the regular programs with important news.*

插队落户 chāduì luòhù
to go and settle in the countryside

The rustication movement during the Cultural Revolution whereby large numbers of urban educated youths were relocated to rural production teams to participate in long-term productive labor.

插杠子 chā gàngzi
to insert a pole

A metaphor for intruding on a smooth-going operation with words or action.

插红旗 chā hóngqí
to plant a red flag

A way of commending superior performance; to establish an advanced model, to attain a victory or commendation. *E.g.* 门门功课插红旗 *to excel in every subject* / 插红旗的地区粮食产量反而下降了。 *In the regions previously designated as advanced, grain production has actually declined.*

插秧机 chāyāngjī
rice seedling planter; rice transplanter

Also called 水稻插秧机 rice seedling planting machine.

插足 chāzú
to insert a foot

A metaphor for joining a certain activity. Now this term often refers to a third party intruding on a marital or romantic relationship. *E.g.* 超级大国已经插足这个地区。 *The superpowers have already intruded into this region.* / 因第三者插足的离婚案比以前多了。 *Divorce cases involving a third party have increased.*

茶吧 chábā
tea bar

茶话会 cháhuàhuì
tea forum; tea party

A forum or symposium with refreshments.

查补 chábǔ
to investigate and exact supplementary payment (of delinquent taxes, etc.)

查处 cháchǔ
investigate and deal with

To investigate the facts of a crime or a mistake, and to take disciplinary action.

查核 cháhé
to examine and check (bills, shipping lists, etc.)

查获 cháhuò
to track down and seize criminals or stolen goods

查苗 chámiáo
to examine seedlings

To check whether seedlings have sprouted uniformly and how well they have grown.

查实 cháshí
to verify

To examine for verification; to be checked and found to be true.

查体 chátǐ
to conduct a physical examination

查证 cházhèng
to investigate and verify

差劲 chùjìn
inferior (referring to personal behavior or ability); **low quality** (referring to goods)

E.g. 那人有点差劲。 *That person is a bit sleazy.* / 你的自行车太差劲了，该换一辆新的。 *Your bicycle is really too bad. You should get yourself a new one.*

差生 chàshēng
low-caliber students

chai

差旅费 chāilǚfèi

expenses for business trips

拆封 chāifēng
to open up a seal (of a door, a letter, etc.)
E.g. 在不拆封的情况下, 对大批成捆的纸币进行消毒处理。 *Without having the seals opened, the big batches of paper money were put through the disinfection process.*

拆借 chāijiè
short-term loan
Originally a dialectal term, referring to a form of short-term loan with a daily interest. Now it refers to a method of transferring funds between various monetary organs to take care of short-term shortages and surpluses.

拆迁 chāiqiān
dismantle and move

拆迁户 chāiqiānhù
households or units relocated due to building demolition

拆装 chāizhuāng
to disassemble and to assemble
E.g. 这种机器拆装很方便。 *This kind of machinery is very convenient to disassemble and reassemble.*

柴油机 cháiyóujī
diesel engine
Also called 狄塞尔机.

chan

掺水股票 chānshuǐ gǔpiào
watered-down stocks
Ordinary stocks that can be bought by persons inside a stock company or a business at a cost lower than their face value.

掺杂兑假 chānzá duìjiǎ
to mix in fake or inferior components (in commodities)

掺沙子 chānshāzi
to have sand mixed in
1) A metaphor for a single element having another element mixed into it. 2) Specifically, when propaganda teams were sent into schools and other territories of the superstructure during the Cultural Revolution, it was called "mixing sand" into the ranks of the intellectuals.

掺杂使假 chānzá shǐjiǎ
to mix in the inferior or fake
To mix something of poor quality in with something of good quality, or to mix something fake into something genuine, lowering the quality for selfish gain.

产成品 chǎnchéngpǐn
finished products

产羔率 chǎngāolǜ
sheep reproduction rate; lambing rate
The percentage of births of lambs per a certain number of sheep.

产假 chǎnjià
maternity leave
A period of leave given to women workers, usually ninety days, before and after they give birth.

产品结构 chǎnpǐn jiégòu
product structure
The composition of products in society and their interconnections. On the basis of the products' usages, capacities, quality or level of processing, they can be divided into many kinds of product structures. For example: the composition of primary and processed products; the composition of intermediate and final

products; and the composition of superior, intermediate, and inferior products.

产前产后 chǎnqián chǎnhòu
before and after production
Pre-production preparation made by agricultural and industrial enterprises (raw material, capital, etc.) and the post-production marketing of goods.
E.g. 建立专业公司，为农业产前产后服务。 *To found a specialized company that serves the pre- and post-production needs of agriculture.*

产销 chǎn xiāo
to produce and market
E.g. 产销淡季 *a low production and marketing season* / 产销目标 *production and marketing targets* / 实行产销直挂 *to implement direct linkage between production and marketing*

产销平衡 chǎn-xiāo pínghéng
equilibrium between production and marketing in the production process
The quantity of commodities produced being basically equivalent to the quantity sold.

产业结构重组
chǎnyè jiégòu chóngzǔ
reorganization of an industrial organization

产业结构升级
chǎnyè jiégòu shēngjí
upgrading of an industrial structure

chang

常规能源 chángguī néngyuán
conventional energy sources
Conventional energy resources such as plant fuels, coal, petroleum, natural gas, hydropower, electrical power, etc.

常规武器 chángguī wǔqì
conventional weapons

常规战争 chángguī zhànzhēng
conventional warfare using conventional (non-nuclear) weapons

常见病 cháng jiànbìng
common illnesses
Ailments that people commonly contract, such as colds, enteritis, etc.

常设 chángshè
established for the long-term; permanent
E.g. 常设机构 *a permanent organization* / 常设委员会 *a permanent committee*

常委 chángwěi
standing committee member (of a committee of a certain organization)
Abbreviation for 常务委员会委员.

常委会 chángwěihuì
standing committee
Abbreviation for 常务委员会.

常智 chángzhì
ordinary intelligence

长话 chánghuà
long distance telephone call
Abbreviation for 长途电话.
E.g. 长话局 *Long Distance Telephone Bureau*

长假 chángjià
long-term leave

长考 chángkǎo
(in the game of Go) to ponder for a long time
E.g. 长考达两个多小时。 *The period of pondering (a move in chess) lasted over two hours.*

长龙 chánglóng

long dragon

A metaphor for a long line (queue).

E.g. 挂号的病人排成了长龙。 *The registered patients formed a long queue.* / 排长龙的现象已得到缓解。 *Queues have become shorter.*

长期共存 chángqī gòngcún
long-term coexistence

The long-term coexistence of the Chinese Communist Party with various other democratic parties. It is the policy, first proposed by Mao Zedong in 1956 in his article "On the Ten Large Relationships", of long-term coexistence of the Chinese Communist Party with various other democratic parties and of their mutual surveillance.

长途 chángtú
long distance (phone calls)

E.g. 挂个长途 *to make a long distance call* / 刚才有人打长途来。 *Just now someone called long-distance.*

长线 chángxiàn
categories in national economic development that are non-urgent or where supply exceeds demand

长线产品 chángxiàn chǎnpǐn
long line products

When economic departments are setting targets for basic construction investments or production, all products that are in abundance – where the supply can meet or even exceed the demand – are called "long line products".

长项 chángxiàng
long suit

Originally referred to a sport in which one was especially strong. Now it is also a metaphor for any activity in which a person or a group enjoys superiority.

E.g. 保守党注意宣传自己在国防外交等方面的长项。 *The Conservative Party makes a point of publicizing its superiority in defense and foreign affairs.*

长效 chángxiào
long-lasting in effectiveness

E.g. 长效复合肥 *compound fertilizer with long-lasting effectiveness*

长余产品 chángyú chǎnpǐn
products whose supply is abundant so that there is a surplus beyond market demands

长征干部 chángzhēng gànbù
Long March cadres

Cadres who participated in the 25,000 *li* Long March of the Chinese Workers and Peasants' Red Army (1934-1936). They totaled almost 30,000 and were the cream of the Chinese Communist Party. Many of them subsequently become leaders or the backbone of the Party's political and military organs.

长治久安 chángzhì jiǔ'ān
political conditions and social order have been stable and tranquil for a long time

厂点 chǎngdiǎn
factory site

E.g. 厂点布局要合理。 *The location of factory sites must be rational.*

厂风 chǎngfēng
factory atmosphere

The atmosphere in a factory, including the work atmosphere, the ideological atmosphere, the management atmosphere, and the daily life atmosphere.

厂家 chǎngjiā
a commodity's production unit; factory

厂矿企业 chǎng-kuàng qǐyè
factory and mining enterprises
The combined term for factory and mining enterprises (as differentiated from transportation and commercial enterprises).

厂礼拜 chǎnglǐbài
factory rest day
The day of the week determined by the factory as a day of rest in lieu of Sunday.

厂情 chǎngqíng
factory situation

厂商 chǎngshāng
factory and store

厂社挂钩 chǎng-shè guàgōu
to link factories with communes
The establishment of permanent links between factories and rural communes for mutual support and cooperation

厂史 chǎngshǐ
factory history

厂校挂钩 chǎng-xiào guàgōu
to link up factories with schools; to form certain cooperative linkages between factories and schools.

A main form of open door education run by urban schools during the Cultural Revolution. Schools and local factories were to establish permanent links. Students were organized into groups to go and labor in the factories so they could understand the situation there, and workers were invited to lecture in the schools on their factory and family histories and on stories of exemplary deeds. This enabled the teachers and students to be "re-educated". The term also means linking together engineering schools and factories for mutual cooperation. For example, schools used the factories as a relatively fixed base for practical training and conducting cultural and technical training classes for the factories' workers and provided certain technical services for the factories.

厂休 chǎngxiū
factory rest day (which may not necessarily be Sunday)
Also called 厂礼拜.
E.g. 今天是我们的厂休。*Today is the day off at our factory.*

场馆 chǎng-guǎn
ground and hall
E.g. 展览场馆 *exhibition halls*

敞开思想 chǎngkāi sīxiǎng
to open up one's thoughts
To dare to speak what is really on one's mind.

唱盘 chàngpán
compact disc (CD)
Musical laser disks.

唱主角 chàng zhǔjué
to play a leading role
A metaphor for shouldering the main responsibilities in a certain situation

倡议书 chàngyìshū
initial written proposal
A document that initiates a proposal to do something.

chao

超编 chāobiān
to exceed quotas in personnel
A military unit or an organization having more personnel than the allocated quota.
E.g. 超编 400 人 *to exceed quota in personnel by 400 persons* / 工作人员超

编。 *The number of workers exceed the allocation.*

超标 chāobiāo

to exceed a standard

E.g. 某些干部的超标新房已被没收。 *The new housing for certain cadres which exceeds the standard has already been expropriated.*

超产 chāochǎn

to overfulfill a production target

To exceed the production quantity stipulated in the original plan.

超产粮 chāochǎnliáng

surplus grain

When the system of centralized grain purchase and sale was in effect, the government set grain production targets, on the basis of each locale's concrete conditions, for units of land that were cultivated by peasant households or by collective production units. Grain produced in excess of government targets was called surplus grain.

超常 chāocháng

surpass the normal or the ordinary

E.g. 超常儿童 *prodigy*

超储 chāochǔ

surplus stockpiles

The situation of supply exceeding demand, causing the stockpiles in warehouses of the commercial sector to exceed the stipulated quotas.

E.g. 1981 年末商业部门库存超储积压的产品有 58 种。 *At the end of 1981, commercial warehouses were overstocked with over fifty-eight major products.*

超导 chāodǎo

superconductivity

E.g. 超导技术 *superconductor technology*

超短波 chāoduǎnbō

ultrashort wave

Also called 米波 metric wave.

超短裙 chāoduǎnqún

mini-skirt

超负荷 chāofùhè

to exceed capacity or weight limit (of an installation or building component); general term for exceeding stipulated work load

E.g. 超负荷工作 *work overload* / 设备超负荷运转。 *The facility is operating beyond capacity.* / 铁路运输严重超负荷。 *Railroad transport is seriously overloaded.*

超纲要 chāo Gāngyào

to surpass the program

To exceed the targets for crop yields stipulated in the National Program for Agricultural Development from 1955 to 1957. (cf. 纲要)

超购加价 chāogòu jiājià

price increase for purchases of commodities surplus to the quota

Agricultural products in excess of the state purchase quota are bought by the state at an increased price.

超购粮 chāogòuliáng

surplus purchase grain

A grain harvest is distributed in the following way: First the portion stipulated for a peasant's personal use is retained. Then the state purchase quota portion is determined and sold to the state. Any portion sold to the state in excess of the quota is called 超购粮。

超耗 chāohào

excess consumption

The consumption of raw materials or

energy in the production process exceeding the stipulated norm.

超级城市 chāojí chéngshì
city with a residential population exceeding 10 million

超级大国 chāojí dàguó
superpower

超级市场 chāojí shìchǎng
supermarket

超龄团员 chāolíng tuányuán
over aged League members
Members of the Communist Youth League who have exceeded the upper age limit of twenty-eight.

超前 chāoqián
to rush to the forefront; ahead of time
E.g. 城市基础建设要超前。*We must carry out basic urban construction ahead of schedule.* / 超前发展 *development ahead of schedule*

超前精神 chāoqián jīngshén
a surpassing spirit
A spirit of having scientific foresight in building up production, of forging ahead, and striving to complete work preparation ahead of schedule.

超前消费 chāoqián xiāofèi
overconsuming
E.g. 人们互相攀比，竞相购置高档商品，一时出现了超前消费的热潮。*People had taken to vying with each other in buying high-grade goods, and this resulted in an upsurge in overconsuming for a period.*

超容 chāoróng
to exceed capacity

超声波 chāoshēngbō
ultrasonic wave

超生 chāoshēng
to exceed the birth quota stipulated by the government
E.g. 超生现象 *the phenomenon of exceeding the birth quota* / 超生的孩子 *children born in excess of the quota* / 杜绝超生 *to stem the breaking of birth quotas* / 超生大户 *a large household which has exceeded the birth quota*

超生游击队 chāoshēng yóujīduì
(sarcastic) exceed birth quota guerrillas
A metaphor for peasants who roam around in order to escape birth quotas and who end up having many children in defiance of regulations.

超市 chāoshì
supermarket
Abbreviation of 超级市场.

超收 chāoshōu
to exceed projected income targets
E.g. 税收系统超收40多亿元。*Tax collection has exceeded the target by over 4 billion yuan.*

超甜玉米 chāotián yùmǐ
super-sweet corn
A variety of corn, called No. 2 sweet corn, that was successfully bred by the Crop Breeding and Cultivation Research Institute of the Chinese Academy of Agricultural Science in the early 1980s. This corn has a high sugar content and is fragrant, sweet, and tender. It can be eaten fresh or frozen, or it can be processed into different kinds of canned corn.

超英赶美 chāo Yīng gǎn Měi
surpass Britain and catch up to the United States
An impractical slogan of the Great Leap Forward in 1958 that called for China to

surpass Britain and rival the United States in the production of important industrial products within a set period of time.

超越遏制 chāoyuè èzhì
beyond containment (Bush's Soviet policy announced in May 1989)

超支户 chāozhīhù
excess household expenditure
Households or units whose expenditure exceeds their incomes.

抄拿 chāoná
to take sth. (property that belongs to others or to the public) **for private use**
E.g. 有人把公家的财物抄拿回家。 *Someone has taken the public property home.*

抄收 chāoshōu
to transcribe (telegram)

钞票挂帅 chāopiào guàshuài
money in command
The perverted attitude and behavior resulting from placing money above all.

潮汐电站 cháoxī diànzhàn
tidal power stations
A power station that uses tides to generate electricity.

炒 chǎo
1) **to profiteer through buying and selling commodities in rapid succession** 2) **to mount aggressive publicity, thereby raise the popularity of someone** (e.g., a performer)
E.g. 新闻媒介爆炒歌星。 *The news media is awash with publicity for a certain singer.*

炒风 chǎofēng
the prevalent practice of engaging in the illegal and opportunistic buying and selling of foreign currency (cf. 炒买炒卖)

炒更 chǎogēng
(Cantonese colloquialism) to hold down a second job in one's leisure time
E.g. 广东青年职工参加炒更活动的人愈来愈多。 *An increasing number of young workers in Guangzhou are engaging in moonlighting activities.* / 炒更者一般都是按劳取酬。 *The income from moonlighting is based on productivity.*

炒股 chǎogǔ
to profiteer with stocks
To buy and sell stocks in rapid succession (for profit).
E.g. 有人炒股暴富。 *Some people become rich overnight through profiteering with stocks.*

炒汇 chǎohuì
to profiteer exchanging foreign currency
To buy and sell foreign currencies in rapid succession (for profit).
E.g. 炒汇者大规模收购外汇。 *Those who profiteer exchanging foreign currency buy it on large scale.*

炒家 chǎojiā
profiteer
Persons who engage in profiteering through buying and selling in rapid succession.

炒冷饭 chǎolěngfàn
to stir-fry cold rice
A metaphor for repeating the same old words and actions without adding new content.

炒买 chǎomǎi
the opportunistic and illegal activity

of buying foreign currency
E.g. 炒买外汇 *to buy foreign currency illegally* (cf. 炒买炒卖)

炒买炒卖 chǎomǎi chǎomài
to stir-fry in buying and selling
The illegal wheelings and dealings in foreign currency, the opportunistic buying and selling of foreign currency for profit.
E.g. 炒买炒卖外汇 *to stir-fry in buying and selling foreign currency*

炒卖 chǎomài
the opportunistic and illegal activity of selling foreign currency
E.g. 炒卖外汇 *to sell foreign currency illegally* / 有人在黑市上炒卖大量美钞、港币。 *There are people selling large amounts of U.S. and Hong Kong currency on the black market.* (cf. 炒买炒卖)

炒作 chǎozuò
profiteering activities
E.g. 炒作之风到处蔓延。 *The vogue of profiteering is spreading rapidly.*

炒鱿鱼 chǎoyóuyú
stir-fry squid
A metaphor for the dismissal or firing of a worker. The term comes from the fired worker having to roll up his bedding, like squid rolling up when fried in the pan.
E.g. 这个厂长在企业竞争中大胆使用"炒鱿鱼"的做法。 *Under the circumstances of competition among enterprises, this factory chief daringly used the method of stir-frying squid.*

che

车匪路霸 chēfěi lùbà
train and highway bandits and robbers

车间主任 chējiān zhǔrèn
workshop director
The person responsible for administering the production work of a workshop. Under the leadership of the factory chief, the workshop foreman organizes and manages all the production activities and is responsible to the factory chief for the workshop's production results.

车况 chēkuàng
condition of a car (vehicle)
E.g. 很多车车况不好。 *Many cars are in poor condition.*

车提 chētí
car profiteer
Someone who profiteers illegally in car sales.

车位 chēwèi
parking space

车组 chēzǔ
the crew or personnel on a train or bus

扯皮 chěpí
to wrangle
To dispute unreasonably, thus preventing something from progressing smoothly.

撤并 chèbìng
to cancel and merge
E.g. 撤并管理机构 *to eliminate and merge management agencies*

撤军 chèjūn
to withdraw troops

chen

尘埃落定 chén'āi luòdìng

dusted down
A metaphor for settling things.

尘封 chénfēng
covered with dust; be dust-laden
A metaphor for things being put aside for a long time.
E.g. 美国宪法中尘封已久的弹劾程序已经再次被启动。*The procedures for impeachment in the American Constitution have accumulated dust over a long period.*

晨练 chénliàn
morning exercise
E.g. 晨练队伍日渐庞大。*The ranks of morning exercisers are growing.* / 晨练者拥入公园大门。*Morning exercisers are pouring into the park.*

晨跑 chénpǎo
morning run
E.g. 他每天坚持晨跑。*He sticks to the practice of running every morning.*

晨运 chényùn
morning exercise
E.g. 做完晨运后吃早饭。*Eat breakfast after doing morning exercise.*

沉淀 chéndiàn
the settling of sediments
A metaphor for something changing from a mobile state into a static state.
E.g. 沉淀资金越来越多。*There is an increasing amount of static capital.*

cheng

城标 chéngbiāo
city emblem
城雕 chéngdiāo
urban sculptures; sculptures placed in urban public areas
城管 chéngguǎn
city administration; urban management
Abbreviation for 城市管理 city administration or urban management.

城际 chéngjì
inter-city
E.g. 城际快车 *inter-city express (buses, trains, etc.)*

城建 chéngjiàn
urban construction
Abbreviation for 城市建设 urban construction.
E.g. 城建部门 *urban development departments*

城郊 chéngjiāo
suburbia

城市规划 chéngshì guīhuà
city planning

城市经济学 chéngshì jīngjìxué
urban economics

城乡分割 chéngxiāng fēngē
urban-rural split
The situation where urban and rural areas have not formed unified economic entities, so that there is an imbalance between cities and the countryside in the supply of raw materials and the marketing of finished goods.

城运会 chéng–yùn–huì
municipal athletics meet
Abbreviation for 城市运动会

成活率 chénghuólǜ
survival rate
The percentage of newly born animals or newly planted seedlings that survive after a certain period.
E.g. 种植一百棵幼苗，成活率是百分之八十。*If a hundred seedlings are planted and eighty survive, the survival rate is eighty per-*

cent.

成龙配套 chénglóng pèitào
to form a dragon by assemblage

Also called 配套成龙 to assemble parts to form the dragon. To form a complete system by fitting the parts together.

成名成家 chéngmíng chéngjiā
to attain renown

To attain renown and to be acclaimed an expert in a field through success in some undertaking or research.

成品粮 chéngpǐnliáng
grain end-product

Also called 加工粮 processed grain.

成人教育 chéngrén jiàoyù
adult education

成人节 chéng rénjié
the activity administering moral education to eighteen-year-olds

成型玻璃 chéngxíng bōli
formed glass

Glass that has been processed according to specifications.

成药 chéngyào
ready-made medicine

Medicine in any form that has been made in a drugstore or pharmacy.

乘警 chéngjǐng
vehicular police

Police responsible for public security work on trains, boats, and airplanes.

乘务员 chéngwùyuán
vehicular attendants

Attendants on trains, boats, airplanes, buses, and trolleys.

程控 chéngkòng
program control

Contraction of 程序控制.
E.g. 程控电话 *program-controlled telephone*

惩办主义 chéngbàn zhǔyì
doctrine of punishment

A manifestation of the leftist opportunist line. In dealing with comrades who have made mistakes, they recklessly use organized methods, and "cruelly struggle against them and mercilessly attack them," rather than adopt an attitude of well-intentioned criticism and aid. This can only damage comrades, weaken the revolutionary strength and destroy the unity of the revolutionary ranks.

惩处 chéngchǔ
to punish; to penalize

惩罚价格 chéngfá jiàgé
penalty prices

Low prices assigned to inferior products by the relevant state authorities to penalise enterprises that manufactured them. These goods can only be sold at much lower prices.

惩前毖后,治病救人
chéngqián bìhòu, zhìbìng jiùrén
punish former, caution future, cure disease, save person

The policy adopted by the Chinese Communist Party toward comrades who have erred. 惩前毖后 means to expose the mistakes of the past without sparing anyone's feelings, and then, with a scientific attitude, to analyze and improve in future work. 治病救人 means that the goal of exposing mistakes and criticizing shortcomings is similar to the goal of a doctor curing a patient; both are committed to curing the person, not to punishing him with death.

承包 chéngbāo
(formerly) a factory or store accepting a project or a large order

Now the meaning of the term has expanded to include any form of contracted project.
E.g. 承包工程 *to contract projects* / 承包合同 *contract (for a project)* / 经营承包 *to engage in business through contracts* / 承包责任制 *the system of contract responsibility (a household or unit that engages in contracted projects)*

承包经营责任制 chéngbāo jīngyíng zérènzhì
Cf. 企业承包经营责任制

承包山 chéngbāoshān
contracted hill

A bare hill contracted out to a production team or an individual. The contracting period, the area to be opened and cultivated, the economic right and interests are all clearly spelled out, so that responsibility, jurisdiction, and benefits are tied together.

承包商 chéngbāoshāng
contractor

承包田 chéngbāotián
contracted field

A field contracted for cultivation by peasants or a production group. The field is owned by the collective, the contractor having only the right of use.

承购 chénggòu
to assume responsibility for purchasing

E.g. 承购包销 *to guarantee the purchase and sale of a certain quantity of goods*

承建 chéngjiàn
to accept a commission for a construction project

E.g. 承建旅游饭店 *to receive a contract for building a tourist hotel*

承销 chéngxiāo
to serve as an agent in selling commodities, bonds, etc.

E.g. 承销团 *a sales agency*

chi

吃大锅饭 chī dàguōfàn
to eat from a big pot

A misguided type of economic eqalitarianism. Under this eqalitarianism, among locales, units, and individuals, those who work hard and those who loaf are treated similarly, as are those who do a good job and those who do a poor job. Those who take on more work do not get greater rewards and those who shirk work do not get penalized. This kind of eqalitarianism completely violates the socialist principle of distribution according to labor, and severely dampens the incentives of the laboring masses.

吃大户 chī dàhù
to eat at the great households

During famines in the old society, peasants banded together and went to rich households to eat or to seize grain. This was a form of peasant initiated struggle. Now it refers to the unethical practice on the part of individuals or units of petitioning for funding (from the government, a collective, or a wealthy party) or of allocating funds illicitly on the pretext of launching an enterprise.

吃喝风 chīhēfēng
the common practice of feasting

1) The perverse practice, on the part of certain organizations or leaders, of seeking every opportunity to squander public funds on large banquets and

feasts. 2) The practice, by certain people, of treating others to meals in order to further their own interests.

吃皇粮 chīhuángliáng

to eat the emperor's grains

A metaphor for living on the fixed income provided by the state.

E.g. 科研单位不能靠吃皇粮过日子。 *Scientific research units cannot just rely on the state for their support.*

吃劳保 chīláobǎo

to live on labor insurance payments

E.g. 他这两年一直生病在家吃劳保。 *These couple of years he's been constantly ill and has been living on labor insurance payments.*

吃老本 chī lǎoběn

to eat on one's principals; to rest on one's laurels

Cadres who do not earnestly seek to upgrade their knowledge, but instead rest on their service record and past achievements or rely on their knowledge and experience.

吃偏饭 chī piānfàn

to enjoy favored treatment

(Metaphor) to enjoy special favorable treatment or help; to place lopsided stress on some aspect (also called 吃偏食).

E.g. 对学习差的学生要帮助，给他吃偏饭。 *We must help those students who are not doing well by giving them special treatment.* / 要给那些"好苗子"、"尖子"吃偏饭，重点培养,早出人才。 *We must provide those excellent "seedlings" and top-notch youths with special care and cultivation in order to develop their talents.*

吃偏食 chīpiānshí

Same as 吃偏饭.

吃请 chīqǐng

to eat on invitation

E.g. 干部不吃请，不受贿，不搞特殊化。 *Cadres do not accept invitations to meals, do not receive bribes, and do not ask for or grant special treatment.*

吃透 chītòu

to know inside-out

To thoroughly comprehend and grasp; to be totally familiar with the actual state of things.

E.g. 吃透中央文件的精神 *to thoroughly grasp the essence of a document from the central authorities*

吃透两头 chītòu liǎngtóu

to have a thorough grasp of both ends

A cadre needs to have, on the one hand, a thorough grasp of the spirit of the directives from the Party Central Committee and the State Council, and on the other hand, a familiarity with the practical conditions in his own unit. He should moreover bring the two together and do a good job.

吃闲饭 chīxiánfàn

having no job or income, simply eating in idleness

E.g. 他表示愿意去工作，不愿呆在家里吃闲饭。 *He indicated that he is willing to work, and was not willing to be supported and stay idle at home.*

吃小灶 chī xiǎozào

to eat from a private stove

Originally the term referred to being treated to the highest collective dining standard. Now a metaphor for leaders or organizations giving special consideration to members of their units.

吃准 chīzhǔn
to understand or grasp (a situation or a sentiment) accurately
E.g. 吃准行情 *to grasp a situation accurately*

持币待购 chíbì dàigòu
waiting to buy with cash in hand

持币抢购 chíbì qiǎnggòu
rushing to buy with cash in hand
A situation where goods are scarce and people compete to buy.

持币选购 chíbì xuǎngòu
to buy selectively with cash in hand
A situation where there is an abundance of goods so that people can selectively buy well designed high quality goods.

持平 chípíng
to hold the line
Not increasing nor decreasing (in quantity), maintaining evenness.
E.g. 第一季度的蔬菜上市量与去年同期持平。*The quantity of vegetables on the market in the first season is at the same level as the same period last year.*

赤潮 chìcháo
red tides (which appear on the ocean)

赤脚兽医 chìjiǎo shòuyī
barefoot veterinarian
Personnel in rural villages who are both farmers and veterinarians.

赤脚医生 chìjiǎo yīshēng
barefoot doctor
Medical workers in rural villages who are both farmers and physicians. This title is no longer used. Since January, 1985, it has been replaced by 乡村医生 country doctor or 卫生员 health worker or a medic.

斥资 chìzī
to allocate and disburse a large amount of funds
E.g. 该公司斥资 700 万元。*That company allocated and disbursed 7 million yuan.*

chong

充电 chōngdiàn
to charge (a battery)
A metaphor for acquiring more knowledge or adding vigor.
E.g. 澳门公务员忙充电。*Civil servants in Macao are busy acquiring new knowledge.*

冲刺 chōngcì
originally, to make a dash toward the finishing line (in a race); now it refers generally to an all out effort to reach one's goal
E.g. 向下一目标冲刺 *to go all out in achieving the next goal* / 工程进入最后冲刺。*The project has entered its final dash toward the goal.* / 这是人生道路上最后的冲刺。*This is the final dash in one's life path.*

冲剂 chōngjì
dissolved medicines
A kind of medicine, usually in powder or pellet form, that is taken after mixing with water.

冲浪运动 chōnglàng yùndòng
surfing

冲销帐目 chōngxiāo zhàngmù
counterbalanced accounts
Also called 冲帐. Revenue and expenditure offsetting each other. The amounts of money the two parties owed each other canceled each other out.

崇洋非中 chóngyáng fēizhōng

worship foreign, repudiate Chinese
To blindly worship things foreign and repudiate things Chinese.

崇洋媚外 chóngyáng mèiwài
worship and toady to things foreign
To worship and fawn on foreign countries.

崇洋哲学 chóngyáng zhéxué
foreign-worship philosophy
The mentality of blindly worshipping foreign countries.

重组 chóngzǔ
to reorganize; recompose; recombine

宠物 chǒngwù
pet (e.g., a cat or a dog)

冲劲 chòngjìn
the vim and vigor for forging ahead

chou

抽测 chōucè
to randomly pick out parts for testing and measuring
E.g. 用雷达测速仪抽测车辆 *to use a radar speed-testing device to spot check vehicles* / 冷饮市场抽测结果,汽水多数不合格。 *The result of the random check on commercial cold drinks shows that the majority of carbonated drinks fall below the standard.*

抽调 chōudiào
to transfer a portion
To transfer a portion (pertaining to personnel or materials).
E.g. 抽调教师 *to transfer a portion of teachers*

抽肥补瘦 chōuféi bǔshòu
draw from the fat to subsidize the lean
To gratuitously deduct money and materials from prosperous production teams and give them to poor production teams. This is a form of equalitarianism that is detrimental to the development of production.

抽检 chōujiǎn
spot check
E.g. 抽检结果表明,商店混有伪劣商品。 *The spot check showed that stocks in stores contained fake and inferior goods.*

抽奖 chōujiǎng
to determine prizes by lottery
E.g. 抽奖仪式 *lottery drawing ceremony*

抽紧 chōujǐn
to tighten up (currency circulating in the market)
E.g. 抽紧银根 *to tighten up the money market*

抽球 chōuqiú
to drive the ball
A way of hitting the ball in the game of ping-pong.

抽试 chōushì
to poll or to test a random sample from a group of people
E.g. 对干部进行抽试 *to carry out a random sample test on cadres*

抽验 chōuyàn
to spot check
To pull out samples for inspection from a batch of goods.
E.g. 消费者协会对一些经营单位进行抽验。 *The Consumers' Association is conducting sample inspections of certain businesses.*

抽样 chōuyàng
to draw a sample

抽酬筹丑臭 chōu – chòu

In the course of practical work, in order to understand and study certain mathematical properties of an object, often only a piece can be extracted from the whole, and used as material for analyzing the entire body. The process of extracting a piece from the whole is called 抽样. Also called 取样 to take a sample.

抽样调查 chōuyàng diàochá
sample investigation
A method of statistical investigation. A certain number of samples are extracted from the object of investigation, on the principle that each unit has equal chance of being selected. The samples are investigated, and from the results, the general state of the entirety is deduced.

酬宾 chóubīn
to sell commodities to customers at a preferential price
E.g. 酬宾展销 an exhibition and sale at discount prices for clients / 商品优惠大酬宾 to give big preferential discounts to clients

筹建 chóujiàn
prepare to build
To make plans and preparations for constructing or establishing something.

筹交 chóujiāo
to collect and pay to the relevant authorities
E.g. 失业保险费由企业统一筹交。Unemployment insurance is deducted (from employees' salaries) and paid to the authorities by businesses collectively.

筹拍 chóupāi
preparations for filming（a movie or television program）

E.g. 电影《三国演义》已开始筹拍。Preparations for filming the "Romance of the Three Kingdoms" have already begun.

筹委会 chóu – wěi – huì
preparation committee
Abbreviation for 筹备委员会 preparation committee.

筹资 chóuzī
prepare funds
Fund raising in preparation for a project.

筹组 chóuzǔ
to prepare and organize
E.g. 由市长负责筹组合作促进会。The mayor is responsible for organizing the Committee for Promoting Cooperation. /《全本三国演义》系列电影筹组顺利。The preparations and organization for filming the series "The Complete Romance of the Three Kingdoms" have proceeded smoothly.

丑闻 chǒuwén
ugly rumors; disgraceful news

丑星 chǒuxīng
clown; buffoon
A performer who specializes in clown roles. The term also refers to uncomely actors.
E.g. 北京是丑星辈出的地方。Countless performers who specialize in clown roles come from Beijing.

臭老九 chòulǎojiǔ
stinking ninth category
The slanderous term applied to intellectuals during the Cultural Revolution by the Gang of Four. The gang placed intellectuals in the ninth position after landlords, rich peasants, counter-revolutionaries, bad elements, rightists,

traitors, spies, and capitalist roaders, and regarded all of them as targets for reform and dictatorship.

臭美 chòuměi

show off one's own attractiveness or ability (a derogatory term)

E.g. 你臭美什么。 *What are you showing off for?* 人家都说他臭美。 *Everyone says she's a show-off.*

chu

初级产品 chūjí chǎnpǐn

relatively unprocessed products (agricultural, wood, mineral, etc.)

Also called 基本产品 basic product or 原始产品 primitive product.

初级社 chūjíshè

elementary cooperative

An elementary level agricultural production cooperative. A semi-socialist economic organization of a collective nature. Cooperative members use their land to become shareholders and unite in management and labor. The major production materials such as land, animals, and heavy farm machinery remain the property of the individual members. The incomes of members are based on how much labor and land they contributed to the collective.

初评 chūpíng

(competition) first round judging; preliminary assessment

E.g. 优秀图书初评工作正在进行。 *The first round of the book competition is in progress.*

出槽 chūcáo

(of pigs) leaving the feeding trough, i.e., heading for slaughter

E.g. 出槽肥猪 *fat pigs heading for slaughter*

出乘 chūchéng

to go out on a vehicle

E.g. 要缩短乘客出乘时间。 *We must shorten the amount of time passengers spend riding in vehicles.*

出工 chūgōng

1) to set out for work

E.g. 明天七点钟出工 *to go to work at 7:00 tomorrow*

2) to turn out for work

E.g. 今天八个人出工。 *Eight people came to work today.*

3) to supply the labor

E.g. 我们出钱，你们出工，咱们一起把这条路修好。 *We'll provide the money, you provide the labor. Together, we will repair this road.*

出口买方信贷 chūkǒu mǎifāng xìndài

export credit for buyers

出口转内销 chūkǒu zhuǎn nèixiāo

(originally) turning products originally designated for export to domestic markets; now, sometimes used as a metaphor for domestic news flowing abroad first, and then flowing back to the domestic public from abroad

E.g. 不要出现新闻出口转内销的现象。 *We don't want to have the phenomenon of having domestic news circulating abroad first, then circling back (to China).*

出栏 chūlán

sold from the farm (of animal stock)

E.g. 生猪出栏头数 *the number of live pigs sold from the farm*

出炉 chūlú

to come out of the stove

A metaphor for making something known to the public.

E.g. 投资保护法细则将在年底之前出炉。 *The detailed rules and regulations of the Investment Protection Law will be promulgated before the end of the year.* / 她关注每一季节新出炉的时装，并努力成为第一个实践者。 *She pays close attention to the new fashions released every season, and tries to be the first to wear them.*

出纳员 chūnàyuán

cashiers; tellers

出气筒 chūqìtǒng

metaphor for a person at whom another's anger and frustration are vented

E.g. 有的父母不顺心时就训斥孩子，拿孩子当出气筒。 *Some parents scold their children when they are unhappy, using them to vent their own anger and frustration.*

出赛 chūsài

to participate in a competition

E.g. 在这场比赛中，最强的选手还未出赛。 *In this tournament, the strongest contender has not yet come into the competition.* / 他出赛了 30 多场。 *He competed in over thirty competitions.*

出山 chūshān

to come out from the mountains

Originally, scholarly recluses coming out of seclusion to assume government office; now the term refers to persons of ability coming out to carry the mantle of leadership.

E.g. 这个厂子，只有请他出山才有可能救活。 *The only way to rejuvenate this factory is to ask him to come out to assume leadership.*

出台 chūtái

to emerge on stage

1) A performer coming onto the stage.
2) A metaphor for publicly carrying out something or acting openly.

E.g. 出台价格 *the disclosed price* / 正式方案不久将出台。 *The formal plan will soon be unveiled.*

出头鸟 chūtóuniǎo

the head of a bird first appeared

A metaphor for someone who stands out from the crowd or who leads a flock.

E.g. 他成了被枪打的出头鸟，受到了批判。 *He was shot at as the head of the flock and was subjected to criticism.* / 要冲破旧体制，敢做出头鸟。 *We must break through old conventions, and dare to stand out from the flock.*

出土文物 chūtǔ wénwù

archeological object

出线 chūxiàn

exceed the line; to attain eligibility

To attain eligibility to participate in the next level in a competition (usually pertaining to athletics).

E.g. 足球队取得了出线权。 *The soccer team passed in the qualifying competition.*

出血 chūxiě

blood-letting

A metaphor for wasting money and resources (usually unwillingly) or shelling out money grudgingly.

E.g. 让他出血 *to make him shell out money* / 我送了不少东西他才给我办这件事，不出血不行。 *I had to give him quite a few things before he was willing to do this for me; nothing can be done without a little blood-letting.* / 有人建议工厂要出点血，订桌饭招待用户。 *Someone suggested that the factory has to give a little blood and put on a banquet for its clients.*

出资 chūzī

to provide investment capital (for an industrial or commercial enterprise); to provide funds (for a project) in general

E.g. 这次比赛是由几个单位出资赞助的。 *This competition was made possible through funding from several units.* / 一位农民出资给学校建了图书馆。 *A peasant donated funds to build a library for the school.*

厨艺 chúyì

culinary art

除草剂 chúcǎojì

weed killer

Also called 除莠剂。

除尘器 chúchénqì

dust remover

Equipment that eliminates dust suspended in the air. This equipment can eliminate dust in exhaust fumes, prevent atmospheric pollution and is sometimes used for recycling materials. Dust removers work on various principles: gravity, centrifugal force, hydraulics, electricity, filter, etc.

除害灭病 chúhài mièbìng

rid scourges, eradicate diseases

Abbreviation for eradicating the four scourges and eliminating serious diseases that plague mankind. This means eradicating rats, bed bugs, flies and mosquitoes, wherever possible, and eliminating, wherever possible, serious diseases that plague mankind, such as schistosomiasis, smallpox, the plague, malaria, kala-azar, hookworm disease, filariasis, infantile tetanus, and venereal disease.

除四害 chú sìhài

to get rid of four scourges

To eradicate rats, bed bugs, flies, and mosquitoes.

储备粮 chǔbèiliáng

stored grain

Grain stored for times of need.

储币待购 chǔbì dàigòu

to save up money for purchases

To save money in order to buy the ideal commodities one needs.

储源 chǔyuán

sources of savings (surplus funds)

E.g. 改革开放使农民收入有了较大增长，扩大了储源。 *Reforms and liberalization led to growth in peasants' incomes and thus expanded the source of savings.*

储运 chǔyùn

storage and transport

E.g. 储运业 *moving and storage enterprise* / 储运能力 *moving and storage capability* / 储运公司 *moving and storage company*

处理品 chǔlǐpǐn

items for disposal

Merchandise that is sold at a discount due to substandard quality or overstocking.

触电 chùdiàn

to receive an electric shock

A metaphor for being associated with the film or television industry.

E.g. 许多朋友都和他谈过"触电"难的经历。 *Many friends have talked to*

him about their difficult experiences of being involved with the film industry.

触及 chùjí
to touch
E.g. 触及灵魂 *to touch one's soul*

触角 chùjiǎo
antenna; sensor
1) Sense organs found on insects, mollusks, and crustaceans. They are usually filaments located on the heads of these animals. 2) A metaphor for intelligence activities carried out by an individual or a group.
E.g. 敌人的触角已伸进我们这个地段了。 *The enemy's sensors have already penetrated our area.*

chuan

穿帮 chuānbāng
Synonymous with 穿梆. (cf. 穿梆)

穿梆 chuānbāng
to commit a faux pas; to be ashamed; to inadvertently divulge information
Also written as 穿帮.

穿梭外交 chuānsuō wàijiāo
shuttle diplomacy
Diplomatic activity involving frequent comings and goings while attempting to solve an international problem.

穿小鞋 chuān xiǎoxié
to wear tight shoes
A metaphor for the situation created by a cadre who uses his authority to retaliate against a comrade toward whom he bears a grudge, making things difficult for the person and moreover making it impossible for him to complain.

穿鞋戴帽 chuānxié dàimào
Same as 穿靴戴帽.

穿靴戴帽 chuānxuē dàimào
to wear boots and hats
A metaphor for the pedantic padding in articles (also called 穿鞋戴帽).

穿新鞋，走老路 chuān xīnxié, zǒu lǎolù
wearing new shoes to walk old paths
Under new situations and circumstances, some people persist in handling matters according to past experiences and old habits.

穿针引线 chuānzhēn yǐnxiàn
to pull with needle and thread
A metaphor for act as go-between or making a linkage.
E.g. 科学技术协会在发展轻工业中发挥了穿针引线的作用。 *In developing light industries, the Science and Technology Association served the function of a go-between.*

传帮带 chuán-bāng-dài
to transmit, aid and lead
Abbreviation for 传授、帮助、带领 transmitting experience, aiding with ideology, and leading the work style. This refers in general to the nurturing, support, and help given to new cadres by old cadres. It also refers to a master nurturing an apprentice.

传播媒介 chuánbō méijiè
mass media; the media
Also called 大众媒介 and 大众传播媒介.

传达报告 chuándá bàogào
reports that transmit (conference proceedings, pronouncements, speeches by leaders, etc.)
E.g. 下午由校长做教育会议传达报告。 *This afternoon, the principal will*

give a report on the proceedings of the education conference.

传感器 chuángǎnqì
sensor; transducer

传呼电话 chuánhū diànhuà
relay telephone
A kind of public telephone system. The person in charge of the phone is responsible for contacting people, receiving call fees and passing on messages. Persons receiving calls must pay a relay fee.

传家宝 chuánjiābǎo
family heirloom
Often used as a metaphor for good revolutionary tradition
E.g. 坚苦朴素是革命的传家宝。
Steadfastness and simplicity are precious characteristics of the revolutionary tradition.

传经送宝 chuánjīng sòngbǎo
transmitting scriptures and delivering treasures
Advanced persons or representatives from advanced units traveling to other units to speak about their experiences, exchange information, and transmit their techniques, as a means of promoting improvements in the other units' work.

传媒 chuánméi
mass media; the media
Abbreviation for 传播媒介.

传声筒 chuánshēngtǒng
sound-transmitting device; megaphone
A metaphor for someone who parrots others.

传统观念 chuántǒng guānniàn
traditional concepts

传统教育 chuántǒng jiàoyù
traditional education
1) Education about the revolutionary tradition. 2) Educational methods that have been handed down from generation to generation. It refers specifically to the European and American classroom educational system, educational theory and methods which are based primarily on Herbart's theory of education.

传统剧目 chuántǒng jùmù
traditional repertoire

传销 chuánxiāo
multi-layer transit sale or a method of direct marketing
The manufacturer develops directly certain transit sale merchants, who in turn develop more transit sale merchants and so on. Transit sale merchants function as the product's salespersons, promoters, and managers, and form a multi-layer network to deliver the product to consumers.

传译 chuányì
translation

传阅 chuányuè
circulate for perusal
E.g. 传阅文件 *documents circulated for perusal* / 传阅材料 *materials circulated for perusal*

传真 chuánzhēn
fax
E.g. 传真系统 *fax system* / 传真机 *fax machine*

船检 chuánjiǎn
to inspect ships

船难 chuánnàn
ship mishap or disaster

串灯 chuàndēng
lights strung together (usually deco-

rative)
串讲 chuànjiǎng
to link and explain; construe
1) To explain the meaning of a text word by word and sentence by sentence in the course of teaching language and literature. 2) To link up and narrate the main ideas of an article or book.

串联 chuànlián
1) **in order to advance a certain project, to contact people individually so that they will work together**
E.g. 土地改革后他们就串联了几户农民，组织起了一个生产互助组。 *After land reform, they linked up several peasant families and organized an agricultural mutual-aid team.*
2) **to connect up several electrical devices or units serially, so that the circuit current will pass through them in order**
The term is also written as 串连.

串联会 chuànliánhuì
linking-up meeting
A meeting convened, for the sake of concerted action, by relevant units or personnel to analyze the situation and discuss tactics.

串味 chuànwèi
the crossing of smells and flavors in different foods or drinks that have been placed together

chuang

窗口 chuāngkǒu
window
A metaphor for places or mechanisms through which things can be exhibited and communication, or transmission of news can occur.
E.g. 特区是新技术的窗口，管理的窗口，知识的窗口，也是对外政策的窗口。 *Special zones are windows for new technology, management techniques, knowledge and China's policies towards the outside world.*

窗口行业 chuāngkǒu hángyè
service industries

床头柜 chuángtóuguì
bedside commode (placed by the head of the bed)

床罩 chuángzhào
bedspread

闯关 chuǎngguān
to break through a pass
Also refers to using illegal means to get through customs.

闯红灯 chuǎng hóngdēng
to run a red light
A metaphor for breaking through obstacles or prohibitions or violating conventions and regulations.
E.g. 改革碰到红灯的时候，要敢于闯红灯。 *When reforms are met with a red light, we must dare to run through it.*

闯将 chuǎngjiàng
pathbreaker
A general who is courageous in charging and shattering enemy positions. Usually used as a metaphor for someone in a certain job situation who is enthusiastic, hardworking, and capable of making a breakthrough.

闯劲 chuǎngjìn
a pathbreaker's spirit
A metaphor for the courageous pioneering and fear-no-difficulties kind of

spirit.

创编 chuàngbiān

to create something in the performing arts (write a script, choreograph a dance, etc.)

E.g. 创编历史剧 to write a historical drama / 创编工作 the work of scriptwriting or choreography / 创编优美而惊险的动作 to choreograph beautiful and astounding feats

创导者 chuàngdǎozhě

prime mover; founder or initiator of a certain cause

创汇 chuànghuì

to earn foreign exchange (through production, sales or other means)

创记录 chuàngjìlù

to set a record

创利 chuànglì

to generate profit

E.g. 这家工厂去年人均创利5万元。Last year, this factory generated a profit of 50,000 yuan per person.

创三好 chuàng sānhǎo

to achieve the three goods (cf. 三好学生)

Young students striving to achieve the status of an advanced individual or group with good ideology, good academic achievements, and good work (身体好,学习好,工作好).

创收 chuàngshōu

to create income (through expanding the scope of a business, providing services to society, etc. (Distinguished from original fixed income)

E.g. 挖掘职工中的潜力,对外提供技术服务,创收提成。Tap the potential of employees and provide technological services to the outside, so as to obtain additional income from a percentage of the gains.

创新 chuàngxīn

to bring forth new ideas; blaze new trails

E.g. 我们一定要有创新精神。We must have a spirit of blazing new trails.

创业精神 chuàngyè jīngshén

enterprising spirit

E.g. 发扬大庆工人坚苦创业的精神 to develop the sedulous enterprising spirit of the Daqing workers

创意 chuàngyì

to create new ideas or concepts

创优 chuàngyōu

to create excellence; to create the best and the exceptionally excellent

E.g. 争先创优 to strive to be advanced and create excellence / 创优活动 the activity of creating excellence

chui

吹风会 chuīfēnghuì

advanced briefing

A meeting to disclose relevant information about a certain project before the project has been formally launched.

吹喇叭 chuīlǎba

to blow the horn

A metaphor for lavishing praises on someone.

E.g. 有的领导干部喜欢别人为他吹喇叭、抬轿子,这样必然脱离群众。Some leading cadres like to have others blow the horn and carry the sedan chair for them; in this way they inevitably become distanced from the masses.

吹冷风 chuīlěngfēng

blow cold wind
A metaphor for circulating negative comments or rumors behind someone's back.

吹奏乐 chuīzòuyuè
wind music

炊拨儿 chuībor
kitchen brush
A metaphor for a lackey.

炊事员 chuīshìyuán
cook; kitchen staff

垂直领导 chuízhí lǐngdǎo
a direct, vertical supervisory relationship

chun

春交会 chūn–jiāo–huì
China's Spring Export Trade Fair
Abbreviation for 中国出口商品春季交易会.

春秋衫 chūnqiūshān
shirts suitable for wearing in spring and autumn

春游 chūnyóu
spring outing (usually organized)

ci

磁带 cídài
recording tape
Audiotapes and videotapes.

磁带录音机 cídài lùyīnjī
tape recorder

磁碟 cídié
(computer) floppy disk
Disk used for storing data. There are two types: hard-style made of lead and soft-style made of plastic.

磁浮列车 cífú lièchē
Same as 磁悬浮列车.

磁浮铁道 cífú tiědào
magnetic suspension rail line
Rail line on which magnetic suspension trains run. (cf. 磁悬浮列车)

磁化杯 cíhuàbēi
magnetic cup (cup made of magnetic material, said to promote good health)

磁卡 cíkǎ
cards with built-in magnetic strips (used in credit cards, calling cards, etc.)

磁卡电话 cíkǎ diànhuà
card-operated telephone
Paid phones accessed by prepaid value cards. (cf. 电话磁卡 telephone card)

磁疗法 cíliáofǎ
magnetic treatment
A method of medical treatment whereby magnetic induction is used to stimulate a certain part of the human body.

磁悬浮列车 cíxuánfú lièchē
magnetic suspension rail car

词典学 cídiǎnxué
lexicography

刺刀见红 cìdāo jiànhóng
close-range bayonet-fighting in warfare
A metaphor for a tenacious indomitable spirit in work.

次文化 cìwénhuà
subculture
Synonymous with 亚文化. (cf. 亚文化)

cong

从群众中来，到群众中去
cóng qúnzhòng zhōng lái, dào qúnzhòng zhōng qù

to come from the masses, to go among the masses

A basic tenet of the Chinese Communist Party's mass line. It consists of gathering the ideas of the masses, transforming them into systematic ideas, then taking these ideas and propagating and explaining them to the masses, transforming them into the masses' ideas again, so that the masses will adhere to them, moreover, testing whether these ideas are correct by the practice of the masses. In this way ideas are circulated in a cycle, and the understanding of the leaders thereby becomes even more accurate, animate, and rich.

从众行为 cóngzhòng xíngwéi
the behavior of blindly conforming to the norm

CU

粗菜 cūcài
coarse vegetables
Vegetables of so-so quality and low price.

粗放经营 cūfàng jīngyíng
(agriculture) a method of increasing yield by applying fixed amounts of labor and capital to an enlarged area

粗放型 cūfàngxíng
extensive form (of agriculture)
A method of farming involving a minimum expenditure of capital and labor and expanding the area under cultivation to increase the total yield. It is the opposite of the intensive form of agriculture.

粗肥 cūféi
coarse fertilizer

A fertilizer that is not very effective in proportion to the volume used.

粗养 cūyǎng
rough and ready animal husbandry
A method of animal husbandry involving little energy and investment and the use of coarse and inexpensive feed.

促进派 cùjìnpài
promoters of progress
Persons or groups that have a motivating and promoting function in the advancement of society and the development of causes. It is the opposite of 促退派 laggards.

促退派 cùtuìpài
laggards
Persons or groups that have a laggardly effect on the advancement of society and the development of causes. It is the opposite of 促进派 promoters of progress.

促销 cùxiāo
to promote sales

cuan

篡党 cuàndǎng
to usurp the leadership of the Party

篡党夺权 cuàndǎng duóquán
to usurp the Party and grab power
To seize power from the Communist Party by using improper means.
E.g. 文革中四人帮企图篡党夺权。 *During the Cultural Revolution, the Gang of Four schemed to usurp the leadership of the Party and to snatch power.*

篡国 cuànguó
to usurp national political power

篡军 cuànjūn

to usurp the military
To seize power from the military by using improper means.

篡政 cuànzhèng
to usurp political power
To seize political power by improper means.

窜升 cuànshēng
to skyrocket (re stock market)
A surge in the price of certain stocks.
E.g. 股市窜升。 *The stock market has skyrocketed.*

cui

催产素 cuīchǎnsù
childbirth inducer

催动 cuīdòng
to spur on; to urge and mobilize
E.g. 催动人们奋发向上 *to spur people on*

cun

村干 cūngàn
village cadre

村民 cūnmín
villagers

村民委员会 cūnmín wěiyuánhuì
villagers' committee
Abbreviated as 村委会.
Mass autonomous organizations in rural areas. The committee members are elected by villagers.
E.g. 村委会主任、副主任和委员，由村民直接选举产生。 *The director, the deputy director and members of the villagers' committee are elected directly by the votes of villagers.*

村史 cūnshǐ
village history

村委会 cūn-wěi-huì
villagers' committee
Abbreviation for 村民委员会.

存车处 cúnchēchù
parking lot (for bicycles)

存储 cúnchǔ
to store data on computer software
E.g. 磁光光盘存储彩色图片质量特别良好。 *Laser disks are superior for storing color images.*

存档 cúndàng
to file

存活 cúnhuó
survival (of newborn domestic animals)
E.g. 今年产仔猪存活10万头。 *The number of survivals from the piglets produced in the entire year is 100,000.*

存栏数 cúnlánshù
the number in a pen
The number of animals that are being raised.

存休 cúnxiū
accumulated vacation or rest time; the number of vacation days or the amount of rest time accumulated
E.g. 他有存休。 *He has some accumulated vacation time.*

寸头 cùntóu
a hair style whereby the hair is only one-inch long

cuo

撮一顿 cuōyīdùn
to have a big meal at a restaurant or someone else's house
E.g. 我们中午撮一顿去。 *Let's go and have a big meal at noon!*

cuò 错

错案 cuò'àn
misjudged case

错漏 cuò-lòu
errors and omissions

错位 cuòwèi
misplacement; dislocation
E.g. 管理体制上下错位。*There are vertical dislocations within the management system.*

D

da

搭班子 dā bānzi
to constitute a group
To form a certain kind of organization to carry out certain tasks.
E.g. 厂领导正在搭班子。*The factory leadership is in the midst of structuring the work force.*

搭车 dāchē
to ride a vehicle
A metaphor for opportunistically and unjustifiably raising the price of certain commodities along with others (that are justified).
E.g. 坚决制止借烟酒调价之机,搭车涨价。*To resolutely curb the opportunistic price increases in the wake of cost adjustments of tobacco and liquor.*

搭卖 dāmài
a merchandising method whereby slow selling goods are packaged with fast selling goods to improve their sale
Same as 搭售.
E.g. 刹一刹菜场的搭卖风 *to put a brake on the prevalent practice of selling off slow moving products as part of a package with fast moving ones.*

搭桥 dāqiáo
to build bridge; to act as go between
A metaphor for making a linkage (between two parties) in order to facilitate something.
E.g. 由于你给我们搭桥,这笔买卖算做成了。*This business deal has come off thanks to you for acting as go-between for us.*

搭桥牵线 dāqiáo qiānxiàn
to build a bridge and pull a line; to help two sides establish linkage
E.g. 对各地区的协作,要做好搭桥牵线工作。*In order to help the various regions cooperate, we must excel in the work of building bridges and pulling lines.* / 她愿为未婚的青年们搭桥牵线。*She wants to build bridges and pull lines for unmarried young people.*

搭售 dāshòu
to sell along with something else
In the process of selling something chosen by a customer, the seller sells him some slow selling item whether the buyer wants it or not.

搭载 dāzǎi
(of vehicles, boats, airplanes, etc.) to pick up extra passengers or freight
E.g. 提倡搭载服务 *to encourage a transport service to take on extra freight* / 搭载试验装置 *to take experimental installations in addition to normal cargo*

达标 dábiāo
to reach the mark
E.g. 学生的体育测验成绩已经达标(达到国家规定的体育锻炼标准)。*The results of the students' athletics tests have already reached the mark*

(reached the standards for athletic training stipulated by the state).

答卷 dájuàn

answer sheet

A metaphor for the attitudes adopted and actions carried out by people in life and work.

E.g. 张海迪以实际行动交了一份令人赞叹的人生答卷。By her concrete actions, Zhang Haidi turned in a laudable answer sheet on life.

答疑 dáyí

to answer or solve difficult questions and problems

打的 dǎdí

to take a taxicab

的 is short for 的士, the term for taxi derived from a Cantonese transliteration of the English word "taxi".

E.g. 打的的人很多。There are lots of people taking taxicabs.

打点滴 dǎ diǎndī

to inject intravenously

To inject a liquid or to drip feed such substances as glucose solution and physiological saline into the body through the veins.

打斗 dǎdòu

to fight

E.g. 电影中有不少打斗的镜头。There are quite a few fighting scenes in the movie.

打翻身仗 dǎ fānshēnzhàng

to fight to change for the better

To work and struggle in order to transform backward or disadvantageous conditions.

E.g. 化肥厂去年亏损，今年大打翻身仗，年终盈利 20 万元。The chemical fertilizer plant took a loss last year. This year it fought to turn around, and by the end of the year, it made a profit of 200,000 yuan.

打非 dǎfēi

to combat illegal publications

E.g. 打非要实行综合治理。In combating illegal publications, we must carry out comprehensive measures.

打棍子 dǎ gùnzi

to hit with a stick

To seize on a person's error, and instead of constructively criticizing and educating him in a seek-truth-from-reality way, gratuitously exaggerating his faults, cooking up charges, attacking and persecuting him on a political and organizational level. (cf. 三不主义)

打击面 dǎjīmiàn

scope of attack

E.g. 要缩小打击面，扩大教育面。We must shrink the scope of attack on a small group of people and improve the education on a large group of people.

打假 dǎjiǎ

to combat counterfeits

To combat the production and sale of counterfeit commodities.

E.g. 打假防劣 to combat and deter counterfeits

打假办 dǎjiǎbàn

Office for Combating Counterfeiting

E.g. 打假办召开了座谈会。The Office for Combating Counterfeiting has convened a seminar.

打卡 dǎkǎ

to stamp a card

打老虎 dǎlǎohǔ

to combat tigers

Tigers being a metaphor for those who engage in such economic crimes as embezzlement, tax evasion, and extortion; to combat them means to expose and investigate them.

打派仗 dǎ pàizhàng
to fight factional wars

During the Cultural Revolution, mass organizations with opposing viewpoints and stances slandered and attacked each other through such means as big character posters, broadcasts, and even armed fighting. This kind of activity was called "fighting factional wars".

打屁股 dǎpìgu
to spank (a form of punishment)

A facetious way of referring to being criticized or penalized.

E.g. 这件事做不好得打屁股。*There will be a "spanking" if this is not done well.*

打前站 dǎ qiánzhàn
to act as an advance party

In a troop maneuver or group outing someone goes in advance to the next rest stop or destination to arrange for food and lodging.

E.g. 这次集体旅游，由小张同志打前站。*In this group trip, Comrade Xiao Zhang acts as the advance party.*

打私 dǎsī
to combat smuggling

To combat the smuggling and sale of illegally imported goods.

E.g. 落实打私会议精神 *to implement the spirit of the Conference on Combating Smuggling*

打死老虎 dǎ sǐlǎohǔ
to beat a dead tiger

1) A metaphor for the opportunistic behavior of not making an effort, but instead seeking to benefit from the work of others.

2) A metaphor for a cowardly person pretending to be a hero, ludicrous behavior.

打头炮 dǎ tóupào
fire the first shot

A metaphor for speaking out first at a meeting or acting first in a certain situation.

E.g. 座谈会开始后没有人打头炮。*At the start of the meeting, no one was willing to speak first.*

打压 dǎyā
to use power to force

E.g. 打压价位 *to force a reduction in price*

打游击 dǎyóujī
to engage in guerrilla activity

A metaphor for work or activities that have no fixed location.

E.g. 学校没有校址，上课到处打游击。*The school has no fixed site, so classes take place here and there.*

打预防针 dǎ yùfángzhēn
to inoculate

A metaphor for alerting others to possible pitfalls.

打砸抢 dǎ-zá-qiǎng
beating, smashing, and looting

The term refers specifically to these activities by rebel factions during the Cultural Revolution.

打砸抢分子 dǎ-zá-qiǎng fènzǐ
elements who committed beating, smashing and looting

One of the three types of people who were active during the Cultural Revolution. They include those who, to a serious degree, framed and persecuted cadres and the masses, conducted interrogations, exacted confessions with torture, and ruined people physically. There were also the primary elements who smashed offices, plundered files, and destroyed public property, as well as those who plotted these things behind the scenes. Lastly there were those elements who plotted, organized, and directed armed fighting and other actions which had grave consequences. (cf. 三种人)

打着红旗反红旗 dǎzhe hóngqí fǎn hóngqí

going against the red flag while holding the red flag

A metaphor for counter-revolutionary activities carried out in the name of the revolution.

大案要案 dà'àn yào'àn

major legal or criminal cases

大巴 dàbā

large-model buses

大帮轰 dàbānghōng

making sound and fury en masse

Also called 大呼隆. (cf. 大呼隆)

大包大揽 dàbāo dàlǎn

to take on in a big way

To take responsibilities and power upon oneself, to maintain control over everything. This term has a derogatory connotation.

大包大统 dàbāo dàtǒng

to consolidate (in a big way) and manage

大包干 dàbāogān

the big responsibility system

1) To take and pledge to fulfill a certain task. 2) Synonymous with 包产到户.

大比武 dàbǐwǔ

a big military match

1) Large-scale training activities involving competition between those taking part to improve performance and skills. 2) Specifically the mass oriented military training movement developed by the Chinese Liberation Army in 1964. At that time, the Central Military Committee of the Communist Party of China issued the directive to popularize the training method created by Guo Xingfu, a commander of a certain Nanjing division. This method took hardship, strictness, and actual warfare as the starting point. Thus a military training movement of a mass character was unfurled. During the Cultural Revolution, Lin Biao and his cohorts repudiated the whole movement and many cadres and soldiers suffered persecution. After the smashing of the Gang of Four, they were redressed and their honor restored.

大辩论 dàbiànlùn

big debates

One of the "four bigs". The various forms of public debates launched by the masses on major issues of right and wrong. They are no longer in vogue. (cf. 四大)

大部头 dàbùtóu

(of book) a huge volume

大参考 dàcānkǎo

nickname for internal publication 参考资料 Reference Material

大操大办 dàcāo dàbàn

to make arrangements on a large scale

To make large-scale arrangements (for a wedding, funeral, etc.)

大吃大喝 dàchī dàhē

to eat and drink in a big way

To eat and drink without restraint, wasting money recklessly in the process.

大串联 dàchuànlián
the big link-up

In the early stages of the Cultural Revolution, teachers, students, and Red Guards from schools in various locales went into society, established ties with various regions and units, incited people to rise in "revolution" and "rebellion," ferreted out and struggled against "capitalist roaders," and thereby disrupted the local Party and political organizations at all levels.

大倒 dàdǎo

Same as 官倒, also called 大倒爷 (cf. 官倒爷).

大道理 dàdàolǐ
great principles

1) Profound principles.

2) A metaphor for important matters that affect the entire situation.

E.g. 小道理要服从大道理。*Small principles must yield to great principles.*

3) Empty rationale and principles that are divorced from practicality.

E.g. 夸夸其谈，光讲大道理，解决不了任何实际问题。*Such extravagant talk, it's all just a bunch of great principles, and cannot solve any practical problems.*

大毒草 dàdúcǎo
big poisonous weed

Synonymous with 毒草.

大而全 dà ér quán
big and complete

The concept that an enterprise should be large in scale, and complete in its technology, divisions, facilities, and mechanical equipment, so that as a unit, it can be an "all-round factory" that does not depend on others for anything. "Big and complete" led to duplication in production, dispersal of capability, and inability to fully give rein to the strengths and potential of each factory. It also impeded the development of specialization in production and mutual cooperation.

大方向 dàfāngxiàng
great direction

The general direction in the development of something.

E.g. 要坚持斗争的大方向。*We must persist in the great direction of the struggle.*

大飞 dàfēi
motorboat with three or more engines.

大干快上 dàgàn kuàishàng
go all out, advance quickly

A slogan popular in the latter period of the Cultural Revolution. That is: work energetically for socialism, advance every task as quickly as possible. Because this slogan was raised under the direction of erroneous leftist ideology, it could not serve any positive function.

大哥大 dàgēdà
cellular phone (nicknamed after a character in a Hong Kong film)

大公共 dàgōnggòng
large bus

Synonymous with 大巴.

大锅饭 dàguōfàn
food prepared in a big pot
(cf. 吃大锅饭)

大轰大嗡 dàhōng dàwēng

much sound and fury

To be grand and spectacular in form, but pay no attention to practical results.

大红伞 dàhóngsǎn
big red umbrella

A metaphor for the protective political umbrella of the proletariat class.

大呼隆 dàhūlóng
making sound and fury all together

Also called 大帮轰. It was a major drawback of centralized labor in rural people's communes before the production responsibility system was implemented. Centralized labor is a simplistic kind of cooperation: it causes workers to lose concern for the work process, creates a situation where everyone waits for others, where people show up for work but exert no effort, reduces the quality of the work, and leads to cadres issuing arbitrary and impracticable directives on production. This state of simplistic cooperation is called 大呼隆.

大户 dàhù
(formerly) big clans such as wealthy, landlord families; (now) households or units with large-scale enterprises; large-scale purchasers

E.g. 养殖大户 *large-scale breeder (of aquatics)* / 专业大户 *large-scale professional organization* / 高损大户 *unprofitable (deficit-taking) large-scale enterprise* / 盈利大户 *profit-making large-scale enterprise* / 用水大户 *big water consumer* / 卖大户 *to sell to large-scale purchasers*

大会战 dàhuìzhàn
big battle

1) A big decisive battle conducted by the main forces of two warring factions at a certain place and time. 2) In the process of socialist construction, to concentrate manpower, materials and financial resources, and to give a big push to the completion of certain important construction projects.

E.g. 大庆油田是用大会战的办法开发出来的。 *The Daqing Oilfield was opened up by the big battle method.*

大集体 dàjítǐ
big collective

1) A type of socialist collective ownership system. In general, it refers to the collectively owned enterprises led and managed by the relevant local district or municipal departments. These enterprises carry out independent accounting, and take responsibility for their own profits and losses. 2) A group on a fairly large scale, in contrast to 小集体 small-scale group.

大轿车 dàjiàochē
big sedan car

A large passenger automobile with a fixed roof.

大节 dàjié
major integrity; political integrity

Integrity manifested by a person when faced with an issue involving a major political principle.

E.g. 一个人不但大节要好，小节也应该好。 *One should have not only political integrity, but also integrity in personal life.* (*cf.* 小节无害论)

大进大出 dàjìn dàchū
large-scale import and export

大考 dàkǎo
final exam; college entrance exam

大款 dàkuǎn
money bag

Someone with loads of money.

E.g. 他是个大款。 *He's a money bag*.

大老粗 dàlǎocū
uncouth fellow

An uncultured person or a person with a relatively low level of education. The term is often used to deprecate oneself.

大礼拜 dàlǐbài
big Sunday

1) Some enterprises and institutions in cities and towns, due to production or work requirements, practice the system of one rest day every two weeks (some have two consecutive rest days). The Sunday that is a rest day is called 大礼拜 big Sunday.

E.g. 今天我们歇大礼拜。 *Today we take a big Sunday rest*.

2) The term is also applied to this kind of system.

E.g. 这个厂实行大礼拜。 *This factory practices the big Sunday system*.

3) After the forty four hour work week was implemented in China, every other weekend became a two day weekend. The two day weekend is called "big Sunday".

E.g. 有了大礼拜，外出旅游就有条件了。 *Since the "big Sunday" came into existence, outings and travel became more feasible*.

大立柜 dàlìguì
wardrobes

大粮食观点 dàliángshi guāndiǎn
the broad view of staple foods

To understand staple foods in a broad sense, to regard all edibles as staple foods. That is, to take not only the grains like rice, flour, corn, and sorghum as the main components of staple foods, but also peanuts, beans, fruits, vegetables, tea, oil., etc., and even foods with relatively high caloric content like meat, eggs, milk, fish, and shrimps.

大梁 dàliáng
major beam in a house, i.e., the one at the apex of the roof

A metaphor for important, mainstay elements.

E.g. 挑起教学大梁 *to be the mainstay on the teaching faculty* / 他是个没挑过大梁的青年演员。 *He is a young actor who has not yet picked up a main role*.

大龄青年 dàlíng qīngnián
"old" unmarried youths

Unmarried men and women in the age range of between twenty eight and thirty five.

大路 dàlù
broad road

A metaphor for common and ordinary commodities.

E.g. 大路产品 *ordinary products* / 大路品种 *ordinary variety*

大路菜 dàlùcài
popular vegetables

Vegetables of middling quality that have relatively big markets.

大路货 dàlùhuò
popular commodities

Commodities of median quality that have a wide market.

大陆 dàlù
mainland; China's mainland (in juxtaposition to Taiwan, Hong Kong, and Macao)

大陆妹 dàlùmèi
a name given by local people to

young mainland Chinese women making their living in Hong Kong and Taiwan

大陆桥 dàlùqiáo
continental bridge
Transcontinental rail transport line, providing land transport to bridge the sea transport at both ends.
E.g. 欧亚大陆桥有能力开办货运。*The Eurasian continental bridge can begin serving cargo transport.*

大帽子 dàmàozi
a big cap
A metaphor for a serious accusation or a very bad reputation.
E.g. 批评要符合实际，不要乱扣大帽子。*The criticism must correspond to reality, we must not recklessly put big caps on people.*

大民主 dàmínzhǔ
big democracy
To conduct class struggle and to resolve society's contradictions by using the method of mass movements. (cf. 四大)

大鸣大放 dàmíng dàfàng
(lit) big voicing, big airing; a free airing of views
I would not cut this out as the term means nothing without it.

大男大女 dànán dànǚ
men and women past the age of marriage
1) Unmarried men and women aged between twenty eight and thirty five. 2) General term for sons and daughters older than fifteen or sixteen who live with their parents.

大农学 dànóngxué
greater agricultural science, a branch of study that includes agri-culture as well as forestry, animal husbandry, and other sidelines
E.g. 大农学专业 *the agricultural profession in the broad sense*

大农业 dànóngyè
greater farming
Farming as understood in the broad sense. That is, farming is not limited to agriculture, but includes agriculture, forestry, stock raising, fisheries, and diversified businesses. Stock raising on the prairies and grasslands, freshwater fisheries and agriculture in lakes and ponds, animal husbandry in villages, bee-keeping, and forestry on hills and plains are all within the scope of greater farming.
E.g. 大农业观点 *the greater farming viewpoint*

大排档 dàpáidàng
large stall
E.g. 广交会不会变成大排档。*The Guangzhou Trade Fair will not become a large stall.*

大批促大干 dàpī cù dà gàn
great criticisms prod great work
A mistaken leftist slogan popular for a time in the latter period of the Cultural Revolution. It means using vigorous criticism of revisionism and capitalism to prod people to work energetically for socialism.

大批判 dàpīpàn
great criticism
A method of the extreme left during the Cultural Revolution. It involved mobilizing the masses to publicly expose and criticize – through such means as meetings, published articles, and big character posters – the so-called "leading

exponents of the bourgeoisie that have infiltrated the Party," "bourgeois reactionary academic authority," and "various reactionary viewpoints."

大批判专栏 dàpīpàn zhuānlán
great criticism column

The wall and board newspapers which various units set up during the Cultural Revolution for the special purpose of publishing articles of criticism. (cf. 大批判)

大破大立 dàpò dàlì
to break and to set up in a big way

A slogan popular during the Cultural Revolution: thoroughly criticize and break old thoughts and old things, resolutely establish new thoughts and things.

大起大落 dàqǐ dàluò
great fluctuations

E.g. 国民经济发展出现了大起大落。 *There were great ups and downs in the development of the national economy.*

大气候 dàqìhòu
greater climate, the climate of a large region

A metaphor for the political and social conditions of a greater sphere (beyond one's own immediate environment).

大钱 dàqián
big money

Originally large coins with a value higher than ordinary coins; now it refers to large sums of money.

E.g. 赚大钱 *to make big bucks* / 挣大钱 *to earn big bucks*

大庆红旗 Dàqìng hóngqí
red banner of Daqing

The Daqing Oilfield was an advanced example of China's industrial enterprises so it served as a symbol and a model. Since Mao Zedong issued the appeal "industries learn from Daqing" in 1954, the oilfield had been eulogized as the "Daqing red banner". (cf. 大庆精神)

大庆精神 Dàqìng jīngshén
spirit of Daqing

The style of thought and work cultivated by the Daqing Oilfeld workers during the process of opening up and building the Daqing Oilfield. Its main features are: work with a will to strengthen the nation, rely on oneself, take real action as worthy of the Chinese people's patriotic spirit and national pride; when faced with serious difficulties, fear nothing, courageously shoulder heavy loads, hold to the revolutionary spirit of relying on one's own two hands to carry out arduous pioneering work; in building up production, be conscientious, meticulous, earnest and responsible, strive to be scientific and hold to the matter-of-fact attitude of doing one's job well; and in one's relationship with the country, hold the overall situation in one's heart, labor selflessly, bear a share of the nation's difficulties, do not fuss over individual gains and losses, and hold to the self-sacrificing spirit, etc.

大庆式企业 Dàqìngshì qǐyè
Daqing-type enterprise

An honorific name – proposed in 1977 – for advanced enterprises. That is, enterprises that are like Daqing in adhering to the socialist direction in enterprise management, in having a scientific management system and strict work style, and in having the main economic and technical targets (cf. 八

项经济技术指标 eight economic and technical targets) reach the advanced level domestically, are eulogistically called Daqing-style enterprises.

大秋作物 dàqiū zuòwù
autumn-harvested crops
Field crops such as sorghum, corn, and rice that are harvested in autumn.

大球 dàqiú
big balls, relatively large balls used in such games as soccer, basketball, and volleyball; the ball games in which the "big balls" are used

大撒把 dàsābǎ
totally laissez-faire
E.g. 计划生育不能大撒把。*We cannot be laissez-faire about birth control.*

大赛 dàsài
large-scale competition, important competition

大三线 dàsānxiàn
big third line
Third line area, the rear area in war strategy. (cf. 三线)

大上大下 dàshàng dàxià
big up and down
1) A job or engineering construction project that has just been started on a large scale and is, for some reason, interrupted or abandoned.
E.g. 新中国成立以来,工业建设有两次大上大下,造成严重损失。*Since New China was founded, industrial construction twice went through a big up and down, with serious losses as a result.*
2) A certain job or production that has achieved much, then experienced a big decline. Also called 大起大落 big rise and big fall.

大是大非 dàshì dàfēi
cardinal questions of right and wrong; major matters of principle
Cardinal issues of right and wrong, usually applied to political matters.

大手术 dàshǒushù
metaphor for major measures adopted to resolve complex problems

大田 dàtián
large field
E.g. 大田作物(包括水稻、小麦、高粱、棉花、牧草等) *big field crops (including rice, wheat, sorghum, cotton, hay, etc.)*

大团结 dàtuánjié
great solidarity
A colloquial term for the Chinese ten-yuan bill, which features a picture of solidarity among the various ethnic groups.
E.g. 他手里拿着十几张"大团结"。*He is holding more than ten great solidarities in his hand.*

大腕儿 dàwànr
big finesse
Movie stars, singers, athletes, etc., who are famous and wealthy. The term also refers to persons with exceptional strength in a particular field.

大休 dàxiū
big rest
After China implemented the forty four hour work week, every other week had a two day weekend, which is called "big rest".
E.g. 这周是大休。*This weekend is a big rest.*

大洋古 dà-yáng-gǔ
large, foreign and ancient

A cover term for three kinds of drama: large-scale, foreign and classical.

大跃进 dàyuèjìn
Great Leap Forward
A movement, carried out in 1958 by the entire nation under the leadership of the Chinese Communist Party, to speed up within a relatively short time industrial and agricultural production. Due to lack of experience in building socialism and the fact that the primary leaders at the time developed proud self-satisfied attitudes, they rushed to seek success, magnified the effect of the subjective will, and did not adequately study or investigate the problems of production. Such leftist errors as overly ambitious targets, arbitrary and impracticable directions ran rampant, leading to serious difficulties in the national economy. However, certain achievements were also made in the socialist reconstruction.

大运会 dà-yùn-huì
college students' athletics meet
Abbreviation for 大学生运动会.

大杂烩 dàzáhuì
hodgepodge
A dish made up of many different kinds of dishes thrown together. A metaphor for a mixture of various things haphazardly thrown together. The term has a derogatory connotation.

大寨县 Dàzhàixiàn
Dazhai-style county
In the 1970s, under the leadership of erroneous leftist thinking, there arose a slogan to build Dazhai-style counties. That is, to spread the Dazhai Brigade's leftist experience to all rural villages of China, so that all levels of leadership and all sectors in every county could carry out their work like the Dazhai Brigade.

大展 dàzhǎn
large-scale exhibition

大专 dàzhuān
1) college for professional training
E.g. 大专生 *a student majoring in a subject*
2) college and technical schools on a par with colleges
E.g. 大专院校 *colleges and technical institutes*

大字报 dàzìbào
big character poster

dai

戴帽小学 dàimào xiǎoxué
capped elementary schools
Certain elementary schools with junior high schools attached.

带电作业 dàidiàn zuòyè
live-wire work
Maintenance work done on charged high voltage electric lines or electrical installations, in order to guarantee uninterrupted supply of electricity to industrial and agricultural production. It can be divided into indirect operations (ground electrical position operations) and direct operations (isoelectric operations).

带钢 dàigāng
belted steel; strip steel
Thin coil or belt shaped steel material.

带头羊 dàitóuyáng
the lead sheep; ringleader
A metaphor for a person who initiates action and mobilizes others. Usually has

a derogatory connotation.

带原 dàiyuán
to carry an infectious virus but not actually develop the disease
E.g. 一名爱滋病带原者 *a HIV carrier*

带职回乡 dàizhí huíxiāng
take along one's position while returning home
Also called 保职回乡 retain position while returning home and 留职停薪回乡 save position stop salary while returning home. National cadres who voluntarily return home to develop enterprises in forestry, stock raising, industrial sidelines, etc., may retain their positions and titles without salary while they are on home leave. This is done by the individual making an application, then having it approved by his leaders. When he returns to his original work post, his salary will be reinstated.

代耕 dàigēng
farming for others
1) A kind of favored treatment given to the families of revolutionary martyrs and soldiers during China's war of revolution; that is each revolutionary base organized peasant masses to help work the land of those families which lacked manpower. The land which was worked on by others was either farmed by workers assigned by the government or by the masses. 2) People make a living farming for others (land owners). 3) Tractor stations working the land for peasant collectives, in accordance with contracted terms, and for a certain fee.

代沟 dàigōu
generation gap
E.g. 不同的思想意识在两辈人之间形成了一条代沟。*The differences in thought and consciousness between the two generations have formed a generation gap.*

代购 dàigòu
purchasing done by an agent
Also called 委托收购 commissioned purchasing. 1) One unit purchasing for another unit, such as China's supply cooperatives purchasing agricultural products or scrap materials for the state's commercial departments. 2) A low level form of national capitalism adopted by China in implementing socialist reforms on national capitalist commerce. The actual practice is: state or cooperative commercial enterprises contract private businesses to purchase commodities from abroad, or to purchase local products or agricultural products domestically. Certain handling fees are paid to the private businesses.

代际 dàijì
inter-generational
Between two generations.
E.g. 代际关系 *inter-generational relationship*

代码 dàimǎ
number code
A number that represents a unit or group.

代培 dàipéi
to train on contract (e.g., an institution undertaking to train members of a work unit)
E.g. 采取代培方式培养人才 *to adopt the method of training-on-contract to train personnel* / 为一些单位代培人才 *to train personnel for certain units*

on contract / 用人单位委托学校代培学生 *employers commissioned schools to train students for them on contract* / 选拔青年职工到大学代培 *to select young workers to receive training by contract at a university*

代培生 dàipéishēng
train-on-contract students

Workers who are being trained by another unit on contract. (cf. 代培)

代销 dàixiāo
to market on commission

1) An enterprise marketing products for another enterprise or individual, as for example, China's supply cooperatives marketing agricultural products for peasants. 2) A lower level form of national capitalism adopted by China in implementing socialist reforms on national capitalist commerce. The actual practice is: a state-managed commercial business signs a marketing commission agreement with a private business to have the latter sell commodities at price set by the state-managed company. A certain handling fee is paid. Marketing agencies are divided into those whose sole function is marketing for others, and those for whom this is only a partial function.

代营食堂 dàiyíng shítáng
commissioned canteens

Synonymous with 街道代营食堂 neighborhood commissioned canteens. They are small restaurants commissioned by state-run restaurants, and managed by workers' families and residents organized by the neighborhood committees in large- and medium-sized cities. Their responsibility is to manage small food items within a certain scale, as a service to residents in the neighborhood.

代职 dàizhí
to perform the duties of a position on an acting basis (e.g., acting president, acting dean)

E.g. 抽调干部到基层工厂代职 *to transfer cadres to grass-roots factories for practical training* / 军事学校抽派学员到前线代职见习。 *The military academy sent students to the front to receive practical training.*

贷学金 dàixuéjīn
student loans (e.g., provided by the state or units to Chinese students studying abroad)

袋装 dàizhuāng
to package in paper or plastic bags

E.g. 袋装食品 *packaged foodstuff* / 袋装牛奶 *packaged milk*

待岗 dàigǎng
be on a waiting post; unemployed and waiting for a new post

待业 dàiyè
awaiting a job assignment

Waiting to take up an occupation.

E.g. 待业青年 *youths awaiting job assignments* / 待业人员 *personnel awaiting job assignments*

dan

单兵教练 dānbīng jiàoliàn
single soldier training

Also called 各个教练 *individual training*, which makes every soldier become thoroughly trained in the basic maneuvres stipulated by the regulations, thus setting the foundation for platoon training.

单兵装备 dānbīng zhuāngbèi
single soldier outfit

The weapons, ammunition, uniform and equipment with which each soldier in the armed forces is outfitted.

单产 dānchǎn
unit production

The yield from a unit area of land in a year or a season. It also means the yield for one crop on one *mu* of land.

单纯任务观点 dānchún rènwù guāndiǎn
the single-minded duty mentality

The mentality of being satisfied with simply completing one's duty, lack of initiative and creativity.

单纯业务观点 dānchún yèwù guāndiǎn
the single-minded professional mentality

The mentality of attending only to a profession and overlooking politics.

单干风 dāngànfēng
the individual work style

A derogatory term which refers to the responsibility-to-the-household system that commune members in certain areas adopted during the economically difficult period from 1959 to 1961. The term was used under the influence of extreme leftist thinking, which took responsibility-to-the-household to mean working singly, and a regression from the collective economy to an individual economy.

单干户 dāngànhù
individual households

Individual rural households that did not join mutual help and cooperative organizations during China's agricultural cooperativization movement. It is also a metaphor for persons who do not wish to work with others, but prefer to complete certain tasks single-handedly.

单缸 dāngāng
single vat

Having only one trough.

E.g. 单缸洗衣机 *single-tub washing machine*

单极世界 dānjí shìjiè
single world power

An international situation in which world affairs are dominated and controlled by one country or one political and military group

单晶炉 dānjīnglú
monocrystal oven

单晶体 dānjīngtǐ
monocrystals

单剧本 dānjùběn
a one off TV program (in contrast to a series)

单卡 dānkǎ
single-cassette (with only one cassette – so it cannot play and record at the same tIme); single-cassette tape player

单列 dānliè
to list as a separate item

E.g. 计划单列 *projected list*

单亲 dānqīn
single parent

Referring to a family with only the father or the mother

E.g. 单亲家庭 *single parent family*

单人宿舍 dānrén sùshè
dormitory for singles

Also called 单身宿舍 singles' dormitory. Collective dormitories set up by enterprises or institutional units for unmarried people or workers whose spouses live in separate places. Each room houses one or more persons.

单身贵族 dānshēn guìzú
single aristocrat
A person who is single and thus has few responsibilities.

单速 dānsù
single speed
Single speed – as opposed to multi-speed – in referring to such things as bicycles and electric appliances.

单向 dānxiàng
one-way; single-facet
E.g. 单向决策 *unilateral decision*

单一经济 dānyī jīngjì
one sided economy; single product economy

单一种植 dānyī zhòngzhí
single cropping
A form of agricultural management whereby only one or two kinds of crops are cultivated.

单元楼 dānyuánlóu
unit buildings
A kind of residential building, composed of several units.

担纲 dāngāng
play (act) a role; take a part in

淡化 dànhuà
to gradually dilute or reduce
E.g. 苦咸水淡化处理 *treatment for reducing acidity of water* / 为人民服务的观念不能淡化。*The concept of serving the people cannot be allowed to diminish.* / 淡化近亲共事的社会现象 *to diminish the social phenomenon of nepotism*

蛋鸡 dànjī
laying hens; layers

dang

当家 dāngjiā
to head a household
A metaphor for playing the key role within a certain realm.
E.g. 他是内当家。*He plays the key domestic role.* / 大白菜是北京地区居民的当家菜。*Chinese cabbage is the main vegetable for the residents of Beijing.* / 当家品种 *the main variety*

当权派 dāngquánpài
the faction in power

党八股 dǎngbāgǔ
(lit.) Party eight-part essay; stereotyped Party writing
A bad writing style within the Chinese Communist Party. The essays and speeches written by certain persons within the revolutionary ranks do not analyze the issues under discussion; technical terms and abstract words are used to create an effect but the essays lack substance and are full of empty talk. This is just like the eight-part essay of the feudal imperial examination era, hence it is called the Party eight-part essay. It is also called 洋八股 modern eight-part essay.

党报 dǎngbào
party newspaper
In China, this term specifically refers to the official newspaper of the Chinese Communist Party.

党代会 dǎng-dài-huì
Congress of Party Representatives
Abbreviation for 党代表大会.

党法 dǎngfǎ
regulations of a certain political party

党费 dǎngfèi

1) a political party's activities funds;
2) fees paid by Party members to the organization

党风 dǎngfēng
party style
1) A political party's work style. 2) The style, customary practices, and character which Chinese Communist Party members have manifested in the various aspects of ideology, politics, work, and life.

党规 dǎngguī
rules and regulations of a political party; specifically the various rules and regulations of the Chinese Communist Party

党纪 dǎngjì
party discipline
The term specifically refers to the discipline of the Chinese Communist Party which every Party member must observe.

党建 dǎngjiàn
(political) party construction; specifically the ideological and organizational construction of the Chinese Communist Party
E.g. 党建理论 *the theory of (communist) party construction* / 党建研究 *the study of (communist) party construction*

党刊 dǎngkāng
party publications
Specifically, they are the publications of the Chinese Communist Party organization.

党课 dǎngkè
party classes
Lectures conducted by the Chinese Communist Party organization to educate Party members on the principles, regulations and policies of the Party. Often non-Party comrades are also drawn in to attend lectures.

党龄 dǎnglíng
party age; party standing
Number of years since one has joined a political party. Specifically it refers to members of the Chinese Communist Party.

党内和平论 dǎngnèi hépínglùn
doctrine of harmony within the Party

党内生活 dǎngnèi shēnghuó
internal life of a party
Specifically, the political life of the Chinese Communist Party. In a broad sense, all party activities are the internal life, such as a meeting of a party group or branch, a party congress, etc.

党票 dǎngpiào
(derogatory) Party membership, qualifications for Party membership
E.g. 坚决顶住利用职权要党票的歪风。 *Resolutely stem the malpractice of abusing one's office to gain Party membership.* / 有的连党票也不要了。 *Some don't even want to be admitted into the Party.* / 不能拿党票作交易。 *One must not use one's Party membership to wheel and deal.*

党群 dǎng-qún
the Chinese Communist Party on the one hand, and the masses outside the Party or non-Party mass organizations on the other

党群关系 dǎngqún guānxì
Party-masses relationship
Specifically, the relationship between the Chinese Communist Party and the masses of people, and the relationship

between Communist Party members and non-Party persons.

党日 dǎngrì

days during which a grass-roots organization of the Party holds collective activities or has its members living collectively

党团 dǎng-tuán

1) the two organizations: the Chinese Communist Party and the Chinese Communist Youth League

E.g. 党团活动 *activities of the Party and the League*

2) The Party leadership organizations set up by state power organizations and citizens' groups before the Seventh Congress of the Chinese Communist Party. These organizations were equivalent to the present-day Party organizations

3) This term refers to a faction of representatives belonging to a single political party in a capitalist country

党团关系 dǎng-tuán guānxì

affiliation with the Party or the Youth League

A person's affiliation with the Chinese Communist Party or the Chinese Communist Youth League. (cf. 组织关系)

党外人士 dǎngwài rénshì

persons outside the Party

Persons of a certain standing and influence in society who are not members of the Chinese Communist Party. They are also called 非党人士 non-Party persons.

党委 dǎngwěi

Party committees

Abbreviated term for the various levels of committees in certain political parties. In China, the term refers specifically to the various levels of committees in the Chinese Communist Party.

党委制 dǎngwěizhì

Party committee system

The collective leadership system of the Chinese Communist Party. The system combines collective leadership exercised by the Party's committees at various levels, and separate responsibilities of individuals. Under this system, all important issues undergo democratic discussion and are decided by the Party's committees.

党校 dǎngxiào

Party school

Schools set up by the Chinese Communist Party to nurture and train the Party's cadres.

党性 dǎngxìng

party character

Political parties of different classes have different party characters. The party character of Chinese Communist Party members is the highest and most focused manifestation of the proletarian class character. It is the yardstick for measuring the level of a Party member's class consciousness and for judging whether his stance is firm.

党章 dǎngzhāng

Party constitution

This term specifically refers to the constitution of the Chinese Communist Party.

党政分开 dǎng zhèngfēnkāi

separation of the functions of the Party and the government (an important element of China's political reform)

党政工团 dǎng–zhèng–gōng–tuán

abbreviation for the four elements which are the Communist Party organization, government, labor unions, and mass organizations

党政机关 dǎng–zhèng jīguān

Party and government organs

The administrative offices of the Chinese Communist Party and the People's Government.

党支部 dǎngzhībù

party branch

Refers specifically to a base level organization of the Chinese Communist Party.

党中央 dǎngzhōngyāng

Party Central Committee

The Central Committee of the Chinese Communist Party, also called "中共中央 Chinese Communist Central Committee".

党总支 dǎngzǒngzhī

Party General Branch

Abbreviation for General Branch Committee of the Chinese Communist Party, one of the base level organizations of the Party.

党组 dǎngzǔ

Party organizations

The Party leadership organizations set up by the Chinese Communist Party in such non-Communist Party leadership bodies as national organizations, citizens' groups, economic organizations, and cultural organizations. Their main responsibilities are to implement Party policies, unite non-Party cadres and the masses, fulfill the tasks assigned by the Party and the nation and direct the work of the Party organizations within non-Party organizations.

档次 dàngcì

grade; rank order

E.g. 提高商品档次 *to raise the caliber of commodities* / 拉开奖金档次 *to widen the differentials in bonuses* / 他们俩不是同一个档次上的人。*The two of them are not of the same caliber.*

dao

倒儿爷 dǎoryé

opportunists who buy up goods in limited supply and coupons from state stores or through other channels and resell them at phenomenal profits

Also written as 倒爷.

倒汇 dǎohuì

to buy and sell foreign currency on the black market

倒买倒卖 dǎomǎi dǎomài

to profiteer by buying and selling

To buy cheap and sell dear, making a huge profit in the process.

E.g. 严厉打击倒买倒卖活动。*We must sternly attack profiteering activities.*

倒卖 dǎomài

to resell at a high price (to gain profit illegally)

E.g. 倒卖文物 *to resell cultural artifacts illegally* / 倒卖外汇 *to resell foreign currency illegally*

倒休 dǎoxiū

(of workers) to exchange days off for work days

E.g. 安排职工倒休 *to arrange for workers to swap their days off for work days* / 今天他倒休。*Today he swapped his day off for a work day.* / 他倒休一天。 *He is swapping one day off for a work day.*

导播 dǎobō
instructor in broadcasting

导购 dǎogòu
to guide customers to particular stores; those who guide customers in selecting merchandise

E.g. 导购小姐 *salesgirls* / 导购业务 *sales work* / 导购小组 *sales committee*

导购员 dǎogòuyuán
shopping assistant; shopping guide

导买 dǎomǎi
Same as 导购.

E.g. 导买服务 *sales service* / 英语导买 *English-speaking salesperson* / 导买既当翻译又当参谋。 *Salespersons serve as both interpreters and consultants.*

导入 dǎorù
to import or introduce from the outside world

导向 dǎoxiàng
to set a certain direction for development; to guide in a certain direction

E.g. 政策导向 *to guide policies in a certain direction* / 市场导向 *to guide the market in a certain direction* / 导向作用 *the effect of guiding something in a certain direction*

导医 dǎoyī
medical referral

To help the sick make contact with hospitals, find physicians, purchase medication, or to provide service personnel.

E.g. 病人希望有个导医服务机构，提供相应的服务。 *The sick hope for a medical referral service organization that can provide the relevant services.*

导游 dǎoyóu
1) to help and guide tourists in their travels and sightseeing; 2) persons who serve as guides and commentators for tourists

到位 dàowèi
to attain a predetermined position; specifically to fulfill a policy or measure

E.g. 中外记者已注册到位。 *Chinese and foreign reporters have all registered and taken up their positions.* / 调整措施要尽快到位。 *The measures for adjustment must be put into place as soon as possible.* / 收购资金已经到位。 *Funds for purchasing the products are already in place.*

倒春寒 dàochūnhán
a cold wave coming after the onset of warm spring weather

A metaphor for a reverse after a turn for the better.

倒错 dàocuò
topsy-turvy

E.g. 体制倒错。 *The system is topsy-turvy.*

倒挂 dàoguà
hanging upside-down

A metaphor for the inverted position of something. For example, if the wholesale purchase price of certain agricultural products paid by a state commercial department is higher than the retail price, it is called price hung upside-down.

倒三七 dàosānqī
to reverse a 3-7 proportion to 7-3; metaphor for a fundamental change in the proportional relationship

between two elements

道德法庭 dàodé fǎtíng
court of ethics
Columns in Chinese newspapers and magazines which criticize unethical conduct. Through publicly exposing and criticizing typical cases which are unethical but not necessarily illegal, they promote righteousness and subject unethical persons to society's opinion and censure.

盗版 dàobǎn
to violate copyright
To illegally reprint a book or manufacture a copy of an audio or videotape.
E.g. 盗版音乐带 *illegal copy of a music tape*

盗伐 dàofá
to fell trees and steal lumber

盗录 dàolù
to dub audio and video tapes illegally (in violation of copyright)
E.g. 这个公司新近出版的录音带被大量盗录。 *The tapes newly published by this company have been massively pirated.*

de

德才兼备 décái jiānbèi
equipped with both ethics and talents
To be equipped with the two aspects of political thought consciousness and professional knowledge.

得主 dézhǔ
one who acquires (something) or wins (some prize)

deng

登山服 dēngshānfú
mountain climbing outfit
Originally cold-resistant clothing with a hood worn by mountain climbers, later a style of winter outerwear (usually a nylon shell filled with down or other fiber)

等额选举 děng'é xuǎnjǔ
the type of election where the number of candidates equals the number of positions to be filled (juxtaposed against 差额选举)

等价交换 děngjià jiāohuàn
equal value exchange
An exchange of commodities based on the principle of equal value.

等量劳动 děngliàng láodòng
equal measure labor
Labor which is equal in quantity and quality.

等身 děngshēn
referring to the voluminousness of a person's works, saying that they are equal in height or weight to his body
E.g. 著作等身。 *The volume of this author's written works can match his own body (in height and weight).*

等外品 děngwàipǐn
substandard commodity
Poor quality commodities which are not classified by grade.

邓选 Dèng-Xuǎn
The Selected Works of Deng Xiaoping
Abbreviation for 《邓小平选集》 *The Selected Works of Deng Xiaoping.*

di

低产 dīchǎn
low productivity; low yield
E.g. 低产田 low-yield field / 低产作物 low-yield crop

低档 dīdàng
low quality (merchandise)

低调 dīdiào
low keyed
A metaphor for taking a cautious and slow approach.
E.g. 销售毒品的大头目最近一直保持低调形象。 The head of the drug trafficking gang has been keeping a low profile recently. / 对事情采取低调处理 to deal with matters in a low keyed way.

低谷 dīgǔ
low valley; a low or stagnant stage in a developmental process
E.g. 出版业走出了低谷。 The publishing business has emerged from a low point.

低耗 dīhào
low consumption (of energy, etc.)

低龄 dīlíng
young in age (compared to the norm), lower than normal age
E.g. 犯罪低龄需引起全社会主意。 The young age of criminals must be drawn to society's attention. / 教育低龄学生要用特殊手段。 Special measures must be used in educating precocious students.

低龄化 dīlínghuà
to become lower in age
The age of a certain category of people becoming lower.
E.g. 目前各国都面临着犯罪低龄化的趋势。 At present, every nation faces the tendency of crimes being committed by younger people.

低聘 dīpìn
a person who had had a high professional position being hired for an inferior position
E.g. 有四人因工作表现差而被低聘。 Four people were assigned to low positions due to their inferior work performance.

低俗 dīsú
low class and vulgar

低质优价 dīzhì yōujià
low quality, high price
Quality low but price very high, in reference to the extremely unreasonable prices of certain commodities.

滴滴涕 dīdītì
DDT

滴灌 dīguàn
trickle irrigation
A method of irrigation whereby water is transported in pipes by pressure and dripped into soil through drip spouts to moisten the roots of crops.

迪斯科 dísīkē
disco

迪斯尼 dísīní
Disney

迪厅 dítīng
discotheque

的哥 dígē
taxi driver brother; male taxi driver

的姐 díjiě
taxi driver sister; female taxi driver

的卡 díkǎ
dacron khaki

Contractions of 的确良卡其.

的确良 díquèliáng
dacron

的士 díshì
taxi

的站 dízhàn
taxi station; taxi stop

敌百虫 díbǎichóng
dipterex
A kind of insecticide high in efficacy and low in toxicity. It is a white or light colored crystal, used in preventing insect damage to vegetables, fruits, grains, cotton, tea, etc.

敌敌畏 dídíwèi
DDVP

敌对分子 díduì fènzǐ
hostile elements
When China became a socialist country, all those who opposed socialist revolution, or harbored a hostile attitude toward socialist construction or undermined it, were hostile elements to the nation and the people.

敌情观念 díqíng guānniàn
awareness of enemy presence
To maintain in one's mind a high degree of vigilance against the enemy.

敌我矛盾 dí-wǒ máodùn
contradictions between the enemy and oneself
Contradictions arising from the basic conflicts of interest between antagonistic classes.

涤纶 dílún
polyester fiber

涤棉 dímián
polyester-cotton blend

底肥 dǐféi
base fertilizer
Fertilizer applied to fields before seeding or transplanting. Fertilizers like barnyard manure, compost, and green manure with latent efficacy are suitable as fertilizers. Also called 基肥 foundation fertilizer.

底价 dǐjià
the lowest possible price in a bid or auction

地霸 dìbà
local tyrant

地板革 dìbǎngé
vinyl flooring materials

地对地导弹 dì-duì-dì dǎodàn
surface-to-surface ballistic missiles

地对空导弹 dì-duì-kōng dǎodàn
surface-to-air ballistic missile

地方国营企业 dìfāng guóyíng qǐyè
local state-operated enterprises
An overall term for all enterprises which are established and managed by provincial, municipal, autonomous, regional, and other local governments at various levels, and which fall under the system of state ownership.

地方民族主义 dìfāng mínzú zhǔyì
local nationalism
Also called 狭隘民族主义 narrow nationalism. A kind of reactionary thinking, manifested by reactionaries among minority peoples in their relationship with the nation. On the pretext of protecting the interests of the minority groups, they undermine national unity and solidarity among the nation's people.

地宫 dìgōng
underground palaces, the tombs of

ancient emperors (excavated and restored)

地滚球 dìgǔnqiú
bowling ball
Also called 保龄球.

地籍 dìjí
record of land condition
E.g. 地籍工作 *the work of recording land condition*

地尽其力 dì jìn qí lì
maximizing land power
To take maximum advantage of the land's potential.

地空导弹 dì-kōng dǎodàn
Abbreviation for 地对空导弹.

地矿 dì-kuàng
geological mineral products
Abbreviation for 地质矿产.

地漏 dìlòu
drainage holes in interior floors (which drain into the sewerage system)

地膜 dìmó
(colloquial) plastic sheets used for covering the ground in agriculture
Also called 农膜.
E.g. 超薄地膜 *super-thin plastic ground cover sheets* / 农田覆盖地膜后增产20%。 *After the fields were covered with plastic sheets, production rose by 20%.*

地膜覆盖 dìmó fùgài
covering with ground sheeting
Abbreviation for 地膜覆盖栽培 *cultivation by covering with ground sheeting.* It is a method of cultivating vegetables. In general, the vegetable bed is covered with a 0.015 millimeter sheet of polyvinyl chloride. According to the distance between rows of vegetables, holes or slits are cut out, then seedlings are transplanted. The sheets' functions are: to promote breakdown of organic fertilizer, decrease the spread of disease, control weed growth, maintain warmth and moisture, reduce heat, prevent over-wetting, and promote the ripening of vegetables. It is very efficient in increasing the yield.

地球村 dìqiúcūn
global village

地球日 dìqiúrì
Earth Day (April 22), a day set aside for activities that publicize the need for global environmental protection

地区霸权主义 dìqū bàquán zhǔyì
regional hegemonism

地热 dìrè
thermal energy in the earth's interior
E.g. 开发地热 *to exploit geothermal energy* / 地热能源 *geothermal energy* / 地热发电站 *geothermal electricity-generation station*

地热田 dìrètián
an area with large amount of underground hot water or steam

地税 dì-shuì
local tax
E.g. 地税部门 *local tax units (department, offices)*

地铁 dìtiě
subway; underground
Abbreviation for 地下铁路 *underground railway (subway).*

地委 dì-wěi
local committee
Abbreviation for 中国共产党地区委员会 *local committee of the Chinese Communist Party.* It is a representative

organ set up by the Chinese Communist Party at the provincial or autonomous regional level.

地下包工队 dìxià bāogōngduì
illegal contract teams
Contract organizations that contract various engineering projects illegally.

地下党 dìxiàdǎng
underground Party
The Chinese Communist Party organization that carried out secret activities in enemy occupied territories before Liberation.

地下党员 dìxià dǎngyuán
underground Party member, specifically Party members engaged in clandestine activities in enemy territory before Liberation

地下工厂 dìxià gōngchǎng
underground factories
1) Factories set up in tunnels. 2) Factories which are set up secretly and operate illegally.

地下工作 dìxià gōngzuò
revolutionary work carried out clandestinely in enemy controlled areas

地下活动 dìxià huódòng
underground activity
1) Revolutionary activities secretly carried out by the Chinese Communist Party organization after it had gone underground as a result of the enemy's white terrorism before Liberation. 2) Secret activities against the organizational principles of the Party.

地下刊物 dìxià kānwù
underground publications; illegal publications

地下人行道 dìxià rénxíngdào
underground pedestrian walkways

地下组织 dìxià zǔzhī
underground organizations
The secret organizations of the Chinese Communist Party which carried out revolutionary activities during the enemy's white terrorism before Liberation.

地效飞机 dìxiào fēijī
land-effect plane
A new means of transport that is neither plane nor ship. Also called "land-effect airship" or "land-effect air-winged ship". It flies near the water surface or 5 to 10 meters above it at a speed of 100 to 500 kilometers per hour.

地缘 dìyuán
geographical affinity or relationship

地缘外交 dìyuán wàijiāo
foreign relations with neighboring countries
E.g. 推行地缘外交 *to promote good relations with neighboring countries*

地震棚 dìzhènpéng
earthquake shelter

地掷球 dìzhìqiú
bowling ball

地主 dìzhǔ
landlord
Those who owned land, did not themselves labor, but relied on renting out land and exploiting peasants as their main source of income.

地主婆 dìzhǔpó
landlord's wife
A colloquial term for the wife of a landlord.

第二产业 dì-èr chǎnyè
secondary industries
指工业(包括采掘业、制造业、自来水、电力、蒸汽、热水、煤气)和建筑业。

Various industries such as mining, manufacturing, building construction; also the supply of running water, generation of electricity, and the reticulation of steam, hot water, and gas.

第二课堂 dì-èr kètáng
second classroom
Various extracurricular activities that promote students' knowledge and abilities; the locations where these activities take place.

第二类物资 dì-èr lèi wùzī
second category of material goods
The material goods that are relatively crucial to the national economy and to the people's livelihood, such things as pork, eggs, Chinese medicinal herbs, brand name bicycles, and domestically-produced color television sets. Because their production is concentrated and their supply targets are broad, or because their production is dispersed and they must meet priority demands or export needs, these items are relatively crucial. The nation administers the policies of unified purchase, assigned purchase, and exclusive marketing toward this type of commodity. With the development of production and a greater diversity of products, specific policies will constantly be revised.

第二世界 dì-èr shìjiè
second world
The economically relatively developed nations which rank between the superpowers and the developing countries.

第二梯队 dì-èr tīduì
second echelon
Persons leading socialist modernization construction who are in their sixties and who occupy the backbone ranks in the Party political leadership.

第二文化 dì-èr wénhuà
second culture
Commputer literacy, the ability to read and write computer programs. People's ability to read and write is called first culture.

第二线 dì-èr xiàn
second line (cf. 第一线)

第二职业 dì-èr zhíyè
second job

第三产业 dì-sān chǎnyè
tertiary industries
The various professions that provide daily-life and production services, such as trade, the food industry, repair businesses, tourism, urban transport, shipping, monetary services, insurance, postal services, information and legal services, cultural and educational enterprises, and scientific research.

第三类物资 dì-sān lèi wùzī
third category of material goods
The various not-so-crucial material goods that fall outside the first and second categories of material goods. (cf. 第一类物资 and 第二类物资)

第三世界 dì-sān shìjiè
third world
指亚洲、非洲、拉丁美洲以及其他地区的发展中国家（总称）。中国属于第三世界。
The developing nations of Asia, Africa, Latin America, and other regions. China belongs to the third world.

第三梯队 dì-sān tīduì
third echelon
Persons in the reserve leadership backbone ranks of those leading socialist

modernization construction. (cf. 三个梯队)

第三线 dì-sān xiàn
third line (cf. 第一线)

第三者 dìsānzhě
1) third party
A person who intrudes into someone else's family and has an improper relationship with the wife or the husband.
E.g. 对于由第三者插足引起的犯罪，一定要依法制裁。*We must impose sanctions against crimes caused by third parties in accordance with the law.*
2) A person or organization besides the two parties involved in an issue

第四产业 dì-sì chǎnyè
quaternary industries based on the production and flow of knowledge and information

第一把手 dì-yī bǎshǒu
first in command
The responsible person among the leadership ranks, such as a Party committee secretary, factory head, principal, etc. Secondary positions are in turn called 第二把手 second in command.

第一产业 dì-yī chǎnyè
primary industries
指农业(包括林业、牧业、渔业等)。
Agriculture in the broad sense, including forestry, animal husbandry, and fisheries.

第一夫人 dì-yī fūrén
the First Lady (wife of the head of state)

第一类物资 dì-yī lèi wùzī
first category of material goods
Also called 统配物资 unified allocation material goods, those goods crucial to the national economy, and to the people's livelihoods, including fuel, primary raw materials, important equipment, grain, etc. This category of material goods is under state unified management. In principle, the food under state unified management is under unified planning, unified pricing, and unified allocation and supply.

第一流 dìyīliú
first class; top-notch (also called 一流)
E.g. 第一流水平 *top-notch level* / 第一流产品 *top-notch products* / 他的技术在全厂是第一流的。 *His skills are the best in the factory.*

第一世界 dì-yī shìjiè
first world
The two superpowers.

第一梯队 dì-yī tīduì
first echelon
Persons leading socialist modernization construction who are in their seventies and who occupy the backbone ranks in the Party political leadership. (cf. 三个梯队)

第一线 dì-yī xiàn
first line
That part of an operation that is most crucial, most basic, and of a day-to-day nature. The other parts are called "second line, or third line" according to their positions. For example, in a production unit, the section engaged directly in production is called first line. Administrative and rear-service units are called second and third lines. Among the various levels of Party political leadership, those who conduct the day-to-day work are called first line, those in consulting positions are called second and

third lines.

递减 dìjiǎn
successively decrease
To decrease each time.
E.g. 劳动生产率提高，产品的成本也随着递减。 The labor production rate has gradually risen, while the production cost of commodities has concurrently decreased.

递增 dìzēng
successively increase
To increase each time.
E.g. 粮食总产量三年平均递增百分之八。 Total grain production over three years has successively increased by 8% annually.

dian

点钞机 diǎnchāojī
money-counting machine (for bills only)

点面结合 diǎn–miàn jiéhé
integration "point" and "sphere"
A Marxist work method. "Point" is a representative unit chosen for a certain objective by the leadership. "Sphere" consists of the other relevant units and places beyond the "point". Integrating "point" and "sphere" means that, at the "point" the leadership intensifies guidance, conducts a deep investigation and study, sums up useful experience, and then extends its findings on recent experience to the "sphere" in a well-planned, step-by-step, positive, steady manner. In the process of extending, they are attentive to the summing up of new experience, in order to revise and amplify the experience obtained from the "point", thereby pushing the work to a new level.

点子公司 diǎnzi gōngsī
ideas company
A type of commercial company that provides ideas and advice for people. Also called 导向公司 directional-guide company or 头脑公司 brain company.

典型试验 diǎnxíng shìyàn
typical case experiment
Also called 典型试点 typical case experiment at a point, 试点工作 experimental work at a point, and 试点 experiment at a point. To conduct experiments on one or two selected and representative units before undertaking a certain project. The experience gained is used to guide the formal opening of the complete project.

典型示范 diǎnxíng shìfàn
to set an example with a model
A kind of work method and technique of leadership which extends step-by-step the advanced experience from the "point" to the "sphere" as described above.

电霸 diànbà
electricity tyrant
A person in the electricity business or electricity supply unit who uses his power to extort and create difficulties for clients.

电传 diànchuán
electrical transmission; telex

电大 diàn–dà
college courses broadcast on television
Abbreviation for 广播电视大学.

电饭锅 diànfànguō
electric rice cooker

diàn 电

Also called 电饭煲 in some areas in South China.

电饭煲 diànfànbāo
electric rice cooker (cf. 电饭锅)

电灌 diànguàn
electrified irrigation
Using electricity to pump water for irrigation.
E.g. 电灌站 *electrified irrigation station*

电光源 diànguāngyuán
a device which converts electricity to light energy (fluorescent)

电话传真 diànhuà chuánzhēn
fax
Using telephone lines to transmit faxes, abbreviated as 传真.

电话磁卡 diànhuà cíkǎ
telephone card
Telephone cards that can be used in lieu of cash at pay phones. Also abbreviated as 磁卡.

电话会议 diànhuà huìyì
telephone conference

电话银行 diànhuà yínháng
telephone bank
A bank that provides a variety of services by phone, such as transfer of funds, information on account balances, payment of bills, etc.

电教 diàn-jiào
education based on electric audio-visual aids
Contraction of 电化教学 electrified education.
E.g. 电教站 *audio-visual education stations* / 电教设备 *audio-visual education facilities*

电教片 diànjiàopiān
educational film

电烤箱 diànkǎoxiāng
electric oven

电老虎 diànlǎohǔ
electricity tiger
1) A machine facility or unit that consumes an inordinate amount of electricity. 2) A metaphor for electricity tyrants. (cf. 电霸)

电猫 diànmāo
electric cat
Colloquial term for electronic automatic mouse traps.

电脑 diànnǎo
computer

电脑病毒 diànnǎo bìngdú
computer virus
Also called 计算机病毒.

电脑犯罪 diànnǎo fànzuì
computer crime

电瓶车 diànpíngchē
bottled electricity vehicle; storage battery car

电热炉 diànrèlú
electric heaters
Appliances and facilities such as electric arc furnaces and resistance furnaces that use electricity to generate heat. They are used for cooking and heating, and in industry for heating, drying, and smelting.

电热褥 diànrèrù
electric blanket
A pad or mat heated by electricity. It is used to warm up a bed.

电褥子 diànrùzi
electric blanket
Same as 电热褥.

电视病 diànshìbìng
television disease, the common

symptoms being aches in the legs, indigestion, back ache, curvature of the spine, near-sightness, etc.

电视传输 diànshì chuánshū
television transmission

电视大学 diànshì dàxué
television college
College courses broadcast on television, a kind of higher education that makes use of television to teach. It is an important form of spare-time education. Abbreviated as 电大.

电视柜 diànshìguì
TV cabinet
A special cabinet for a television set.

电视机 diànshìjī
television set

电视剧 diànshìjù
television theater

电视片 diànshìpiān
television movies

电视墙 diànshìqiáng
television wall, a wall full of television monitors showing different images simultaneously

电视塔 diànshìtǎ
television tower (for transmission)

电视文化 diànshì wénhuà
television culture, the phenomenon of using the television as the source of information regarding politics, economics, science, and the arts

电衙门 diànyámen
electricity yamen
A metaphor for the electricity management departments that take advantage of their power to extort and cause difficulties for clients. (衙门 yamen was the term for government offices in feudal China.)

电影周 diànyǐngzhōu
film week (certain types of films are gathered and shown within a certain week)

电针疗法 diànzhēn liáofǎ
electrical acupuncture method
An acupuncture treatment method which combines Chinese and Western medicine. When the needle has produced tingling and swelling sensations at the acupuncture point, an electrical current is sent through the needle, to continuously stimulate the point in order to attain the goal of the treatment.

电针麻醉 diànzhēn mázuì
electrical acupuncture method of anesthesia
Basically the same as 电针疗法 electrical acupuncture method, but is used as a method of anesthesia.

电子报刊 diànzǐ bàokān
electronic news bulletins
News and information transmitted to readers through multi-media facilities.

电子表 diànzǐbiǎo
electronic watch or meter

电子秤 diànzǐchèng
electronic scale
It is used to weigh, tally the cost, and show the result by using liquid crystals.

电子地图 diànzǐ dìtú
electronic map
A map displayed by an electronic technique.

电子货币 diànzǐ huòbì
electronic currency
Circulation of currency in trade by means of ATM, magnetic cards, etc.
E.g. 以电子货币代替传统的硬币、纸币 *to replace traditional coins and*

paper money with electronic currency

电子货币工程 diànzǐ huòbì gōngchéng
electronic currency engineering
A major engineering project to modernize the management and flow of money electronically for businesses and individuals.

电子计算机 diànzǐ jìsuànjī
electronic computer

电子计算器 diànzǐ jìsuànqì
electronic calculator
Also called 袖珍计算机 pocket calculators.

电子琴 diànzǐqín
electronic organ; electronic keyboard

电子商务 diànzǐ shāngwù
e-business; e-commerce
Any business or trade done through the internet, including advertising, booking, making payments, customer's service and marketing research and analysis, providing financial access, and arranging production.

电子数据交换业务 diànzǐ shùjù jiāohuàn yèwù
electronic data interchange service

电子台灯 diànzǐ táidēng
electronic lamp

电子玩具 diànzǐ wánjù
electronic toy

电子显微镜 diànzǐ xiǎnwēijìng
electron microscope

电子信箱 diànzǐ xìnxiāng
e-mail box
E.g. 美国总统克林顿设有电子信箱。*American President Clinton has an e-mail box.*

电子音乐 diànzǐ yīnyuè
electronic music

电子银行 diànzǐ yínháng
electronic banking
Banks that provide services and conduct transactions electronically. The client can hook up with the bank and conduct business through a terminal with a keyboard.

电子邮件 diànzǐ yóujiàn
e-mail
E.g. 人们将用电子邮件取代普通邮件。*People will be replacing ordinary mail with e-mail.*

电子邮局 diànzǐ yóujú
e-post office
Commercial companies which provide a service receiving and delivering e-mail for customers.

电子游戏 diànzǐ yóuxì
electronic game; computer game

电子自由职业经济 diànzǐ zìyóu zhíyè jīngjì
the e-lance economy

店风 diànfēng
shop atmosphere
The ideology and management attitude of personnel in stores, hotels and restaurants.

店堂 diàntáng
salesroom

殿堂 diàntáng
palace or temple hall
A metaphor for an elegant and magnificent place, or a refined spiritual or cultural realm.
E.g. 音乐殿堂 *palace of music* / 艺术殿堂 *palace of art* / 知识殿堂 *palace of knowledge* / 文学殿堂 *palace of literature*

diao

吊运 diàoyùn
hoist and transport
To hoist up and deliver goods by machine or manpower.

钓鱼工程 diàoyú gōngchéng
angling engineering projects
During the period of basic construction, in order to get state approval and funding, some project organizers underestimated costs and did not include the necessary support facilities in their proposals. After the engineering projects received approval, the organizers would ask the state for a supplementary investment.

调拨 diàobō
transfer and allocate (mostly material goods)
E.g. 调拨款项 *transfer and allocate funds* / 调拨粮食 *transfer and allocate grains*

调档 diàodàng
to extract files for reading, specifically in reading school entrance exams, to extract those which meet certain minimum standards for further scrutiny
E.g. 调档的最低成绩叫调档线。 *The lowest score that qualifies an exam for further consideration is called the "file extraction line".*

调度员 diàodùyuán
dispatcher; controller
Personnel responsible for the management and allocation of work, manpower, vehicles, etc.

调干生 diàogànshēng
cadre college student
Students who were national cadres and who were admitted, either through assignment by their units or examination, to institutions of higher learning in their own fields.

调干生助学金 diàogànshēng zhùxuéjīn
financial aid for cadre college student
Aid for living expenses given by the state to cadre students on the basis of their concrete situations. This financial aid is generally higher than that enjoyed by other students in the same fields.

调干学员 diàogàn xuéyuán
cadre student
In-service cadres who have been chosen to attend various levels of spare-time schools or training classes. In general, they participate in cultural studies, advanced studies in their speciality, or certain speciality training.

调离 diàolí
transfer out
To transfer a worker to another job, causing him to leave his original work post.

调派 diàopài
allocate and dispatch
E.g. 上级决定调派一批干部支援大西北建设。 *The superiors decided to allocate and dispatch a group of cadres to assist in the construction in great northwest China.*

调赛 diàosài
to bring together athletes or athletic teams under an organization's jurisdiction for competition, for the purpose of exchange or selection
E.g. 他去参加全国调赛了。 *They went to participate in the national ath-*

letics competition.

调演 diàoyǎn

to transfer and perform

The management sector gathering various relevant performance groups together so that they can view each other's programs, emulate each other and share experiences. The practice is intended to promote the development of the arts.

调阅 diàoyuè

to extract documents and files for reading or investigation

E.g. 调阅档案 *to extract files for reading* / 调阅材料 *to extract material for reading*

调运 diàoyùn

to allocate and transport

E.g. 调运工业品下乡 *to allocate and ship industrial products to the countryside*

die

跌幅 diēfú

range of a price drop

跌势 diēshì

(of prices) falling trend

E.g. 抑止美元的跌势 *to stem the depreciation of the US dollar* / 扭转跌势 *to turn the downward trend around*

ding

丁克族 dīngkèzú

DINKS

指夫妻双职双收入不抚养孩子的上班族。也称丁克家庭。也写作顶客。

A short term for dual income, no kids.

钉子户 dīngzihù

recalcitrants

1) The recalcitrant elements among the enemy during the war years. A policy of eradication was adopted toward them. 2) Squatters who occupy construction sites and refuse to move in accordance with government ordinances or related agreements, and who extort from state construction units. 3) All those units or individuals who have no regard for the law, and who sabotage and impair national welfare.

钉子精神 dīngzi jīngshén

spirit of the nail

A metaphor for a spirit of assiduous study whereby one grasps and uses every available minute and second.

顶班 dǐngbān

substituting in the ranks

A cadre going down to the grass-roots to participate in productive labor, taking over the work of a regular worker.

E.g. 李厂长经常在车间顶班劳动。*Factory Manager Li often labors as a substitute in the ranks in the workshop*.

顶峰论 dǐngfēnglùn

theory of pinnacle

The theory advocated by Lin Biao which claims that "Mao's thought is the contemporary pinnacle of Marxism-Leninism". It is anti-Marxist-Leninist, and an unscientific fallacy.

顶岗 dǐnggǎng

to work regular shifts; to work full time

Same as 顶班.

顶换 dǐnghuàn

to take someone's place (in a job); to replace

Same as 顶替.

顶级 dǐngjí
top level; the highest level; topmost
E.g. 顶级人才 *best talent*; *top personnel*

顶尖 dǐngjiān
topmost; top level
E.g. 顶尖科学家 *top level scientist* / 顶尖名医 *top level doctor* / 顶尖人物 *topmost figure*

顶冒 dǐngmào
to pass off a counterfeit as the real thing
E.g. 顶冒牌号 *to counterfeit a name brand*

顶门杠 dǐngméngàng
door bolt
Originally a thick pole used for buttressing a door. Now a metaphor for cadres in leadership positions who adopt an attitude of resistance toward the orders and directives of superiors in times of reform or other activities.

顶替工 dǐngtìgōng
replacement workers
According to relevant stipulations of the Chinese government, a son or daughter of a worker who retires or resigns may be admitted into the work force and become a regular employee of the state. They are called replacement workers. This method was implemented for a time in the past.

定编 dìngbiān
personnel allocation
Determining the setup of departments, personnel quotas, and assignments to positions of responsibility.

定产 dìngchǎn
production quota (cf. 三定)

定点 dìngdiǎn
fixed location
1) At a fixed location or unit.
E.g. 粮食定点供应。 *Staples are supplied at fixed locations.*
2) To determine a place.
E.g. 定点建房 *to determine a place to build housing*

定调子 dìng diàozi
to set a tune
A metaphor for leaders or relevant persons stipulating in advance through various methods the attitude to be shown toward a certain issue, so that others can all accordingly publicize that view. It usually has a pejorative connotation.

定额包工 dìng'é bāogōng
job contract with quota
A system of job contracts in which certain production tasks are to be accomplished according to quotas.

定额计酬 dìng'é jìchóu
quota remuneration
To calculate remuneration according to the stipulated amount of work completed by the laborer.

定额记分 dìng'é jìfēn
record work points according to quota
The practice, on the part of certain collective agricultural units, of recording work points according to a stipulated amount and quality of labor completed by the individual worker.

定岗 dìnggǎng
determining posts
The colloquial way of referring to the establishment of the system of responsibility for each post within a Party political organization, a mass organization, or a professional unit.

定购 dìnggòu
purchase with a quota; rationed purchase (cf. 三定)

定评 dìngpíng
fixed assessment
A generally accepted assessment of a person or a matter.

定势 dìngshì
set tendency
(Re peolpe's views) a tendency formed over a long period.
E.g. 长期的宣传工作在人们头脑中形成的认识定势。*The way of thinking entrenched in people's minds by propaganda over a long period of time.*

定位 dìngwèi
to determine a position
1) To determine the location of objects.
2) To assign to a fixed work station.
E.g. 教师定位 *to assign teachers to positions*

定息 dìngxī
fixed interest rate
After China's private industrial and commercial enterprises became government-private co-management, the government determined the capital of the capitalist and paid interest at fixed time intervals according to a fixed rate.

定向 dìngxiàng
to determine direction
To determine, stipulate, or gauge the direction of a thing.
E.g. 教师定向 *determining the direction of teachers* / 导弹定向装置 *direction finding equipment of guided missiles* / 用指南针定向 *to gauge direction by a compass*
This term is also used as a modifier meaning having direction.

E.g. 定向天线 *directional antenna*

定向分配 dìngxiàng fēnpèi
fixed direction allocation
The method of allocation whereby students in institutions of higher learning are given job assignments after graduation at the places from which they originally came.

定向广播 dìngxiàng guǎngbō
fixed direction broadcast
Breacast station broadcasting programs to a particular country or area. This type of broadcast has fixed directions, hence the term "fixed direction broadcast".

定向培养 dìngxiàng péiyǎng
fixed direction training
Schools training students according to the nature of the work and the needs of the employing units.

定向销售 dìngxiàng xiāoshòu
fixed direction marketing
High demand merchandise is specially sold to certain people.
E.g. 这次展销的彩电采取定向销售的办法，对象是模范教师。*This trade fair of color TV sets adopted the measure of fixed direction marketing for model teachers.*

定向招生 dìngxiàng zhāoshēng
directioned recruitment of students
The practice in certain institutions of higher learning whereby students are recruited from designated areas and sectors. For example, schools may recruit a portion or a majority of their students from agricultural villages, mining districts, military bases, oilfields, geological teams, etc. After the students graduate, they generally return to their original areas or units to work.

定销 dìngxiāo
rationed marketing (cf. 三定)

定心骨 dìngxīngǔ
same as 主心骨 **backbone, mainstay; metaphor for someone or something reliable; metaphor for a definite idea or plan**

定员 dìngyuán
stipulated number of persons
The quota of personnel in an organization or department, or the quota of passengers on a train, bus, boat, etc.

dong

东风压倒西风 dōngfēng yādǎo xīfēng
east wind prevailing over west wind
A metaphor for the revolutionary or progressive forces prevailing over the reactionary forces.

东盟 Dōng-Méng
Association of Southeast Asian Nation (ASEAN)
Abbreviation for 东南亚国家联盟.
Formed in Bangkok on August 8, 1957, it is comprised of Indonesia, Thailand, the Philippines, Singapore, Malaysia, and Brunei.

东西对话 dōng-xī duìhuà
East-West dialogue
Cooperation between China's economically more developed eastern areas and her resource-rich western areas.

冬奥会 Dōng-Ào-Huì
Winter Olympics
Short for 冬季奥运会.

动迁 Dòngqiān
to relocate due to building demolition
E.g. 明天开始动迁。 *Tomorrow, the relocation will begin.* / 召开动迁工作动员大会 *to convene a conference to mobilize people for relocation work* / 动迁5,000多户人家 *to relocate over 5,000 households* / 动迁居民对居住地段要求很高。 *The relocated residents made high demands regarding their residential area.*

动迁户 dòngqiānhù
relocated households
Households or units relocated due to building demolition.

动手术 dòng shǒushù
to operate on a patient
A metaphor for a major reform or measure carried out to solve an entrenched problem.
E.g. 工厂里改革,首先对人事制度动手术。 *In reforming the factory, the first place to be operated on is the personnel system.*

动态 dòngtài
trends
1) The circumstances concerning the development and transformation of things.
E.g. 科技动态 *trends in science and technology* / 经济动态 *economic trends*
2) Dynamic, or from the perspective of dynamics.
E.g. 动态电流 *dynamic electric current* / 动态分析 *dynamic analysis*

冻雨 dòngyǔ
sleet

dou

斗批改 dòu-pī-gǎi
to struggle, criticize, and reform

This was the one-phrase mission for the Cultural Revolution resolved at the Eleventh Plenary Session of the Eighth Central Committee of the Chinese Communist Party. "Struggle" is beating down the "capitalist roaders in power," "criticize" is criticizing the "bourgeois reactionary academic authority," and criticizing the ideology of the bourgeois and all exploitative classes; "reform" is the reform of education, literature and art, and all the superstructures inappropriate to a socialist economic foundation. "Struggle, criticize, and reform" is an abbreviation.

斗批会 dòupīhuì
struggle and criticism meeting

A term of the Cultural Revolution. It is a meeting to struggle against and criticize the so-called "capitalist roaders" and "reactionary academic authority". Also called 批斗会.

斗私批修 dòu sī pī xiū
struggle against privatism and criticize revisionism

In September of 1957, Mao Zedong issued a directive to "struggle against privatism and criticize revisionism". This means people should struggle against their own selfish thoughts and criticize revisionism.

斗妍 dòuyàn
to vie in beauty, i.e., gorgeous; often used in describing many flowers blooming together, as if in a beauty contest

Also called 斗艳.

斗艳 dòuyàn
Same as 斗妍.

E.g. 争奇斗艳 *to compete in bizarrerie and to vie in beauty.*

斗争会 dòuzhēnghuì
struggle meeting

The masses' meeting to attack hostile and bad elements by means of reasoning, exposure, and accusations. Also called 斗争大会 big struggle meeting.

斗争哲学 dòuzhēng zhéxué
philosophy of struggle

A popular term during the Cultural Revolution – to advocate struggle in every realm and as a result, create disorder in the entire nation.

豆腐老虎 dòufu lǎohǔ
beancurd tiger

A metaphor for a person or group which has a strong and fierce exterior but actually has very little strength. It is synonymous with 纸老虎 paper tiger.

豆腐帐 dòufuzhàng
beancurd account

An account which is simple and recorded at any time. It is a metaphor for simply enumerating facts without making any deep analysis.

豆腐渣工程 dòufuzhā gōngchéng
bean dregs project

A metaphor for inferior quality buildings.

E.g. 不能再搞豆腐渣工程。 *No more inferior quality projects.*

豆制品 dòuzhìpǐn
bean products

Various foods manufactured from beans, such as beancurd, dried beancurd, etc.

du

督查 dūchá
to supervise and inspect

督导 dūdǎo
to supervise and direct
E.g. 督导人员 *supervisory personnel* / 督导培训班 *course for training supervisors*

督学 dūxué
supervise learning
People who are responsible for the supervision and evaluation of education.

督政 dūzhèng
to supervise and guide the management of a school

毒草 dúcǎo
poisonous weeds
A metaphor for views and written works that are harmful to the people and to socialist work. It is the opposite of 香花 fragrant flowers.

毒枭 dúxiāo
drug trafficker

渎职罪 dúzhízuì
dereliction of duty (by someone in an important government office) – a criminal act

独立国家联合体 dúlì guójiā liánhétǐ
the Commonwealth of Independent States (cf. 独联体)
A political entity made up of former states of Soviet Union.

独立王国 dúlì wángguó
independent kingdom
A metaphor for a local organization with political power or a unit within the revolution which does not obey the central government or leadership, and goes off on its own.

独立性 dúlìxìng
independence
The characteristic of not relying on other people and not being influenced by external factors.

独立自主 dúlì zìzhǔ
independent and self-directed

独联体 Dú–Lián–Tǐ
the Commonwealth of Independent States
Abbreviation for 独立国家联合体.

独生子女 dúshēng zǐnǚ
single child
China is promoting the policy of one child per couple. The single child born to a pair of parents is called "single child".

独生子女证 dúshēng zǐnǚzhèng
single child certificate
The certificate issued to couples with just one child by the government. It entitles the single child to enjoy certain advantages.

独资 dúzī
capital invested by one party (in contrast to 合资 joint-venture)
E.g. 他独资创办一所大学。*He single-handedly funded the founding of a university.* / 独资兴办企业 *to put up capital for an enterprise single-handedly* / 独资企业 *wholly-owned enterprise*

读卡机 dúkǎjī
magnetic card reading machine
A machine that can read magnetic codes on cards and send out commands.

读书班 dúshūbān
study class
Short term study class organized for cadres or workers.

读书无用论 dúshū wúyònglùn
the theory that studying is useless
During the Cultural Revolution, due to the policy of keeping the people in

ignorance propagated by Lin Biao and the Gang of Four, cultural and educational work was disrupted causing some people to develop the idea that studying is useless.

赌风 dǔfēng
the common and unhealthy practice of gambling

度假村 dùjiàcūn
vacation villa

duan

短程 duǎnchéng
short distance (traveling); short process
E.g. 决策短程化 to shorten the process of making a policy decision / 短程导弹 short-distance guided missiles

短池 duǎnchí
short-distance swimming pool
E.g. 巴黎短池泳赛我获金银牌各一。 In the short-distance swimming contest in Paris, our team won a gold and a silver medal.

短尺少秤 duǎnchǐ shǎochèng
short yard stick and light scale
A sales clerk giving less than the purchased amount to the customer. Short yardstick means the length is insufficient; light scale means the weight is insufficient.

短导 duǎndǎo
short-range guided missile (with a range of less than 1,000 kilometers)
Abbreviation for 短程导弹.

短斤缺两 duǎnjīn quēliǎng
short on the catty and lacking on the ounce
A sales clerk giving the customer less than the purchased amount.

短平快 duǎn-píng-kuài
short, adaptable, and fast
Originally, a specialized term used in volleyball. Now the term is applied to technological items. "Short" means that the turn around time for commercializing a new technology is short; "adaptable" means that it is adaptable to the technological level of small and medium-sized enterprises; "fast" means that economic benefits are quickly attained.

短期行为 duǎnqī xíngwéi
short-sighted behavior, concerned with only the present without consideration of long-term effects

短线 duǎnxiàn
short line
1) A relatively weak aspect.
E.g. 能源、交通是短线。 Energy resources and transportation are short lines.
2) In relatively short supply.

短线产品 duǎnxiàn chǎnpǐn
goods that are in short supply

短线专业 duǎnxiàn zhuānyè
specialities that are in short supply
Professional fields where schools and research institutes are temporarily unable to satisfy society's needs, and therefore must develop vigorously.

短效 duǎnxiào
short-term effects
E.g. 短效口服避孕药 contraceptive pills with a short-term effect

短训班 duǎnxùnbān
short-term speciality training class
Abbreviation for 短期专业训练班.

断档 duàndàng
severed shelf; sold out

The situation where commodities of a certain grade are completely sold out.

断线 duànxiàn
line breakage (e.g., telephone disconnected)
A metaphor for breakdown in a contact or connection.

断想 duànxiǎng
incoherent, unsystematic thinking; fragmentary thought
E.g. 富民政策断想。 *The policy for enriching the people is incoherent.* / 思想工作断想。 *The ideological work is incoherent.*

断指再植 duànzhǐ zàizhí
reconnecting a severed finger or toe

dui

兑换券 duìhuànquàn
abbreviation for 外汇对换券 foreign exchange certificates (FEC)
Also called 外汇券. (cf. 外汇券)

队友 duìyǒu
team buddies
Mutual appellation for members of an athletic or investigative team.

对不上号 duì bù shàng hào
unable to match up the numbers; to have a discrepancy
Two numbers not corresponding to each other. For example, if an auto's license does not correspond to the number on the vehicle, it can be said that the license and the vehicle cannot be matched in number. The term is also a metaphor for two aspects with discrepancies.
E.g. 他说的和做的根本对不上号。*There are huge discrepancies between his words and his deeds.*

对调 duìdiào
to interchange
E.g. 对调工作 *to interchange jobs*

对话 duìhuà
dialogue
Specifically an exchange of ideas between leading cadres and representatives of the masses in which problems of the masses are discussed in an atmosphere of equality and mutual respect.
E.g. 召开对话会 *to have a dialogue meeting*

对讲机 duìjiǎngjī
intercom
A setup used for short-distance communications. There are two types: wired intercoms and wireless intercoms.

对接 duìjiē
to connect; to link up
1) Two objects connecting horizontally.
2) Two objects connecting head-to-tail.
E.g. 联盟号飞船与礼炮6号空间站对接。 *The spaceship Soyuz and the space station Salyut VI have connected.*

对抗性矛盾 duìkàngxìng máodùn
antagonistic contradictions
Contradictions that require an external clash for them to be resolved, such as the contradictions between ourselves and an enemy, etc.

对口 duìkǒu
to match
Concordance in the work content and nature of two mutually related parties.
E.g. 工作对口 *the job matches (one's skills, etc.)* / 专业对口 *the speciality matches (the work unit's needs, the individual's interests, etc.)*

对口词 duìkǒucí

dialogue

A new form of oral performing art. It is performed by two persons, one speaks and the other responds. It has characteristics of a poetry reading. A performance by more than two persons is called 群口词 group dialogue or 多口词 many-mouths dialogue.

对口支援 duìkǒu zhīyuán
matched assistance

Mutual assistance of two units with the same responsibilities.

对立面 duìlìmiàn
antithesis

The two aspects of mutual dependence and mutual contention within an entity. It also refers to an aspect which differs from one's own opinions, views, and standpoint.

对立统一规律 duìlì tǒngyī guīlǜ
law of unity of opposites

The fundamental law of materialist dialectics. It states that all things are unities of opposites; all things contain contradictions. The antithesis of contradictions unite as well as contend, and under certain conditions mutually transform, promoting the development of things. With respect to any concrete matter, the unity of opposites is conditional, temporary, and transitional, and is therefore relative; but antagonistic contention is unconditional and absolute.

对台九条 duì Tái jiǔtiáo
nine articles toward Taiwan

即1981年9月30日全国人民代表大会常务委员会委员长叶剑英提出的关于台湾回归祖国，实现和平统一的九条方针政策。主要内容是：要尽早结束中华民族分裂的不幸局面，建议国共两党举行对等谈判，实行通邮、通航、通商。国家实现统一后，台湾可作为特别行政区，享受高度的自治权，现行社会、经济制度、生活方式不变，台湾当局和各界代表可担任全国性政治机构的领导职务，参与管理国家。

The nine guiding policies proposed by Ye Jianying, chairman of the Standing Committee of the National People's Congress, on September 30, 1981, concerning Taiwan returning to the motherland and the realization of peaceful reunification. The main contents are: The unfortunate state of national division must end as soon as possible. It is suggested that the Nationalist and Communist Parties conduct reciprocal negotiations. The two sides should implement postal services, air traffic, and commerce. After the nation is re-unified, Taiwan can become a special administrative region and enjoy a high level of autonomy. The current social, economic system, and life style can remain unchanged. The Taiwan regime and representatives from various levels may assume leadership positions in national political organizations and participate in the management of the nation.

对象 duìxiàng
target; object

1) A person or matter that serves as the object in an action or thought.

E.g. 革命对象 *target of revolution* / 研究对象 *research target*

2) Special reference to the target of one's love.

E.g. 找对象 *to find a match* / 他有对象了。 *He has a match now.*

对着干 duìzhegàn
to do in opposition; to act in opposition to a certain way
E.g. 不能和上级领导对着干。*One cannot oppose upper level leadership.*

dun

吨公里 dūngōnglǐ
ton-kilometer
A unit of the measure for the transport of goods, i.e., transporting one ton of goods a distance of one kilometer.

吨粮田 dūnliángtián
grain fields which attain a per-acre yield of one ton

吨粮县 dūnliángxiàn
a county where the average per-acre grain yield reaches one ton

蹲点 dūndiǎn
squat at a point
A cadre going to a grass-roots unit to participate in actual labor or conduct investigative studies.

蹲点跑面 dūndiǎn pǎomiàn
squat at a point and run through the sphere
A leader goes to the grass-roots, delves deeply into a unit, sums up advanced model experience, then promotes the method to a broader sphere. The leader must do the work at the point (a concrete unit) well and also give consideration to the work at the sphere (the entire situation). Point and sphere are to be united, with the point leading the sphere, so that the work will gradually deepen and continuously improve.

duo

多吃多占 duōchī duōzhàn
to eat and hog up a large amount
Before rural villages implemented the remuneration-related-to-output responsibility system, certain commune and brigade cadres on their own authority monopolized the collective properties of commune members, and used public funds for feasting, etc.

多发 duōfā
frequently occurring
E.g. 事故多发地区 *high accident zone*

多发病 duōfābìng
prevalent illnesses
Illnesses that occur frequently among certain groups of people, such as colds, chronic tracheitis, asthma, etc. There are different prevalent illnesses in different regions, as a result of different living conditions, and different seasons.

多管齐下 duōguǎn qíxià
to fell a multitude with a multibarrel gun
A metaphor for implementing something from various angles simultaneously. Also called 数管齐下.
E.g. 多管齐下,刹住走私歪风。 *We must combat the rampant smuggling from many angles and put a stop to it.*

多国公司 duōguó gōngsī
multi-national corporations

多极化 duōjíhuà
multipolarization
The phenomenon of a few powerful nations or blocs dominating international affairs.

E.g. 国际形势出现了多极化格局。 *There emerged on the international scene the pattern of multipolarization.*

多极性 duōjíxìng
multipolarized

Being led (dominated) by several forces.

E.g. 多极性世界 *multipolarized world*

多快好省 duō-kuài-hǎo-shěng
greater, faster, better, more economical

A substantive point of the overall path of socialist construction which was ratified at the Second Plenary Session of the Eighth Central Committee of the Chinese Communist Party in May, 1958. It means that within socialist construction, the quantity should be large, the quality should be good, the pace should be speedy, and expenses should be low. It also means that the people's work is guaranteed to be of high quality and quantity, as well as speedy and economical.

多劳多得 duōláo duōdé
more labor more benefits

The more one labors (quantity large, quality good), the more remuneration one receives.

多媒体 duōméitǐ
multi-media

High-level media that combine the technology of computers, television, sound recorders, etc.

多面手 duōmiànshǒu
jack of all trades

Someone with many different skills.

多速 duōsù
multi-speed (referring to bicycles, electric appliances, etc.)

多种经营 duōzhǒng jīngyíng
diversified production

The mode of production in which there are one or two main products and some secondary ones.

夺杯 duóbēi
to seize the cup; to win the championship

E.g. 中国女排曾多次夺杯。 *China's women's volleyball team has won the championship many times.* / 这次比赛古巴队志在夺杯。 *In this competition, the Cuban team aspires to win the championship.*

夺标 duóbiāo
to win the trophy

夺冠 duóguàn
to win the championship

夺魁 duókuí
to win first place in a competition; to win the championship

E.g. 中国队19次夺魁，名列榜首。 *The Chinese team won the championship nineteen times, so it's listed at the top of the roster.* / 北大辩论队在亚洲大专辩论会中夺魁。 *The Beijing University Debating Team won the championship at the Asian Colleges' Debate.*

躲让 duǒràng
to dodge; to avoid

E.g. 一辆汽车冲来，人们纷纷躲让。 *A car dashed over, the people scrambled to dodge it.*

E

e

额度 édù
limit in number or amount
E.g. 国家拨给一定额度的费用。
The state allocated funds for a certain expenditure.

恶补 èbǔ
to force to take a cramming course (students)

恶性案件 èxìng ànjiàn
pernicious case
An illegal matter with extremely serious consequences.

恶性差错 èxìng chācuò
pernicious error
An error with extremely serious consequences.

恶性循环 èxìng xúnhuán
vicious cycle
E.g. 有些地方因粮食不足则毁林开荒，结果造成恶性循环，水土流失，气候受到影响，使粮食生产受到严重损失。 *In certain areas, due to a shortage of food, forests were destroyed and a wilderness created, resulting in erosion of soil, and climatic changes, which in turn caused an even greater loss in food production.*

恶战 èzhàn
fierce, cruel battle; fierce competition
E.g. 两个球队展开了一场恶战。 *The two teams are engaged in a fierce competition.*

厄尔尼诺现 È'ěrnínuò xiànxiàng
the El Niño phenomenon
A warm in shore current that originates near Ecuador and sometimes leads to a global climatic effect (a year in which this phenomenon occurs is called an El Niño year).

en

恩格尔系数 ēngé'ěr xìshù
Engel's coefficient
The coefficient of relations between income and money spent on meals and living expenses.
E.g. 我国大城市的人均恩格尔系数大约在0.5左右。 *The average Engel's coefficient in the big cities of China is about 0.5.*

er

儿童剧 értóngjù
children's drama

儿童片 értóngpiān
films or television movies made especially for children

耳针疗法 ěrzhēn liáofǎ
ear acupuncture treatment method
Acupuncture treatment in which a needle is placed in a certain point of the earlobe (called acupoint) to treat an illness in an internal part of the body.

211工程 Èryīyī gōngchéng
211 project

A systematic project to raise the level of the entire higher educational system in China. That is, with an eye toward the twenty-first century, to build about 100 universities and a batch of key research units over the next ten years or more. The universities originally designated as "key" by the State Education Commission will remain unchanged. The goal is to raise the caliber of higher education and scientific research, and increase the efficiency of school management.

二把手 èrbǎshǒu
second in command

The second responsible person in a unit, such as deputy secretary, vice-principal, deputy factory manager, etc.
E.g. 他是工厂的二把手。*He is the second man in the factory.*

二百方针 èrbǎi fāngzhēn
the two hundred guiding principle

Also called 双百方针 double hundred guiding principle. (cf. 百花齐放, 百家争鸣)

二遍苦 èrbiànkǔ
second time bitterness

To suffer bitter hardships a second time. A term used in promoting education about class struggle. It means: if capitalism is revived in China, the laboring peoples would perhaps again suffer the bitter hardships which they experienced in the old society.

二部制 èrbùzhì
two-shift educational system whereby students are divided into two groups – morning and afternoon, or every other day (in order to accommodate a teacher or make up for shortages of classrooms)

二茬罪 èrcházuì
second crop of suffering

Synonymous with 二遍苦.

二传手 èrchuánshǒu
second transmitter

A term in volleyball designating the player who functions as the pivot between defensive and offensive; a person or thing that serves a pivotal or intermediary role.
E.g. 发挥二传手的作用 *to bring the role of pivot into play* / 当好二传手 *to play the pivotal role well*

二道贩子 èrdào fànzi
two-way merchants

Merchants who take advantage of the differential between the government fixed price and the free market price, and illegally buy from one and in turn sell in the other in order to make a profit.

二等残废 èrděng cánfèi
(jocular) secondary handicap, i.e., shorter than normal height (in youths)

二等公民 èrděng gōngmín
second class citizen

二地主 èrdìzhǔ
second landlord

Before Liberation, those persons whose main source of livelihood came from renting large amounts of land from landlords and subletting it to others, not cultivating the land themselves.

二哥大 èrgēdà
similar to 大哥大 cellular phone, but can be used only for one-way trans-

mission.

二锅饭 èrguōfàn

second pot

This term is derived from the term 大锅饭 big pot. It refers to the problem of equalitarianism which the "team responsibility system" was unable to totally eliminate. The "team responsibility system" overcame the equalitarianism of all teams eating out of the same big pot, but within individual teams, the labor-reward system in some locations remained one in which work points are based on labor time or "the same bottom line". This is still a kind of equalitarianism, which commune members call "second pot of rice".

二级市场 èrjí shìchǎng

secondary market

Arena where commodities, bonds, etc., circulate a second time.

E.g. 投机者在二级市场上买卖国债。*Opportunists buy and sell national bonds on the secondary market.*

二进宫 èrjìngōng

to enter the palace a second time

Someone with a past criminal record again commits a crime, and is convicted and put into a correctional institution.

E.g. 他因窃车"二进宫"。*He stole a car and entered the "palace" a second time.*

二炮 Èr-Pào

Second Artillery

Abbreviation for 中国人民解放军第二炮兵 the Second Artillery of the People's Liberation Army.

二汽 Èr-Qì

Second Auto Factory

Abbreviation for 第二汽车制造厂 the Second Auto Factory.

二手 èrshǒu

second-hand

E.g. 二手货 *second-hand goods*

二手车 èrshǒuchē

second-hand vehicle

二手烟 èrshǒuyān

second-hand smoke

The smoke exhaled by smokers which is in turn inhaled by others.

二为 èr-wèi

serve the people and serve socialism

Abbreviation for 为人民服务、为社会主义服务 serve the people and serve socialism.

二为方向 èrwèi fāngxiàng

the two "for" directions

Literature and art following the directions of serving the people and serving socialism.

二五普法 èrwǔ pǔfǎ

second five-year period for propagating basic legal knowledge

二线 èrxiàn

second line (cf. 第一线)

二野 Èr-Yě

Second Field Army

Abbreviation for 中国人民解放军第二野战军 the Second Field Army of the People's Liberation Army.

二月逆流 èryuè nìliú

February Adverse Current

指1967年2月前后，中共中央政治局和中央军委的几位领导人谭震林、陈毅、叶剑英、李富春、李先念、徐向前、聂荣臻等，在不同的会议上对"文化大革命"的错误作法提出强烈的批评，当时被诬为"二月逆流"，并受到压制和打击。

Around February of 1967, leaders of the Political Bureau and the Military Commission of the Central Committee of the Chinese Communist Party Tan Zhenlin, Chen Yi, Ye Jianying, Li Fuchun, Li Xiannian, Xu Xiangqian, Nie Rongzhen, etc., fiercely criticized at various meetings the erroneous methods of the Cultural Revolution. At the time, they were vilified as the "February adverse current", and suffered suppression and attacks.

二月提纲 èryuè tígāng
February Outline

指 1957 年 2 月中共中央发出的《关于当前学术讨论的汇报提纲》，简称"二月提纲"。"提纲"强调了社会主义时期在学术领域清除资产阶级和其他反动思想的重要性，要求通过斗争锻炼出一支又红又专的学术队伍，要求坚持"放"的方针，坚持实事求是，在真理面前人人平等的原则。1957 年 5 月 15 日，中共中央发出通知，批判"二月提纲"的所谓十大错误，并决定撤销这个提纲。

This is the abbreviated term for the "Outline of the Report on Discussions Concerning the Current Academic Scene" issued by the Chinese Communist Party Central Committee in February 1955. The outline emphasized the importance of eradicating bourgeois and other reactionary ideology from the academic sphere during the socialist period, demanded that, through struggle, an academic contingent that is both red and expert be trained, demanded adherence to the "open" policy, and adherence to the principle of seeking truth from reality, and asserted that everyone was equal before the truth. On May 15, 1955, the Chinese Communist Party Central Committee issued a notification criticizing the "February Outline", and resolved to rescind it.

F

fa

发案 fā'àn
case occurrence
E.g. 发案率 rate of occurrence of cases

发达国家 fādá guójiā
developed countries
Second World countries with relatively developed economies and cultures (as compared with developing countries). (cf. 三个世界)

发寄 fājì
to mail out
E.g. 有些报刊由报刊社自己发寄。 Some newspapers organize their own distribution and mailing. / 邮件由发寄局到投递局，中间要经过多次分拣。 In the process of mailing out and delivery, newspapers must go through several sortings.

发烧友 fāshāoyǒu
people who are captivated by acoustic equipment; also refers to music buffs
E.g. CD 发烧友 people who are captivated by CD players

发运 fāyùn
dispatch (goods); to dispatch and ship out
E.g. 那批货物已提前发运。 That batch of merchandise has already been dispatched ahead of schedule.

发债 fāzhài
to put bonds on sale
E.g. 发债机构 Organizations that distribute bonds

发展中国家 fāzhǎnzhōng guójiā
developing countries

罚没 fámò
to fine and confiscate (money and property)
E.g. 罚没款要全部上交。 The fine must be paid in its entirety. / 罚没办公室 the office in charge of fines and confiscations / 罚没管理工作 fine and confiscation management work

法盲 fǎmáng
legal illiterates
People who have no understanding of legal matters.

法塔赫 Fǎtǎhè
巴勒斯坦民族解放运动的简称。在阿拉伯文中，"法"、"塔"、"赫"分别是"巴勒斯坦"、"解放"、"运动"三个字的首个字母，故名。
Abbreviation for the Palestinian Liberation Movement; the characters "法" "塔" "赫" represent the three lead syllables of the abbreviated Arabic term.

发廊 fàláng
hair dresser; beauty parlor (usually referring to small-scale private enterprise)

发乳 fàrǔ
hair cream

发屋 fàwū
beauty parlor (usually referring to small-scale private enterprise)

发型 fàxíng
hair style

fan

帆板运动 fānbǎn yùndòng
wind surfing
Also called 风冲浪板运动 wind surge wave board sport.

翻车 fānchē
car turning over
A metaphor for failure or setback.
E.g. 在改革中有人政绩平平, 甚至翻车落马。 *In the reform process, some people's performances were mediocre, a small number even fell by the wayside.*

翻船 fānchuán
boat capsizing
A metaphor for failure or setback.
E.g. 美国女排险些翻船。 *The American women's volleyball team almost "capsized" (suffered an upset).*

翻斗车 fāndǒuchē
tip truck

翻番 fānfān
to double
Abbreviation for 翻一番 to increase twofold.
E.g. 产值不断翻番 *to double production value*

翻改 fāngǎi
to alter
To take apart a completed garment (usually old) and remake.

翻建 fānjiàn
to renovate; to rebuild on an old foundation
E.g. 翻建工程 *renovation project* / 全市有 2000 多间亟待翻建的危房。 *In this city, there are over 2,000 hazardous housing units awaiting renovation.* / 去年翻建了 10 所幼儿园。 *Last year, ten nursery schools were renovated.*

翻老帐 fānlǎozhàng
to turn up old accounts; to bring up old scores
A metaphor for bringing up matters that have happened long ago.

翻录 fānlù
to dub an audio or videotape
E.g. 要坚决制止和打击违章翻录、销售音像制品的活动。 *We must resolutely stem the illegal dubbing and sale of audio tapes and videotapes.*

翻牌公司 fānpái gōngsī
flipped sign company
Referring to certain enterprises that were formerly government organs, but which have changed into companies in the reforms of the economic system. The various functionaries of the original government organs remain in the same offices within these companies.

翻身 fānshēn
to turn over
To turn over one's body while lying down. 1) A metaphor for being liberated from oppressed, exploited conditions. 2) A metaphor for changing a backward or disadvantaged condition.

翻身斗争 fānshēn dòuzhēng
struggle to turn over
Revolutionary struggle carried out by the people to liberate themselves from oppression and exploitation.
E.g. 土改时广大农民群众积极参加翻身斗争。 *During land reform, the broad masses of peasants actively partic-*

ipated in the struggle to turn over.

翻身户 fānshēnhù

households that have turned over

Peasants households that have been liberated from the oppression and exploitation of old society.

翻身农民 fānshēn nóngmín

peasants that have turned over

Peasants who have been liberated from the feudal exploitative system through land reform.

翻身农奴 fānshēn nóngnú

serfs that have turned over

Serfs in the Tibetan Autonomous Region and other minority regions who were liberated from feudal serfdom through democratic reforms.

翻身奴隶 fānshēn núlì

slaves that have turned over

Former slaves in the Tibetan Autonomous Region and certain other minority areas that were liberated from feudal serfdom after these areas had undergone democratic reformation.

繁体字 fántǐzì

complex characters

Characters that have already been replaced by simplified forms, as "漢" is the complex form of "汉", "體" is the complex form of "体".

凡是派 fánshìpài

die-hard followers of Mao's words

Persons who maintain the "two any-and-alls" point of view. (cf. 两个凡是)

反霸 fǎnbà

resist hegemonism

1) To resist the hegemonism of the superpowers. 2) The struggle to settle accounts of the crimes of despotic landlords during the land reform movement in China.

反差 fǎnchā

(originally) the black and white contrast in photographs and scenes; (now) the degree of contrast in some dissimilar aspect of related things

E.g. 物质上富有，精神上贫乏，这两方面形成一大反差。*Materialistically rich but spiritually impoverished, herein lies the difference.*

反潮流 fǎncháoliú

to go against the current

1) To go against the social current, usually referring to erroneous social currents. 2) Specifically, the movement developed in China in 1973 to counter the return of the so-called revisionist line. Actually it was the Gang of Four and their cohorts countering the correct measures adopted by Premier Zhou Enlai in political, economic, cultural, and educational realms in order to salvage or minimize the damage done by the Cultural Revolution.

反党 fǎndǎng

anti-Party

Speccifically, to oppose the Chinese Communist Party.

E.g. 反党分子 *anti-Party elements*

反党集团 fǎndǎng jītuán

anti-Party clique

Those cliques within the Chinese Communist Party which manifest themselves in various forms and which use devious tactics to oppose the guiding principles, directions, and policies of the Chinese Communist Party.

E.g. 林彪和"四人帮"两个反党集团 *the two anti-Party cliques of Lin Biao and the Gang of Four*

反导弹体系 fǎndǎodàn tǐxì
antiballistic system

反帝 fǎn-dì
anti-imperialism
Abbreviation for 反对帝国主义 anti-imperialism.

反动学术权威 fǎndòng xuéshù quánwēi
reactionary academic authority (cf. 资产阶级反动学术权威)

反对党 fǎnduìdǎng
(political) opposition party

反腐蚀 fǎnfǔshí
anti-corruption
To oppose the corrupting influence of bourgeois thoughts and life style on the proletarian political party and on revolutionaries.

反革命分子 fǎngémìng fènzǐ
counter-revolutionary elements
Those who oppose revolutionary political forces, carry out acts of sabotage, and scheme to overthrow revolutionary political forces. There is the distinction between historical counter-revolutionary elements and contemporary counter-revolutionary elements. The former are those who suppressed or disrupted revolutionary work, such as secret agents and core members of counter-revolutionary parties. The latter are those who carried out activities after the establishment of the People's Republic of China. Their aims were to overthrow the people's democratic dictatorship and the socialist system, which makes them a danger to the nation.

反革命两面派 fǎngémìng liǎngmiànpài
counter-revolutionary double-faced elements
Those who infiltrate revolutionary ranks and pretend to be revolutionaries, but actually oppose and disrupt revolutionary work.

反攻倒算 fǎngōng dàosuàn
counter-attack and ounter-liquidate
Originally this term referred to the activities of the landlord class which had already been defeated by the Chinese revolution, but tho used counter-revolutionary forces to turn around, counter-attack and persecute the peasants, and snatch back land and property which had been allocated to peasants by the revolutionary political authority. Later, the activities of all previously defeated class enemies who intended to exact revenge and attack the people and the masses were called "counter-attack, counter-liquidate". **反骄破满** fǎnjiāo pòmǎn
to oppose and destroy arrogance and complacency

反馈 fǎnkuì
feedback
Feedback originally used scientifically, now used more broadly.
E.g. 信息反馈 *information feedback*. *Also called* 回轮 *wheel back or* 回授 *give back*.

反冒进 fǎnmàojìn
opposition to premature advances
The opposition raised by the Chinese Communist Party in 1955, to the phenomenon of premature and unrealistic advances that surfaced in socialist construction work.

反面教材 fǎnmiàn jiàocái
negative teaching material

Discourse used by the enemy in attacking the revolution, and material that is politically reactionary, erroneous, or negative. Because this material is a negative example in the education of the revolutionary political party and the people, it is called "negative teaching material".

反面教员 fǎnmiàn jiàoyuán
negative teacher

This term generally refers to enemies, but also to people whose thoughts and political characters are evil and who have committed evil deeds that are harmful to the Party and the people. These people are negative examples in the education of the revolutionary political party and the people, therefore they are called "negative teachers".

反面人物 fǎnmiàn rénwù
negative character

反批评 fǎnpīpíng
counter criticism

Criticisms of criticisms.

反社会主义分子 fǎnshèhuì zhǔyì fènzǐ
anti-socialist element

反思 fǎnsī
(originally used in philosophical parlance) to reflect; to recall and evaluate the past

E.g. 对文化进行反思 *to reflect upon and evaluate a culture* / 觉悟始于反思。*Consciousness begins with reflection.*

反贪 fǎntān
to combat graft

To investigate and penalize cases of graft within governmental sectors.

反弹 fǎntán
to rebound; metaphor for prices rising again after a fall

E.g. 价格反弹 *the rebounding of prices*

反特 fǎntè
to oppose the sabotage of secret agents

反修 fǎnxiū
to oppose revisionism

反右 fǎnyòu
to oppose rightism

1) To oppose rightist opportunism. 2) The 1957 movement conducted in China to oppose bourgeois rightists. (cf. 反右派斗争)

反右防左 fǎnyòu fángzuǒ
to oppose the right and guard against the left (cf. 反左反右)

反右派斗争 fǎnyòupài dòuzhēng
struggle against rightists

Also called 反右斗争. In the summer of 1957, an extremely small minority of bourgeois rightist elements took advantage of the Chinese Communist Party's rectification movement to advocate a great airing of views; they wildly attacked the Party's newborn socialist system, and vainly attempted to take over the leadership of the Communist Party. In June the Chinese Communist Party Central Committee resolved to carry out counter-attacks on the rightist elements' attacks; this was basically concluded in October. But the anti-rightist struggle went too far and a group of intellectuals, patriots, and Party cadres were erroneously identified as "rightist elements", with unfortunate results. From

1959 to 1964, the majority of rightist elements were exonerated. In 1978, the Chinese Communist Party Central Committee made a resolution to exonerate all rightist elements, and moreover, in a practical and realistic manner, redressed all those who had been wrongly marked as rightist elements.

反右倾 fǎnyòuqīng
to oppose rightist tendencies

1) The struggle to oppose rightist opportunism. 2) The struggle conducted by the Chinese Communist Party in the summer of 1959 to oppose rightist opportunism. In July 1959, during the enlarged conference of the Chinese Communist Party Central Political Bureau (Lushan Conference), Peng Dehuai wrote a letter to Mao Zedong describing his views on the leftist errors since 1958. Mao Zedong treated it as an attack on the Party, and claimed the letter represented anti-Party principles of rightist opportunism. In the latter part of the conference, Mao Zedong initiated criticism of Peng Dehuai, which grew to become the entire Party's "anti-rightist" campaign. The result was serious damage to the democratic life within the Party. Economically, the leftist errors persisted through an even longer period.

反殖 fǎn-zhí
anti-colonialism

Abbreviation for 反对殖民主义.

反左防右 fǎnzuǒ fángyòu
to oppose the left and guard against the right

In the process of revolution and construction, while opposing erroneous leftist tendencies, one must pay attention to guarding against the emergence of erroneous rightist tendencies. While opposing the erroneous rightist tendencies, one must pay attention to guarding against the emergence of erroneous leftist tendencies. Only then will work advance in the right direction.

返销 fǎnxiāo
reselling grains and other agricultural products purchased by the state to the countryside; exporting products made using imported technology and raw materials

E.g. 改革前有少数农村吃粮靠返销。 *Before the reforms, a small number of agricultural villages relied on grains resold by the state.* / 这个工厂引进设备，迅速更新产品，当年就能返销。 *After this factory brought in new equipment, it rapidly renewed its products, and began exporting them within the same year.*

返销粮 fǎnxiāoliáng
resold grain

Grain that has been purchased by the state from rural villages and sold back to rural villages, for all kinds of reasons.

范读 fàndú
model reading

A teacher giving students a demonstration on how to read.

贩私 fànsī
illegal vending; to sell illegal commodities

饭票 fànpiào
meal tickets

Tickets used by employees and cadres in the dining halls of their work units. In general the tickets are divided into two kinds: grain coupons (for purchasing

泛方房防 fàn – fáng

the main staple) and "dish" tickets (for purchasing non-staple dishes).

泛读 fàndú
extensive reading
1) To read in only a general way books and articles on a variety of subjects, not mulling over them in detail, in order to obtain a wide range of knowledge and broaden one's field of vision. 2) Students reading certain texts in only a general way, in order to review and consolidate material that has already been learned. It is the opposite of intensive reading.

泛光灯 fànguāngdēng
floodlight

fang

方便面 fāngbiànmiàn
convenient noodles; instant noodles
A kind of pre-cooked dried noodle. The noodles only need to be soaked in boiling water for a few minutes or cooked briefly before being served. They are relatively convenient to serve and take on a trip, hence the name.

方便食品 fāngbiàn shípǐn
convenient foods (fast and easily prepared)

方城 fāngchéng
square city wall
Jocular term for majong, derived from the fact that in the game the tiles are arranged in a square.
E.g. 他又去大战方城了。 *He has again gone to fight the square city wall.*

方队 fāngduì
square formation
A square formation prepared for inspection (as in a military parade). It can be composed of personnel, decorated vehicles, military equipment, etc.

房贷 fángdài
housing loans

房改 fánggǎi
housing system reform
Abbreviation for 住房制度改革.
E.g. 房改工作 *housing reform* / 房改部门 *housing reform agencies* / 房改单位 *housing reform work units* / 房改配套措施 *comprehensive set of measures for housing reform*

房改房 fánggǎifáng
housing reform houses
Houses bought at cost price or a standard price by employees according to the relevant regulations concerning housing reform and house selling.

房管 fáng–guǎn
real estate management
Abbreviation for 房地产管理.
E.g. 房管职工 *real estate management workers* / 房管系统 *real estate management system* / 房管部门 *real estate management sectors*

房管所 fáng–guǎn–suǒ
urban real estate management organs

房老虎 fánglǎohǔ
housing tigers
Departments or people in the housing management business who take advantage of their professional authority to extort, cheat, and cause difficulties for clients in the process of allocating and managing housing.

房市 fángshì
housing market

防雹 fángbáo
hail-damage prevention

E.g. 防雹研究 hail-damage prevention research / 防雹区 hail-damage prevention district / 防雹炮弹 hail prevention rockets

防暴 fángbào
riot protection
To prevent riots taking place.
E.g. 防暴队 riot protection team / 防暴警察 riot police; riot squad

防风林 fángfēnglín
wind-break forests

防寒服 fánghánfú
cold-resistant clothing

防护林带 fánghù líndài
shelter belts
Belt forests planted to regulate climate, and to alleviate or eliminate natural damage caused by rainfall, drought, wind, and sand.

防盲 fángmáng
blindness prevention
E.g. 全国防盲治盲基层保健系统已形成。 The basic system for the prevention and treatment of blindness throughout the nation is in place.

防沙林 fángshālín
sand-break forests

防特 fángtè
to guard against secret agents

防治 fángzhì
prevent and cure

仿冒 fǎngmào
counterfeits
Fraudulent imitations (of brand name products).
E.g. 谨防仿冒 to guard against counterfeits

仿生学 fǎngshēngxué
bionics

仿真 fǎngzhēn
to make a replica of the original object
E.g. 仿真机 replicating machine / 北京仿真中心 Beijing Replicating Center

访贫问苦 fǎngpín wènkǔ
to visit the poor and interview the bitter
A method used to arouse the masses in rural class struggle. That is, going among the masses to visit those poor, lower, and middle peasants who have suffered great hardships and who harbor deep grievances, to understand their bitterness, thereby arousing their class consciousness and organizing them to throw themselves into the struggle.

访视 fǎngshì
to visit a patient at home

访谈 fǎngtán
to interview and to discuss
To conduct a special interview on a particular subject and to add commentary or critique.
E.g. 焦点访谈 an interview discussion on a hot topic / 访谈录 record of an interview discussion

放飞 fàngfēi
release to fly
1) To release a bird from a cage. 2) To let an airplane take off.

放活 fànghuó
to loosen and enliven
To loosen up a policy and to enliven the economy.
E.g. 放活经济 to loosen up and enliven the economy

放开 fàngkāi
to remove restraints or limitations; to set free

E.g. 放开干 *to work without constraints* / 放开价格 *to remove price controls* / 放开手脚,大胆改革 *to untie the hands and courageously carry out reforms*

放空 fàngkōng
to let production resources lie idle
E.g. 生产能力放空。 *Production capabilities are lying idle.*

放空炮 fàngkōngpào
to fire off an empty bomb
A metaphor for expressing pointless opinions and viewpoints, or empty talk.

放宽政策 fàngkuān zhèngcè
to relax policies
After the Third Plenary Session of the Eleventh Central Committee of the Chinese Communist Party, China adjusted its internal policies, canceled various restrictions of the previous period when leftist ideology held sway, and changed the conditions in various realms, such as the overly restrictive conditions in agriculture, in order to bring into full play the initiatives of the masses in production, thus allowing the four modernizations to speedily get on the track of healthy development.

放疗 fàngliáo
radiation treatment
Abbreviation for 放射线疗法.
E.g. 病人愿意接受放疗。*The patient consented to radiation treatment.*

放权 fàngquán
transfer power to a lower level; to give greater power to lower or local levels

放卫星 fàngwèixīng
to launch a satellite
A metaphor for a certain job breaking a new record, or accomplishing something startling.

放下包袱 fàngxià bāofu
to put down a burden
A metaphor for getting rid of the burden which influenced one's thoughts and actions.

放下架子 fàngxià jiàzi
to relinquish haughty airs; to get off one's high horse
A metaphor for getting rid off conceited and pretentious airs.
E.g. 领导者必须放下架子,才能和群众打成一片。 *Leaders must relinquish their haughty airs before they can merge with the masses.*

放眼 fàngyǎn
to open up one's vision
E.g. 放眼世界 *to open up one's vision onto the whole world.*

放羊 fàngyáng
herd sheep
A metaphor for letting things drift.

放养 fàngyǎng
to cultivate (certain fish, bees, etc.)
To put certain economically valuable animals such as fish, bees, and tussah silkworms at certain locations and allow them to breed.

放音机 fàngyīnjī
tape player

放足鞋 fàngzúxié
shoes for released bound feet
Shoes especially made for women whose feet were bound in the old society. Although these women had stopped binding their feet long ago, their feet had become deformed and they could no longer wear ordinary shoes.

fei

非党群众 fēidǎng qúnzhòng
non-Party masses
Also called 党外群众 outside party masses. It specifically refers to people who have not joined the Chinese Communist Party.

非党人士 fēidǎng rénshì
non-Party personages
Persons who are not Chinese Communist Party members but who have a certain social influence and prestige.

非对抗性矛盾 fēiduìkàngxìng máodùn
non-antagonistic contradictions
Contradictions that can be resolved without external conflicts. In a class society, they are the contradictions that exist on a foundation of basically homogeneous class interests, such as the contradictions between laboring peoples. It is the opposite of 对抗性矛盾 antagonistic contradictions.

非官方 fēiguānfāng
non-official
E.g. 非官方关系 *non-official relationship* / 非官方报纸 *non-official newspaper* / 非官方消息 *non-official information*

非婚性行为 fēihūn xìngxíngwéi
extra-marital sexual activity
All forms of sexual activity outside of marriage.
E.g. 非婚性行为是传播性病、艾滋病的主要原因。 *Extra-marital sexual activity is a major cause of venereal disease and AIDS.*

非贸易外汇收入 fēimàoyì wàihuì shōurù
non-trade foreign currency income
The portion of foreign currency income not derived from trade. In general, it refers to international tourism, export of labor, remittance by overseas Chinese and other private foreigners, etc.

非农化 fēinónghuà
de-agriculturalize, the process of turning agricultural labor into non-agricultural employment

非欧佩克 fēi'ōupèikè
oil-producing nations and regions outside of OPEC
指欧佩克（石油输出国组织）以外的石油出产国家和地区

非书资料 fēishū zīliào
non-print materials
Information not in printed form, such as audio and videotapes, slides, microfilms, models, and educational toys.

非斯计划 Fēisī Jìhuà
the Fez Plan
一项解决巴勒斯坦和中东问题的阿拉伯方案。1982年在摩洛哥非斯城阿拉伯国际首脑会议上通过。
A plan for resolving the Palestinian and Middle East problem, drawn up by the Arab states in Fez in 1982.

非组织观点 fēizǔzhī guāndiǎn
non-organizational viewpoint
The erroneous idea and opinion within revolutionary ranks that there is no need for organizational (political party, group) leadership or for organizational discipline.

非组织活动 fēizǔzhī huódòng
non-organizational activity
Activities within the revolutionary ranks which go against the organizational (political party, group) principle and

organizational discipline, and which are carried out behind the back of the organization, and which are harmful to revolutionary interests.

绯闻 fēiwén
gossip concerning sexual relations
E.g. 演员常受绯闻的困扰。 *Performers are often plagued by gossip about their sexual relationships.*

飞碟 fēidié
UFO; flying saucer; frisbee
1) A saucer-shaped flying object of unidentified origin. Also called 不明飞行物 unidentified flying object. 2) A saucer-shaped flying object used in a sport. It is thrown and caught by two or more players.
E.g. 飞碟射击比赛 *frisbee contest*

飞鸽牌 fēigēpái
flying pigeon brand
Originally a brand of bicycle, now a metaphor for someone unable to stay long at a certain location.
E.g. 他是飞鸽牌,在这待不长。 *He's the flying pigeon type, and would not stay here long.*

飞过海 fēiguòhǎi
to fly overseas
A phenomenon during the Cultural Revolution whereby individuals bypassed the Party organizations in their own units when they would not admit them into the Party. They used their prerogatives and connections and went to other Party organizations to be admitted into the Party.

飞迁 fēiqiān
(of flocks of birds and swarms of flying insects) to migrate
E.g. 成群的飞蛾是从江淮一带飞迁来的。 *The swarms of moths migrated here from the Yangtze River and Huai River region.*

飞人 fēirén
flying person, someone who runs especially fast or jumps especially high or far

飞行集会 fēixíng jíhuì
a type of demonstration march that can be organized and dispersed quickly

飞行器 fēixíngqì
all flying machines and devices (two types: those used in air travel and those used in outer space, the latter are also called 航天器)

飞行物 fēixíngwù
flying objects (usually refers to UFO's)

飞行药检 fēixíng yàojiǎn
fly-in drug inspection
A method used by international athletic organizations to inspect athletes for banned drug use; the organization dispatches inspectors to the site where the athletes are stationed and where they can carry out their inspection without prior notice.

肥力 féilì
fertility
The degree of soil fertility.

肥水 féishuǐ
rich water
A metaphor for benefits and advantages.
E.g. 肥水不落外人田。 *Life giving water does not fall on someone else's field.*

肥皂粉 féizàofěn
soap powder; detergent
Also called 洗衣粉 clothes-washing

powder.

肥皂剧 féizàojù

soap opera

A radio or television serial in America. The content mostly concerns family problems portrayed in the form of melodrama or farce. Soap companies often use these serials to promote their products, hence the name "soap opera".

肥猪粉 féizhūfěn

pig-fattening powder

A drug which promotes the growth of fat and meat in pigs. It can suppress thyroid functioning and decrease metabolism, causing a great amount of fat to accumulate in the body.

沸腾炉 fèiténglú

boilers

Also called 沸腾锅炉, a new kind of coal-burning stove. The coal pellets are blown up by air, then churned in the stove as they burn. It is like water boiling, hence the name. There are two types: total boiler and semi boiler.

fen

分贝 fēnbèi

decibel (now often used to measure sound pollution)

分餐 fēncān

divided meals

(Meals served at home or at party) Each person having a set of eating utensils and an individual serving of food.

分成 fēnchéng

percentage allotment

To be allotted a certain percentage of the total income (a portion of the money or goods).

分导 fēndǎo

to guide separately

E.g. 分导式多弹头导弹 *multi-headed ballistic missiles with each warhead guided separately*

分类排队 fēnlèi páiduì

to categorize and prioritize matters; to analyze employees' political and professional qualities

分裂主义 fēnliè zhǔyì

splittism; separatism

A manifestation of opportunism and revisionism in an organization. It consists of forming cliques to seek private interests, discriminating against those with different views, engaging in secret factional activities, alienating cadres from the masses, factionalizing the proletarian political party, even setting up a separate central government, vainly attempting to change the Party's line and policy, and undermining proletarian revolutionary work.

分流 fēnliú

(originally) to divert the flow of a river or flood; (now) to divert the flow of traffic

E.g. 开展公路铁路分流 *to open up the diversion of traffic to highways and railways* / 开辟长途客运分流线 *to open up branch lines for long-distance passenger transport*

分秒必争 fēnmiǎo bìzhēng

must grasp every minute and second

Using every second.

分配式 fēnpèishì

method of allocation

The method of equalized allocation of commodities from top to bottom, which was practiced in the commercial sector before the Third Plenum of the Eleventh Party Central Committee. This method did not allow retailers and grass-roots supply and marketing units to freely choose the sources of their commodities, the variety of goods, or their specifications or quantity. This turned the economic relationships between enterprises into those between a superior and an inferior, which was detrimental to the flow of commodities.

分片包干 fēnpiàn bāogān
divide up into pieces and assign responsibility

Also called 包片儿 take responsibility for pieces. It consists of delineating certain responsibilities according to the area or scope of a job, then assigning them to individuals or units, who pledge satisfactory completion.

分权 fēnquán
to disperse centralized political, economic, and military power to local or subsidiary units

E.g. 中央和地方适当分权。 *Power should be divided between the central and local governments.*

分散主义 fēnsàn zhǔyì
decentralism

An erroneous tendency which damages the centralized unified leadership of the proletarian political party and the socialist nation. Its chief manifestations are: not accepting the unified leadership of the Party, going against democratic centralism, and taking the attitude of going off on one's own and implementing one's own policies, irrespective of the Party's directives and the resolutions of the central government and the authorities.

分食 fēnshí
i.e. 分餐 divided meal, where each person has individual servings of food

分数挂帅 fēnshù guàshuài
to put grades in command

The erroneous tendency and method of the educational sector of seeking high grades on exams, and not attending to the actual quality of education. This term is no longer used.

分数线 fēnshùxiàn
grade cut-off point

Abbreviation for 录取分数线 acceptance cut-off point. This is the point on school entrance exams, which marks acceptance and non-acceptance. The examination subjects and the requirements of the schools vary, therefore the grade cut-off point also varies.

分税制 fēnshuìzhì
system of divided taxation

A system of taxation whereby the central and local governments have jurisdiction over different types of taxes.

分灶吃饭 fēnzào chīfàn
divide up the stove and eat

对"划分收支、分级包干"财政体制的比喻说法。中国从1980年起实行这种体制，即：按照经济管理体制规定的隶属关系，明确中央和地方的收支范围。各省、市、自治区根据国家的方针、政策和统一的计划，统筹安排本地区的生产建设事业和财政支出。中央各企业、事业主管部门，对于应当由地方安排的各项事业，不再归口安排处理，也不再向地方分配财政支出指标。但应提出指导方针和工作方向，制定政策措施，检查经济效果。"分灶吃饭"的体制能调动各级政府当家理财的积极性。
A metaphor for the fiscal system of delineating income and expenditure, and letting each level take responsibility for itself. Since 1980, China has adopted this type of system. Based on the jurisdictions as determined by the economic management system, the income and expenditure spheres of the central and local governments are clearly delineated. Each province, city, and autonomous region is responsible for overall planning of production and fiscal expenditure but this should accord with national directives and the policies of a unified plan. Management departments of the central government no longer manage the enterprises that now fall under local jurisdiction, nor do they direct local fiscal expenditure. They should, though, suggest guidelines, stipulate policies, and monitor economic performance. The system of "divide up the stove and eat" can mobilize the initiative of various levels of government in taking charge and managing finances.

分子生物学 fēnzǐ shēngwùxué
molecular biology

粉尘 fěnchén
dust
A dust-like waste product from burning or from an industrial production process.
E.g. 粉尘作业 *dust work*

粉领工人 fěnlǐng gōngrén
pastel-collar workers, those employed in female-dominated professions such as salesclerks, teachers, and secretaries

粉领族 fěnlǐngzú
pink-collar tribe
Women who play major roles in certain professions such as office workers, secretaries, models, airline hostesses, etc.

粉碎机 fěnsuìjī
pulverizer

奋飞 fènfēi
to take off with great speed
A metaphor for rapid development.

奋进 fènjìn
to advance courageously

份儿饭 fènrfàn
table d'hôte meal; set meal

氛围 fènwéi
atmosphere; sentiment

丰产田 fēngchǎntián
bumper harvest field

封顶 fēngdǐng
to seal the top
To put a seal on the top (of house, cellars, stoves, etc.). A metaphor for stipulating the maximum of certain quantities.
E.g. 奖金上不封顶,下不保底。 *The bonus has no seal on the top (has no ceiling) and no guaranteed minimum.*

封冻 fēngdòng
ice-sealed

封镜 fēngjìng
The completion of the filming of a movie or television program.
E.g. 那部八集连续剧已经封镜。 *The filming of that eight-part serial drama has already finished.*

封盘 fēngpán
(terminology used in board game competitions such as chess) to record the location of the pieces in an unfinished game, which will be

continued later

封杀 fēngshā
to forbid; to ban
E.g. 非法经营出境旅游机构被封杀。 *Companies operating without government approval to send tourist groups abroad were banned.*

封山育林 fēngshān yùlín
seal off the mountain to cultivate forests
A measure to protect the maturation of forest. It forbids grazing and tree-cutting on mountains with young forests or a potential forest within a certain period.

封资修 fēng-zī-xiū
feudalism, capitalism, and revisionism
Contraction of 封建主义 (feudalism), 资本主义 (capitalism), and 修正主义 (revisionism).

蜂王浆 fēngwáng jiāng
queen bee pulp
A highly nutritious substance produced by worker bees' salivary glands, used as a tonic, also known as royal jelly.

蜂窝煤 fēngwōméi
beehive coal
A type of household cooking fuel made of coal mixed with other ingredients and shaped into beehive-like drums.

蜂窝通信 fēngwō tōngxìn
cellular communications

风纪扣 fēng jìkòu
discipline button
The hook and eye that close the collar on a military uniform or Zhongshan suit.

风景线 fēng jǐngxiàn
scenic view; attractive scenery or phenomenon
E.g. "浙江村"的第一道风景线是窗帘店多。 *The first thing seen in "Zhejiang Village" is a large number of curtain shops.*

风幕 fēngmù
wind screen
A kind of formless screen wall, which utilizes wind as a barrier.
E.g. 风幕机 *wind screen machine*

风能 fēngnéng
wind energy (usually captured by windmills and transformed into mechanical energy)

风派 fēngpài
opportunists (who shift directions with the wind)
E.g. 不要做风派。 *Don't be an opportunist.*

风派人物 fēngpài rénwù
persons of the "wind clique;" wavering fence-sitter
指"文化大革命"中某些搞政治投机的人。他们时刻窥测政治风向，哪边风硬，就倒向哪边，故称为"风派人物"。
Political opportunists of the Cultural Revolution. They always watched which way the political wind was blowing and bent to the strongest. Hence the term "persons of the wind clique".

风头主义 fēngtóu zhǔyì
limelightism
To be fond of being in the limelight, and of showing off.

风味小吃 fēngwèi xiǎochī
local-flavor snacks

风险投资 fēngxiǎn tóuzī
risk investment

风衣 fēngyī
wind-breaker (type of clothing)

风雨衣 fēngyǔyī

trench coat
A full-length coat capable of warding off wind and rain.

fu

肤色 fūsè
color of the skin

扶本 fúběn
to nurture the basics (cf. 扶志)

扶标 fúbiāo
to aid with targets
The opposite of 扶本 to nurture the basics. That is, to render assistance in secondary areas. To aid poor households in rural villages in only monetary ways, with the result that they are unable to fundamentally alter the conditions that cause poverty.

扶贫 fúpín
to aid the poor
To give support to poor households in developing production and changing the conditions that cause poverty. The term also refers specifically to aiding the relatively poor rural households, which have been slow in their development after the Third Plenary Session of the Eleventh Central Committee of the Chinese Communist Party (where the new responsibility system was promulgated).

扶贫小组 fúpín xiǎozǔ
aid-the-poor committees
Organizations formed to aid poor households in developing production and changing the conditions that cause poverty after China's rural villages implemented the remuneration-related-to-output responsibility system.

扶优限劣 fúyōu xiànliè
to nurture well-managed enterprises and curtail the inferior ones

扶正祛邪 fúzhèng qùxié
to nurture healthy tendencies and to eliminate unhealthy ones
E.g. 干部要带头扶正去邪。 *Cadres must take a lead in nurturing healthy tendencies and eliminating the unhealthy ones.*

扶志 fúzhì
to nurture the will
To render assistance in the most basic areas. To support the poor households in China's rural villages to strengthen their faith in developing production and changing the conditions that cause poverty. It consists primarily of publicizing the policy of enriching the people promulgated since the Third Plenary Session of the Eleventh Central Committee of the Chinese Communist Party, and helping them to analyze the various benefits of developing production, thus allowing them to find a way to attain wealth.
E.g. 扶贫要先扶志。 *In aiding the poor, we must nurture the will.*
E.g. 分享福祉 *to share happiness*

辐照 fúzhào
irradiation
E.g. 辐照一次性医疗器 *disposable (only used once) irradiation medical device*

服软 fúruǎn
to relent
To submit to a certain force and to relent.
E.g. 他终于服软。 *He finally relented.*

服务费 fúwùfèi

service fee

Service fees collected from customers in certain food and drink establishments.

服务态度 fúwù tàidu

service attitude

The attitude of service personnel toward customers.

服务行业 fúwù hángyè

service professions

Professions that serve people and provide conveniences in people's lives, such as the staff of a hotel, a barber, and businesses that repair articles of everyday use. Also called 服务业 service professions.

服务员 fúwùyuán

service personnel

1) Persons who do odd jobs in organizations. 2) Workers who serve customers in hotels, restaurants, and other service professions.

浮动工资 fúdòng gōngzī

fluctuating wages

A wage system whereby the workers' wages can fluctuate up or down according to how good business is, the quality of the work, and price fluctuations.

浮夸风 fúkuāfēng

atmosphere of exaggeration

The common practice of not basing truth on reality and exaggerating, which surfaced in 1958 during the Great Leap Forward and the communization movement.

福利院 fúlìyuàn

welfare institutions

福祉 fúzhǐ

happiness

辅导员 fǔdǎoyuán

counselors

Persons who help or direct political thought education in schools.

E.g. 少先队辅导员 counselor for the Young Pioneers / 政治辅导员 political counselor.

辅料 fǔliào

supplementary materials

Various ingredients that have a supplementary function in the production of commodities.

腐化变质分子 fǔhuà biànzhì fènzǐ

degenerate elements

Persons within revolutionary ranks whose ideology has degenerated, whose lives have become dissolute, and who have lost the character of the proletarian laboring people.

副标题 fùbiāotí

subheading

Also called 副题 subtitle.

副食本 fùshíběn

supplemental food card

A certificate for purchasing various non-staple food items.

副食关系 fùshí guānxì

supplementary food relationship

Practice in the first years after liberation, the relationship between citizens and the local supplier of non-staple food. Residents had to buy non-staples from appointed suppliers. If they moved they would have to form a relationship with a new supplier in the new locality.

副食商店 fùshí shāngdiàn

supplementary food stores; grocery

Stores that sell supplemental food items such as fish, meat, and vegetables.

副研 fù-yán

associate researcher

Abbreviation for 副研究员.

E.g. 申请副研 *to apply for the professional title of associate researcher*

覆盖率 fùgàilǜ
ratio of ground cover
The ratio of land area which is covered with vegetation.

复读 fùdú
(students destined to graduate from elementary or secondary schools) to repeat the last year of schooling due to failure to graduate to the next level

复读班 fùdúbān
a class composed of students repeating the last year of schooling

复读生 fùdúshēng
a student repeating the last year of schooling

复关 fùguān
to be restored to the position of a signatory nation to GATT
E.g. 中美将磋商中国复关协议书。*China and the U.S. are negotiating on the protocols of restoring China to GATT.*

复旧 fùjiù
reverting to the old
To revert to old customs, concepts, system, etc.

复课 fùkè
to resume classes
To resume classes after they have been stopped for some reason.

复垦 fùkěn
to re-open fallow land for cultivation

复录 fùlù
to dub tapes (same as 翻录)

复贫 fùpín
to fall back into poverty after having risen above it for a period

复式住宅 fùshì zhùzhái
a type of residential housing that maximizes usable space by increasing the number of two storey buildings

复述 fùshù
to reiterate
1) To retell something that has been said by someone else or by oneself. 2) A practice method used in language teaching whereby students retell in their own words the content of reading materials.

复退军人 fù-tuì jūnrén
abbreviation for 复员退伍军人 **demobilized servicemen**

复印机 fùyìnjī
xerox machine
Also called 静电复印机 electrostatic copier.

复制 fùzhì
to replicate
To replicate an original item (usually a work of art), to reprint a book, etc.

复种 fùzhòng
multiple crops
A method of cultivation whereby two or more crops are cultivated on the same land within a year.
E.g. 复种面积 *multiple crop area (acreage)* / 复种指数 *multiple crop index*

复转军人 fù-zhuǎn jūnrén
armymen demobilized or transferred to civilian work
Contraction of 复员军人 and 专业军人.

复壮 fùzhuàng
to rejuvenate (agriculture)
To recover the original superior characteristics of a certain species (of crop)

and to raise the vitality of the seeds.
E.g. 品种复壮 *to recover the strength of the species* / 某些春播作物进行冬播可以使种子复壮。*Sowing in winter can rejuvenate the seeds of certain spring crops.*

父子党 fùzǐdǎng
father-son party
A phenomenon of the international communist movement whereby the communist party of a big nation treated the communist parties of the other nations in an unegalitarian way. It issued orders at will, and ruled as if it was the head of the household. This relationship was like that of father and son, hence the term "father-son party".

负面 fùmiàn
reverse side; negative aspect
E.g. 负面影响 *negative reaction* / 负面效应 *negative effect*

富国 fùguó
rich nations; to make a nation rich and powerful
E.g. 富国强兵 *enrich the nation and strengthen the military* / 富国利民 *enrich the nation and bring benefits to the people*

富民 fùmín
to make the people rich and prosperous

富民政策 fùmín zhèngcè
policy of enriching people
国家为引导人民勤劳致富而制定的有关政策。
Policies established by the state for the purpose of leading the people to attain riches through hard work.

富农 fùnóng
rich peasants
Those people in rural villages before Liberation who based their livelihood primarily on exploiting hired labor, lending money at high interest and renting out part of their land. In general they owned land, the better tools of production, and mobile capital. They may themselves have participated in labor, but their income derived primarily from exploitation. They were the bourgeoisie in rural villages.

富裕中农 fùyù zhōngnóng
rich middle peasants
Relatively rich middle peasants who held a relatively large quantity of production materials, and who practiced a small degree of exploitation. Also called 上中农 upper middle peasants.

附加工资 fùjiā gōngzī
supplementary wages
Also called 活工资 flexible wages and 暂时增发工资 temporary wage supplements. Wages in addition to standard regular wages. This was a temporary measure adopted during the Cultural Revolution after bonuses were stopped. Following the reinstitution of bonuses and piece rate wages, supplementary wages were gradually eliminated as workers were promoted.

附捐邮票 fùjuān yóupiào
postal stamps whose cost and face value include a component that is donated to an organization (the post office disperses the donations to the beneficiary organizations)

附中 fùzhōng
attached middle school
A middle school attached to a university.

E.g. 北大附中 *Beijing University's attached middle school*

妇产医院 fùchǎn yīyuàn
obstetrics-gynecology hospital

妇代会 fù – dài – huì
Women's Congress
Abbreviation for 妇女代表大会.

妇联 fù – lián
Women's Federation
Abbreviation for 妇女联合会.

妇男 fùnán
a facetious term for men who take primary responsibility for domestic chores

妇幼保健站 fù – yòu bǎojiànzhàn
women and children's health station
A medical facility for protecting the health of women and children.

G

gai

改产 gǎichǎn
to change production by abandoning former products for new ones
E.g. 帮助他们改产 to help them change their products / 改产人民需要的产品 to change manufacturing to products that people need

改制 gǎizhì
to reform the system

概念车 gàiniànchē
concept cars
体现设计思想的样品车。
Refers to sample cars revealing the ideas of designers.

概念化 gàiniànhuà
generalization
A bad tendency in literary and artistic works which lack profound concrete depiction, and which use abstract generalizations instead of individual characterization.

盖 gài
to surpass; to exceed
E.g. 他每次考试都盖我一等。On every exam, he surpasses me by a notch.

盖饭 gàifàn
covered rice
A meal sold in portions. It consists of rice in a bowl or dish with vegetables and sometimes meat on top. Also called 盖浇饭.

盖浇饭 gàijiāofàn
(simple meal in eateries) rice in a bowl or dish topped with vegetables
Abbreviated as 盖饭.

盖了 gàile
exceedingly good

盖洛普 gàiluòpǔ
Gallup Poll
音意词。意指民意测验。

盖帽儿 gàimàor
(basketball) defense player knocking down a ball shot at the basket by an opponent
Also called 盖了帽儿.

gan

干货 gānhuò
dried fruit (prunes, raisins, etc.); solid stuff with padding and moisture removed

干扰素 gānrǎosù
interferon

干鲜果品 gānxiān guǒpǐn
composite term for dried and fresh fruit

干洗 gānxǐ
dry-cleaning

干预生活 gānyù shēnghuó
to intercede on life
The exposure of the dark aspects of social life in works of literature and art. Such works may affect the politics of the

times, so that such negative aspects are overcome.

甘居中游 gānjū zhōngyóu
content to swim in the middle
Being content to be in a middling position, being neither advanced nor backward.
E.g. 甘居中游思想 *content-to-swim-in-the-middle mentality*

肝功 gāngōng
the function of the liver
E.g. 肝功正常。*The functioning of the liver is normal.*

赶超 gǎnchāo
to catch up and surpass (a certain level)
E.g. 赶超先进 *to catch up with and surpass the advanced*

感冒 gǎnmào
(originally) flu; jocular term for having positive feelings or an interest
E.g. 厂长治厂无方，工人普遍对他不感冒。*The factory manager is incompetent at his job, so the workers generally don't have positive feelings toward him.*

敢于斗争 gǎnyú dòuzhēng
dare to struggle
To have the determination and courage to struggle against enemies, evil persons and bad things. In the process of transforming natural conditions, having the determination and courage to overcome difficulties can also be called "daring to struggle".

敢于胜利 gǎnyú shènglì
dare to triumph
In a struggle, one must have the determination and courage to attain victory, and one must have faith that victory will be attained.

干部服 gànbùfú
cadre suit
The top of the suit has two pockets on either side, each with a flap and a button. The bottom is a pair of Western-styled trousers. Also called 中山装 Zhongshan suit in China.

干部路线 gànbù lùxiàn
guideline on cadres
The fundamental principles and channels followed in appointing cadres to positions.

干部下放 gànbù xiàfàng
to send down cadres
To arrange for national cadres to go work at grass-roots units, or to participate in labor and life in rural villages or factories. This can be short-term or long-term. It is also called 下放干部.

干部责任制 gànbù zérènzhì
cadres' responsibility system
A system that clearly stipulates the professional responsibilities of cadres and the standards relating to rewards and punishment.

干革命 gàn gémìng
to carry out revolutionary work

干警 gànjǐng
cadre and police
Cadres and policemen of the Public Security Office.
E.g. 公安干警提高了政治素质和业务水平。*The public security cadres and police have raised their political caliber and professional standards.*

干龄 gànlíng
number of years as cadre

干群关系 gàn-qún guānxì
the relationship between cadres and

the masses

干校 gàn-xiào

cadre school

1) Schools that specialize in cultivating and training various kinds of cadres.
E.g. 政治干校 *political cadre school* / 煤炭干校 *School for the cadres from coal industry*
2) It refers specifically to the May Seventh Cadre School that surfaced during the Cultural Revolution. (cf. 五．七干校)

干休所 gàn-xiū-suǒ

cadres' sanitarium

Establishments specifically for retired, old, weak, sick, and invalid cadres to rest and receive medical treatment. They are also called 干休所.

gang

钢城 gāngchéng

steel cities

Cities where steel production is relatively concentrated and a high quantity is produced.

钢领工人 gānglǐng gōngrén

steel-collar worker; robots

An appellation for robots in Western societies. It is derived from the terms blue-collar workers and white-collar workers.

纲要 Gāngyào

Guiding Principles

《1955年到1957年全国农业发展纲要》的简称。该文件是1955年1月中共中央根据毛泽东的倡议提出，1950年4月经第二届全国人民代表大会第二次会议讨论通过。《纲要》全文共40条。也简称农业发展纲要或纲要。

Abbreviation for "Guiding Principles for National Agricultural Development for 1955-1957. This document was proposed by the Chinese Communist Party Central Committee in January 1955 on the basis of Mao Zedong's recommendation, and resolved after deliberation at the Second Session of the Second National People's Congress in April 1950. The "Guiding Principles", consisting of forty articles, are also abbreviated as 农业发展纲要 Guiding Principles for Agricultural Development or simply 纲要 Guiding Principles.

岗位责任制 gǎngwèi zérènzhì

work post responsibility system

A system used in China's socialist enterprises whereby the function and responsibility of each work post are clearly stipulated. This responsibility system is also being tried in institutional units.

港澳 Gǎng-Ào

composite term for 香港 **Hong Kong and** 澳门 **Macao**

港府 Gǎngfǔ

Hong Kong local government

港人 Gǎngrén

Hong Kong residents

港衫 Gǎngshān

a style of summer shirt in China imported from Hong Kong

港商 Gǎngshāng

Hong Kong businessmen and merchants

港式 Gǎngshì

Hong Kong style (usually of clothing and make-up)

港事 Gǎngshì

Hong Kong affairs

E.g. 中国方面提出设立港事顾问的构想。 *The Chinese side proposed establishing a Hong Kong Affairs Consultative Office.*

港属 Gǎngshǔ

relatives of Hong Kong compatriots in China

港台 Gǎng-Tái

composite term for 香港 **Hong Kong and** 台湾 **Taiwan**

港星 Gǎngxīng

Hong Kong stars, popular entertainers in Hong Kong

杠杠 gànggang

bat

Certain limits and stipulations.

E.g. 年龄杠杠 *age limit*

gao

高层 gāocéng

(of buildings) tall; high-ranking

E.g. 高层建筑 *tall buildings* / 高层领导人 *high-ranking leaders* / 高层会晤 *meeting of high-ranking leaders*

高产田 gāochǎntián

high-yield fields

高产稳产 gāochǎn wěnchǎn

high production and steady production

The per-area production of agricultural fields is high and stable.

高大全 gāo-dà-quán

tall, big, and perfect

指"文化大革命"期间，某些文艺作品中按照"四人帮"的文艺"理论"所塑造的脱离现实生活、虚假的"英雄人物"形象。这种所谓的"英雄人物"形象，比其他人物都要"高大"而且"完美无缺"，故称"高大全"。"高大全"也指"四人帮"的这种塑造人物的荒谬理论和创作方法。

Nonexistent heroic figures, divorced from real life and fabricated in certain literary and art works according to the Gang of Four's theory of literature and art during the Cultural Revolution. These "heroic" figures were taller and bigger than normal human beings, and were perfect, hence the term "tall, big, and perfect". The term also refers to this absurd theory of characterization and this method of creation by the Gang of Four.

高低柜 gāodīguì

uneven cabinet

A cabinet made up of components the tops of which are at different levels.

高发 gāofā

high incidence (of disease)

E.g. 癌症高发地区 *area of high incidence of cancer* / 肝炎高发区 *area of high incidence of hepatitis*

高法 gāo-fǎ

the Supreme Court of the People's Republic of China

Abbreviation for 中华人民共和国最高人民法院.

高分低能 gāofēn dīnéng

to have high academic marks but low practical ability

高峰 gāofēng

(mountain) peak; pinnacle (in metaphorical sense)

E.g. 每天上下班高峰时，开辟10条高峰线。 *During peak rush hours, ten rush hour (express) lines or lanes are opened.* / 早晚是学生用厕高峰时间。 *Morning and evening are peak toilet usage times for students.* / 春节铁路运输高峰推迟。 *Peak demand for railroad transportation over the Spring Festival holidays is near at hand.*

高峰会议 gāofēng huìyì
summit meeting
Meeting of heads of states.

高干 gāo-gàn
high level cadre
Abbreviation for 高级干部.
E.g. 高干子弟 *children of high level cadres*

高工 gāo-gōng
high level engineer
Abbreviation for 高级工程师.

高级社 gāojíshè
high level cooperatives
The full term is 高级农业生产合作社 high level agricultural production cooperatives. A type of socialist collective economic organization formed in China's agricultural collectivization process. They were larger in scale than the elementary level cooperatives. Their special characteristics were: land, and production materials such as farm animals and large-scale agricultural implements all belonged to the collective; land ownership was rescinded; the principle of allocation according to labor was instituted.

高级知识分子 gāojí zhīshi fènzǐ
high level intellectuals
Persons with relatively profound scientific or cultural knowledge. In general, the term refers to intellectuals at or above the associate professor level.

高技术 gāojìshù
high-tech industry
Abbreviation for 高技术产业, industries in which the proportionate investment in technology vs. capital or labor is high.

高价 gāojià
high cost

高架公路 gāojià gōnglù
elevated highway
A road structure which is elevated from the ground to facilitate traffic flow. Also called 高架道路 or 高架路 elevated road.

高架路 gāojiàlù
overhead road; elevated road (highway)

高精尖 gāo-jīng-jiān
high, refined, and peak
Scientific technology or products that are of a high quality, perfected, and the most advanced.
E.g. 高精尖产品 *high, refined, peak products*

高举 gāojǔ
to raise high
E.g. 高举红旗 *to hold high the red flag*

高考 gāokǎo
college entrance examination
The unified examination for admission to institutions of higher learning.

高空作业 gāokōng zuòyè
aerial work
Work done at a high location, on top of scaffolding, etc. Constructing tall buildings or bridges, erecting electricity pylons, etc., all involve this type of work.

高难 gāonán
(of technology) high caliber and high degree of difficulty
E.g. 高难动作 *difficult movements that require superior skills* / 高难技巧 *a superior and difficult technique* / 高难度格斗 *wrestling at a high degree of*

skill and difficulty

高能燃料 gāonéng ránliào
high power fuel

高能物理学 gāonéng wùlǐxué
high energy physics

高聘 gāopìn
to be appointed to a high position
To appoint someone in a low professional position to a high position.
E.g. 他被推荐到厂部高聘。*He was recommended for a high-level appointment in the factory.*

高企 gāoqǐ
(prices) to maintain an upward trend
E.g. 日元高企给日本带来不利影响。 *The continuous rise of the Japanese yen has had a deleterious effect on the Japanese economy.* / 今年度世界棉花价格高企不下。 *This year the price of cotton on the world market has risen continuously without any sign of a drop.*

高师 gāoshī
abbreviated term for teacher-training institutions at the secondary and tertiary levels

高速公路 gāosù gōnglù
super highways

高速铁路 gāosù tiělù
high-speed railroad
Rail lines that carry trains traveling at over 200 kilometers per hour; they have the advantages of large transport capacity, speed, and safety.

高危 gāo–wēi
high and dangerous
High in number and in danger.
E.g. 儿童是铅污染的高危人群。 *Children are a large and endangered group of people affected by lead pollution.*

高消费 gāoxiāofèi
high consumption

高校 gāo–xiào
abbreviated term for institutions of higher education

高效节能 gāoxiào jiénéng
energy-efficient
Highly economical in energy consumption.

高新技术 gāoxīn jìshù
advanced high technology
E.g. 高新技术产业开发区 *development zone for high and new technology industries*

高薪 gāoxīn
high salary

高薪阶层 gāoxīn jiēcéng
high-salary stratum

高压锅 gāoyāguō
pressure cooker

高压手段 gāoyā shǒuduàn
high pressure tactics
Dictatorial, peremptory, and cruel methods of forcing other people to submit.

高研 gāo–yán
high-level researcher
Abbreviated term for 高级研究员.

高知 gāo–zhī
high-level intellectual
Abbreviated term for 高级知识分子.

高指标 gāozhǐbiāo
high target
Targets proposed in the production process that exceed realistic possibilities. The term refers specifically to the unrealistic targets proposed in the 1958 Great Leap Forward communization movement under erroneous leftist influence.

高姿态 gāozītài

magnanimous behavior

搞对象 gǎo duìxiàng

to be occupied with finding a match (marriage partner)

A young man or woman occupied with finding a match.

E.g. 他正忙着搞对象。*He is busy finding a match.*

搞活 gǎohuó

to enliven

E.g. 搞活企业 *to enliven enterprises* / 搞活流通 *to enliven the flow* / 搞活经济 *to enliven the economy* / 搞活市场 *to enliven the market*

搞通思想 gǎotōng sīxiǎng

to get through to someone

To bring about a thorough understanding and acceptance of some issue that is hard to understand.

搞卫生 gǎo wèishēng

to do cleaning work

E.g. 今天下午搞卫生。*Cleaning will be done this afternoon.*

搞小圈子 gǎo xiǎoquānzi

to be involved in a small circle

(cf. 小圈子)

告败 gàobài

to declare failure

告吹 gàochuī

to fizzle out

A relationship falls apart or something fails.

E.g. 恋爱告吹。*The romance has fallen apart.*

ge

歌后 gēhòu

"queen of songs", famous female music star

歌迷 gēmí

music aficionado

歌坛 gētán

world of vocal music

歌王 gēwáng

king of songs

Famous male music star.

歌星 gēxīng

singing star

A popular singing performer.

鸽派 gēpài

the dove faction

割尾巴 gē wěibā

to cut off the tail

A metaphor for eradicating erroneous things. The term also means cutting off the capitalistic tail. (cf. 割资本主义尾巴)

割资本主义尾巴 gē zīběn zhǔyì wěibā

to cut off the capitalist tail

During the Cultural Revolution, the counter-revolutionary group of Lin Biao and Jiang Qing undermined the rural economic policy, and regarded commune members' domestic sidelines, private plots, private animals, and rural trade as a capitalistic economy. They eliminated these practices and called it "cutting off the capitalist tail".

革命传统 gémìng chuántǒng

the revolutionary tradition

The excellent tradition formed by the Chinese Communist Party and the People's Army in the long revolutionary struggle. It includes such things as relating intimately to the masses, relating theory to reality, self-criticism, not fearing sacrifices, struggling under hardship, and serving the people with one's heart and mind.

革命闯将 gémìng chuǎngjiàng
pathbreaker for the revolution
Persons who are full of vitality in their revolutionary work. They have no fear of difficulties, they dare to break new ground, and they have attained outstanding achievements.

革命发展阶段论 gémìng fāzhǎn jiēduànlùn
theory of stages of revolutionary development
The Marxist theory that the different developmental stages of the proletarian revolution are distinct and connected. Revolution is made up of stages. The continuous revolutionary process consists of stages with different characteristics, and each stage is connected to its adjacent stages. The previous stage is the necessary precursor for the following stage, and the following stage is the inevitable trend of the previous stage.

革命化 gémìnghuà
to revolutionize
To make one's thoughts and actions conform to the requirements of revolutionary work. The essentials are upholding the socialist path and the leadership of the Chinese Communist Party, hard work and plain living, relating theory to reality, and maintaining close links with the masses. Revolutionization is the primary requirement of a cadre; and combined with "youth-ization", "knowledge-ization", and specialization, the four are called the four "cadre-izations".

革命接班人 gémìng jiēbānrén
successors of the revolution
The thousands of revolutionaries who will carry on the revolutionary work started by the older generation of proletarian revolutionaries.

革命浪漫主义 gémìng làngmàn zhǔyì
revolutionary romanticism

革命乐观主义 gémìng lèguān zhǔyì
revolutionary optimism
A manifestation of the proletarian world view: being filled with faith in the future of life and the revolutionary cause. Even if one encounters temporary difficulties in the revolutionary struggle and in the cause of national construction, or suffers frustrating circumstances, one is able to maintain a positive and optimistic attitude and a vigorous spirit to persist in the struggle unswervingly, and to overcome all difficulties in striving for victory.

革命派 gémìngpài
revolutionaries
Those who dedicate their lives to the revolutionary cause. It also refers specifically to the rebels during the Cultural Revolution, who were the antithesis of the conservatives. (cf. 造反派)

革命气概 gémìng qìgài
revolutionary mettle
The spirit and momentum, manifested in revolutionary work; not fearing difficulties and hardships, daring to struggle and to triumph.

革命前辈 gémìng qiánbèi
revolutionaries of the older generation
Old cadres who joined revolutionary work early and have made important

contributions.

革命热情 gémìng rèqíng
revolutionary fervor

Ardent feelings toward revolutionary work.

E.g. 满怀革命热情 *to be filled with revolutionary fervor in one's heart*

革命人道主义 gémìng réndào zhǔyì
revolutionary humanitarianism

Interpersonal ethical principles proposed in the years of the revolutionary war. They are closely tied with the revolutionary struggle. Revolutionary humanitarianism takes the interests of the masses of people as a principle in dealing with interpersonal relationships, opposes obliterating people's class character and opposes abolishing class struggle and violent revolution.

革命熔炉 gémìng rónglú
the revolutionary crucible

A metaphor for revolutionary struggle. It can temper a person, uplift his consciousness, strengthen his revolutionary will, and nurture him to become a mature revolutionary.

E.g. 在革命熔炉里锻炼成长 *to be tempered and matured in the revolutionary crucible*

革命圣地 gémìng shèngdì
sacred place of the revolution

Locations that have important historical significance and through their role in the course of the revolution, for example, Yan'an in Shaanxi Province.

革命委员会 gémìng wěiyuánhuì
revolutionary committee

Temporary authority organs of local administration during the Cultural Revolution. The various levels of local revolutionary committees were the various levels of local people's government. In October of 1982, the term "revolutionary committee" was abolished and the term "people's government" was reinstated.

革命文物 gémìng wénwù
artifacts of the revolution

Artifacts remaining from the revolutionary struggle which are of great value to researchers of revolutionary history, such things as buildings, stone inscriptions, implements, weapons, letters and documents.

革命现实主义 gémìng xiànshí zhǔyì
revolutionary realism

革命样板戏 gémìng yàngbǎnxì
revolutionary model theater

"文化大革命"中经常上演的《红灯记》、《沙家浜》、《白毛女》、《红色娘子军》等8出现代题材的京剧和舞剧，当时因被树为戏剧改革的样板而称革命样板戏。

Abbreviated as 样板戏 model theater. During the Cultural Revolution, the modernized Beijing operas "The Red Lantern", "Shajiabang", and the modern ballet dramas "White Hair Girl" and "The Red Detachment of Women" were models for theater reform, and they were collectively called "revolutionary model theater".

革命英雄主义 gémìng yīngxióng zhǔyì
revolutionary heroism

The lofty spirit which represents the interests of the progressive class and the laboring people and which dares to carry out a staunch struggle against the reactionary conservative forces in society and against the obstacles of the natural world.

革委会 gé-wěi-huì
revolutionary committee
Abbreviation for 革命委员会. (cf. 革命委员会)

隔离带 gélídài
dividing strip, specifically the lines separating fast and slow lanes on a road

隔离审查 gélí shěnchá
(during political movements) to isolate and interrogate

个案 gè'àn
individual case (involving special circumstances)

个股 gègǔ
individual share

个人崇拜 gèrén chóngbài
to deify and worship an individual (national leader, etc.); individual superstition

个人电脑 gèrén diànnǎo
personal computer
E.g. 美国推出最快个人电脑。
America brought out the fastest personal computer.

个人迷信 gèrén míxìn
individual superstition; personality cult
Also called 个人崇拜 individual worship or superstition. To inappropriately magnify the impact of an individual, to deify and idolize an individual. This goes against historical materialism.

个体户 gètǐhù
households engaged in individual enterprises
Workers who own certain production resources and manage small-scale businesses, such as individual farmers, individual craftsmen, individual retailers.

个体经济 gètǐ jīngjì
individual economy
Economy founded on individual ownership of production resources and individual labor, including individual agriculture, handicrafts, retailing, and services. Individual economy has special characteristics: it is small in scale, dispersed in management, and economically unstable. Within a socialist society, a certain amount of individual economy is allowed to supplement the economy of public ownership.

个体经营户 gètǐ jīngyínghù
individually managed establishments
Same as 个体户. In present-day China, this term refers to those workers engaged in small-scale handicrafts, businesses, services, and transport.

个体劳动 gètǐ láodòng
individual labor
To engage in productive labor with the individual or household as the unit.

个体农户 gètǐ nónghù
individual agricultural household
Farmers who have not joined collective economic organizations, and who engage in production with the household as the unit.

个体商贩 gètǐ shāngfàn
individual retailers
Workers engaged in small-scale commercial activities with the individual or the household as the unit.

个体所有制 gètǐ suǒyǒuzhì
individual ownership
Abbreviation for 个体劳动者所有制

individual worker ownership system. It is a form of economy whereby a household owns certain production resources and constitutes a unit of production.

个展 gèzhǎn
one-man exhibition
An exhibition of a single artist's calligraphy, paintings, etc.

gei

给出路 gěichūlù
to provide a way out
An important policy of the Chinese Communist Party. In dealing with members of the overturned reactionary class and reactionaries, as long as they don't rebel or create a disturbance, opportunities for earning a living are provided. They are allowed to be reformed through labor into workers who support themselves through their own work. The term also refers to providing opportunities in work and life for those who have committed serious errors, helping them to correct their errors and to continuously make progress.

gen

根雕 gēndiāo
root carvings
E.g. 根雕作品 a work of root carving / 他从事根雕只有三年。 He has been practicing root carving for only three years.

根红苗壮 gēnhóng miáozhuàng
roots are red and the seedling is sturdy
A metaphor for someone with a good family background and who grew up under the nurture and education of the Chinese Communist Party and the People's Government.
E.g. 他自以为根红苗壮，就不注意思想改造。 He takes himself to be red roots and sturdy seedling, and therefore pays no attention to thought reform.

根植 gēnzhí
to take root

根子正 gēnzizhèng
roots are straight
Someone with a good family background (laboring people or revolutionary family), or who has had rather negative experiences (suffered great bitterness or grievances, or joined the revolution early in life).

跟班劳动 gēnbān láodòng
to labor in the ranks
A cadre or person from a leadership organization going to the grass-roots to work with the workers or peasants, in order to form ties with the masses, to understand their circumstances, and to help the grass-roots level carry out their work.

geng

耕读小学 gēngdú xiǎoxué
farm-study elementary schools
(cf. 耕读学校)

耕读学校 gēngdú xuéxiào
farm-study schools
Rural schools where students study and participate in agricultural production at the same time.

更年期 gēngniánqī
transition from adulthood to old age;

menopause

更新换代 gēngxīn huàndài
to replace with the new
1) To phase out outdated production facilities and technology and to adopt advanced facilities and technology. 2) In production, to continuously create new products to replace the old products.

gong

工程语言学 gōngchéng yǔyánxué
engineering linguistics

工代会 gōng–dài–huì
employees' representatives union
Abbreviation for 职工代表大会 employees' representatives union. It is China's basic form of the democratic management of enterprises, and it is the organization that empowers the workers in decision making, management, and supervision of cadres.

工读生 gōngdúshēng
(originally) students who support themselves through work; (now) students in work-study institutions (cf. 工读学校)

工读学校 gōngdú xuéxiào
work-study school (reformatory)
Schools that specialize in educating, redeeming, and reforming juvenile delinquents. The students consist primarily of youths who have committed misdemeanors and who are difficult for regular schools to handle. All of them board at the schools and both work and study. The schools emphasize ideological education, study of cultural knowledge, and productive labor, with the goal of establishing a foundation for academic advancement and a future vocation.

工分 gōngfēn
work points
Abbreviation for 劳动工分 labor work points. They are the units of measurement used in collective agricultural enterprises for their members' work and for labor remuneration. In general, the various labor quotas and work points for completing the various quotas are based on such factors as the level of skill for the type of work, the amount of labor, and its importance to production. In the end of the year accounting, each member's labor remuneration is based on his total number of work points and the work point value of that particular collective economic unit.

工分挂帅 gōngfēn guàshuài
to make work points a priority

工行 gōng–háng
Abbreviation for 工商银行 Industrial and Commercial Bank.

工号工程师 gōnghào gōngchéngshī
project engineer

工间操 gōngjiāncāo
workbreak calisthenics
Calisthenics practiced daily during working hours by workers.

工交 gōng–jiāo
composite term for 工业 **industry and** 交通 **transport**

工交口 gōng–jiāo–kǒu
industrial and communications offices
A cover term for organizations that manage industries, communications, and transportation.

工交战线 gōng–jiāo zhànxiàn
industrial and communications fields
A cover term for working departments

involved in industry, communications and transportation.

工纠队 gōng-jiū-duì
abbreviated term for 工人纠察队 **worker pickets (group organized by workers for maintaining security and order)**

工均 gōngjūn
average work load
The average per-day work load.
E.g. 工均分配值 *the assigned value of an average per-day work load.*

工矿企业 gōng-kuàng qǐyè
factories and mining enterprises
A cover term for factory and mining enterprise units.

工贸 gōng-mào
industry and commerce
Short for "工业 industry" and "贸易 commerce".
E.g. 工贸系统 *industrial and commercial systems* / 工贸结合 *integration of industry and commerce*

工农兵学员 gōng-nóng-bīng xuéyuán
worker, peasant, soldier students
Workers, peasants and soldiers of the Liberation Army who were admitted, during the Cultural Revolution, to institutions of higher learning, not through examination, but through the tri-pronged process of recommendation by the masses, approval by the leadership, and review by the school.

工农干部 gōngnóng gànbù
worker, peasant cadres
Cadres who come from a worker or peasant background.

工农讲师团 gōngnóng jiǎngshītuán
worker-peasant lecture teams
Lecture teams composed of workers and poor, lower and middle peasants. They operated during the Cultural Revolution and conducted propaganda education in various kinds of schools. Primarily they reported to students and intellectuals about "class struggle" and "contrasts between past misery and present happiness", thereby raising their political consciousness.

工农速成中学 gōngnóng sùchéng zhōngxué
worker-peasant accelerated high schools
Schools founded in the early 1950s to provide accelerated education to train workers, peasants, and worker-peasant cadres in scientific and cultural knowledge. They had the characteristics of ordinary high schools, and covered middle-level basic scientific and cultural knowledge. In general students attended them for three years. They ceased recruiting new students in the fall of 1955.

工农中学 gōngnóng zhōngxué
worker-peasant high schools
Schools founded in the 1950s which drew their students mainly from the ranks of workers, peasants, and their children.

工农子弟 gōngnóng zǐdì
the children of workers and peasants

工农子弟兵 gōngnóng zǐdìbīng
soldiers of worker-peasant children
Abbreviated as 子弟兵 children soldiers. It is a term of endearment for China's People's Liberation Army. The Liberation Army is an army for protecting the interests of the masses of workers

and peasants; the majority of them come from workers and peasants, hence the term.

工青妇 gōng-qīng-fù
composite term for 工会 the Trade Union, 共青团 the Communist Youth League, and 妇联 the Women's Federation

工人工程师 gōngrén gōngchéngshī
worker engineers
Engineers trained from the ranks of workers. Workers with actual work experience who have studied assiduously, and have been certified by examination as having reached the caliber of engineers.

工商联营 gōng-shāng liányíng
combined management of industry and commerce
To combine the management of the production of industrial products with their marketing, in order to coordinate production and sales, and to enliven the economy.

工属 gōngshǔ
employees' families
Contraction of 职工家属 family dependents of employees.

工薪阶层 gōngxīn jiēcéng
officially paid class
People who work in government organs, offices and state-run enterprises or institutions and who are paid a salary.

工休 gōngxiū
work recess

工休日 gōngxiūrì
rest day
The weekly rest day of a factory or enterprise unit.

工宣队 gōng-xuān-duì
worker propaganda teams
即"工人毛泽东思想宣传队",是"文化大革命"期间被派往大中城市的大、中、小学领导学校工作的工作队。
Worker teams for propagandizing Mao Zedong Thought. They were the work teams sent during the Cultural Revolution to colleges, middle and elementary schools in large and medium-sized cities to lead the work of the schools.

工业工程 gōngyè gōngchéng
industrial engineering

工业券 gōngyèquàn
industrial product coupons
A coupon used in China's cities in the 1950s and 1970s for purchasing certain high-demand industrial products.

工运 gōng-yùn
workers' movement
Abbreviated term for 工人运动.

工转干 gōng zhuǎn gàn
worker turned cadre

工仔面 gōngzǎimiàn
(Hong Kong slang) instant noodles (called 方便面 "convenient noodles" in China's mainland)

工作餐 gōngzuòcān
meals provided by certain work units; meals provided by state units to workers on business trips

工作队 gōngzuòduì
work teams
Relatively small groups organized especially to carry out certain functions. Most of them are dispatched by leadership organizations.
E.g. 四清工作队 *"Four Cleanups" work teams*

工作面 gōngzuòmiàn

work range

Location of open cast mining or rock quarrying, which shifts as the mining progresses. The term also refers to the part of a component which is undergoing machine-processing.

工作室 gōngzuòshì
studio

工作烟 gōngzuòyān
work cigarettes

Cigarettes used to facilitate interpersonal interaction in the work place, particularly in Party and government organizations, and in industrial and mining enterprises.

工作组 gōngzuòzǔ
work groups

Small groups formed especially to carry out certain tasks. They are usually set up by leadership organizations.

攻博 gōng-bó
studying for the Ph.D. degree

Abbreviated term for 攻读博士学位.

攻关 gōngguān
to tackle a critical point

To concentrate essential manpower and material resources to work intensively on the completion of a certain task.

E.g. 技术攻关 *to tackle a certain task with technology*

功夫片 gōngfupiān
kungfu film

功能结构主义语言学 gōngnéng jiégòu zhǔyì yǔyánxué
functional structural linguistics

供不应求 gōng bù yìng qiú
supply not meeting demand

The supply (of a commodity) cannot satisfy the demand for it.

E.g. 目前市场上名牌自行车供不应求。 *At present, the supply of name brand bicycles on the market cannot meet the demand.*

供给制 gōngjǐzhì
system of rations

A system of allocation whereby resources for daily life are provided directly according to roughly equal standards.

供暖 gōngnuǎn
heating

E.g. 供暖设备 *heating equipment* / 供暖时间 *heating time periods*

供气 gōngqì
gas supply

E.g. 供气设备 *gas supply facility*

供热 gōngrè
same as 供暖 to provide heating

E.g. 供热系统 *heating system* / 发展城市集中供热 *to develop a system of urban centralized heating*

供销社 gōngxiāoshè
supply and marketing cooperative

Abbreviated term for 供销合作社.

供应学派 gōngyìng xuépài
supply school economics

An American school of economics. It advocates reducing taxes, allowing personal and enterprise income to increase in order to encourage an increase in savings and investments, thereby stimulating the entire economy.

公安部队 gōng'ān bùduì
public security force

公安部门 gōng'ān bùmén
public security sector

公办 gōngbàn
publicly administered

Initiated by the state or by a collective, or salaries paid by the state.

E.g. 公办教师 *teachers who are paid*

by the state

公车 gōngchē

public (as opposed to private) vehicles; (in Taiwan) buses

公厕 gōng-cè

public toilets

Abbreviated term for 公共厕所.

公厕广告 gōng-cè guǎnggào

public toilet ads

Advertisements pasted or drawn on the walls inside and outside of public toilets.

公方 gōngfāng

(in state-private joint ventures) the side representing the state (as opposed to 私方 the private side)

公费医疗 gōngfèi yīliáo

medical services at state expense

Medical services entirely at the state's expense. In China, all cadres in national organizations and regular personnel in state enterprises and institutions enjoy medical services at the state's expense.

公共积累 gōnggòng jīlěi

common accumulation; accumulated public money or materials

公共课 gōnggòngkè

courses required of all students in a secondary or tertiary school regardless of their majors, such as political theory, a foreign language, and physical education

公共食堂 gōnggòng shítáng

public dining hall

A dining hall provided for members of a certain organization or group.

公关 gōng-guān

public relations

E.g. 公关部门 departments of public relations / 公关小姐 young woman engaged in public relations

公积金 gōngjījīn

accumulated funds

公检法 gōng-jiǎn-fǎ

a cover term for the public security organization, the people's procuratorate, and people's court.

公交 gōng-jiāo

public transportation

Abbreviated term for 公共交通.

公决 gōngjué

public adjudication; communal decision

E.g. 全民公决 a decision made by the entire citizenry / 公决投票在全国开始。 Voting to decide issues has begun throughout the nation.

公派 gōngpài

to be sent abroad (for study or work) by the state or one's unit

E.g. 公派出国留学人员 persons sent abroad by the state to study (at the state's expense)

公平秤 gōngpíngchèng

fair scales

Scales set up in certain stores specifically for customers to examine the weight of their purchases.

公平尺 gōngpíngchǐ

fair yardsticks

Yardsticks set up in certain stores specifically for customers to examine the lengths of the fabrics they are purchasing.

公勤人员 gōngqín rényuán

office attendants

Personnel in offices who carry out odd jobs.

公社 gōngshè

commune

Abbreviation for 人民公社 people's commune. (cf. 人民公社)

公社化 gōngshèhuà
communization

The movement launched in 1958 in China's rural areas to create people's communes, i.e., to establish people's communes throughout the country.

公社史 gōngshèshǐ
commune history

During the "Four Cleanups" movement, commune histories were widely written to carry out class and line (political) education for the masses.

公式化 gōngshìhuà
formulism

The unhealthy tendency in literary and art creations of mechanically using certain fixed formulas to depict actual life and human characters. The term also means mechanically applying certain fixed methods in dealing with problems rather than taking into account the concrete circumstances.

公私合营 gōng-sī héyíng
public-private joint management

The superior form developed in China through socialist reform of national capitalist industrial and commercial enterprises. It is divided into the two forms: public-private joint management of a single enterprise and public-private joint management of an entire industry.

公文旅行 gōngwén lǚxíng
travel of documents; bureaucratic red-tape

The bureaucratic practice in leadership organizations of procrastination in handling matters. In certain leadership organizations, due to overstaffing, one document is sent from one person to another so that responsibility for it is shifted, documents are perused at various levels and they are signed and altered arbitrarily. The result is long delays in dealing with the documents.
E.g. 大家对公文旅行,解决问题慢,意见很多。 *Everyone has criticisms of the phenomenon of travel of documents and the slow resolution of matters.*

公务员 gōngwùyuán
government employee

E.g. 公务员制度 *civil service system* / 公务员考核试点 *civil service examination sites* / 实行公务员招聘制度 *to implement a system of recruiting public servants*

公休 gōngxiū
holiday stipulated by a work unit

E.g. 公休日 *a day off from work stipulated by one's work unit*

公烟 gōngyān
public cigarettes

Cigarettes purchased with public funds intended for use in treating guests.
E.g. 主人以整条公烟相送。 *The hosts gave whole cartons of publicly funded cigarettes to each other.*

公养 gōngyǎng
public raising (of animals)

Raising of domestic animals by the collective.

公益广告 gōngyì guǎnggào
public-interest ads

Publicity exhorting the public to behave in certain positive ways for the benefit of society.

公益金 gōngyìjīn
public welfare funds

A fixed percentage drawn annually by China's socialist collective economic organizations from incomes. The funds are used mainly for social security and collective welfare, such as managing a cooperative health care system, child care facilities, kindergartens, and support for poor households and "five-guarantees" households (childless and infirm old persons guaranteed of the five necessities of life).

公益劳动 gōngyì láodòng
volunteer labor
Labor for collective welfare without remuneration.

公用月票 gōngyòng yuèpiào
public monthly ticket
A bus or trolley car ticket purchased on a monthly basis, which may be used by any members of a work unit.

公照 gōngzhào
to use public funds to take photos for personal reasons
E.g. 公照非常流行。 *The practice of taking personal photos with public funds is very prevalent.*

共产风 gòngchǎnfēng
communist style
A method of equalitarianism that surfaced in the early period of the 1958 movement to establish people's communes. Its chief characteristic was that it placed everyone on an equal footing no matter how hard they worked or how much they contributed to production. Some people have linked this method of equalitarianism with communism, hence the term communist style.

共产主义道德 gòngchǎn zhǔyì dàodé

communist ethics
The ethics of struggle for the sake of realizing the cause of communism. Its distinctive features are collectivism, benefiting solely others and not oneself, and serving the people with one's heart and soul. In China, the most basic communist ethical norm that the entire population should follow is loving the motherland, the people, labor, science, and socialism.

共产主义劳动大学 gòngchǎn zhǔyì láodòng dàxué
communist labor university
Abbreviated as 共大 communist university. It was an agricultural school system of half study founded in Jiangxi Province in 1958. It had one main campus and more than a hundred branch campuses were scattered in various mountains of the province, with a small number also on the plains. The students were mostly youths, but some of them were middle-aged cadres.

共产主义青年团 gòngchǎn zhǔyì qīngniántuán
Communist Youth League
Abbreviated as 共青团. It is a mass organization of progressive youths under the leadership of the Chinese Communist Party. When it was founded in May, 1922, it was named the Chinese Socialist Youth League. It is a powerful assistant to the Chinese Communist Party. It unites and educates the younger generation to struggle for the cause of communism.

共建 gòngjiàn
to build together
Often refers to soldiers and civilians

jointly engaging in activities to promote spiritual culture.

E.g. 军民共建 *joint construction carried out by soldiers and civilians* / 警民共建 *joint projects carried out by the public security forces and citizens* / 军地共建 *joint projects carried out by the military and the local people* / 共建小组 *joint project committee* / 共建委员会 *joint project commission* / 共建活动 *joint project activities*

共青团 gòng-qīng-tuán
Communist Youth League

Abbreviation for 中国共产主义青年团.

共识 gòngshí
jointly-held views; an agreed-upon or unanimous understanding

共同纲领 gòngtóng gānglǐng
Common Program

《中国人民政治协商会议共同纲领》的简称。1949 年 9 月 29 日中国人民政治协商会议第一届全体会议上通过。它规定了新中国的国家性质和基本的方针政策。在 1954 年《中华人民共和国宪法》颁布前,起了临时宪法的作用。

Abbreviation for "Common Program of the Chinese People's Political Consultative Conference". This was ratified at the first plenary session of the Chinese People's Political Consultative Conference on September 29, 1949. It formulated New China's national character and her basic directive policies. Before the Constitution of the People's Republic of China was promulgated in 1954, it served as a temporary constitution.

共运 gòng-yùn
communist movement

Abbreviated term for 共产主义运动.

gou

狗崽子 gǒuzǎizi
(derogatory) children of "curs"

"文化大革命"中对家庭出身不好的人的蔑称。During the Cultural Revolution children of "bad elements" were called the children of "curs".

构想 gòuxiǎng
conceptualization

Contraction of 构思 to conceive and 设想 to contemplate.

E.g. 一个国家,两种制度的构想 *the concept of two systems within one nation*

购货本 gòuhuòběn
"purchase books" – voucher booklets for purchasing rationed commodities

购粮本 gòuliángběn
vouchers used by urban residents for purchasing grains

购物中心 gòuwù zhōngxīn
shopping center

购销联社 gòu-xiāo liánshè
joint purchase-sale commissary

An economic organization in management that is involved in both purchase and sales.

够意思 gòuyìsi
to have reached a high caliber or standard (used mostly in praise)

gu

估产 gūchǎn
yield estimate

估价师 gūjiàshī

appraiser professionals who evaluate the prices which real estate can realistically fetch.
Also called 房地产估价师 real estate appraisers.

鼓劲 gǔjìn
to drum up energy and enthusiasm
E.g. 给大家鼓劲 *to give everybody some vim* / 说几句鼓劲的话 *to say a few encouraging things* / 鼓劲前进 *to drum up the energy and enthusiasm to go forward*

鼓足干劲 gǔzú gànjìn
to go all out
To exert one's utmost strength in a task, and to persevere in carrying it out to the end.
E.g. 鼓足干劲，争取最后的胜利。 *Go all out and strive for final victory.*

古为今用 gǔ wèi jīn yòng
using the ancient in the present
To absorb the quintessence of the ancient cultural heritage and let it serve in the developing and prospering modern culture.

骨干 gǔgàn
backbone
1) The central section of long bones, connected at the two ends to epiphyses.
2) A metaphor for persons or matters that serve a main function in an overall scheme.
E.g. 骨干产品 *backbone commodity* / 骨干工程 *backbone engineering project* / 骨干企业 *backbone enterprise* / 骨干项目 *backbone item* / 骨干分子 *backbone element*

谷底 gǔdǐ
lowest part of a valley; metaphor for the nadir in a transition
E.g. 美元跌价已近谷底。 *The depreciation of the U.S. dollar has hit bottom.* / 这个工厂扭亏为盈走出谷底。 *This factory turned their deficit around and thus emerged from their lowest point.*

谷地 gǔdì
valley
A metaphor for adverse or difficult circumstances
E.g. 走出谷地 *to emerge from difficult circumstances*

股潮 gǔcháo
stock market wave
A metaphor for the situation in which droves of people are buying stocks and engaging in stock market activities.

股份合作制 gǔfèn hézuòzhì
stock cooperative system
A new system of economic organization whereby the stock system is applied to a cooperative enterprise. It entails shareholding within or between different ownership systems in the various essential elements of production such as capital, facilities, site, and labor.

股份制 gǔfènzhì
shareholding system
A business management system whereby the capital of an enterprise is distributed as stocks to employees or society at large, and representatives of stockholders organize a board of trustees and appoint a manager to manage the enterprise.
E.g. 实行企业股份制 *to carry out a shareholding system for enterprises*

股盲 gǔmáng
stock illiterate
People who know absolutely nothing

about stocks.

股民 gǔmín
stock buyers; people who own stocks or shares

股权 gǔquán
stockholders' rights

股市 gǔshì
stock market
Abbreviated term for 股票市场.

股灾 gǔzāi
stock disasters
The disasters caused by the erratic rise and fall of stock prices.
E.g. 股灾不断出现。*Stock disasters keep occurring.*

股指 gǔzhǐ
stock market index
E.g. 股指快速下探。*The stock market index is falling rapidly.*

顾大局 gù dàjú
to consider the overall scheme
In thought, speech and action, to consider the benefit of the entirety, and not to proceed from an individual or partial standpoint.

固定工 gùdìnggōng
employees occupying positions officially authorized by the state or an organization

固体水库 gùtǐ shuǐkù
solid reservoir
A metaphor for frozen rivers.

固体饮料 gùtǐ yǐnliào
solid drinks

雇佣观点 gùyòng guāndiǎn
hired-hand mentality
The negative attitude of doing no more work than what one is paid for; lacking the attitude of being one's own master in one's work.

雇佣思想 gùyòng sīxiǎng
hired-hand thinking (cf. 雇佣观点)

gua

刮风 guāfēng
to stir up a wind
A metaphor for seeking to imitate the outward form and to do something in a boastful, exaggerated, and superficial way.
E.g. 用刮风的办法纠正不正之风，效果不好。*Using the "stir up a wind" method to correct unhealthy tendencies will not yield sound results.*

瓜菜代 guācàidài
using melons and vegetables as substitutes for staples (in times of grain shortage)
A metaphor for substituting and making do with substandard personnel or things.
E.g. 没有粥吃就搞瓜菜代。*If there's no porridge, then melons and vegetables can be used as substitutes.* / 瓜菜代的生活和精神已成为历史。*The life and spirit of using melons and vegetables as substitutes for staples is already a thing of the past.*

挂钩 guàgōu
to link up
1) Using hooks to connect two cars (as in railroad cars). 2) A metaphor for linking up.
E.g. 厂校挂钩 *link up a factory with school* / 产销挂钩 *link up a production with marketing*

挂钩会 guàgōuhuì
link-up meeting

Meeting convened by certain units or sectors in order to establish linkages in production or work.

挂靠 guàkào

adjunct

A unit appended to another by name, organization, or funding.

E.g. 老舍研究会挂靠在北京语言文化大学。*The Lao She Research Society is an adjunct of the Beijing Language and Culture University.*

挂靠户 guàkàohù

an adjunct organization

(cf. 挂靠)

挂历 guàlì

hanging calendars

Calendars hung on walls.

挂拍 guàpāi

to hang up the paddle

A ping-pong player ending his career, and ceasing to participate in formal competitions and training.

E.g. 乒坛名将曹燕华挂拍退役，告别乒坛。*The ping-pong star Cao Yanhua is about to hang up the paddle and retire (from ping-pong), thus saying farewell to the world of ping-pong.*

挂牌 guàpái

to hang out a sign (for opening a business or some other purpose)

E.g. 挂牌行医 *to hang up a shingle and practice medicine* / 商店挂牌公布了议价商品的价格。*The store hung up signs and announced the negotiated prices (as opposed to prices stipulated by the state) of goods.* / 有些国家实行挂牌办公。 *Some state agencies have begun hanging out signs while carrying out their business.*

挂牌售货 guàpái shòuhuò

hang signs in selling goods

For the sake of improving the service attitude and facilitating supervision by customers, the names of sales clerks and concrete specifications and guarantees of the commodities are shown on signs.

挂起来 guàqǐlai

to suspend

Before a person's problem (political, historical, or other) has been thoroughly investigated and clarified, to treat it as an open question, not making any premature conclusions or judgments.

挂线疗法 guàxiàn liáofǎ

ligating methods of treatment

One of the operations practiced in Chinese medicine, suitable for treatment of such ailments as anal fistula and mastitis. It involves passing a rubber band around the affected passage, and tightening it to constrict blood flow and bring about necrosis. Then the tube is cut open and medication applied, allowing the opening to close up.

挂鞋 guàxié

to hang up shoes

Soccer players, track stars, etc., ending their careers in sport, ceasing to participate in formal competitions and training.

E.g. 日本女排由于三位主将"挂鞋"，实力明显减弱。*Because three star players in the Japanese women's volleyball team have hung up their shoes, the strength of their team has manifestly diminished.*

挂靴 guàxuē

same as 挂鞋 to hang up shoes

A metaphor for an athlete retiring.

E.g. 刘易斯参加下届奥运会后将挂靴。 *Louis will retire from his sport after participating in the next Olympics.*

挂职 guàzhí
to suspend duties

To retain one's position in one's original work unit while going to a subsidiary unit to work or train for a short period, or going to a different unit (filling a certain post) for a short term to carry out work or study.

E.g. 选拔优秀青年干部挂职下放 *to select superior young cadres and suspend their duties and send them down* / 大医院的技术专家到基层挂职。 *Specialists from major hospitals suspend their duties to go down to the grass roots.*

guai

拐棍 guǎigùn
walking stick; cane

A metaphor for a source of support.

拐卖 guǎimài
to ensnare sb. and sell

E.g. 拐卖妇女儿童 *to kidnap and sell women and children*

怪圈 guàiquān
something spellbinding or bewitching

guan

关爱 guān'ài
to love and care (for)

关门办学 guānmén bànxué
to run schools with closed doors

A policy for running schools which departs from social reality.

关门读书 guānmén dúshū
to study with closed doors

To be unconcerned with the world, and to merely bury one's head in studies. It is an unhealthy style of learning that departs from social reality.

关门整风 guānmén zhěngfēng
to rectify work style with closed doors

When the Chinese Communist Party rectified its internal work style, certain grass-roots organizations would not listen to the opinions of the masses and non-Party persons. This was a mistake.

关门主义 guānmén zhǔyì
closed-door-ism

The erroneous proposition of certain people during the revolutionary struggle of opposing the establishment of a broad united front, refusing to unite all the people and strengths that could be united, but rather shutting them outside the gate of revolution. The term also refers to the erroneous practice of keeping those who qualify for admission into the Communist Party or the Youth League outside the gate of the Party or League organization.

关停并转
guān–tíng–bìng–zhuǎn
close, stop, merge, and shift

根据调整国民经济的需要，对一些亏损企业分别不同情况采取4种处理方法，即有的关闭，有的停产整顿，有的与其他企业合并，有的则转产其他物品，简称关停并转。

In response to the need to adjust the national economy, four different methods have been adopted for enterprises with deficits. Some are closed down, some are temporarily stopped for reorganization, some are merged with other enterprises, and some shift to producing other products. The four are abbreviated as 关停并转 close, stop, merge, and shift.

关系方 guānxìfāng

prescriptions obtained through special, "back-door" connections

关系户 guānxìhù

parties of connection

In the context of economic activity or professional transactions, units or individuals who take advantage of the prerogatives of their positions or job, and through improper means make promises and help each other for personal gain. The two sides are thus parties of connection.

E.g. 他通过关系户从外地买来一批紧俏商品。 *Through connections, he purchased a batch of high-demand commodities from another part of the country.*

关系网 guānxìwǎng

connection network

A system of mutual connections formed by units or individuals-an unhealthy tendency.

E.g. 要敢于打破"关系学",冲破"关系网"。 *We must courageously destroy "the practice of using connections for one's own advantage" and break through the connection network.*

关系学 guānxìxué

practice of using connections for one's own advantage

In the context of social transactions, the method or trick of building improper connections with various sectors, disregarding principles and violating relevant rules and regulations in the process, in order to attain benefits for oneself or a small group. This is a derogatory term for this phenomenon.

官办 guānbàn

(formerly) managed by government officials; (now) funded and managed by the state.

E.g. 官办企业 *state-managed enterprises*

官本位 guānběnwèi

the yardstick of administrative rank whereby the status, authority, and political and economic treatment of an individual or a unit are determined

E.g. 官本位制 *system of ranking of officials* / 官本位意识 *rank consciousness*

官兵一致 guān–bīng yīzhì

equality between officers and soldiers

Within the Chinese People's Liberation Army, between superiors and underlings, between cadres and soldiers, there is political equality, solidarity and love, sharing of happiness and suffering. Democracy with leadership is put into practice, and self-conscious discipline is established.

官倒爷 guāndǎoyé

persons or organizations in government and business conspiring to buy and resell short-supply high-demand goods for huge profits

Also called 官倒 or 大倒.

官工作风 guāngōng zuòfēng

work style of a servant in old officialdom

Certain employees in state enterprises

lack the spirit of being master of one's own work; they lack sense of responsibility, and are unconcerned with the management of the enterprises, as if they were merely servants in the officialdom of the old society.

官暮骄娇四气 guān-mù-jiāo-jiāo sìqì
the four airs of bureaucratism, lethargy, haughtiness, and squeamishness

指官气、暮气、骄气和娇气。这些都是党政干部中存在的不良作风。官气是指严重脱离群众做官当老爷;暮气是指缺乏革命朝气,工作没有干劲,疲疲沓沓;骄气是指骄傲自满,缺乏谦虚谨慎的态度;娇气是指革命意志脆弱,不能吃苦耐劳。

The four unhealthy attitudes that exist among cadres in the Party and the government system. Bureaucratism means acting like a lord, seriously alienated from the masses; lethargy means having no enthusiasm for work, being slack, lacking revolutionary vigor; haughtiness means being snobbish and self-satisfied, lacking humility and circumspection; squeamishness means being frail in will, lacking in tempering, unable to endure hardship.

官商 guānshāng
state-run business

A derogatory term for state-run businesses and their employees, which are notorious for their poor management style and attitude to service.

官商作风 guānshāng zuòfēng
bureaucratic business style

The work style of certain state-run stores whereby they hold iron rice bowls in their hands (are guaranteed their jobs), do not actively upgrade their business management or raise their business effectiveness, and would rather sit and wait for customers to come to them.

官瘾 guānyǐn
(sarcastic) yen to be an official

E.g. 他的官瘾很大。 *He has a longing to be an official.*

观潮派 guāncháopài
onlookers

A derogatory title which emerged in the 1958 Great Leap Forward. It was wrongly used on those who expressed disagreement or correctly criticized. 观潮 means to stand on the sidelines, regarding mass movements.

观摩演出 guānmó yǎnchū
performances for viewing and emulation

Performances of various theater arts organized specifically for the artists to see each other's accomplishments, to exchange experiences, and to learn from each other.

观瞻服 guānzhānfú
uniform used in a group performance (such as marching bands)

观照 guānzhào
observation and portrayal of things

E.g. 影片观照现实生活。 *The film portrays life realistically.* / 小说有时代的观照。 *The novel is a reflection of the times.*

管护 guǎnhù
caretaking (of horticulture)

To take care of and manage flowers, grass, trees and shrubs.

E.g. 管护任务 *the duty of taking care of the grounds*

管件 guǎnjiàn

various pipes and their fittings used in industry or construction

E.g. 大型电站管件研制成功。*The study and the manufacture of pipe for large-scale electrical plants were successful.*

管教 guǎnjiào

to control and educate

E.g. 管教干部 *cadres engaged in the work of controlling and educating*

管教所 guǎnjiàosuǒ

reformatory

Reformatory for juvenile delinquents, a kind of labor reform facility. It accommodates youths from fourteen to eighteen years of age. In actual practice, it follows the principle of reform primarily through education, supplemented by light labor.

管界 guǎnjiè

sphere of jurisdiction

管卡压 guǎn-qiǎ-yā

control, block, suppress

指单凭行政手段来压服人的管理方法，即管人、卡人、压制群众。"文化大革命"期间，在极"左"错误影响下，把合理的规章制定都诬称为管卡压。

Control and block people, and suppress the masses. During the Cultural Revolution, under the erroneous influence of the extreme left, reasonable rules and regulations were vilified as "control, block, and suppress".

管片 guǎnpiàn

a section (of an area) under one's management

管线 guǎnxiàn

pipeline

Pipes laid according to a certain path.

E.g. 高压煤气管线 *high-pressure gas line. Also refers to the various pipelines and electric cables buried underground.*

管制劳动 guǎnzhì láodòng

labor under surveillance

A form of punishment. The criminal is not imprisoned, but is limited in his freedom of movement. He undergoes reform by participating in collective labor, during which time he is under the surveillance of the masses.

罐装 guànzhuāng

to can

To pack in an airtight metal (as aluminum) can or ceramic crock.

E.g. 罐装食品 *canned food*

惯骗 guànpiàn

chronic swindler

灌录 guànlù

to make sound recordings

E.g. 灌录故事卡带 *to make audio tapes of story readings*

灌区 guànqū

irrigated district

Area benefiting from an irrigation construction project.

E.g. 韶山灌区 *Shaoshan irrigated district*

灌制 guànzhì

to make sound recordings

E.g. 灌制外语教学留声片 *to make audio tapes for foreign language instruction*

灌装 guànzhuāng

to bottle

To pour liquid into a narrow-mouthed container.

E.g. 灌装液化石油气钢瓶 *to bottle liquified petroleum gas (LPG) in steel bottles*

guang

光彩事业 guāngcǎi shìyè
noble undertaking
Activities directed at helping poverty-stricken areas which are conducted through community channels and in a form determined by the people (i.e., non-governmental).

光导纤维 guāngdǎo xiānwéi
light-transmitting fiber

光电话 guāngdiànhuà
photo-telephone

光电技术 guāngdiàn jìshù
photoelectric technology

光杆儿司令 guānggǎnr sīlìng
single commander
A leader who operates alone without assistants.

光缆 guānglǎn
light cable
E.g. 光缆通讯 *communications by light cable*

光亮派 guāngliàngpài
luminous schools (of architecture); the glass and chrome school
A style of architecture popular in the West. Its distinctive feature is using a large amount of glossy materials, such as aluminum alloys, stainless steel, plastics, and various reflective, semi-reflective, and semi-translucent materials. The buildings' exteriors are attractive, bright as mirrors, and sparkling, hence the term the luminous school.

光脑 guāngnǎo
photon brain (machine)
A machine which relies on photons to deliver information. It's better than a computer because its speed of calculation is faster, it generates less heat, and it has a greater capacity for storing information.
E.g. 光脑将于2010年前后问世。 *Photon machines will be produced in about the year 2010.*

光盘 guāngpán
laser disk
E.g. 中国光盘存储技术已跨入世界先进行列。 *China's laser disk technology is already among the world's more advanced.*

光荣榜 guāngróngbǎng
posted honor roll often with photographs and descriptions of deeds being honored

光荣院 guāngróngyuàn
institutes for the glorious; nursing homes
Nursing homes established by certain local civil administration departments for old childless Red Army soldiers, solitary, aged retired veterans, and solitary aged members of revolutionary martyrs' families.

光通讯 guāngtōngxùn
photocommunications

光纤 guāng-xiān
light-transmitting fiber
Abbreviation for 光导纤维 light-transmitting fiber.

广播讲话 guǎngbō jiǎnghuà
broadcast speeches
Speeches broadcasted by radio, television or wired broadcasting.

广播体操 guǎngbō tǐcāo
broadcast calisthenics
Body-building calisthenics with directions on radio or television broadcasts.

They are usually accompanied by music.

广而告之 guǎng ér gào zhī
to publicize widely

广告躲避 guǎnggào duǒbì
advertisement avoidance
The phenomenon of people rejecting and resisting advertisements due to their overkill in terms of both quantity and substance.

广告人 guǎnggàorén
advertisers
People who create ads. The term also refers to those who disseminate ads.

广交会 Guǎng-Jiāo-Huì
Guangzhou Trade Fair
Abbreviation for 广州中国出口商品交易会 Guangzhou Chinese Commodities Fair. It is conducted in Guangzhou twice a year, in the spring and in the fall. Its main functions are to display and market export commodities and to allow people in business to negotiate with clients.

广开 guǎngkāi
to open up broadly; to widen
E.g. 广开门路 *to broaden outlets* / 广开渠道 *to broaden channels*

广种薄收 guǎngzhòng bóshōu
broad sowing but meager harvest
A method of cultivation whereby the cultivated area is large but the per-unit yield is relatively low.

gui

规模经营 guīmó jīngyíng
Controlled-scope management
To keep an operation within a certain sphere as a means of increasing efficiency.

规模效益 guīmó xiàoyì
in economic activities, the benefits achieved at a certain scale

硅谷 guīgǔ
Silicon Valley

归档 guīdàng
to file documents

归口 guīkǒu
channel to the proper authorities (on the basis of jurisdiction)
To take a certain area of work and uniformly turn it over to a certain department.
E.g. 归口部门 *the department with jurisdiction (over certain matters)* / 归口管理 *to channel to the appropriate department for management* / 归口包干 *to channel a certain matter and give full responsibility for it to the appropriate department*

归侨 guīqiáo
returned overseas nationals
Overseas Chinese who have returned to reside in China.

轨道站 guǐdàozhàn
orbit station
Also called 空间轨道站 outer space orbit station.

柜员 guìyuán
counter clerk
Tellers who work at bank counters.

柜员机 guìyuánjī
(banking) automated teller machine

gun

滚打 gǔndǎ
undergo training; be trained

E.g. 在生活中滚打 *to be trained in the school of life* / 在阶级斗争的风雨中滚打 *to be trained amidst the storms of class struggle*

滚雪球 gǔnxuěqiú
(metaphorical) to snowball

棍子 gùnzi
metaphor for accusations or tactics used in attacking someone

guo

国奥队 Guó–Ào–Duì
the National Olympics Team
Abbreviation for 国家奥林匹克队.

国办 Guó–Bàn
the General Office of the State Council
Abbreviation for 国务院办公厅.

国宾馆 guóbīnguǎn
guest house for top-level guests of the state

国道 guódào
major highways under the jurisdiction of the State Central Transportation Department

国防科委 Guófáng Kēwěi
State Commission of Science for National Defense
Abbreviation for 国防科学委员会.

国格 guógé
national honor
The character and dignity of a nation.

国合商业 guóhé shāngyè
combined term for 国营商业 state-managed businesses and 合作商业 cooperative businesses

国计民生 guójì mínshēng
the national economy and the people's livelihood

国际笔会 guójì bǐhuì
International Pen (an international writers' association)

国际大循环 guójì dàxúnhuán
great international cycle
Applying China's rural labor force to produce labor-intensive export items, using the foreign exchange thus generated to aid basic industries, and then using the capital generated by industrial development to aid agriculture.

国际共运 guójì gòngyùn
international communist movement
Abbreviation for 国际共产主义运动 international communist movement.

国际回信券 guójì huíxìnquàn
a type of monetary certificate issued by the International Postal Alliance; it can be purchased domestically and used abroad; this type of certificate may be exchanged for stamps in post offices throughout the world

国际社会 guójì shèhuì
international society
An overall term for the various nations and societal organizations of the world, and the opinions of international society.

国家队 guójiāduì
national team
Now often used as a metaphor for enterprises that play a key role in developing the national economy

国家公园 guójiā gōngyuán
national park (minimum size of 10,000 hectares by internationally-recognized standards)

国脚 guójiǎo
national feet, the most outstanding

soccer players in the nation

国库券 guókùquàn
treasury bill (T.B.)

国民经济恢复时期 guómín jīngjì huīfù shíqī
period of the national economic recovery
The period from the founding of the People's Republic of China to the end of 1952. Its central mission was to restore the national economy.

国啤 guópí
homemade beer; Chinese made beer
E.g. 国啤和洋啤质量差不多。*The quality of homemade beer and foreign made beer is more or less the same.*

国企 guó-qǐ
state enterprise
Enterprise owned or managed by the state.
E.g. 国企税负十分沉重。*The tax burden of state enterprises is extremely heavy.*

国手 guóshǒu
national champion (in any kind of endeavor)

国税 guó-shuì
national tax
E.g. 国税局 *National Tax Bureau*

国土规划 guótǔ guīhuà
programs for national lands
Programs for developing the nation's land resources, their use, management, and protection. They include two categories: regional programs and special topical programs.

国土经济学 guótǔ jīngjìxué
economics of national lands

国威 guówēi
national ascendancy
A nation's prestige and power in the international arena.
E.g. 给我们国家壮一壮国威 *to strengthen our national ascendancy*

国务委员 guówù wěiyuán
State Council member
A member of the Standing Committee of the State Council of the People's Republic of China. The position is equivalent to the rank of vice-premier of the State Council. A State Council member, on mandate from the Premier or State Council, takes responsibility for work in a certain area or for a specific important task. He can represent the government in carrying out various types of diplomatic work, and on a mandate from the Premier may represent the Premier in carrying out important activities.

国营经济 guóyíng jīngjì
state-operated economy
An economy based on socialist ownership by all the people. Included are modern major industries, communication and transportation enterprises, postal and telephone-telegraph services, major commercial enterprises, banking, and a portion of the modern farms. The state-operated economy is the guiding force of the national economy.

国营农场 guóyíng nóngchǎng
state farm

国营企业 guóyíng qǐyè
state-operated enterprise
Enterprises that rely on state investment and management, such as factories, mines, railroads, etc. Enterprises with investment and management by various departments of the central government

are called central state-operated enterprises. Enterprises with investment and management by local people's government at or above the district level are called local state-operated enterprises.

国优 guóyōu
(products) national excellence
A title accorded to products that have been rated "excellent" in a nationwide competition
E.g. 国优产品 *products rated as excellent nationally* / 产品全部获国优。*All the products were rated as excellent nationally.* / 创国优 *to create products that are rated as excellent nationally.*

国资局 guó-zī-jú
the State (National) Assets Bureau
Abbreviation for 国家资产局.

国嘴 guózuǐ
national mouth, a top-ranking broadcaster in the country

果茶 guǒchá
fruit drinks
Beverages made from the pulp and juice of fruits, plus sugar, etc.

果农 guǒnóng
fruit farmer

果珍 guǒzhēn
powdered fruit drink
A quick dissolving beverage powder made from sugar, lemon essence, vitamins, food coloring, etc.

过长江 guò Chángjiāng
crossing the Yangtze River
According to stipulations of the "National Program for Agricultural Development from 1955 to 1957", areas north of the Yangtze River with an average annual per-*mu* yield of 400 and 500 catties could achieve the annual per-*mu* yield of 800 or more catties of areas south of the Yangtze River. Hence it was called "crossing the Yangtze River". (cf. 纲要)

过得硬 guòdeyìng
able to stand up to a rigorous trial

过电影 guòdiànyǐng
metaphor for reflecting upon various past experiences in one's mind
E.g. 十年前的事情都在脑中过电影。*The experiences and events of ten years ago were all replayed in one's mind.*

过渡时期总路线 guòdù shíqī zǒnglùxiàn
general line for the transitional period
即中国共产党制定的从中华人民共和国成立到社会主义改造基本完成这段过渡时期的总路线。具体内容是：在一个相当长的时期内，基本上实现国家工业化和对农业、手工业、资本主义工商业的社会主义改造。
The general line formulated by the Chinese Communist Party for the transitional period from the founding of the People's Republic of China to the time when socialist reforms were basically completed. Its concrete contents are: over a relatively long period to basically realize national industrialization and socialist reform of agriculture, handicrafts and capitalist industrial and commercial enterprises.

过伐 guòfá
to exceed a certain limit in cutting down timber

过关思想 guòguān sīxiǎng
over-the-crisis thinking

The mentality of those who, having committed a crime or done some misdeed, hold an indifferent attitude toward criticism and investigations, and want to get the matter over with as quickly as possible.

过街天桥 guòjiē tiānqiáo
pedestrian overpass
Also called "步道桥" pedestrian bridge.

过滤嘴 guòlǜzuǐ
filter tip (of cigarettes)
The filter part on cigarettes. Also cigarettes with filters.

过热 guòrè
(economics) overheated
Economy developing too rapidly or on too large a scale, thus exceeding objective realistic possibility
E.g. 经济过热。 *The economy is overheated.*

过失犯罪 guòshī fànzuì
crimes of negligence
Actions that one should have foreseen as being detrimental to society, but did not because of carelessness, or did but did not think that they could be avoided.

过头粮 guòtóuliáng
purchase of grain allotted for peasants' basic needs
When the grain requisitioned (by rationed purchase) by the state from a rural area exceeds what the area can supply, the amount by which the requisition dips into the grain allotted to the peasants for their basic needs is called 过头粮.
E.g. 不向农民征过头粮。 *In the rationed purchase of grain (by the state), do not dip into the grain allotted to peasants for their basic needs.* / 不许购过头粮。 *Purchase of grain allotted for peasants' basic needs is not permitted.*

H

ha

蛤蟆夯 hámáhāng
frog rammer
A machine for tamping earth. Its action is like that of a frog jumping.

哈达 hǎdá
Tibetan sash used as gift or token of tribute
E.g. 敬献哈达 *to present a Tibetan sash (as tribute)* / 赠送哈达 *to give (as a gift) a Tibetan sash*

hai

海基会 Hǎi-Jī-Huì
the Taibei-based Straits Exchange Foundation
Abbreviation for 台湾海峡交流基金会.

海监 hǎijiān
maritime patrol
E.g. 海监飞机 *maritime patrol planes* / 海监船 *maritime patrol ships*

海绵田 hǎimiántián
sponge fields
Agricultural fields that have undergone intensive transformation. They have a flat surface, high humus content, a thick layer of top soil, and a loose soft texture.

海南 Hǎinán
abbreviation for 海南岛 **Hainan Island or** 海南省 **Hainan Province**

海难 hǎinàn
sea disaster
A disaster that occurs to a ship at sea.

海瑞罢官 Hǎi Ruì bàguān
The Dismissal of Hai Rui
A historical drama written by Wu Han in 1950, this play commends the morally honorable spirit of Hai Rui who never stooped to flattery, spoke honestly, and struggled against corrupt officials. It also extols his attitude, which showed sympathy and concern for the people, and his efforts to promote their interests. The drama was originally well received but was criticized during the Cultural Revolution and Wu Han was hounded to death because of it.

海瑞精神 Hǎi Ruì jīngshén
the spirit of Hai Rui
The spirit of the upright Ming Dynasty official Hai Rui, who never stooped to flattery, dared to speak honestly, was concerned with the people's sufferings, and struggled against corrupt officials.

海外关系 hǎiwài guānxì
overseas connections
Social relationships between people in China's mainland and people overseas.

海峡 hǎixiá
straits
Specifically refers to the Taiwan Straits

海协会 Hǎi-Xié-Huì
Association for Relations Across the

Taiwan Straits

Abbreviation for 海峡两岸关系协会. Also called 海协.

海洋经济学 hǎiyáng jīngjìxué

marine economics

The science which studies marine economic relationships and marine economic activities. It includes primarily the study of the basic conditions of the oceans, ways and means of raising the oceans' economic utility, marine economic policy, marine laws and regulations, and the forecasting of marine economic activities.

海政 Hǎi-Zhèng

the Chinese People's Naval Political Department

Abbreviation for 中国人民解放军海军政治部.

E.g. 海政文工团 *The cultural troupe of the Naval Political Department*

海滋 hǎizī

(Shandong patois) **an odd phenomenon, in reality a kind of mirage**

han

含金量 hánjīnliàng

gold content

Originally it referred to the amount of gold contained in something. Now a metaphor for the value or importance of something.

E.g. 要知道,这一席话的"含金量"有多重。*You should know the gold content of these words.(You should know how important these words are.)* / 这个职位的"含金量"不断增加。*The gold content of this position (job) is increasing.*

涵盖 hángài

to encompass, to cover

函大 hán-dà

correspondence university

Contraction of "函授大学 correspondence university".

函调 hándiào

correspondence investigation

Investigation conducted through correspondence.

函授大学 hánshòu dàxué

correspondence university

Abbreviated as 函大.

函索 hánsuǒ

to collect (publications, etc.) through requests sent in the mail

E.g. 本厂备有产品说明,函索即可。*This factory has prepared explanatory brochures of its products, which can be obtained by postal requests.*

旱冰 hànbīng

roller-skating

旱冰场 hànbīngchǎng

roller-skating rink

旱冰馆 hànbīngguǎn

indoor roller-skating rink

旱冰鞋 hànbīngxié

dry ice shoes (roller skates)

旱涝保收 hàn-lào bǎoshōu

guaranteed harvest despite drought and flood

Agricultural production was not affected by drought or flood, and a certain harvest could be guaranteed. It is also a metaphor for the equalitarianism, which plagued state-operated enterprises before reforms were instituted; that is, no matter how well or poorly an enterprise was managed, all could receive certain material guarantees from the state.

汉堡包 hànbǎobāo
hamburger

汉语拼音方案 Hànyǔ Pīnyīn Fāng'àn
Scheme for the Chinese Phonetic Alphabet

The plan to provide Chinese characters with phonetic notations and to use a phonetic script for the standard language. It was promulgated at the Fifth Session of the First National People's Congress on February 11, 1958. This plan adopted the Roman alphabet, supplemented by diacritics to indicate the tones. It is a tool for helping the learning of characters and for popularizing the standard language.

汉字信息处理 hànzì xìnxī chǔlǐ
Chinese character coding

To dissect Chinese characters according to the characters' roots (structural components), stroke numbers, or phonetic spelling, transforming them into corresponding letters or numbers; they are then put into a computer through a foreign language keyboard, and the computer will store or print the Chinese characters. It can be used in such technology for machine translations and ordering items on listings.

hang

航保 hángbǎo
navigation protection

E.g. 航保部门 *the navigation protection sector*

航测 hángcè
aerial survey and mapping (done with equipment on an airplane)

航空港 hángkōnggǎng
air harbor

Airports with a large capacity for passenger and cargo transport.

航空器 hángkōngqì
air vehicle; any flying machine that operates in the earth's atmosphere

航模 háng-mó
airplane and ship models; games or sports that involve airplane and ship models

E.g. 航模选手 *Contestants in a sport involving airplane and ship models*

航母 háng-mǔ
aircraft carrier

Abbreviation for 航空母舰的简称.

E.g. 现在除了航母,我们能造的舰艇品种已相当齐全。 *Now we can build a complete variety of naval vessels except for aircraft carriers.*

航拍 hángpāi
aerial filming (for movies and television programs)

E.g. 电视航拍在国外已广泛使用,而我国近几年才较多使用。 *Aerial television-videotaping is already widely used abroad, yet it's only in recent years that it came to be used in our country.*

航摄 hángshè
aerial photography

Abbreviation for 航空摄影.

E.g. 航摄任务 *aerial photography assignment* / 航摄结果 *aerial photographic results*

航天 hángtiān
space flight

E.g. 航天工业 *space engineering* /

航天技术 space technology

航天飞机 hángtiān fēijī
space shuttles
Their formal name is 空间运输系统 space transport system.

航天服 hángtiānfú
space suit
Synonymous with 太空服 space suit. (cf. 太空服)

航天器 hángtiānqì
any manned or unmanned space vehicle that can orbit the earth or travel to another celestial object, such as man-made satellites, spaceships, space stations, etc.

航天站 hángtiānzhàn
space station

hao

豪的 háodí
luxury taxi

豪华型 háohuáxíng
deluxe (in reference to automobiles, hotels, etc.)
E.g. 豪华型小轿车 *deluxe sedans (automobiles)* / 豪华型旅馆 *deluxe hotels*

好八连 hǎobālián
Good Eighth Company
Also called the Good Eighth Company of Nanjing Rd. A model company of the People's Liberation Army garrisoned on Nanjing Rd. in Shanghai. It was given this honorary appellation on April 25, 1953 by the Department of Defense.

好处费 hǎochùfèi
favor fees
1) (Monetary) gift paid or received for a favor. 2) Tips.
E.g. 这个单位规定外出办事人员不许收取好处费。*This unit has a rule to the effect that their personnel on business trips may not receive favor fees.*

好人主义 hǎorén zhǔyì
nice-guy-ism; goody-goody-ism
A worldly-wise and play-it-safe kind of individualism. It means having no principles in dealing with people and matters, not daring to struggle against wrongs, so as not to offend others, and hoping to use this method to smooth over relationships with other people.

耗电 hàodiàn
to consume electricity

耗能 hàonéng
energy consumption
E.g. 耗能量 *quantity of energy consumption*

号型 hàoxīng
size and type
Size and type specifications of a product.

he

喝墨水 hē mòshuǐ
to drink ink
A facetious way of referring to studying

喝西北风 hē xīběifēng
to drink the northwest wind
A metaphor for having no income or for suffering from lack of food.
E.g. 粮食快吃完了,下个月就得喝西北风。*Our provisions will soon be exhausted. Next month we will have nothing to eat.*

荷兰豆 hélándòu
peas (a Cantonese word)

核霸权 hébàquán
nuclear hegemony

核霸王 hébàwáng
nuclear hegemony

核保护伞 hébǎohùsǎn
"nuclear umbrella", the protective effect given by the nuclear power of a nation to other nations or regions

核备战 hébèizhàn
preparation for nuclear war

核裁军 hécáijūn
nuclear disarmament

核查 héchá
examine and verify
Contraction of 审核查对 examine and verify.
E.g. 美国人民上报的所得税必须经税收部门核查。 *The income tax reports submitted by Americans must be examined and verified by the tax collecting agency (i.e., the IRS).*

核冲突 héchōngtū
nuclear conflict

核大国 hédàguó
nuclear power

核导弹 hédǎodàn
nuclear ballistic missiles

核电 hédiàn
electricity generated by nuclear energy

核电厂 hédiànchǎng
nuclear electricity generation plant

核电站 hédiànzhàn
nuclear power station

核冬天 hédōngtiān
nuclear winter
The cold climate which scientists predict will result from nuclear warfare.

核动力 hédònglì
nuclear motive force

核讹诈 hé'ézhà
nuclear blackmail

核发 héfā
to examine (applications) and issue (a permit, license, etc.)
E.g. 核发营业执照 *to examine applications and issue permits for businesses*

核反应堆 héfǎnyìngduī
nuclear reactor
Also called 原子反应堆 atomic reactor.

核废料 héfèiliào
nuclear waste
All waste materials derived from use of nuclear energy, including nuclear testing, and medical and industrial applications. Also called 核废物 and 核垃圾 or 放射性垃圾 radioactive waste.

核基地 héjīdì
nuclear base

核军备 héjūnbèi
nuclear armament

核恐怖 hékǒngbù
nuclear terror

核扩散 hékuòsàn
nuclear proliferation

核力量 héliliàng
nuclear power

核垄断 hélǒngduàn
nuclear monopoly

核能 héněng
nuclear energy

核骗局 hépiànjú
nuclear fraud

核试验 héshìyàn
nuclear tests
Abbreviation for 核武器试验 testing of nuclear weapons.

核算单位 hésuàn dānwèi

accounting unit

An organization within the production management sector used for checking and calculating all the incomes and expenditure, profits and losses.

E.g. 人民公社以生产小队为基本核算单位。 *People's Communes take the production team as the basic accounting unit.*

核谈判 hétánpàn

nuclear arms negotiations

核糖核酸 hétánghésuān

RNA（ribonucleic acid）

核威慑 héwēishè

nuclear deterrence

核威胁 héwēixié

nuclear threat

核武库 héwǔkù

nuclear arsenal, nuclear stockpile

核武器 héwǔqì

nuclear weapons

They are also called 核子武器 nuclear weapons or 原子武器 atomic weapons.

核心家庭 héxīn jiātíng

nuclear family

A family consisting of husband, wife and unmarried children.

核心人物 héxīn rénwù

key figure; core person

The person within an organization who holds authority and makes policy decisions.

核心小组 héxīn xiǎozǔ

core group

The leading group composed of a small number of persons within a unit, department, or organization that has the authority to make policy decisions.

核牙齿 héyáchǐ

nuclear teeth

核优势 héyōushì

nuclear superiority

核战争 hézhànzhēng

nuclear war

核装置 hézhuāngzhì

nuclear device

核资 hézī

to check over capital funds and assets

E.g. 清仓核资 *to make an inventory of the warehouse and to check over capital funds and assets*

和风细雨 héfēng xìyǔ

gentle winds and fine rain

A metaphor for a gentle, relaxed and smooth manner.

和美 héměi

congenial（in reference to interpersonal relationships）

和平队 hépíngduì

peace corps

和平改造 hépíng gǎizào

peaceful reform, i.e., to transform a capitalist economy to a socialist one through peaceful means

和平攻势 hépíng gōngshì

peaceful（non-military）offensive

In international relations, a nation or bloc using non-military means such as public opinion to attack an opponent, putting it in a disadvantageous position.

和平共处 hépíng gòngchǔ

peaceful coexistence

Nations with different social systems using peaceful methods to resolve mutual conflicts, and to develop economic and cultural relations on the basis of equality and mutual benefits.

和 平 共 处 五 项 原 则 hépíng

gòngchǔ wǔxiàng yuánzé
Five Principles of Peaceful Coexistence

由中国倡导的处理国家相互关系的重要原则。即①互相尊重主权和领土完整；②互不侵犯；③互不干涉内政；④平等互利；⑤和平共处。这五项原则在国际关系中得到越来越广泛的承认和应用。

The important principles in handling relationships between nations that China initiated. They are: 1) mutual respect for sovereignty and territorial integrity, 2) mutual non-aggression, 3) non-interference in each other's internal affairs, 4) equality and mutual benefits, 5) peaceful coexistence. These five principles have increasingly received wide recognition and application in international relations.

和平过渡 hépíng guòdù
peaceful transition

The thesis raised by some in the international communist movement that a capitalist society can enter socialism through peaceful means.

和平解放 hépíng jiěfàng
peaceful liberation

To change the political leadership authority of a region by non-military means (such as negotiations).

E.g. 西藏和平解放 *the peaceful liberation of Tibet*

和平竞赛 hépíng jìngsài
peaceful competition

The competition, proposed by some within the international communist movement, between the two systems of socialism and capitalism, which will elevate people's material life and spiritual welfare. They believe that through this kind of competition, socialism can triumph over capitalism.

和平演变 hépíng yǎnbiàn
peaceful evolution

The subversion of socialist nations and restoration of capitalism by imperialist nations through non-military means. That is, using all propaganda tools and artistic works such as literature and art to disseminate bourgeois reactionary thoughts and corrupt life style, in order to poison the thoughts of the people, dissipate their revolutionary will, making the people of socialist countries, especially the young generation, grovel before the bourgeois "civilization". Furthermore to cause those with authority to completely relinquish the principles of Marxism-Leninism, and to surrender to imperialism, so that capitalism can be restored in socialist nations.

合成革 héchénggé
synthetic leather

A leather-like product made from synthetic materials. It has the ability to breathe and absorb moisture. It is usually made of a synthetic fiber base with a dyed or pasted-on surface. It can be used instead of leather in the manufacture of shoes, suitcases, bags, etc.

合成军 héchéngjūn
combined arms unit

1) A military unit formed from combining several kinds of troops. 2) An army (military unit) formed by integrating several kinds of troops.

合成师 héchéngshī
combined division

A division formed by combining several

kinds of troops.

合成纤维 héchéng xiānwéi
synthetic fibers

合二为一 hé èr wéi yī
to unit two into one
原为古代哲学术语，现在是对矛盾同一性的通俗概括和表达。基本含义是对立中有同一，差别中有联结；强调矛盾着的双方互相联系、互相渗透构成统一事物。也叫"合二而一"。
Originally a term from ancient philosophy. It is now a common generalization and expression of the unity-in-contradictions phenomenon. The basic meaning is that there is unity in opposites, and ties in differences; it stresses that the two contradictory sides seek connections and infiltrations with each other in order to become a united entity. This is also called 合二而一 combining two to become one.

合法斗争 héfǎ dòuzhēng
legal struggles
This term usually refers to the struggle engaged in by the proletarian political party within the scope permitted by the laws of the reactionary ruling class. These activities include participating in meetings, organizing strikes and conducting marches and demonstrations, publishing books and disseminating revolutionary propaganda.

合伙企业 héhuǒ qǐyè
partnership enterprise
An enterprise formed by two or more parties who agree to jointly put up the capital and manage the enterprise, and to share the profits and losses.

合理化建议 hélǐhuà jiànyì
reasonable suggestion
Suggestions that are feasible, and can advance work or promote production.

合拍 hépāi
to collaborate in making a film or television program
A metaphor for compatibility of ideas or methods.
E.g. 合拍电影 *to collaborate in making a film* / 合拍一张照片 *to take a photograph together* / 他们两人工作不合拍。 *The two of them are professionally incompatible.* / 工作和生活安排得很合拍。 *One's work and life are arranged very compatibly.*

合同工 hétónggōng
contract workers
Workers who are employed under a contract system.

合同医院 hétóng yīyuàn
contract clinic
A clinic with which one's unit has a medical service contract and where one may have an account.

合同制 hétóngzhì
labor contract system
(cf. 劳动合同制)

合同制工人 hétóngzhì gōngrén
contract worker
Also called 劳动合同制工人 and abbreviated as 合同工 (cf. 合同工)

合议庭 héyìtíng
a court composed of judges or a judge and jurors

合资 hézī
joint-capital (in setting up an enterprise), as opposed to single-capital
E.g. 合资开发自然资源 *to develop natural resources with joint capital*

合资经营 hézī jīngyíng
business corporations

Enterprises invested in and managed jointly by two or more parties. There are corporations of private individuals, of individuals and a collective or individuals and the state. They can also consist of a collective and the state, and even of foreign and Chinese enterprises.

合资企业 hézī qǐyè
joint-capital enterprises

合作化 hézuòhuà
cooperativization

To organize dispersed individual labor and private ownership into an organized form of cooperatives.

合作商店 hézuò shāngdiàn
cooperative store

A form of economy with collective ownership by the working masses. A number of small shop owners and peddlers, voluntarily pool their capital funds, unite in management, do accounting independently, and share gains and losses.

合作社 hézuòshè
cooperatives

劳动人民根据互助合作的原则自愿建立起来的经济组织。合作社根据经营业务的不同,可分为生产合作社、消费合作社、供销合作社、信用合作社等。

Economic organizations formed voluntarily by working people on the principle of mutual aid and cooperation. According to the various businesses engaged, cooperatives can be categorized into production cooperatives, consumers' cooperatives, supply and marketing cooperatives, credit cooperatives, etc.

合作医疗 hézuò yīliáo
cooperative health care; cooperative medical service

盒饭 héfàn
boxed meals

Meals packaged in boxes sold by the portion.

盒式磁带 héshì cídài
cassette tape

盒式录音机 héshì lùyīnjī
cassette tape recorder

河肥 héféi
river fertilizer

Sludge from rivers, lakes, and ponds used as fertilizer.

河网 héwǎng
river network

A system formed by many criss-crossing waterways.

E.g. 河网化 *to create a network of waterways*

贺卡 hèkǎ
greeting cards

Greeting cards used for New Year's, birthdays, etc.

E.g. 今年贺卡的价格与去年基本平衡。 *The cost of greeting cards this year is basically the same as last year.*

贺岁片 hèsuìpiān
New Year greeting film

Films shown during New Year's Day and the Spring Festival. Characteristically the films are comedies, or films with happy endings and films with many movie stars. There is a specified screening time.

hei

黑八论 hēibālùn
the eight black doctrines

林彪、江青一伙于1955年2月提出的所谓8种资产阶级、修正主义文艺思想的代表性论点，即"写真实"论、"现实主义广阔的道路"论、"现实主义的深化"论、反"题材决定"论、"中间人物"论、反"火药味"论、"时代精神汇合"论和"离经叛道"论，统称为黑八论。其目的是为了彻底否定建国后17年文艺工作的成绩。

The eight so-called representative bourgeois and revisionist doctrines of literature and art identified for criticism by Lin Biao, Jiang Qing, and their cohorts in February of 1955. The eight doctrines – depicting reality, the broad path of realism, deepening realism, opposing predetermined themes, middle-of-the-roaders, opposing "smell of gunpowder", integrating the spirit of the times, and departing from the classical and orthodox (the beaten track) – were lumped together and called the eight black doctrines. Their objective was to thoroughly negate the literary and artistic accomplishments of the seventeen years since the founding of the People's Republic.

黑白电视 hēibái diànshì

black and white television

黑白机 hēibáijī

black and white television set

黑帮 hēibāng

black clique; sinister gang

All reactionary groups and their members. An overall term for those forming a gang to foment reactivity in politics, using sinister means. In the Cultural Revolution, Lin Biao, Jiang Qing and their cliques vilified many Party and political leaders calling them "black cliques" and "black clique elements".

黑潮 hēicháo

black waves (on the ocean)

黑车 hēichē

vehicles that engage in illegal businesses

黑道 hēidào

a criminal society

黑洞 hēidòng

black hole

This term originally refers to the hypothetical collapsed star to which all celestial matters gravitate; now a metaphor for hidden dangers in economic activities.

E.g. 国有企业在经营中存在潜亏的黑洞。*There exists in state enterprises the black hole of latent losses.*

黑孩 hēihái

unregistered child

A child whose birth is hidden from the government, mainly because the birth does not accord with China's childbirth policy.

黑户口 hēihùkǒu

unregistered household; unregistered resident

Mostly the population of unregistered children, who have not been entered into the official population register.

E.g. 有些孩子已十岁多了，至今还是黑户口。*Some children already over ten years old have not been entered into the official population register.*

黑货 hēihuò

illegal commodities; contraband or commodities that have evaded taxation

A metaphor for opinions or writings that are politically reactionary.

黑金政治 hēijīn zhèngzhì
black money politics

指官府与黑社会势力、商人互相勾结,进行权钱交易。

Refers to the collusion between government officials and criminals or merchants in an illegal deal involving power and money.

黑经济 hēijīngjì
illegal economic activities

黑客 hēikè
hacker

Originally it referred to a computer programmer of great skill. Now it refers to people who use their computer skills to steal information and commit crimes on computer networks.

黑六论 hēiliùlùn
the six black doctrines

指"文化大革命"中强加给原中国国家主席刘少奇的所谓修正主义5种代表性论点,即:阶级斗争熄灭论、驯服工具论、群众落后论、入党做官论、党内和平论、公私溶化(即吃小亏占大便宜)论。1980年2月中共中央十一届五中全会通过决议为刘少奇平反昭雪,这些不实之词全部推倒。

The six so-called representative doctrines of revisionism that the late Chairman of the People's Republic of China Liu Shaoqi was forcibly charged with during the Cultural Revolution. They are the doctrines of: extinguishing the class struggle, docile tools, backwardness of the masses, joining the Party to become an official, harmony within the Party, and melding the public with the private (that is, accept small losses to attain large gains). In the Fifth Plenary of the Eleventh Central Committee of the Communist Party of China in February of 1980, it was resolved to redress and restore honor to Liu Shaoqi, and all these false accusations were overturned.

黑马 hēimǎ
black horse (an unexpected and hitherto unknown winner in a competition)

黑牌 hēipái
black label, used to signify a penalty

黑七类 hēiqīlèi
seven black elements

"文革"中的7种人,即:地主、富农、反革命分子、坏分子、右派分子、资产阶级分子和走资派,以及上述7种人的子女。

(Cultural Revolution terminology) "seven black elements": landlords, rich peasants, counter-revolutionaries, bad elements, rightists, capitalists, and capitalist-roaders; also the children of the above seven categories of people.

黑社会 hēishèhuì
criminal society

黑手 hēishǒu
black hand

A metaphor for a criminal with a reactionary political goal, who is manipulated by someone backstage to participate in a certain activity, or to join a certain organization to engage in sabotage.

黑手党 hēishǒudǎng
Black Hand, an international terrorist and criminal cartel

黑条子 hēitiáozi
black slips

Receipts for medicine, travel expenses, even daily-life sundries for which certain persons of power use to extort "reimbursal" from businesses under their jurisdiction.

黑五类 hēiwǔlèi
the five black elements
"文化大革命"中用语。指地主、富农、反革命分子、坏分子、右派分子及其子女。
Terminology of the Cultural Revolution in reference to landlords, rich peasants, counter-revolutionaries, bad elements, rightists, and all their children.

黑匣子 hēixiázi
black box

黑线 hēixiàn
the black line
Terminology of the Cultural Revolution in reference to the so-called revisionist line. It is the opposite of the "red line".

黑线人物 hēixiàn rénwù
black line characters
Terminology of the Cultural Revolution in reference to those who carried out the so-called revisionist line and their associates.

黑线专政 hēixiàn zhuānzhèng
dictatorship of the black line
This term was first used by Lin Biao, Jiang Qing, and their cohorts to vilify the literary and artistic works of the first seventeen years after the founding of the People's Republic. They asserted that, since the founding of the nation, "the literary and artistic fields were under the dictatorship of an anti-Party anti-socialist black line which opposed Chairman Mao's thought". Later, Lin Biao, Jiang Qing, and their cohorts extended "dictatorship of the black line" to education, publishing, athletics, health care, public security, the Party's organizational work, propaganda, work of the United Front, and other Party political work. This kind of ridiculous assessment which turned truth upside-down was a main tenet of the Cultural Revolution.

黑箱作业 hēixiāng zuòyè
black case work
To work in secret and let nobody know. Also called 暗箱操作.

黑样板 hēiyàngbǎn
black models
Terminology of the Cultural Revolution. "Black" meant erroneous or reactionary things; "model" meant models to emulate. During the Cultural Revolution, some originally progressive persons or groups were vilified as "black models" who carried out the "revisionist line".

黑字 hēizì
black figure
(in business accounting) a positive balance between income and expenditure.

heng

横扫 héngsǎo
operation mop-up; to force the eradication of or clean-up
E.g. 横扫一切牛鬼蛇神 to eradicate all the monsters and demons

横向 héngxiàng
parallel (in rank, relationship, etc.)
E.g. 横向经济联系 parallel economic connections / 横向协作 parallel cooperation / 横向比较 parallel comparisons

横向联合 héngxiàng liánhé
horizontal linkage

Horizontal economic linkages is a system by which, under the principle of voluntary mutual benefits for enterprises and districts, barriers between districts, departments, and ownership systems are removed. This is intended to forge linkages in the economy which should lead to the establishment of new enterprise complexes or collectives.

hong

哄动效应 hōngdòng xiàoyìng
a huge reaction in society (referring usually to the effect of a literary or artistic work)
哄闹 hōngnào
to raise a ruckus
E.g. 中国足球队以一比二负于对方，大批观众在看台上哄闹。 *When the Chinese soccer team lost by one to two, a section of the spectators raised a ruckus.*
哄抢 hōngqiǎng
looting
Many people grabbing and taking things in a frenzy.
E.g. 哄抢事件 *a looting incident* / 哄抢公共财物 *to loot public property*
哄抬 hōngtái
(referring to opportunistic merchants) to create a disturbance and thereby raise prices
E.g. 哄抬物价 *to create turmoil on the market so as to raise prices*
洪峰 hóngfēng
flood peak
1) The water level reached by a river at its peak. It also refers to the highest lever reached in a flood. 2) The entire process of a river from its rise in a flood to its return to the original level.
宏富 hóngfù
grand and rich (i.e., abundant)
宏观管理 hóngguān guǎnlǐ
macroscopic management
宏观经济 hóngguān jīngjì
macro-economic
弘扬 hóngyáng
to carry to new heights, to greatly enhance
E.g. 弘扬民族文化 *to carry national culture to new heights* / 弘扬民魂 *to carry the national spirit to new heights* / 弘扬孙中山先生的伟大精神 *to carry the great spirit of Sun Yat-sen to new heights*
红包 hóngbāo
red packets (of money)
Traditionally, the bonuses given out at the end of the year or other special occasions; now it refers to the extra remuneration given to cadres and workers (amounts are confidential); sometimes it refers to money used for bribes.
红宝书 hóngbǎoshū
precious red book
Terminology of the Cultural Revolution in reference to the writings of Mao Zedong, including Selected Works and Quotations.
红茶菌 hóngchájūn
fermented tea
Originally called 海宝. A beverage made by fermenting a sugared tea with a bacterium. It is rich in such nutrients as vitamin C, vitamin B, and organic acids. It can promote metabolism and regulate human physiological functions.
红潮 hóngcháo

red surge

A sudden proliferation of certain floating plants in the ocean, causing the sea water to turn reddish, brownish, greenish, or yellow. Also called 赤潮.

红筹股 hóngchóugǔ
red chip stocks

Shares in Hong Kong companies controlled by Chinese capital equal to or exceeding 30%.

E.g. 红筹股频频出击。 *Red chip stocks are proliferating in droves.*

红道 hóngdào
legal society

A person or a group which relies on or has the support of the government.

红灯 hóngdēng
red light

Originally a red traffic light, now also used metaphorically to mean a barrier.

E.g. 闯过红灯 *to run a red light* / 不要给改革设置红灯。 *Don't set up red lights in the path of reforms.*

红灯区 hóngdēngqū
red light district

红管家 hóngguǎnjiā
red housekeepers

Persons who are conscientious, hardworking, and frugal in managing the materials and life of a collective group.

红海洋 hónghǎiyáng
red sea

An extremely leftist kind of behavior in the early period of the Cultural Revolution. It consisted of writing quotations from Mao in red on all buildings and public places, or painting them red, displaying an expanse of red everywhere, in order to symbolize the revolution.

红会 hónghuì
the Red Cross

Abbreviation for 红十字会.

红领巾 hónglǐngjīn
red scarf

A kind of red triangular scarf, which represents one corner of the Red Flag. It is the insignia of a member of the Chinese Young Pioneers. The term also means a Young Pioneer.

红领人 hónglǐngrén
red-collared persons

Party, political, and sci-tech cadres.

E.g. 红领人是一个高素质的阶层。 *Red-collared persons belong to a high rank.*

红领章 hónglǐngzhāng
red collar badge

A red badge worn as an insignia on uniform collars by soldiers of the People's Liberation Army.

红帽子 hóngmàozi
red cap

Refers to the reputation a private enterprise enjoys by becoming attached to a government department and doing business in the name of a state-run or collective-run enterprise.

红娘 hóngniáng
Hongniang; matchmaker; go-between

Originally the name of a maid in the traditional tale "West Chamber" who successfully maneuvered the union of her mistress with her lover; later the term was applied to a person who helps a couple form a happy marital union; now the term is extended to mean any person or unit that serves as a bridge in helping two sides link up.

红牌 hóngpái
red card

Originally card used by referees in sporting events to signal a penalty; now also a metaphor for any signal that indicates cancellation of the right to participate or continue in a certain activity. *E.g.* 9号运动员受到红牌处罚。 *Player 9 was removed from play as a penalty.* / 裁判员出示了红牌。 *The referee flashed his red card (to signal a penalty).*

红旗 hóngqí
red flag

A metaphor for being progressive or revolutionary. *E.g.* 他是班上的一面红旗。 *He is a red flag in the class.*

红旗单位 hóngqí dānwèi
red flag unit

A progressive unit. A unit which has been appraised and is recognized as being progressive in production or other areas is given the title "red flag unit" and is awarded a red silk banner.

红旗竞赛 hóngqí jìngsài
red flag competition

Socialist labor competition. It consists mainly of competing to be progressive, emulating the progressive, catching up with the progressive, helping and supporting each other, trying to overtake each other in friendly emulation. The most progressive is appraised as a red flag unit, and is awarded a red silk banner to provide further encouragement.

红旗手 hóngqíshǒu
red-banner pacesetter; advanced worker

An honorary name given to progressive persons who have attained outstanding achievements in their work.

红热线 hóngrèxiàn
infrared ray

Synonymous with 红外线 infrared ray.

红色保险箱 hóngsè bǎoxiǎnxiāng
red safe

1) A metaphor for having a good family background. From the 1950s to the 1960s, some young people from families of workers, poor, lower, and middle peasants, revolutionary cadres, and revolutionary martyrs regarded their families as red safes. This meant that if one came from a good family, then he was a born revolutionary, would always be a revolutionary, his revolutionary character would never change, and therefore he had no need to reform his thoughts. 2) A metaphor for sectors in good political standing, such as important Party and government organs, and military units. This means that when a person joined one of these units, politically he would have reliable guarantees, and would not get into trouble, and the issue of being "red" would naturally be resolved. This type of thinking was totally erroneous.

红色政权 hóngsè zhèngquán
red political authority

Revolutionary political authority, the opposite of white political authority.

红色种子 hóngsè zhǒngzi
red seeds

Those who disseminated revolution within areas under the rule of a reactionary government. The term also refers to the offspring of revolutionaries.

红哨兵 hóngshàobīng

red sentries

During the Cultural Revolution, persons assigned to certain factories and schools with the specific responsibility of examining the work. Their job was to examine what was being produced as well as, the work, study, or life, so that those aspects which did not meet with requirements, could be corrected.

红条子 hóngtiáozi
red slip

Receipt (from the fact that the writing and lines on receipts are red).

红头文件 hóngtóu wénjiàn
red-headed documents

Documents issued by the central government and top level provincial and municipal Party and government organs. The documents use large red characters for headings, hence the term.

红透专深 hóngtòu zhuānshēn
to become thoroughly red and profoundly expert

To continuously elevate one's political ideology and knowledge of one's specialty, in order to attain the highest standards. (cf. 又红又专)

红卫兵 hóngwèibīng
Red Guards

A mass organization formed by school youths during the Cultural Revolution. Their earliest activities were primarily to destroy the four olds and establish the four news. Later they were drawn into factional wars, involved in fighting, break-ins, and lootings.

红五类 hóngwǔlèi
the five red elements

"文化大革命"中对工人、贫下中农、革命干部、革命军人及革命烈士子女的统称。

The cover term used during the Cultural Revolution for the children of workers, poor, lower and middle peasants, revolutionary cadres, revolutionary soldiers, and revolutionary martyrs.

红五月 hóngwǔyuè
Red May

Revolutionary May. Because the May Fourth Movement and the May Thirtieth Revolutionary Movement both occurred in May, the month is called "Red May".

红线 hóngxiàn
the red line

1) Specifically the revolutionary line, the opposite of "black line". 2) Lines marked in red on a map. 3) A metaphor for the main theme running through an article.

红小兵 hóngxiǎobīng
little red soldiers

A children's organization in elementary schools during the Cultural Revolution. It also refers to elementary school children in general.

红小鬼 hóngxiǎoguǐ
little red devil

A term of endearment for youths who participated in the revolutionary war (on the communist side)

红心 hóngxīn
red heart

A metaphor for dedication to the proletarian revolutionary cause and serving the people wholeheartedly.

E.g. 一颗红心为人民 *to serve the people with a red heart*

红眼病 hóngyǎnbìng
red eye disease

1) Acute conjunctivitis. 2) A metaphor

for jealousy and jealous behavior toward others.

红专 hóngzhuān
red and expert
"Red" means political consciousness; "expert" means knowledge in a speciality and specialized skills.
E.g. 红专道路 *the red and expert course* / 红专关系 *the relationship between red and expert*

红专大学 hóngzhuān dàxué
red and expert university
Work-study schools founded by some factories in 1958. They required students to study both professional knowledge and politics, so that would become both red and expert.

hou

猴市 hóushì
monkey market
The situation of stock prices fluctuating wildly the same day.

厚爱 hòu'ài
profound love
A term of respect used in referring to the concern and care bestowed by someone on oneself.
E.g. 学生感谢老师对他们的厚爱。 *The students are grateful for the profound love bestowed on them by their teacher.*
E.g. 观众的厚爱自然是促进艺术家创作的一种动力。 *The love and appreciation of an audience is naturally a motivation for artists to be creative.*

厚古薄今 hòugǔ bójīn
to stress the ancient, not the present
In academic studies, to emphasize the ancient and pay scant attention to the present.

厚今薄古 hòujīn bógǔ
to stress the present, not the ancient
In academic studies, to emphasize the modern and place the ancient in a secondary position.

候补委员 hòubǔ wěiyuán
alternate committee member
A committee member who is waiting to fill a vacancy.
E.g. 中共中央候补委员 *alternate member of the Chinese Communist Party Central Committee* / 团中央候补委员 *alternate member of the Youth League Central Committee* / 市委候补委员 *alternate member of a municipal Party committee*

候诊室 hòuzhěnshì
waiting room of a clinic
A room set up in a clinic especially for patients waiting for treatment.

后备干部 hòubèi gànbù
reserve cadres
Cadres prepared to take up certain jobs or vacancies.

后处理 hòuchǔlǐ
after treatment
The recycling of useable residual materials from fuels used in nuclear electric generation stations.

后发性 hòufāxìng
effects or characteristics that surface slowly in the development of a certain matters
Also called 滞后性.

后进 hòujìn
backward
To advance relatively slowly and to be at a relatively low level. The opposite of 先

进 advanced.

E.g. 先进帮后进。*The advanced help the backward.*

后进队 hòujìnduì
backward team

Production teams in people's communes that lag behind in production and whose members have lower living standards.

后门 hòumén
backdoor

A metaphor for going through irregular channels and using connections.

后市 hòushì
future market

后现代 hòuxiàndài
later modern

后现代主义 hòuxiàndài zhǔyì
later modernism

hu

呼姐 hūjiě
pager girl

Girl who works at pager stations.

呼拉圈 hūlāquān
hula-hoop

E.g. 五十年代呼拉圈风靡于欧美。*In the fifties, hula-hoops were a fad in Europe and America.* / 似乎一夜间北京各大街小巷都转起了呼拉圈。*Hula-hoops popped up on every street and alley of Beijing overnight.*

胡吃海塞 húchī hǎisāi
to recklessly stuff oneself with food

胡子 húzi
beard, moustache or whiskers

A metaphor for something dragging out beyond a reasonable time.

胡子工程 húzi gōngchéng
dragging constructions

Construction work that proceeds at a snail's pace, is repeatedly delayed and takes a long time to complete.

E.g. 改革以后,基本上杜绝了胡子工程。*After the reform, dragging constructions have basically ended.*

胡子牌 húzipái
dragging brands

A sarcastic term for commodities that remain for long periods in the testing stage and cannot be put into regular production.

湖吃海喝 húchī hǎihē
to eat and drink a huge amount

护航 hùháng
to guard ships and airplanes during a flight or trip

A metaphor for supporting and protecting the development of a certain project.

E.g. 军队要积极为沿海改革开放保驾护航。*The Army must actively provide navigation protection along the coast for the sake the of reforms and liberalization process.*

护林员 hùlínyuán
forest ranger

Personnel set up by appropriate departments in forest regions to guard and protect forests.

护苗 hùmiáo
seedling-protection

To protect plant seedlings.

E.g. 护苗工作 *seedling-protection work*

护嫂 hùsǎo
married nurse

Refers to nurses more than 25 years old who are married.

护田林 hùtiánlín

field-protection woods

Protective trees planted around agricultural fields, usually consisting of entire rows of trees or bushes. Their main function is to protect agricultural fields, and to guard against such natural adversities as wind and sand.

互补 hùbǔ
complementary

E.g. 互补互利，共同繁荣。 *to supplement and benefit each other, and to prosper together* / 海峡两岸经济具有互补性。 *The economies on the two sides of the Taiwan Straits are complementary in nature.*

互访 hùfǎng
reciprocal visit

互教互学 hùjiāo hùxué
to teach and learn reciprocally

To teach each other knowledge and skills and to learn from each other.

互联网 hùliánwǎng
Internet

互市 hùshì
to buy and sell commodities to each other

互助组 hùzhùzǔ
mutual aid teams

1) Small mutual aid teams in production, work, or study. 2) The early form of agricultural cooperation in China. They were voluntarily groups organized by peasant households to facilitate cooperation in labor resources, use of farm implements, domestic animals, etc.

户均 hùjūn
household average

The average per household.

E.g. 户均收入 5000 元。 *The average household income is 5,000 yuan.*

户售 hùshòu
household sale

Sold by each household.

E.g. 平均户售粮食 2000 斤。 *The average per household grain sale is 2,000 catties.*

户营 hùyíng
managed by a household

Managed independently by a peasant household.

E.g. 户营农机 *household-managed farm machine*

户造户管 hù zào hù guǎn
planted and managed by a household

A term for afforestation. Trees planted by a particular household that will manage them.

hua

花岗岩脑袋 huāgāngyán nǎodài
granite-like skull

A metaphor for being incorrigibly obstinate.

E.g. 他是花岗岩脑袋。 *He's got a granite-like skull.*

花架子 huājiàzi
pretty appearance (lit., flower frame)

A metaphor for a work style that seeks show off superficial form and pays no attention to actual accomplishments.

E.g. 不追求花架子。 *Do not seek only a pretty appearance.*

华人 huárén
Chinese people; also refers to foreign citizens of Chinese ancestry

华文 huáwén
the Han (Chinese) language, especially the written language

华语 huáyǔ

the Chinese language; sometimes this term refers specifically to the standard common Chinese language

华约 Huá-Yuē

Warsaw Treaty

Abbreviation for 华沙条约组织 Warsaw Treaty Organization.

滑草 huácǎo

grass skating

A newly-merged sport in which one slides down a grassy slope wearing grass-skating boots. Standing on grass skates, and holding a pole in each hand.

滑坡 huápō

landslide; also used metaphorically to refer to a rapid or dramatic decline

E.g. 昨天出现一起山体大滑坡。 *Yesterday, there was a major mountain landslide.* / 工业生产连续滑坡。 *There is a continuous and drastic decline in industrial production.*

滑水 huáshuǐ

water-skiing

滑雪衫 huáxuěshān

snow-suit or snow-jacket (usually made of a nylon shell filled with down)

画圈圈 huà quānquan

to circle

When leaders have read certain documents, they circle their names to indicate that they have read them.

画坛 huàtán

(of art) painting circles

画展 huàzhǎn

painting exhibition

划拨 huàbō

to transfer

1) To transfer funds or accounts from a certain unit to another.
E.g. 这笔款子由银行划拨。 *This sum of money will be transferred by the bank.*
2) To separate out and appropriate.
E.g. 把机器结余的钢材划拨给农具厂。 *To transfer the machine factory's surplus steel materials to the agricultural implements factory.*

划成分 huà chéngfèn

to assign class status

To assign a person to a class status on the basis of that person's economic position in society, such as worker, poor peasant, landlord, capitalist, etc.

划圈 huàquān

to draw a circle to indicate that one has read the document

Also written as 画圈 or 画圈圈.
E.g. 有的人工作中只划圈不拍板。 *Some people, in their work, only draw circles (on documents to indicate that they have read them) without giving any verdicts.* / 有的事划圈划了半年还解决不了。 *Some issues have been passed around for half a year without arriving at any resolution.*

划线 huàxiàn

to draw a line, i.e., to categorize people or things according to certain criteria

E.g. 以派划线 *to draw factional lines* / 以人划线 *to draw lines according to personal preferences* / 按年龄划线 *to draw lines according to age*

划线排队 huàxiàn páiduì

to draw lines and to line up

Terminology of the Cultural Revolution.

To "draw lines" means to use certain standards to clearly delineate whether something is correct or erroneous, whether it is revolutionary or counter-revolutionary; to "line up" means to assign people to one of the three categories of "left, center, and right" on the basis of their attitudes and political opinions.

化肥 huàféi
chemical fertilizer
Abbreviation for 化学肥料 chemical fertilizer.

化工 huàgōng
chemical industry
Abbrevation for 化学工业.

化公为私 huà gōng wéi sī
transfoming the public to the private
To make a publicly owned thing privately owned

化解 huàjiě
to resolve or end a conflict
E.g. 化解矛盾 to resolve a conflict

化疗 huà-liáo
chemotherapy
Abbreviation for 化学疗法.

化纤 huà-xiān
chemical fiber
Abbreviation for 化学纤维.

话路 huàlù
talk lines
Lines that transmit speech in a communication set-up.

话亭 huàtíng
telephone booth

话筒 huàtǒng
1) mouthpiece of a telephone; 2) microphones; 3) a loud hailer
Also called 传声筒 voice-transmitting tube.

话务员 huàwùyuán
switchboard operator

huai

坏分子 huàifènzǐ
bad elements
Robbers, swindlers, murderers, arsonists, gangsters, and other kinds of people who seriously undermine social order.

坏头头 huàitóutou
(Cultural Revolution terminology) bad leaders (of groups, cliques, or organizations)

huan

欢宴 huānyàn
welcome feast
To put on a feast to welcome someone.
E.g. 美国总统欢宴中国总理。The president of the United States gave a welcoming feast to the premier of the People's Republic of China.

环保 huán-bǎo
environmental protection
Abbreviation for "环境保护 environmental protection".
E.g. 环保工作 environmental protection work

环保部门 huán-bǎo bùmén
environmental protection organizations

环保工业 huán-bǎo gōngyè
environmental protection industries (which produce and market equipment and products for use in protecting the environment)

环发 huán – fā
environment and development
E.g. 环发大会 Conference on Environment and Development

环幕电影 huánmù diànyǐng
circular movie screen (a screen that fully surrounds the viewer)

环委会 huán – wěi – huì
Environmental Committee
Abbreviation for 环境委员会.

环卫 huán – wèi
environmental sanitation
Abbreviation for 环境卫生.
E.g. 环卫工作 environmental sanitation work

环卫工人 huán – wèi gōngrén
environmental sanitation workers
Workers responsible for environmental sanitation in cities. Also called 清洁工 sanitation workers.

缓建 huǎnjiàn
to delay construction
E.g. 缓建工程 a delayed construction project

缓解 huǎnjiě
to relax
A tense situation becoming relaxed and taking a turn for the better.
E.g. 两国关系有了缓解。 The relationship between the two nations is relaxed.

缓行 huǎnxíng
to walk or travel slowly; to slow down or temporarily delay implementation

换工 huàngōng
to exchange work
In agricultural production, production units or peasant households exchanging labor on a voluntary basis.

换汇 huànhuì
to exchange currency
Using export commodities to trade for foreign currency.

换届 huànjiè
to change personnel upon completion of a term of office
E.g. 政府年底换届。 The government personnel will change at the end of the year as their terms expire. / 人民代表换届选举工作已结束。 The election of People's Representatives to replace those, whose terms have expired, has already been completed.

换马 huànmǎ
(derogatory) to change horse i.e., to change personnel

换脑筋 huànnǎojīn
to change brains
A metaphor for changing one's thinking or consciousness.
E.g. 改变机制，首先要换脑筋。 In order to change the mechanism, one must first change people's thinking.

换休 huànxiū
to change the day off
The workers of an enterprise or unit changing their regular day off for another day.
E.g. 那个工厂实行换休制。 That factory is implementing the system of changing the day off.

换血 huànxiě
to change blood (used both literally and figuratively)
E.g. 中国女排大换血。 The Chinese Women's Volleyball Team is undergoing a major turnover of players. / 老企业正在进行换血。 Old enterprises are undergoing major turnovers.

huang

荒诞派 huāngdànpài
the absurdist school of art, in reference particularly to the theater, as in "theater of the absurd"

黄潮 huángcháo
pornographic wave
The wave of pornographic publications, VCDs, and videotapes that has flooded society.

黄带 huángdài
pornographic audio tapes and videotapes

黄昏恋 huánghūnliàn
twilight romance, romance of the elderly

黄金 huángjīn
gold
A metaphor for something extremely valuable.
E.g. 黄金时代 *golden era* / 黄金时间 *golden time* / 黄金水道 *precious waterways*

黄金海岸 huángjīn hǎi'àn
gold coast
A coastline that has become economically valuable through the development or tourism.

黄牛 huángniú
originally a type of ox, now it refers to profiteers who deal in train tickets, boat tickets, etc., or engage in similar activities

黄牌 huángpái
yellow card
Originally an emblem used by referees in sporting events to signal a warning; now used metaphorically for any warning signal.

E.g. 黄牌警告 *a yellow card warning* / 出示黄牌 *to show the yellow card (to indicate a warning in a sport)* / 亮出黄牌 *to flash the yellow card*

黄皮书 huángpíshū
yellow paper; yellow book
Refers to documents on important political or foreign affairs and financial issues.

黄条 huángtiáo
yellow slips
Notes for postponing the cashing of checks and money orders used by banks (due to problems in cash flow). These notes are yellow, hence the term.
E.g. 打黄条现象已制约企业的发展。 *The phenomenon of handing out yellow slips has already put a damper on the development of enterprises.*

皇粮 huángliáng
emperor's grains
Originally the salaries paid by the emperor, now also a metaphor for the national government's revenue

hui

灰领工人 huīlǐng gōngrén
grey-collar workers
Workers in maintenance services, such as auto mechanics, electrical repairmen, etc.

灰色经济 huīsè jīngjì
gray economy
The various shenanigans in economic activities, such as the trading of power, improper competition, sale of fake products, etc.

灰色收入 huīsè shōurù
improper income (derived from tax

evasion, embezzlement, etc.)

灰色消费 huīsè xiāofèi
gray expenditure
Expenditure in enterprises that violate regulations.
E.g. 灰色消费迅速膨胀。 *Gray expenditure is increasing rapidly.*

徽标 huībiāo
emblem
An emblem that symbolizes a unit or group. Synonymous with 徽记.

徽记 huījì
emblem
Synonymous with 徽标.

回潮 huícháo
tide reversion
Something that has been dried in the sun or toasted dry becoming wet again. It is also a metaphor for the reappearance of an error or a bad ideological tendency.

回顾展 huígùzhǎn
retrospective exhibition

回归 huíguī
to return
1) To retreat.
E.g. 回归线 *line of retreat*
2) To revert.
E.g. 香港回归祖国。 *Hong Kong reverts to the motherland.*

回炉 huílú
return to the oven
The original literal meaning has been extended to the metaphorical meaning of retraining personnel.
E.g. 让教师回炉一年。 *Let teachers be retrained for a year and have them return to school for further education.*

回收 huíshōu
1) to recycle discards; 2) to collect previously distributed goods; 3) to return a man-made satellite to earth by remote control
E.g. 回收空酒瓶 *to recycle empty wine bottles* / 剩余材料按制度回收 *to systematically recycle remnant materials* / 试验卫星回收成功。 *The recovery of the experimental satellite was successful.*

回乡知青 huíxiāng zhīqīng
educated youths who return to the countryside
Abbreviation for 回乡知识青年.

回乡知识青年 huíxiāng zhīshí qīngnián
educated youths who return to the countryside
Youths from agricultural villages who have completed high school education in cities and then returned to their own home areas to work in agricultural production.

回忆录 huíyìlù
memoirs

会倒 huìdǎo
to collect high expenses on the pretext of convening or participating in conferences

会道门 huìdàomén
superstitious sects and secret societies
Abbreviation for 会门 and 道门. These are all superstitious feudal organizations in the old society. Most of them were exploited by the ruling class to carry out activities harmful to the people.

会风 huìfēng
habit of meetings
The bad habit on the part of some departments or systems of frequently holding meetings with no practical purpose.

会海 huìhǎi
ocean of meetings, i.e., huge number of meetings

会荒 huìhuāng
dearth of meetings
Referring to the dearth of meetings in a certain organization or unit.
E.g. 广大农村的基层出现了严重的会荒。*In rural areas, there is a dearth of meetings at the grass-roots level.*

会考 huìkǎo
assembled exam
An exam in which examinees from various schools in a region are gathered together.

会来事 huìláishì
adroit at handling interpersonal relationships

会签 huìqiān
two or more parties cosigning a document

会堂 huìtáng
meeting hall
E.g. 人民大会堂 *Great Hall of the People* / 科学会堂 *Science Hall*

会演 huìyǎn
joint performance (cf. 汇演)

会战 huìzhàn
to join in a battle
1) The chief forces of two warring sides fighting a decisive battle. 2) To gather all available strength and make an intense effort to complete a certain task.
E.g. 石油大会战 *a great battle for oil*

会诊 huìzhěn
to join in treatment
Several physicians jointly diagnosing a difficult and complicated illness.

汇报思想 huìbào sīxiǎng
to report one's own thoughts
To report truthfully to Party political leadership about one's own thoughts and views on matters, so that the leadership can understand and help.

汇价 huìjià
currency exchange rate
Also called 汇率.

汇款单 huìkuǎndān
money order

汇路 huìlù
channels through which banks remit funds
E.g. 要保证汇路畅通。*We must ensure that the remittance channels are flowing smoothly.*

汇演 huìyǎn
joint performance
Also called 会演 joint performance. Various units from various locations put together their theatrical programs and perform them singly or together. It serves the function of reporting, learning from each other, and exchanging experience.

绘制 huìzhì
drawing (chart or diagram)

hun

婚补 hūnbǔ
wedding ceremony remedy
Ceremonies for middle aged or old couples who have been married many years. Activities include taking pictures, wearing wedding gowns and presenting jewelry to each other. The ceremonies are intended to heal past differences and deepen the love between

the couples.
E.g. 婚补消费正在都市悄然兴起。*There has been a slight increase in spending on wedding ceremony remedies.*

婚假 hūnjià
marriage leave

婚检 hūnjiǎn
pre-marital physical exam

婚恋 hūnliàn
marriage and romantic love

婚外恋 hūnwàiliàn
extramarital love
E.g. 婚外恋是不道德的。*To love a third party is immoral.*

婚育期 hūnyùqī
marriage and childbirth period
Periods in the human life cycle recognized in physiology as suitable for marriage and childbirth.

混纺 hùnfǎng
to blend and weave
1) To weave two or more different fibers together. Blended fabrics can economize on more expensive materials or give the fabric new properties. 2) Fabrics made by blending.

混关 hùnguān
to smuggle through customs
To violate regulations and smuggle items through customs.
E.g. 混关行为 *smuggling through customs*

混级抬价 hùnjí táijià
to pass off as higher grade and raise the price
To pass off low-grade commodities as high grade, in order to raise their prices.

混凝剂 hùnníngjì
coagulant

混双 hùn-shuāng
mixed doubles
Abbreviation for 混合双打 mixed doubles (in sports).

huo

活靶子 huóbǎzi
live target
People or issues chosen and used as the direct targets in the criticism of certain errors or reactionary thought. This term was more widely used during the Cultural Revolution.

活标本 huóbiāoběn
living specimen
A metaphor for the most practical material which can help people analyze and understand certain matters.

活化石 huóhuàshí
living fossil

活教材 huójiàocái
live teaching material
1) The antithesis of fixed teaching material. It is teaching material that can be altered any time in accordance with need. 2) The antithesis of book teaching material. It is teaching material taken from life in its most practical aspects, which can increase the student's knowledge.

活命哲学 huómìng zhéxué
philosophy of survival (saving one's neck); save one's skin
The base thought of clinging to life instead of braving death, of caring for nothing else but saving one's life, even selling out one's comrades and the interests of revolution.

活神仙 huóshénxiān
live immortal

A metaphor for a carefree untrammeled person.

活思想 huósīxiǎng
live ideology

People's newly arisen, most realistic kind of ideology, in contrast to ideology that is out-dated or in books only. This term was widely popular during the Cultural Revolution.

活学活用 huóxué huóyòng
live learning, live usage

The study of theory must be combined with practicality, one must combine learning with usage and emphasize application. This saying was widely used during the Cultural Revolution.

活样板 huóyàngbǎn
live model

The most realistic model that can be provided for learning.

活愚公 huóyúgōng
live Foolish Old Man

A metaphor for a person who has the spirit of unswerving determination, of overcoming a myriad of difficulties, and of pursuing the revolutionary cause to the end. (cf. 愚公精神)

火 huǒ
booming; prosperous

E.g. 服装卖的很火。 *The sale of clothing is sizzling.*

火电 huǒdiàn
1) generating electricity by burning fossil fuels, abbreviation for 火力发电; 2) the electricity thus generated

火箭干部 huǒjiàn gànbù
rocket cadre

An ordinary worker or cadre who was elevated to a top position overnight during the Cultural Revolution.

火炬计划 huǒjù jìhuà
torch plan

A developmental plan that was promulgated in August 1988 in order to promote the development of high technology

火线入党 huǒxiàn rùdǎng
admitted to the Party in the firing line

During the war years, those who experienced the test of life or death in the firing line, who were courageous in killing the enemy, had no fear of sacrificing their own life, and had performed outstandingly, could be admitted to the Party right at the battle front. Those persons at the front line of production and work, who have undergone unusual tests and have performed outstandingly, are immediately admitted to the Chinese Communist Party, and are also called "admitted to the Party in the firing line".

火药味 huǒyàowèi
smell of gunpowder

A metaphor for views or articles with very fierce and militant content.

E.g. 他的发言充满火药味。 *His speech was permeated with the smell of gunpowder.*

获选 huòxuǎn
to be elected; to win an election

和稀泥 huòxīní
to mix mud

A metaphor for having no principles, merely making concessions and compromises in face of contradictions.

E.g. 处理问题要有原则，不要和稀泥。 *In dealing with issues, we must not*

be mixing mud.

货币主义学派 huòbì zhǔyì xuépài
the currency doctrine school of economics

A philistine school of economics that surfaced in the United States in the 1950s and 1960s. It took the simplistic quantity of currency as its theoretical basis, insisting that shifts in the currency supply was the most basic cause of shifts in price levels and in economic activity. It advocated implementing the "single-rule" currency policy, hence it was called the "currency doctrine school".

货仓式商店 huòcāngshì shāngdiàn
stockroom-style stores

Synonymous with 仓储式商店. (cf. 仓储式)

货的 huòdí
taxi lorry

货柜 huòguì
container

货机 huòjī
cargo aircraft

货流 huòliú
flow of goods

The quantity of goods transported in a certain direction within a certain amount of time. By getting a handle on the pattern of the flow of goods, the irrational transport phenomena of counter-flow and surplus flow can be overcome, and a rational system of transport can be organized.

货运 huòyùn
transport of goods

E.g. 货运量 *transport capacity*

ji

跻身 jīshēn
to elevate oneself (to a certain rank or realm)

E.g. 跻身于开拓者的行列 *to elevate oneself to the ranks of pioneers* / 跻身国际市场 *to elevate oneself into the international market* / 跻身世界强队 *to elevate oneself to be among the strong teams of the world* / 跻身世界经济强国 *to elevate oneself to an international economic power*

击剑衫 jījiànshān
fencing shirt

A jacket-like top modeled after shirts used in the sport of fencing.

基本工资 jīběn gōngzī
basic wages

Money paid to employees at fixed intervals according to the job level. It is distinguished from supplemental wages, allowances for certain posts, grain and oil subsidies, bonuses, etc.

基本功 jīběngōng
basic ability

The basic knowledge and skills necessary for a certain kind of work.

基本核算单位 jīběn hésuàn dānwèi
basic accounting unit

A unit which carries out independent accounting, is responsible for its own gains and losses, and directly organizes production and allocation. For example, in the people's commune, the production team generally is its basic accounting unit.

基本建设经济学 jīběn jiànshè jīngjìxué
economics of capital construction

A newly arisen field of study that delves into such issues as the nature and scope of capital construction, its function and position in social production and reproduction. It involves such sectors as national economic construction plans, public finances, banking, material allocation and supply, and construction projects. It is an inter-disciplinary synthesized field of study formed in the wake of developments in socialist economic construction.

基本口粮 jīběn kǒuliáng
basic grain ration

The standard grain ration provided to each person by the state according to differences in age and nature of work. It does not include the supplemental grain rations for those in certain specialized work.

基本劳动日 jīběn láodòngrì
basic work days

The minimum stipulated number of days per year or month that each person must participate in work in a rural collective production system.

基本路线 jīběn lùxiàn

basic line

The line which is basic and has decisive function.

E.g. 党的基本路线 *the Party's basic line*

基本矛盾 jīběn máodùn

basic contradictions

Contradictions which determine the nature of a matter's entire developmental process, and moreover determine and influence the existence and development of other contradictions in this process.

基本群众 jīběn qúnzhòng

basic masses

The broad proletarian masses who are trusted and relied upon in the work and struggles of the proletarian political party.

基层政权 jīcéng zhèngquán

grass-roots political authority

State organs at the lowest administrative districts. Grass-roots political authority carries out work within its area of jurisdiction and within the limits of authority as prescribed by law. An example is the government of a rural village.

基础工业 jīchǔ gōngyè

basic industries

Industrial sectors that primarily provide raw materials, energy, and technology to the various sectors of the national economy. They include such industries as steel, petroleum, coal, electrical power, chemistry, and machinery.

基础科学 jīchǔ kēxué

basic science

基干民兵 jīgàn mínbīng

basic core people's militia

The basic and backbone force within people's militia organizations. Their ages are eighteen to twenty-eight for men and eighteen to twenty-five for women. They are distinct from 普通民兵 ordinary people's militia.

基建 jī-jiàn

capital construction

Abbreviation for 基本建设, construction which involves increasing fixed assets in the various sectors of the national economy.

E.g. 基建战线 *the capital construction front* / 基建项目 *capital construction item* / 基建工程 *capital construction engineering project*

基因 jī yīn

gene

基因工程 jīyīn gōngchéng

genetic engineering

Also called 脱氧核糖核酸重组技术 DNA restructuring technology.

机播 jī-bō

seed-sowing by machine

Abbreviation for 机器播种.

E.g. 机播面积 *acreage sown by machinery*

机插 jī-chā

planting rice sprouts by machinery

机电 jīdiàn

mechanical and electrical

A cover term for machinery and electric power facilities.

E.g. 机电产品 *mechanical and electrical products* / 机电公司 *mechanical and electrical company*

机顶盒 jīdǐnghé

set-top box

连接在电视机上的盒式设备，能收看数字电视节目，连上电话线能上网,享受各种服务。

An attachment to a TV set which allows it to receive digital TV programs. It also connects the internet through the telephone and provides other services.

机动车 jīdòngchē
motor vehicle
A vehicle propelled by a motor, such as an automobile or motorcycle.

机帆船 jīfānchuán
motorized sailboat

机耕 jīgēng
mechanized farming
To farm with machines.
E.g. 机耕队 *mechanized farm team* / 机耕面积 *acreage under mechanized farming*

机工 jīgōng
mechanic; machinist

机关党委 jīguān dǎngwěi
Communist Party committees set up at the various Party and government organizations

机灌 jīguàn
agricultural irrigation by machinery

机井 jījǐng
motor-pumped well
A deep well that utilizes a pump to draw water.

机具 jījù
machines and tools
A cover term for machinery and tools.

机库 jīkù
airplane hangar

机器人 jīqìrén
robot
Also called 机械人 mechanical human.

机器手 jīqìshǒu
mechanical hand
Also called 机械手 mechanical hand.

机务 jīwù
machine operation and maintenance professions
E.g. 机务员 *machine operators and maintenance personnel* / 机务段 *machine operation and maintenance sector*

机务人员 jīwù rényuán
flight personnel
Personnel on airplanes responsible for navigation, communications, mechanical maintenance, etc.

机械臂 jīxièbì
mechanical arm
Synonymous with 机械手 mechanical hand.

机械人 jīxièrén
robot

机修 jīxiū
machine maintenance
E.g. 机修工 *machine repair personnel* / 机修车间 *machine repair shop*

机恤 jīxù
a new style of machine-knitted shirts

机载卫星电话 jīzài wèixīng diànhuà
in-flight satellite phones
Phones installed on airplanes, which can be used to communicate with earth via satellite transmission.

机制 jīzhì
(originally) 1) a mechanical system; 2) the structure, function, and relationship among organisms; (new extended meaning) the complex functional relationship among all things
E.g. 运行机制 *system of movement* / 经营机制 *management system* / 竞争机制 *system of competition*

机组 jīzǔ

flight crew; unit; set

1) The entire group of personnel on an airplane.

E.g. 机组人员 *personnel of a flight crew*.

2) A complete integrated system composed of various machines.

E.g. 发电机组 *electricity-generating set*

积案 jī'àn

cumulative unresolved cases

积代会 jī-dài-huì

conference of activist representatives

Abbreviation for 积极分子代表会议.

积淀 jīdiàn

accumulated sediments

E.g. 文化积淀 *cultural sediments*

积非成是 jīfēi chéngshì

a continuous long-term error eventually leading to the erroneous assumption that it is correct

积极分子 jījí fènzǐ

activists

Persons who seek political advancement, who are active and responsible in their work, or who are especially enthusiastic about certain activities in the literary, art, or athletic spheres.

E.g. 党的积极分子 *Party activists* / 体育积极分子 *athletic activists*

激光 jīguāng

laser

It is also called 莱塞、镭射.

E.g. 激光武器 *laser weapons* / 激光测量 *laser gauge* / 激光通信 *laser communication* / 激光导航 *laser navigation*

激光视盘 jīguāng shìpán

laser disk

Also called 影碟.

绩优股 jīyōugǔ

blue chip stocks

Stocks of a corporation with a good record of performance and growth potential.

缉毒 jīdú

to investigate and arrest drug traffickers

吉祥物 jíxiángwù

mascot

An emblematic animal or creature signifying good fortune.

极端分子 jíduān fènzǐ

extremists

Persons whose opinions, views, or behavior have exceeded the proper limits and have become extreme. The term has a derogatory connotation.

极端民主化 jíduān mínzhǔhuà

extremist democracy

The unhealthy tendency of wanting democracy and not centralism, wanting freedom and not discipline.

极右 jíyòu

extreme right

To be extremely conservative in thought or politically extremely reactionary.

极左 jízuǒ

extreme left

Leftist opportunism which exceeds objective reality and which has the semblance of being revolutionary but is in reality completely against the basic principles of Marxism-Leninism.

极左思潮 jízuǒ sīcháo

extreme leftist ideological trend

The ideological trend of using radical revolutionary rhetorics, of going all out in advocating leftist opportunism, which exceeds objective reality and which adopts blind risk-taking measures.

集餐 jícān
people coming together to dine

集成板 jíchéngbǎn
integrated circuit board
Abbreviation for 集成电路板.

集成电路 jíchéng diànlù
integrated circuits

集贸市场 jímào shìchǎng
collective household market
A rural or urban market place with stalls selling various agricultural products and handicrafts.

集市贸易 jíshì màoyì
fair trade
Trade activities in markets held at periodic intervals in urban and rural areas. (cf. 自由市场)

集体户 jítǐhù
collective household (organized by urban educated youths sent to the countryside)

集体化 jítǐhuà
collectivization
To join together many individual components and form an organized whole.

集体经济 jítǐ jīngjì
collective economy
Socialist collective economy, the kind of economy that takes the socialist laboring masses' collective ownership as its foundation. Its production materials and products of labor are the collective properties of the workers. This system accepts the leadership of state planning, makes its own production arrangements, does independent accounting, and takes on responsibility for gains and losses.

集体宿舍 jítǐ sùshè
collective dormitory
Dormitory for single employees in enterprises or institutions, or for live-in students. In general several persons share one room.

集体所有制 jítǐ suǒyǒuzhì
collective ownership system
Abbreviation for 社会主义劳动群众集体所有制 socialist working masses' collective ownership system. It is a form of socialist public ownership whereby the production resources belong to the laboring masses collectively, and the collective ownership enterprises carry out independent accounting, take responsibility for their own gains and losses, and remunerate in accordance with the work performed. Relative to ownership by the whole people, it is a low level form of socialist public ownership.

集体英雄主义 jítǐ yīngxióng zhǔyì
collective heroism
The proletarian thought consciousness of relying on collective strength, overcoming difficulties, and courageously struggling for the people and the revolutionary cause. It is the antithesis of individual heroism.

集体主义 jítǐ zhǔyì
collectivism
The proletarian thought consciousness, which takes the collective as the starting point for everything, and puts collective interests above individual interests. It is the basic spirit of socialism and communism.

集约化经营 jíyuēhuà jīngyíng
intensive management
Synonymous with 集约经营. (cf. 集约经营)

集约经营 jíyuē jīngyíng
intensive management
A method of agriculture that increases total production by increasing the productivity per unit of land area through applying a relatively large proportion of production resources and labor to the same area of land, and by applying advanced techniques, cultivating intensively and meticulously. It is the opposite of extensive management.

集装箱 jízhuāngxiāng
container

集装运输 jízhuāng yùnshū
container shipping

集资 jízī
to concentrate funds
To collect together funds, pulling together scattered money for use in economic construction and social services.

挤提 jǐtí
a rush of withdrawals from a bank
E.g. 挤提风波 *a wave of bank withdrawals*

挤牙膏 jǐyágāo
to squeeze out toothpaste
A metaphor for extracting information bit by bit through interrogation.

挤占 jǐzhàn
to jostle and occupy
To force one's own entry or to force out others and to occupy.
E.g. 挤占房屋 *to force one's way in and occupy housing* / 挤占发明权 *to vie for the claim on inventor's rights* / 挤占市场 *to squeeze in and corner a market* / 挤占学生的课余时间 *to squeeze in and occupy students' out-of-class time* / 非法挤占流动资金 *to take over circulating funds illegally*

技改 jì-gǎi
technology reform
Abbreviation for 技术改革.

技工 jìgōng
skilled worker; technician; mechanic

技术第一 jìshù dì-yī
skills first
A term that emerged under the influence of Leftist errors. The erroneous viewpoint that overlooks political thought, believing that professional skills can determine everything and are higher than everything.

技术服务专业户 jìshù fúwù zhuānyèhù
technical service speciality household
Agricultural households in China's rural villages that specialize in agricultural scientific and technical services, such as seeds, cultivation techniques, disease immunization and treatment of domestic animals, provision and repair of farm machinery, and transport of farm products.

技术经济学 jìshù jīngjìxué
technological economics
Also called 经济效果学 the study of economic utility. It is a science which studies the economic patterns of production, technological development, and the theories, methods, and applications of calculating, analyzing, and evaluating the effectiveness of society's various policies, plans, and measures regarding technology. It can be divided into macro and micro technological economics in accordance with the content. It can also be categorized by economic sectors.

技术密集型 jìshù mìjíxíng

technology-intensive (referring to a mode of production)

技术入股 jìshù rùgǔ
investment in technology

技术市场 jìshù shìchǎng
technology market
An arena where technologies are circulated and traded as commodities.

技术职称 jìshù zhíchēng
technical titles
Professional titles for workers with specialized technical skills. For example, among technical engineering personnel, there are technicians, assistant engineers, engineers, and senior engineers.

技校 jì-xiào
technical school
Abbreviation for 技工学校 or 技术学校.

季节工 jìjiégōng
seasonal workers
Temporary workers employed for certain seasons, such as temporary boiler operators in the winter.

寄销 jìxiāo
to sell on consignment
Also called 寄售 and 寄卖. To give or take articles on consignment for sale.

计划单列 jìhuà dānliè
to be listed as an independent item in the national plan

计划调拨 jìhuà diàobō
planned transfer
To transfer and allocate raw materials or products as stipulated in economic planning.

计划生育 jìhuà shēngyù
planned births
To adopt scientific methods in giving birth to children according to a plan.

计划外用工 jìhuàwài yònggōng
extrinsic employment; extrinsically employed personnel
Hiring and retention of workers by a state-managed unit which is beyond its personnel plan.

计经委 jì-jīng-wěi
planned economy committee
Abbreviation for 计划经济委员会.

计时工资 jìshí gōngzī
hourly wage

计算机 jìsuànjī
computer

计算机病毒 jìsuànjī bìngdú
computer virus

计算器 jìsuànqì
calculator

计委 Jì-Wěi
the State Planning Commission
Abbreviation for 国家计划委员会.

记工本 jìgōngběn
work record book
A book used by a production team to record the work points of its members.

记工员 jìgōngyuán
work point recorders
Personnel in rural collective production who have responsibility for recording the members' work attendance, work time, and amount of work.

记实小说 jìshí xiǎoshuō
record of reality fiction
A genre of fiction based on real people and events.

记协 Jì-Xié
Journalists' Association
Abbreviation for 新闻工作者协会.

继往开来 jìwǎng kāilái
to continue the past and open up the

future

To continue the work of predecessors and to open up paths for the future.

继续教育 jìxù jiàoyù
continuing education

纪检 jì-jiǎn
to inspect discipline
E.g. 纪检部门 *the department for inspecting discipline*/ 纪检工作 *inspecting discipline*

纪念币 jìniànbì
commemorative coins

纪念封 jìniànfēng
commemorative envelopes (issued by the postal service)

纪念邮票 jìniàn yóupiào
commemorative stamps

纪委 jì-wěi
discipline committees
Abbreviation for 纪律检查委员会 the various levels of commissions for inspecting discipline in the Chinese Communist Party.

jia

夹缝 jiāfèng
crevice
Metaphor for a tight spot or difficult circumstances
E.g. 在夹缝中生活 *to live in straightened circumstances* / 跳出夹缝，摆脱困境 *to escape from a tight spot and to cast off straightened circumstances*.

夹生饭 jiāshēngfàn
half-cooked rice
Rice which has not been thoroughly cooked. A metaphor for a lack of thoroughness in performing a task, and falling short of expectations.

佳绩 jiājī
excellent performance
E.g. 选手要发挥高超技术水平，争取佳绩。*The contestant must use his best techniques, so as to achieve an excellent performance.*

家电 jiā-diàn
electrical home appliances
Abbreviation for 家用电器.

家访 jiāfǎng
home visit
To visit someone's home as a part of one's work, such as a teacher visiting a student's home, to report on the student's in-school performance, and to understand the student's home situation.

家肥 jiāféi
domestic fertilizer
Fertilizer collected and made by farm families, such as barnyard manure and compost formed by mixing human and animal excrement, corral soil, and grass.

家教 jiājiào
home education
The education of children by parents; the term also refers to tutors (tutoring is usually done in the student's home).

家居 jiājū
residence; the term also refers to family life

家史 jiāshǐ
family history

家属工厂 jiāshǔ gōngchǎng
family dependents' factory
A factory managed by a certain unit, and employs only the family dependents of that unit's employees.

家属宿舍 jiāshǔ sùshè

family dependents' dormitory

A dormitory provided by military units or enterprise and institutional units specifically for the soldiers or employees, and their family members.

家属委员会 jiāshǔ wěiyuánhuì
family dependents' committee

A self-governing organization of a mass character formed by a work unit's employees' families. It assists the concerned sectors in developing their work in civil administration, public order, employment, sanitation, everyday life services, etc.

家庭病床 jiātíng bìngchuáng
home sickbeds

Sickbeds set up by hospitals in the homes of the patients. For patients who cannot stay in hospitals (or cannot be accommodated because of a shortage of sickbeds, or cannot conveniently stay in hospitals), hospitals will send out medical personnel to the patients' homes to administer systematic treatment.

家庭出身 jiātíng chūshēn
family background

The class status of the family to which one is born. In China, this term refers generally to the social status of one's family before one has attained economic independence.

家庭副业 jiātíng fùyè
domestic sideline

The economic activities carried out at home by peasants aside from their main production responsibilities, such as cultivating their private plots, working their private hills, domestic livestock-raising, weaving and knitting, embroidery, collecting edible or medicinal plants, fishing and hunting, etc.

家庭妇女 jiātíng fùnǚ
housewife

Women who do only domestic work and do not have employment in society.

家庭工业 jiātíng gōngyè
household industry

Small-scale industrial production conducted with a family as the unit. In general, this is linked with a collective enterprise whereby the collective enterprise distributes the processing of certain components to families.

家庭经济 jiātíng jīngjì
family economies

The individual ownership economic activities conducted with the family as the unit. They supplement China's socialist public ownership system. They are very small proportion of all the economic activities, and serve only an auxiliary function.

家庭劳动服务介绍所 jiātíng láodòng fúwù jièshàosuǒ
domestic work service agency

A work service organization that takes families as its clientele. It is responsible for training, introducing, and supervising service personnel to carry out long-term or short-term domestic work.

家庭联产承包责任制 jiātíng liánchǎn chéngbāo zérènzhì
household joint production contract responsibility system

The full name of the rural contract system promulgated in 1978 whereby families or collective units agree to produce a certain amount of commodities for the state, retaining the surplus for their own use, in exchange for allotments of land

and other resources.

家庭学 jiātíngxué
family studies

A branch of social science that studies family structures, functions, origins, evolution and developments.

家庭影院 jiātíng yǐngyuàn
home theater

Home audio and video systems with high quality sound effects and screen pictures.

家委会 jiā-wěi-huì
family dependents' committee

Abbreviation for 家属委员会.

家长制 jiāzhǎngzhì
patriarchal system

The family organization system in a slave society and feudal society. The male who is the head of household has all the economic power and is in the position to allocate within the family, and all other members obey him absolutely. The term is also a metaphor for a collective group where the leader has sole power and all the members obey him absolutely.

家装 jiā-zhuāng
home decoration

E.g. 家装公司 *home decoration company* / 家装咨询洽谈活动 *home decoration consulting activities*

加班 jiābān
to work overtime

Extra work time or shift beyond the regular work time.

加班费 jiābānfèi
overtime pay

Remuneration paid to overtime workers.

加班加点 jiābān jiādiǎn
to work overtime

E.g. 他经常加班加点修车出车。*He often works overtime repairing vehicles and making runs.*

加餐 jiācān
to add a snack

In certain urban elementary schools, students are given a simple snack during a recess around 10 a.m.

E.g. 课间加餐关系到孩子的成长。*A snack in between classes has an impact on the growth of children.*

加工订货 jiāgōng dìnghuò
processing and ordering goods

Generally, the term means to perform various processes with raw materials or semi-finished products according to certain specifications and to pre-order commodities. Specifically, the term refers to the measures adopted by the state in the 1950s to implement socialist reforms in private enterprises. That is, the state signed processing contracts with private enterprises, providing them with raw materials and semi-finished products and paid them a processing fee to perform processing tasks. Or the state signed contracts with private enterprises to pre-order commodities and to pay certain prices (when necessary, a portion of the payment was paid in advance as a deposit, or a portion of the raw materials was rationed out). Hence, a limit was placed on capitalist exploitation, and private enterprises began to be brought into the orbit of national planning.

加盟 jiāméng
to join (an organization or collective) and form an alliance; now usually refers to joining an athletic team in a competition

加密 jiāmì
set up a secret number (code)
E.g. 存款加密比较安全。 *It's rather safe to have a secret number for a saving card.*

加塞儿 jiāsāir
to butt into a line; to jump the queue
To disregard order and cunningly get into a line that has already been formed.

加速器 jiāsùqì
accelerator

加温 jiāwēn
to heat up
Metaphor for taking measures to generate development or transformation in something.
E.g. 为农业加温 *to generate developments in agriculture*

夹克 jiákè
jacket

贾桂思想 Jiǎ Guì sīxiǎng
Jia Gui mentality
Slave mentality. Jia Gui is a character in Peking opera 法门寺; he was a personal slave of the eunuch Liu Jin. He was content to be ordered around by others, and abetted a bad person in doing evil.

甲肝 jiǎ–gān
hepatitis A
Abbreviation for 甲型病毒性肝炎.

甲型肝炎 jiǎxíng gānyán
hepatitis A

假大空 jiǎ–dà–kōng
false, big, and empty
To talk in a hyperbolic and empty way.

假劣 jiǎ–liè
(of commodities) fake or low-quality

假冒 jiǎmào
to fake (something real or higher-grade)
E.g. 假冒商品 *fake commodities* / 假冒行为 *deceptive behavior*

假性近视 jiǎxìng jìnshì
pseudo near-sightedness

假条 jiǎtiáo
absence slips
Slips requesting leave. Slips of paper submitted by employees, cadres, or students to the leadership requesting leave. Reasons and duration are stated on the slips.
E.g. 病假条 *sick leave slip* / 事假条 *personal business leave slip*

价差 jiàchā
price differential

价改 jiàgǎi
price reform
E.g. 油粮价改 *price reform on oil and grains*

价格补贴 jiàgé bǔtiē
subsidized price
Financial subsidy provided by the state in cases where a policy decision has led to a sale price lower than that of the purchase price, or to a loss. For example, subsidized pricing is carried out for agricultural products that are intimately related to the people's livelihood.

价位 jiàwèi
standard price; level of a price

价值工程 jiàzhí gōngchéng
value engineering
Value analysis. To seek the lowest expenditure in obtaining the highest value through analysis of a product's material quality, construction, craftsmanship, etc.

架构 jiàgòu
frame structure
E.g. 理论架构 *theoretical framework* / 和平架构 *a framework for peace*

架空 jiàkōng
to prop up in mid-air
To appear to support but secretly undermine and cause loss of actual power.

驾校 jià-xiào
driving school
Abbreviation for 驾驶学校.

驾照 jià-zhào
driving license
Abbreviation for 驾驶执照.

jian

监测 jiāncè
observe and measure
E.g. 环境监测 *observation and surveying of the environment* / 地震监测 *earthquake observation and measurement* / 自动监测仪器 *automatic monitor*

监督电话 jiāndū diànhuà
supervision telephones
Phone lines set up for people to report on the work performance of certain service units to their superiors (the phone numbers are usually publicized in newspapers and the various relevant units).

监管 jiānguǎn
to supervise and control (prisoners or commodities)
E.g. 监管单位 *parole unit* / 监管改造 *parole reform*

监控 jiānkòng
supervise and control
Contraction of 监视 supervise and 控制 control.

监理 jiānlǐ
to supervise and control
E.g. 交通监理人员 *traffic supervisory and control personnel* / 公路交通监理站 *highway traffic control station*

监审 jiānshěn
to supervise and investigate
E.g. 对生活必需品的价格要进行监审。*We must carry out supervision and investigation of the prices of life's daily necessities.*

监事 jiānshì
personnel with supervisory responsibilities in banks and monetary organs

监听 jiāntīng
using radio facilities to monitor (to listen in on) others' conversations or radio signals
E.g. 监听站 *radio monitoring station* / 监听敌人的情况 *to monitor the enemy's situation via radio*

坚挺 jiāntǐng
robust
Solid and strong, often used in reference to a currency that is stable and rising on the international exchange.
E.g. 美元坚挺。*The American dollar is robust.*

尖刀班 jiāndāobān
dagger squad
A metaphor for the squad that first invades enemy territory in a battle.

尖端 jiānduān
peak; acme
A metaphor for the highest level (scientific, technological, etc.)
E.g. 尖端技术 *top-notch skill* / 尖端产品 *top-notch product* / 尖端工业 *most advanced industry*

尖端科学 jiānduān kēxué

most advanced science

New branches of science at the forefront of scientific development, that synthesize various technologies, and have important significance and influence. Examples are microelectronics, optical communications, hereditary engineering, developing new materials, energy, and space science.

尖子 jiānzi

cream of the crop

Originally this term meant the sharp tip of an object. It is now a metaphor for a person especially outstanding in some respect.

E.g. 技术尖子 *the one with the highest skills* / 业务尖子 *professionally the best one*

尖子班 jiānzibān

advanced class

A class consisting of students with superior achievements. The pace is faster and the standards are higher.

检测 jiāncè

to examine and determine

E.g. 检测试验 *to inspect the experiment* / 检测中心 *inspection center* / 检测手段 *methods of inspection* / 检测技术 *techniques of inspection* / 检测线 *inspection line*

检察院 jiǎncháyuàn

procuratorate

The state organization which has responsibility for investigating and approving arrests, investigating and determining suits, and attending court in support of public prosecutions.

检举箱 jiǎnjǔxiāng

accusation letter box

A box set up by state organizations or units for receiving letters from people exposing criminal acts. The contents are opened and read at fixed intervals by designated persons.

检索 jiǎnsuǒ

to search

To examine and search for (data, publications, etc.) manually or with automated equipment.

检修 jiǎnxiū

to examine and repair

To examine and repair (machinery, equipment, housing, etc.)

检疫 jiǎnyì

quarantine

To investigate for diseases; a preventive measure to guard against the spread of contagious human, animal, and plant diseases from outside to a local area. For example, to examine and disinfect persons and goods entering from areas with contagious diseases, or to adopt quarantine measures, etc.

简报 jiǎnbào

brief report

E.g. 新闻简报 *news briefing* / 工作简报 *brief work report* / 会议简报 *brief report of a meeting*

简并 jiǎnbìng

to simplify and merge

E.g. 简并企业所得税 *to simplify and merge income tax on businesses*

简化汉字 jiǎnhuà hànzì

simplified characters

1) To simplify the strokes of characters such as simplifying "禮" to "礼", and "動" to "动"; meanwhile to reduce the number of characters. 2) Characters that have undergone the simplifying process, such as "礼" and "动".

简介 jiǎnjiè
brief introduction

简历 jiǎnlì
concise biography; curriculum vitae

简明新闻 jiǎnmíng xīnwén
concise and clear news; news in brief

简写 jiǎnxiě
simplified writing

The simplified way of writing characters. An example is "刘", the simplified way of writing "劉".

简易房 jiǎnyìfáng
simple spartan housing

简政放权 jiǎnzhèng fàngquán
decentralize authority

精简机构下放权力。指中国经济体制改革中要改变过去机构臃肿，权力集中，统的过死的经济管理体制，把财权、人权、经营自主权等下放给基层生产单位，充分发挥企业的主观能动性，把企业搞活。

To streamline organizations and transfer power to lower levels. In the post-Mao era, China's economic management system is being reformed to do away with bureaucratic overstaffing, excessive centralization of power, and inflexible uniformity. Authority over funds, personnel, and management autonomy has been transferred to grass-roots production units, so that enterprises will develop their own initiatives and dynamics, and will thus be enlivened.

剪刀差 jiǎndāochā
scissors differential

The differential between the costs of industrial products and those of agricultural products when the former is much higher than the latter. On statistical diagrams, the differential often forms the shape of opened scissors, hence the term "scissors differential".

减肥 jiǎnféi
to reduce weight

减幅 jiǎnfú
scope of reduction

E.g. 机构设置由原来的 291 个精简为 214 个，减幅达 25.5%。 *The facilities of the organization are being reduced from 291 to 214, so the scope of reduction is 25.5%.*

减负 jiǎnfù
to lighten the burden

E.g. 减负的根本目的是要增加农民收入。 *The real purpose of lightening the burden is to increase farmers' income.*

减缓 jiǎnhuǎn
reduce and decelerate

To reduce the quantity or degree, and to delay the implementation date.

减亏 jiǎnkuī
to reduce loss

减税 jiǎnshuì
tax reduction

减员 jiǎnyuán
personnel reduction

A reduction in the established personnel of a group for a reason.

减灾 jiǎnzāi
to reduce natural disasters

鉴证 jiànzhèng
to inspect and verify such documents as deeds and contracts

E.g. 劳动合同鉴证 *to inspect and verify labor contracts*

见缝插针 jiànfèng chāzhēn
to insert a needle wherever a crevice is seen

A metaphor for making maximum use of space and time.

见马克思 jiàn Mǎkèsī
to see Marx
A jocular way of referring to the death.

见习工程师 jiànxí gōngchéngshī
probational engineer

件次 jiàncì
total number of items from successive events
A compound measure expressing the total number from several successive events. For example, if there were two fashion shows, with two hundred garments exhibited in the first and three hundred in the second, the total is 五百件次 five hundred items.

毽球 jiànqiú
shuttlecock ball
A sport similar to volleyball and badminton in which the opponents kick a ball similar to a shuttlecock; the ball used in this sport.

健美 jiànměi
healthful beauty
1) To be physically strong and beautiful.
E.g. 体操有健美作用。 Gymnastics can promote healthful beauty.
2) The style of music or dance being healthy and esthetically pleasing.
E.g. 舞蹈的风格健美明快。 The style of dance is beautiful and sprightly.

健美操 jiànměicāo
body-building exercises
Exercises to develop muscle tone and a well-proportioned physique.

健身 jiànshēn
body-building
E.g. 健身运动 body-building exercise / 健身器材 body-building equipment / 健身营养食品 nutritional food for body-building

健身球 jiànshēnqiú
health ball
A small ball that one holds and revolves around in the palm of the hand. The movement of the finger joints enhances good health by promoting blood circulation and regulation of the nerves. It is used by elderly people.

溅落 jiànluò
splash down
A heavy object falling into a body of water. Specifically, it refers to an object such as a man-made satellite or spaceship returning to earth and falling into the ocean.

建材 jiàncái
construction materials

建材工业 jiàncái gōngyè
building material industries
All industries that produce building materials, including concrete, plate glass, bricks, tiles, bathroom tiles, non-metallic building materials (such as asbestos and plaster), new lightweight materials, concrete components, etc.

建党学说 jiàndǎng xuéshuō
theory of founding a party

建构 jiàngòu
to establish and form

建行 jiàn–háng
the Construction Bank
Abbreviation for 建设银行.

建军节 jiànjūnjié
Army Day
A day for commemorating the founding of the army. It refers specifically to the birth of the Chinese People's Liberation

Army on August 1, 1927, hence it is also called "August First Army Day".

建设公债 jiànshè gōngzhài
public bonds for construction
"National Economic Construction Bonds" issued in China in the 1950. They were issued in the mass fund-raising for opening the economic developments of the first five-year plan, which followed the completion of tasks of the economic recovery period.

建设周期 jiànshè zhōuqī
construction cycle
The entire period from the beginning of a construction project to its completion (when it is put to use).

建委 jiàn-wěi
abbreviation for 建设委员会 **the Construction Committee**

建销 jiànxiāo
to construct and sell
E.g. 建销豪华住宅 *to construct and sell luxurious residential housing*

jiang

将军肚 jiāngjūndù
general's paunch
A jocular way of referring to a fat belly.

奖金挂帅 jiǎngjīn guàshuài
placing a premium on bonuses
The concept and method of using mainly bonuses to motivate people in production and work. It is no longer used.

奖励工资 jiǎnglì gōngzī
reward wages
A form of payment that combines basic wages with bonuses. On top of the basic wages for the respective ranks, certain bonuses are paid in accordance to production and work performance (such as completing targets, economizing, etc.). There are two forms: time reward wages and piece work reward wages.

奖牌 jiǎngpái
award plaque
A commemorative plaque awarded to a prizewinner or an individual or group who have made outstanding contributions. There are three types of plaques: gold, silver, and bronze.

奖旗 jiǎngqí
award banners

奖勤罚懒 jiǎngqín fálǎn
reward the diligent and punish the lazy
To reward those who work diligently and industriously, and punish those who are lazy and shirk work.

奖售 jiǎngshòu
a sale in which the buyer can receive a discount or win something

奖学金 jiǎngxuéjīn
monetary academic prize; scholarship

奖优罚劣 jiǎngyōu fáliè
to reward the superior ones and to penalize the inferior ones

讲排场 jiǎng páichǎng
to be ostentatious
Pertaining to formality or through extravagance at an occasion.

讲评 jiǎngpíng
narration and critique
E.g. 作文讲评 *description and critique of an essay* / 考试讲评 *description and critique of an exam* / 比赛讲评 *narration and critique of a competition*

讲师团 jiǎngshītuán

lecture team

Specifically, in recent years, the Central Committee of the Communist Party of China has fostered the improvement of the educational level of primary and middle schools of each province by commissioning staff members from departments under the Party Central Committee to teach or train teachers in the various localities. Namely, 中央讲师团 the Lecture Team of the Party Central Committee.

讲用 jiǎngyòng
to relate one's practical experience in applying one's learning or theories

讲用会 jiǎngyònghuì
meeting for discussing application

A meeting for individuals or groups to talk about their experiences and thoughts derived from the process of learning and applying theory to practice. This was popular in the early 1950s when Lin Biao put out the so-called 活学活用 live learning, live usage.

讲桌 jiǎngzhuō
lectern

A desk in a classroom or meeting hall used by the teacher or speaker.

降幅 jiàngfú
degree of reduction

降解 jiàngjiě
(plastics) to bio-degrade

E.g. 降解塑料 bio-degradable plastic

降温 jiàngwēn
temperature reduction; reduction of enthusiasm or momentum

E.g. 大风降温 *drop in temperature due to great winds* / 基本建设应该降温。 *There should be a cooling-off in basic construction.*

降下帷幕 jiàngxià wéimù
to lower the curtain

To conclude a conference, an exhibition, or an activity (also called 落下帷幕).

jiao

焦裕禄精神 Jiāo Yùlù jīngshén
the spirit of Jiao Yulu

Jiao Yulu (August 1922 to May 1954) was a Party secretary of Lankao County in Henan Province. He disregarded his cancer, led cadres and the masses to struggle relentlessly against natural adversities such as floods, wind, sand, and salinization; through three years of hard struggle, they transformed the backward state of Lankao County. His proletarian revolutionary spirit of not seeking fame and fortune, not fearing difficulty or sacrifice, and serving the people with all his heart and mind has come to be called the spirit of Jiao Yulu.

胶球 jiāoqiú
(physics) colloidal ball

A particle formed by the coalescing of colloids.

胶子 jiāozǐ
colloid

交白卷 jiāo báijuàn
to hand in a blank exam (unable to answer any item on an exam)

A metaphor for not completing a project according to specifications.

交班 jiāobān
to change shift

To transfer work to the following shift.

交叉科学 jiāochā kēxué

intersecting sciences

Newly-arisen branches of learning that intersect the natural and social sciences.

交代历史 jiāodài lìshǐ

to give an account of one's history

The narration of a person's history and problems given by an individual under investigation.

交待问题 jiāodài wèntí

to give an account of the problem

An accounting, given by an individual under investigation to the relevant unit or organization, of the errors or crimes he has committed.

交待政策 jiāodài zhèngcè

to lay out the policy

To inform an individual under investigation of the Party and state's policy, in order to dispel his misgivings, so that he can explain his own problems or crimes, and seek magnanimous treatment.

交电 jiāodiàn

communications and electrical equipment

E.g. 北京交电公司 *Beijing Municipal Communications and Electrical Equipment Company* / 交电市场 *the communications and electrical equipment market*

交工 jiāogōng

to hand over a completed project

A construction unit handing over a completed construction project to the unit that commissioned the construction.

交际舞 jiāojìwǔ

social dancing

交警 jiāo-jǐng

traffic police

Abbreviation for 交通警察.

交流学者 jiāoliú xuézhě

exchange scholars

交售 jiāoshòu

to sell (to the state)

A production unit selling products to the state in accordance with the quota assigned by the state.

E.g. 交售任务 *the duty of sale*

交心 jiāoxīn

to reveal what's in one's heart

To speak without reservation of the thoughts in the depth of one's heart.

E.g. 向党交心 *to tell the Party what's in one's heart* / 相互交心 *to share with each other thoughts from the heart*

交学费 jiāoxuéfèi

to pay for tuition

A metaphor for making sacrifices or paying a price for something.

交谊舞 jiāoyìwǔ

friendship dance

Social dancing, by men and women in pairs.

跤坛 jiāotán

wrestling circles

郊县 jiāoxiàn

suburban counties that fall under the jurisdiction of the municipality

浇灌 jiāoguàn

irrigation

1) To water, to irrigate.

E.g. 浇灌面积 *irrigated acreage*

2) Pour a fluid into a mould.

E.g. 浇灌混凝土 *to pour concrete*

浇注 jiāozhù

to pour into a mould

角刺人物 jiǎocì rénwù

prickly characters

Persons who have horns on their heads and thorns on their bodies, a metaphor for people who make difficulties for others. The term is used specifically in reference to those who, during the Cultural Revolution, revolted, seized power and committed all kinds of outrages.

绞肉机 jiǎoròujī

meat grinder

A kitchen machine that uses grinding blades to grind meat.

教参 jiào – cān

reference material used in teaching

E.g. 教参销售量最大。 *The sales volume of reference material for teaching is the largest.*

教代会 jiào – dài – huì

school personnel representative assembly

An assembly of representatives of the teachers and other school staff members. The assembly is a body formed for the democratic management of the school.

教改 jiào – gǎi

educational reform

Reform of the education system or teaching methods.

教改组 jiào – gǎi – zǔ

educational reform groups

Departments, set up in schools during the Cultural Revolution, which were responsible for teaching and its reform.

教工 jiào – gōng

teachers and staff

Teachers and other employees of a school.

E.g. 教工篮球队 *teachers and staff basketball team*

教龄 jiàolíng

years of service as a teacher

E.g. 教龄津贴 *subsidy based on years of service as teacher* / 教龄补贴 *supplement based on years of service as teacher* / 这里的教师都有十年以上的教龄。 *The teachers here have all been in service for more than ten years.*

教师节 jiàoshījié

Teachers' Day

September 10, the day designated to celebrate teachers. This day was reinstituted in 1985.

教条主义 jiàotiáo zhǔyì

doctrinairism

A manifestation of subjectivism, whereby a person separates theory from reality, does not analyze the transformation and development of matters, does not study the special characteristics of contradictions in matters and treats Marxism as a metaphysical viewpoint, taking it to be an ossified dogma and applying it mechanically to everything.

教委 jiào – wěi

education commission

Abbreviation for 国家教育委员会 the State Education Commission and 教育委员会 the education commissions at the various local levels.

教务处 jiàowùchù

dean's office

A department in institutions of higher learning responsible for academic affairs.

教务长 jiàowùzhǎng

dean of studies

An administrative leader, directly under the leadership of the president of an institution of higher learning, who is responsible for overall supervision of the academic matters of the entire school.

教学大纲 jiàoxué dàgāng
syllabus

教学医院 jiàoxué yīyuàn
teaching hospital

A hospital attached to a medical school which serves teaching and practical training needs.

教研室 jiàoyánshì
teaching and research divisions

Teaching and scientific research divisions set up in various departments of institutions of higher learning according to specialties or curricula. Their main functions are to lead and organize teaching and scientific research work, academic activities, teachers' advanced studies, and graduate students' work. They are also responsible for the laboratories for the work of these two constituents and the building and management of reference collections, etc. Also organizations for the study of teaching set up by the education bureau of government departments.

教研组 jiàoyánzǔ
teaching and research group

Teaching research units set up according to the various curricula. Their main functions are to research teaching materials and teaching methods, and to upgrade the level of teaching.

教育附加费 jiàoyù fùjiāfèi
educational expense subsidy

Funds from sources other than the government which contribute toward educational enterprises.

教育面 jiàoyùmiàn
sector to be educated

In the proletarian struggle and political activities, the sector of the population to win over, to unite, and to educate.

E.g. 扩大教育面，缩小打击面。
Expand the sector to be educated, reduce the targets of attack.

教职工 jiào-zhí-gōng
faculty, staff, and workers (at a school)

教职员工 jiàozhíyuángōng
teachers, staff, and workers

The cover term for the entire work force of a school, including teachers, staff, and workmen.

叫花子主义 jiàohuāzi zhǔyì
beggarism

The philosophy of relying on charity to live.

叫卖语言 jiàomài yǔyán
sales pitch

叫响 jiàoxiǎng
loudly lauded

To receive commendation for an outstanding performance.

jie

揭丑 jiēchǒu
to expose errors or the dark side of things

E.g. 主动揭丑不护短 *to voluntarily reveal errors and not shield shortcomings.*

揭盖子 jiē gàizi

to uncover

To remove from a device the cover which conceals a function. A metaphor for removing all obstacles, so that hidden things are exposed.

揭老底 jiēlǎodǐ

to expose the ins and outs of someone or something

揭秘 jiēmì

to reveal the secrets

E.g. 人们最爱看的节目是魔术揭秘。*The program people like to watch most is the one in which the secrets of magic are revealed.*

揭牌 jiēpái

to lift the cloth cover to reveal a sign (for a business or organization)

Also a metaphor for the official opening of a certain enterprise.

E.g. 金融系统首家"青年示范行'揭牌'"。*The first Youth Demonstration Bank of the financial conglomerate officially opened for business.*

揭批 jiēpī

to expose and criticize

E.g. 揭批四人帮 *to expose and criticize the Gang of Four*

接班人 jiēbānrén

successors

People who take over the work of the previous shift. Young people or successors of the revolutionary cause taking over from the older generation.

接待日 jiēdàirì

days set aside by certain cadres to receive people who come to see them

接访 jiēfǎng

to receive and visit the people

E.g. 接访群众 *to receive visits from the masses*

接轨 jiēguǐ

to connect the tracks

Originally, to connect two sections of railroad. Now the term is used mostly as a metaphor for connecting two things of similar nature.

E.g. 把我们的管理、生产、检验与国际接轨。*We should connect our management, production, and inspection to international standards.*

街道办事处 jiēdào bànshìchù

street agencies

Administrative bodies under the grass-roots political authority in China's cities which are responsible for the residents' affairs.

街道服务站 jiēdào fúwùzhàn

street service stations

Organizations under the street agencies which provide services for the residents' everyday life. They wash, sew, and mend clothing, distribute milk, transmit telephone calls, etc.

街道工厂 jiēdào gōngchǎng

street factories

街道企业 jiēdào qǐyè

street-enterprises

街景 jiējǐng

street scene

E.g. 丰富街景 *to enrich the street scene* / 街景规划 *a plan for the street scene*

阶级报复 jiējí bàofù

class revenge

The deliberate sabotage, committed out of class hatred by groups or individuals of the overturned exploitative class, of the people's property, or of revolutionary or construction tasks.

阶级成分 jiējí chéngfèn

class status

The class position of an individual or family in society. Class status is determined by the nature of one's primary means of livelihood in a certain period of time. There is a difference between a person's own status (the individual's status) and his family's status (based on one's family background).

阶级敌人 jiējí dírén

class enemy

阶级斗争熄灭论 jiējí dòuzhēng xīmièlùn

the theory that class struggle will die out

The view that class struggle will not resurface in a socialist society. During the Cultural Revolution, Liu Shaoqi was accused of holding this view, which was listed as one of the "six black doctrines". (cf. 黑六论)

阶级队伍 jiējí duìwù

class rank and file

Revolutionary ranks the people organized to engage in revolutionary struggle and national construction.

阶级分化 jiējí fēnhuà

class polarization

The phenomenon whereby, under certain socio-economic and political conditions, elements from certain classes or strata shift into other classes or strata due to changes in their positions. Transformations in the middle class or stratum tend to be the most striking. For example, as a result of the development of capitalism, a small proportion of the petty bourgeoisie were elevated to the bourgeoisie, while the great majority gradually became poor and destitute, and joined the ranks of the proletarian class.

阶级分析 jiējí fēnxì

class analysis

A basic method of Marxism-Leninism of using class and class struggle as a means of observing and studying the social phenomena of a class society.

阶级观点 jiējí guāndiǎn

class viewpoint

The Marxist-Leninist viewpoint concerning class and class struggle. It is also the basic viewpoint and attitude that each class has.

阶级教育 jiējí jiàoyù

class education

Propaganda and education about Marxist theories concerning class struggle.

阶级觉悟 jiējí juéwù

class consciousness

Also called 政治觉悟 political consciousness. The term is usually used to mean the proletarian class' knowledge of its position, responsibilities, basic interests and historical mission. Class consciousness of the proletarian class is not born of itself, but is gradually cultivated under the leadership and education of the proletarian political party, through the practice of struggle, and the study of Marxism as related to practical reality.

阶级苦 jiējíkǔ

class bitterness

The bitterness of laboring and peasant masses under the oppressive exploitative system.

阶级烙印 jiējí làoyìn

iron brand of a class

The inherited marks of a class which are

reflected in the people's ideological consciousness, political attitudes, and life style.

阶级立场 jiējí lìchǎng
class standpoint

Abbreviated as 立场 standpoint. It is the basic attitudes of a member of a certain class, which reflect the interests and requirements of that class. Different class standpoints determine people's basic viewpoints, ways of thinking, political attitudes, and class feelings. Discerning to which class interests, a person's thoughts, views, and actions correspond is the main means of determining his class standpoint.

阶级路线 jiējí lùxiàn
class line

The basic line followed by the proletarian political party, based on the nature and mission of the revolution, in analyzing the economic positions of society's various classes and their attitudes toward the revolution, distinguishing the relationships among enemies, friends, and ourselves, thereby determining on whom to rely, with whom to form an alliance, and whom to attack. Because each historical period has different revolutionary missions, the content of class line likewise varies.

阶级矛盾 jiējí máodùn
class contradictions

Contradictions among the different socio-economic classes arising out of their different interests and requirements. The term refers primarily to the contradictions between the exploitative class and the laboring class due to their basic conflict of interests.

阶级调和论 jiējí tiáohélùn
theory of class conciliation

阶级性 jiējíxìng
class character

The manifestation of class nature, which is determined by the socio-economic position and material life conditions of each class. In class societies, due to the fact that people have different long-term class statuses, they develop their own life styles, interests and requirements, psychology, ideology, habits, viewpoints, styles, etc., thus forming different class natures. The nation, political parties, politics, law, philosophy, literature, art, etc., are all affected by class nature.

阶级兄弟 jiējí xiōngdì
class brothers

People from the same class ranks.

阶级异己分子 jiējí yìjǐ fènzǐ
alien-class elements

People of an enemy class who have sneaked into revolutionary ranks but who persist in holding a reactionary standpoint.

阶级阵线 jiējí zhènxiàn
class alignment

A metaphor for the camps formed by antagonistic classes in their struggle.

截留 jiéliú
to retain a cut

To take a cut from the profits or funds, that should be submitted to higher-ups, and retain it for one's own use.

截流 jiéliú
to stop the flow

To cut off the flow of water.

截瘫病人 jiétān bìngrén
paraplegics

劫机 jiéjī
to hijack an airplane
E.g. 劫机事件 *hijacking incident* / 劫机分子 *hijacking elements* / 劫机者 *hijacker*

节电 jiédiàn
to conserve electricity
E.g. 节电量 *amount of electricity conserved*

节假日 jié-jiàrì
holidays and vacations

节流 jiéliú
to reduce the flow
To economize on the flow of water. A metaphor for economizing on expenditure.

节煤 jiéméi
to conserve coal

节能 jiénéng
to save energy
To economize on energy resources.

节能灶 jiénéngzào
energy-saving stove
A stove that is economical on fuel. It is contrasted with stoves that burn a large amount of coal or firewood.

节水 jiéshuǐ
to conserve water

节育 jiéyù
birth control
E.g. 节育技术 *techniques of contraception* / 节育手术 *sterilization*

节育环 jiéyùhuán
IUD (a birth control device)

节支 jiézhī
economize on expenditure
Contraction of 节省开支 *economize on expenditure*.

节资 jiézī
to conserve capital
E.g. 节资3万元 *to have saved 30,000 yuan in capital*

结党营私 jiédǎng yíngsī
to form cliques for private gain
To form cliques or small groups in order to seek private gain.

结对子 jiéduìzi
to form a collaborative relationship
E.g. 学校和工厂结对子，开展共建活动。 *The school and the factory are collaborating in developing joint activities.*

结构工资制 jiégòu gōngzīzhì
composite wage system
指由不同成分构成工资整体的制度。一般由固定工资和变动工资两大部分组成。固定工资又分为基本生活工资（由工龄长短体现）和劳动技能工资；变动工资又可分为超额劳动工资（由劳动效果决定）和职能岗位工资。

A system whereby the total wages are composed of various components. In general, they consist of two major parts: a fixed wage and a variable wage. A fixed wage is in turn divided into a basic living wage (reflecting the length of employment) and a labor skill wage. The variable wage can be divided into an above-quota labor wage (determined by labor output) and function post wage.

结构主义语言学 jiégòu zhǔyì yǔyánxué
structural linguistics
Also called 结构语言学 structural linguistics.

结汇 jiéhuì
to settle a foreign exchange account

An enterprise or individual buying or selling foreign exchange at a bank according to the foreign exchange rate.

结扎手术 jiézhā shǒushù
ligation operation

An operation to block a certain passage by tying it with a special suture. The term refers specifically to birth control operations such as of vasectomy or tuboligation.

结转 jiézhuǎn
to settle and transfer an account

To settle accounts at fixed times, and on the basis of receiving or paying, to transfer and record the account in another account book.

解冻 jiědòng
to thaw (literal and figurative)

解读 jiědú
to decode

Also called 破译 to break through and interpret.

解放干部 jiěfàng gànbù
liberated cadres

指"文化大革命"中让被打倒或离开工作岗位"靠边站"的干部重新出来工作。Cadres who were overthrown, or left their posts to "stand aside" during the Cultural Revolution and who later returned to work.

解放军 jiěfàngjūn
liberation army

An army organized to liberate the masses of people. It refers specifically to the Chinese People's Liberation Army.

解放区 jiěfàngqū
liberated areas

Areas where the reactionary government had been overthrown and people's political authority had been established. The term refers specifically to the areas liberated, during China's War of Resistance Against Japan and places liberated in the war between the army of the Chinese Communist Party and the puppet nationalist government.

解放思想 jiěfàng sīxiǎng
liberate ideology

This term refers specifically to the policy, resolved at the Third Plenum of the Eleventh Party Central Committee, of liberating ideology. It demanded that people be liberated from the extreme leftist line of the Cultural Revolution and from modern superstition, that they return to the scientific track of Marxism-Leninism and Mao's thoughts. The term refers generally to breaking the bondage of force of habit and subjectivism, studying new conditions, and solving new problems.

解放战争 jiěfàng zhànzhēng
liberation war

War conducted by an oppressed people and class in striving for independence, freedom, and liberation. The term refers specifically to China's third internal revolutionary war (1945-1949).

解禁 jiějìn
to lift a ban

E.g. 被封存的奶粉及乳制品将有条件解禁。*The ban on milk powder and dairy products, which have been sealed up for safekeeping, will be lifted.*

解教 jiě–jiào
to release from education through labor

Abbreviation for 解除劳动教养. A form of re-education for young offenders.

E.g. 解教人员 personnel that have been released from labor reform / 争取早日解教 to strive for an early release from labor reform

解困 jiěkùn
to resolve problems
E.g. 制定解困办法 to formulate a method of resolving problems

解困房 jiěkùnfáng
problem solving houses
Houses built by the local governments to solve the special housing problems of local citizens.

解剖麻雀 jiěpōu máquè
dissecting a sparrow
A metaphor for analyzing a typical case. There is a Chinese saying "The sparrow may be small, but it has all the five vital organs". The sparrow is small, so it is convenient; it has all the five organs, so it is representative and typical. "Dissecting a sparrow" means to investigate a typical case, to find a common pattern from individual cases, in order to provide guidance for the overall work.

解释学 jiěshìxué
deconstructionism
A school of literary analysis that focuses on interpretation of the text itself.

解危 jiěwēi
to solve the problem of unsafe housing
E.g. 加快住房解危步伐 to step up the pace of solving the problem of unsafe housing

解押 jiěyā
to send (a prisoner or captive) under escort; to escort
E.g. 潜逃了三年的重大贪污犯在检察机关的人员解押下，沮丧地走下舷梯。 The embezzler who had escaped for three years is walking down the boarding ramp looking depressed, escorted by people from the procuratorial office.

戒毒 jièdú
to quit drug abuse

戒毒所 jièdúsuǒ
drug rehabilitation center (where drug addicts are helped or forced to quit drugs)

界定 jièdìng
boundaries and regulations; to set boundaries and formulate regulations

借调 jièdiào
to transfer on loan (temporarily)
E.g. 借调干部 to transfer a cadre on loan

借东风 jièdōngfēng
taking advantage of the east wind
A metaphor for taking advantage of favorable circumstances or conditions (in developing or pushing forward a certain task).

借读 jièdú
to study at a school on a "loan" basis
Elementary or secondary students who, for some reason, are unable to attend schools at their regular residential locations and instead attend schools at other locations.

借鸡下蛋 jièjī xiàdàn
to borrow a hen to lay an egg
A metaphor for using external conditions to advance one's own projects.

借考 jièkǎo
to take the national college entrance exam in a district other than where

one is registered

E.g. 有的职工子女要求在外地借考。 *Some children of workers requested to take the exam outside their own districts.*

jīn

金边债券 jīnbiān zhàiquàn
national bonds

Because national bonds are secure, low-risk, and their interest rates are stable, they are euphemistically called "gold-rimmed bonds". They are also called "no-risk bonds".

金卡工程 jīnkǎ gōngchéng
gold card engineering

The national electronic money engineering project aimed at building a system for transferring funds electronically in order to replace traditional cash exchange. (cf. 电子货币工程)

金领工人 jīnlǐng gōngrén
gold collar workers

High-level professionals such as engineers, lawyers, analysts, editors, programmers, planners, etc.

金霉素 jīnméisù
aureomycin

金农 jīnnóng
"gold peasants"

Peasants who pan for gold or work at gold mines.

金牌 jīnpái
gold medal, top athletic prize

E.g. 亚运会在最后两天将决出40块金牌。 *Forty gold medals will be determined in the final two days of the Asian Olympics.* / 他获得两枚金牌。 *He won two gold medals.*

金融工程 jīnróng gōngchéng
financial project

A new type of financial service project involved in designing and developing financial products and financial equipment.

金三角 jīnsānjiǎo
golden triangle

金珠玛米 jīnzhūmǎmǐ
Tibetan term for the People's Liberation Army

紧跟 jǐngēn
to follow closely

Metaphor for slavishly adhering to certain directives.

E.g. 紧跟中央政府的部署。 *Strategic plans that adhere closely to directives of the central government.*

紧迫感 jǐnpògǎn
feeling of urgency

A feeling that a job assignment is urgent and cannot be delayed.

紧俏 jǐnqiào
to sell well (commodities)

E.g. 紧俏物资 *goods and materials that sell well.*

紧俏商品 jǐnqiào shāngpǐn
high demand merchandise

Merchandise of superior quality, also in high demand.

紧缺 jǐnquē
shortage

Insufficient supply of goods.

E.g. 紧缺物资 *materials in short supply*

紧张 jǐnzhāng
tense; shortage

1) To be at a high level of anticipation, excitement and agitation.

E.g. 心情有些紧张 *to be in an ex-*

cited mood

2) Fierce and urgent, causing one to be tense or excited.

E.g. 物资的短缺造成一些生活困难 an insufficiency that makes it difficult to meet demand

E.g. 电力紧张 There is a shortage of electrical power / 物资紧张 There is a shortage of material goods

锦标主义 jǐnbiāo zhǔyì

trophy mania

Unscrupulous thoughts or behavior in a competition, solely going after victory.

锦纶 jǐnlún

polymide fiber

进尺 jìnchǐ

footage advanced

The rate of progress in such work as mining and drilling.

E.g. 掘进工作面的月进尺 the footage advanced monthly in the tunnel drilling face / 钻机钻探的年进尺 the footage advanced annually by the drilling machine

进宫 jìngōng

(traditionally) to enter the palace; now a metaphor for being arrested by the police (jocular)

E.g. 他多次作案,"进宫"三次。 He committed crimes repeatedly and has been arrested three times.

进贡 jìngòng

(traditionally) to submit tributes or gifts to the emperor; now a metaphor for sending "gifts" or bribes in order to "grease the wheels"

进销 jìnxiāo

to stock up and to sell

E.g. 进销物资 to stock up (for sale) on goods and materials

晋职 jìnzhí

promotion (to a higher office)

禁毒 jìndú

drug prohibition

禁区 jìnqū

forbidden zones

1) Areas where entry is forbidden to ordinary people.

E.g. 军事禁区 forbidden military zone

2) Areas that receive special protection due to their special scientific or economic value.

3) In medicine, the areas of the body where an operation or acupuncture is forbidden because of high risk.

4) A metaphor for issues that cannot be touched on due to various reasons.

E.g. 思想禁区 ideological forbidden zone

禁赛 jìnsài

to bar from competition

E.g. 禁赛处分已经解除。 The penalty of being barred from competition is already over.

禁运 jìnyùn

embargo

One or several nations prohibiting the movement of commodities and other material goods to and from a certain country.

E.g. 禁运法 embargo law / 禁运物资 materials prohibited from being imported or shipped across certain borders

尽如人意 jìn rú rén yì

to be completely as one wishes

To meet with people's wishes.

E.g. 我们的工作还不能尽如人意。 Our work is still not as good as we would like it to be.

劲射 jìnshè
(soccer) a sudden shot at the goal

E.g. 劲射破门 *to make a sudden shot at the goal* / 起脚劲射入网 *to suddenly kick right into the net*

劲舞 jìnwǔ
rap dancing

A dance popular among young people. It is characterized by speed and variety of movements.

E.g. 风靡美国的现代劲舞深受喜爱现代舞蹈的年轻人欢迎。 *Rap dancing is widespread in the States and is popular with young people who are greatly excited by modern dance.*

jīng

晶体管 jīngtǐguǎn
transistors

京官 jīngguān
(traditionally) officials at the capital

A metaphor for high level cadres who hold offices in the capital.

京郊 jīngjiāo
suburbs of the capital

京剧革命 jīngjù gémìng
revolution in Peking opera

Reforms that took place in traditional Peking opera in the early 1950s. Modern Peking opera created and performed according to the principle of "using the ancient for the present" to reflect China's revolutionary themes.

精兵简政 jīngbīng jiǎnzhèng
to replace with more efficient troops and simplify administration

A metaphor for increasing efficiency in a work unit.

精读 jīngdú
intensive reading

To read and study meticulously. Those portions of liberal arts teaching materials intended for in-depth study and mastery. It is the opposite of extensive reading.

E.g. 精读课 *intensive reading course*

精简机构 jīngjiǎn jīgòu
to streamline organizations

To reduce organizations. To do away with unnecessary organizations through dismantling, compression, and merging, retaining only that which are necessary.

精讲多练 jīngjiǎng duōliàn
to lecture or explain clearly and thoroughly, then to follow up with lots of exercises

精料 jīngliào
refined fodder

Also called 精饲料 refined feeding material and 浓厚饲料 condensed feeding material. It is selective or processed vegetable feed with a high nutritional value. It includes seeds, grains, and their processed by-products (such as bean cakes and bran). Sometimes it contains meat-derivatives with protein and calcium phosphate content. It is the opposite of coarse fodder.

精煤 jīngméi
refined coal

Coal that has gone through the selection (washing) process, so that impurities such as dust and sulfur have been reduced. The resultant coal is of high grade and good quality, and meets certain specifications.

精品 jīngpǐn
exquisite works of literature or art

E.g. 艺术精品 *exquisite works of art*

精神产品 jīngshén chǎnpǐn
spiritual products
Literary and artistic works that satisfy the needs of mankind's spiritual life, such as novels, films, dramas, music, dance, photography, and works of art.

精神公害 jīngshén gōnghài
public spiritual poison
Erroneous or reactionary theories, literature and art which are detrimental to ideology, morality and the social climate.

精神贵族 jīngshén guìzú
intellectual aristocracy
A metaphor for people who hold themselves above the masses, who see themselves as having a monopoly on culture and knowledge, and who look down on the masses, as if they were feudal aristocrats with special privileges.

精神枷锁 jīngshén jiāsuǒ
spiritual shackles
A metaphor for the psychological oppression and restrictions that people suffer.

精神食粮 jīngshén shíliáng
spiritual food
A metaphor for reading materials that satisfy the needs of mankind's spiritual life, such as newspapers and magazines, theoretical books, and literary works.

精神万能 jīngshén wànnéng
spiritual omnipotence
An idealistic viewpoint, which boundlessly exaggerates the function of the spirit, and believes that the spirit can determine everything.

精神文明 jīngshén wénmíng
spiritual civilization
The spiritual assets created in the social history of mankind, including thought, education, ethics, customs, science, and culture. It can be contrasted with "物质文明 material civilization".

精神污染 jīngshén wūrǎn
spiritual pollution
The corrosion of the people's thoughts by the reactionary corrupt thoughts of the bourgeois and other exploitative classes.

精神武器 jīngshén wǔqì
spiritual weapon
A metaphor for the scientific theories that people use as a guide in their participation in society.

精神鸦片 jīngshén yāpiàn
spiritual opium
A metaphor for the reactionary corrupt thoughts, theories, literary works, etc., that numb people's spirits and corrode their souls.

精神原子弹 jīngshén yuánzǐdàn
spiritual atomic bomb
Spiritual weapon of great strength. A metaphor for certain theories and doctrines that guide people's thoughts and actions.

精神支柱 jīngshén zhīzhù
spiritual pillars
Beliefs, ideals, theories, etc., that support people's spirits.

精瘦 jīngshòu
extremely lean

精饲料 jīngsìliào
animal feed which has high nutritional value
Abbreviated as 精料.

精选 jīngxuǎn

to select or screen very carefully

E.g. 这幅画是从900幅作品中精选出来的。 *This painting was exclusively selected from 900 works.* / 《精选英汉汉英词典》 *Concise English-Chinese Chinese-English Dictionary*

精养 jīngyǎng
punctilious animal husbandry

To punctiliously adopt scientific methods in raising animals. This includes selecting superior breeds, using refined fodder, preventing diseases, using scientific management, etc. It is the opposite of 粗养 unpunctilious animal husbandry.

精英 jīngyīng
elite

Talented people who stand out from the crowd in certain respects.

精制 jīngzhì
to make with extra care

To apply processing to coarsely made items, to make with great care.

E.g. 精制盐 *refined salt* / 精制品 *finely made items*

腈纶 jīnglún
acrylic fibers

经办 jīngbàn
to handle a matter

E.g. 经办人员 *personnel who handle matters*

经风雨，见世面 jīngfēngyǔ, jiànshìmiàn
to experience wind and rain, and to see the ways of the world

To engage in the struggle of the masses in order to be tempered, to grow in knowledge and ability, and to understand the conditions of the struggling masses.

经互会 Jīng-Hù-Huì
CMEA; Comecon

Abbreviation for Council of 经济互助委员会 Mutual Economic Assistance. Originally it was a regional economic organization involving the Soviet Union and Eastern European countries, and later joined by Mongolia, Cuba, and Vietnam. Its charter stipulates that "total economic cooperation" will be developed on the basis of the principle of "international division of labor". Later, through many resolutions concerning "economic integration" some transnational organizations and bilateral and multilateral "united companies" were established.

经济动物 jīngjì dòngwù
economic animal

A derogatory term applied by certain people to Japan in respect to that country's intention of pursuing rapid economic development.

经济杠杆 jīngjì gànggǎn
economic levers

经济核算 jīngjì hésuàn
cost accounting

A mode of enterprise management whereby cost is used to measure the economic efficiency of labor and material consumption, in order to strive for the most cost effective way of combining the use of labor, technological facilities, materials, energy, etc.

经济合同 jīngjì hétóng
financial agreement

经济基础 jīngjì jīchǔ
economic foundation

经济计量学 jīngjì jìliàngxué
econometrics

Also called 计量经济学.

经济结构 jīngjì jiégòu
economic structure

1) Economic structure of a society, the economic foundation (sum total of all production relationships) at a certain stage in the historical development of mankind. The economic structures of societies are different; social systems are also different. 2) The composition of the various sectors of the national economy and of the various aspects of social production, including the structure of property, the structure of allocation, the structure of exchanges, the structure of consumption, and the structure of technology.

经济开发区 jīngjì kāifāqū
economic development zones

In implementing the policy of opening up to the world, China has set up clearly demarcated areas outside of cities. In these zones basic facilities have been installed and they are set aside to attract Sino-foreign joint-capital businesses, cooperative businesses, and foreign-capital-only business enterprises. Certain special economic zone policies give them preferential treatment. These zones are called economic development zones.

经济立法 jīngjì lìfǎ
economic ordinances

Laws, decrees, rules and regulations drawn up and promulgated to regulate and correctly deal with the relationships between the various aspects of society's economic life.

经济联合体 jīngjì liánhétǐ
economic coalition

A form of economic union organized by various nations, regions, sectors, or enterprises. The union is carried out on the basis of the members' needs to develop production, and in accordance with an agreement. China currently has many different forms of economic coalitions at different administrative levels, such as specialized companies, incorporated factories, agricultural-industrial-commercial joint enterprises, Sino-foreign joint-capital business enterprises, etc.

经济林木 jīngjì línmù
economic woods

Woods and trees which are of relatively great economic value, such as those that produce fruits, oils, industrial raw materials, and medicines. Used broadly, the term includes woods that produce lumber.

经济民主 jīngjì mínzhǔ
economic democracy

One of the three aspects of the Chinese People's Liberation Army's internal democratic life. An economics committee, elected by each company's soldiers at large, assists the company commander in managing food and agricultural sideline production, in supervising economic expenditure, in preventing embezzlement and waste, etc.

经济区划 jīngjì qūhuà
division into economic districts

To divide the entire nation or a region into several economic districts according to the differences in labor, and economic conditions, the special characteristics of economic contacts in districts; and the extent and direction of their development in specialization. The division into economic districts of a socialist country is an important measure in formulating and implementing the national economy, and in rational development of production. It is also an important basis for studying the national economic management system and adjusting administrative divisions.

经济圈 jīngjìquān
economic circle

(In economic development) a broad zone with inter-related areas and segments.

经济人 jīngjìrén
people who carry on economic activity for the sole purpose of seeking personal gain

经济渗透 jīngjì shèntòu
economic infiltration

The economic expansion conducted covertly by capitalist nations on other nations or regions in order to vie for markets, raw materials, and investment. For example, they export capital and commodities to developing countries in the name of economic assistance and technical assistance. Due to an imbalance in the economic development of the capitalist nations, there is fierce competition among them for markets, and therefore they conduct economic infiltration.

经济师 jīngjìshī
financial officer

A mid-level position in China, comparable to lecturer in a university.

经济实体 jīngjì shítǐ
economic entity

A unit that independently carries out economic accounting and economic activities. An economic entity is independent and determines its own business management. It has power over the organization of production, supply, and sale, and over the allocation of manpower, funds, and materials. It is a legal independent economic unit, and in its economic relationships with other enterprises, it has the responsibility of completing economic agreements.

经济适用房 jīngjì shìyòngfáng
economic houses

Low profit houses built by the state which provides the land and remits taxation for a large group of middle and low income people.

经济手段 jīngjì shǒuduàn
economic measure

Also called 经济方法 economic method. Seen from the perspective of all economic activities, it includes economic levers, such as price control, taxes, credit, and interest rates, that have a function in adjusting the economy. Seen from the perspective of business administration, it is primarily the methods that link the results of operating the enterprise with economic benefits, and that tie together responsibility, power, and benefits. These measures include enterprise funding, percentage division of profits, floating wages, subsidies for certain posts, bonuses, etc. Economic measures correspond to administrative measures.

经济特区 jīngjì tèqū
special economic zones

Designated zones – such as Shenzhen and Xiamen – where special economic policies and management systems are put into practice.

经济体制 jīngjì tǐzhì
economic system

Abbreviation for 经济管理体制 economic management system. The overall term for the regulations, forms, and methods of management that govern the entire national economy.

经济效益 jīngjì xiàoyì
economic efficiency
The ratio between labor consumption and productivity in economic activity, which reflects the utilitarian effectiveness of manpower, materials, and funds within each link in social production. Also called 经济效果.

经济协作区 jīngjì xiézuòqū
economically coordinated regions
Also called 经济区 economic regions. Economic regions demarcated according to the requirements of economic districting and which have certain production specializations. Among the economically coordinated regions, the production sectors maintain comprehensive balanced development, take proper consideration of the people's conditions, and in as far as possible seek concordance with administrative districting.

经济一体化 jīngjì yītǐhuà
economic unification
An overall term for the implementation of economic unity among several nations, who adopt joint economic principles, policies and measures to link their national economies into a unit, and form a regional economic community. An example is the European Economic Community of Western Europe. As another example, the Soviet Union proposed at the Council of Mutual Economic Assistance (CMEA or Comecon) to do away with national boundaries and establish a united, coordinated, comprehensive economic entity. Some developing nations have also formed regional economic collectives and implemented measures for economic unity.

经济员 jīngjìyuán
financial clerk
A low-level position in China, comparable to "teaching assistant" in a university.

经济责任制 jīngjì zérènzhì
economic responsibility system
The system in socialist economic life whereby the state, the collective, and the individual must each assume certain duties and responsibilities toward each other. This includes the duties and responsibilities between the state and enterprises, among enterprises themselves, among the various levels of organization within an enterprise, and among the various sectors. The economic responsibility system has legal efficacy, it is linked with the principle of material benefits and rewards and penalties.

经济帐 jīngjìzhàng
the financial perspective on a certain matter

经济支柱 jīngjì zhīzhù
economic pillars
Industries that form the foundation for economic development, such as agriculture and stock-raising, energy sources, power, etc. Once these industries are established other industries can be developed, thus promoting economic prosperity.

经济作物 jīngjì zuòwù
economic crops
Agricultural crops that serve as industrial raw materials. They are also called

工业原料作物 industrial raw material crops or 技术作物 technological crops. According to their usage, they can be divided into the following kinds: fiber, oil, sugar, starch, rubber, dyes, medicines, beverages, and luxury goods (tobacco, alcohol), etc.

经济增长点 jīngjì zēngzhǎngdiǎn
growth engines

经警 jīng-jǐng
police in charge of economic affairs
Abbreviation for 经济警察.

经贸 jīng-mào
economics and commerce
Contraction of 经济贸易 economics and commerce.
E.g. 经贸系统 *economic and commercial system*

经委 Jīng-Wěi
Economic Commission
Abbreviation for 国家经济委员会 the State Commission for the Economy of the People's Republic of China.

经销专业户 jīngxiāo zhuānyèhù
households specializing in marketing
The households that specialize in marketing agricultural products after the implementation of the responsibility contract system in China's rural areas.

经营层次 jīngyíng céngcì
management tiers
An overall term in the context of management activities for the related organizations at various levels.

经营承包制 jīngyíng chéngbāozhì
management contract system
A form of economic responsibility system implemented by enterprises. It is divided into two types: contracts that enterprises have with the state, and contracts with an enterprise. In the first type, an enterprise contracts for the profits after paying the taxes stipulated by regulations; in the second type, an economic responsibility system is instituted within an enterprise; it includes not only profit targets, but also various other economic targets. The management contract system ties responsibility, power, and benefits together, and bestows rewards and penalties according to the circumstances in which the terms of the contract were carried out.

经营方向 jīngyíng fāngxiàng
management direction
The aims of an enterprise operation.

经营思想 jīngyíng sīxiǎng
management philosophy
The guiding philosophy in managing an enterprise.

经营性亏损 jīngyíngxìng kuīsǔn
losses of a management nature
Losses caused by reasons of poor enterprise management, excessive consumption of raw materials, fuel, and power, poor quality products, high production costs, lack of markets, etc. This is the opposite of losses due to policy. (cf. 政策性亏损)

经营责任制 jīngyíng zérènzhì
management responsibility system
The various economic responsibility systems implemented in the management of enterprises. (cf. 经济责任制 and 经营承包制)

经营作风 jīngyíng zuòfēng
management style
The guiding philosophy, service attitude, work performance, etc., reflected in the management of an enterprise.

经援 jīngyuán
economic aid
Contraction of 经济援助 economic aid.
E.g. 对外经援工作 *economic aid to foreign countries*

井灌 jǐngguàn
well irrigation
To irrigate farmland with well water.

井喷 jǐngpēn
blowout
The sudden blowout of subterranean high-pressure oil and natural gas from a well opening when an oil well is being drilled.

警车 jǐngchē
police car

警督 jǐngdū
police supervisor
It refers to public security personnel who are in charge of supervising policemen's conduct.

警徽 jǐnghuī
policeman's badge

警阶 jǐngjiē
ranks within the police force
E.g. 中国决定在人民警察中实行警阶制。 *China decided to implement a system of ranks in the People's Police.*

警力 jǐnglì
police force
Abbreviation for 警察力量.
E.g. 接到报警，公安局立即组织精干警力追击。 *After receiving the report, the public security bureau immediately organized an intelligent and capable force of police to chase the criminals.*

警民 jǐng-mín
the police and the people
E.g. 警民关系 *relationship between the police and the people* / 警民共建 *jointly built by the police and the people*

警容 jǐngróng
police decorum

警嫂 jǐngsǎo
(a polite term for a) policeman's wife

警亭 jǐngtíng
police kiosk
A kiosk at an intersection or gate for the use of on-duty traffic police or guards.

警务 jǐngwù
police affairs

警衔 jǐngxián
various ranks of the officers and men of the police force

警政 jǐngzhèng
police administration, i.e., duties and affairs of the police sector

景点 jǐngdiǎn
scenic spot
E.g. 旅游景点 *scenic tourist spot* / 景点建筑 *a building at a scenic spot*

景观 jǐngguān
exceptional natural scenery and famous historical relics
E.g. 自然景观 *natural scenic wonder* / 人文景观 *man-made cultural wonder* / 建筑景观 *architectural wonder*

景区 jǐngqū
scenic area

静止轨道 jìngzhǐ guǐdào
static orbit; synchronous orbit

境外 jìngwài
beyond national boundaries; abroad

敬老院 jìnglǎoyuàn
respect-the-elderly institution; old folks' home
Also called 养老院 nursing home. A kind of social welfare organization, managed by the public or by a collec-

tive, for taking care of lone elderly people.

敬业 jìngyè
to respect and love one's profession

竞投 jìngtóu
to compete in bidding (for a contract, etc.)

竞赛 jìngsài
to compete; to contend
E.g. 军备竞赛 *competition in a military build-up*

净菜 jìngcài
cleaned vegetables (readied for market)

净化 jìnghuà
to purify
E.g. 净化污水 *purification of waste water* / 净化灵魂 *to purify the soul* / 净化社会空气 *to purify the societal atmosphere (to improve people's morals)*

净空 jìngkōng
cleared sky
Refers to the sky above a special area such as an airport where flying objects are forbidden to enter.

jiu

揪斗 jiūdòu
to drag (someone) out for criticism and struggle

纠风 jiū-fēng
to rectify corrupt tendencies
Abbreviation for 纠正行业不正之风 的简称.
E.g. 纠风工作要抓紧。*We must take a firm hand in rectifying corrupt tendencies.*

纠风办 jiū-fēng-bàn
Bureau for the Rectification of Corrupt Tendencies
Abbreviation for 纠正行业不正之风办公室的简称.
E.g. 中央成立了纠风办。*The central government established the Bureau for the Rectification of Corrupt Tendencies.*

九大 Jiǔ-Dà
the Ninth National Congress of the Chinese Communist Party
Abbreviation for 中国共产党第九次全国代表大会 (April 1-24, 1959, in Beijing).

九二米 jiǔ'èrmǐ
the kind of rice from which 92 catties of white rice can be extracted from 100 catties of unpolished rice

九三 Jiǔsān
the September Third Learned Society
Abbreviation for 九三学社. One of China's Patriotic Democratic Parties (originally called 民主科学社 Democratic Scientific Society, it was renamed the September Third Learned Society on September 3, 1945).

九一三事件 Jiǔ-yīsān shìjiàn
the September Thirteenth Incident
The incident which occurred on September 13, 1971: After the plot by Lin Biao's reactionary clique to engineer a revolutionary military coup d'etat was exposed, Lin Biao and his cohorts tried to flee the country, with the result that they fell to their death at Ondorhaan in Mongolia.

旧框框 jiùkuàngkuang
old restrictions, old conventions

旧社会 jiùshèhuì
old society
The society before the founding of the

People's Republic of China in 1949.

ju

居留证 jūliúzhèng
residence card (I.D. card issued to foreign residents in China)
居民大院 jūmín dàyuàn
large residential compounds
Compounds in cities and towns ocupied by several residential families.
居民身份证 jūmín shēnfènzhèng
residence I.D.card (issued by the government)
居民委员会 jūmín wěiyuánhuì
residential committees
The grass-roots self-governing organizations formed by citizens in China's cities and towns in their own residential districts. The term is abbreviated to 居委会 residential committees. They manage public affairs and public welfare work of their local residential districts, mediate disputes among the residents, assist in maintaining social order, and transmit the people's opinions and requests, and make suggestions, to the government as well.
居室 jūshì
1) residential rooms
E.g. 他们家是一套两居室的房子。 *Their living quarters consist of a two-room suite.*
2) residential housing
居委会 jū–wěi–huì
residential committees
Abbreviation for 居民委员会 (cf. 居民委员会).
局麻 jú–má
local anesthesia
Abbreviation for 局部麻醉.
举报 jǔbào
to report an offense to the authorities, to lodge an accusation
E.g. 举报中心 center for reporting complaints / 举报站 station for reporting complaints / 举报电话 hot lines for reporting complaints / 举报人 a person reporting a complaint / 举报揭发贪污受贿行为 *to report and expose corruption and acceptance of bribes*
举借 jǔjiè
to borrow funds from others
举旗抓纲 jǔqí zhuāgāng
to raise the flag and grasp the guiding principles
"举旗"是指高举毛泽东思想伟大红旗;"抓纲"是指抓阶级斗争(阶级斗争曾被认为是一切工作的总纲)。这是中共十一届三中全会以前和"文化大革命"期间流行的一句"左"倾错误口号。
To "raise the flag" means to raise aloft the great red flag of Mao Zedong Thought; to "grasp the guiding principles" means to grasp class struggle (class struggle had been recognized as the overall guiding principle for all work). This was an erroneous leftist slogan popular before the Third Plenum of the Eleventh Party Central Committee and during the Cultural Revolution.
举坛 jǔtán
weight-lifting circles
巨无霸 jùwúbà
the giant; the extra large
Originally a name for an ancient person who was tall and strong, and so energetic that no one could compete with

him. Now it means a giant and also refers to a super burger.

句型 jùxíng
sentence patterns

句型教学 jùxíng jiàoxué
the teaching of sentence patterns
A method of teaching language guided by the theories of structural linguistics which emphasizes sentence patterns in learning a language. Practitioners believe that every language has a certain number of sentence patterns, and that through extensive substitution drills, a student can master the patterns and learn that language.

剧减 jùjiǎn
dramatic reduction
E.g. 耕地面积剧减 *The cultivated acreage plummeted.*

剧评 jùpíng
drama review

剧坛 jùtán
the theatrical world

剧协 jù-xié
Dramatists Association
Abbreviation for 戏剧家协会.

剧运 jù-yùn
drama and athletics
Abbreviation for 戏剧运动.

剧增 jùzēng
sudden increase
To increase rapidly and suddenly.
E.g. 贺年片销量剧增。*There is a sudden rise in the sale of New Year's cards.*

剧展 jùzhǎn
theatrical exhibitions
Abbreviation for 戏剧展览.

剧组 jùzǔ
theater group
The complete cast and staff involved in the production of a movie, television program, or theater performance.
E.g. 剧组全体人员 *all persons of the theater group*

juan

捐资 juānzī
to donate funds
E.g. 捐资创办医院 *to donate funds for the founding of a hospital* / 捐资办学 *to donate funds for schools*

卷扬机 juǎnyángjī
reel and lift machine; hoist
A weight-lifting device, constructed of a reel, steel cables, and electric motor, used in mining and construction projects. Also called 绞车 winch.

jue

角色 juésè
role (in a play, a profession, society, or life)
E.g. 扮演……角色 *to play the role of...* / 进入角色 *to get into a role*

角逐 juézhú
to contend
Originally referred to fighting physically, now it refers to all forms of struggle.
E.g. 经过激烈角逐，北京队夺取冠军。*After intense struggle, the Beijing team won the championship.* / 角逐场地 *arena of fierce contention*

决策机构 juécè jīgòu
strategy decision organ
An office that determines strategies and methods.

决心书 juéxīnshū

written pledge

A report or letter expressing one's firm determination to accomplish a certain task.

绝对平均主义 juéduì píngjūn zhǔyì

absolute equalitarianism

Extreme equalitarianism. It is the philosophy that advocates uniform treatment of people in material distribution regardless of their labor and contribution to society. It maintains that only absolute equalization can be counted as equality. This mentality was the pipe dream of those engaged in individual handicrafts and small agricultural economics.

绝对权威 juéduì quánwēi

absolute authority

A popular term of the Cultural Revolution. It means that the leader has the highest authority and is subject to no restrictions under any circumstances, that the leader's words are the highest directives, have the highest prestige and the greatest power, and that every word is truth. This was an erroneous view.

绝活 juéhuó

unique skill（i.e., having no competition in that particular skill）

绝情 juéqíng

to break off friendship; to have absolutely no friendly feelings

绝育 juéyù

sterilization

jun

均衡裁军 jūnhéng cáijūn

equibalanced disarmament

The proposition that, in disarmament, both sides must maintain an equal balance in their military capabilities.

军兵种 jūn–bīngzhǒng

categories of troops

军种和兵种的统称。军种如陆军、海军、空军。兵种是军种内部的分类，如步兵、炮兵、骑兵、装甲兵、通信兵、工程兵、防化兵、空降兵、海军航空兵等。

An overall term for military service categories and their subtypes. 军种 include army, navy, and air force. 兵种 are the subcategories within each service category, such as infantry, artillery, cavalry, armored forces, signal corps, engineering corps, antichemical warfare corps, paratroopers, naval air force, etc.

军博 Jūn–Bó

Military Museum of the Chinese People's Revolution

Abbreviation for 中国人民革命军事博物馆.

军地两用人材 jūndì liǎngyòng réncái

Cf. 两用人才

军工 jūngōng

military industry

Abbreviation for 军事工业 military industry.

E.g. 军工部门 *the military industrial sector* / 军工产品 *military industrial products*

军管 jūn–guǎn

military control

军事管制的简称。国家在战争或其它特殊情况下采取的一种措施，由军事部门暂时接管特定的单位、局部地区，以至国家政权。特指"文化大革命"中的军管。(参见"三支两军")
Abbreviation for 军事管制 military control. Measures adopted by a nation at war or under special circumstances, whereby the military sector would take temporary control over designated units, local areas, and even national political power. The term also refers specifically to military control during the Cultural Revolution.(cf. 三支两军)

军管会 jūn-guǎn-huì
Military Control Committee
Abbreviation for 军事管制委员会.

军婚 jūnhūn
military marriage (one or both of the spouses being in military service)

军垦农场 jūnkěn nóngchǎng
army reclamation farm
Farms established by the Chinese People's Liberation Army through reclamation. After the War of Liberation was won, a portion of the People's Liberation Army reclaimed uncultivated land in the border regions and coastal areas, established farms, carried out self-sufficient production, and provided the state with a large quantity of marketable grains and economic crops.

军控 jūnkòng
armament control

军列 jūnliè
train cars designated for military use
Abbreviation for 军用列车.

军令状 jūnlìngzhuàng
military command contract
A pledge written by an officer after receiving a military order. A metaphor for the guarantee contract submitted by a responsible person or the leadership of an enterprise unit to the higher-up supervisory department.(cf. 责任状)

军贸 jūnmào
arms trade, i.e., sale and purchase of military weapons

军民共建 jūn-mín gòngjiàn
joint construction between the army and the people of a spiritual and material civilization
Abbreviation for 军民共建两个文明. *E.g.* 军民共建活动 *the joint construction activity between the army and the people* / 军民共建点 *the joint construction station of the army and the people*

军民一致 jūnmín yīzhì
unity between the army and the people
One of the three basic principles of the Chinese People's Liberation Army's political work, and a glorious tradition of the army. It requires the troops to love the people, protect the people's interests, abide by policies and ordinances, respect local cadres, establish rigorous discipline in their dealings with the masses, direct propaganda toward the people as well as organize and arm them, assist and participate in socialist revolution and socialist construction.

军品 jūnpǐn
military ware
1) Items produced by the military industrial sector. 2) Items for military use.

军企 jūnqǐ
military-run enterprise

军容 jūnróng
military decorum (of a military division or an individual)

军嫂 jūnsǎo

honorific appellation for the wives of military personnel

军事民主 jūnshì mínzhǔ
military democracy
One of the three aspects of the internal democratic life of the Chinese People's Liberation Army. In practical terms, military democracy means that in military training, cadres and soldiers are mobilized to discuss how to accomplish military missions; and after the battle, they conduct a critique and summarize their experience.

军售 jūnshòu
arms sale
E.g. 该地区为一大潜在的军售市场。*This region is a potentially large market for arms sales.*

军体 jūn-tǐ
military physical education

军威 jūnwēi
military prestige
The command and prestige of the military.
E.g. 国庆检阅时,一定要走出样子来,壮我国威、军威。*We must give a good showing in the National Day parade, so as to strengthen our national ascendancy and military prestige.*

军委 Jūn-Wěi
Military Commission
"中央军事委员会"的简称。也叫"中央军委"。有中华人民共和国中央军委和中国共产党中央军委。
Abbreviation for 中央军事委员会 Military Commission of the CPC Central Committee. Also called 中央军委.

军宣队 jūn-xuān-duì
army propaganda teams
中国人民解放军毛泽东思想宣传队的简称。是"文化大革命"期间,被派往学校、机关、工厂等部门执行"三支两军"任务的解放军工作队。
Abbreviation for the Mao Zedong Thought Propaganda Teams of the Chinese People's Liberation Army. They were work teams sent by the Chinese People's Liberation Army during the Cultural Revolution to schools, government offices, factories, etc., to carry out the duties of the 三支两军 three supports and two militaries.(cf. 三支两军)

军运 jūn-yùn
military transport
E.g. 军运任务 *military transport mission*

军政训练 jūnzhèng xùnliàn
military and political training

军转 jūnzhuǎn
the transfer of military personnel to civilian work
E.g. 军转干部 *cadres who were formerly military personnel* / 军转安置工作 *the work of placing military personnel in civilian work*

K

ka

咖啡伴侣 kāfēi bànlǚ
coffee mate
A substance made from powdered milk that is mixed in coffee.

卡巴迪 kǎbādí
a team sport popular in Southeast and South Asia
In this sport, the two teams are separated by a line; a player who crosses the line to touch an opponent without being caught wins a point for his team.

卡介苗 kǎjièmiáo
Bacille Calmette – Guerin vaccine

卡拉 OK kǎlā OK
(originally Japanese) Karaoke, entertainment whereby a performing patron sings to music and words on a television screen

kai

开村 kāicūn
to build and open up a village (community) for the use of athletes in an international athletics competition such as the Olympics
E.g. 亚运村昨天举行开村仪式。
The Asian Games Village conducted its opening ceremony yesterday.

开顶风船 kāi dǐngfēngchuán
to operate a ship against the wind
A metaphor for struggling against prevalent or powerful but erroneous ideas or trends.

开发区 kāifāqū
development zone
An area designated for development.

开发性承包 kāifāxìng chéngbāo
developmental contract
Farmers independently or jointly contracting to manage and develop hitherto unexploited agricultural resources, such as mountainous areas, hills, grasslands, water surfaces, coastal beaches.

开发性生产 kāifāxìng shēngchǎn
developmental production
To open up new productive territory. That is, aside from cultivating the existing land, farmers develop on a large scale such natural resources as uncultivated areas, hills, grasslands, hills of spoil, water surfaces, and hydropower, in order to increase production and raise economic efficiency.

开放大学 kāifàng dàxué
open university
Where students are taught through television programs, radio broadcasts, correspondence, etc.

开放政策 kāifàng zhèngcè
open policy
After the Third Plenary Session of the Eleventh Central Committee of the Chinese Communist Party, concomitant with the domestic policy of invigorating the economy, the open foreign policy

was implemented. That is, on the basis of independent self-determination and self-reliance, and according to the principle of equality and mutual benefits, China will actively draw in foreign capital and advanced scientific technology, strengthen economic cooperation with foreign countries, and take full advantage of beneficial international factors to serve the four modernizations.

开关 kāiguān
the opening of a new customs office

开馆 kāiguǎn
the opening of a new embassy, library, exhibition hall, museum, etc.

开后门 kāihòumén
to open a back door

To provide conveniences for those who use improper tactics to seek selfish ends.

开机 kāijī
starting to film a movie or television program

E.g. 连续剧《武则天》开机。*The filming of the serial drama "Wu Zetian" has started.*

开架 kāijià
open shelves

A bookstore or library that allows readers to go to the shelves and select books they need.

开镜 kāijìng
Same as 开拍。(cf. 开拍)

E.g. 电影《红楼梦》昨日在京开镜。*The filming of "Dream of the Red Mansions" began yesterday in Beijing.*

开具 kāijù
to write out (a receipt, affidavit, etc.)

E.g. 开具发票 *to write out a receipt*

开卷考试 kāijuàn kǎoshì
open-book examination

A type of examination where the questions are made public and those taking the exam may have free access to relevant materials. It is the opposite of closed-book examination.

开考 kāikǎo
to hold an exam

E.g. 全国计算机等级考试今年将在北京开考。*The national computer ranking examination will be conducted in Beijing this year.*

开口子 kāi kǒuzi
to open a loophole

The leadership or a leadership organ creating openings for acts that violate regulations.

开绿灯 kāi lǜdēng
to turn on the green light

A metaphor for providing conveniences so that certain affairs can proceed smoothly.

开门办学 kāimén bànxué
open-door school management

A method of operating schools prevalent during the Cultural Revolution. For the majority of their time, students left traditional classroom and engaged in learning activities in factories, rural villages, and armed forces. Workers, poor lower middle peasants, officers and soldiers of the Liberation Army were invited to the schools to participate in teaching activities. It lopsidedly emphasized practice, and neglected the teaching of systematic theoretical knowledge. As a result, the level of education seriously declined.

开门红 kāiménhóng
off to a good start
A metaphor for attaining notable achievements at the beginning of the year or at the start of a task.
E.g. 全国工业生产开门红，元月工业总产值比去年增长 8%。 *Production in the entire nation's industries is off to a good start. In the first month, the total industrial output increased 8% over the same period last year.*

开门整党 kāimén zhěngdǎng
open-door rectification of the Party
When the Chinese Communist Party underwent rectification of its work style, it invited non-Party professionals and the masses to participate in meetings and criticisms, and listened to opinions and suggestions from outside the Party.

开门整风 kāimén zhěngfēng
open-door rectification of work style
Synonymous with 开门整党. (cf. 开门整党)

开拍 kāipāi
to begin filming a movie or television program
E.g. 电影《西游记》开拍。 *The filming of "Journey to the West" has begun.*

开取 kāiqǔ
to open up and take out
E.g. 信箱开取时间 *time of mail pick-up at a mailbox*

开司米 kāisīmǐ
cashmere
Also transliterated as 开士米.

开拓型 kāituòxíng
pioneering
Pertaining to persons who dare to break through various unreasonable regulations and systems and outdated ideas and traditions, and who, in striving to create the new, attain certain achievements.
E.g. 选拔开拓型的人才 *to promote talented pioneering persons*

开小灶 kāi xiǎozào
favored treatment (lit., open a private kitchen)
Originally, the term meant giving someone favored treatment, catering to his taste, and making especially good food for him. Now the term is a metaphor for giving special support to a certain project or constituency.

开院 kāiyuàn
the opening of a new hospital
E.g. 新建医院举行开院典礼。 *The newly constructed hospital conducted its opening ceremony.*

kan

刊大 kān-dà
universities that teach through publications
Abbreviation for 刊授大学. (cf. 刊授大学)

刊授大学 kānshòu dàxué
universities that teach through publications
A kind of correspondence university in which courses on certain specialities are taught through publications sent periodically to students. An organized form of open-style teaching carried out by the editorial departments of publications through published materials. Appropriate personnel are hired to provide the necessary tutoring for registered stu-

dents. The courses are primarily self-taught. This is a new form of education for employed adults.

侃 kǎn

Cf. 侃大山 below; also written as 砍.

侃大山 kǎndàshān

(Beijing patois) to shoot the breeze

To chat about anything under the sun, including far-out things; also written as 砍大山.

侃价 kǎn–jià

to bargain

侃爷 kǎnyé

"granddaddy of chat"

Someone especially adept at chatting up a storm; someone skilled at story-telling. *E.g.* 作家王朔被称谓侃爷。*The writer Wang Shuo has been dubbed the granddaddy of chat.*

砍 kǎn

Cf. 砍大山; also written as 侃.

砍大山 kǎndàshān

Same as 侃大山 above.

看跌 kàndiē

to anticipate a falling trend in market value

E.g. 美元继续看跌。*Anticipation of a decline in the value of the US dollar continues.*

看好 kànhǎo

to anticipate an upturn

E.g. 赛前行情看好。*An upturn is anticipated in the pre-race scores.* / 市场形势看好。*An upturn in market conditions is anticipated.*

看涨 kànzhǎng

to anticipate a rising trend in market value

E.g. 行市看涨。*A rise in market prices is anticipated.* / 运动衣价格看涨。*A rise in the cost of sports attire is anticipated.*

kang

康复车 kāngfùchē

"health restoration vehicle"

Automobiles specifically for the use of the handicapped.

康复国际 Kāngfù Guójì

Health Restoration International

致力于残疾人全面康复、充分参与社会生活的国际组织。1922年成立,总部设在美国纽约。

An international organization founded in 1922 to promote the welfare of the handicapped (its headquarters are in New York).

康帕斯 kāngpàsī

transliteration of an acronym

An organization for promoting the development and utilization of land and natural resources.

康体 kāngtǐ

health fixing (building)

E.g. 康体休闲活动 *health building leisure time activities*

抗大 Kàng–Dà

Resistance University

The full name is 中国人民抗日军事政治大学 Chinese People's Anti-Japan Military and Political University, also called 抗日军政大学 Anti-Japan Military and Political University. The name was changed from that of Chinese Anti-Japan Red Army University at the beginning of 1937. It was the school in which the Chinese Communist Party trained military and civil cadres to resist Japan. The school was located in Yan'an.

抗洪 kànghóng
to resist floods
To adopt measures to guard against the danger and damage inflicted by floods.

抗美援朝 kàng Měi yuán Cháo
resist America, aid Korea
The mass movement carried out by the Chinese people in the early 1950s to resist the aggression of American imperialism and to aid the Korean people. On June 25, 1950, American imperialists launched a war and made incursions into the People's Democratic Republic of Korea, and moreover drew the flames of war toward the Chinese border. In response to Chairman Mao Zedong's call to "resist America and aid Korea, protect home and nation", the Chinese people organized a volunteer army that went to the Korean battle front on October 25 to fight side by side with the Korean People's Army and to resist American military aggression. The people at home carried out a movement to increase production and practiced frugality, contributed airplanes and guns, and supported the war at the front. The American imperialists suffered repeated defeats, and were forced to sign the cease-fire treaty in July 1953. The resist-America-aid-Korea movement concluded victoriously.

抗上 kàngshàng
to defy or to stand up to one's superior

抗生菌 kàngshēngjūn
antibiotic bacterium

抗税 kàngshuì
to refuse to pay taxes
E.g. 抗税不缴 to refuse to pay taxes / 抗税案件 a case of refusal to pay taxes

抗灾 kàngzāi
to fight (to prevent or alleviate the effects of) natural calamities
E.g. 抗灾保苗 to fight natural disasters and to protect seedlings / 抗灾夺丰收 to fight natural disasters and strive for a bumper harvest / 抗灾抢险 to fight natural disasters and rush to deal with emergencies

炕肥 kàngféi
fertilizer from a heatable brick bed
In north China, the fertilizer made from the materials in the dismantled base of a heatable brick bed and the ashes remaining under the brick bed.

kao

考本 kǎoběn
to take the relevant exam in order to obtain a driver's license

考博 kǎobó
to take the entrance examinations for a doctor's degree

考点 kǎodiǎn
location of an examination

考风 kǎofēng
the atmosphere at an examination hall or room

考级 kǎojí
grade examination
E.g. 音乐考级 grade examination for music

考纪 kǎojì
examination discipline (rules and regulations)
E.g. 考纪必须常抓不懈。 The examination rules must be stressed frequently.

考量 kǎoliàng

to consider

考评 kǎopíng

evaluation (of one's professional work)

To investigate and make an evaluation. To make an appraisal of a staff member's professional knowledge and actual work.

考区 kǎoqū

examination area; place to take an examination

考务 kǎowù

examination affairs (administration)

E.g. 要严格考务管理。 *The administration of an examination should be strict.*

考研 kǎo-yán

to take the graduate school entrance exam

E.g. 他们不想考研。 *They don't want to take the graduate school entrance exam.*

考照 kǎozhào

to have (take) driving license tests

烤箱 kǎoxiāng

oven

靠边儿 kàobiānr

keep to the side

Cadre leaders who are not up to par being relieved of their duties or transferred out of their leadership posts. This is different from 靠边站 (stand aside) of the Cultural Revolution period, when competent cadres were pushed aside for erroneous political reasons.

靠边站 kàobiānzhàn

to stand aside; to stand off to the side

A metaphor for vacating one's post or losing power (usually not by one's own choice but due to external pressure).

ke

科幻小说 kēhuàn xiǎoshuō

science fiction; sci-fi

Short for 科学幻想小说.

科技 kējì

science and technology

E.g. 科技领域 *the realm of science and technology* / 科技人员 *scientific and technical personnel*

科技户 kējìhù

sci-tech household

Also called 农科户 agricultural scientific household. Rural households that use scientific methods in managing production. They include primarily households that breed improved strains, cultivate high-yield grains and cotton, or lead in agricultural technology, members of the Science Dissemination Association, households with members educated elsewhere, and households that carry out scientific experiments assigned from above.

科技示范户 kējì shìfànhù

sci-tech model household

Advanced households in rural villages that apply and popularize new scientific agricultural technology. The relevant departments provide the sci-tech model households with special guidance in technology, and give them priority in the supply of capital, good seeds, and fertilizer. After they have attained results, they will disseminate the new technology to the other peasant households and the masses, and serve as models.

科教片 kējiàopiān

science education films

Abbreviation for 科学教育影片.

科考 kē-kǎo
scientific investigation

科盲 kēmáng
blind to science

A metaphor for people with no understanding of science.

科贸 kē-mào
sci-tech and trade

E.g. 科贸街 *Sci-tech and Trade Street*

科普 kē-pǔ
dissemination of science

E.g. 科普协会 *Science Dissemination Association* / 科普刊物 *popular science publications*

科普读物 kē-pǔ dúwù
reading materials for disseminating scientific knowledge to the populace

科室 kē shì
departments and offices

The overall term for the various management departments and offices in an enterprise or organization.

E.g. 科室人员 *departmental and office personnel*

科坛 kētán
scientific circles

科委 kē-wěi
science and technology commission

Abbreviation for 科学技术委员会; specifically the 国家科学技术委员会 National Science and Technology Commission.

科协 Kē-Xié
China's Science and Technology Association

Abbreviation for 中国科学技术协会.

科学城 kēxuéchéng
science town

An area with a concentration of scientific research facilities and corresponding residential facilities.

E.g. 北京中关村科学城 *the science town of Zhongguancun in Beijing (near Beijing University)*

科学学 kēxuéxué
the study of science

A new composite discipline that studies the developmental patterns of science; also called 科学的学科 the science of science.

科学种田 kēxué zhòngtián
scientific farming

Using scientific methods to carry out agricultural production.

科研 kēyán
scientific research

E.g. 科研工作 *scientific research work* / 科研人员 *scientific research personnel*

科影厂 Kē-Yǐng-Chǎng
the Science Education Film Studio

Abbreviation for 科学教育电影制片厂

可比产品 kěbǐ chǎnpǐn
comparable products

Products produced regularly by an industry or enterprise in the preceding year or the last few years, and which continue to be produced in the current year, and moreover have records of production costs that can be compared. The term is the opposite of 不可比产品 incomparable products.

可比经济指标 kěbǐjīngjì zhǐbiāo
comparable economic targets

The various economic technical targets for production carried out regularly by an industry or enterprise in the preceding year or recent years, which continue to be carried out in the current year, and moreover have records that can be compared.

可比能耗 kěbǐ nénghào
comparable energy consumption
The fuel consumption per unit of a product produced regularly by an enterprise in the preceding year or recent years, which continues to be produced in the current year, and moreover has records that can be compared.

可持续发展 kěchíxù fāzhǎn
sustainable development

可的松 kědìsōng
cortisone

可读性 kědúxìng
readability

可控硅 kěkòngguī
silicon controlled rectifier (SCR)

可口可乐 kěkǒukělè
Coca-Cola

可乐 kělè
Cola
E.g. 天府可乐 Tianfu Cola / 蜜茶可乐 Honey Tea Cola

可视电传 kěshì diànchuán
visual fax
Also called 传真.

可视电话 kěshì diànhuà
videophone; viewphone

可行性研究 kěxíngxìng yánjiū
feasibility study
Also called 可行性分析 feasibility analysis.

克格勃 Kègébó
the KGB
Acronym for the transliteration of the Soviet Union's Committee of State Security.

克隆 kèlóng
clone
E.g. 克隆羊的诞生震惊了世界。
The birth of the cloned sheep has shocked the world.

克星 kèxīng
conquering star
Something that can thoroughly overcome something else.

刻瓷 kècí
carved porcelain
Calligraphy or picture carvings on the glaze of porcelain. The artist needs many skills — drawing, engraving, calligraphy, epigraphy, etc.

客队 kèduì
(in sports) visiting team

客饭 kèfàn
guest meals
1) Meals prepared on special occasions by dining halls of institutions or offices for guests. 2) Meals sold by the portion in restaurants, trains, and boats.

客房 kèfáng
guest room
1) Rooms for putting up guests of institutions, agencies, and military units. 2) Rooms for travelers in hotels.

客户 kèhù
client, customer
E.g. 国内外客户 domestic and foreign clients

客里空 kèlǐkōng
Krikun
A transliteration of Krikun from Russian. A metaphor for the unhealthy style in news reporting that deceives and goes against objective reality. Its source is the famous Soviet play "The Front" by Korneychuk. In the play, Krikun is a reporter skilled at fabricating facts. The

term also refers in general to people who are flashy but have no substance, and who love to tell lies.

客流 kèliú
flow of travelers
The number of travelers going in a certain direction within a certain time period.
E.g. 客流量 *"volume" of travelers*

客隆 kèlóng
open storage shop

客源 kèyuán
supply of passengers (visitors, tourists)
E.g. 客源充足。 *There is an ample number of tourists.* / 承揽客源 *to contract to supply a number of tourist groups*

客座教授 kèzuò jiàoshòu
visiting professor

课间餐 kèjiāncān
recess snack
The snack taken by some elementary and secondary school students in mid-morning after their second period.

课间操 kèjiāncāo
recess calisthenics
Calisthenics done in schools in the between-class recesses.

ken

肯德鸡 kěndéjī
Kentucky fried chicken

垦区 kěnqū
reclamation area
An area of wasteland delineated for opening up to cultivation and production.

恳谈 kěntán
sincere and candid dialogue

恳谈会 kěntánhuì
frank discussion meeting
A meeting which convenes people from various sectors to hold frank discussions on one or several particular issues.

keng

坑骗 kēngpiàn
to entrap and to deceive
E.g. 坑骗群众 *to entrap and deceive the masses* / 坑骗消费者 *to entrap and deceive consumers*

kong

空播 kōngbō
aerial sowing

空对空 kōng-duì-kōng
airy, not realistic; air-to-air (missile)
E.g. 理论要密切联系实际，不要空对空。 *Theory must be closely linked to reality, and must not be airy.* / 空对空导弹 *air-to-air missiles*

空防 kōng-fáng
air transport safety patrol

空港 kōnggǎng
airport (cf. 航空港)
E.g. 北京空港配餐有限公司开始营业。 *The Beijing Airport Meal Service Company, Ltd. has begun its operation.*

空间渡船 kōngjiān dùchuán
nickname for spaceship

空间技术 kōngjiān jìshù
space technology

空间科学 kōngjiān kēxué
space science

空间垃圾 kōngjiān lājī

waste materials (discarded flying objects, etc.) in outer space

空间站 kōngjiānzhàn

space station (cf. 航天站)

空姐 kōngjiě

stewardess (on airplanes)

Abbreviation for 空中小姐.

空难 kōngnàn

space disaster

E.g. 这是一次最大的空难. *This was one of the greatest space disasters.*

空气浴 kōngqìyù

air bath

A method of body-building by exposing the body to fresh air.

空勤 kōngqín

air duty

The various kinds of jobs in aviation carried out in the air (distinguished from 地勤 ground duty).

空气质量和排放标准 kōngqì zhìliàng hé páifàng biāozhǔn

air quality and emission standards

空嫂 kōngsǎo

middle-aged female flight attendants

空天飞机 kōngtiān fēijī

a type of flying vehicle that can travel in the atmosphere as well as outer space (still being developed)

空调 kōngtiáo

air conditioning

E.g. 空调设备 *air conditioning equipment* / 自动空调 *automatic air conditioning*

空调器 kōngtiáoqì

air-conditioner

Abbreviated as 空调.

空头政治 kōngtóu zhèngzhì

phony politics

A metaphor for a style which departs from reality, indulges in empty political rhetoric and slogans, and does not solve any practical problems.

E.g. 空头政治家 *phony politician*

空域 kōngyù

space territory

The air space that belongs to a certain district or region.

E.g. 上海空域 *Shanghai air space territory*

空政 Kōng-Zhèng

the Air Force Political Department of the PLA

Abbreviation for 中国人民解放军空军政治部.

空中大学 kōngzhōng dàxué

air wave university

A type of university in which teaching is conducted by radio and television broadcasts.

空中公共汽车 kōnzhōng gōnggòng qìchē

air bus

Also called 空中客车.

空中教育 kōngzhōng jiàoyù

air wave teaching

A mode of education in which teaching is conducted by satellite, television, and radio.

空中客车 kōngzhōng kèchē

air bus

Also called 空中公共汽车.

空中小姐 kōngzhōng xiǎojiě

airplane stewardess

Abbreviated as 空姐.

空中预警飞机 kōngzhōng yùjǐng fēijī

early warning planes

空中走廊 kōngzhōng zǒuláng

air corridor

A certain space along which planes can fly.

孔塔多拉集团 Kǒngtǎduōlā Jítuán
the Contadora Bloc

Formed by Mexico, Venezuela, Colombia, and Panama in 1983 (Contadora is an island of Panama).

控办 kòng-bàn
Office for Controlling the Purchasing Power of Societal Blocs

Abbreviation for 控制社会集团购买力办公室.

控编 kòng-biān
to control the authorized size of a work unit's personnel

控产压库 kòng-chǎn yā-kù
to control and reduce the production and stockpiling of overstocked goods

控购 kòng-gòu
to control purchases (mainly refers to controlled commodities); **to control the purchasing power of societal blocs**

控股 kòng-gǔ
to control stocks or stock certificate rights

E.g. 国家要控股。 *The state must control stocks and stock certificate rights.*

控股公司 kòng-gǔ gōngsī
a company which has gained control of one or more companies through holding a certain percentage of the other companies' stocks or stock certificate rights

控诉会 kòngsùhuì
accusation meeting

A mass meeting where the people accuse the ruling class or a reactionary authority of oppression, exploitation, and persecution. This was one method by which class education was conducted.

kou

抠机 kōujī
"call" device

A device which transmits call signals. 抠 is a transliteration of the English word "call".

口 kǒu
departments

An overall term for the organs and departments of a certain sector.
E.g. 文教口 *cultural and educational departments* / 农林口 *agricultural and forestry departments* / 工交口 *industrial and transportation departments*

口头革命派 kǒutóu gémìngpài
lip-service revolutionaries

口子 kǒuzi
an opening; a crack

A metaphor for an opening which allows some people to overcome certain regulations or restrictions.
E.g. 他不敢开劳动力合理流动的口子。 *He doesn't dare to create an opening for reasonable labor mobility.*

扣帽子 kòu màozi
to put a hat on someone; to label someone

To label (e.g., backward element, bureaucratism, anti-Party, anti-socialism, etc.) someone or something without investigation, study, or careful analysis.

扣球 kòuqiú
to smash a ball

To hit a ball with a strong downward

stroke (volleyball, ping pong, badminton, etc.)

扣子 kòuzi
button; knot
A metaphor for an unresolvable ideological problem.
E.g. 解扣子 *to untie a knot (metaphorical)*

ku

苦大仇深 kǔdà chóushēn
sufferings great, hatred deep
Sufferings and difficulties were tremendous, and the hatred ran deep. This term usually refers to the sufferings of the laboring people in the old society.

苦果 kǔguǒ
bitter fruit
1) Bad outcome, painful result.
E.g. 他不得不吞下这形式主义的苦果。*He has no choice other than to swallow the bitter fruit from formalistic procedures.*
2) Insult and injury.
E.g. 任何外国不要指望中国会吞下损害自己利益的苦果。*No nation can count on China swallowing bitter fruit when something infringes her national interests.*

库区 kùqū
(water) reservoir area

库容 kùróng
capacity of a reservoir, warehouse, granary, freezer, etc.

裤袜 kùwà
pantyhose

酷 kù
cool
A metaphor for someone who is good looking, natural and unrestrained.
E.g. 他打扮得很酷。*He looked very cool.* / 小姐穿这衣服一定很酷。*Miss, you will be very cool if you try these clothes on.*

kua

夸海口 kuāhǎikǒu
"hyperbolic mouth"
Speaking in wildly exaggerated terms.

夸克 kuākè
(physics) quark (tiny particles from which matter is constituted)

跨纲要 kuà Gāngyào
to exceed the Program targets
指粮食生产平均亩产量超过《1956年到1967年全国农业发展纲要》规定的指标。(参见"纲要")
The average per-mu grain yield exceeding the targets stipulated in the National Program for Agricultural Development from 1956 to 1967. (cf. 纲要)

跨国公司 kuàguó gōngsī
transnational corporations
Also called 多国公司 multi-national corporations and 国际公司 international corporations.

跨黄河 kuà Huáng Hé
to surpass the Yellow River
The average annual per-mu grain yield in the region north of the Yellow River exceeded the 400 catties targeted in the National Program for Agricultural Development from 1955 to 1957, and reached or exceeded the 500 catties stipulated for regions south of the Yellow River. (cf. 纲要)

跨世纪 kuàshìjì
trans-century

kuai

快班 kuàibān
accelerated class
A class in a school, composed of students with strong academic foundations, which proceeds at a fast pace and has high academic requirements. After the Cultural Revolution, this method was adopted for a time as a means of recovering and developing education as quickly as possible. This term is the opposite of 慢班 decelerated class.

快餐 kuàicān
fast meals
Simple ready-made foods which save meal time, such as apportioned self-served meals, boxed meals, and packaged foods.

快递 kuàidì
express delivery
E.g. 快递邮件 express mail

快货 kuàihuò
quick-selling merchandise

快件 kuàijiàn
express mail
E.g. 快件汇款 remittance by express mail (express postal money order)

快捷 kuàijié
(Taiwan usage) express delivery
Same as 快递.
E.g. 快捷邮件 express mail

快克 kuàikè
crack (the narcotic drug)

快克婴儿 kuàikè yīng'ér
crack infants (infants with congenital effects resulting from the mother's use of crack)

快人快语 kuàirén kuàiyǔ
straightforward talk from a straightforward person

快相 kuàixiàng
instant photographs
1) Photographs that are developed immediately after exposure. 2) Photographs which customers can get from the studio as soon as possible after they are taken.

快译通 kuàiyìtōng
electronic bilingual dictionary

快硬水泥 kuàiyìng shuǐní
quick hardening cement

快中子 kuàizhōngzǐ
fast neutrons

块块 kuàikuai
blocks
A system of enterprise management by various levels of local government. (cf. 条条块块)

kuan

宽带通信 kuāndài tōngxìn
wideband connections

宽松 kuānsōng
(clothing) wide and loose; affluent; lenient, relaxed, easy-going
E.g. 报刊言论有了宽松。The standards for views published in newspapers and magazines are now more relaxed. / 电影审查标准会进一步宽松。Standards for film censorship will be relaxed one more notch.

宽限期 kuānxiànqī
grace period; day of grace

宽银幕 kuānyínmù
wide movie screen

宽展期 kuānzhǎnqī
grace period

E.g. 给商标注册六个月的宽展期 *to give a six-month period of grace for trademark registration*

款爷 kuǎnyé
granddaddy of money
Someone especially rich. Synonymous with 大款.

kuang

匡算 kuāngsuàn
rough estimate
To calculate roughly.

框架 kuāngjià
framework
1) The main structure of buildings, furniture, etc. 2) The basic concept of something or the basic conceptualization of a literary or artistic work.

框框 kuāngkuāng
framework; conventions; restrictions
Now often used as a metaphor for unreasonably restrictive rules and conventions.
E.g. 破除框框 *to eliminate strictures* / 不要受老框框束缚 *to refuse to be shackled by old strictures*

矿管 kuàng-guǎn
legal management of mining
Abbreviation for 矿业法制管理.

矿泉壶 kuàngquánhú
mineral water pot
A water-purifying device which improves the quality of drinking water by killing germs, removing minerals, etc.
E.g. 矿泉壶走俏市场。 *Mineral water pots are selling like hot cakes on the market.*

矿泉水 kuàngquánshuǐ
mineral water

矿务局 kuàngwùjú
mining bureau

kui

亏损包干 kuīsǔn bāogān
loss contract system
A kind of contractual responsibility system implemented in deficit enterprises. Within a certain period, a quota on a subsidy is applied. Enterprises that reduce their deficits, and turn their deficits into profits ahead of schedule receive the pre-determined loss subsidy or a percentage of it. Those that exceed their loss quotas are not given an additional subsidy.

kun

昆交会 Kūn-Jiāo-Huì
the Commodities Exchange Fair in Kunming, China
Abbreviation for 中国昆明商品交易会.

困退 kùntuì
to withdraw due to difficulties
To return personnel sent to other locales or urban educated youth sent to the countryside to their original location as a result of certain difficulties.

kuo

扩大内需 kuòdà nèixū
to expand domestic demand

扩大企业自主权 kuòdà qǐyè zìzhǔquán
to expand enterprise autonomy

To give enterprises greater autonomy (under the directions of the national plan) in their utilization of manpower, material and financial resources, production management, and supply and marketing. For example, after guaranteed completion of required state-assigned tasks, enterprises may arrange their own production according to market demands, take on cooperative tasks, adopt a floating wage system, etc. Abbreviated as 扩权 to expand power.

扩股 kuògǔ
to enlarge the number of shares
E.g. 增资扩股 *to increase investment and enlarge the number of shares*

扩建 kuòjiàn
to expand (a building)

扩权 kuòquán
to expand power
Abbreviation for 扩大企业自主权 to expand enterprise autonomy. (cf. 扩大企业自主权)

扩容 kuò-róng
to expand capacity
E.g. 股市扩容。 *The stock market is expanding its capacity.*

扩音机 kuòyīnjī
amplifier
Also called 扩音器.

扩印 kuòyìn
to enlarge and print (photographs)

扩展 kuòzhǎn
to expand
To enlarge or extend outward.
E.g. 扩展马路 *to expand a road* / 扩展厂房 *to expand a factory building*

扩招 kuò-zhāo
to increase enrollment
E.g. 大学扩招是为了鼓励教育消费。 *To increase college enrollment is to encourage education.*

扩种 kuòzhòng
to expand cultivation
To expand the area under cultivation.

L

la

垃圾学 lājīxué
waste science

The study of the management and use of waste materials.

拉帮结派 lābāng jiépài
to form cliques

A manifestation of bourgeois factionalism within revolutionary ranks. Some people, for the sake of self interest, go against the principles of the organization and come together to form cliques. They practice nepotism, exclude outsiders, split the revolutionary ranks, and damage revolutionary interests. The source of this mentality is the extreme individualism and anarchism of the exploitative class.

拉出去，打进来 lā chūqù, dǎ jìnlái
to draw out and to make incursions

敌人用软硬兼施的手段把革命队伍中意志薄弱者变为蜕化变质分子或成为敌方人员，称为拉出去；敌人用派遣特务或伪装革命等手段钻进革命队伍，从事破坏活动，称为打进来。

"To draw out" means the use of soft and hard tactics by the enemy to transform weak-willed individuals within the revolutionary ranks into regressive degenerate elements or into enemy agents. "To make incursions" means such enemy tactics as sending agents or pretending to be revolutionary to infiltrate the revolutionary ranks and to conduct sabotage.

拉关系 lā guānxì
to form connections; to cultivate relations with someone

拉锯战 lājùzhàn
seesaw battle

The back-and-forth warfare between opposing sides over certain territory.

拉开帷幕 lākāi wéimù
to open the curtains

To begin a conference or event.

拉力赛 lālìsài
(loan word from English) endurance race

E.g. 汽车拉力赛 *long-distance automobile race*

拉练 lāliàn
camp and field training

Troops leaving the barracks, and carrying out training such as long-distance marching and camping, in accordance with battle requirements.

拉尼娜 lānínà
La Nina

紧跟在厄尔尼诺现象之后的一种使气候发生骤变的现象。厄尔尼诺通常是将一个地区一贯的气候特征给打乱，而拉尼娜只是加强该地区的气候特征，使干旱的土地变得更加干旱，潮湿的土地变得更加潮湿。该词来自西班牙语,意思是小女孩。

A climatic change which may follow El

Niño. El Niño often disturbs the normal characteristics of a climate in a region, while La Nina accentuates the climate's characteristics, making dry climates drier and moist ones wetter.

拉山头 lāshāntóu
factionalism
A kind of sectarianism within revolutionary ranks. It is the behavior of going against the principles of the organization, forming a clique, cultivating individual power, and dominating a certain area.

拉下马 lāxiàmǎ
to pull off the horse; to depose
To pull someone with an official title down from his throne, i.e., to cause someone to fall from power.

拉下水 lāxiàshuǐ
to pull into the water
A metaphor for luring someone to commit a bad deed. Also called 拉人下水 pulling someone into the water.
E.g. 被资产阶级拉下水 *to be pulled into the water by the bourgeoisie*

喇叭裤 lǎbākù
bell-bottom pants

lai

来件装配 láijiàn zhuāngpèi
assembling imported parts
A form of economic cooperation whereby components are provided from another source or from a foreign country, and assembled into finished products in local factories. The local factories earn a certain processing fee.

来料加工 láiliào jiāgōng
processing imported materials
To have foreign businesses provide the raw materials, and to employ domestic facilities and labor to carry out processing and manufacturing in accordance with the foreign specifications, thereby earning a processing fee.

来样加工 láiyàng jiāgōng
processing according to a foreign specimen
A form of supplemental trade. To manufacture a product according to specimens and materials supplied by a foreign business, then the products are turned over to the other party to market or sold directly to the other party.

lan

蓝筹股 lánchóugǔ
blue chip
High-quality, high-priced stocks.
E.g. 四川长虹股有"中国第一蓝筹股"的美誉。 *The Sichuan Long Rainbow stocks have the reputation of being "China's first blue chip stocks".*

蓝领工人 lánlǐng gōngrén
blue-collar worker

蓝帽子 lánmàozi
blue caps
Machine-maintenance technicians in textile factories (as opposed to weavers, who wear white caps).

蓝色农业 lánsè nóngyè
sea agriculture

拦洪 lánhóng
to hold back a flood
To hold a flood back and not allow it to cause a disaster, moreover to as far as possible, create benefits from damage.

篮坛 lántán

basketball circles (people)

揽储 lǎnchǔ
to control savings
To attract capital to savings accounts of a bank by using a high interest rate.
E.g. 高息揽储问题得到了控制。
The problem of controlling savings by using high interest rates has been brought under control.

览胜 lǎnshèng
to sightsee
E.g. 颐和园览胜 *Sightseeing at the Summer Palace*

懒汉鞋 lǎnhànxié
loafers
Synonymous with 松口鞋 shoes with a loose opening. (cf. 松口鞋)

烂摊子 làntānzi
shambles
A metaphor for a situation which is difficult to rectify.

滥发 lànfā
to send out indiscriminately
E.g. 滥发奖金 *to indiscriminately pay out bonuses* / 滥发学历证书 *to indiscriminately send out academic transcripts* / 滥发复印材料 *to indiscriminately distribute review materials*

lang

狼孩 lánghái
wolf child
A child raised by wolves.

lao

捞稻草 lāodàocǎo
to clutch at a straw
Derived from the saying "a drowning person will clutch at even a straw". A metaphor for struggling in vain.

捞油水 lāoyóushuǐ
to sponge off
A metaphor for improperly reaping benefits or extra income for oneself.

捞资本 lāozīběn
to dredge for capital
To resort to all methods to attain private objectives. It has a pejorative connotation.

劳保 láo-bǎo
abbreviation for 劳动保护 **labor protection or** 劳动保险 **labor insurance**

劳保所 láo-bǎo-suǒ
Institute of Labor Protection Science
Abbreviation for 劳动保护科学研究所.

劳动保护 láodòng bǎohù
labor protection
The various measures adopted to protect workers' safety and health at work. Abbreviated as 劳保.

劳动保险 láodòng bǎoxiǎn
labor insurance
A system whereby cadres and workers are guaranteed the necessities of life in case of illness, old age, disability, or other special circumstances. Abbreviated as 劳保.

劳动定额 láodòng dìng'é
labor quota
1) The standard manpower needed to complete a certain production task using certain production technology and under certain production organizational conditions. In industry, it is generally called 生产定额 production quota. In agriculture, it is usually called "工作定额

work quota". 2) The quantity of work to be accomplished by an average worker in one day of normal work, under certain production conditions and according to certain quality standards.

劳动镀金论 láodòng dùjīnlùn
philosophy of laboring for sake of gold plating

A term used during the Cultural Revolution. A cadre or intellectual participating in labor without sincerely tempering and reforming himself, and only for the sake of attaining the glory of laboring, so as to show himself off as being ideologically revolutionary.

劳动服务公司 láodòng fúwù gōngsī
employment service company

A social work organization that deals with the employment of urban youths. Its main tasks are to register and supervise youths awaiting employment, provide vocational training and a referral service, and to assist youths awaiting employment to start up collective or individual businesses.

劳动改造 láodòng gǎizào
labor reform

In sentencing counter-revolutionary criminals and other criminal offenders, China forces all those who are able-bodied to work in order to reform themselves and to become new persons. This is an important measure that China uses to transform the majority of criminal offenders into law abiding, self supporting workers.

劳动观点 láodòng guāndiǎn
attitude toward labor

In general, the attitude toward physical labor. The term also refers to the correct attitude toward physical labor, which is to fervently love labor.

E.g. 劳动观点很强。 *The labor attitude is very strong.* / 没有劳动观点 *lacking (a positive) labor attitude*

劳动合同制 láodòng hétóngzhì
labor contract system

The system of implementing contract agreements in productive labor. The agreements clearly state the rights and responsibilities of both parties, and are binding on the parties involved. The conditions must be agreed upon by both parties. The labor contract system may be implemented between enterprises or between enterprises and labor.

劳动化 láodònghuà
laborization

The laborization of intellectuals. That is, intellectuals must participate in productive labor and integrate themselves with the masses of workers and peasants, so that they will be transformed into persons who have both book knowledge and the ability to do productive labor. This was a slogan voiced in the 1950s.

劳动教养 láodòng jiàoyǎng
labor education

A kind of compulsory educational reform used in China for persons who violated laws but shirked responsibility for their offenses, and who are able-bodied. The term of labor education is one to three years, and can be extended one year if necessary. Labor education follows the guiding principle of combining labor production and thought education. After the term of labor education is completed, the reformed offender is not discriminated against in employment or in schooling.

劳动力市场 láodònglì shìchǎng
labor market

A site where labor is traded like a commodity. A labor market can be tangible or intangible.

劳动密度 láodòng mìdù
labor intensity

The amount of labor expended in certain production work.

劳动密集型 láodòng mìjíxíng
labor-intensive (as opposed to capital-intensive)

E.g. 劳动密集型产品 *labor-intensive product* / 劳动密集型产业 *labor-intensive industry*

劳动密集型行业 láodòngmìjíxíng hángyè
labor-intensive professions

Professions that require a relatively large amount of manpower, such as the service professions, and arts and crafts factories.

劳动模范 láodòng mófàn
labor model

An honorary title given by China to advanced persons who have made significant contributions to socialist construction. Abbreviated as 劳模.

劳动人事部门 láodòng rénshì bùmén
personnel departments

Administrative departments specifically responsible for job assignments, transfers, wages, benefits, dismissals, rewards and penalties of cadres and workers.

劳动日 láodòngrì
labor days

1) A yardstick for calculating the amount of labor and remuneration of peasants in the rural socialist collective economy. One labor day is the equivalent of the average amount of agricultural work accomplished by an average worker in one day. One labor day normally consists of ten work points. Labor remuneration is determined partly by the number of labor days and partly by the unit value of a labor day. 2) Labor day is another name for a work day; it is a unit used in calculating the amount of labor time. In general, eight hours is one labor day.

劳动英雄 láodòng yīngxióng
labor hero

An honorary title given to those who have accomplished much and contributed to industrial or agricultural production of the revolutionary regime at the revolutionary base before liberation.

劳动致富户 láodòng zhìfùhù
households that have prospered through labor

Also called 冒尖户 stand-out households. They are the agricultural households that have done especially well in production after the rural responsibility system was instituted. They have very high incomes and enjoy a standard of living above the ordinary.

劳动组合 láodòng zǔhé
labor constitution

Making employees efficient.

劳动组合制 láodòng zǔhézhì
a system of building a labor organization

That is, within an enterprise, the leaders and employees of various units select each other and voluntarily sign an agreement stating the rights, responsibilities, and benefits of each party, and thereby build a labor organization to engage in production.

劳改 láo-gǎi
labor reform
Abbreviation for 劳动改造.(cf. 劳动改造)

劳改犯 láo-gǎifàn
criminal sentenced to labor reform

劳教 láo-jiào
labor education
Abbreviation for 劳动教养.(cf. 劳动教养)
E.g. 劳教人员 labor education personnel

劳教所 láo-jiào-suǒ
labor reformatory

劳均 láojūn
average per worker
E.g. 劳均收入 average income per worker

劳模 láo-mó
labor model
Abbreviation for 劳动模范.(cf. 劳动模范)
E.g. 劳模大会 labor model conference

劳损 láosǔn
strain due to over-exertion
E.g. 肌肉劳损 muscle strain

劳务 láowù
service professions
A term in political economics. Also called 服务 services. The work of persons engaged in service professions, such as medical workers, who cater to special needs of people, not in a material way, but in the form of a service.

劳务出口 láowù chūkǒu
to export services
Also called 无形出口 invisible exports. It refers to the export of non-material things, which include mainly scientific and technological know-how, maritime and air transport services, insurance and travel services, cultural arts, and manpower. Compared with the export of commodities, export of services involves little investment and costs little, but yields fast returns and high profits.

劳务费 láowùfèi
payment for a service

劳务合作 láowù hézuò
service cooperation
Through friendly commercial exchanges, and in an organized, planned manner, to undertake certain contracted engineering projects abroad for a fee, or to provide services for foreign contractors.

劳务旅行 láowù lǚxíng
working tourism
Tourism which includes working at a locale, whereby the tourist is immersed in that society.

劳务市场 láowù shìchǎng
employment market
A place where potential employers and employees can meet and negotiate; fields that have employment openings.

劳逸结合 láoyì jiéhé
integrating labor and leisure
To arrange appropriately the two aspects of labor and rest, so that they are well balanced.

劳资处 láozīchù
payroll office
Abbreviation for 劳动工资处.

劳资科 láozīkē
payroll department
Abbreviation for 劳动工资科.

老八路 lǎobālù
old Eighth Route
Eighth Route was the Eighth Route Army, people's militia led by the Chinese Communist Party during the War of Resistance Against Japan. Old Eighth Route is a term of endearment that people later gave to the Eighth Route Army cadres and soldiers who had fought in the War of Resistance Against Japan, and who had endured the test of long-term hardship and struggle.

老保 lǎobǎo
old conservatives
During the Cultural Revolution this term was applied to those persons who did not actively adhere to the leftist ways and whose thoughts were said to be "conservative".

老大难 lǎo-dà-nán
old, big, and difficult
指长期存在、影响很大而又不能解决的问题。也指存在这种问题的单位。 Problems that have existed for a long time, that have a major impact, and that cannot be solved. The term also refers to units with these kinds of problems.
E.g. 老大难单位 *an old, big, and difficult unit*

老干部 lǎogànbù
old cadre
Cadres who are advanced in age or seniority, particularly those who joined the revolution before October 1, 1949.

老革命 lǎogémìng
old revolutionary
A revolutionary cadre who joined the revolution early and has experienced many struggles.

老红军 lǎohóngjūn
old Red Army
Someone who has participated in the Agrarian Revolutionary War (1927-1937) and has been in the Red Army.

老虎 lǎohǔ
tiger
1) A metaphor for someone with vitality. 2) Facilities that consume a great amount of energy or raw materials, or that lead to serious waste or damage, e.g., coal tiger, electricity tiger. 3) Persons who commit graft, theft, or tax evasion in a big way.
E.g. 那小伙子干劲十足,有点小老虎的味道。 *That young fellow is so energetic that he exudes the spirit of a little tiger.* / 在五十年代贪污1千元以上是"小老虎",1万元以上是"大老虎"。 *In the 1950s, a person who embezzled more than 1,000 yuan was called a "little tiger" and if he embezzled more than 10,000 yuan he was called a "big tiger".* / 他多占住房严重,人们称他为房老虎。 *He hogs up housing in a serious way, so the people dubbed him "housing tiger".* / 投机倒把的粮老虎 *opportunistic profiteering "grain tiger"* / 那种船是耗油量很大的油老虎。 *That kind of ship is an "oil tiger" as it consumes a great deal of oil.*

老虎屁股 lǎohǔ pìgu
tiger's rump
A metaphor for a fierce difficult-to-deal-with person. It has a pejorative connotation.

E.g. 那人是老虎屁股，摸不得。 *That person is a tiger's rump, he cannot be touched.*

老化 lǎohuà
to age (referring to material things, living organisms, people, knowledge and techniques, etc.)
E.g. 细胞老化 *aging of cells* / 人口老化 *aging of the population* / 领导班子老化 *aging of the leadership ranks* / 知识老化 *aging of knowledge* / 设备老化 *aging of facilities*

老黄牛 lǎohuángniú
old ox
A metaphor for an honest, sincere, hardworking and selfless person.

老框框 lǎokuāngkuang
old conventions
E.g. 打破老框框 *to destroy old conventions*

老龄 lǎolíng
elderly, persons who have reached a certain age
E.g. 老龄问题全国委员会 *National Commission on the Problems of the Elderly* / 老龄活动站 *senior citizens' activities center* / 老龄婚姻介绍所 *senior citizens' marriage agency* / 老龄大学 *senior citizens' university*

老龄化 lǎolínghuà
age-ization
Too high a ratio of elderly in the population (over 20%) or within the leadership ranks.

老龄问题 lǎolíng wèntí
societal problems of the elderly

老冒 lǎomào
extremely dimwitted
E.g. 他因太老冒又吃亏。*Because he is extremely dimwitted, people always take advantage of him.*

老年型国家 lǎoniánxíng guójiā
elderly nation
Often refers to a nation with more than 7% of its population over sixty-five or more than 10% of its population over sixty.

老区 lǎoqū
old areas
Old liberated areas. Areas that had been liberated and established a revolutionary regime long before 1949.

老弱病残 lǎo-ruò-bìng-cán
(abbreviation) the old, weak, sick, and handicapped

老三届 lǎosānjiè
people who were in middle school during the first three years of the Cultural Revolution (1966-1968)

老三篇 lǎosānpiān
three old essays
指毛泽东的三篇文章。即《为人民服务》、《纪念白求恩》和《愚公移山》。
Three articles by Mao Zedong: "Serve the People", "In Memory of Norman Bethune" and "The Foolish Old Man Removes the Mountain". (cf. 老五篇)

老少边穷（地区）lǎo-shǎo-biān-qióng (dìqū)
old, minority, border, and poor (areas)
Old revolutionary base areas, minority peoples' areas, border regions and poor areas.
E.g. 要帮助老少边穷地区发展经济。*We must help the old, minority, border, and poor areas develop their economies.*

老鼠会 lǎoshǔhuì
to take advantage of a pyramid sale;

to engage in the opportunistic marketing of goods

老帅 lǎoshuài
honorific appellation for the noble and prestigious marshals of the Chinese People's Liberation Army

老外 lǎowài
colloquial term for foreigners or outsiders

老五篇 lǎowǔpiān
five old essays
指毛泽东的五篇文章, 即《为人民服务》、《纪念白求恩》、《愚公移山》、《关于纠正党内的错误思想》和《反对自由主义》。
Five articles by Mao Zedong: "Serve the People", "In Memory of Norman Bethune", "The Foolish Old Man Removes the Mountain", "On Correcting Mistaken Ideas in the Party" and "Combating Liberalism". (cf. 老三篇)

老中青 lǎo-zhōng-qīng
(abbreviation) old, middle-aged, and young persons

老中青三结合 lǎo-zhōngqīng sānjiéhé
integration of the old, middle-aged, and young
指领导班子要由老干部、中年干部和年轻干部结合组成。The leadership ranks should be formed by joining together old, middle-aged, and young cadres.

老子党 lǎozǐdǎng
paternalistic party
A kind of big power chauvinism in the international communist movement. It means that in its relations with the other fraternal parties, the Communist Party of a large country does not respect other parties, and takes on the role of father in directing and ordering around other parties.

老字辈 lǎozìbèi
the older generation
Those who are older and have substantial qualifications and experience.
E.g. 老字辈要扶持小字辈。The older generation should support and nurture the younger generation.

lei

雷打不动 léidǎ bùdòng
unmoved by thunder
A metaphor for absolute steadfastness or immutability

雷锋精神 Léi Fēng jīngshén
the spirit of Lei Feng
Lei Feng was a model soldier of the Chinese People's Liberation Army. He died in action on August 15, 1952. The spirit of Lei Feng consists mainly of: a class stance that clearly distinguishes love from hate, a revolutionary spirit with deeds matching words, a communist style of being public minded with no regard for the self, and a proletarian fighting will that defies personal danger.

雷区 léiqū
mine field zone
(Originally) mine field zone, now used metaphorically in referring to dangerous circumstances.
E.g. 公司误入雷区。The company mistakenly entered a land mine zone.

雷射 léishè
laser
Transliteration of "laser", also called

激光. Also written as 镭射.
E.g. 雷射唱片 laser disc

镭射唱片 léishè chàngpiān
laser disc

镭射电影 léishè diànyǐng
movie projected from a laser disk
Also called 镭射片.

镭射影碟 léishè yǐngdié
laser disk
Also called 激光视盘.

leng

冷巴 lěngbā
air conditioned bus

冷板凳 lěngbǎndèng
cold bench
A metaphor for an indifferent post or a cold reception; being cold-shouldered or slighted.

冷背 lěngbèi
commodities that attract no buyers and are passed over
E.g. 冷背商店 commodities not in demand / 冷背书 books not in demand

冷处理 lěngchǔlǐ
cooling treatment
(Originally) a cooling off process in manufacturing; now also a metaphor for putting off dealing with a problem until the heat of the moment has subsided.

冷点 lěngdiǎn
cool spots
Places or things that have not yet attracted popular attention.
E.g. 开辟旅游冷点 to develop cool spots for tourism

冷柜 lěngguì
cold locker (for food storage)

冷库 lěngkù
cold storage
Also called 冷藏库.

冷门货 lěngménhuò
goods that are not much in demand

冷销 lěngxiāo
commodities moving very slowly
Opposite of 热销 hot selling.
E.g. 近年凉席是冷销货。 In recent year cool mats (straw mats used on beds) have been slow selling.

冷饮 lěngyǐn
cold drinks

li

离经叛道 líjīng pàndào
to rebel against orthodoxy
Formerly, this meant to rebel against the tenets of the feudal ruling class. Now it means repudiating socialist direction and rebelling against the principles of Marxism-Leninism and Mao Zedong Thought.

离任 lírèn
to leave a post
To transfer out of one's original work unit.
E.g. 中国驻美大使将离任回国。 The Chinese ambassador to the United States is about to leave his post and return to China.

离土不离乡 lítǔ bù líxiāng
to leave the land but not the home
Peasants who engage in industry, commerce, mining, transportation, and other professions, but still reside in the rural villages. Their families still cultivate a portion of the land, and produce a portion of their foodstuff. This type of peasants is said to "leave the land but

not the home".

离休 líxiū
retirement
Abbreviation for 离职休养 leave a position to rest. It is a system for settling retiring old cadres who took part in revolutionary work before the founding of PRC, or who have lost the ability to work. After cadres retire, their basic political treatment remains unchanged, and they receive favorable welfare benefits. When they retire, old cadres receive honorary retirement certificates.
E.g. 离休干部 *retired cadre*

离职 lízhí
to leave one's job
To leave one's job due to old age, illness, or other reasons.
E.g. 离职休养 *to leave one's job in order to recuperate* / 文化水平低的干部要离职学习。 *Cadres of a low cultural level must leave their jobs and undertake studies.*

理疗 lǐliáo
physiotherapy
Abbreviation for 物理疗法 physiotherapy.

理论界 lǐlùnjiè
theoretical realm

理论至上 lǐlùn zhìshàng
theory in command
To one-sidedly emphasize the importance of theory, seeing it as more important than practical experience, and to deny the dependence of theory on practice. This is an erroneous viewpoint.

理念 lǐniàn
idea; thought
E.g. 资本经营理念 *capital management idea*

理赔 lǐpéi
insurance compensation
An insurance company compensating an insured client for losses sustained.

理顺 lǐshùn
to straighten and smooth out
To straighten and smooth out something that is jumbled.
E.g. 理顺经济关系 *to straighten and smooth out economic relationships*

礼宾司 lǐbīnsī
Department of Protocol

历史反革命 lìshǐfǎngémìng
old-line or historical counter-revolutionaries
Historical counter-revolutionary elements, persons who suppressed or sabotaged the revolutionary cause before liberation, such as secret agents who organized, led, or participated in espionage organizations, reactionary Party and Youth League core members, heads of reactionary secret societies, local tyrants, bandits, etc.

利多 lìduō
policy or news that causes a rise in the stock market index or in a particular stock

利改税 lìgǎishuì
(pertaining to enterprises) to change the form of payment to the state from a percentage of the profit to taxes

利好 lìhǎo
profitable; good
E.g. 股市利好。 *The stock market is profitable.* / 有利好消息传来。 *Here comes the good news.*

利空 lìkōng
policy or news that causes a dip in the stock market index or in a par-

ticular stock

E.g. 深圳股市受到利空传言的打击。 *The Shenzhen stock market suffered a drop due to rumors of a new policy.*

利民活动 lìmín huódòng

people benefitting activities

Activities beneficial to the people.

利润挂帅 lìrùn guàshuài

profits in command

Under the erroneous influence of the extreme left, the profit principle of production in enterprises was denied. Emphasis on the profit principle was vilified as 利润挂帅 putting profit in command, and it was criticized as "revisionism". This was erroneous.

利润留成 lìrùn liúchéng

retained proportion of the profit

Also called 利润分成 shared proportion of the profit and 利润提成 lifted out proportion of the profit. The profit realized in a state-managed enterprise is in part turned over to the state, and according to regulations, another part called "retained proportion of the profit," is retained by the enterprise to allocate as it wishes. Funds from the retained proportion of the profit are used for developing production, operating collective welfare work, and issuing workers' bonuses.

利税 lì shuì

profit and taxes

例会 lìhuì

regular meetings

Meetings held according to a regular schedule.

例假 lìjià

regular holidays

Days stipulated as holidays, such as New Year's Day, Spring Festival (China's New Year), May First, National Day, etc. 2) A euphemism for menstruation and the menstrual period.

立党为公 lìdǎng wèigōng

establish the Party for the public

Organizing and joining the Communist Party solely to seek benefits for the majority of the people. It is the opposite of 立党为私 establish the Party for private gains.

立党为私 lìdǎng wèisī

establish the Party for private gains

Organizing and joining the Communist Party with the goal of seeking private gains for oneself or for a few people. It is the opposite of 立党为公 establish the Party for the public.

立等可取 lìděng kěqǔ

to be finished while you wait

Pertaining to developing photos, repairs, etc.

立交工程 lìjiāo gōngchéng

overpass project

Abbreviation of 立体交叉工程.

立交桥 lìjiāoqiáo

cloverleaf bridge

Abbreviation for 多层立体交叉桥 multi-level three dimensional interchange bridge.

立体电影 lìtǐ diànyǐng

3-D movie

立体农业 lìtǐ nóngyè

an intensive form of farming whereby aspects of agriculture and animal husbandry are dovetailed to yield maximum productivity

立体声 lìtǐshēng

stereo sound

E.g. 立体声收录机 *stereo radio-tape*

player

立体种植 lìtǐ zhòngzhí

an intensive form of agricultural production whereby different crops are interwoven to maximize productivity

立足点 lìzúdiǎn

foothold

A standpoint taken in observing or dealing with a certain issue. Also a location relied upon for survival and development.

力挫 lìcuò

to defeat with utmost effort

E.g. 中国队力挫日本队获冠军。*The Chinese team defeated the Japanese team with great effort and thus won the championship.*

力度 lìdù

extent of merit; degree of strength

E.g. 拳头的力度 *strength of the fist* / 这是一部有力度的作品。*This is a meritorious work (of literature).*

力克 lìkè

to overcome with effort

To attain success through struggle.

力争上游 lìzhēng shàngyóu

to strive for the best; to aim high

To work hard to reach the front or to attain the most advanced standards.

E.g. 鼓足干劲, 力争上游, 多快好省地建设社会主义。*Go all out, aim high, and achieve greater, faster, better and more economical results in building socialism.*

力作 lìzuò

magnum opus

lian

联办 liánbàn

to collaborate in setting up

E.g. 联办企业 *collaborative enterprise* / 两个单位联办一所学校。*Two units collaborate in managing a school.*

联播 liánbō

to broadcast over a network

Several radio or television stations simultaneously relaying the same program.

联产承包 liánchǎn chéngbāo

production related contracting

A production team contracts out land and production work to peasants or small teams, using the method of calculating remuneration in relationship to output. It is also called the 联产承包责任制 production related contract responsibility system or 包干到户 work contracted to the household. (cf. 包干到户)

联产承包责任制 liánchǎn chéngbāo zérènzhì

Same as 家庭联产承包责任制.

联产到户 liánchǎn dào hù

production related household contract system

Synonymous with 联产到劳 production related laborer contract system.

联产到劳 liánchǎn dào láo

production related laborer contract system

One form of the agricultural production responsibility system. It is also called the 统一经营, 联产到劳责任制 unified management, production related, laborer responsibility system. It involves contracting the production work directly to the laborer to complete, and calculating the remuneration in the contract or paying according to the output. (cf. 五定一奖)

联产到人 liánchǎn dào rén
production related individual contract system
Synonymous with 联产到劳 production related laborer contract system.

联产计酬 liánchǎn jìchóu
calculating remuneration in relation to output
The remuneration-related-to-output production responsibility system. It links up production responsibility, fiscal responsibility, and individual distribution. Simply, it calculates remuneration according to output. That is, it takes the quantity and value of the products as the basis for calculating remuneration. This system overcomes equalitarianism in distribution, and better implements the principle of distribution according to labor. The remuneration-related-to-output production responsibility system has many forms, such as contracting jobs, production contracted to households, work contracted to households, speciality contracts, etc.

联动 liándòng
unified action

联购联销 liángòu liánxiāo
joint purchasing and marketing
A method of joint management by commercial units. That is, they join together in purchasing and marketing commodities.

联合体 liánhétǐ
an economic entity made up of various components

联户 liánhù
joint households
Several peasant households organizing and joining together to manage enterprises.
E.g. 联户林场 *joint-household tree farm* / 联户选购 *joint household purchasing*

联机检索 liánjī jiǎnsuǒ
online information retrieval

联检 lián-jiǎn
combined inspection
E.g. 联检制度 *combined inspection system* / 联检单位 *combined inspection unit*

联赛 liánsài
league matches
A competition between three or more comparable teams in such sports as basketball, volleyball, and soccer.

联社 liánshè
an organization made up of two or more cooperatives

联手 liánshǒu
to link hands; to join closely together

联体 liántǐ
Same as 连体.

联网 liánwǎng
to network, to link related matters by computer into one system

联销 liánxiāo
two or more independent businesses joining together to sell goods

联谊 liányì
friendship ties
To make friendly contacts, to form friendships.
E.g. 联谊活动 *activities for developing friendship ties* / 联谊晚会 *evening get-together for developing friendships*

联谊会 liányìhuì

parties
Recreational activities which give the opportunity to make friendly contacts and form friendships.

联姻 liányīn
linked by marriage
(Originally) two families linked by marriage. Now often used metaphorically to mean two parties forming a close relationship.
E.g. 新技术与土特产联姻。*New technology and the production of local specialities have resulted in a close relationship.*

联营 liányíng
two or more parties jointly managing an enterprise

联营户 liányínghù
joint management households
Households that join together in managing a certain enterprise.

联展 liánzhǎn
two or more units setting up an exhibition (may include selling)
E.g. 举办联展 *to put on a joint exhibition*

连队 liánduì
company (a military unit)
The customary term for a particular military unit and units comparable to it.

连冠 liánguàn
to win the championship successively
E.g. 中国女排五连冠。*The Chinese women's volleyball team won five successive championships.*

连锁店 liánsuǒdiàn
chain store
A retail store belonging to a chain and managed by a company.

连体 liántǐ

Siamese twins
Twins with a certain part of the body connected together. Also written as 联体.
E.g. 连体婴儿 *infants with a linked body part*

连续剧 liánxùjù
serial play

连续片 liánxùpiān
serial movie

连轴转 liánzhóuzhuàn
to turn the axle continuously
To work without pause within a certain period.
E.g. 他二十多天连轴转，没有休息。*He worked non-stop for over twenty days.*

廉政 liánzhèng
honest and clean politics; political honesty
E.g. 廉政建设 *construction (of a nation, city, etc.) with a honest policy* / 廉政制度 *honest policy system* / 廉政监督员 *honest policy supervisor*

恋情 liànqíng
romantic love

恋人 liànrén
men and women in love

练摊 liàntān
to operate a stall (for business)
E.g. 这老外来咱中国练摊。*This foreigner came to China to learn how to operate a stall.*

liang

粮管所 liángguǎnsuǒ
the office of grain and oil management

Abbreviation for 粮油管理所.

粮票 liángpiào
grain coupons

Coupons for purchasing grains and grain products issued by China's grain department as a means of guaranteeing the planned supply of grains. They are divided into two types: coupons usable nationally and coupons usable only in stipulated locales.

粮油补贴 liáng-yóu bǔtiē
grain and oil subsidy

When the costs of grain and oil purchased by the state exceed the ration prices of the grain and oil necessary for people's livelihoods, the differential is subsidized by the state, and is called the farmers' "grain and oil subsidy". This policy is enacted to increase income but not affect people's livelihoods.

粮油关系 liáng-yóu guānxì
the grain and oil source

The source that provides the grain and oil for an individual or a group. That is, the provision store that supplies their grain and edible oil. When one's residence changes, one's grain and oil source will correspondingly be in another location.

粮状元 liángzhuàngyuán
number one in grain production

A person who has attained outstanding achievements in grain production. ("状元 Number One Scholar" was a title conferred on the candidate who came first in the highest imperial examination.)

良性循环 liángxìng xúnhuán
beneficial cycle

A certain system with internal links that form a circle of movements and transformations that produce good results. For example, in agriculture, by fully utilizing human and animal excrement and animal and plant waste, to promote the development of agriculture, forestry, animal husbandry, fisheries and other sidelines, a beneficial cycle within the agricultural system can by maintained.

两保一挂 liǎngbǎo yīguà
two guarantees and one linkage

实行企业承包经营责任制的一种形式。两保是：保证照章纳税和完成上缴利润；保证完成经国家批准的企业技术改造任务。一挂是：实行职工工资总额与经济效益挂钩，工资总额随效益增减。

Measures that govern the enterprise responsibility system. The "two guarantees" are guaranteeing the payment of profit and taxes to the state and guaranteeing the completion of technological reforms approved by the state. The "one linkage" is the direct link between the workers' wages and the profits generated by the enterprise.

两报一刊 liǎngbào yīkān
two newspapers and one magazine

指《人民日报》、《解放军报》和《红旗》杂志。"文化大革命"期间，两报一刊常联合发表在当时具有权威性的社论和文章。

The two newspapers, *People's Daily* and *Liberation Army News*, and the magazine *Red Flag*. During the Cultural Revolution, these two newspapers and one magazine often jointly published editorials and articles that were authoritative at the time.

两不变 liǎngbùbiàn

the two immutables

指1982年4月全国农村工作会议上提出的两不变政策,即土地等基本生产资料公有制长期不变和集体经济要建立生产责任制长期不变。

A policy, proposed at the National Conference on Rural Work in April 1982, whereby two things will remain unchanged over a long period: the public ownership of the basic means of production such as land, and the institution of the production responsibility system in the collective economy.

两参一改三结合 liǎngcān yīgǎi sānjiéhé

two participations, one reform, tripartite unity

两参是干部参加劳动,工人参加企业管理;一改是改革不合理的规章制度;三结合是领导干部、技术人员和工人群众相结合。(参见《鞍钢宪法》)

The two participations are cadres participating in labor and workers participating in enterprise management; the one reform is reforming unreasonable regulations and systems; the tripartite unity is unity of cadre leaders, technical personnel, and workers.(cf. 鞍钢宪法)

两弹 liǎngdàn

the "two bombs," i.e., atomic bomb and hydrogen bomb

两弹一星 liǎngdàn yīxīng

two bombs and one satellite

Abbreviation for atomic bomb, hydrogen bomb, and man-made satellite. "Two bombs and one satellite" is symbolic of the accomplishments of China's science and technology.

两点论 liǎngdiǎnlùn

the two aspects doctrine

唯物辩证法的思想方法。要求用一分为二的观点去全面地、本质地分析研究事物。如既要看到事物的正面,又要看到事物的反面;既要看到事物的本质、主流方面,又要看到事物的非本质、非主流方面。

The dialectical materialist way of thinking. It requires one to use the "one divides into two" perspective to comprehensively and fundamentally analyze and study matters. That is, one must see the two sides of things; and one must see the non-essential, non-mainstream aspects of things as well as the essential mainstream aspects.

两定一奖 liǎngdìng yījiǎng

two fixeds and one bonus

指牧区实行的定工、定产、超产奖励的责任制,后来改为"大包干"。

The responsibility system implemented in pastoral areas whereby there were fixed quotas for work and production, and bonuses for exceeding production quotas. Later on, the system was changed to 大包干 the big responsibility system.

两分法 liǎngfēnfǎ

method of dividing into two

毛泽东对辩证法或其对立统一规律的一种通俗的说法。是"两点论"的同义语。(见"两点论")

A colloquial way of referring to Mao Zedong's dialectics or his theory of the unity of opposites. It is a synonym for 两点论 the two-aspects doctrine.(cf. 两点论)

两个凡是 liǎnggè fánshì

two "any-and-alls"

"凡是毛主席作出的决策,我们都坚决拥护;凡是毛主席的指示,我们都始终不渝地遵循。"这是毛泽东逝世以后"左"倾思想严重的人所坚持的错误主张。
"We will resolutely uphold any and all policy decisions made by Chairman Mao; we will unswervingly adhere to any and all of Chairman Mao's directives." This was an erroneous stance held by those with serious leftist tendencies after the death of Mao Zedong.

两个估计 liǎnggè gūjì
two assessments
即"四人帮"于1971年在全国教育工作会议纪要中提出的对"文化大革命"前17年教育战线形势的"估计"。具体内容是 1)认为教育战线在17年中是"资产阶级专了无产阶级的政",党的教育路线"基本上没有得到贯彻执行"。2)认为学校教师队伍中的大多数和17年培养出来的大多数学生的"世界观基本上是资产阶级的",是"资产阶级知识分子"。"两个估计"完全是颠倒黑白,违背事实。
The assessments, given by the Gang of Four in 1971 in the "Minutes of the National Conference on Educational Work" of the educational front in the seventeen years prior to the Cultural Revolution. The concrete details are: 1) The educational front in those seventeen years was a case of "the bourgeoisie usurping the dictatorship of the proletarian class", and a claim that the Party's line on education was "basically not carried out". 2) The world view of the majority of those in the ranks of school teachers and the majority of the students nurtured in those seventeen years was basically that of the bourgeoisie, and they were "bourgeois intellectuals". The "two assessments" completely turned black into white, and was removed from reality.

两个基本点 liǎnggè jīběndiǎn
the "two basic points"
中国共产党十三大制定的党的基本路线的两个基本内容,即坚持四项基本原则;坚持改革开放的方针。
The two main directives promulgated by the Thirteenth National Congress of the Chinese Communist Party, i.e., adhering to the four "basic original principles" and at the same time upholding the policy of reform and liberalization.

两个积极性 liǎnggè jījíxìng
two initiatives
指领导干部的积极性和广大群众的积极性。又指中央的积极性和地方的积极性。
The initiative of the cadre leaders and the initiative of the broad masses. Also the initiative of the central government and local areas.

两个离不开 liǎnggè líbùkāi
two inseparables
指汉族离不开少数民族,少数民族离不开汉族。
The Han people are inseparable from the minority peoples, and the minority peoples are inseparable from the Han people.

两个文明 liǎnggè wénmíng
two civilizations
指社会主义的精神文明和物质文明。
Material civilization and spiritual civilization of socialism.

两户 liǎnghù
two kinds of households
指农村专业户和重点户。(参见"专业户"和"重点户")

Speciality households and key households. (cf. 专业户 and 重点户)

两户一体 liǎnghù yītǐ
two kinds of households and one entity
农村专业户、重点户和经济联合体的简称。
Abbreviation for speciality and key households in agriculture and forestry, and the economically integrated entity.

两会 liǎnghuì
the two conferences
全国人民代表大会和全国人民政治协商会议。
The National People's Congress and the National People's Political Consultative Conference.

两极分化 liǎngjí fēnhuà
polarization
Something developing and transforming in two opposite directions. It refers specifically to the polarization between the poor and the rich peasants that occurred after China's rural land reform in the 1950s.

两快一慢 liǎngkuài yīmàn
two quicks and one slow
护士注射时的操作规则。即"进针快、出针快、推药慢"。
The rule followed by nurses in giving injections. That is "needle in quickly, needle out quickly, inject the serum slowly".

两劳人员 liǎngláo rényuán
two labor persons
指劳动改造和劳动教养人员。(参见"劳动改造"和"劳动教养")
Those who work under labor reform and the labor education system (usually criminals). (cf. 劳动改造 and 劳动教养)
E.g. 个体户中有些以前是两劳人员。Some of the individual households were previously two labor persons.

两类矛盾 liǎnglèi máodùn
two types of contradictions
指敌我矛盾和人民内部矛盾。这是性质完全不同的两类矛盾，解决的方法也不同。(参见"敌我矛盾"和"人民内部矛盾")
Contradictions between the enemy and the self and the people's internal contradictions. These two types of contradictions are entirely different in nature, and the methods for their resolution are also different. (cf. 敌我矛盾 and 人民内部矛盾)

两论起家 liǎnglùn qǐjiā
to build from two theories
指中国石油工人学习运用毛泽东的两篇哲学著作《实践论》和《矛盾论》，指导开发大庆油田，取得了胜利。
Chinese petroleum workers learning to apply two philosophical works of Mao Zedong – 实践论 "On Practice" and 矛盾论 "On Contradictions" which guided them in opening up the Daqing Oilfield and helped them to achieve success.

两平一稳 liǎngpíng yīwěn
two equilibriums and one stability
指财政上收支平衡、银行信贷平衡和市场物价稳定。
Fiscally, equilibrium between income and expenditure, between bank accounts and loans, and stability in market prices.

两权分离 liǎngquán fēnlí
separation of two rights
特指中国在改革中实行的企业所有

权与经营权分开的原则。
(Pertaining to China's economic reforms) the principle of separating the right of enterprise ownership from that of management.

两山 liǎngshān
two mountains
指自留山和责任山。
The privately owned mountain and the contract responsibility mountain.

两手抓 liǎngshǒuzhuā
grasp with both hands
Metaphor for putting an effort into building both a material civilization and a spiritual civilization.
E.g. 在工作中要坚持两手抓、两手硬。*In our work, we must persevere in grasping with both hands and being firm with both hands.*

两田制 liǎngtiánzhì
the two fields system
指某些农村在大包干的基础上,实行的口粮田和责任田分别承包的制度。
The system, practiced in certain villages, on the basis of the contract responsibility system, of contracting the grain ration fields and the responsibility fields separately.

两条道路 liǎngtiáo dàolù
two paths
指社会主义道路和资本主义道路。
The paths of socialism and capitalism.

两条路线 liǎngtiáo lùxiàn
two lines
指共产党内部的正确路线和错误路线。(参见"路线斗争")
The correct and erroneous lines within the Communist Party.(cf. 路线斗争)

两条腿走路 liǎngtiáotuǐ zǒulù
to walk on two legs
对"同时并举"的建设方针的形象比喻。基本内容是:工业和农业同时并举,重工业和轻工业同时并举,中央工业和地方工业同时并举,大型企业和中小型企业同时并举,洋法生产和土法生产同时并举。这如同人走路,两条腿才走得好。
A metaphor for upholding simultaneously two guiding principles for construction. The basic content is: to uphold simultaneously industry and agriculture, heavy and light industries, centralized industries and local industries, large-scale enterprises and medium, and small enterprises, and foreign and domestic methods of production. This is like walking, which is best done on two legs.

两头在外 liǎngtóu zàiwài
two ends abroad
中国发展沿海地区经济的措施之一。指把生产经营过程中购买原材料和销售产品这头尾两个环节都放到国际市场上去。
In China's export-oriented economic development raw materials from abroad pass through coastal regions and are processed into products which are then sold abroad.
E.g. 要实现国际大循环,两头在外,大进大出。*We must realize the great international circulation, two ends abroad, to import and export on a large scale.*

两忆三查 liǎngyì sānchá
two remembrances and three examinations
1950年中国人民解放军开展的一项阶级教育活动。两忆是忆阶级苦、民族苦;三查是查立场、查斗志、查工作。1970年解放军又开展两忆三查活动,内容是忆阶级苦、民族苦;查思想、查工作、查作风。

A class education campaign inaugurated by the Chinese People's Liberation Army in 1950. The two remembrances are remembering class bitterness and national bitterness; the three examinations are examining stand, will to fight, and work. In 1970 the Liberation Army again inaugurated the "two remembrances and three examinations" campaign. Its contents were: remembering class and national bitterness; and examining thought, work, and style.

两用人才 liǎngyòng réncái
double-function talents

指中国人民解放军培养的既能打仗,又能搞社会主义建设的军队和地方都需要的人才。

Persons with ability, in both the military arts and socialist construction, chosen by the Chinese People's Liberation Army to serve military and local needs.

两用衫 liǎngyòngshān
two-way shirts

Shirts that can be worn with collars open or closed.

两张皮 liǎngzhāngpí
two skins

比喻有关联的两个事物或两个方面彼此脱节,互不联系,不协调的现象。

A metaphor for two related matters or aspects becoming disjointed and uncoordinated.

E.g. 要克服整党与经济工作两张皮的现象。 *We must overcome the opposing tension between the two facets of rectification within the Party and economic work.* / 不要把科研和生产对立起来,搞成两张皮。 *We must not let scientific research and production become antithetical and thus become two opposing facets.*

两种基数,三种价格 liǎngzhǒng jīshù, sānzhǒng jiàgé
two kinds of base figures, three kinds of prices

指计划收购基数,外调计划基数;计划价、超购价、浮动价。

Planned state-purchase base figure and planned transfer out base figure; planned price, surplus purchase price, and floating price.

两种教育制度 liǎngzhǒng jiàoyù zhìdù
two educational systems

即全日制学校和半工半读、半农半读两种教育制度,二者同时存在,互相补充,互相促进。

The two educational systems. One, full time schooling, and the other half work, half study. The two coexist, they supplement and promote each other.

两种劳动制度 liǎngzhǒng láodòng zhìdù
two labor systems

1) 指八小时的劳动制度和半工半读的制度。2) 指固定工、临时工和合同工并存的制度。1958年提出。实行这种制度就是提倡多用临时工、合同工,少用固定工。

1) The eight-hour labor system and the half-time work and study system. 2) The coexistent systems of fixed (permanent) labor and temporary or contract labor proposed in 1958. Implementing the two systems means advocating using temporary or contract labor more, and using fixed labor less.

两种生产 liǎngzhǒng shēngchǎn
two kinds of production
指人类自身的生产和人类进行的物质资料的生产。
The production of mankind itself (through human reproduction) and the production of material resources by mankind.

两种市场 liǎngzhǒng shìchǎng
two kinds of markets
Domestic and international markets.

两种责任制 liǎngzhǒng zérènzhì
two responsibility systems
指农业生产责任制和计划生育责任制。
The responsibility systems of agricultural production and planned human reproduction.

两种资源 liǎngzhǒng zīyuán
two kinds of resources

量化 liànghuà
to illustrate something by using figures or statistics
Domestic and international resources.

量刑 liàngxíng
measure of a penalty
The type and degree of punishment for a criminal determined by a judicial body.

亮丑 liàng chǒu
to publicly reveal one's own shortcomings or mistakes
E.g. 主动亮丑 *to voluntarily reveal the ugly side* / 敢揭问题，不怕亮丑 *to have the courage to reveal problems and not be afraid of revealing the ugly side*

亮底牌 liàng dǐpái
to reveal the ins and outs (often pertaining to how something began or one's actual strength)

亮点 liàngdiǎn
shining point; bright spot
Hopeful or good outlook.
E.g. 首份年报带出市场亮点。*The bright spot of the first annual report was the good outlook regarding markets.*

亮短 liàng duǎn
to voluntarily reveal one's own shortcomings

亮红灯 liàng hóngdēng
to show the red light
A metaphor for an injunction.

亮丽 liànglì
bright and pretty
Also a metaphor for a flourishing career.

亮牌子 liàng páizi
to show the plate
A metaphor for indicating one's status or office.

亮相 liàngxiàng
to pose
1) The momentary pose struck by an opera performer as he enters or exits the stage, or by a dancer in the midst of a dance movement. The purpose is to highlight the emotions of the character or to intensify the mood of the scene.
2) A metaphor for expressing one's attitude publicly and making one's viewpoint clear.

亮证经营 liàngzhèng jīngyíng
to display a certificate in doing business
A small retailer displaying his license or certificate, to show that he is legal and responsible.

liao

疗程 liáochéng
treatment periods

In medical treatment, the continuous treatment periods stipulated for certain illnesses.

疗效 liáoxiào

efficacy of treatment

E.g. 疗效显著 *marked efficacy of a treatment*

疗效食品 liáoxiào shípǐn

curative foods

Foods with medicinal properties which are effective in curing certain illnesses.

疗养院 liáoyǎngyuàn

sanatorium

燎原计划 liáoyuán jìhuà

a plan to cultivate skilled professionals in the rural areas

撂荒 liàohuāng

abandoned land; deserted land

1) Abandoned land once used for cultivation.

E.g. 粮价太低,农民只好撂荒。*The farmers had to abandon the land because the price of grain was too low.*

2) It also means to waste assets and not conduct business any more.

E.g. 国有资产被撂荒。*National assets are wasting.*

撂挑子 liào tiāozi

to throw down a shoulder pole; to put down one's shoulder pole

A metaphor for relinquishing a responsibility that one should bear, and washing one's hands of a job.

料理 liàolǐ

cuisine

A term derived from Japanese.

料子服 liàozifú

woolen clothing

lie

列车员 lièchēyuán

train attendants

列车长 lièchēzhǎng

train crew captain

列支 lièzhī

to list as an expenditure

To include in the list of expenditures.

E.g. 排污费从生产成本中列支。*The pollutant drainage fee paid by enterprise units can be listed as an expenditure in the production costs.*

裂变 lièbiàn

nuclear fission

A metaphor for a series of major transformations within something.

E.g. 科技界在改革中发生大裂变。*The field of science and technology, in the process of reform, underwent a great fission.*

劣品 lièpǐn

low-quality products

劣生 lièshēng

inferior genes

To give birth to inferior children, as opposed to 优生 eugenics.

E.g. 人口素质下降的原因在于劣生。*The reason for the decline in the caliber of the population is inferior genes.*

劣质 lièzhì

low in quality

E.g. 劣质产品 *inferior products*

劣质低价 lièzhì dījià

poor quality, low price

Poor quality commodities will have correspondingly lower prices.

猎头公司 liètóu gōngsī

head hunting agency; head hunter
E.g. 北京是1993年开始有了第一家私营性质的猎头公司。 *The first private head hunting agency started in Beijing in 1993.*

猎装 lièzhuāng
hunting costume

lin

林带 líndài
forest belt
E.g. 防风林带 *wind-prevention forest belt* / 防沙林带 *sand-prevention forest belt*

林科户 línkēhù
scientific forestry household
An agricultural household that uses scientific methods in managing forestry.

林片 línpiàn
forest tract
A tract of forest planted to ward off wind and sand.

林权证 línquánzhèng
certificate of forest rights
A document which certifies the ownership of a forest. For the sake of encouraging peasants to plant trees and forests, the relevant departments in certain areas issue certificates of forest rights for trees planted by peasants on their privately owned hills, so that peasants are reassured of harvesting the products of their labor.

林网 línwǎng
forest network
A system of forests which crisscross and links up many forest tracts and forest belts. It serves the function of protecting farm lands and water resources.

林业专业户 línyè zhuānyèhù
forestry speciality households
Agricultural households that expend the majority of their labor and time in forestry work, and derive their family incomes primarily from forestry.

临门 línmén
(soccer) close to the goal
E.g. 临门一脚 *a kick close to the goal (in soccer)*

临时工 línshígōng
temporary worker (usually paid by the day)

临战 línzhàn
close to battle
A metaphor for nearing the start of a project.

ling

零部件 língbùjiàn
spare parts and components

零料 língliào
odd materials
Scattered raw materials in small quantities.

领办 lǐngbàn
to take the lead in setting up something
E.g. 领办乡镇企业 *to take the lead in setting up and managing enterprises in villages and towns*

领导班子 lǐngdǎo bānzi
leadership ranks
An organization composed of persons responsible for leadership roles within units.

领导骨干 lǐngdǎo gǔgàn
leadership backbone

A cadre within a unit or organization who serves a leadership function. The term also refers to a cadre within the leadership ranks who plays a main role.

领导核心 lǐngdǎo héxīn

core of a leadership group; leading nucleus

Primary persons within the leadership ranks.

另起炉灶 lìngqǐ lúzào

to fire up a separate stove

A metaphor for starting a task anew, for setting up a separate sector, or for having a separate setup.

另行 lìngxíng

to do separately

E.g. 另行规定 *to make separate regulations (disregarding the pre-established regulations)*

liu

溜门撬锁 liūmén qiàosuǒ

to break in (robbery)

溜拍 liūpāi

to fawn on

Contraction of 溜须拍马 to fawn on, metaphor for flattery and toadying.

溜派 liūpài

slinkers

Those who followed the counter-revolutionary clique of Lin Biao and the Gang of Four during the Cultural Revolution and committed many evil deeds. They refused to own up to their crimes after the downfall of Lin Biao and the Gang of Four and tried to place the blame on others scheming to slink away themselves.

溜撬 liū-qiào

to break in

Same as 溜门撬锁.

留成 liúchéng

to retain from the profits

(Pertaining to a state-managed enterprise) to retain from the profits submitted to the state a fixed portion for the unit itself to allocate; the funds from the retained proportion.

E.g. 利润留成 *a reserved proportion of the profit* / 留成比例 *the proportion of the reserved portion* / 用利润留成发奖金 *to use a reserved proportion of the profit for bonuses*

留党察看 liúdǎng chákàn

on probation within the Party

A measure used by the Chinese Communist Party to discipline its members. A party member on probation has no right to vote, elect, or be elected. If the member on probation has truly mended his ways, his membership rights are restored. If he persists in his errors, he will be expelled from the Party. The maximum probation period is two years.

留后路 liúhòulù

to leave a way open to retreat; to leave a way out

留后手 liúhòushǒu

to leave room for future maneuvering

留言簿 liúyánbù

comments notebook

A notebook for visitors to write comments in. These notebooks are often set up in bus stations, docks, trains, hotels, and exhibitions, so that travelers and visitors may write comments when they leave.

留余地 liúyúdì

to leave some leeway, i.e., not push things to the extreme

留职停薪 liúzhí tíngxīn
retain job, stop salary （cf. 保职停薪）

流动电影队 liúdòng diànyǐngduì
mobile movie projection team
A movie projection team that changes its locale frequently.

流动服务 liúdòng fúwù
mobile service
A service that shifts its work location in response to needs.

流动红旗 liúdòng hóngqí
floating red flag
A red flag is an award for superior achievers. A floating red flag is one that does not stay permanently with any unit, but changes its location according to the performances of different units.
E.g. 卫生流动红旗 *sanitation floating red flag*

流动售货 liúdòng shòuhuò
mobile vending
Venders taking merchandise in vehicles from shops to residential areas to sell, and not staying at a fixed location.

流动站 liúdòngzhàn
mobile station
A scientific research organization with researchers traveling from place to place.
E.g. 博士后流动站 *post-doctoral mobile research station*

流氓团伙 liúmáng tuánhuǒ
hoodlum gangs

流脑 liúnǎo
epidemic meningitis
Abbreviated term for epidemic cerebro-spinal meningitis.

流生 liúshēng
school dropouts
Also called 流失生.

流食 liúshí
liquid foods
Foods in liquid form, such as milk, rice broth, thin gruel, and fruit juices.

流通领域 liútōng lǐngyù
circulation domain

流向 liúxiàng
direction of flow; direction in which commodities, capital, personnel, etc., flow
E.g. 商品流向 *directions in which commodities flow, i.e., markets for commodities*

流行色 liúxíngsè
faddish colors

六个优先 liùgè yōuxiān
six priorities
中国政府为保证轻工业的发展，在六个方面采取的优先措施。即在原材料和能源供应、银行贷款、挖革改（参见"挖革改"）、基本建设、利用外资和引进技术、交通运输六个方面优先保证轻工业的发展。
The prior measures adopted by the Chinese government in six areas to guarantee the development of light industries. The six areas are: supply of raw materials and energy; bank loans; measures to tap the productivity of existing enterprises, to innovate the technology of production, and to reform production techniques and old enterprises(cf. 挖革改); capital construction; use of foreign capital and imported technology; and transport.

六害 liùhài

six scourges in society
指社会上的六中丑恶现象：卖淫、嫖娼、制作贩卖传播淫秽物品、拐骗妇女儿童、私种吸食贩运毒品、聚众赌博、利用封建迷信骗财害人。
Prostitution, pornography, kidnapping of women and children, narcotics abuse and trade, organized gambling, swindling by taking advantage of feudal superstition.

六好企业 liùhǎo qǐyè
six goods enterprise
指达到"六好要求"的国营企业。"六好要求"是：国家、集体、职工个人三者利益兼顾好，产品质量好，经济效益好，劳动纪律好，文明生产好，政治工作好。
A state-managed enterprise that has done well in the six requirements, which are: taking into consideration the benefits to the nation, the collective, and individual workers; quality products; economic efficiency; labor discipline; civilized production; and political work.

六好职工 liùhǎo zhígōng
six goods worker
即在商业部门六个方面都做的比较好的职工。这六个方面是：政治思想好，执行政策完成任务好，团结互助服务态度好，爱护公共财物好，业务技术好，经常学习好。
A worker in the commercial sector who has done well in the following six areas: political ideology; carrying out policies in completing tasks; showing an attitude of solidarity, mutual assistance and service; cherishing public property; acquiring professional skills; studying and learning frequently.

六条政治标准 liùtiáo zhèngzhì biāozhǔn
six political standards
指毛泽东在《关于正确处理人民内部矛盾的问题》一文中指出的中国社会主义时期从政治上判断言论和行动的是非的标准。即：1)有利于团结全国各族人民，而不是分裂人民；2)有利于社会主义改造和社会主义建设，而不是不利于社会主义改造和社会主义建设；3)有利于巩固人民民主专政，而不是破坏或者削弱这个专政；4)有利于巩固民主集中制，而不是破坏或者削弱这个制度；5)有利于巩固共产党的领导，而不是摆脱或者削弱这个领导；6)有利于社会主义的国际团结，而不是有损于这个团结。这六条标准中，最重要的是社会主义道路和党的领导两条。
The standards, enunciated by Mao Zedong in his article "On the Correct Handling of Contradictions Among the People" by which views and actions are to be evaluated politically during China's socialist period. Views and actions: 1) Conducive to uniting all the ethnic groups of the nation, and not to dividing the people; 2) Beneficial, rather than detrimental, to socialist reform and construction; 3) Conducive to consolidating the people's democratic dictatorship, and not to damaging or weakening this dictatorship; 4) Conducive to consolidating democratic centralism, and not to damaging or weakening this system; 5) Conducive to consolidating the leadership of the Communist Party, and not to casting off or weakening this leadership; 6) Conducive to international socialist unity, and not damaging to this unity. Among these six standards, the most important two are the ones

relating to the socialist path (2 above) and the Party's leadership (5 above).

六五计划 Liù-Wǔ Jìhuà
the Sixth Five-Year Plan
Abbreviation for 中华人民共和国国民经济和社会发展第六个五年计划 the Sixth Five-Year Plan (1981-1985) for National Economic and Social Development of the People's Republic of China; also called 六五.

遛早儿 liùzǎor
(Beijing colloquialism) to take an early morning walk

long

龙头 lóngtóu
dragon's head
A metaphor for something that occupies an initiating position and plays a key role in a matter.
E.g. 这家企业以优质名牌产品为龙头进行组织。*The focal point around which this enterprise is organized is its high-quality name brand products.*

聋童 lóngtóng
deaf child

隆乳 lóngrǔ
breast enlargement

陇兰经济带 Lǒnglán Jīngjìdài
Longhai-Lanxin Economic Belt
The east-west economic belt along the Lianyungang-Lanzhou and Lanzhou-Xinjiang railway lines.

lou

楼群 lóuqún
building project, cluster of multi-storied buildings

楼堂馆所 lóu-táng-guǎn-suǒ
buildings, halls, hotels (for foreigners), and guest houses
Abbreviation for 大楼、礼堂、宾馆、招待所.

楼宇 lóuyǔ
buildings

漏斗户 lòudǒuhù
funnel households
A metaphor for those economically disadvantaged peasant households that remain in poverty in spite of having repeatedly received aid from the state and the collective.
E.g. 对漏斗户，不能单纯地给救济，要扶本，帮助他们发展生产，改变贫困面貌。*In dealing with funnel households, we cannot simply give them aid, but must nurture the basics and help them develop production so that they can escape their state of poverty.* (cf. 扶本 and 扶志)

漏划地主 lòuhuà dìzhǔ
a landlord who escaped being classified as such
During the time of land reform, those persons who should have been classified as landlord elements but escaped being classified as such.

漏判 lòupàn
(in a sports competition) referee failing to call a foul
E.g. 以手触球的事裁判员经常漏判。*Referees often neglect to call when football players handle the ball.*

lu

路风 lùfēng
transportation work style

The collective work style of personnel in the railroad, highway, intra-city transportation sector.
E.g. 我们要努力造成良好的路风。 *We must strive to create a good transportation work style.*

路肩 lùjiān
shoulder (along a road or a railroad)

路警 lùjǐng
(abbreviation) railroad police

路考 lùkǎo
road test
A test for a driver's license in which the examinee actually operates an automobile on a road.

路线斗争 lùxiàn dòuzhēng
line struggle
The struggle between the correct and incorrect lines within the proletarian political party.

路障 lùzhàng
road block
A metaphor for a person or a thing that blocks forward movement of traffic.
E.g. 设置路障 *to set up roadblocks* / 警戒路障 *to be on the alert against roadblocks*

录放机 lùfàngjī
audio or video tape recorder-player

录入员 lùrùyuán
computer input technicians

录像 lùxiàng
videotaping

录像带 lùxiàngdài
videotape

录像机 lùxiàngjī
video recorder
A mechine for recording television images and sounds so that they may be replayed. Video tape recorders are the most common type.

录音本 lùyīnběn
taped books

录制 lùzhì
to make audio tapes or videotapes
E.g. 录制流行歌曲 *to manufacture tapes of popular songs* / 录制电视连续剧 *to tape television serials*

lǚ

旅行车 lǚxíngchē
tour bus

旅行剪 lǚxíngjiǎn
travel scissors
Scissors suitable for use during travel. They are small, light, and easy to carry.

旅游 lǚyóu
tourism
Travel and sightseeing.
E.g. 旅游事业 *the tourist enterprise*

旅游车 lǚyóuchē
Same as 旅行车 tour bus.

旅游经济学 lǚyóu jīngjìxué
economics of tourism

旅游图 lǚyóutú
tour maps

旅游鞋 lǚyóuxié
travel shoes

滤嘴香烟 lǜzuǐ xiāngyān
filter-tipped cigarette

绿党 lǜdǎng
Green Party
A political party whose platform is ecological protection.

绿化工程规划 lǜhuà gōngchéng guīhuà

green engineering program (such as planting trees)

绿卡 lǜkǎ
green card
Nickname for the US permanent residence card for aliens (formally named Resident Alien Registration Receipt Card).

绿色 GNP lǜsè GNP
GNP
The net gross national product after the cost of environmental damage caused by human activities has been taken into account.

绿色产品 lǜsè chǎnpǐn
green product

绿色长城 lǜsè chángchéng
green Great Wall
Also called 绿色万里长城 green ten thousand li Great Wall. The large scale forest belt, being planted to ward off wind and stop sand incursion, extending from Xinjiang in the west to Heilongjiang in the east. This forest belt approximates the route and length of the Great Wall, hence its name.

绿色革命 lǜsè gémìng
the green revolution
The development of new varieties of food plants through technological advances that resulted in dramatic crop yields.

绿色食品 lǜsè shípǐn
green foods
Foods that are safe, nutritious, and harmless to the public.
E.g. 已有多种食品获得绿色食品标志。 *Many foods have already been awarded the "green food" label.*

绿色塑料 lǜsè sùliào
green plastic
Also called "bio-degradable plastic" made of amylum other organic materials. This kind of plastic will bio-degrade in one year, and will not cause environmental pollution.

绿色照明 lǜsè zhàomíng
energy conservation lighting

绿色证书 lǜsè zhèngshū
green certificate
Certifying that the individual has attained a certain level of technical competence in agriculture.
E.g. 很多农民获得了绿色证书。 *Many farmers have been awarded the Green Certificate.*

绿条 lǜtiáo
green slip
Postal money order slip. It is so called because the characters and lines printed on it are green. Also called 绿条子.

绿委会 lǜ-wěi-huì
the Afforestation Commission
Abbreviation for 绿化委员会.

绿衣使者 lǜyī shǐzhě
envoy dressed in green, i.e., a mailman

绿茵 lǜyīn
green carpet, i.e., grass lawn; (by extension) soccer field, the sport of soccer
E.g. 我国绿茵姑娘出国与敌手较量。 *Our nation's women soccer players went abroad to compete with strong teams.* / 绿茵小将羊城一战 *The young soccer star played a game in Guangzhou.*

绿茵场 lǜyīnchǎng
grass lawn soccer field

绿证 lǜzhèng
green certificate

Abbreviation for 绿色证书.

lüe

掠影 lüèyǐng
glimpses (written)
Written sketches of visits or trips, similar to sketches of impressions, often used as headings in articles.
E.g. 访美掠影 *sketches of a trip to America*

lun

轮次 lúncì
the number of round trips of a boat or plane

轮伐期 lúnfáqī
lumber rotation period
Cyclical period in lumbering. The trees in a forest cannot all be felled at one time, but must be felled on a rotational basis according to a cycle. This method is beneficial to the protection of forest resources and to forest regeneration while providing lumber.

轮岗 lúngǎng
change one's (working) post
E.g. 国家公务员要实行轮岗。*State civil servants change their posts within a certain period.*

轮滑 lúnhuá
roller blade skating
E.g. 轮滑大赛 *roller blade skating competition*

轮换工 lúnhuàngōng
mining laborers recruited from ranks of peasants on a rotational basis

轮休 lúnxiū
days off in rotation
Workers taking days off in rotation. The term also refers to the period when crops are not cultivated on a certain field to help retain fertility.

轮训 lúnxùn
training in rotation
To train workers on a rotational basis.

轮作 lúnzuò
crop rotation
To rotate in a fixed order several different crops on the same field. This method can improve soil fertility and eliminate the bacteria in the soil which are harmful to certain crops.

论资排辈 lùnzī páibèi
to go according to seniority
The erroneous view and method of going purely on seniority in appointing cadres to positions and assigning jobs to them.
E.g. 论资排辈的思想做法成了破格提拔干部的严重障碍。*Going by seniority has become a serious obstacle to making exceptions in promoting cadres.*

luo

裸露土地 luǒlù tǔdì
naked land
Land not covered with vegetation.

裸戏 luǒxì
films or television programs that contain nude scenes; nude scenes in films or TV shows

落标 luòbiāo
to lose a bid (for a contract)
E.g. 他在竞争中落标了。*He lost the bid in the competition.*

落地灯 luòdìdēng
floor lamps

落地扇 luòdìshàn
standing fan (height adjustable)

落马 luòmǎ
to fall off the horse
A metaphor for losing a race.

落幕 luòmù
to lower the curtains, i.e., to conclude a show or event

落聘 luòpìn
to lose out on an appointment (to a position or job)

落实 luòshí
to solidly implement
To thoroughly investigate a policy, plan, or measure, to be certain that it is practicable, and then to carry it out.
E.g. 落实政策 *to ascertain and carry out a policy* / 落实计划 *to ascertain and carry out a plan*

落下帷幕 luòxià wéimù
to lower the curtains, i.e., to conclude a conference, exhibition, or some other event

M

ma

妈妈桑 māmasāng
head waitress in a place of entertainment such as karaoke bar

马鞍形 mǎ'ānxíng
saddle-shaped
A metaphor for things that are high at two ends and low in the middle.
E.g. 1956年至1958年，中国农业生产出现了马鞍形。 *From 1956 to 1958, there appeared a saddle shape in China's agricultural production.*

马大哈 mǎdàhā
careless
To be careless and negligent. Persons who are careless and negligent.

马蜂窝 mǎfēngwō
wasp nest
Dwelling of wasps. A metaphor for fierce persons or units that one dare not provoke.

马钢宪法 Mǎ-Gāng Xiànfǎ
the Ma-Steel Charter
The enterprise management methods of the Soviet Magnitogorsk Steel Company.

马列 Mǎ-Liè
Marxism-Leninism
Abbreviation for 马克思列宁主义 Marxism-Leninism; the classics of Marxism-Leninism.

马路新闻 mǎlù xīnwén
hearsay and rumors

马屁精 mǎpìjīng
fawning expert

马太效应 mǎtài xiàoyìng
the Matthew effect
美国社会学家罗伯特·默顿指出的一种规律性现象，即科学家荣誉越高就越易得到新的荣誉，反之，成果越少就越难创造新成果。《马太福音》中说："凡有的，还要加给他，叫他有余；没有的，连他所有的，也要夺过来。"故名。
A phenomenon in scientific circles whereby one's accomplishments and reputation tend to snowball, and those with meager accomplishments have greater difficulty achieving accomplishments (named after a line in the Book of Matthew in the Bible).

马王堆汉墓 Mǎwángduī hànmù
Han Dynasty tombs excavated in present-day Mawangdui (near Changsha in Hunan Province)

马约 Mǎ-Yuē
the Maastrichit Agreement
Abbreviation for 马斯里赫特条约, the Maastrichit Agreement.

蚂蚁啃骨头 mǎyǐ kěngǔtou
ants gnawing at a bone
In the absence of large-scale facilities, to use small-scale machine tools to process a large component, like ants gnawing at a large bone. Also, to work strenuously, bit by bit, in order to complete a large assignment.

骂娘 màniáng

cursing someone's mother
To curse someone's mother because of anger toward someone or something. (A phenomenon akin to the use of the term "s.o.b" in American English.)

mai

埋头业务 máitóu yèwù
to bury head in profession
The bad tendency of being concerned solely with one's profession and not being concerned with politics.

埋线疗法 máixiàn liáofǎ
the suture-burying treatment method
An acupuncture method which treats an illness by burying catgut in the relevant acupoints to maintain stimulation, in order to open up channels and facilitate the flow of vital energy and blood. It is suitable for treating digestive ulcers, polio vestiges, etc.

买单 mǎidān
restaurant bill
(From Cantonese dialect) Bill presented at the end of a restaurant meal.

买方市场 mǎifāng shìchǎng
buyer's market

买家 mǎijiā
purchaser; buyer; customer

麦当劳 màidāngláo
MacDonald's
An American fast-food chain.

麦饭石 màifànshí
a type of stone, shaped like a kind of wheat dumpling, which has a health function

麦乳精 màirǔjīng
extract of malt and milk
A nourishing beverage that comes in solid or powder form, and is easily dissolved in water. Its major components are malt extract, milk, eggs, and glucose.

卖大号 màidàhào
selling big
State-managed stores violating regulations and selling, on a wholesale basis, certain high-demand commodities designated for retail to parties with whom they have special connections.

卖大户 màidàhù
to sell (a retail store) to a big business; to sell big sizes
E.g. 狠刹行业中卖大户的歪风。 to fiercely demolish the corrupt trend of selling to big business.

卖方市场 màifāng shìchǎng
seller's market

卖家 màijiā
seller

卖招纸 màizhāozhǐ
to sell covers for audio tape boxes (to attract buyers)

man

瞒报 mánbào
to make a deceptive report

满产满报 mǎnchǎn mǎnbào
to fulfill production and sales targets

满点 mǎndiǎn
to reach the stipulated number of hours
E.g. 干满点 to fulfill the stipulated hours of work.

满负荷工作 mǎnfùhè gōngzuò
full operating capacity
An enterprise attaining maximum productivity in terms of labor, materials,

满勤 mǎnqín
perfect work-attendance record

E.g. 出满勤 *to have perfect work attendance* / 保证满勤 *to guarantee perfect work attendance*

满堂灌 mǎntángguàn
to stuff to the gills

A teaching method in which facts are rigidly stuffed into students, not allowing them leeway to contemplate or digest, and not caring whether they can comprehend or grasp the facts. (cf. 填鸭式教学法)

满堂红 mǎntánghóng
red all over

To be totally victorious or flourishing everywhere.

满天飞 mǎntiānfēi
(lit., fly all over the sky) innumerable, existing everywhere; to travel everywhere

满园春色 mǎnyuán chūnsè
the garden is filled with spring airs

Depicting a lively flourishing scenario.

满员 mǎnyuán
filled to capacity

To reach the stipulated number of people, as applied to passengers on a train, persons in a military unit, etc.

慢班 mànbān
slow class

A class where the students are of a lower caliber and the pace is slower.

慢件 mànjiàn
(rail transport) slow items

Baggage or parcels not accompanying passengers and which are longer in transit.

慢镜头 mànjìngtóu
(in a film or TV show) slow motion

mang

盲打 mángdǎ
blind typing

To type up words on the computer without regard to punctuation, paragraphing, or format.

盲流 mángliú
blind flow; unauthorized move

1) The movement of people without government sanction.

E.g. 饥荒的那二年,城内盲流特别多。 *In those two famine years, there was an exceptionally large number of people in cities who had moved there without government sanction.*

2) Persons who moved without government sanction.

E.g. 他 1960 年盲流到黑龙江省。 *He moved to Heilongjiang Province without government sanction in 1960.*

盲校 mángxiào
school for the blind

忙音 mángyīn
(telephone) busy signal

mao

猫儿腻 māornì
cat grime

A metaphor for secretive, improper matters (also called 猫腻儿).

E.g. 这里有点猫儿腻。 *There is something fishy here.* / 不要玩猫儿腻。 *Don't play any fishy tricks.*

猫耳洞 māoěrdòng
cat earholes

Semi-circular holes dug on either side of

a trench for protection (used in warfare).

毛哔叽 máobìjī
woolen serge

毛孩 máohái
hairy child

毛片 máopiān
films awaiting inspection (by censors) and revision; also refers to pornographic films

毛选 Máo–Xuǎn
Selected Works of Mao Zedong
Abbreviation for 毛泽东选集.

毛泽东思想 Máo Zédōng Sīxiǎng
Mao Zedong Thought

毛泽东思想体系 Máo Zédōng Sīxiǎng tǐxì
Mao Zedong Thought system

毛泽东思想宣传队 Máo Zédōng Sīxiǎng xuānchuánduì
Mao Zedong Thought propaganda teams
Mao Zedong Thought propaganda teams made up of workers and soldiers of the Liberation Army. They were the work teams dispatched to the cities during the Cultural Revolution to lead the work in primary and secondary schools, as well as in colleges and universities.

毛著 Máo–Zhù
writings of Mao Zedong
Abbreviation for 毛泽东著作.

矛盾上交 máodùn shàngjiāo
passing the buck
Certain cadres or organizations reporting hard-to-solve and hard-to-deal with problems to higher authorities and letting them take responsibility for them. This is an irresponsible attitude.

矛头向上 máotóu xiàngshàng
to point the spearhead upward
The fallacy, on the part of the counter-revolutionary clique of Lin Biao and Jiang Qing during the Cultural Revolution, of advocating pointing the spearhead of struggle at upper level cadre leaders. In essence, they were inciting the masses to rise and rebel, to overthrow revolutionary cadre leaders, in order to realize their vicious ambition of usurping the Party and seizing power.

冒富 màofù
to become rich
To have a much higher income and living standard than the average, to become richer than one's peers.

冒富大叔 màofù dàshū
Uncle Maofu
Originally the male protagonist Jiang Maofu in the movie "Laughter at Moon Bay". People affectionately called him Uncle Maofu. Now the term refers in general to village folks who have prospered through labor.

冒尖儿 màojiānr
to stand out
To be superior or outstanding.

冒尖儿队 màojiānrduì
stand-out teams
Production teams that have actively implemented the Party's guiding policies, developed production quickly, greatly increased the income of peasants, and prospered before other.

冒尖儿户 màojiānrhù
stand-out households
Also called 劳动致富户 households that have prospered through labor. Agricultural households that have prospered through labor, and whose standard of

living is above the ordinary.

冒领 màolǐng
to pose as someone else in claiming something

冒傻气 màoshǎqì
to appear muddle headed or dumb

冒失鬼 màoshīguǐ
a rash, careless person

贸促会 Mào-Cù-Huì
China's Commission for the Promotion of International Trade
Abbreviation for 中国国际贸易促进会.

贸发会议 Mào-Fā-Huìyì
United Nations Trade Development Conference
Abbreviation for 联合国贸易发展会议.

贸易保护主义 màoyì bǎohù zhǔyì
trade protectionism

贸易货栈 màoyì huòzhàn
commercial warehouse
An intermediary commercial agency which engages primarily in commercial service activities such as organizing buyers and sellers to make transactions directly, and serving as an agent for purchase, sale, storage, and transport. Some commercial warehouses also manage some businesses of their own.

贸易战 màoyìzhàn
trade war; struggle to gain a world market

mei

煤倒 méidǎo
to improperly resell coal at a profit; coal profiteer

煤老虎 méilǎohǔ
coal tigers
1) Boilers with low coal burning efficiency and high coal consumption. 2) Units or individuals who hold power over the supply of coal, and who abuse this power for private gain, committing extortion and blackmail in the process.

煤气罐 méiqìguàn
gas bottle
A sealed bottle for liquefied petroleum gas (LPG).

煤质 méizhì
quality of coal

煤砖 méizhuān
coal bricks; briquet
Brick-shaped coal pieces made from coal dust mixed with water. They are used as a fuel.

没戏 méixì
hopeless; no good prospects
E.g. 他以为没戏了。 *He thought it was hopeless.*

媒体 méitǐ
media, material or facility for transmitting sound waves, light waves, magnetic waves, and information

美编 měi-biān
art editing
Abbreviation for 美术编辑.

美餐 měicān
to have a wonderful meal
E.g. 美餐一顿 *a marvelous meal* / 一顿美餐 *a wonderful meal*

美发 měifà
to beautify hair; to have a hairdo
E.g. 美发表演 *hair-dressing performance* / 为职工义务美发 *to provide a free hair-dressing service to employees*

美发厅 měifàtīng

měi

beauty parlor (for hairdos)

美化 měihuà
to beautify
E.g. 美化环境 *to beautify the environment*

美联储 Měi–Lián–Chǔ
American Federal Reserve Committee
Abbreviation of 美国联邦储备委员会.

美容 měiróng
to improve one's appearance; to have cosmetic treatment
E.g. 美容高手 *cosmetic expert* / 美容美发保你漂亮。*Cosmetic treatment and hair dressing will guarantee that you will be beautiful.*

美食 měishí
gourmet food
E.g. 很多种上乘美食 *many kinds of high-class gourmet foods*

美食家 měishíjiā
a gourmet

美食街 měishíjiē
gourmet street
A street with many different restaurants.

美院 měi–yuàn
academy of fine arts
Abbreviation for 美术学院.

美展 měizhǎn
art exhibition
Abbreviation for 美术作品展览.

媚俗 mèisú
(re literary works) catering to the readership's poor taste
E.g. 文学不能媚俗。*Literature must not cater to the reader's poor taste.*

men

门店 méndiàn
shops (that sell goods or provide services)

门将 ménjiàng
gate general
The goalie in certain sports.

门镜 ménjìng
door peephole

门前三包 ménqián sānbāo
three responsibilities in front of the gate
指各单位负责门前和所在地段环境卫生的责任制,"三包"是包卫生、包绿化、包秩序。
A responsibility system whereby each unit is responsible for environmental sanitation in its own area and the area outside its gate. The three responsibilities are: sanitation, landscaping, and orderliness.

门球 ménqiú
a croquet-like team sport with five players on each team

闷棍 mèngùn
a sudden strike of a club
A metaphor for a sudden unexpected blow.
E.g. 挨了闷棍 *to have suffered an unexpected blow*

meng

蒙混过关 ménghùn guòguān
to attempt to pass an investigation by being evasive

蒙在鼓里 méng zài gǔlǐ
sealed in a drum
A metaphor for being kept in the dark

about something occurring right under one's nose.

E.g. 他们仍然蒙在鼓里。 *They are still in the dark.*

朦胧诗 ménglóngshī
murky poetry

Poetic works of an obscure style which appeared in China's poetry circles in the late 1970s and early 1980s. Their characteristics are: thematic ideas not obvious, poet's train of thought unclear, not easily understandable.

蒙古大夫 Měnggǔ dàifu
a quack

猛增 měngzēng
dramatic increase

E.g. 销量猛增。 *Sales volume has skyrocketed.* / 产值猛增。 *Output value has skyrocketed.* / 赤字猛增。 *The deficit has increased drastically.*

孟泰精神 Mèng Tài jīngshén
the spirit of Meng Tai

The working class' spirit of being the master of one's own affairs, manifested by loving the factory as one's own family, struggling assiduously, and striving to build the nation. Meng Tai is a worker in the Anshan Steel Works in the northeast, a model worker, and a Communist Party member. He loves the factory as his own family, works assiduously and has achieved outstanding accomplishments for China's economic recovery and socialist construction. He has been repeatedly elected model worker.

mi

迷彩 mícǎi
camouflage colors (used in warfare)

迷彩服 mícǎifú
clothing in camouflage colors

迷你 mínǐ
(transliteration) mini

迷你裙 mínǐqún
mini skirt

迷思 mísī
myth; unknown field or phenomenon

谜团 mítuán
something elusive

E.g. 千古谜团 *an age-old riddle* / 解不开的谜团 *an unsolvable riddle*

米袋子 mǐdàizi
rice bag

A metaphor for primary foods like rice, wheat, and other products.

E.g. 要解决好人民群众的米袋子问题。 *We must solve the problem of the people's rice bags (i.e., supply of staples).* / 稳住米袋子 *to stabilize the supply of staples*

密报 mìbào
secret report

Abbreviation for 秘密报告.

密集劳动 mìjí láodòng
labor intensive

Cf. 劳动密集型

密码箱 mìmǎxiāng
case with a combination lock; suitcase with a combination lock

密商 mìshāng
secret negotiations

Abbreviation for 秘密商量.

密植 mìzhí
dense planting

To appropriately reduce the space between rows and between individual plants on a unit area of land, to increase the quantity sown, or to increase the number of saplings.

mian

棉白糖 miánbáitáng
powdered white sugar

棉府绸 miánfǔchóu
cotton poplin

棉花糖 miánhuātáng
cotton-like candy

棉华达呢 miánhuádání
cotton gabardine

棉茧绸 miánjiǎnchóu
cotton-silk fabric

棉农 miánnóng
cotton farmers

面包车 miànbāochē
minibus

面的 miàndī
mini-van taxi cab

面对面 miàn-duì-miàn
face to face; to do something right in front of the person concerned
E.g. 面对面批评 to criticize face-to-face / 面对面评议领导 to critique the leadership face-to-face

面料 miànliào
surface fabric
Materials used for the outside of jackets and quilts. They can be cotton, wool, silk, or synthetic.

面面观 miànmiànguān
multi-perspective (used in titles of articles and books)
E.g. 买书难面面观 the many facets of the problems in purchasing books / 世界人口面面观 the many facets of the world's population / 高速公路面面观 the many facets of super-highways

面世 miànshì
to emerge
To emerge in society.
E.g. 一种新试制的涂料将面世。A new experimental paint is about to come out.

面市 miànshì
to appear on the market
E.g. 新产啤酒下月面市。The new beer will appear on the market next month.

面试 miànshì
to examine by interview
To carry out an examination through an interview.
E.g. 对考生要增加面试。We should increase the use of the interview format in examining students.

面授 miànshòu
to teach or explain face-to-face
E.g. 面授机宜 to brief (someone) on how to act / 函授与面授相结合 to combine teaching through correspondence with face-to-face sessions / 组织面授 to organize face-to-face instruction

面向 miànxiàng
1) to face; in the direction of
E.g. 面向生产 to face production / 面向社会 to face society / 面向现实 to face reality
2) to cater to; to meet the needs of

面向农村 miànxiàng nóngcūn
to meet the needs of rural villages
E.g. 毕业分配的原则是面向农村。The principle in job assignments for graduates is to meet the needs of rural villages.

面向群众 miànxiàng qúnzhòng
to cater to the needs of the masses

E.g. 宣传工作要面向群众。*Propaganda work should be directed at the masses.*

面值 miànzhí
face value
The surface monetary value of a certificate or coupon with a certain unit of value. This face value may be different from its actual value.
E.g. 面值两角的邮票 *a stamp with a face value of twenty cents (but maybe worth much more on the philatelic market)*

miao

苗床 miáochuáng
seedbeds
Fields for cultivating crop seedlings. Those which use artifcial heating to spur growth are called warm beds; those which use only such things as glass and solar heat to maintain warmth are called cold beds.

苗木 miáomù
nursery stock
Cultivated tree saplings. They are usually planted in nurseries. They can be grown from seeds, or by grafting, cuttings, etc.

苗期 miáoqī
seedling period
Growth period for seedlings.

苗禽 miáoqín
poultry chicks
Specially bred chickens and ducklings.

苗情 miáoqíng
seedling condition
The growth condition of seedlings.

苗子 miáozi
seedlings; young successors
Metaphor for young people destined to be successors to certain tasks.

庙堂 miàotáng
altar hall in a temple
A metaphor for a sacred place or realm.
E.g. 艺术庙堂 *sacred hall for the arts*

mie

灭虫宁 mièchóngníng
bephenium

灭资兴无 miè zī xīng wú
eradicate capitalism and foster proletarianism
To destroy bourgeois ideology and establish proletarian ideology. The term was popular before and during the Cultural Revolution. It is no longer used. Same as 兴无灭资.

min

民办 mínbàn
founded and managed by private citizens
E.g. 民办公助 *privately managed but assisted by the state* / 民办科技机构 *privately managed sci-tech organization* / 民办高等教育 *privately managed higher education*

民办教师 mínbàn jiàoshī
citizen-managed teachers
Teachers in rural citizen-managed or state-managed schools who do not receive the normal remuneration from the government. These teachers are mostly educated youths in rural villages. Their remuneration is in the form of work points for comparable manual labor in

production teams. They participate in the distribution system along with peasants, and receive a certain amount of cash as subsidy.

民兵工作三落实 mínbīng gōngzuò sānluòshí
three solid implementations for militia work
Militia work must be solidly implemented organizationally, politically, and militarily. (cf. 落实)

民兵师 mínbīngshī
militia divisions
Militia organizations in communes and large enterprises and institutional units organized along the lines of level one military divisions.

民代国储 mín dài guó chǔ
storage of national grains by citizens
The storage of agricultural products purchased by the state by peasants individually or collectively, as a way of alleviating the state's shortage of storage facilities. The relevant government agencies pay the peasants reasonable fees according to the quantity and length of time of storage. This method of grain storage has been practiced in China in recent years.

民倒 míndǎo
to profiteer by improper buying and reselling on the part of ordinary citizens (as opposed to 官倒, the same kind of profiteering on the part of officials)

民革 Mín-Gé
Revolutionary Committee of the Chinese Kuomintang
Abbreviation for 中国国民党革命委员会, one of China's patriotic parties, founded on January 1, 1948, in Hong Kong.

民工潮 míngōngcháo
the phenomenon of a wave of peasants flooding urban areas in search of work
E.g. 每年春节前后都出现民工潮。 There is a wave of peasant workers flooding the urban areas every year around Chinese New Year time.

民柬 Mín-Jiǎn
Democratic Kampuchea
Abbreviation for 民主柬埔寨.

民建 Mín-Jiàn
China Democratic National Construction Association
Abbreviation for 中国民主建国会, one of China's patriotic democratic parties, founded in December 1945 in Chongqing.

民进 Mín-Jìn
China Association for Promoting Democracy
Abbreviation for 中国民主促进会, one of China's patriotic democratic parties, founded in December 1945 in Shanghai.

民警 mínjǐng
people's police
Abbreviatioon for 人民警察.

民盟 Mín-Méng
China Democratic League
Abbreviation for 中国民主同盟, one of China's patriotic democratic parties, founded in Chongqing in 1941, adopted its present name in 1944.

民品 mínpǐn
civilian goods; civilian products
Abbreviation for 民用产品. The term can be compared with 军品 military goods.

民调 mín–diào
public opinion research; poll
Mediation of disputes among citizens.
E.g. 民调工作 *civil mediation work*

民企 mín–qǐ
public-run enterprise

民庭 mín–tíng
civil court
Abbreviation for 民事法庭. It is responsible for adjudicating civil cases.

民委 Mín–Wěi
ethnic affairs commission
Abbreviation for 民族事务委员会, specifically the State Ethnic Affairs Commission.

民意测验 mínyì cèyàn
opinion survey; opinion poll

民营 mínyíng
(enterprise) managed by private citizens (either collectively or individually)
E.g. 民营运输 *privately-operated transport* / 民办民营 *set up and operated privately*

民用三表 mínyòng sānbiǎo
three meters for citizens' use
指居民日常生活所用的电表、水表、煤气表。
The three meters for measuring electricity, water, and gas which residents use in their daily lives.

民运会 mín–yùn–huì
Minorities Traditional Sports Meeting
Abbreviation for 少数民族传统体育运动会.

民政 mínzhèng
civil administration
A component of domestic administration. In China, this includes elections, administrative districting, local governments, residency administration, national citizenship administration, mobilization of workers for public projects, marriage registration, registration of mass organizations, support for revolutionary martyrs and servicemen (veterans administration), relief work, etc.

民主办社 mínzhǔ bànshè
democratic management of a collective organization
To use democratic methods to manage collective economic organizations, such as agricultural collectives, people's communes, and supply cooperatives. For example, the cadres of these organizations are chosen through elections by members, members – in a variety of ways – participate directly in management, and financial matters are reported to members periodically.

民主党派 mínzhǔ dǎngpài
democratic parties
指在长期革命斗争中，同情和支持中国共产党领导的人民革命，中华人民共和国成立后，拥护社会主义制度，接受中国共产党的领导，积极参加社会主义建设的其他政党。这些政党是：中国国民党革命委员会、中国民主同盟、中国民主建国会、中国民主促进会、中国农工民主党、中国致公党、九三学社、台湾民主自治同盟。各民主党派都是中国人民政治协商会议的组成成员和中国共产党领导的爱国统一战线的组成部分。
China's political parties, other than the Communist Party, that empathized with and supported the Chinese Communist Party's leadership of the people's revolution during the long revolutionary

struggle, and which, after the founding of the People's Republic of China, supported the socialist system, accepted the leadership of the Chinese Communist Party, and actively participated in socialist construction. These political parties are: Revolutionary Committee of the KMT, China Democratic League, China Democratic National Construction Association, China Association for Promoting Democracy, Chinese Peasants' and Workers' Democratic Party, China Zhi Gong Dang, Jiu San Society, and Taiwan Democratic Self-Government League. Each democratic party is a member of the Chinese People's Political Consultative Conference and a component of the patriotic united front led by the Chinese Communist Party.

民主改革 mínzhǔ gǎigé
democratic reforms

Social reforms which eradicate the feudal system and establish a democratic system. They include reforms in the areas of land ownership, enterprise management, marriage system, as well as liberation of serfs and slaves in certain minority areas.

民主管理 mínzhǔ guǎnlǐ
democratic management

To use democratic methods in managing enterprises; that is, in socialist enterprises, to implement democratic centralism, to allow workers to exercise their rights as masters of their own affairs and to participate in enterprise management. There are workers' representative associations in enterprises; grass-roots cadres in enterprises are chosen through democratic elections; within enterprises, democracy is practiced in the areas of administration, technology, and economics.

民主集中制 mínzhǔ jízhōngzhì
democratic centralism

A system which combines centralism on the basis of democracy and democracy under centralized leadership. It is the organizational principle of the proletarian political party, socialist state organizations, and citizens' groups.

民主人士 mínzhǔ rénshì
democratic personages

Patriotic public figures with a certain amount of renown and societal influence who are not members of any political party, and who, in China's revolutionary period, empathized with and supported the propositions of the Chinese Communist Party and participated in patriotic democratic activities, and after the founding of the People's Republic accepted the leadership of the Chinese Communist Party and supported socialism.

民主生活 mínzhǔ shēnghuó
democratic life

The term usually refers to the political and organizational life within the Communist Party and the Youth League. It fully promotes democracy, appropriately initiates criticism and self-criticism, upholds truth, and corrects errors.

E.g. 党的民主生活正常进行，有利于党的团结与统一，保证党的方针政策顺利进行。 *The normal practice of the Party's democratic life is beneficial to the unity and solidarity of the Party, and ensures the smooth implementation of the Party's policies.*

民主生活会 mínzhǔ shēnghuóhuì
democratic life meetings

Small scale meetings convened occasionally within a class or a section of an organization. In a democratic manner, they initiate criticisms and self-criticism in relation to problems that exist in people's work or life, in order to attain the goals of self-education and continuous advancement. These democratic life meetings are often convened within such organizations as the Communist Party, the Youth League, and political work sections.

民族大家庭 mínzú dàjiātíng
the big family of ethnic groups
The various ethnic groups are equal regardless of their size. There are unity, love, and fraternity among them, just like a harmonious family.

民族隔阂 mínzú géhé
estrangement between ethnic groups
The mutual mistrust, antagonism, and enmity that exist among ethnic groups within a nation. This estrangement is created by the reactionary ruling class.

民族区域自治 mínzú qūyù zìzhì
autonomy of minority areas
To establish autonomous organs within ethnic minority regions, to exercise autonomous rights, and under the unified leadership of the State Council, to manage the internal local affairs of ethnic minorities.

民族学院 mínzú xuéyuàn
national minority institutes
Colleges and universities established in China primarily for cultivating minority cadres. Their primary functions are to recruit minority students, cultivate minority cadres, and conduct scientific research into minority issues. There are Central University of Nationalities and local minority institutes.

ming

明白人 míngbairén
sensible persons
Persons who know and understand certain issues. In the context of reforms, the term refers to persons who are supportive of the Party's line, knowledgeable, vigorous, proficient in their professions, able to manage, and courageous in breaking new ground.

明补 míngbǔ
to openly subsidize; subsidy disbursed to individuals directly

明贴 míngtiē
Synonymous with 明补 above.

鸣放 míngfàng
to air views
To fully express one's opinions and views.

名模 míngmó
famous model

名声大振 míngshēng dàzhèn
reputation suddenly soaring

名特 míngtè
a famous speciality of a certain locale; a famous special product of a certain locale
E.g. 名特产品 *famous local products*

名优 míngyōu
(traditionally) famous actor; famous high quality brand; well-known and superior
A contraction of 名牌 brand name and 优质 high quality.
E.g. 名优产品 *quality brand name*

products

明细 míngxì

detailed; in detail; clear and detailed

E.g. 明细帐 *subsidiary ledger* / 明细的管理条例 *detailed management regulations*

命令主义 mìng lìng zhǔyì

commandism

The style of leadership which loses touch with reality and with the masses, and which relies solely on enforcing orders to expedite work. This is one manifestation of bureaucratism.

mo

摸底 mōdǐ

to touch the bottom

To understand all the details.

E.g. 大家的思想情况,他都摸底。 *He understands all the details in others' thinking.*

摸老虎屁股 mō lǎohǔ pìgu

to touch the tiger's rump

A metaphor for having the courage to cross paths with those who are fierce hard to deal with, and ideologically problematic.

摸论 mōlùn

the method of crossing a river by feeling for the rocks

Jocular term for the saying: 摸着石头过河 crossing a river by feeling for the rocks.

E.g. 只有摸论还不够。 *Using only the "crossing a river by feeling for the rocks" method is far from adequate.*

摸透 mōtòu

to understand clearly

To have a thorough and clear understanding of certain situations through in-depth investigation or study.

摸着石头过河 mōzhe shítou guòhé

to cross a river by feeling for the rocks

To proceed with extreme caution in dealing with an unfamiliar or uncertain matter.

蘑菇云 móguyún

mushroom cloud

模糊语言 móhu yǔyán

fuzzy language

磨合 móhé

grind together; meshing together

This term originally referred to the process of having the components of a new piece of machinery grind together to get a smooth fit; now it's a metaphor for the process of different matters mutually adjusting and meshing together.

E.g. 传统伦理观念与现代家庭意识正在磨合。 *Traditional moral concepts and concepts of the modern family are meshing together to find a compromise.*

摩的 módí

rental motorcycles

魔方 mófāng

magic cube (Rubik's cube)

魔棍 mógùn

magic stick

魔球 móqiú

magic ball

末班车 mòbānchē

the last train or bus

A metaphor for the last opportunity or occasion.

mou

谋职 móuzhí
to seek employment
E.g. 很多大学生到国营大中型企业谋职。 *Many university graduates seek employment in large and medium-sized state-owned enterprises.*

mu

亩产 mǔchǎn
yield per *mu*
The crop yield per *mu* of land.

亩均 mǔjūn
average per *mu*
The average yield or income from each *mu* of land.

母老虎 mǔlǎohǔ
tigress
A metaphor for a fierce woman, a shrew.

母夜叉 mǔyèchā
a malevolent spirit in Buddhism
A metaphor for an ugly and ferocious woman.

墓群 mùqún
a group of tombs; a tomb complex

幕墙 mùqiáng
screen wall
A wall made of a series of screens (often with inlaid glass).
E.g. 幕墙玻璃 *glass used in screen walls* / 玻璃幕墙 *glass screen walls*

木卡姆 mùkǎmǔ
(Uygur word) musical suite

目标管理 mùbiāo guǎnlǐ
goal management
A theory and method of management widely practiced in the United States. It was first proposed in 1954 by an American. According to this theory, the most important factor in motivating workers is to have them take pleasure in their work, and to have them derive satisfaction from their accomplishments. When individual employees attain their goals and aspirations, the goals of the entire enterprise are attained concurrently. The method entails transforming the overall goals of the enterprise into individuals' small goals, and to integrate the process of attaining individuals' small goals with the management process.

目无组织 mùwú zǔzhī
to defy organizational discipline
The abominable behavior of an arrogant conceited individual who disregards the organization and its discipline, takes himself to be infallible, and holds himself above the Party or Youth League organization.

牧工商联合企业 mù‐gōng‐shāng liánhé qǐyè
integrated stock-raising-industry-commerce enterprise
An economic organization which links together stock-raising, processing, and marketing.

N

na

拿牌 nápái
to take the medal; to win an athletic event

呐喊助威 nàhǎn zhùwēi
to cheer loudly in order to boost morale

那达慕 nàdámù
Nadam Fair
A Mongolian traditional fair including archery, horse racing, and wrestling.

纳米 nàmǐ
nanometer (nm)
A unit of measurement. $1 \text{ nm} = 10^{-9} \text{m}$.

纳新 nàxīn
to take in the fresh
This term originally meant to inhale fresh air; it is now a metaphor for taking in new Party or Youth League members. (cf. 吐故纳新)

nai

奶山羊 nǎishānyáng
milk goats
Goats used specifically for producing milk.

nan

南北对话 nán-běi duìhuà
North-South dialogue
Also called 南北会议 North-South conferences, international economic conferences in which developing nations and industrialized nations conduct dialogues. The term is derived from the fact that the developing nations are mostly in the Southern Hemisphere and the industrialized nations are mostly in the Northern Hemisphere.

南北合作 nán-běi hézuò
North-South cooperation
Economic cooperation between the developed and developing nations of the world.

南粮北调 nánliáng běidiào
transferring southern grain to the north
Because south China produces a surplus of grain and the north has a grain shortage, a portion of the grain produced in the south is allocated and shipped to northern cities or areas with a grain shortage.

南南对话 nán-nán duìhuà
South-South dialogue
Conferences convened by developing nations to coordinate their respective stands. The term is derived from the fact that the majority of the developing nations are in the Southern Hemisphere.

南南关系 nán-nán guānxì
South-South relations
The economic relationships among the

developing nations.

南南合作 nán-nán hézuò
South-South cooperation
Economic cooperation between developing nations.

南泥湾精神 Nánníwān jīngshén
the spirit of Nanniwan
The revolutionary spirit of relying on oneself, working hard for the prosperity of the nation, and transforming conditions of poverty. In the spring of 1941, the officers and men of Brigade 359 of the Eighth Route Army, guided by the slogan, "with a hoe and a gun, produce for self-sufficiency and protect the Party Central Committee", garrisoned at Nanniwan (southeast of present-day Yan'an in Shaanxi Province), opened up and cultivated waste land, and carried out the three-in-one task of military combat, production, and work. Though three years of hard work, they attained total fiscal and material self-sufficiency, turned in over 500,000 kilograms of public grain, and transformed Nanniwan into the south China of northern Shaanxi.

南水北调 nánshuǐ běidiào
to transfer southern water to the north
To divert water from the Yangtze River to areas lacking water in the north.

男保姆 nánbǎomǔ
male nannies
Male hired domestic workers

男单 nán-dān
men's singles
Men's singles in ping-pong, badminton, tennis, etc.

男科 nánkē
male department (in a hospital or clinic), which specializes in men's diseases

男篮 nán-lán
men's basketball
Abbreviation for 男子篮球队.

男女同酬 nán-nǚ tóngchóu
equal pay for men and women

男女作风 nánnǚ zuòfēng
improper relationship between a man and a woman
Also called 生活作风.
E.g. 他有男女作风问题。 *He has a moral problem in his relationship with a woman (or women).*

男排 nán-pái
men's volleyball
Abbreviation for men's volleyball or men's volleyball team.
E.g. 男排决赛 *men's volleyball finals* / 国家男排 *national men's volleyball team*

男朋友 nánpéngyǒu
boyfriend

男士 nánshì
(honorific) men

男双 nán-shuāng
men's doubles
Men's doubles in ping-pong, badminton, tennis, etc.

男童 nántóng
boy

男团 nán-tuán
competition between male teams
Abbreviation for 男子团体赛.

男子汉 nánzǐhàn
men (in referring specifically to their masculine characteristics)

男子气 nánzǐqì

masculinity

难产 nánchǎn
difficult labor (in childbirth)
A woman in confinement having difficulty giving birth. Also a metaphor for having difficulty in completing a literary work or a project.

nao

脑库 nǎokù
consulting company

脑瘫 nǎotān
brain failure; brain paralysis; stroke

脑体倒挂 nǎo-tǐ dàoguà
brain-brawn upside-down
The pay for manual labor being higher than that for mental labor.

闹待遇 nào dàiyù
to fuss over remuneration
A manifestation of individualism. The behavior of being dissatisfied with one's remuneration, making unreasonable demands, and quibbling endlessly.

闹独立性 nào dúlìxìng
to assert one's independence
To request improper special privileges, in order to cast off the organization's restrictions, so that one can do as one wishes and place oneself above it.

闹翻身 nào fānshēn
to fight for emancipation
To carry out revolutionary struggle, in order to be liberated from exploitation and oppression.

闹革命 nào gémìng
to make revolution
To be engaged in revolution and to carry out the revolutionary struggle.

闹工资 nào gōngzī
to fuss over wages
To be dissatisfied with one's wages or with the fact that one has not been given a raise, and to make unreasonable demands.

闹情绪 nào qíngxù
to be disgruntled
To be unhappy or restless because of dissatisfaction with one's work or studies.

nei

内参 nèicān
internal reference
Printed material to be read internally by a certain circle of people.
E.g. 这条消息登在内参上。 *This piece of information was published in the internal reference (news).*

内查外调 nèichá wàidiào
to investigate internally and externally
The relevant department conducting investigation and verification within and without the unit to which the person in question belongs. The matters being investigated can be current violations or criminal offenses, or problems from the past.

内定 nèidìng
to decide internally
To be decided internally (usually in reference to personnel decisions).

内斗 nèidòu
internal conflict or struggle

内功 nèigōng
exercises to benefit the internal organs
(Originally) a form of exercises or

qigong that strengthens one's internal organs. Now often used metaphorically in referring to the internal operations of an enterprise or group.

E.g. 调整机构，苦练内功，加快培育市场。*We must restructure the organization, strenuously practice "internal qigong", and accelerate the cultivation of a market.*

内耗 nèihào
internal waste
E.g. 要解决内部长期不团结的内耗问题。*We must solve the problem of internal waste due to endemic internal discord.*

内核 nèihé
inner core; inner essence
E.g. 观察问题要深入事物的内核。*In observing an issue, we must get to the core of the matter.*

内画 nèihuà
painting drawn on the inside of an artistic container

内紧外松 nèijǐn wàisōng
seemingly liberal but internally strict (pertaining to implementation of policies)

内控 nèikòng
controlled from the inside (i.e., not allowing those on the outside to take part)
E.g. 内控规定 *internal control regulations* / 内控对象 *targets of internal control*

内联 nèilián
intra-connections
E.g. 内联企业 *enterprises with internal connections*

内联单位 nèilián dānwèi
allied hinterland units
Shanghai and other coastal cities have assisted the development of hinterland enterprises by implementing effective economic alliances. The hinterland enterprises that have formed such linkages with coastal cities are called hinterland units.

内联外挤 nèilián wàijǐ
to ally internally and to press externally
指上海等沿海城市生产发展的战略方针。1983年提出。"内联"是：同内地要实行有效的经济联合，为发展内地经济服务，带动内地共同提高；"外挤"是：要挤进国际市场，发展对外贸易，加强国际经济合作和技术交流，提高科学技术和经济管理水平。也称"外挤内联"。

A strategy proposed in the beginning of 1983 for the development of production in Shanghai and other coastal cities. To "ally internally" means to implement effective economic linkages with the interior, in order to develop its economic services, to give it impetus, and to advance together. To "press externally" means to expand onto the international market, to develop external trade, to strengthen international economic cooperation and exchanges of technology, and to upgrade science, technology, and management standards. Also called 外挤内联 *to press externally and to ally internally*.

内留私分 nèiliú sīfēn
to retain internally and to divide up privately
To retain products within a unit and to privately divide them up among individuals, which entails violating state regulations and deceiving higher-ups.

内贸 nèimào
domestic commerce

Commerce conducted in the country or within the local area, as opposed to 外贸 foreign trade.
E.g. 内贸部 *Internal Trade Bureau*

内企 nèiqǐ
enterprises launched with domestic capital

内伤 nèishāng
internal injury (physical)

Now also a metaphor for the internal damage to a certain work, company or to damage a person's psyche.

内退 nèituì
early retirement

Employees in enterprises arranging to retire before the normal retirement age.
E.g. 男职工 50, 女职工 45, 都可以办理内退。 *Male employees aged 50 and female employees aged 45 may arrange for early retirement.*

内向型 nèixiàngxíng
domestically-oriented (pertaining to a business or an enterprise)

内销 nèixiāo
to market domestically or locally

内需 nèixū
domestic demand (in a market)

E.g. 扩大内需 *to increase (expand) domestic demand* / 内需增长率 *increasing rate of domestic demand*

内招 nèizhāo
to recruit (workers or students) from within (i.e., from the family members of existing employees)

内装修 nèizhuāngxiū
interior trimmings (walls, floor, lighting, etc.)

内资 nèizī
domestic capital

E.g. 内资企业 *enterprises operated on domestic capital*

neng

能官能民 néng guān néng mín
able to be both an official and a citizen

Able to assume the role of a cadre leader or to be an ordinary worker. It means that when one is a cadre, one should carry out one's duties and responsibilities fully, and to serve the people with one's heart and mind; and when one is not a cadre, one should be a good ordinary citizen, and be amenable to others' leadership.

能耗 nénghào
energy consumption

The consumption of energy in industrial production or transportation.
E.g. 能耗水平 *level of energy consumption*

能级 néngjí
level of competence

E.g. 能级标准 *proficiency standards* / 技术能级 *technical proficiency*

能上能下 néng shàng néng xià
able to go up or down

Synonymous with 能官能民 able to be both an official and a citizen. (cf. 能官能民)

能源 néngyuán
energy resource

能源结构 néngyuán jiégòu
energy resource structure

The proportional capacities of the various energy resource sectors in the total capacity of the entire energy resource industry.

ni

泥饭碗 nífànwǎn
clay rice bowl (in contrast to iron rice bowl)
A metaphor for farming (as a profession) and unstable professions.

泥足巨人 nízú jùrén
clay-footed giant
A metaphor for something that is huge but in reality is very weak.

尼龙 nílóng
nylon
E.g. 尼龙伞 *nylon umbrellas* / 尼龙袜子 *nylon stockings*

逆反 nìfǎn
to run counter to convention, tradition, the norm, or the expected

逆反心理 nìfǎn xīnlǐ
negativistic mentality

逆向 nìxiàng
in the opposite direction

逆序词典 nìxù cídiǎn
a dictionary which lists terms by their last characters

溺弃 nìqì
to drown and abandon (often said of infants)
E.g. 溺弃女婴 *to drown or abandon female infants*

nian

年报 niánbào
annual report
The report on an entire year's fiscal situation made to higher-ups by a finance department in the end of the year accounts.

年检 niánjiǎn
annual check-up
E.g. 年检工作 *annual check-up work*

年均 niánjūn
annual average
E.g. 年均收入 *average annual income* / 年均增产 *average annual increase in production*

年历工资 niánlì gōngzī
wages based on seniority and education
Wages determined by formal education and years on the job.

年龄结构 niánlíng jiégòu
age structure
The proportions of elderly, middle aged and young in the total population.

年轻化 niánqīnghuà
youth-ization
A leadership body or a group composed of younger people.
E.g. 干部队伍要年轻化。 *We must youth-ize (inject more young people into) the ranks of the cadres.*

年资 niánzī
age and qualifications (for a job)
E.g. 年资结构 *system of seniority* / 打破年资框框 *to break through the seniority strait jacket*

niang

娘家 niángjia
maternal home
(Originally) a married woman's natal family; now a metaphor for a place where one has lived, studied, or worked for a considerable length of time in the past, a unit in charge of personnel or work arrangements, a place of origin of a certain product.

E.g. 作家把长期生活的地方叫娘家。*Writers dub the locales where they have been brought up their maternal homes.* / 妇联是妇女的娘家。*The Women's Federation is the maternal home for women.* / 把劣质货退回娘家去 *to return inferior goods to their original source*

ning

宁左勿右 nìng zuǒ wù yòu
rather be overly left than right

The behavior of some people, in political movements or political struggles, whereby they prefer to err on the side of being to the left rather than to be seen as conservative, backward, or to risk erring on the right. They believe that left is better than right, that being left is a problem of perception whereas being right is a problem of stance. Actually, leftist and rightist errors are equally detrimental to the revolutionary cause.

niu

牛鼻子 niúbízi
muzzle of an ox (to which a rope can be tied to tame and manipulate the ox)

A metaphor for the key aspect of a matter or of a conflict.
E.g. 牵住企业改革的牛鼻子 *to grab hold of the key to reforms in enterprises*

牛鬼蛇神 niúguǐ shéshén
monsters and demons

The term originally meant strange demonic forms. It is now used as a metaphor for the various kinds of evil people and all repulsive things.

牛郎织女 niúláng zhīnǚ
the cowherd and the weaving maid

Characters in a traditional Chinese tale about a pair of lovers separated by a god and allowed to meet only once a year; now a metaphor for a couple working and living in two different places.
E.g. 很多对牛郎织女得到了团聚。*Many pairs of lovers long separated were able to be united.*

牛棚 niúpéng
cowshed

A term used during the Cultural Revolution to designate places in various units used temporarily for locking up and putting under surveillance the so-called "monsters and demons". The "monsters and demons" were the Party, government, and military cadre leaders, the intellectuals, and the ordinary citizens who were labeled traitors, secret agents, counter-revolutionaries, capitalist-roaders, etc.

牛气 niúqì
bull market

A rising trend in the stock market.
E.g. 纽约股市牛气冲天。*The New York stock market is extremely bullish.*

牛市 niúshì
(re stock market) bull market

牛仔裤 niúzǎikù
jeans

扭亏为盈 niǔkuī wéiyíng
to turn losses into gains

扭亏增盈 niǔ kuī zēng yíng
to turn a loss around and to increase profit

To turn a deficit around, and to enable

an enterprise to increase its profit.

扭曲 niǔqū

to twist out of shape; to distort (now also used figuratively)

E.g. 自行车已扭曲变型。The bicycle has been twisted out of shape. / 扭曲价格 to distort prices / 扭曲人性 to distort human nature

扭送 niǔsòng

to send (a criminal) under escort

E.g. 小偷当场被扭送到公安局。The thief was seized on the spot and handed over to the Public Security Bureau.

nong

农办 nóng-bàn

office of agriculture

Abbreviation for 农业办公室.

农大 nóng-dà

agricultural university

Abbreviation for 农业大学.

农代会 nóng-dài-huì

congress of peasant representatives

Abbreviation for 农民代表大会.

农贷 nóng-dài

agricultural cash loan

Abbreviation for 农业贷款.

农电 nóngdiàn

use of electricity in agriculture

农副产品 nóng-fù chǎnpǐn

agricultural products

Agricultural products and products from agriculture-related sidelines, such as grains, cotton, oils, pigs, eggs, chickens, ducks, wool, etc.

农工 nónggōng

peasants and workers; agricultural workers; peasants hired temporarily for other jobs

农工党 Nónggōngdǎng

Chinese Peasants and Workers Democratic Party

Abbreviation for 中国农工民主党. One of the patriotic democratic parties, founded in 1930 under the name of Provisional Action Committee of the Chinese Kuomintang (中国国民党临时行动委员会), adopted its present name in February 1947.

农工商联合企业 nóng-gōng-shāng liánhé qǐyè

integrated farm-industry-commerce enterprise

An economic organization which links together agricultural production, processing of agricultural products, and marketing of products.

农行 Nóng-Háng

Agricultural Bank of China

Abbreviation for 中国农业银行.

农机 nóngjī

agricultural machinery

Abbreviation for 农业机械.

农机户 nóngjīhù

agricultural machinery households

Agricultural households that cultivate others' land for a fee with their own agricultural machinery.

农技 nóngjì

agricultural technology

Abbreviation for 农业技术.

农家肥 nóngjiāféi

agricultural domestic fertilizer

Natural fertilizer, as opposed to chemical fertilizer.

农科户 nóngkēhù

agricultural scientific households

Agricultural households that use scientific methods to manage production. They include: households that breed superior strains, households that take on scientific experiments assigned by higher-ups, households that raise high-yield grains and cotton, households that lead in agricultural technology, members of the Science Dissemination Association, and households with educated students who have returned.

农科示范户 nóngkē shìfànhù
agricultural science model households

Also called 科技示范户 sci-tech model households. Advanced agricultural households that promote applied agricultural science and technology. These agricultural households have experience, sufficient manpower, and prestige; they are knowledgeable about techniques and readily receptive to new ideas. The state gives them priority in the supply of superior seeds, fertilizers, capital, and technical materials; it provides them with guidance in the dissemination of new applied technology; and allows them to go one step ahead of others. After they have attained results, they will then disseminate the new techniques to ordinary agricultural households and the surrounding masses. In this way, they effectively carry out their function as models.

农科所 nóng-kē-suǒ
institute of agricultural science

Abbreviation for 农业科学研究所.

农科院 nóng-kē-yuàn
Chinese Academy of Agricultural Science

Abbreviation for 中国农业科学研究所.

农垦 nóngkěn
agricultural reclamation

To reclaim wasteland for the development of agricultural production.

E.g. 农垦局 *Bureau of Agricultural Reclamation* / 农垦部门 *agricultural reclamation department*

农口 nóngkǒu
agricultural agencies

An overall term for organizations responsible for work in the field of agriculture.

农林牧副渔 nóng-lín-mù-fù-yú
agriculture, forestry, animal husbandry, sidelines, and fisheries

Abbreviation for 农业、林业、畜牧业、副业和渔业.

农贸 nóng-mào
agriculture and commerce; trading of agricultural products

E.g. 农贸结合 *to link agriculture with commerce*

农贸市场 nóngmào shìchǎng
farmers' market

Synonymous with 自由市场 *free market*.

农门 nóngmén
the field of agriculture

Work in the area of agricultural production.

E.g. 鼓励人才进农门 *to encourage talented people to enter the agricultural field*

农民工 nóngmíngōng
peasants who have migrated to urban areas to work

Also called 农工.

农民意识 nóngmín yìshí
peasant mentality

Such weaknesses as conservatism, narrow-mindedness, and selfishness which may characterize individual peasants who are small producers.

农膜 nóngmó
protective plastic film used in agriculture

农轻重 nóng-qīng-zhòng
agriculture, light industries, and heavy industries

Abbreviation for 农业、轻工业、重工业.

农区 nóngqū
agricultural district

农委 nóng-wěi
agricultural committee

Abbreviation for 农业委员会.

农业八字宪法 nóngyè bāzì xiànfǎ
the Eight-Point Charter for Agriculture

即毛泽东1958年提出的农作物增产技术措施的八个方面，概括为八个字，即土、肥、水、种、密、保、管、工。土(深耕、改良土壤、土壤普查和土地规划)、肥(合理施肥)、水(发展水利和合理用水)、种(推广良种)、密(合理密植)、保(植物保护、防治病虫害)、管(田间管理)、工(工具改革)。简称"八字宪法"。

The eight technological measures proposed by Mao Zedong in 1958 to increase agricultural production. They are summarized by the eight characters meaning "soil, fertilizer, water, seeds, density, protection, management, equipment", which mean: soil-improvement, rational application of fertilizers, development of waterworks, rational use of irrigation, improvement of seed strains, rational dense planting, crop protection, field management, improvement of farm implements.

农业队 nóngyèduì
agricultural team

A production team that specializes in managing crops. It is distinguished from teams engaged in sidelines, forestry, and fishery.

农业工程 nóngyè gōngchéng
agricultural engineering

A field of study concerned with agricultural biology, agricultural economics, and rural services. It coordinates such engineering sciences as mechanics, waterworks, electrical facilities, construction, chemical engineering, and electronics with agriculture in an organic way, enabling them to develop agricultural production techniques that lead to rapid growth, high yields, superior quality, and low consumption.

农业合作化 nóngyè hézuòhuà
agricultural cooperativization

Using as model the organizational form of cooperatives to create large-scale, collective, socialist agricultural economies from individual, dispersed agricultural economies. Also called 农业集体化 agricultural collectivization.

农业集体化 nóngyè jítǐhuà
agricultural collectivization

Synonymous with 农业合作化 agricultural cooperativizaton.

农业老四化 nóngyè lǎosìhuà
the old four "izations" in agriculture

即农业机械化、水利化、化肥化、园田化。The cover term for agricultural mechanization, irrigation, fertilzation, and garden-style cultivation.

农业区划 nóngyè qūhuà
agricultural districting

The districting of agricultural production areas. After comprehensive systematic investigation, management by districts is implemented in agriculture, forestry, animal husbandry, and fishery on the basis of the natural conditions of the various areas, their natural resources, and such societal economic factors as united labor force, material and technological facilities, and transportation facilities. In general, this includes: natural divisions, departmental divisions, and divisions according to agricultural technological reforms. China's agricultural districting occurs at four different levels: the nation, the province (region), the locality (city), and the county.

农业社 nóngyèshè
agricultural production cooperative

Abbreviation for 农业生产合作社.

农业生产合作社 nóngyè shēngchǎn hézuòshè
agricultural production cooperative

Abbreviated as 农业社. The collective economic organizations formed by China's peasants, under the guidance of the Chinese Communist Party, along the principle of voluntary sharing of mutual benefits. There were two types: the semi-socialist elementary agricultural production cooperatives and the fully socialist advanced agricultural production cooperatives.

农业生产责任制 nóngyè shēngchǎn zérènzhì
agricultural production responsibility system

A system in agricultural production that clearly stipulates the producers' responsibilities, production duties, attainable material benefits, and methods of rewards and penalties. The responsibility system links the peasants' labor intimately with their material benefits, facilitates the implementation of distribution-according-to-labor (to each according to his work) principle, and motivates the peasants' enthusiasm for production. The agricultural production responsibility system takes in various forms, such as contracts for subsections, production contracted to the household, production contracted to the team, production-related laborer contract system, production-related team contract system, and the responsibility system.

农业信用合作社 nóngyè xìnyòng hézuòshè
agricultural credit cooperatives

Collective economic organizations established after land reform by the broad masses of peasants on a voluntary basis. Their property, such as stocks and accumulation of credit, belong to the members of the cooperatives collectively. The credit cooperatives organize collective and individual savings, issue collective and individual credits. Through these activities, they help commune production teams develop agricultural sidelines, and help individual members overcome difficulties in production and everyday life.

农业中学 nóngyè zhōngxué
agricultural middle school

Vocational schools set up by China's rural people's communes. They were first founded in 1958. The schools operated on a half-study half-farming basis. Their main function was to cultivate farmers with socialist consciousness, impart general knowledge, and know-how in modern science and technology, and to train elementary level personnel in agricultural technology and management.

农艺师 nóngyìshī
masters of agricultural skills
Persons with such specialized agricultural skills as crop cultivation and seed-selection.

农运会 nóng-yùn-huì
peasants' athletic meet
Abbreviation for 农民运动会.

农展馆 Nóng-Zhǎn-Guǎn
China's National Agriculture Exhibition Hall
Abbreviation for 全国农业展览馆.

农中 nóng-zhōng
agricultural middle school
Abbreviation for 农业中学.

农转非 nóng zhuǎn fēi
change from rural to non-rural
Abbreviated term for changing from a rural residence registration to a city, town, or other non-rural residence registration. China's rural population is 80% of the entire nation's population. Rigorous restrictions are placed on changing rural residence registrations. Only those who are admitted to the military, recruited for jobs, admitted to educational institutions, or promoted to cadre ranks can change their registration.

农资 nóngzī
agricultural production resource materials, or materials for agricultural use
Abbreviation for 农业生产资料 or 农用物资.
E.g. 农资企业 *enterprises engaged in producing resource materials for agricultural production* / 农资部门 *sectors engaged in producing resource materials for agricultural production*

nu

奴才哲学 núcái zhéxué
lackey's philosophy
The mentality of being content to be ordered around by others, listening only to the master's commands, not distinguishing right from wrong, and even abetting evil acts.

奴隶主义 núlì zhǔyì
slavishness
The mentality of not thinking independently about matters, having no views of one's own, always nodding and yessing to higher-ups, and believing blindly.

nü

女单 nǚ-dān
women's singles
Women's singles in ping-pong, badminton, tennis, etc.

女将 nǚjiàng
female general
A metaphor for a women of exceptional talent and ability.
E.g. 排球女将 *female volleyball kingpin*

女篮 nǚ-lán
women's basketball
Abbreviation for 女子篮球队.

女垒 nǚ-lěi
women's softball team
Abbreviation for 女子垒球队.

女能人 nǚnéngrén
superwoman
Also called 女强人.

女排 nǚ-pái
women's volleyball
Abbreviation for women's volleyball or women's volleyball team.
E.g. 女排决赛 *women's volleyball finals* / 国家女排 *national women's volleyball team*

女强人 nǚqiángrén
(formerly) female robbers; (now) superwoman

女双 nǚ-shuāng
women's doubles
Women's doubles in ping-pong, badminton, tennis, etc.

女童 nǚtóng
girl, female child

女团 nǚ-tuán
women's team competition
Abbreviation for 女子团体赛.

女足 nǚ-zú
women's soccer team
Abbreviation for 女子足球队.

nuan

暖身 nuǎnshēn
to warm up (cf. 热身)

nuo

挪占 nuózhàn
to misappropriate
To embezzle (public funds or property) for private use.

O

OU

欧安会 Ōu-Ān-Huì
European Security and Cooperation Conference
Abbreviation for 欧洲安全与合作会议.

欧币 Ōu-bì
European currencies

欧共体 Ōu-Gòng-Tǐ
the European Community
Abbreviation for 欧洲共同体.(cf. 欧洲共同体)

欧盟 Ōuméng
European Union
Abbreviation for 欧洲联盟.

欧佩克 Ōupèikè
OPEC (the Organization of Petroleum Exporting Countries)
E.g. 欧佩克成员国 *a member nation of OPEC*

欧元 Ōuyuán
Eurodollar
E.g. 1999 年 1 月 1 日,欧元开始在欧盟 11 国正式使用。The Eurodollar was officially circulated in eleven countries of the European Economic Community on January 1, 1999.

欧洲共同体 Ōuzhōu Gòngtóngtǐ
the European Community
Composite term for 欧洲经济共同体 European Economic Community, 西欧共同市场 European Common Market, 欧洲煤铁联营 European Coal and Steel Community and 欧洲原子能联盟 European Atomic Energy Community, abbreviated as 欧共体.

偶像明星 ǒuxiàng míngxīng
idol star (movie or pop star)

P

pa

趴窝 pāwō
to be grounded
Fowls or domestic animals lying prone in their nests or pens. A metaphor for automobile breakdowns, causing them to be immobilized.
E.g. 经过抢修，趴窝的两辆汽车又开动起来了。 *After a rush-repair job, the two grounded automobiles were started again.*

扒窃 páqiè
to pickpocket
E.g. 扒窃分子 *pickpocket elements* / 扒窃活动 *pocket picking activity* / 扒窃犯 *pickpockets*

爬格子 págézi
to crawl the squares
A metaphor for writing (emphasizing the tedious aspect of writing).
E.g. 费尽心血去爬格子 *to exert oneself in the tedious task of writing*

爬坡 pápō
to climb uphill
A metaphor for struggling to advance.
E.g. 爬坡精神 *the spirit of struggling to advance* / 奋力爬坡 *to spare no effort in struggling to advance*

爬行哲学 páxíng zhéxué
crawler's mentality (cf. 爬行主义)

爬行主义 páxíng zhǔyì
crawler's mentality
To underestimate one's own capabilities in science and technology, to blindly worship the ideas from Western capitalist nations, to believe that Chinese science and technology can only follow others' beaten paths and crawl step by step behind others.

怕字当头 pàzì dāngtóu
the word "fear" hanging over one's head
The mentality of being timid and full of worries when faced with matters. The opposite of 敢字当头 the word "dare" hanging over one's head.

pai

拍板 pāibǎn
to beat the clappers; to call the shots
1) To rap a clapper to indicate the clinching of a deal; formerly used in auctions at trading companies, a metaphor for decision making by the person in charge.
2) To beat time with clappers.
E.g. 你唱，我拍板。 *You sing, I will beat time with the clappers.*

拍马 pāimǎ
to fawn on
Abbreviation for 拍马屁.

拍让 pāiràng
to auction off
E.g. 公开拍让 *public auction*

排挡 páidàng
stalls

排放 páifàng
to release
E.g. 排放废气 to release waste gas / 工业污水排放标准 the standard for releasing industrially polluted water

排灌 páiguàn
drainage and irrigation
The drainage and inflow of water.
E.g. 机械排灌 mechanized drainage and irrigation / 排灌机械 drainage and irrigation machinery

排灌站 páiguànzhàn
drainage and irrigation station

排涝 páilào
to drain waterlogged fields

排难解忧 páinán jiěyōu
to resolve or relieve difficulties and anxieties

排坛 páitán
world of volleyball

排头兵 páitóubīng
soldier at the head of the line
A soldier who stands in front of a lineup of troops. A metaphor for an advanced individual in a unit or group who is worthy of being emulated by others.
E.g. 他是我们单位的排头兵。 He is the soldier at the head of the line in our unit.

排污 páiwū
to get rid of filth
A metaphor for getting rid of polluted thought and behavior.
E.g. 排污费 fee for debris removal / 排污单位 debris-removal unit / 思想上也要排污。 Thoughts and behavior also need to be cleansed (to be rid of "pollution").

排险 páixiǎn
to eliminate risk or danger

排序 páixù
order of rank
E.g. 全国最大200家轻工企业排序 the order of rank of the nation's 200 largest light industrial enterprises

排忧解难 páiyōu jiěnán
to relieve worries and overcome difficulties
Contraction of 排除忧患 relieve worries and 解除困难 overcome difficulties.

牌号 páihào
(originally) name or trademark of a store; (now) name and grade designation of a commodity

派 pài
manner; "air" (often derogatory)
E.g. 那风度真够派。 That person sure shows off a high style! / 照片照得真好，真有派。 The photograph is really well done, it shows the person off in high style.

派出机构 pàichū jīgòu
agency
A representative agency set up in certain districts to facilitate the work of certain administrative organs. For example, a provincial government may set up administrative offices in counties to serve as its agencies.

派饭 pàifàn
arranged meals
Meals in peasants' homes arranged for cadres sent to work in rural areas for short periods. The boarders pay the peasants a stipulated amount of grain coupons and cash.
E.g. 吃派饭 to eat arranged meals

派购 pàigòu
assigned purchasing
The policy adopted by the Chinese gov-

ernment toward important agricultural products, such as pork and eggs, for which demand exceeds supply. The policy is to assign certain quotas to rural production teams or individual peasants to be sold to the state. (cf. 统购统销)

派活 pàihuó
to assign work

派售 pàishòu
superiors assigning marketing responsibilities for certain commodities to subordinates

派送 pàisòng
to send (an envoy)

派性 pàixìng
factionalism
The separating out of small groups in various mass organizations during the Cultural Revolution. The characteristics of the small group are: taking the faction as central, using the selfish interests of the individual or the small group as the point of departure in everything, engaging in political fragmentation and organizational factionalism, and carrying out destructive activities.

派仗 pàizhàng
factional wars (cf. 打派仗)

派驻 pàizhù
to dispatch to a post
To dispatch personnel to station at a certain location.
E.g. 联合国派驻贝鲁特的观察员有50人。 *The United Nations has dispatched fifty observers to station at Beirut.*

pan

攀比 pānbǐ
to vie
To imitate as examples those instances that are advantageous to oneself, in order to seek certain benefits in an improper way.
E.g. 不少机关单位在滥发奖金和实物方面互相攀比。 *Quite a few organizations and units have taken to vying with each other in distributing bonuses and material rewards indiscriminately.*

攀升 pānshēng
to climb; to rise continuously
E.g. 日元继续攀升。 *The Japanese yen is rising continuously.*

盘菜 páncài
food dish
Semi-precooked food sold by the dish.

盘档 pándàng
(re stock market) the periodic process of inventory and inspection

盘活 pánhuó
to enliven an enterprise (to make an enterprise thrive) through proper management
E.g. 盘活国有企业 *to enliven state-owned enterprises through proper management*

盘整 pánzhěng
stock prices in a relatively stable state, i.e., not subject to sharp rise or fall

判读 pàndú
machine reading

叛党 pàndǎng
to betray or rebel against the Party
Often referring specifically to the Chinese Communist Party.
E.g. 叛党卖国 *to betray the Party and the country*

叛国 pànguó
to betray one's country
叛逃 pàntáo
to betray (one's own country) and flee (to another country)
叛徒哲学 pàntú zhéxué
renegade philosophy

pao

抛荒 pāohuāng
to abandon the land and let it go fallow
E.g. 有的地方出现了耕地抛荒的现象。In some areas, agricultural land has been allowed to go fallow.

跑火 pǎohuǒ
(re business) flourishing; hot
E.g. 目前最跑火的行业是酒楼和舞厅。The hottest business these days is restaurants and dance halls.

跑冒滴漏 pǎo-mào-dī-lòu
to escape, emit, drip, and leak
原指化工生产中的浪费现象，把有用的物资从烟囱中跑了冒了，从各种漏洞里滴了漏了。也指财政收入中的各种损失。如偷税，漏税，税率偏低，截留上缴利润等。
Originally this term referred to the phenomenon of waste in chemical industries, whereby useful materials were allowed to escape, go up the chimney and to drip and leak. Now this term also means the various revenue losses due to tax evasion, tax leakage, illegal reduction of tax rates, interception of profits to be turned in, etc.

跑面 pǎomiàn
to investigate the conditions at various locales and units, and then to disseminate and promote a certain tested method on a broad scale (cf. 蹲点跑面)

泡吧 pàobā
to kill time in a bar (internet or wine)
E.g. 青年人喜欢泡吧。Young people like to kill time in a bar.

泡病号 pàobìnghào
to shirk work on the pretext of illness; malinger

泡沫经济 pàomò jīngjì
bubble economy
An economy that manifests deceptive prosperity. This kind of economy, like bubbles, expands rapidly but will suddenly burst after reaching a certain stage.

泡沫灭火器 pàomò mièhuǒqì
styrofoam fire extinguisher
Also called 泡沫灭火机.

泡沫塑料 pàomò sùliào
foam plastic; styrofoam

泡汤 pàotāng
(literal) to soak in soup; (figurative) waterlogged (of land); to dawdle (at work); to fall through (of a project or matter)
E.g. 这块地一下雨就泡汤。This land gets waterlogged every time it rains. / 改革后泡汤的就吃不开了。After reforms, those who dawdle (at work) no longer got off easy. / 计划全部泡汤。The plan fell through completely. / 奖金泡汤。The bonus fell through.

炮打 pàodǎ
to strike with cannon; to attack

炮轰 pàohōng
to bombard by cannon; to fiercely

and openly criticize someone

pei

培干 péi-gàn
to train cadres
Contraction of 培训干部.

陪餐 péicān
to be a secondary guest at a banquet
Also called 陪吃 or 陪吃陪喝.

陪床 péichuáng
to be by someone's bedside
To visit someone (a family member, relative, friend, or colleague) in hospital to keep him company and to take care of him.

陪斗 péidòu
to accompany in struggle
Terminology of the Cultural Revolution. When a primary targeted person was criticized and struggled against, some other peripheral targets of criticism and struggle were brought in. The criticism of the primary target served as a warning to the peripheral targets. They stood to the side to keep the primary target company.

陪读 péidú
to accompany and aid someone in his studies; specifically the status of accompanying spouses of Chinese students studying abroad
E.g. 政府允许配偶到国外陪读。 *The government permits spouses to go abroad with students.* / 父母望子成龙心切, 有的夜夜陪读。 *Parents all hope fervently that their children will be successful,, to the point that some study with their kids every night.*

陪风 péifēng
habit of being attended
An unhealthy habit on the part of certain cadre leaders of needing to be attended by people in every move, so that they can parade their stature and show off their prestige.

陪护 péihù
to accompany and care for a hospitalized patient
E.g. 陪护人员 *personnel who accompany and care for hospital patients*

陪酒女 péijiǔnǚ
bar girls (who keep customers company)

陪练 péiliàn
to accompany athletes in training; accessory athletes
E.g. 陪练队员 *accessory teammates* / 男篮在赛前需要陪练。 *The men's basketball team needs to train with accessory teams before the meet.* / 有的拳手用机器人陪练。 *Some boxers use robots as training accessories.*

陪审员 péishěnyuán
jurors
E.g. 人民陪审员 *people's jurors*

陪宴 péiyàn
to be a secondary guest at a banquet

陪夜 péiyè
to accompany and care for a hospitalized patient overnight
E.g. 丈夫病重住院, 妻子去医院陪夜。 *The husband is critically ill in the hospital, so the wife went there to stay with him overnight*

陪住 péizhù
to stay in a hospital in order to accompany and care for a hospitalized patient
E.g. 在病房陪住 *to stay with a pa-*

tient overnight / 陪住三天 *to stay and live with (a patient) for three days*

配餐 pèicān
special diet meals
Meals made up of foods with various nutrients according to the special needs of individuals.

配电 pèidiàn
electricity distribution
To deliver electric power from electricity generator or transformers to consumers.

配额 pèi'é
allocated quota

配发 pèifā
to allocate and distribute
E.g. 配发鞋袜 *to distribute shoes and socks*

配歌 pèigē
to compose songs for films and TV programs
E.g. 为电影配歌 *to compose songs for a film*

配给制 pèijǐzhì
ration system
Also called 配售制 allocated sale system and 统销 centrally-controlled sale (planned supply). It is a method of supplying certain commodities. In general, the government stipulates quotas and issues coupons to those in need of the commodities, the coupons are then used in making purchases.

配购 pèigòu
to purchase rationed commodities (especially necessities of life)
E.g. 对农副产品实行统购、配购 *to purchase agricultural side-products on a government-monopoly or rationed basis*

配股 pèigǔ
to allocate stocks
A company allocating stocks to its original stockholders. The term also refers to the stocks thus allocated.

配送 pèisòng
to select (goods) and deliver (to customers)
E.g. 配送的实质是一种规模经营。 *The essence of selecting and delivery is a large run of business.*

配送中心 pèisòng zhōngxīn
selecting and delivery center
Also called goods transportation center. An agency which purchases from production enterprises, and then selects and supplies goods to retail enterprises.

配演 pèiyǎn
to play a supporting role; supporting actor/actress
E.g. 此戏因无人配演而停止。 *This play was discontinued because it lacked a supporting cast.*

配种站 pèizhǒngzhàn
breeding station
An organ that specializes in merging the male and female reproductive cells of animals in order to generate offspring. The work includes natural mating and artificial insemination.

pen

喷灌 pēnguàn
spray irrigation
An irrigation method that uses mechanized devices to spray water through a nozzle into the air, which then descends like rain onto fields.

喷浆 pēnjiāng
to spray a thick liquid
A painting method whereby machinery is

used to spray paint throitugh a nozzle onto a wall. The term also means 井喷, the sudden blowout of subterrranean high-pressure oil and natural gas from a well opening when an oil well is being drilled.

喷气式 pēnqìshì
jet-propelled
Airplanes powered by jet engines. It is also a kind of corporal punishment used during the Cultural Revolution, in which one is bent forward, with the head raised high, and both arms stretched toward the back, in the form of a jet plane.

喷云吐雾 pēn-yún tǔ-wù
depiction of fog or smoke being emitted (by a smoker, etc.)

盆花儿 pénhuār
potted plants

盆栽 pénzāi
to plant in pots; potted plants
E.g. 在这里梅花只能盆栽。 *At this location, plum blossoms can only be planted in pots.* / 盆栽葡萄 *grapes grown in pots*

peng

棚户 pénghù
families that live in shacks; shacks

膨化 pénghuà
to expand (through heat, pressure, etc., as in popcorn)

膨化食品 pénghuà shípǐn
inflated food
A food product made dampening a food, subjecting it to pressure and heat, then suddenly releasing the pressure, allowing the food to expand and to take on a crisp texture. This kind of food is crispy and easy to digest. An example is popcorn.

捧杯 pěngbēi
to take the cup; to win a competition (often athletic)
E.g. 中国女排捧杯。 *The Chinese women's volleyball team won the cup.*

碰克 pèngkè
punk
Also transliterated as 朋克.

碰碰车 pèngpèngchē
bumper cars

碰碰船 pèngpèngchuán
bumper boats

碰软 pèngruǎn
to uphold principles and handle matters judiciously in dealing with insidious breaches of the law carried out through corrupt underhanded measures
E.g. 碰软需要韧性。 *It takes resilience to uphold principles and handle matters judiciously in dealing with insidious breaches of the law carried out through corrupt underhanded measures.*

碰头会 pèngtóuhuì
brief meeting
A brief, small-scale, informal meeting with no fixed agenda, the main purpose of which is to exchange information.

碰硬 pèngyìng
to confront firmly
In dealing with unhealthy tendencies, violations, or breaches of discipline, to abide by principles, to not give in to personal considerations, and to carry out a determined struggle.
E.g. 敢于碰硬 *dare to confront firmly*

pi

霹雳舞 pīlìwǔ
break dancing
E.g. 有的地方跳霹雳舞成风。*Break dancing became a common practice in some places.*

批捕 pībǔ
to sanction an arrest
E.g. 办理批捕手续 *to go through the procedures for sanctioning an arrest*

批次 pīcì
number of batches
E.g. 全天检验出口商品50批次。*Today fifty batches of export commodities were examined.*

批调 pīdiào
approved transfer
The transfer of materials from one unit to another after it has been approved by the department in charge.

批斗 pīdòu
to criticize and struggle against
Contraction of 批判 and 斗争.

批购户 pīgòuhù
businesses which make wholesale purchases from state-owned stores and resell the goods at retail prices

批件 pījiàn
documents already responded to or to be responded to (by supervisors)

批量 pīliàng
batch size
The quantity of identical products produced in one batch. In the course of production, batch size is a fact or in the labor-production ratio, the production cycle period, and the amount of capital involved.

E.g. 批量生产 *to produce in batches* / 批量接待旅游团 *to receive tour groups in batches* / 批量作价 *to set wholesale prices* / 批量上市 *to come onto the market in batches* / 批量投放市场 *to release onto the market in batches*

批林批孔 pī Lín pī Kǒng
criticize Lin Biao and Confucius
The movement to criticize Lin Biao and Confucius conducted by Jiang Qing's counter-revolutionary clique in the latter period of the Cultural Revolution. In reality, they were pointing the spearhead of the struggle at Premier Zhou Enlai.

批判会 pīpànhuì
criticism meeting
A meeting convened specifically to conduct systematic analysis and show disapproval of persons with erroneous thoughts, words, and deeds.

批判现实主义 pīpàn xiànshí zhǔyì
critical realism

批售 pīshòu
wholesale
E.g. 批售权 / *wholesale license* / 向外商批售 *to sell wholesale to foreign businessmen*

批条 pītiáo
(person in charge) writing a response on a note requesting instructions; a note responding to a request for instructions
Also called 批条子.
E.g. 烟厂党委决定任何领导不准给关系户批条买好烟。*The Party committee of the tobacco factory decided that no leader is permitted to give others with connections approval (priority) to*

purchase quality cigarettes.

批文 pīwén

written response from a superior or a managing department

批销 pīxiāo

wholesale business; to purchase wholesale and to sell by retail

E.g. 批销户 *wholesalers* / 批销中心 *wholesale center* / 批销关系 *wholesale connections*

批修整风 pīxiū zhěngfēng

criticize revisionism and rectify trends

The movement to criticize revisionism and to rectify trends within the Party which gained ground within the entire Party and the entire nation after the 1970 Second Plenum of the Ninth Party Central Committee. Criticism of revisionism was actually criticism of Chen Boda, therefore, it was also called 批陈整风 criticize Chen and rectify trends.

批转 pīzhuǎn

to write comments and transmit

A superior writing comments or instructions on a document or notification submitted by a subordinate, and then transmitting it to appropriate quarters.

啤酒肚 píjiǔdù

beer belly

E.g. 只要调整食物结构,增加摄取复合碳化合物,就能消除啤酒肚。*As long as food intake is measured and carbohydrates are assimilated, one's beer belly can be eliminated.*

皮包公司 píbāo gōngsī

briefcase company

A business that operates out of a briefcase, with business cards, contracts, purchase agreements, etc., but no capital, no fixed location, and no inventory

皮包商 píbāoshāng

briefcase businessmen those engaged in briefcase company business

(cf. 皮包公司)

皮草 pícǎo

fur; fur coat

皮试 píshì

skin test

A test for allergies whereby allergens are injected into the skin.

匹料 pǐliào

bolt materials

Fabrics (cotton, silk, dacron, woolen, etc.) that come in bolts.

痞气 pǐqì

riffraff aura or ways

pian

偏饭 piānfàn

favorable treatment

E.g. 吃偏饭 *to enjoy favorable treatment*

偏科 piānkē

lopsided concentration

The phenomenon of students concentrating in one or a few courses, and neglecting others.

E.g. 现在中小学里是不允许偏科的。*Lopsided concentration is not permitted in elementary and secondary schools now.*

偏食 piānshí

Synonymous with 偏饭. (cf. 偏饭)

偏题 piāntí

catch exam questions

Out of the way and catch questions in an exam.

偏远地区 piānyuǎn dìqū
out-of-the way areas
Remote and outlying areas.

片儿警 piànrjǐng
police responsible for a certain neighborhood or area

片面观点 piànmiàn guāndiǎn
one-sided view (cf. 片面性)

片面性 piànmiànxìng
one-sidedness
In observing and dealing with issues, instead of looking at the entire matter and grasping the various aspects of a contradiction, to see only one side of the matter and not the other side, to see only the tree and not the forest.

片商 piànshāng
film distributors

片约 piànyuē
film contract (between an actor and a film producer)

骗买骗卖 piànmǎi piànmài
to use deceptive tactics in business

骗赔 piànpéi
to defraud an insurance company; to file a false claim for compensation

骗销 piànxiāo
fraudulent marketing
To sell commodities through deceptive tactics.

piao

票霸 piàobà
ticket racketeers
Those who buy tickets in high demand and resell them at extortionate prices

票贩子 piàofànzi
racketeers who deal in tickets, ration coupons, I.D. cards, etc.

票房价值 piàofáng jiàzhí
box office income
Income from sale of tickets. It is one index of the audience's attitude toward a performing work of art and performers.

票提 piàotí
ticket profiteer
People who find tourists for tourist buses and make a profit by selling tourists bus tickets (fares).

票证 piàozhèng
coupons
All certificates for purchasing commodities controlled by government supply planning, such as oil and grain coupons, and purchase certificates. There are two types of coupons: those with prices and those without.

pin

拼搏 pīnbó
to fight with all one's might
To go all out in a struggle, even risking one's life.
E.g. 奋勇拼搏 *to courageously fight with all one's might*

拼搏精神 pīnbó jīngshén
the spirit of fighting with all one's might
The athlete's spirit of going all out, training assiduously, and fighting tenaciously. It also means the indomitable, courageous, and tenacious spirit in any kind of endeavor.

拼抢 pīnqiǎng
to exert to one's utmost in a competition
E.g. 在赛场上拼抢凶猛。 *The*

competition in the arena is fierce.

拼杀 pīnshā

to go all out — even risking death — in combat (literal or figurative)

拼死拼活 pīnsǐ pīnhuó

to exert to one's utmost in a struggle or work, even to the point of risking one's life

E.g. 在田里拼死拼活 to give one's all in working in the fields / 男篮拼死拼活也要得这块金牌。The men's basketball team is sparing no effort in fighting for the gold medal.

拼音字母 pīnyīn zìmǔ

phonetic alphabet

The alphabet of any phonetic writing system. Used specifically, it means the twenty-six letters of the Roman alphabet in the Chinese phonetic alphabet scheme for writing Chinese phonetically.

拼装 pīnzhuāng

to assemble from odd parts

To make something by assembling components that do not belong to a set.

E.g. 拼装自行车 to put together a bicycle from odd parts

贫牧 pínmù

poor herdsmen

Abbreviation for 贫苦牧民.

贫下中牧 pín-xiàzhōngmù

poor and lower middle herdsmen

Contraction for poor herdsmen and lower middle herdsmen.

贫下中农 pín-xiàzhōngnóng

poor and lower middle peasants

Contraction for poor peasants and lower middle peasants.

贫下中农讲师团 pín-xiàzhōngnóng jiǎngshītuán

poor and lower middle peasant lecture teams

Propaganda teams composed of poor and lower middle peasants that were stationed in schools to re-educate intellectuals during the Cultural Revolution.

贫下中农协会 pín-xiàzhōngnóng xiéhuì

poor and lower middle peasant associations

Abbreviated as 贫协. Class organizations of a mass nature organized voluntarily by poor and lower middle peasants under the leadership of the Chinese Communist Party.

贫下中渔 pín-xiàzhōngyú

poor and lower middle fishermen

贫协 pín-xié

poor and lower middle peasant associations

Abbreviation of 贫下中农协会.

贫宣队 pín-xuān-duì

poor, and lower middle peasants Mao's thought propaganda team

(Cultural Revolution terminology) Abbreviation for 贫下中农毛泽东思想宣传队.

贫渔 pínyú

poor fishermen

Abbreviation of 贫苦渔民.

品牌 pǐnpái

brand of merchandise

品味 pǐnwèi

to taste the flavor; to meticulously discern and appreciate (as a connoisseur)

E.g. 品味人生 to savor life

品位 pǐnwèi

(of mineral ores) grade; the percentage of mineral contained in the ore; (figuratively) the net value or

function of a certain matter

E.g. 文化品位 cultural taste

品种花样 pǐnzhǒng huāyàng

varieties and styles

All the varieties and styles of products or commodities.

聘期 pìnqī

term (period) of employment

E.g. 聘期一年。 The term of the appointment is one year.

聘任 pìnrèn

to appoint

To appoint someone to take on a certain job.

E.g. 聘任书 appointment contract / 聘任制 system of appointment

聘选 pìnxuǎn

to select and appoint (to positions)

E.g. 聘选制 system of selection and appointment / 聘选领导人员 to select and appoint personnel to leadership positions

聘用 pìnyòng

to appoint and employ

E.g. 聘用制 system of employment by appointment / 聘用干部 to appoint a cadre

聘约 pìnyuē

appointment contract

E.g. 订立聘约 to settle an appointment contract

聘职 pìnzhí

to recruit (for certain professional positions)

ping

乒联 pīng-lián

the Ping-Pong Association

Abbreviation for 乒乓球联合会.

乒坛 pīngtán

the world of ping-pong

平板三轮 píngbǎn sānlún

flat-board tricycle

Also called 平板车 flat-board cart. It is a kind of tricycle used for transporting goods, with the goods-carrying part being a flat board.

平暴 píngbào

to quell a rebellion or riot

平调 píngdiào

to possess gratis the fruit of other's work

平调 derives from 一平二调. (cf. 一平二调)

平衡生产 pínghéng shēngchǎn

balanced production

The production of various goods is in accordance with a ratio determined by laws governing the production of material resources and concrete conditions concerning the time and place. Thus, the various runs of production can be well coordinated, so that they can proceed smoothly.

平均主义 píngjūn zhǔyì

equalitarianism

平叛 píng-pàn

to suppress rebellion

Contraction of 平定叛乱.

平绒 píngróng

velveteen

平销 píngxiāo

parity sale

To sell at no profit and no loss.

平抑 píngyì

to suppress; to calm down

E.g. 平抑物价 to suppress prices (curb inflation)

平战结合 píng-zhàn jiéhé
to link up peace and war

To link military training during peace with the actual needs in a time of war. Only in this way can the troops' ability to meet attacks be upgraded.

瓶插 píngchā
the art of flower arranging (in vases); flower arrangements

E.g. 瓶插用花 *flowers used in flower arranging* / 到集市上去买瓶插 *to sell flower arrangements at the open-air market*

瓶颈 píngjǐng
(figurative) bottleneck

评比 píngbǐ
to compare and evaluate

To evaluate level and quality through comparison.

E.g. 评比生产成绩 *to compare and evaluate production achievements*

评法批儒 píng Fǎ pī Rú
to evaluate the Legalists and criticize the Confucians

The conspiratorial activities, plotted by Jiang Qing and her cohorts in 1974, to evaluate the Legalists and criticize the Confucians. This movement was actually a disguised attack on Premier Zhou Enlai.

评功摆好 pínggōng bǎihǎo
to elaborate on someone's merit and to display his superiority; to speak of someone in glowing terms

评工记分 pínggōng jìfēn
to evaluate work and record work points

A method used in rural people's commune production teams and other collective enterprises to evaluate members' labor and to calculate labor remuneration. On the basis of labor quantity and level of skill, labor quotas and the number of work points are determined. Then after an evaluation of the extent to which each member has completed work, a certain number of work points is recorded. In year-end accounting, remuneration for labor is distributed on the basis of the work point value of that unit and the total number of work points of each member.

评估 pínggū
to appraise and estimate (the value of something)

E.g. 评估标准 *standard of appraisal* / 进行评估 *to conduct an appraisal* / 综合评估 *overall appraisal*

评级 píngjí
rank evaluation

To evaluate and determine the administrative or salary ranks of cadres.

评教评学 píng jiào píng xué
to evaluate teaching and learning

Teachers and students together evaluating the strengths and weaknesses in their teaching and learning, and summarizing their experience, in order to upgrade the effectiveness of their teaching and learning.

评介 píngjiè
to review

To criticize and introduce (books, movies, etc.).

评卷 píngjuàn
to evaluate examination papers

E.g. 高考评卷委员会 *Committee for Evaluating University Entrance Exams*

评考 píngkǎo
evaluation test

E.g. 现在的评考太重文凭和外语。*The present evaluation test places too much emphasis on qualifying and foreign languages.*

评模 píngmó

to appraise and select the outstanding ones to be models

E.g. 评模会议 *meeting to appraise and select models*

评聘 píngpìn

to evaluate and appoint (to positions of employment)

E.g. 职务评聘 *to evaluate a candidate for an appointment to a job*

评审 píngshěn

to appraise and examine

Contraction of 评选 appraise and select and 审定 examine and approve.

E.g. 评审1984年国家重大发明奖。*To judge and determine the 1984 national awards for important inventions.*

评委 píng-wěi

(abbreviation) same as 评委会 (see below); a member of 评委会.

评委会 píng-wěi-huì

Abbreviation for all the following three: 评选委员会 evaluation and selection committee, 评审委员会 evaluation and adjudication committee, 评议委员会 deliberations committee.

评薪 píngxīn

salary evaluation

To evaluate work and determine wages.

评选 píngxuǎn

to elect through appraisal

To compare, evaluate, and elect.

E.g. 评选先进工作者 *to evaluate and elect advanced workers*

评优 píngyōu

to appraise and select the most outstanding or the highest quality

E.g. 产品评优 *to appraise products and select the outstanding ones*

评职 píngzhí

professional evaluation

Abbreviated term for evaluation of people's professional work.

评传 píngzhuàn

critical biography

屏幕 píngmù

screen on a television or monitor

po

婆婆 pópo

mother-in-law (of a woman)

(Figurative) a cadre or managing organization with jurisdiction over one (often applied to those that are overly demanding or rigid).

E.g. 环节多，婆婆也多，办事就很困难。*There are many steps and many supervisory units, so it is very difficult to get anything done.*

婆婆嘴 pópozuǐ

mother-in-law's mouth; long-winded garrulous meddlesome people

E.g. 他是个婆婆嘴，爱管爱说。*He is a long-winded garrulous meddlesome fellow, and loves to talk and meddle in others' affairs.*

破罐破摔 pòguàn pòshuāi

throwing a broken jar around

A broken jar is broken whether or not it is thrown around. It cannot be fixed, and there's no point in fussing over it. It is a metaphor for the negative resigned attitude of people who have erred. They feel that they will always carry a black mark, so they have no incentive to correct their errors, and simply allow themselves to fall further behind or continue on an erroneous path.

破旧立新 pòjiù lìxīn
destroy the old and establish the new
E.g. 破旧立新，移风易俗 *to destroy the old and establish the new, to change customs and habits*

破私立公 pòsī lìgōng
to destroy the private and establish the public
To overcome selfishness and to foster a spirit of serving the public wholeheartedly.

破四旧，立四新 pò sìjiù, lì sìxīn
to destroy the four olds, establish the four news
指"文化大革命"中提出的破除剥削阶级的旧思想、旧文化、旧风俗、旧习惯，树立无产阶级的新思想、新文化、新风俗、新习惯。
The idea, advocated during the Cultural Revolution, of destroying the old thoughts, culture, customs and habits of the exploitative class, and of establishing the new thoughts, culture, customs and habits of the proletarian class.

破译 pòyì
to crack a code
To analyze and decipher a certain telegraphic code.

破中有立 pò zhōng yǒu lì
to establish amidst destruction
To establish the new in the process of destroying the old.

破字当头，立在其中 pòzì dāngtóu, lì zài qízhōng
to establish (the new) in the midst of confronting destruction (of the old)
To courageously destroy the old, and to establish the new in the process of destroying the old.

迫降 pòjiàng
forced landing

迫降 pòxiáng
forced surrender

pou

剖腹产 pōufùchǎn
caesarean birth

pu

铺路 pūlù
(literal and figurative) to pave a road; to pave the way
E.g. 懂得"关系学"的人，常用烟酒铺路。 *Those who understand the importance of the "science of connections" often use cigarettes and liquor to pave the way.* / 为学生的勤工助学活动铺路搭桥。 *We should pave the way and build bridges for students to work in order to support their studies.*

铺路石 pūlùshí
road-paving stone
(Figurative) a person or an organization that made contributions or sacrifices so that others might succeed.

普测 pǔcè
general exam
A general exam for testing learning achievement or proficiency. It also means general surveys or inspections done with instruments or other methods.

普法 pǔfǎ
to disseminate the law
To disseminate general knowledge about

legal matters.

E.g. 普法教育 *law dissemination education* / 普法手册 *law dissemination handbook*

普高 pǔ-gāo
ordinary senior high schools
Abbreviation for 普通高级中学.

普惠制 pǔhuìzhì
system of generalized preferential treatment in custom duties

普建 pǔ-jiàn
to establish universally or widely

普教 pǔ-jiào
common education; universal education
Contraction of 普通教育.

E.g. 普教工作 *common education work*

普九 pǔ-jiǔ
to make nine-year compulsory education universal; to popularize nine-year compulsory education
Abbreviation for 普及九年义务教育.

普六 pǔ-liù
universalizing the six-year compulsory education system
Abbreviation for 普及六年义务教育.

普调 pǔ-tiáo
to make an upward adjustment across the board

E.g. 给职工普调一级工资 *to raise the salary of all employees by one grade*

普通话 pǔtōnghuà
standard speech
The modern standard Han language, which takes the speech of Beijing as the standard for pronunciation, the northern dialect as the basic dialect, and model modern vernacular writings as the standard for grammar.

普校 pǔ-xiào
ordinary schools

普治 pǔzhì
universal cure
To cure certain diseases universally.

蹼泳 pǔyǒng
snorkeling

Q

qi

期房 qīfáng
forward delivery housing
Housing expected to be made available in a limited time according to the contract.
E.g. 期房交易 *forward delivery housing deal*

期市 qī-shì
(re stocks) futures market
Abbreviation for 期货市场.
E.g. 期市窄幅滑坡。 *The market for futures is going down a narrow slope.*

期望值 qīwàngzhí
level of expectation
E.g. 毕业生要调整自己的期望值。 *Graduating students must adjust their expectations (i.e., be more realistic).*

欺行霸市 qīháng bàshì
to bully others in the trade and to ruthlessly dominate the market

栖居 qījū
(of birds and other animals) to perch; to rest
E.g. 小鸟晚上都栖居在树上。 *Small birds all perch on trees at night.* / 秦岭是大熊猫的重要栖居地。 *The Qin Mountain is an important habitat of the giant panda.*

妻管严 qīguǎnyán
Cf. 气管炎

七·二一大学 qī èryī dàxué
July 21st University
Workers' universities founded on the directive issued by Mao Zedong on July 21, 1968. The students are drawn from the ranks of workers and are trained to become university level skilled professionals, who then return to serve in their original units or systems. The training is divided into two types: total leave and semi-leave from regular work. The term for total-leave students is two to three years, that for semi-leave students is accordingly extended. The students recruited are superior workers with practical experience; their educational level is comparable to high school graduates.

七·一 Qī Yī
July 1
The commemorative day of the Chinese Communist Party. On July 1, 1921, the Chinese Communist Party convened its first national representatives meeting in Shanghai and announced the formal founding of the Chinese Communist Party.

七千人大会 Qīqiānrén Dàhuì
the conference of the seven thousand
The enlarged work conference convened by the Chinese Communist Party Central Committee in Beijing from January 11 to February 7, 1962. The conference summed up work experience since the founding of the People's Republic; unified the understanding of the entire

Party; strengthened solidarity, discipline, democratic centralism, and centralized unity; mobilized the entire Party to carry out the Eight-Character Principle for adjusting the national economy (cf. 八字方针) and to turn the difficult national economic situation around. At this conference, Liu Shaoqi and Deng Xiaoping tried to rectify the detrimental leftist tendencies of the previous several years. More than seven thousand persons attended the conference, hence it was called the conference of the seven thousand.

七五 Qī-Wǔ
the Seventh Five-Year Plan
Abbreviation for 七五计划 the Seventh Five-Year Plan.

七五计划 Qī-Wǔ Jìhuà
the Seventh Five-Year Plan
Abbreviation for 中华人民共和国国民经济和社会发展第七个五年计划 the Seventh Five-Year Plan (1986-1990) for National Economic and Social Development of the People's Republic of China; also called 七五.

棋圣 qíshèng
chess saint
Honorific appellation for someone who is exceptionally outstanding in chess (all varieties, including go).

棋坛 qítán
world of chess (of various kinds, including go)

奇缺 qíquē
in extraordinarily short supply
E.g. 住房奇缺 dire shortage of housing / 市场商品奇缺。There is a dire shortage in the supply of commodities. / 政法人才奇缺。There is a dire shortage of persons trained in political science and law.

奇谈怪论 qítán guàilùn
strange illogical opinions and views

奇效 qíxiào
extraordinary result or effect

齐飞 qífēi
to advance shoulder to shoulder; to develop together
E.g. 农牧齐飞。Agriculture and animal husbandry are developing side by side. / 两类人才齐飞。Two kinds of talented people are developing side by side.

旗帜鲜明 qízhì xiānmíng
clear banner; clear-cut stand
A metaphor for having a very clear-cut political attitude, idea, or viewpoint.

骑警 qíjǐng
horseback police
E.g. 太原市已设立骑警。The city of Taiyuan has already established a contingent of police on horseback.

起飞 qǐfēi
to take off
1) A plane taking off from the ground.
2) A metaphor for a certain task or matter beginning to develop rapidly.
E.g. 经济起飞。The economy is taking off.

起获 qǐhuò
to ferret out (ill gotten funds, stolen goods, etc.)
E.g. 起获赃款 to ferret out money from bribes and embezzlement

起居室 qǐjūshì
living room

企划 qǐhuà
a plan comprised of creative ideas

企业承包经营责任制 qǐyè

chéngbāo jīngyíng zérènzhì
the enterprise contract management responsibility system (China's solution to economic reform under socialist principles)
Also called 承包经营责任制.

企业党组织 qǐyè dǎngzǔzhī
the Communist Party organization within an enterprise, including the Party committee, general Party branch, and Party branch

企业电视 qǐyè diànshì
enterprise television
Television programs made and broadcasted by enterprises for internal use.

企业法 qǐyèfǎ
enterprise laws
Specifically the 中华人民共和国全民所有制工业企业法 Law of the People's Republic of China Governing Industrial Enterprises under the System of National Ownership.

企业集团 qǐyè jítuán
enterprise group
A production and management entity formed by several enterprises joining together.

企业家 qǐyèjiā
expert entrepreneurs
E.g. 农民企业家 *agri-businessmen* / 企业家阶层 *entrepreneurial strata* / 企业家队伍 *ranks of entrepreneurs* / 中国企业家协会 *Chinese Entrepreneurs' Association*

企业素质 qǐyè sùzhì
quality of an enterprise
The survival and developmental abilities of an enterprise under certain socialist production conditions. These abilities of a socialist enterprise include feedback ability, competitiveness, adaptability, and developmental ability.

企业文化 qǐyè wénhuà
enterprise culture
The value system, moral standards, and behavioral standards shared by those in a certain enterprise.

企业下放 qǐyè xiàfàng
to place an enterprise under a lower level of administration
To transfer an enterprise from one level of administration to a lower one, such as changing an enterprise from national central jurisdiction to local jurisdiction.

气粗 qìcū
coarse in temperament and mannerisms or bombastic in speech
E.g. 他没有文化，就是气粗。 *He lacks cultivation and is a rather coarse person.* / 财大气粗 *great in wealth and big in voice*

气垫船 qìdiànchuán
(hydrofoil, hydroplane) hovercraft
Also called 腾空船.

气功疗法 qìgōng liáofǎ
treatment method based on a system of *qi*
A method of treating illness by using a system which mobilizes the *qi* within the body (involving deep breathing). One type is self-treatment by having the patient practice *qi* exercises over a period of time. Another type is having a *qi*-exercise master send out *qi* to treat the patient.

气管炎 qìguǎnyán
bronchitis; under petticoat government
A play on words. 气管炎 is an ailment, it sounds the same as 妻管严 the

wife's control is stern, hence the term is a jocular way of saying that the husband is henpecked.

E.g. 现在盛行一种"气管炎"。 *Presently, a type of "bronchitis" henpecking is prevalent.*

气区 qìqū
gas area

气田 qìtián
gas field

qia

卡脖子 qiǎbózi
to take hold by the neck
(Figurative) to have a grip on something.

洽购 qiàgòu
to arrange a purchase
Contraction of 接洽购买.
E.g. 洽购粮油 *to arrange a purchase of grain and oil*

洽谈 qiàtán
to talk over
Contraction of 接洽 to take up a matter and 商谈 to discuss.
E.g. 洽谈业务 *to talk over a professional matter*

洽谈会 qiàtánhuì
negotiation meeting (for business)
E.g. 日用品洽谈会 *trade negotiation meeting concerning daily-use commodities* / 技术协作洽谈会 *technical co-operation negotiation meeting*

qian

牵头 qiāntóu
to pull people together (lit., to lead in heads)
To provisionally have a certain person take responsibility for gathering people together and making contacts.
E.g. 由厂长牵头。 *The factory head will pull people together.*

牵线搭桥 qiānxiàn dāqiáo
to pull strings and build bridges
To promote the development of linkages between two sides.

千里马 qiānlǐmǎ
a horse that can run a thousand *li* in a day
(Figurative) an exceptionally capable and talented person.

千年虫 qiānniánchóng
millennium bug; Y2K
E.g. 千禧一刻的到来,千年虫没有发作。 *Y2K didn't affect all the computers when the moment of new millennium arrived.*

千禧婴儿 qiānxǐ yīng'ér
millennium infant (baby)
Baby born on the first day of 2000. (cf. 世纪婴儿)

迁建 qiānjiàn
to relocate and to build anew
E.g. 迁建工程 *a project to relocate and rebuild*

迁装 qiānzhuāng
to dismantle, relocate, and reassemble (equipment)
E.g. 迁装工期 *The period during which equipment is relocated and reassembled* / 迁装施工 *to implement the relocation and reassemblage of equipment*

签批 qiānpī
to approve and issue (a document, license, certificate, etc.)

签约 qiānyuē
to sign a contract

前科 qiánkē
prior criminal record
E.g. 前科犯罪 *a convict with a prior criminal record* / 有前科的人 *persons with prior criminal records* / 有诈骗前科 *to have a record for fraud*

前卫 qiánwèi
the most advanced; the most fashionable; ahead of time
E.g. 电子消费属于比较前卫的消费方式。 *Electronics consumption is regarded as a rather advanced form of consumption.* / 她言谈举止都大胆前卫。 *Her speech and deportment are bold and fashionable.* / 他担心我过于前卫。 *He's afraid that I'm too advanced.*

前沿科学 qiányán kēxué
front line sciences
Acadmic fields, such as biological engineering, information science, and materials science, that serve a leading function in the development of science.

前瞻性 qiánzhānxìng
predictive; foresight; farsightedness

潜地导弹 qián-dì dǎodàn
submarine-to-land guided missiles

潜返 qiánfǎn
to return to a locale clandestinely (to infiltrate and sabotage)

潜科学 qiánkēxué
latent science
It is the opposite of 显科学 manifested science.

潜亏 qiánkuī
hidden loss
Losses that are not obvious on accounts. *E.g.* 企业存在潜亏。 *There are hidden losses in the enterprise.*

潜能 qiánnéng
potential (re ability and talents)
E.g. 发挥潜能 *to give rein to one's potential*

潜水器 qiánshuǐqì
general term for underwater devices
Also called 潜器.

潜质 qiánzhì
hidden potential
A person's abilities that have not yet been shown or developed.

遣俘 qiǎnfú
to repatriate POW's
To send prisoners of war back to their homelands.

欠产 qiànchǎn
production shortfall
Production falling short of the stipulated quota.

欠佳 qiànjiā
not good enough
E.g. 成绩欠佳。 *The achievements are not good enough.* / 性能欠佳。 *The performance (of a product) is not good enough.*

欠税 qiànshuì
to default on or to be in arrears with tax payments

qiang

枪击 qiāngjī
gunfire
E.g. 枪击事件 *incidence of gunfire* / 遭到枪击 *to fall victim to gunfire*

墙布 qiángbù
wall fabric (used as wallpaper)

强化 qiánghuà
to strengthen

E.g. 强化训练 *to strengthen the training* / 强化管理 *to strengthen management*

强化食品 qiánghuà shípǐn
condensed foods
Foods that have been reduced in volume and increased in nutritional content.

强加于人 qiángjiā yúrén
to impose opinions on others
To force others to accept certain opinions or ways.

强劳 qiángláo
forced labor
Abbreviation for 强制劳动教养 forced labor education. (cf. 劳动教养)

强人 qiángrén
strong men
1) Formerly, the term meant robbers.
2) Now the term refers to persons with special ability who have made outstanding achievements in certain areas.

强身 qiǎngshēn
body strengthening
E.g. 强身健体 *body-strengthening* / 强身呼吸法 *a body strengthening method of breathing* / 具有强身功效 *to possess body building efficacy*

强势 qiángshì
powerful trend; strong impetus (or momentum)

强手 qiángshǒu
strong hand
Persons with extraordinary skills.
E.g. 超过名将强手 *to outdo the super stars*

强项 qiángxiàng
(in sports) forte; strong suit

强买强卖 qiángmǎi qiángmài
a kind of hegemony in marketing whereby a party forces others to buy or sell

强制机关 qiángzhì jīguān
institutions of law enforcement
Organizations that carry out the functions of proletarian dictatorship, such as courts, the procuratorate, and public security.

强制劳动 qiángzhì láodòng
forced labor
A measure applied by the state to reform criminals in accordance with the law. That is, criminals are compelled to participate in labor, and through labor to reform themselves and to become new persons.

抢点 qiǎngdiǎn
(in soccer) to grab the perfect moment to shoot for the goal; (when behind schedule) to rush in order to make up for lost time
E.g. 包抄抢点非常及时。*The team grabbed the perfect moment to outflank the opponent.* / 上下班不抢点骑快车。*One should not speed (in riding a bike) during rush hour (going to and from work)*

抢红灯 qiǎnghóngdēng
to run a red light
E.g. 他多次骑自行车抢红灯。*He ran a red light many times while riding his bike.*

抢建 qiǎngjiàn
to charge ahead in constructing
E.g. 抢建码头 *to charge ahead in building a wharf*

抢拍 qiǎngpāi
to grab the perfect moment or angle to shoot a photo; to rush ahead to photograph
E.g. 抢拍雪景 *to grab the perfect*

angle in photographing a snow scene / 抢拍不少镜头 to have grabbed quite a few perfect moments or angles in photographing

抢收 qiǎngshōu
rushed harvest
Quickly, and with an all out effort, to harvest ripened crops to avoid possible damage (due to natural disasters, etc.)

抢手 qiǎngshǒu
(re high-demand commodities) being snapped up quickly (by buyers)
E.g. 彩电在市场上抢手一时。*For a time, color televisions on the market were being snapped up.* / 布鞋很抢手。*Cloth shoes are in high demand (on the market).*

抢手货 qiǎngshǒuhuò
grabbed items
Commodities in high demand which people compete to purchase. Synonymous with 热门货 hot items.

抢险 qiǎngxiǎn
to rush to the rescue

抢种 qiǎngzhòng
rushed planting
To grasp the right moment and go all out in planting.

qiao

敲定 qiāodìng
to nail down; to make the final decision

侨办 Qiáo-Bàn
Office of Overseas Chinese
Abbreviation for 国务院华侨事务办公室 Office for Overseas Chinese Affairs under the State Council.

侨胞 qiáobāo
compatriots living abroad

侨汇 qiáohuì
remittance by overseas nationals
Money remitted to the home country by nationals living abroad.

侨汇券 qiáohuìquàn
overseas Chinese money certificate
Abbreviation for 侨汇物资供 materials supply certificate for overseas Chinese, also called 侨汇证. It is issued by the Bank of China. With this certificate, one can purchase commodities that are in high demand, under state supply planning, or at a preferential price (discount) at overseas Chinese stores or other designated stores.

侨眷 qiáojuàn
relatives of overseas Chinese
Contraction of 华侨眷属. People in China who are the spouses or direct relatives of overseas Chinese, indirect relatives of overseas Chinese that are often supported by the overseas relatives, or indirect relatives who have not yet divided family property with overseas relatives, though they are not supported by them.

侨联 Qiáo-Lián
Overseas Chinese Federation
Abbreviation for 归国华侨联合会 Repatriated Overseas Chinese Federation, a mass organization. At the national level, there is the organization, called 中华全国归国华侨联合会 All-China Federation of Repatriated Overseas Chinese which is abbreviated as 全国侨联. Corresponding local organizations have also been founded in areas with concentrated populations of

repatriated Chinese and their relatives.

侨领 qiáo-lǐng
leader of overseas Chinese
Abbreviation for 华侨领袖.

侨商 qiáoshāng
compatriots abroad engaged in business; overseas Chinese businessmen

侨属 qiáoshǔ
families and relatives (in China) of compatriots living abroad

侨委 Qiáo-Wěi
Overseas Chinese Council
Abbreviation for 国家华侨事务委员会 State Overseas Chinese Affairs Commission, also called 国家侨委.

侨乡 qiáoxiāng
overseas Chinese hometowns
Areas with a concentration of overseas Chinese (now residing abroad) and relatives of overseas Chinese, such as certain areas of Guangdong and Fujian provinces.

侨资 qiáozī
overseas Chinese funds
Various funds deposited in China by overseas Chinese.

翘尾巴 qiàowěiba
stuck-up (lit., tail stuck-up)
A metaphor for being snobbish and self-important.

俏货 qiàohuò
hot commodities
Commodities that sell well and are popular with customers.

俏色 qiàosè
popular colors; pretty colors

qie

窃密 qièmì
to steal secret information or confidential materials

qin

侵权 qīnquán
to infringe on the legal rights of another person or unit
E.g. 侵权行为 *behavior that infringes on others' rights*

亲等 qīnděng
levels of kinship

亲系 qīnxì
blood relationship between or among kin

秦俑 Qínyǒng
Qin dynasty tomb figures (of soldiers and horses)

勤工助学 qíngōng zhùxué
work-study
A system whereby students enrolled in schools do part-time work or a social service in a systematic way, so that they receive a certain income and gain practical knowledge.
E.g. 勤工助学活动出现了蓬勃发展的新局面。 *Work-study activities have brought about a new flourishing development.*

勤俭办社 qínjiǎn bànshè
to run an organization industriously and frugally
To manage a cooperative or people's commune on the principles of industriousness and frugality.

勤俭建国 qínjiǎn jiànguó
to build the nation industriously and frugally
To build the nation with a guiding ideology of industriousness and frugality.

勤杂工 qínzágōng
odd-jobber
A worker who handles odd jobs in a unit.

勤政 qínzhèng
diligent and expeditious administration (of government workers)

禽场 qínchǎng
poultry farm
A place for raising poultry.

禽苗 qínmiáo
poultry chicks
The young of domestic birds, such as chicks, ducklings, and goslings.

qing

青春偶像 qīngchūn ǒuxiàng
adolescent idol
Movie stars, singers, etc., who are idolized by adolescents.
E.g. 青春偶像评比活动 *a contest among adolescent idols*

青工 qīng-gōng
young worker
Contraction of 青年工人.

青联 Qīng-Lián
Youth Federation
Abbreviation for 中华全国青年联合会 All-China Federation of Youth, a coalition of youth organizations, which is guided by the Chinese Communist Party and which derives its core strength from the Chinese Communist Youth League.

青料 qīngliào
green fodder
Synonymous with 青饲料. (cf. 青饲料)

青霉素 qīngméisù
penicillin
Also called 盘尼西林.

青饲料 qīngsìliào
green fodder
Green animal feeds, such as fresh wild grass and green leaves.

青运会 qīng-yùn-huì
youth athletics conference
Abbreviation for 青年体育运动会.

青贮饲料 qīngzhù sìliào
silage; preserved green fodder
Feed made from burying green fodder and allowing it to ferment. Being cut off from air, it produces an organic acid, which serves as a preservative and reduces loss of nutrition.

轻纺 qīng-fǎng
light and textile industries
Composite term for 轻工业 and 纺织工业; the textile industry among light industries.
E.g. 轻纺工业 *light and textile industries* / 轻纺消费品 *light industrial and textile commodities* / 轻纺产品 *light industrial and textile products*

轻轨交通 qīngguǐ jiāotōng
light rail traffic
Light rails are fast, quiet, energy-saving, economical to build, have high transport capacity, and the tracks are versatile (can be built on the ground, underground, or on scaffolds).

轻机产品 qīngjī chǎnpǐn
light industrial machine products

轻骑 qīngqí
light cavalry
1) Lightly outfitted cavalry. 2) Also lightweight motorcycles.

轻骑兵 qīngqíbīng
light cavalry

Synonymous with 轻骑. Also a metaphor for compactly organized, highly mobile literary and art propaganda teams.

E.g. 文艺轻骑兵 *light literary and art "cavalry"*

轻音乐 qīngyīnyuè
light music (such as light rock)

轻重缓急 qīngzhòng huǎnjí
non-essential and essential, relaxed and urgent

Matters are differentiated by being classified non-essential or essential, relaxed or urgent.

E.g. 做工作要注意轻重缓急。 *In work, we must pay attention to the difference between non-essential and essential, between relaxed and urgent.*

轻装上阵 qīngzhuāng shàngzhèn
to go into battle lightly out-fitted

Originally, this meant going into battle in ancient times without wearing armor, so that movements could be agile. Now the term is a metaphor for getting rid of the various kinds of ideological baggage when pitching into revolutionary work.

倾斜 qīngxié
to tilt in a certain direction (literal and figurative)

E.g. 社会收入分配过于向个人倾斜。 *The allocation of social income is overly tilted toward the individual.*

清仓查库 qīng cāng chá kù
to take an inventory of warehouse stock

To sort out periodically and put in order goods stored in a warehouse.

清仓挖潜 qīng cāng wā qián
to take an inventory and dig out buried goods

To take an inventory of warehouse stock and to tap latent resources. That is, to take out and use overstocked goods.

清查 qīngchá
to check

To examine thoroughly.

E.g. 清查户口 *to check residence card*

清产核资 qīng chǎn hé zī
to take an inventory of property and to make an account of funds

清场 qīngchǎng
to clear out or clean up a gathering place (theater, arena, athletic field, etc.)

清队 qīng-duì
to purify the ranks

Abbreviation for 清理阶级队伍 to purify the class ranks, an activity carried out during the Cultural Revolution. That is, to ferret out the so-called class enemies that have wormed their way into the revolutionary ranks and to clear them out, in order to purify the proletarian ranks.

清洁工 qīngjiégōng
sanitation workers

Workers responsible for public environmental sanitation.

清经济 qīng jīngjì
to clear up finances

To sort out and put in order financial matters, including checking accounts, making inventories, making an account of property, and sorting out work points. (cf. 四清)

清理阶级队伍 qīnglǐ jiējí duìwu
to purify the ranks

Abbreviated as 清队. (cf. 清队)

清思想 qīng sīxiǎng

to clean up ideology

To examine and to clean up ideology. That is, to remove all non proletarian ideas from one's ideology. (cf. 四清)

清退 qīngtuì
to clear up and return
1) After sorting out and verifying, to return private property that was erroneously turned over to higher authorities during certain movements (particularly the Cultural Revolution). 2) After an investigation, to return property belonging the state or a collective that certain cadres or workers had appropriated. 3) After an investigation, to dismiss personnel that had been inappropriately recruited or employed.

清污 qīngwū
to clean up pollution; to purge spiritual pollution

清运 qīngyùn
to clean up and remove (garbage, discards, etc.)
E.g. 清运垃圾 *to clean up and remove garbage* / 清运工作 *garbage removal work*

清障 qīngzhàng
to clean out obstructing materials from waterways (to enhance water flow)
E.g. 河道清障 *to clean waterways of obstructing materials* / 清障方案 *a plan to clean waterways of obstructing materials* / 清障领导小组 *committee of leaders in the business of cleaning waterways*

清资 qīngzī
to put property or assets in order

清组织 qīng zǔzhī
to clean up the organization

To investigate and clean up the cadre ranks within the Party or a political organization. That is, to clean out the enemies, class dissidents, and degenerates that have wormed their way into the Party and government cadre ranks, in order to ensure that political power is in the hands of reliable revolutionaries who are loyal to the proletarian cause.

情结 qíngjié
emotional ties; deep emotions associated with something

情人节 qíngrénjié
Valentine's Day
A traditional Western holiday on February 14.

情商 qíngshāng
sensibility quotient
The term 情商 sensibility quotient is modeled after the term 智商 intelligence quotient. It refers to the degree of responsiveness to feelings of faith, optimism, anxiety, fear, and intuition, etc.

情治 qíngzhì
intelligence and security (情报与治安 often used in the national sense)
E.g. 情治人员 *intelligence and security personnel* / 情治单位 *intelligence and security units*

请吃 qǐngchī
to invite someone to a meal (to promote a relationship)

请调 qǐngdiào
to apply for a work transfer
E.g. 请调报告 *an application for work transfer* / 请调人员 *workers applying for transfer*

请战 qǐngzhàn
request a battle

Requesting to participate in a battle; also a metaphor for requesting to fulfill certain work assignment.

qiong

穷棒子精神 qióngbàngzi jīngshén
spirit of paupers
The spirit, manifested by China's peasants in the process of collectivization, of relying on oneself, working assiduously for material prosperity, frugal management, and hard struggle. (cf. 穷棒子社)

穷棒子社 qióngbàngzishè
paupers' cooperative
A name given to Jianming (Build Brightness) agricultural production cooperative led by Wang Guofan and situated in Pu Village forty *li* west of the county town of Zunhua in Hebei Province. Paupers was the disdainful appellation in northern villages for impoverished poor peasants. When Wang Guofan's cooperative was founded in 1952, they had only twenty-three households of poor peasants and three donkey legs (they owned three-quarters of a donkey, the other quarter belonged to others); they had no capital and no farm tools; thus they were ridiculed as Paupers' Cooperative. In 1955, Mao Zedong praised their spirit of hard work and frugality, and introduced them to the whole nation as an advanced model, hence they became famous.

穷过渡 qióngguòdù
to make a transition in poverty
The method of equalization practiced by the Gang of Four during the Cultural Revolution. The substance of it was: to disregard the level of development of productivity, and subjectively force collective agricultural accounting units to make the transition overnight from production teams to production brigades; to disregard the discrepancy between poor and rich teams and their economic contradictions, and force them to equalize, advocating the slogan "poor teams must rely on the spirit of poverty to make the transition". The term also applies to the attempt of the 1958 communization movement to prematurely enter communism under a very low level of development of productivity.

qiu

秋后算帐派 qiūhòu suànzhàngpài
the post-autumn book keeping sect (doing book keeping after the harvest is in)
Also called 算帐派 book keeping sect. A derogatory term that emerged during the 1958 Great Leap Forward. It was wrongly labeled on those who did not believe a false and boasting report, but the square accounts after the autumn harvest.

秋游 qiūyóu
autumn outing (often an organized outing)

秋杂 qiūzá
autumn sundries
A cover term for the multifarious agricultural products harvested in autumn, such as corn, sorghum, and beans.

球风 qiúfēng
style of play (in a ball game)

球籍 qiújí

global citizenship

E.g. 被开除球籍 *to be stripped of global citizenship (jocular)*

球龄 qiúlíng

number of years a ball player has been engaged in a game

E.g. 他已有十年的球龄了。*He has been a player (in a ball sport) for ten years.*

球幕电影 qiúmù diànyǐng

Same as 全景电影. (cf. 全景电影)

球手 qiúshǒu

(re sports) ball player

球坛 qiútán

world of various types of ball games

球王 qiúwáng

"ball king", a champion or superstar in a certain ball game

球星 qiúxīng

a star in a certain ball game

球员 qiúyuán

(re sports) a ball player

求实精神 qiúshí jīngshén

pragmatic attitude

An attitude of being concerned with practicalities.

E.g. 必须把革命干劲和求实精神结合起来。*We must combine revolutionary enthusiasm with a pragmatic attitude.*

求职 qiúzhí

look for a job; apply for a job

E.g. 网上求职 *to look for a job on the internet*

qu

趋利避害 qūlì bìhài

to pursue benefits and avoid damage

趋同 qūtóng

to tend to conform; to incline to the same conclusions

E.g. 要警惕高新技术产业趋同。*We should be alert that high and new technological industry tends to be similar.*

趋同化 qūtónghuà

to standardize

E.g. 各行业产品结构趋同化。*The production structure of all trades and professions are standardized.*

区段 qūduàn

a section

A certain area under the jurisdiction of a traffic control department.

区间 qūjiān

a sectioned-off route of a train or bus

A train route that has been sectioned off in order to manage train runs, usually the line between two regular stops. Certain routes that have been sectioned off from regular routes in intra-city buses and trolley cars according to management needs are also called sectioned-off routes. The sectioning-off is done to accommodate the needs of heavily used portions of routes, etc.

区间车 qūjiānchē

shuttle train or bus

A public vehicle that travels only the sectioned-off portion of a route. (cf. 区间)

区委 qūwěi

district committee

A 区 district is an administrative unit. It includes an autonomous region, a district under a municipality or under a county government. A Communist Party committee set up at the district level is called a district committee.

区位 qūwèi
regional location
The location of a certain region.
E.g. 利用区位优势,加快经济发展 *to use an advantageous location to speed up economic development*

区域经济 qūyù jīngjì
regional economics

区域旅游 qūyù lǚyóu
regional tourism
For example, the east China regional tourist route consisting of Shanghai, Jiangsu, Zhejiang, and Anhui; the southwest regional tourist route consisting of Guangdong, Guilin, and Nanning.

区域自治 qūyù zìzhì
regional autonomy
Also called 民族区域自治 autonomy of minority areas.

屈居 qūjū
to be in a demeaning position
E.g. 中国队屈居亚军。 *The Chinese team is in the inferior position of second place.*

驱赶 qūgǎn
to drive out; to chase out

曲库 qǔkù
music library
A large-scale audio-visual product that includes various kinds of music, drama, and performing folk art forms.
E.g. 这套曲库是由国家教委艺术教育委员会编制的。 *This music library was compiled by the Arts Education Committee of the State Education Commission.*

曲坛 qǔtán
world of popular performing art
曲协 qǔ-xié
Chinese Ballad Singers Association
Abbreviation for 曲艺家协会.

取经 qǔjīng
to obtain sacred texts
The term originally referred to Buddhist going to India to seek sacred Buddhist texts. Now it is a metaphor for absorbing experiences from advanced persons, units, or regions.

取向 qǔxiàng
the direction taken
The viewpoint and attitude adopted toward certain matters.
E.g. 青少年的价值取向 *the value concepts of youths* / 行为取向 *direction of behavior* / 取向不同。 *The direction is not the same.*

取消主义 qǔxiāo zhǔyì
liquidationism
An anarchist trend of thought which advocates abolishing all existing systems, regulations, required qualifications, and rights, regardless of whether they are reasonable or not.

取信于民 qǔxìn yúmín
to attain the people's trust

取证 qǔzhèng
to gather evidence
E.g. 现场调查取证 *to make an on-the-spot investigation and to gather evidence*

去粗取精 qù cū qǔ jīng
to get rid of the coarse and obtain the refined
To get rid of the coarse portions, retaining only the quintessence.

去伪存真 qù wěi cún zhēn
to rid the fake and retain the genuine
To get rid of the fake, retaining only the genuine.

quan

圈定 quāndìng

to draw a circle on a document to indicate agreement with a decision; (generally) to determine

E.g. 圈定干部 to designate cadres / 圈定典型 to determine the typical form

圈护 quānhù

to encircle or fence in order to protect

E.g. 园林有围墙圈护。The garden is encircled by a fence.

圈批 quānpī

a draw a circle on a document to indicate approval

E.g. 那项工程是由最高领导人圈批的。 That project was approved by the highest-level leadership.

圈阅 quānyuè

to read and circle

After a leader has read and examined a document, he draws a circle by his name to indicate that he has read it.

E.g. 文件已由主要领导人圈阅过。 The document has been read by the main leaders.

权股 quángǔ

power stocks

The stocks amassed by Party and political cadres by abusing their power in the stock market.

E.g. 权股现象十分严重。 The "power stocks" phenomenon is very serious.

权位 quánwèi

power and position; powerful position

E.g. 提高权位 to elevate one's power and position / 被拉下权位 to be demoted in power and position

权欲 quányù

lust for power

全方位 quánfāngwèi

all the various directions and positions; all the facets (of a matter)

E.g. 全方位对外开放 to open up all aspects to the outside / 全方位思考 to consider from all angles

全方位外交 quánfāngwèi wàijiāo

multi-faceted diplomacy

Also called 多方位外交 multi-bearing diplomacy.

全国粮票 quánguó liángpiào

national grain coupons

Grain coupons that could be used anywhere in the nation (as opposed to those with geographic restrictions). They were issued by the Grains Department of the People's Republic of China, and came in denominations of half *shijin* (a unit of measure equivalent to half a kilogram), one *shijin*, three *shijin*, five *shijin*, etc.

全国一盘棋 quánguó yīpánqí

whole nation as one chess game (to coordinate all the activities of the nation like pieces in a chess game)

A metaphor for the need to take the entire nation's situation as the point of departure in socialist construction. That is, under the nation's centralized leadership, to put into place comprehensive arrangements, rational distribution, assured priority to key places, and mutual assistance, so that manpower, material and financial resources will be utilized more rationally.

全会 quán–huì

meeting of the entire group or body

Abbreviation for 全体会议 meeting of the entire group or body.

E.g. 中共十一届三中全会 *the Third Plenary Session of the Eleventh Central Committee of the Chinese Communist Party*

全景电影 quánjǐng diànyǐng
cinepanoramic

全劳力 quánláolì
fully able bodied laborer

Also called 全劳动力. A person with full physical strength who is capable of various light and heavy physical labor (usually in reference to agricultural labor).

全面开花 quánmiàn kāihuā
(figurative) to open up or develop all the various aspects.

E.g. 技术推广全面开花 *to totally open up in popularizing technology*

全面专政 quánmiàn zhuānzhèng
total dictatorship

The reactionary theory, proposed by the Gang of Four during the Cultural Revolution, that total dictatorship must be exercised over the so-called bourgeoisie in all realms and stages. In actuality, this was a counter-revolutionary fascist dictatorship exercised over the broad masses of people.

全民皆兵 quánmín jiēbīng
an entire nation in arms; every citizen a soldier

Every citizen in the entire nation should receive certain military training, so that in the event of war, everyone can carry a gun and go to the battle front.

全民文艺 quánmín wényì
art and literature for the entire citizenry

A school of thought on art and literature which transcends class. It advocates that art and literature should serve all the people in a class society.

全能运动 quánnéng yùndòng
all-round athletic event

全勤 quánqín
perfect work attendance

To have a perfect work attendance, so that work is not held up due to tardiness, early withdrawal, absence due to illness or other matters. It is the opposite of 缺勤 to be absent from work.

全球定位系统 quánqiú dìngwèi xìtǒng
GPS (global positioning system)

全塑汽车 quánsù qìchē
an automobile whose body is made of plastic materials

Abbreviated as 全塑车.

全天候飞机 quántiānhòu fēijī
all-weather aircraft

全托 quántuō
total child care

Also called 整托 full child-cared. It is a system of child care for infants and young children in kindergartens and child care centers. The parents pay a certain fee and the kindergartens and child care centers take full responsibility for the children's room and board. In general, the children are sent on Monday mornings and are taken home on Friday afternoons.

全息 quánxī
holographic

E.g. 全息影像 *holographic image* / 全息技术 *holographic technology* / 全息显微 *holography microscopy* / 全息缩微存储 *holographic microfilm stor-*

age / 全息电影 *holographic movie* / 全息摄影 *holography* / 全息照相 *holography* (*Synonymous with* 全息摄影)

全优 quányōu
all-round excellence

To be excellent in all areas of academic work. Also, to attain the level of excellence in every target in the production process.

全优工程 quányōu gōngchéng
all-round excellent project

Also called 国家优质工程 national project of excellent quality. In accordance with the stipulations of the relevant departments, any project, such as a factory, mine, road, bridge, harbor, dam, power station, large-scale public project, or civilian building complex, that has attained the level of all-round excellence in terms of quality, efficiency, consumption, capital, safety, and project completion date, and that is significant in developing the national economy, is called all-round excellent project and is awarded a 国家优质工程项目金质奖 prize for national project of excellent quality.

全优工号竞赛 quányōu gōnghào jìngsài
all-round excellent project competition

即1974年在全国基本建设战线开展的"全优工号"社会主义劳动竞赛。它规定对达到"质量、效率、消耗、成本、安全和竣工"六项全优标准的单位实行"全优综合超额奖"。

The socialist labor competition conducted on the national basic construction front in 1974. It stipulated that an "all-round excellence surpass-multi-targets prize" be awarded to units that have attained all-round excellence in the six areas of quality, efficiency, consumption, capital, safety, and project completion.

全员 quányuán
full number of persons

The number of persons reaching the stipulated quota (in reference to personnel in a military unit, passengers on a train or boat, etc.).

E.g. 全员培训 *training of the entire staff* / 全员劳动生产率 *productivity of full labor capacity* / 全员劳动合同制 *full labor capacity contract system*

全运会 quán-yùn-huì
National Games

Abbreviation for 全国运动会.

全脂奶粉 quánzhī nǎifěn
whole milk powder

拳头产品 quántou chǎnpǐn
"fist" commodities

Refers to competitive products. Their quality and specifications meet the requirements of the market, and their supply source is in equilibrium. These commodities compete well on the market.

劝退 quàntuì
to persuade someone to resign

1) The Chinese Communist Party or the Chinese Communist Youth League persuading members who are not up to standards to voluntarily withdraw from the organization. 2) A work unit persuading members who do not meet the requirements to voluntarily resign and leave.

que

缺编 quēbiān
understaffed
The number of workers short of the authorized staff quota.

缺档 quēdàng
out of stock; to lack certain sizes or grades (of a commodity)
E.g. 缺档产品 *out of stock commodities* / 纺织品缺档 *textile products are out of stock*

缺斤短两 quējīn duǎnliǎng
to short charge a customer on the weight of a purchase
Same as 缺斤少两.

缺斤少两 quējīn shǎoliǎng
short on the catty and the ounce
The amount of merchandise sold short of the measured quantity.

缺门 quēmén
gap
A department or category with a void.
E.g. 填补缺门 *to fill a gap* / 缺门技术 *a technological gap*

确保 quèbǎo
to ensure; to guarantee
E.g. 加强田间管理，确保粮食丰收。 *to strengthen the management of agricultural fields and to ensure a bumper harvest of grain*

qun

裙裤 qúnkù
culottes
群雕 qúndiāo
an related group of sculptures
E.g. 一组群雕 *a group of sculptures* / 青年运动史群雕 *a group of sculptures on the sports history of youths*

群防群治 qúnfáng qúnzhì
prevention and cure by the masses themselves (often pertaining to public security)

群体 qúntǐ
an integral entity
1) An entity created by the process of individual biological entities of the same species forming physiological connections, such as sponge and coral in the animal kingdom and certain algae in the plant kingdom.
2) A group formed from things of the same kind.
E.g. 群体产量 *productivity of the group (the integral entity)* / 群体建筑 *modular building (composed by a grouping of modules)* / 英雄群体 *heroic group (made up of a group of individuals)*
3) Abbreviation for 群众体育活动 mass sports activities.

群言堂 qúnyántáng
to rule by the voice of many (lit., multi-voiced hall)
The opposite of 一言堂 to rule by the words of one. A work style of cadre leaders which consists of: following the mass line, fully developing a democratic style, allowing everyone to speak out, listening to the ideas of the masses, and being able to pull together the correct viewpoints.

群英会 qúnyīnghuì
a gathering of heroes
A gathering of many heroes. Originally a traditional repertoire item in Peking opera which takes its source from the

story of Sun Quan and Liu Bei uniting to resist Cao in the historical novel *Romance of the Three Kingdoms*. Now, the term refers to a meeting of heroic model persons or representatives from advanced groups.

群众工作 qúnzhòng gōngzuò
mass work

The work of Party and government cadres and Party members in penetrating the masses, forming intimate ties with the masses, understanding and resolving the problems existent in the work, studies, ideology, and life of the masses.

群众关系 qúnzhòng guānxì
relationship with the masses

The state of an individual's relationships with the people around him.

群众观点 qúnzhòng guāndiǎn
the mass viewpoint

The attitude which the proletarian political party should maintain toward the masses. That is: to persist in the mass line, to consider the masses to be the true heroes, to trust and rely on the masses, to respect the pioneering spirit of the masses, to be concerned with the hardships of the masses, to serve the people with one's heart and mind, and to be a humble student of the masses.

群众路线 qúnzhòng lùxiàn
the mass line

The basic path for all the work of the Chinese Communist Party. On the one hand, in all work or struggle, it requires the Party to trust and rely on the masses, and to organize the masses to use their own capabilities to solve their own problems. On the other hand, it requires the leadership to carry out the principle of "come from the masses, go to the masses". That is, to formulate guiding principles and policies on the foundation of the collective views of the masses, then to turn them over to the masses to discuss and implement, and in the process of discussion and implementation, to make revisions based on the opinions of the masses in order to gradually perfect the principles and policies.

群众团体 qúnzhòng tuántǐ
mass organizations

Organizations formed by the masses, such as labor unions, the Women's Federation, and the Communist Youth League, which do not have the character of state political authority.

群众性 qúnzhòngxìng
of a mass character

Matters in which the broad masses participate and that are relevant to the interests of the broad masses.

群众专政 qúnzhòng zhuānzhèng
dictatorship of the masses

The erroneous way of the Cultural Revolution period whereby mass organizations usurped the functions of the nation's organs of dictatorship.

群众组织 qúnzhòng zǔzhī
mass organizations

1) Synonymous with 群众团体.
2) Specifically, "rebel" organizations formed by groups of people with similar views during the Cultural Revolution.

R

ran

燃爆 ránbào
to ignite and explode; an explosion caused by ignition

rang

让步政策 ràngbù zhèngcè
policy of making concessions
The policy, used by the feudal ruling class in historical periods to consolidate its dominant position, by reducing its oppression and exploitation of the peasant class under "certain conditions" and "certain premises", such as reducing taxes, restraining bullies, remitting land tax, and constructing irrigation projects. This is an issue in historical research which is still being debated.

让渡 ràngdù
to give someone else the right to use funds in a bank account

让利 rànglì
to offer advantages; to offer discounts
E.g. 产品降价让利 *the products have been discounted* / 向顾客让利 *to give clients discounts*

让贤 ràngxián
to yield one's own position to one who is virtuous and talented

rao

扰民 rǎomín
to harrass or disturb the people

re

热 rè
fad; popular
E.g. 体育热 *sports fad* / 出国热 *fad of going abroad* / 文化热 *cultural fads* / 体育运动的一些冷门项目逐渐热起来。 *Some hitherto unpopular sports have gradually become popular.* / 水产养殖业又成了热。 *The enterprise of raising aquatic products is again becoming popular.*

热岛效应 rèdǎo xiàoyìng
tropical island effect
The phenomenon of rising temperatures in a city or a localized area arising from the deterioration of the ecological environment.

热得快 rèdékuài
popular nickname for a gadget that heats liquids

热点 rèdiǎn
hot spots
1) Places or issues that are politically rather sensitive and prone to result in conflicts. 2) Places with a preponderance of tourists.
E.g. 热点城市 *hot spot cities*

热狗 règǒu
hot dog

热核武器 rèhé wǔqì
hydrogen bomb

热门股票 rèmén gǔpiào
hot stocks
Ordinary stocks distributed by a booming enterprise. These stocks are expected to maintain a steady and high growth rate.

热门话题 rèmén huàtí
hot subject of conversation

热门货 rèménhuò
hot merchandise

热启动 rèqǐdòng
to reset
原指计算机在死机时用最简便、迅速的方法启动。又指尽快开始进行某项事情。
A term originally is used in computer. It also refers to start doing something quickly.
E.g. 商业医疗保险，期待"热启动"。*Commercial medical insurance is expected to start.* / 贷款消费热启动 *to reset the mortgage (loan) consumption*

热气球 rèqìqiú
hot air balloon

热钱 rèqián
hot money (money attained illegally)

热区 rèqū
tropical zone
E.g. 云南热区总面积达一亿一千七百零七万亩。*The tropical area in Yunnan Province is 117.07 million mu.*

热身 rèshēn
warm up (prior to physical exercise or a sport competition)
E.g. 热身训练 *warm up exercises* / 中国队第一场热身失利。*The Chinese team made a poor showing in the first warm up round.* / 足球队在天津热身。*The soccer team is warming up in Tianjin.*

热身赛 rèshēnsài
warm up competition
E.g. 明晚是他们出征前的热身赛。*Tomorrow evening they will have their warm up competition before they go out to battle.*

热水器 rèshuǐqì
water heater

热土 rètǔ
hot land
1) A place which one loves and remembers fondly.
E.g. 他真心爱上北京了这块热土。*He fell in love with Beijing as his beloved land.*
2) A place with great potential for economic development and is a hot spot for investors.
E.g. 荒滩变成了投资者的热土。*The desert became a hot spot for investors.*

热线 rèxiàn
hot line
1) Infrared ray. 2) Telephone lines for urgent use by national leaders. 3) Phone lines dedicated to specific usages, particularly in emergencies, also a metaphor for a direct line to information or a secret informant. 4) A heavily used transportation route.
E.g. 苏美两家之间建立了热线。*An emergency telephone line has been established between the United States and the Soviet Union.* / 保持热线联系 *to*

maintain hot line contact / 旅游热线 *tourist hot line*

热销 rèxiāo
selling hot
Commodities welcomed by buyers and selling fast.
E.g. 领带热销。 *Neckties are selling hot.* / 热销产品 *hot-sale products* / 热销货 *hot-sale commodities*

热战 rèzhàn
hot war
War that involves actual combat (as opposed to a cold war).

ren

人才库 réncáikù
talent bank, a unit or locale with a concentration of talented people

人才流动 réncái liúdòng
mobility of talents
To reform the system of ownership of talents by work units, so that persons with certain specialized skills or with both ability and political integrity may change their work units on the basis of their special abilities and society's needs. In this way, people can give full play to their talents, and talents can be put to maximum use. Mobility of talents takes on such forms as selective transfer, loan, recruitment, imports (from another location), concurrent posting, etc.

人才学 réncáixué
the study of human ability
A discipline which studies the patterns of the development and cultivation of human ability. It can be divided into three categories: 1) natural scientific study of human ability, which investigates the physical catalysts which raise human intelligence through studying brain physiology, prenatal development, heredity, eugenics, and nutrition; 2) study of individual human ability, which investigates individual self-cultivation and the general patterns of maturation of abilities in individuals; 3) sociological study of human ability, which uses the perspective of social structure and management to investigate society's ability to develop human capabilities. That is, it studies the investment and development of human intelligence including such issues as, how to discover, distinguish, promote, rationally utilize, and effectively cultivate talent.

人产 rénchǎn
per-person production
The average per-person production yield.
E.g. 他们村人产粮食已达千斤。 *Their village has already attained a per-person grain yield of a thousand catties.*

人潮 rénchāo
human tide

人大 rén-dà
People's Congress
Abbreviation for 人民代表大会, the organ through which the Chinese people exercise their state power. Representatives to the National People's Congress and the local People's Congresses at various levels are all elected by democratic consultation. The National People's Congress is the organ of highest power, its permanent body is the Standing Committee of the National People's Congress. The local People's

Congresses at various levels are local organs of the state. Those at or above the county level have standing committees. The term 人大 is also used in referring to 中国人民大学 Chinese People's University.

人大常委会 rén–dà cháng–wěi–huì
Standing Committee of the People's Congress

Abbreviation for 人民代表大会常务委员会.

人大会堂 Rén–Dà Huìtáng
the Great Hall of the People

Abbreviation for 人民大会堂. (cf. 人民大会堂)

人代会 rén–dài–huì
People's Congress

Abbreviation for 人民代表大会. (cf. 人大)

人防 rén–fáng
civil air defense

Abbreviation for 人民防空.

E.g. 人防教育 *civil air defense education*

人防工程 rén–fáng gōngchéng
civil air defense constructions

Above ground and underground facilities constructed for civil air defense, such as air-raid shelters, underground shelters, underground shops, and tunnels.

人工合成胰岛素 réngōng héchéng yídǎosù
synthetic insulin

A chemically synthesized protein. Because protein and the phenomenon of life are intimately linked, synthetic proteins have great significance. In 1965, for the first time in the world, China synthesized a biological protein, crystalline bovine insulin.

人工湖 réngōnghú
man-made lakes

人工流产 réngōng liúchǎn
induced abortion (lit., artificial miscarriage)

Also called 堕胎 drop the fetus, or more popularly, 打胎 strike the fetus.

人工器官 réngōng qìguān
artificial organs

人工生态 réngōng shēngtài
artificial ecology

人工智能 réngōng zhìnéng
artificial intelligence

Also called 智能模拟 simulated intelligence.

人海战术 rénhǎi zhànshù
huge-crowd strategy

A work method which relies on concentrating a large amount of manpower to complete certain tasks. The term is usually applied to large construction projects.

人机对话 rén–jī duìhuà
man machine interaction

Also called 自然语言理解 natural language comprehension.

人际 rénjì
interpersonal; between persons

E.g. 人际关系 *interpersonal relationship*

人居 rénjū
man's residence (dwelling)

E.g. 我国又获两项人居奖。 *China has won two Habitat Awards.*

人均 rénjūn
per capita

The average for the population.

E.g. 人均收入 *per-capita income /*

人均销售 per-capita sale / 人均增长 per-capita growth / 人均增产 per-capita production increase

人口高峰 rénkǒu gāofēng
population peak
The period with the highest total population.

人口经济学 rénkǒu jīngjìxué
population economics

人口普查 rénkǒu pǔchá
census

人口素质 rénkǒu sùzhì
characteristics of a population
Certain characteristics of a particular population, such as the intelligence, physique, cultural level, skills, culture, and the population composition.

人口学 rénkǒuxué
demography

人口质量 rénkǒu zhìliàng
quality of a population
The scientific and cultural attainments, work skills, physique and level of health of a population.

人口自然增长率 rénkǒu zìrán zēngzhǎnglǜ
rate of natural population increase (usually in terms of a certain number per thousand per year)

人类工程学 rénlèi gōngchéngxué
human engineering

人流 rénliú
1) abortion
Abbreviation for 人工流产.
E.g. 做人流 to perform an abortion / 人流手术 abortion operation
2) human flow (a mass of people moving in a certain direction)
E.g. 疏导人流 to direct the flow of people

人民币 rénmínbì
RMB (the Chinese currency)
Its basic unit is 元 yuan.

人民大会堂 Rénmín Dàhuìtáng
the Great Hall of the People
A place where the People's Congress meets, built in 1959, on the west side of Tian'anmen Square

人民代表大会 rénmín dàibiǎo dàhuì
People's Congress
Abbreviated as 人代会 or 人大. (cf. 人大)

人民公社 rénmín gōngshè
people's communes
Rural people's communes. Originally, they were the basic organizations in China's rural areas which integrated government administration and commune management. They appeared in 1958, and were formed by uniting advanced agricultural production cooperatives. The 1982 Constitution of the People's Republic of China established the principle of separating government administration and commune management, so that people's communes came to exist only as collective economic organizations.

人民民主专政
rénmín mínzhǔ zhuānzhèng
people's democratic dictatorship
The people's democratic political authority which is led by the working class (through the Communist Party), and which takes the coalition of workers and peasants as its foundation. People's democratic dictatorship has undergone two different developmental stages. Before liberation, the people's democratic

dictatorship of the revolutionary base carried the mission of the democratic revolution of the bourgeoisie. It was the dictatorship of several revolutionary classes, led by the proletarian class and based on the coalition of workers and peasants, over the running dogs of imperialism, the bureaucrat-comprador class, and the feudal landlord class. After the founding of the People's Republic in 1949, the people's democratic dictatorship carried out the mission of socialist revolution and socialist construction, in reality it was the dictatorship of the proletarian class.

人民内部矛盾 rénmín nèibù máodùn
contradictions among the people

Contradictions that exist within the premise of basic unity in the people's interests. They are non-antagonistic contradictions, and are the opposite of 敌我矛盾 contradictions between the enemy and ourselves.

人民陪审员 rénmín péishěnyuán
people's assessors

Personnel elected by the people to participate in judicial activities of the court. During their term of office, people's assessors are members of the court and enjoy equal authority with the judges.

人民调解委员会 rénmín tiáojiěwěiyuánhuì
people's mediation committees

Mass organizations for resolving the people's internal disputes. They work under the leadership of grass-roots people's governments and grass-roots people's courts. Their responsibilities are to mediate general civil disputes among the people and disputes that involve misdemeanors, and to publicize and educate the people on policies and laws. People's mediation committees are formed through democratic elections by the masses.

人民团体 rénmín tuántǐ
people's organizations

People's (non-governmental) organizations, such as the Red Cross, China's Medical Association, and the Chinese People's Association for the Study of Foreign Relations.

人民委员会 rénmín wěiyuánhuì
people's committee

Abbreviated as 人委. The various levels of local people's government. During the Cultural Revolution, the term 革命委员会 revolutionary committee was used. Now the term 政府 government is used uniformly.

人民性 rénmínxìng
affinity to the people

Reflections on the life, thoughts, feelings and aspirations of the masses of people in literature and works of art.

人民英雄纪念碑 Rénmín Yīngxióng Jìniànbēi
Monument to the People's Heroes

Built in 1952-1958 to commemorate the heroes of the various revolutions between 1840 and 1949, another landmark in Tian'anmen Square.

人民战争 rénmín zhànzhēng
people's war

A revolutionary war led by the proletarian class and joined by the broad masses of people, with the people's army as their backbone. The term is also a

metaphor for a mass movement.
E.g. 打了一场挑水点种的人民战争 *to have fought a people's war of carrying water for dibbling seeds*

人平 rénpíng
per person
To average out according to the population. Synonymous with 人均.
E.g. 人平收入 1000 元。 *The per-person income is 1,000 yuan.*

人气 rénqì
people's (public) attitude, enthusiasm or assessment of something
E.g. 市场人气转弱。 *People's enthusiasm for the market is less than it was.*

人情方 rénqíngfāng
favor prescription, a prescription for hard to obtain medication written by a doctor as a favor to someone covered by state-funded medical care
E.g. 医院不准开人情方。 *The hospital or clinic has a regulation against providing prescriptions as favors.*

人情味 rénqíngwèi
human touch
E.g. 此人没有一点人情味。 *This person shows no vestige of human touch.*

人蛇 rénshé
illegal immigrant
指偷渡者。

人事处 rénshìchù
personnel offices
Offices in enterprises and institutional units – such as government agencies, factories and mines, military units, and schools – which are responsible for the hiring, training, transfer, reward and punishment of employees. The smaller units are called 人事科 personnel sections; the larger units with more personnel are called 人事处 personnel offices.

人事调动 rénshì diàodòng
personnel transfer
Workers changing work units because of job requirements, including transferring in, transferring out, dismissal, promotion, and demotion.

人事科 rénshìkē
personnel department (cf. 人事处)

人事制度 rénshì zhìdù
personnel system
The state's regulations regarding the employment, training, transfer, reward, punishment, and dismissal of employees, cadres, and other relevant personnel.

人售 rénshòu
per-person sale
The average amount sold by each person.
E.g. 全县人售余粮两千斤。 *The average per-person sale of surplus grain in the county was two thousand catties.*

人梯 réntī
human ladder
In the literal sense, a ladder made up of humans. The term is also a metaphor for people who sacrifice themselves for a revolutionary cause, who foster others so that they may achieve something.
E.g. 甘当人梯 *willing to be a human ladder (stepping stone) for others*

人头粮 réntóuliáng
head-count grain rations
The system of grain rations in rural areas whereby each person, regardless of age and amount of need, received an average amount of grain ration. This was

also a form of equalitarianism.

人委 rén-wěi
people's committee
Abbreviation for 人民委员会. (cf. 人民委员会)

人卫 rén-wèi
artificial satellite
Abbreviation for 人造卫星.
E.g. 人卫系统 *the system of artificial satellites*

人武 rén-wǔ
people's armed forces
Abbreviation for 人民武装 people's armed forces.

人武部 rén-wǔ-bù
people's armed forces department (of a commune, country, etc.)
Abbreviation for 人民武装部.

人行横道 rénxíng héngdào
pedestrian crossing

人造地球卫星 rénzào dìqiú wèixīng
artificial earth satellite

人造革 rénzàogé
synthetic leather

人造棉 rénzàomián
synthetic cotton

人造器官 rénzào qìguān
man-made organs
Synonymous with 人工器官 artificial organs.

人造卫星 rénzào wèixīng
artificial satellite

人造纤维 rénzào xiānwéi
synthetic fiber

人造小平原 rénzào xiǎopíngyuán
man-made small plain
A small flat piece of land created through human labor, such as leveling small hills and filling in ponds and bays.

人造胰岛素 rénzào yídǎosù
synthetic insulin
(cf. 人工合成胰岛素)

人治 rénzhì
government by individuals (as opposed to government by law)
E.g. 人治与法制并存。*The rule of man and the rule of law exist side by side.*

人字呢 rénzìní
herringbone
A woolen fabric with a weave shaped like the character "人". It has a thick and dense texture and is usually used for uniforms and overcoats.

韧劲儿 rènjìnr
tenacity
Synonymous with the second meaning of 韧性 below.

韧性 rènxìng
toughness
1) The quality of being pliable but strong, not easily torn or snapped.
E.g. 薄膜韧性好。*The thin membrane is very tough.*
2) An indomitable and resilient spirit.
E.g. 革命韧性 *indomitable and resilient revolutionary spirit*

任教 rènjiào
to serve in the capacity of a teacher or coach

任聘 rènpìn
to appoint someone to a position
E.g. 任聘教练 *to appoint a coach*

任务观点 rènwù guāndiǎn
the get-it-over-and-done-with attitude
The erroneous work attitude of simply completing the duties assigned by one's

superiors, not paying any attention to the quality of the job.

认捐 rènjuān

to pledge a donation; to agree to donate money

E.g. 认捐数额 *the amount pledged as a donation* / 认捐十万元美金 *to pledge a donation of US $ 100,000*

认同 rèntóng

to approve; to endorse

认养 rènyǎng

to provide a needy child with regular support through a children's foundation

This arrangement does not entail legal relationships between the benefactor and the child, the child does not live with the benefactor, no change in census registration is involved. Aside from providing support on a regular schedule, and expressing love and concern for the child, the benefactor has no legal responsibilities.

认指 rènzhǐ

to identify and point out

Contraction of 辨认 and 指出.

ri

日光灯 rìguāngdēng

fluorescent lamp; daylight lamp

It is also called 荧光灯 fluorescent lamp.

日光浴 rìguāngyù

sun-bathing

日均 rìjūn

daily average

日托 rìtuō

day-care

A kindergarten and child-care center system whereby children are taken care of only in day time. Usually the children come to the kindergarten or child-care center each morning and are taken home by their parents each evening. This system is distinguished from 全托 total child-care.

日杂 rì-zá

sundries for everyday use

Abbreviation for 日用杂货.

E.g. 日杂公司 *sundries company* / 日杂商店 *sundries store*

rong

荣获 rónghuò

to attain with honor

E.g. 荣获冠军 *to win (attain the honor of) the championship* / 荣获最佳男演员 *to win the best male performer award*

荣民 róngmín

(Taiwan terminology) honored citizens

荣退 róngtuì

honorable discharge; to be honorably retired from a post

荣退军人 róng-tuì jūnrén

disabled soldiers and veterans

Composite term for 荣誉军人 and 退伍军人.

融通 róngtōng

to put capital funds and assets into circulation (to enliven the economy)

E.g. 融通资金 *to put capital into circulation* / 提高资金融通效果 *to raise the effectiveness of capital circulation*

融物 róngwù

(re economics) to put goods and materials into circulation; goods and materials put into circulation

融资 róngzī

to put capital into circulation

E.g. 进行融资 to carry out capital circulation / 扩大融资规模 to expand the scale of capital circulation / 实行横向融资 to carry out traverse capital circulation

容留 róngliú

to take in and accommodate

冗余 rǒngyú

surplus; excess; superfluous

rou

肉鸽 ròugē

pigeon raised for meat

肉鸡 ròujī

chicken raised for meat

肉牛 ròuniú

beef cattle

肉票 ròupiào

meat ration coupons

肉兔 ròutù

rabbit raised for meat

肉鸭 ròuyā

ducks raised for meat

肉羊 ròuyáng

sheep raised for mutton

ru

儒法斗争 Rú-Fǎ dòuzhēng

struggle between the Confucianists and the Legalists

The contention between the Confucianists and the Legalists during China's Spring and Autumn and Warring States periods. During the Cultural Revolution, the Gang of Four, spurred by political motivation, made the absurd assertion that the struggle between the Confucianists and the Legalists ran through all of Chinese history, and that the struggle was between conservatives and the progressives, and between the reactionaries and the revolutionaries.

儒商 rúshāng

intellectual businessmen

Intellectuals that have gone into business professions.

乳制品 rǔzhìpǐn

dairy products

The various products made from milk, such as milk powder, butter, cheese, milk skin (from boiled milk), etc.

入场券 rùchǎngquàn

entrance ticket

A metaphor for qualifying to enter a certain competition.

入党 rùdǎng

to join a party

To join a party organization. The term refers specifically to joining the Chinese Communist Party.

E.g. 他 1925 年入党。 He joined the Party in 1925.

入党申请书 rùdǎng shēnqǐngshū

Party membership application

A written application submitted to a grass-roots organization of the Party by someone requesting to be admitted to the Party.

入党志愿书 rùdǎng zhìyuànshū

application form for Party membership

A form filled out by someone wishing to

be admitted to the Chinese Communist Party. In the form, there are portions to be filled out separately by the applicant, the sponsor, the grass-roots organization and the upper level approval organ.

入档 rùdàng

to place material into files; to put on file

E.g. 整理资料入档 *to organize and file materials*

入关 rùguān

to enter one of the gates of the Great Wall from the outside; to be admitted to GATT

E.g. 洋货价格将随入关下降。*After being admitted to GATT, the price of imported commodities will fall.*

入库 rùkù

to place (grains, commodities, funds, etc.) into granaries, warehouses, treasury, etc.; to enter data into computer files

E.g. 产品入库 *to warehouse products* / 入库进度 *warehouse or storage rate* / 把信息归档入库 *to put data into files*

入脑 rùnǎo

to inscribe in the memory

E.g. 文章读后能够入脑 *able to inscribe an article in one's memory after reading it* / 学习文件要入耳入脑。*In studying a document, one must hear it and inscribe it in one's mind.*

入世 rù-Shì

to access to the WTO

入团 rùtuán

to be inducted into the Chinese Communist Youth League

入托 rùtuō

to put (a child) into a day care facility

E.g. 入托婴幼儿 *to place a child in a day care facility* / 解决入托难的问题 *to solve the problem of placing children in day care*

入伍 rùwǔ

to join the military; (specifically) to join the Chinese People's Liberation Army

入藏 rù Zàng

to enter Tibet

入主 rùzhǔ

to get into (a place or situation) and take charge

E.g. 执政党连续三届入主白宫。*The ruling party took charge of the White House (occupied the presidency) for three successive terms.*

ruan

软班子 ruǎnbānzi

feeble ranks

A leadership group that is timid, weak, ineffectual, lacking in principles, and unable to properly perform the work of its unit.

软包装 ruǎnbāozhuāng

to soft pack; to package foodstuff and other commodities in soft materials such as plastic; soft packaging material

E.g. 软包装牛奶 *soft-pack milk*

软赤字 ruǎnchìzì

soft deficit

The deficit shown in the difference between revenue and expenditure without taking into account income from debt collection.

软贷款 ruǎndàikuǎn
soft loan

Loan with a low rate of interest.

软雕塑 ruǎndiāosù
soft sculpture

Indoor three dimensional ornaments handmade from cotton, hemp or wool.
E.g. 软雕塑作品已开始进入家庭。*The soft sculptural works have begun to appear in family homes.*

软工厂 ruǎngōngchǎng
soft factory

Also called digitized factory, a factory that relies mainly on software and computers for its production, where workers are the main force, and robots play secondary role.

软广告 ruǎnguǎnggào
soft advertisement

The advertising of commodities through dialogues, props, and stage setting in television programs.
E.g. 电视剧中开始出现软广告。*The phenomenon of soft advertisements is beginning to appear in television programs.*

软环境 ruǎnhuánjìng
soft environment

The social conditions including system of organization, laws, working efficiency, etc. It's the opposite of 硬环境.
E.g. 厦门采取一个窗口对外，简化手续，大力改善外商投资的软环境。*Xiamen provides a window for foreigners by simplifying formalities and devoting much effort to the improvement of the soft environment for the convenience of foreign investors.*

软技术 ruǎnjìshù
soft technology

The organizational management of science, technology, and economics, including methods of management and policies on technology.

软件 ruǎnjiàn
software

Also called 程序系统 program system or 软设备 soft facility.

软开业 ruǎnkāiyè
soft founding of a business

Different units, academic fields, and personnel coming together to form a company that researches, produces, and designs new technological products.

软科学 ruǎnkēxué
soft science

Refers to social sciences.

软懒散 ruǎn-lǎn-sǎn
soft, lazy, and diffused

指一些单位的领导班子怕犯错误，意志衰退，团结涣散的不正常现象。软，就是怕字当头，丧失原则，顶不住，跟着别人跑；懒，就是意志衰退，不读书，不看报，不动脑筋，不下部队，好吃懒做；散，就是争权夺利，搞不团结，捏不到一起。

The unhealthy phenomenon in some units where the leadership ranks are fearful of making errors (too timid), weak in will, and lack cohesion. "Soft" means being timid, lacking in principles, unable to withstand pressure, and following after others; "lazy" means being weak willed, not reading books and newspapers, not exercising one's brain, not going down among the ranks, and loving to eat but too lazy to work; "diffused" means to contend for power and benefits, and to have no unity.

软任务 ruǎnrènwu
soft tasks
Tasks that are not taken seriously; they are not considered urgent so no time limit is placed on them. They are the opposite of 硬任务 hard (serious) tasks.
E.g. 有人把教育工作当作软任务。*Some people consider education to be a soft task.*

软商品 ruǎnshāngpǐn
soft commodities
The products of third enterprises, i.e., service enterprises. (cf. 第三产业)

软设备 ruǎnshèbèi
software (cf. 软件)

软生产 ruǎnshēngchǎn
soft production
Production activities of a soft factory. (cf. 软工厂).

软投入 ruǎntóurù
soft investment
General term for investment in intellectual property, including scientific and technical know-how, management, market research, etc.

软卧 ruǎnwò
soft berth
A relatively comfortable and soft bunk on a train where a passenger may sleep.

软席 ruǎnxí
soft seat
A relatively comfortable and soft seat or bunk on a train.

软饮料 ruǎnyǐnliào
soft drinks

软指标 ruǎnzhǐbiāo
soft targets
Targets with no time limit or rigid requirements. They are the opposite of 硬指标 stiff targets.

软着陆 ruǎnzhuólù
soft landing
The successful landing of a man-made satellite or spaceship of the surface of the earth or another celestial body. In this process, certain equipment is used to change the orbit and to slow down the speed of descent.

软座 ruǎnzuò
soft seat
A relatively comfortable and soft seat. The term refers specifically to the soft seats on a train.

ruo

弱化 ruòhuà
to weaken
E.g. 弱化财产所有权 *to weaken property ownership* / 基础教育呈现弱化。*Basic education is showing signs of weakening.*

弱能 ruònéng
mentally or physically handicapped persons
E.g. 香港有弱能人士28万余人。*There are over 280,000 mentally and physically handicapped people in Hong Kong.*

弱势 ruòshì
weak trend
Generally refers to a weak currency.
E.g. 美元弱势难改。*The weak trend of the American dollar is difficult to turn around.*

弱视 ruòshì
weak eyesight

弱项 ruòxiàng
an athletic event in which an indi-

vidual competitor or team is weak
弱智 ruòzhì
retarded (lit., weak intelligence)
To be below normal intelligence.
E.g. 弱智儿童 retarded children / 弱智教育 education for the retarded
弱质 ruòzhì
low quality; low profitability
E.g. 农业是弱质产业。Agriculture is a low profit enterprise.

S

sai

赛场 sàichǎng
competition arena
Contraction of 比赛场地.

赛程 sàichéng
date or procedure of a competition; route of a race

赛风 sàifēng
sportsmanship and deportment manifested by athletes in a competition

赛区 sàiqū
the region in which a regional competition takes place

赛事 sàishì
arrangements for a competition
Short for 比赛事宜.
E.g. 北京赛区的赛事结束了。*Arrangements for the competition in the Beijing district have concluded.*

赛势 sàishì
how things stand in a competition

赛艇 sàitǐng
racing boats; to have a boat race

赛制 sàizhì
system of competition; regulations of a competition

san

三八红旗集体 sānbā hóngqí jítǐ
March 8 red flag organizations
An honorific title for advanced organizations, composed primarily of women, which have made outstanding contributions on the various fronts of socialist construction. (March 8 is International Women's Day.)

三八红旗手 sānbā hóngqíshǒu
March 8 red flaggers
An honorific title for women who have made extraordinary achievements and outstanding contributions on the various fronts of socialist construction.

三八式干部 sānbāshì gànbù
cadres of the 1938 era
Cadres who went to Yan'an and other resistance bases during the War of Resistance Against Japan (1937-1945) to participate in revolutionary work.

三八线 sānbāxiàn
the 38th parallel (boundary between North and South Korea)
A metaphor for an inviolable boundary.

三八作风 sānbā zuòfēng
the three-eight working style
指毛泽东针对军队提出的三句话和八个字。三句话是坚定正确的政治方向，艰苦朴素的工作作风，灵活机动的战略战术；八个字是团结、紧张、严肃、活泼。简称"三八作风"。现已不用。
The three sayings and eight characters with which Mao Zedong admonished his troops. The three sayings are: firm and correct political direction, tough and plain work style, and agile and flexible

strategy. The eight characters are: 团结 unity, 紧张 alertness, 严肃 solemnity, and 活泼 liveliness. Together they are summed up as the "three-eight working style". The term is no longer used.

三班倒 sānbāndǎo
three shifts

The system of three shifts used in factories whereby workers take turns working the early, middle, and night shifts.

三班制 sānbānzhì
three-shift system (covers 24 hours)

三包 sānbāo
three guarantees

工厂为了取信于用户，对自己出售的产品实行"包修、包退、包换"的办法，简称"三包"。

The three guarantees – guaranteed repairs, guaranteed returns, and guaranteed exchange – that factories apply to their products to gain the trust of customers. They are summed up as the "three guarantees".

三包一奖 sānbāo yījiǎng
three responsibilities and one reward

中国高级农业生产合作社时实行的一项基本的生产责任制，即"包工、包产、包成本和超产奖励"的制度。简称"三包一奖"。

A production responsibility system implemented in China's advanced agricultural production cooperative. The three responsibilities involve labor, production, and production costs, and the one reward is for surplus production. They are summed up as "three responsibilities and one reward".

三保 sānbǎo
three guarantees

指对产品提供服务的三项保证措施：即优质产品、优质配件和良好的技术服务。

Guarantees providing customers with high quality in three areas: products, parts, and technical services.

三保三压 sānbǎo sānyā
three protections and three suppressions

指基建工作中保计划内项目，压计划外项目；保生产性建设，压非生产性建设；保重点建设，压非重点建设。也说三压三保。

(In capital construction) three protections (protecting: projects within the plan, constructions geared toward production, and key constructions) and three suppressions (suppressing: projects not within the plan, constructions not geared toward production, and non-key constructions). Also called 三压三保.

三保田 sānbǎotián
three-conservation fields

指保水、保肥、保土的田地。

Fields where conservation of water, fertilizer and soil is practiced.

三北地区 sānběi dìqū
the three north areas

东北、华北、西北三个地区的统称。

A cover term for the northeast, north, and northwest areas of China.

三边工程 sānbiān gōngchéng
three-concurrents construction

指边勘察、边设计、边施工的工程。这是一种违反科学的作法。

A construction project in which surveying, designing, and constructing are carried out concurrently (rather than in rational stages). This is an unscientific method.

三不政策 sānbù zhèngcè
three-nots policy
Synonymous with 三不主义 three-nots-ism.(cf. 三不主义)

三不主义 sānbù zhǔyì
three-nots-ism
即不抓辫子、不戴帽子、不打棍子。意思是禁止任意夸大一个人的错误，罗织成为罪状，并给予政治上、组织上的打击甚至迫害。
Not pulling someone's pigtail (i.e., not seizing on someone's mistakes), not putting a cap on someone (assigning a bad name to someone), and not coming down with a big stick. This means prohibiting the deliberate exaggeration of someone's mistakes, framing them in a crime, or subjecting a person to political and organizational attacks or persecution.

三材 sāncái
three materials
指建筑上常用的三种材料：钢材、木材和水泥。
The three materials most commonly used in construction: steel, wood, and concrete.

三大差别 sāndà chābié
three big differences
指社会主义阶段存在的工农差别、城乡差别、脑力劳动和体力劳动的差别。
The three differences that exist in the socialist stage: between industry and agriculture, between town and country, and between manual and mental labor.

三大法宝 sāndà fǎbǎo
three big wonder working weapons
指统一战线、武装斗争和党的建设。这是中国共产党在中国革命中战胜敌人的三条主要经验。
The three main means by which the Chinese Communist Party triumphed over the enemy in China's revolution: united front, armed struggle, and Party construction.

三大改造 sāndà gǎizào
three reforms
指中国在1956年底完成的国家对农业、手工业和资本主义工商业的社会主义改造。
Three reforms (the socialist reforms in agriculture, handicrafts, and capitalist industry and commerce completed in 1956).

三大革命实践 sāndà gémìng shíjiàn
three great revolutionary practices
指阶级斗争、生产斗争和科学实验。
Class struggle, production struggle, and scientific experimentation.

三大革命运动 sāndà gémìng yùndòng
three great revolutionary movements
Also called 三大革命实践 three big revolutionary practices.(cf. 三大革命实践)

三大纪律，八项注意 sāndà jìlǜ, bāxiàng zhùyì
Three Main Rules of Discipline and Eight Points for Attention
指毛泽东在第二次国内革命战争中为中国工农红军制定的纪律。1947年10月10日，中国人民解放军总部统一规定，将其作为中国人民解放军的纪律。三大纪律是：(一)一切行动听指挥；(二)不拿群众一针一线；(三)一切缴获要归公。八大注意是：(一)说话和气；(二)买卖公平；(三)借东西要还；(四)损坏东西要赔；(五)不打人骂人；(六)不损坏庄稼；(七)不调戏妇女；(八)不虐待俘虏。

The disciplinary code that Mao Zendong formulated for the Chinese Workers' and Peasants' Red Army during the Second Revolutionary Civil War. On October 10, 1947, the Chinese People's Liberation Army Headquarters adopted it as its code. The Three Main Rules of Discipline are as follows: obey orders in all your actions; don't take a single needle or piece of thread from the masses; turn in everything captured. The Eight Points for Attention are as follows: speak politely; pay fairly for what you buy; return everything you borrow; pay for everything you damage; don't hit or swear at people; don't damage crops; don't take liberties with women; don't ill-treat captives.

三大件 sāndàjiàn
three big items

过去指"自行车、手表、缝纫机"为生活中的三大件。现指"电风扇、洗衣机、电冰箱"为三大件。通称为新老三大件。

In the past, the three big items in everyday life were a bicycle, watch, and sewing machine. Now they are an electric fan, washing machine, and refrigerator. The two sets are called the old and the new three big items respectively.

三大领主 sāndà lǐngzhǔ
three kinds of estate-holders

指西藏民主改革前(1959年)的官家(封建政府)、寺庙和贵族。

The feudal government, the monasteries and the nobles of Tibet in the days before democratic reform (1959).

三大民主 sāndà mínzhǔ
democracy in three main fields

指在中国人民解放军内实行的政治民主、经济民主和军事民主。

The political, economic, and military democracy practiced within the Chinese People's Liberation Army.

三大平衡 sāndà pínghéng
three big equilibriums

指国民经济中的物资平衡、财政平衡和信贷平衡。

Equilibrium in three areas of the national economy: material goods, public finance, and credit.

三大球 sāndàqiú
three major ball games

Basketball, volleyball and football.

三大任务 sāndà rènwu
three big tasks

中国人民解放军担负的三大任务是指"打仗、做群众工作和生产建设"。中国人民八十年代的三大任务，一是在国际事务中反对霸权主义，维护世界和平；二是台湾回归祖国，实现祖国统一；三是加紧经济建设，就是加紧四个现代化的建设。

The three big tasks shouldered by the Chinese People's Liberation Army are: fighting, mass work, and building up production. The three big tasks before the Chinese people in the 1980s were: to oppose hegemonism on the international scene and to safeguard world peace, to return Taiwan to the motherland and to unite the nation, to intensify economic construction, i.e., to intensify the construction of the four modernizations.

三大实践 sāndà shíjiàn
three great practices
Synonymous with 三大革命实践 and 三大革命运动. (cf. 三大革命实践, 三大革命运动)

三大运动 sāndà yùndòng
three big movements
指抗美援朝、土地改革和镇压反革命运动。

The three big movements are: resisting the United States and aiding Korea, land reform, and suppressing counter-revolutionaries.

三大战役 sāndà zhànyì
three big military campaigns
指1948年9月至1949年1月先后进行的辽沈战役、淮海战役、平津战役。

Three big military campaigns (between September 1948 and January 1949: the Liaoning-Shenyang Campaign, the Huai-Hai Campaign, and the Beiping (Beijing)-Tianjin Campaign).

三大作风 sāndà zuòfēng
three main work styles
即理论和实践相结合的作风，和人民群众紧密地联系在一起的作风，以及批评和自我批评的作风。这是中国共产党倡导的党的作风。

The three work styles of: linking theory with practice, relating intimately with the masses, and criticizing oneself. These are the work styles advocated by the Chinese Communist Party.

三点式 sāndiǎnshì
three-point bathing suit (bikini)
Also called 三点装 three-point suit and 比基尼泳装 bikini bathing suit.
E.g. 三点式游泳装 *bikini*

三定 sāndìng
three fixeds
中国实行粮食统购统销制定的定产、定购、定销的政策，即定粮食产量、定粮食收购量，定粮食统销指标,简称"三定"。工矿企业中实行的定机(机器)、定人、定活(加工对象)的办法,也简称三定。

Abbreviated term for the Chinese policy of fixing targets for the production, government purchase and sale of grains. The term also refers to the system, practiced in industrial and mining enterprises, of fixing the amount of machinery, manpower, and work.

三多一少 sānduō yīshǎo
three increases and one decrease
即"流通渠道增多、经营方式增多、经营成分增多和流通环节开始减少。"这是十一届三中全会以后在经济领域里出现的生动局面，是搞活经济的重要标志。

An increase in the circulatory channels (for capital, production resources, products, etc.), management methods, and economic components (various kinds of ownership and responsibility systems, etc.), and the start of a decrease in the circulatory segmentation (multiple levels of authority, segmentation in the flow of resources and products, etc.). This was the lively situation that surfaced in the economic realm after the Third Plenary Session of the Eleventh Central Committee of the Chinese Communist Party, and was an important factor in enlivening the economy.

三番两次 sānfān liǎngcì
repeatedly
Also called 三番五次.

三反 sānfǎn

three oppositions

指 1951 年底至 1952 年秋在党内和国家机关内部开展的"反贪污、反浪费、反官僚主义"的三反运动。

The movement against three evils, launched within the Party and government organs from the end of 1951 to the fall of 1952, to counter corruption, waste, and bureaucracy.

三反分子 sānfǎn fènzǐ
three-opposition elements

"文化大革命"期间把所谓"反对毛主席、反对毛泽东思想、反对毛泽东的革命路线"的人称为三反分子。

A name given during the Cultural Revolution to those who allegedly opposed Chairman Mao, opposed Mao Zedong Thought, and opposed Mao Zedong's revolutionary line.

三反运动 sānfǎn yùndòng
movement against three evils (cf. 三反)

三废 sānfèi
three wastes

指工业上的废气、废水、废渣。

Three kinds of industrial wastes: gases, liquids, and residues.

三风五气 sānfēng wǔqì
three styles and five airs

指 1958 年"双反"运动中提出的要通过运动揭露一些干部在思想作风上存在的"主观主义作风、官僚主义作风、宗派主义作风"和打掉他们身上存在的"官气、暮气、阔气、骄气和娇气"。简称三风五气。

An abbreviated term for the characteristics of certain cadres that were targeted for exposure in the 1958 "double opposition" movement. The "three styles" were the subjectivism, bureaucratism, and sectarianism, and the "five airs" were bureaucratic airs, lethargy, extravagance, arrogance, and squeamishness.

三高 sāngāo
three highs

指农村实行责任制后,"两户"(即专业户和重点户)大量涌现,农村经济中出现的"劳动生产力高、商品率高、经济收益高"。

The high labor production, high commodities rate, and high economic efficiency which occurred in the rural economy when the "two kinds of households" (cf. 两户) surfaced in large numbers after the responsibility system was implemented in rural areas.

三高政策 sāngāo zhèngcè
policy of three highs

指在"左"倾错误思想影响下提出的批判所谓高薪金、高稿酬、高奖金的政策。

The policy of so-called high salaries, high manuscript fees, and high bonuses which was criticized under the influence of erroneous leftist ideology.

三搞一篡 sāngǎo yīcuàn
three carryings-on and one usurping

即搞修正主义、搞分裂、搞阴谋诡计,妄图篡夺党和国家的领导权。这是四人帮反革命集团在中国搞反革命活动的实质。

To carry on revisionist separatism, and devious schemes, and to vainly attempt to usurp the leadership power of the Party and the nation. These were the counter-revolutionary activities of the counter-revolutionary Gang of Four group in China.

三个不变 sān gè bùbiàn

three immutables

即农村实行"统一经营、联产到劳"责任制以后实行的生产资料集体所有制不变、生产队统一分配不变、基本核实单位不变的政策。

After the "centralized management, production-related laborer contract" responsibility system was implemented in rural villages, three things remained unchanged. These were: collective ownership of production resources, centralized allocation by the production team, and the basic unit of accounting.

三个好转 sān gè hǎozhuǎn
three turns for the better

即中国共产党第十二次全国代表大会中提出的今后五年争取实现的"国家财政经济状况的根本好转、社会风气的根本好转和党风的根本好转"。

At its Twelfth National Congress, the Chinese Communist Party proposed to strive, within the next five years, to make a fundamental turn for the better in these three areas: the state of national public finance and economy, the general mood of society, and the atmosphere within the Party.

三个面向 sān gè miànxiàng
three directions to face

指"教育要面向现代化,面向世界,面向未来"。这是 1983 年 9 月邓小平给景山学校的题词。它概括了中国在新的历史时期教育的战略方针和前进方向。

The three directions toward which education should be geared: modernization, the world, and the future. These were Deng Xiaoping's words to Beijing's Jingshan School in September of 1983. They summarized the strategic principle and direction for education to advance in China's new historical period.

三个面向,五到现场 sān gè miànxiàng, wǔdàoxiànchǎng
face three directions and achieve five matters on site

"三个面向"是:面向群众,面向基层,面向生产。"五个现场"是:政治工作到现场,生产指挥到现场,原材料供应到现场,计划、科研到现场,生活服务到现场。这是大庆油田机关革命化的优良作风。

The three directions to face are: the masses, the grass roots, and production. The five matters to achieve on site are: political work, instructions for production, supply of raw materials, planning and scientific studies, and everyday life services. These points constitute the outstanding revolutionary style of the Daqing Oilfield organization.

三个世界 sān gè shìjiè
three worlds

1974 年,毛泽东根据当时世界各种基本矛盾的发展变化,提出划分三个世界的论断。即苏联和美国两个超级大国是第一世界;亚、非、拉美及其他地区中的发展中国家、被压迫民族和被压迫国家构成第三世界;处于这两者之间的发达国家是第二世界。

In 1974, Mao Zedong postulated the division into three worlds according to the developments and transformations in the various basic contradictions in the world at that time. That is, the two superpowers – the Soviet Union and the United States – were the first world; the developing nations of Asia, Africa, Latin America, and other areas, as well as oppressed peoples and nations were the third world; the developed nations in between these two worlds were the second world.

三个市场 sān gè shìchǎng
three markets

The rural market, urban market, and international market.

三个梯队 sān gè tīduì
three echelons

"三个梯队"是中共中央对领导班子建设的设想。即一些老一辈无产阶级革命家担任国家领导职务，运筹帷幄，决定大政方针，这是第一梯队。第二梯队是处在国家领导机构第一线的同志，他们是负责实际工作的中坚力量。而第三梯队则指具备"四化"条件的中青年干部，这是充实各级领导班子的后备力量。

An idea concerning the leadership ranks which the Chinese Communist Party Central Committee conceptualized. The first echelon is the older generation of proletarian revolutionaries who take leadership responsibilities for the nation, devise strategies in the inner circle, and make policy decisions. The second echelon consists of comrades at the front line of the nation's leadership organizations; they are the force responsible for the practical work. The third echelon consists of middle-aged and young cadres with four-modernization qualifications; they are the reserve force for filling up the leadership ranks at various levels.

三过思想 sānguò sīxiǎng
three-passing mentality

指一些人头脑中存在的"思想上过得去、工作上过得硬、生活上过得好"的思想。

The mentality of indifference that some people have. People who are content to just get by on ideology, be competent in their job, and to have a comfortable life.

三好学生 sānhǎo xuéshēng
three-goods students

An honorific title given to students that are good in the three areas of physical health, academic studies, and work.

三和一少 sānhé yīshǎo
three reconciliations and one modicum

指"对帝国主义、现代修正主义和各国反动派要和，对世界民族解放斗争的支援要少"，简称为"三和一少"。这是"文化大革命"中强加给刘少奇等国家领导人的诬蔑不实之词。

The slanderous accusations, forced on Liu Shaoqi and other national leaders during the Cultural Revolution, who were accused of reconciling with imperialism, revisionism, and the various nation's reactionaries, and of wanting to give only a modicum of aid to the liberation struggles of the world's peoples.

三户两场 sānhù liǎngchǎng
three kinds of households and two kinds of tree farms

指林业实行责任制以后出现的"林业专业户、重点户、林业科学户和集体林场、联户林场"。简称为"三户两场"。

A cover term for the kinds of households and tree farms that developed after the implementation of the responsibility system in forestry. These are: forestry speciality households, key households, forestry science households, collective tree farms, and joint household tree farms.

三化 sānhuà
three "-ations"

指工矿企业中产品的"标准化、系列化和通用化（统一化）"。

The standardization, seriation, and unification of industrial and mining products.

三荒 sānhuāng
three barren areas

指荒山、荒坡和荒滩。

Barren hills, barren slopes, and barren beaches.

三会一课 sānhuì yīkè
three kinds of meetings and one kind of class

The system of meetings and Party classes for the Chinese Communist Party's grass-roots organizations. The "three kinds of meetings" are general meetings of all members, branch committee meetings, and Party group meetings. The "one kind of class" refers to Party education classes conducted for Party members.

三基 sānjī
three basics

Basic theory, basic knowledge, basic skills

三机一扇 sānjī yīshàn
three machines and one fan

The electrical home appliances that have become popular with the Chinese people: televisions, washing machines, tape recorders, and electric fans.

三级过渡 sānjí guòdù
transition in three stages

指从生产队核算过渡到生产大队核算，从生产大队核算过渡到公社核算，再从公社核算过渡到全民所有制。简称为"三级过渡"。这是人民公社化运动时提出的农村集体所有制过渡为全民所有制的方式，是一种不切实际的提法。

An unrealistic formulation proposed during the People's Communization Movement for the transition from rural collective ownership to ownership by the whole people. The three stages proposed are: transition from the production team to the production brigade as the unit of accounting; transition from the production brigade to the commune as the unit of accounting; and transition from the commune to ownership by the whole people.

三级体制 sānjí tǐzhì
tri-level system

The tri-level system: ownership by the production team, ownership by the production brigade, and ownership by the commune-practiced in rural areas.

三家村 sānjiācūn
Three Family Village

指"文化大革命"前邓拓、吴晗、廖沫沙三人在《前线》杂志"三家村札记"专栏上所发表的文章。"文化大革命"中遭受批判。

The name given to the series of articles written by Deng Tuo, Wu Han, and Liao Mosha in the *Three Family Village Notes* column of the magazine *Battle Front* before the Cultural Revolution. These articles were criticized during the Cultural Revolution.

三讲 sān–jiǎng
three stresses

指讲学习、讲政治、讲正气。

To stress learning, to stress politics, and to stress a healthy atmosphere.
E.g. 要以整风的精神开展"三讲"教育。*We should carry out education on three stresses in a spirit of rectification.*

三兼顾 sānjiāngù
three considerations
指兼顾国家、集体和劳动者个人三者的利益。也叫"三兼顾"原则,这是处理社会主义经济利益的根本原则。
The basic principle in dealing with socialist economic benefits; giving consideration to the interests of the nation, the collective, and the working individual.

三结合 sānjiéhé
three-way integrations
"三结合"指三种不同类型的人或三种不同事物、三种不同方面的结合,如在"四清"运动中提出群众、干部、工作队要三结合;在企业管理和科学技术工作中实行的"干部、工人、技术人员"的三结合;"文化大革命"中建立"革委会"时,实行"解放军、革命领导干部和革命群众"的三结合;在领导班子的组成中,又提出"老、中、青"三中不同年龄的干部的三结合等。
The integration of three different types of people, three different kinds of matter, or three different aspects. For example, during the Four Cleanups Movement (cf. 四清), the three-way integration of the masses, the cadres, and the work teams was proposed; in enterprise management and scientific technological work, the three-way integration of cadres, workers, and technical personnel was implemented; when revolutionary committees were formed during the Cultural Revolution, three-way integration of the Liberation Army men, revolutionary cadre leaders, and revolutionary masses was carried out; in the composition of leadership ranks, the three-way integration of old, middle-aged and young cadres was proposed.

三就方针 sānjiù fāngzhēn
the three-local guiding principle
即"就地取材,就地生产,就地销售"的方针。
The guiding principle of using local materials, producing locally, and marketing locally.

三居室 sānjūshì
a three-room apartment

三开人物 sānkāi rénwù
people favored in all three periods
1) 指国民党统治时期吃得开,在所谓修正主义路线统治时期也吃得开,在左倾路线时期仍吃得开的人。2)泛指不管什么时期,不管哪些人当权,都能受到重用的人。
1) People who enjoyed favored positions in the period under KMT rule, in the period dominated by the pragmatists' line, and in the period dominated by the leftist line. 2) In general, the term refers to people who enjoy prominence regardless of the period and regardless of the people in power.

三靠队 sānkàoduì
three-way dependent teams
即农村中"吃粮靠返销,生产靠贷款,生活靠救济"的穷生产队。
Poor production teams in rural villages that depend on resold grain for staples, depend on loans for production, and depend on relief funds for daily life.

三靠社 sānkàoshè
three dependence communes
Communes that rely on resold (submitted to the state and later resold to the commune) grains for food, loans for production, and relief funds to survive.

三宽 sānkuān
three kuans
指宽容、宽厚、宽松。
Tolerant, generous, and lenient (these three words share the morpheme 宽 broad).

三来一补 sānlái yībǔ
three importeds and one compensatory
Abbreviation for 来样加工 processing according to a foreign specimen, 来料加工 processing imported materials, 来件装配 assembling imported parts, and 补偿贸易 compensatory trade. This is an important way of using the rich source of labor, to increase the export of concentrated labor products.
E.g. 放手扩大"三来一补"业务。*To go all out to enlarge the business of "three importeds and one compensatory"*

三老四严 sānlǎo sìyán
three honests and four yans, (严 Yan is the first character in the bi-syllabic word meaning strict, tight, solemn, etc.)
"三老"指对待革命事业要"当老实人、说老实话、办老实事"。"四严"指对待革命工作要"严格的要求、严密的组织、严肃的态度、严明的纪律"。这是大庆油田职工首先倡导并一直坚持的优良作风。
With regards to revolutionary work, the "three honests" are being an honest person, speaking honest words, and doing honest work; the "four yans" are strict requirements, tight organization, solemn attitude, and strict discipline. These constitute the outstanding work style first advocated and thereafter upheld by the Daqing Oilfield workers.

三联单 sānliándān
triplicate form
A blank form that comes in triplicates. A number and seal are placed at the perforations. After the triplicate form is filled out, one copy is filled in the original unit and the other two copies are sent to relevant departments. In China, the form which civil servants take with them to clinics to receive medical treatment is usually also called "triplicate form".

三连冠 sānliánguàn
three successive championships
To win the championship in three successive competitions. This term refers specifically to China's national women's volleyball team, which won the World Cup championship in 1981, the World Title championship in 1982, and the Olympic championship in 1984.

三料 sānliào
three materials
The three vital materials in rural areas: fertilizer, fodder, and fuel.

三乱 sānluàn
three recklesses
Recklessly collect fees, exact fines, and apportion funds.

三轮摩托车 sānlún mótuōchē
motor tricycle

三轮汽车 sānlún qìchē
three-wheel automobile

三论 sānlùn
the three old theories

System theory, information theory, and control theory.

三麦 sānmài
three grains

A cover term for wheat, barley, and naked barley (hordeum vulgare var. nuda).

三门干部 sānmén gànbù
three-gate cadre

指那些自幼读书,从家门到学校门,毕业后又从学校门进入机关(包括学校和工矿企业、研究单位等)门的人。

Someone who has been educated since early childhood, and went from the gate of his home to the gate of a school, then after graduation went from the school's gate to the gate of an employing organization (including school, industrial or mining enterprise, or research unit).

三面红旗 sānmiàn hóngqí
three red banners

The three aims formulated in 1958: the general line for socialist construction, Great Leap Forward, and the people's commune.

三明治 sānmíngzhì
sandwich

三名三高 sānmíng sāngāo
three kinds of celebrities and three highs

"三名"指"名作家、名演员、名导演";"三高"指"高薪金、高稿酬、高奖金"。在极左错误思想影响下,"三名三高"曾被作为修正主义的东西加以批判。

The "three kinds of celebrities" are famous writers, famous actors, and famous movie directors. The "three highs" are high salaries, high manuscript fees, and high bonuses. Under the influence of erroneous extreme leftist ideology, the "three kinds of celebrities and three highs" were criticized as revisionist phenomena.

三年困难时期 sānnián kùnnan shíqī
three-year difficult period

The 1959 to 1961 period when China's national economy experienced serious difficulties.

三农 sānnóng
three agricultures

Agricultural administrative management sector, agricultural research units, and agricultural schools.

三跑田 sānpǎotián
three runoff fields

Agricultural fields where there are runoffs of water, fertilizer, and soil. It is the opposite of 三保田.

三陪 sānpéi
three companionships

The profession of drinking, dancing, and sitting with guests of the opposite sex at certain entertainment arenas.

E.g. 要彻底制止三陪。 *We must thoroughly eradicate the three companionships.* / 三陪女深入到各大宾馆去拉客。 *Women engaging in the three companionships have become entrenched in the major hotels.*

三朋四友 sānpéng sìyǒu
the various friends one makes in society

三七开 sānqīkāi
proportion of three to seven

The acceptable proportion of errors to achievements in a person's whole lifetime, which is 70% achievements and

30% errors.

E.g. 一个人能够三七开就很好了。 *Being able to attain three-seven proportion in one's life is reckoned to be quite good.*

三气 sānqì
three emotions

指人们在受到不公正待遇时所产生的"怨气、泄气、不服气"三种情绪。

The three emotions of resentment, disheartenment, and non-acceptance that arise in those who have suffered unjust treatment.

三秋 sānqiū
three autumn activities

Autumn harvesting, tilling, and planting (or sowing).

E.g. 三秋大忙季节 *a season busy with the three autumn activities*

三缺户 sānquēhù
three-lack households

Households in rural villages that lack manpower, capital, and production tools.

三热爱 sānrè'ài
three loves

"热爱中国共产党、热爱祖国、热爱社会主义"的简称。

Abbreviation for loving the Chinese Communist Party, the motherland, and socialism.

三 S sān S
Three S

中国的三位国际友人: 史沫特莱、斯特朗和斯诺的代称。

China's three international friends: Agnes Smedley, Anna Louise Strong, and Edgar Snow.

三三制 sān–sānzhì
three-thirds system

A system of dividing things into three parts or forming things from three components. The actual substance of the system varies. For example, during the Cultural Revolution, some leadership organizations divided their cadres into three groups: one third of them went down to labor, one third went down to conduct investigations, and one third carried out routine work.

三史 sānshǐ
three histories

指家史、村史、公社史。"四清"运动中提倡写"三史"。目的是通过回忆过去的历史，使广大社员对新社会更加热爱。

Family history, village history, and commune history. The writing of the Three Histories was advocated during the Four Cleanups (cf. 四清) movement. The aim was to have the broad masses of commune members recall the past and thereby develop even greater love for the new society.

三铁 sāntiě
three irons

指铁饭碗、铁交椅、铁工资。

Iron rice bowl, iron armchair, and iron wages (guaranteed job, position, wages).

三通 sāntōng
three exchanges

即中华人民共和国中央政府向台湾提出的"通邮、通商、通航"的建议，简称"三通"。

The proposal, made by the central government of the People's Republic of China to Taiwan, to establish a postal service, air and shipping services and trade between the two regimes.

三通四流 sāntōng sìliú

the three opening-ups and four flows
指大陆和台湾的通邮、通商、通航和探亲旅游、开展学术、文化、体育交流,简称"三通四流"。
Between China's mainland and Taiwan the three opening-ups (postal, trade, and shipping) and four flows (visiting relatives and traveling, academic, cultural, and athletic exchanges).

三同 sāntóng
three togethers
Cadres who go to rural villages must do three things together with the peasants: eat, live, and work.

三突出 sāntūchū
three standouts
"文化大革命"中,四人帮炮制的文艺创作的模式。即要求文艺作品中,在所有的人物里突出正面人物,在正面人物中突出主要英雄人物,在主要英雄人物中突出最主要的中心人物。这是极"左"思想在文艺创作中的反映。
The formula for literary and art creations which the Gang of Four tried to implement during the Cultural Revolution. The formula required literary and art works to have positive characters that stand out from other characters, then main heroic characters that stand out from the positive characters, and finally, a most important central character that stands out from the main heroic characters. This was a reflection of extreme leftist ideology in literary and art creation.

三脱离 sāntuōlí
three separations
指脱离劳动、脱离工农群众、脱离实际。
To drop out of manual labor, to cut oneself off from the masses of workers and peasants, and to lose contact with reality.
E.g. 三脱离干部 *three-separation cadres*

三无企业 sān-wú qǐyè
three-no-enterprises
It refers to enterprises with no capital, no plant, and no administrative structure. Also called 皮包公司 briefcase company.

三五普法 sān-wǔ pǔ-fǎ
the third five-year popularization of education on knowledge of law program

三西地区 sānxī dìqū
the three-xi (three-west) areas
The three areas of 河西 Hexi and 定西 Dingxi in Gansu Province and 西海固 Xihaigu in Ningxia Hui Autonomous Region. These are all remote areas in northwestern China.

三夏 sānxià
three summer activities
Summer harvest, summer planting, and summer field management.

三线 sānxiàn
third line
1)指三线地区。60年代初期,从战备需要出发,根据战略位置不同,将中国各地区分为一、二、三线。"三线"地区是全国的战略大后方。2)也指一些老干部离休后所处的不再担任任何职务的地位。
1) Third line area. In the early 1960s, as a result of the need for defense preparations, the various areas of China were divided into first (front), second, and third lines on the basis of their

strategic positions. The "third line" was the strategic rear of the whole nation. 2) The term also means the position of old retired cadres, who no longer carry on their duties.

E.g. 退居三线 *to retire to the third line*

三降一灭 sānxiáng yīmiè
three surrenders and one extinguishing

"投降帝国主义、投降修正主义、投降反动派、扑灭世界革命"的简称。这是"文化大革命"中诬蔑外事工作的用语。

Abbreviation for "surrendering to imperialism, revisionism, and reactionism, and extinguishing world revolution". This was a slanderous terminology used during the Cultural Revolution to vilify diplomatic work.

三项建设 sānxiàng jiànshè
three build-ups

指在企业整顿中要做好的三个方面的工作。即"逐步地建立起一种又有民主、又有集中的领导体制;逐步地建设起一支又红又专的职工队伍;逐步地建设起一套科学文明的管理制度。"简称为"三项建设"。

The three aspects that must be attended to in overhauling enterprises: to build up step by step a leadership system that is both democratic and centralized; to build up step by step a red and expert work force; and to build up step by step a scientific and enlightened management system.

三要三不要 sānyào sānbùyào
three dos and three don'ts

"要搞马克思主义,不要搞修正主义;要团结,不要分裂;要光明正大,不要搞阴谋诡计。"简称为"三要三不要"。这是毛泽东在1971年针对林彪等人的阴谋活动提出的。

Abbreviation for "do engage in Marxism, don't engage in revisionism; do unite together, don't practice separatism; do be open and honest, don't engage in devious scheming". This was said by Mao Zedong in 1971 in regard to the devious activities of Lin Biao and his cohorts.

三野 Sān-Yě
the Third Field Army of the Chinese People's Liberation Army

Abbreviation for 中国人民解放军第三野战军.

三优 sānyōu
three excels

To strive for excellence in giving birth, rearing, and nurturing children.

E.g. 要抓好三优 *We must get a firm grip on the three excels.*

三优一学 sānyōu yīxué
three excels and one emulate

指1983年"全民文明礼貌月"期间开展的比"优质服务、优良秩序、优美环境和学习雷锋、学习先进的竞赛活动"。简称"三优一学"。

The competitions, held during the National Enlightenment and Courtesy Month in 1983, to excel in service, orderliness, and environmental beautification, and to emulate Lei Feng and those who are advanced.

三灶 sānzào
three stoves

指煤气灶、太阳灶、省柴灶。

Methane gas stove, solar stove, and firewood-economizing stove.

三支两军 sānzhī liǎngjūn

three supports and two militaries

指"文化大革命"期间,人民解放军到地方支左(支持当时被称为左派的人们)、支农(支援农业)、支工(支援工业)和军管(对一些地区、部门和单位实行军事管制)、军训(对学术进行军事训练)。简称"三支两军"。

Abbreviation for the activities carried out by the People's Liberation Army in local areas during the Cultural Revolution. The activities were: supporting the left (supporting those who were called leftists at the time), supporting agriculture, supporting industry, carrying out military control (in certain areas, departments, and units), and conducting military training (for students).

三忠于四无限 sānzhōngyú sìwúxiàn

three loyalties and four unlimiteds

"忠于毛主席、忠于毛泽东思想、忠于毛主席的无产阶级革命路线"。简称"三忠于"。"无限热爱毛主席、无限信仰毛主席、无限忠于毛主席、无限崇拜毛主席"。简称"四无限"。这是"文化大革命"中大搞现代迷信活动时流行的一种形式主义的口号。

The "three loyalties" were loyalty toward Chairman Mao, loyalty toward Mao Zedong Thought, and loyalty toward Chairman Mao's proletarian revolutionary line. The "four unlimiteds" were unlimited love for Chairman Mao, unlimited faith in Chairman Mao, unlimited loyalty to Chairman Mao, and unlimited worship of Chairman Mao. This was a slogan prevalent in activities associated with Mao's personality cult during the Cultural Revolution.

三种人 sānzhǒngrén

three types of people

即在"文化大革命"中追随林彪、江青反革命集团造反起家的人,帮派思想严重的人,打砸抢分子。"三种人"中造反起家的人,是指那些在"文化大革命"期间,紧跟林彪、江青一伙拉帮结派,造反夺权,升了官,干了坏事,情节严重的人。帮派思想严重的人,是指那些在"文化大革命"期间,极力宣扬林彪、江青反革命集团的反动思想,拉帮结派干坏事,粉碎"四人帮"以后,明里暗里继续进行帮派活动的人。打砸抢分子,是指那些在"文化大革命"期间,诬蔑迫害干部、群众,刑讯逼供,摧残人身,情节严重的人;砸机关、抢档案、破坏公私财物的主要分子和幕后策划者;策划、组织、指挥武斗造成严重后果的分子。

Three types of people during the Cultural Revolution: those who made their way up by following the counter-revolutionary Lin Biao-Jiang Qing clique by creating disruption, those with a serious cliquish mentality, and those elements who took part in beating, vandalism and looting. The first followed the Lin Biao-Jiang Qing clique closely, engaged in factionalism, carried out sabotage, usurped power, rose in rank, and committed evil deeds. The second glorified the reactionary ideology of the counter-revolutionary Lin Biao-Jiang Qing clique, formed factions and committed evil deeds; after the downfall of the Gang of Four, they continued their factional activities both overtly and covertly. The third were those who vilified and persecuted cadres and the masses, extorted confessions by torture and destroyed people physically. This group includes the main characters and instigators behind the smashing of organizations, looting of files, and destruction of public and private property; and finally it also includes the elements who plotted, organized, and directed armed fighting.

三转一响 sānzhuàn yīxiǎng
three things that turn and one thing that makes a noise

指人们日常生活用品中的"手表、自行车、缝纫机和收音机"。曾有一个时期，随着人们生活水平的提高而争相购买。

These following items in people's everyday life: watch, bicycle, sewing machine, and radio. At one time, they were much sought after.

三资企业 sānzī qǐyè
three investment enterprises

Abbreviation for 中外合资企业 Sino-foreign joint investment enterprises, 中外合作经营企业 Sino-foreign joint management enterprises and 外商独资企业 foreign-funded enterprises.

E.g. 充分利用外资，积极发展"三资企业" *to make full use of foreign funds in actively developing three investment enterprises.*

三自一包 sānzì yībāo
three zis and one contract

A policy initiated by Liu Shaoqi to rejuvenate agricultural production after people's communes were founded. The "three zis" were 自由市场 free markets, 自留地 private plots, and 自负盈亏 self-responsibility for gains and losses. The "one contract" was 包产到户 the system of contracting responsibility for production to the household. During the Cultural Revolution, under the baneful influence of extreme leftist ideology, the three zis and one contract were criticized as capitalist phenomena.

三总部 sān-zǒng-bù
three headquarters

Composite term for: 总参谋部 Headquarters of the General Staff, 总政治部 Headquarters of the Political Department, and 总后勤部 Logistical Headquarters (of PLA).

三座大山 sān zuò dàshān
the three great mountains

A metaphor for the three reactionary forces that pressed on the Chinese people in old China. They were: imperialism, feudalism, and bureaucratic capitalism.

散货 sǎnhuò
scattered merchandise

散记 sǎnjì
narrative essay

An essay which records and narrates an event.

散件 sǎnjiàn
unassembled components of a certainly entity

散客 sǎnkè
scattered, individual travelers (vs. tour groups)

E.g. 要注意日益庞大的散客市场。 *We must pay attention to the growing individual travelers' market.*

散手 sǎnshǒu
karate

E.g. 散手曾被列为比赛项目。 *At one time, karate was listed as an important tournament event.*

sang

桑拿按摩 sāngná ànmó
sauna massage

桑拿浴 sāngnáyù
sauna bath
E.g. 1985 年北京清华池浴池开设了第一家桑拿浴室。 In 1985, the Qinghua Bathhouse in Beijing opened up the first sauna.

桑塔纳 sāngtǎnà
Brand name of a car. Transliterated from German, the term means the people.

sao

扫毒 sǎodú
to eradicate the production, processing, selling, and imbibing of narcotics

扫黄 sǎohuáng
to wipe out pornography

扫盲运动 sǎománg yùndòng
literacy movement
A movement to eradicate illiteracy.

扫描 sǎomiáo
scanning
Originally used in its technical sense, using a certain device to traverse a surface (in a certain direction, and in an ordered manner) with a beam of light or electrons and reproduce the shape of an object. Now it is also used meta-phorically — mostly in titles — to mean observe and depict.
E.g. 都市婚庆扫描 glimpses of urban wedding celebrations

扫尾工作 sǎowěi gōngzuò
rounding-off work
To finish the final portion of a certain task or movement. Also called 收尾工作.

se

色拉 sèlā
salad
Also called 沙拉.

色狼 sèláng
sex wolf
A man who takes sexual advantage of women.

sen

森警 sēnjǐng
forest patrol (i.e., ranger)
Abbreviation for 森林警察.

森林公园 sēnlín gōngyuán
forest reserves used as parks

sha

砂洗 shāxǐ
sand wash
A textile treatment process designed to give the fabric a slightly worn and handcrafted feel.

杀关管 shā–guān–guǎn
execution, imprisonment, and surveillance
新中国成立后，对一些罪大恶极分子实行的惩处政策。根据罪行大小，分别决定处死（杀）、关押（关）和管制（管），简称为杀、关、管。
After the founding of New China, three forms of punishment – execution, im-

prisonment, and surveillance – were meted out to serious criminals according to the crime.

杀手 shāshǒu
assassin
A metaphor for life-threatening things.

刹车 shāchē
to brake
1) Originally to stop a car, a boat, etc., by using the brake. 2) Now, a metaphor for immediately stopping something.
E.g. 对中央严令禁止的事要立即刹车。
We must immediately put a stop to things that the central government has prohibited.

傻大黑粗 shǎ-dà-hēi-cū
stupid, big, black, and coarse (depicting the big, awkward, or clumsy appearance of a product)

傻蛋 shǎdàn
blockhead; simpleton

傻瓜相机 shǎguā xiàngjī
simpleton's camera
A fully automatic camera.

傻冒 shǎmào
blockhead; simpleton; foolishness; to exude foolishness
Also written as 傻帽儿 or 傻冒儿.

shai

筛选 shāixuǎn
to sift through a sieve; to screen and select
E.g. 筛选垃圾 *to sift through garbage* / 筛选词条 *to sift through vocabulary items* / 对信息资料进行筛选 *to sift through data sources* / 经过筛选，确定10名为干部推荐对象。*After a selection process, ten persons were nominated for cadre positions.*

色酒 shǎijiǔ
colored wine, especially wine made from fruit

shan

山地车 shāndìchē
mountain bikes
A kind of bicycle designed for rough mountain terrain. It is light-weight, has thick tires, and is equipped with gears.

山海经 shānhǎijīng
a well-known ancient Chinese book on geography; a plan or blueprint for developing the natural resources of mountains and waters
E.g. 念好山海经 *to carry out a good study on the plans for developing natural resources*

山姆大叔 shānmǔ dàshū
Uncle Sam

山头主义 shāntóu zhǔyì
mountain stronghold mentality
A form of selfish departmentalism and sectarianism, manifested by attaching great weight to one's own mountain stronghold, not being able to unite with other comrades, and excluding others' influence in order to establish one's own prestige.

煽情 shānqíng
to incite or to stir up emotions
E.g. 这是一部很煽情的作品。*This is a very emotional (moving) work.*

闪光灯 shǎnguāngdēng
flashlamp
1) A light installed on a shore or a water

surface and used as a marker or signal.
2) A lighting device for photography.

善待 shàndài

to treat well; to take good care of

shang

伤残 shāngcán

damaged or maimed (of things or humans); to damage or maim

伤残人 shāngcánrén

physically disabled or handicapped persons

伤痕文学 shānghén wénxué

scar literature

Literary works reflecting the scars inflicted on people's psyches by the Cultural Revolution. This kind of literature, which appeared in great quantity after the downfall of the Gang of Four, is represented by the short story "Scar".

商潮 shāngcháo

business wave

The phenomenon of a great number of people taking up commercial businesses.

商城 shāngchéng

shopping mall

商调 shāngdiào

to negotiate and transfer

To transfer personnel after negotiations.
E.g. 为解决职工夫妻分居问题，各省市正在召开商调会。*To solve the problem of married couples living apart due to their job locations, the various provinces and municipalities are holding meetings to negotiate the transfer of personnel.*

商海 shānghǎi

commercial sea

Refers to commercial activities involving unpredictable changes.
E.g. 商海是一个陷阱。*The commercial sea is a trap.*

商函 shānghán

business correspondence

E.g. 商函订货 *to order goods by correspondence*

商机 shāngjī

business opportunity

Opportunity to transact business.
E.g. 不要贻误商机。*Don't bungle a business opportunity.*

商检 shāngjiǎn

inspection of commercial products

Abbreviation for 商品检查.
E.g. 商检工作 *commercial products inspection work* / 商检部门 *sectors engaged in the inspection of commercial products* / 商检局 *Bureau for the Inspection of Commodities*

商流 shāngliú

commodities exchange; circulation of commodities

商贸 shāng-mào

commercial

E.g. 商贸集团 *a commercial conglomerate*

商品畜 shāngpǐnchù

commodity animals

Domestic animals raised to be sold as commodities.

商品房 shāngpǐnfáng

commercial residential building

It refers to buildings developed by real estate firms and sold to the public.

商品化 shāngpǐnhuà

commercialism

To consider everything from the angle of merchandising (i.e., buying and selling, money, monetary value, etc.).

商品经济 shāngpǐn jīngjì
commodities economy

商品粮 shāngpǐnliáng
commodity grain

Grain sold as commodity. In China, the chief source of commodity grain is the grain which peasants turn in to the state (agriculture tax) and the surplus grain sold by peasants. The grain which the state supplies to urban residents and workers is also called commodity grain.
E.g. 商品粮基地 *commodity grain base*

商品棉 shāngpǐnmián
cotton produced for commercial purposes

商嫂 shāngsǎo
(a polite term for) a married female shop assistant

商社 shāngshè
company

A loan word from Japanese meaning a commercial company.
E.g. 北京饭店里有一些外国的长住商社。*At the Beijing Hotel, there are some foreign businessmen who are long-term residents.*

商摊 shāngtān
vendor's stand, booth, or stall

商亭 shāngtíng
vendor's kiosk

商厦 shāngshà
large commercial building

商业街 shāngyèjiē
commercial street; business district

商展 shāngzhǎn
commodities exhibition; trade fair

商战 shāngzhàn
trade war; price war

上传下达 shàngchuán xiàdá
to transmit to those above and those below

To report the ideas of the masses to the leadership, and to transmit the leadership's directives and orders to the masses.

上大课 shàngdàkè
to hold an enlarged class

A teaching method whereby several classes are combined.

上调 shàngdiào
to transfer up

To transfer (funds and materials) to a superior or a superior unit; To be promoted (in a profession) or to be transferred from a rural area to a city or factory.
E.g. 有的单位担心财物上调。*Some units are worried that funds and materials may be transferred to superior units.* / 上调到城里工作 *to be transferred to a job in the city*

上访 shàngfǎng
to meet with the higher authorities

Individuals from the ranks of the masses, of their own initiative, going to a high level Party (all the way to the Central Committee) or state organ to report on a situation, to appeal for redress of a wrong, to make a request, to expose misdeeds or wrong-doers, or to criticize and make suggestions about the nation's work, work personnel, or leaders. (cf. 信访工作 information visitation work)

上浮 shàngfú
to float upward (re prices, interest rates, wages, etc.)

E.g. 利率上浮。 *The interest rate is floating upward.* / 工资上浮一级。 *Wages floated upward by one notch.*

上钢 Shàng-Gāng
Shanghai Iron and Steel Company
Abbreviation for 上海钢铁公司.

上纲 shànggāng
to elevate an issue to the level of principles
E.g. 无限上纲 *to exaggerate matters to the level of principles* / 不要把学术问题上纲为政治问题。 *Don't elevate an academic viewpoint to that of a political issue.*

上纲上线 shànggāng shàngxiàn
heighten to the level of principles and ideology
A phenomenon of the Cultural Revolution whereby an individual's flaws, errors, or mistakes in work – regardless of their magnitude – were casually heightened to the level of class and ideological struggle, and were dealt with accordingly. This method was a product of extreme leftist ideology.

上岗 shànggǎng
to go to one's assigned work station; to begin one's duties at one's work station

上挂下联 shàngguà xiàlián
hook up with above and link up with below
Terminology from the Cultural Revolution. It refers to the practice, used in struggle sessions, of hooking up (the accused) with the biggest capitalist roaders or high level leaders, and linking up with the specific persons and issues at the local unit or department.

上管改 shàng-guǎn-gǎi
to attend, manage, and reform
指"文化大革命"期间工农兵学员进入大学后的任务，即所谓"上大学、管大学、用毛泽东思想改造大学"。 During the Cultural Revolution, these were the tasks to be performed by the worker-peasant-soldier students after they entered the universities: attend universities (academic work), manage universities, and reform universities along the lines of Mao Zedong Thought.

上馆子 shàngguǎnzi
to go and eat at a restaurant
Also called 下馆子.

上环 shànghuán
installing an I.U.D
A method of birth control whereby a contraceptive ring is installed in the uterus to prevent conception.

上机 shàngjī
to operate computers
E.g. 上机费 *computer operation fee* / 上机时间 *computer operation time*

上山下乡 shàngshān xiàxiāng
go up to the mountains and down to the countryside
Urban educated youths going to and settling in rural areas to join in labor. This was a policy rigorously carried out during the Cultural Revolution.

上市公司 shàngshì gōngsī
on the market company
A limited-liability joint stock company which sells its stocks on the stock market.

上市股票 shàngshì gǔpiào
on the market stocks
Stocks that can be bought and sold openly in the stock market. Also called 挂牌股票 hung-sign stocks.

上台阶 shàngtáijiē
to be elevated to a new height; to achieve a new level in caliber
E.g. 工业生产又上新台阶。 *Industrial production again rose to a new height.*

上调 shàngtiáo
upward adjustment (in prices, interest rates, etc.); to raise (prices, interest rates, etc.)
E.g. 商品价格普遍上调。 *Commodity prices rose sharply.*

上网 shàng wǎng
to connect internet; connected internet
To engage in the activities of the internet.

上扬 shàngyáng
(re prices, etc.) to rise
E.g. 美元汇价上扬。 *The exchange rate of the US dollar rose.*

上影 Shàng-Yǐng
Shanghai Film Studio
Abbreviation for 上海电影制片厂.

上游企业 shàngyóu qǐyè
upper reaches enterprise; raw material processing enterprise; elementary (extensive) processing enterprise

shao

烧烤 shāokǎo
barbeque

烧香 shāoxiāng
(originally) to burn incense (in front of gods or ancestors)
Now a metaphor for activities involved in begging favors from individuals or units.
E.g. 请他办事非烧香磕头才行。 *In asking him to do something, one must beg him as though he's some god.*

少而精 shǎo ér jīng
concise and quintessential
A principle of education which advocates that the curriculum and material content must not be excessive or overly complex, and that the teacher must lecture on and practice the essentials, so that the students will grasp what is essential.

少慢差费 shǎo màn chà fèi
little, slow, poor, and wasteful
1) The opposite of 多快好省 more, faster, better, and more economical. It means doing little work and being slow or poor in quality, and costing too much. This is an unhealthy tendency in the activities of socialist economic construction. 2) The term also refers in general to a work style that is poor and inefficient.

少代会 shào-dài-huì
Conference of Young Pioneers Representatives
Abbreviation for 少年先锋队代表会议.

少工委 shào-gōng-wěi
Youth and Children's Work Committee
Abbreviation for 少年儿童工作委员会.

少管 shào-guǎn
juvenile reform
Abbreviated term for 少年犯管教 the reform and education of juvenile delinquents. The guiding principle of juvenile reform is that reform through education is primary and light labor is sup-

plementary. It provides juvenile delinquents with an education in political morality, basic knowledge, and production skills.

少管所 shào-guǎn-suǒ
juvenile reformatory
Abbreviation for 少年犯管教所.

少年宫 shàoniángōng
children's palace

少年庭 shàoniántíng
juvenile court

少先队 shào-xiān-duì
Young Pioneers
Abbreviation for 少年先锋队, a mass organization of children in China aged from 6 to 14.

she

蛇皮袋 shépídài
snake-skin bag (made of snake skin or woven from snake skin like plastic strips)

蛇头 shétóu
snake head
The heads or key figures in organizations that smuggle illegal immigrants.

摄录 shèlù
to photograph and to videotape

摄录机 shèlùjī
video camera
Synonymous with 摄像机.

摄像机 shèxiàngjī
video camera
It comes in black and white, color, or 3-D.

摄制 shèzhì
to make a film or television program

射门 shèmén
to shoot the goal
To shoot the ball toward the goal in sports such as soccer and ice hockey.

涉外单位 shèwài dānwèi
foreign affairs unit
A unit frequently involved in the work of foreign affairs.

涉外婚姻 shèwài hūnyīn
marriages between a nation's citizens and foreign nationals

涉外税收 shèwài shuìshōu
foreign tax
Tax levied on foreigners, Sino-foreign joint-capital enterprises, and enterprises in China funded solely by foreign capital.

社办企业 shèbàn qǐyè
commune-managed enterprises
Socialist collectively owned enterprises, founded and managed by rural people's communes, which operate independently and assume responsibility for their own gains and losses. (cf. 社队企业 and 乡镇企业)

社队 shè-duì
commune and team
Contraction of 人民公社 people's commune and 生产队 production team.

社队企业 shè-duì qǐyè
commune- or team-managed enterprises
Socialist collectively owned enterprises, founded and managed by communes, brigades, or production teams, which operate independently and assume responsibility for their own gains and losses. After the separation of government administration from communes in the early 1980s, this term was changed to 乡镇企业 village and town en-

terprises. (cf. 乡镇企业)

社会工程 shèhuì gōngchéng
social engineering

A technical field, which deals with the organization and management of socialist construction, i.e., it applies control theory to the activities of the entire national economy. It lies within the sphere of systems engineering.

社会工作 shèhuì gōngzuò
work in service to society

Work in service to the masses without remuneration. It is distinguished from regular work.
E.g. 他担任了许多社会工作。*He has taken on much work in service to society.*

社会关系 shèhuì guānxì
social relationships

A person's relationships with relatives and friends. Also the mutual relationships formed between people in the process of shared activities. Of all the social relationships, the most basic ones are production relationships, i.e., economic relationships; the nature of all other political and legal relationships is determined by production relationships.

社会集团 shèhuì jítuán
societal groups

A cover term for offices, groups, enterprises, schools and other organizations.
E.g. 社会集团购买力 *the purchasing power of a societal group*

社会青年 shèhuì qīngnián
youths in society

Youths in society who are not in school and have no vocation.

社会语言学 shèhuì yǔyánxué
sociolinguistics

社会渣滓 shèhuì zhāzǐ
dregs of society

Bad elements that disrupt the order and security in society, such as hoodlum gangs, thieves, swindlers, etc.

社会主义初级阶段 shèhuì zhǔyì chūjí jiēduàn
elementary stage of socialism

This term refers specifically to that certain stage that China – under the circumstances of backward productivity and an underdeveloped commodity economy – must undergo in building socialism. From the basic completion of socialist reform in ownership of production resouces of the 1950s to the realization of socialist modernization – which requires at least 100 years – all belong to the elementary stage of socialism.

社会主义大院 shèhuì zhǔyì dàyuàn
socialist compounds

Also called 向阳院 sun-facing compounds. They were a kind of mass organization that surfaced during the Cultural Revolution with residential compounds or dormitory buildings as units. Management committees were formed by employed workers, retired workers, neighborhood cadres, and youth representatives. Their main activities were to strengthen out of school education for youths in the local areas, and to organize youths to participate in beneficial activities, thus helping them to develop morally, intellectually, and physically.

社会主义改造 shèhuì zhǔyì gǎizào
socialist reform

A form of socialist revolution in which, under the dictatorship of the proletarian class, non-socialist economic elements are reformed to accord with socialist principles. For example, through the route of cooperativization, the individual economies of peasants and handicrafters were gradually transformed into socialist economies, and through the various forms of national capitalism, the capitalist economy was gradually transformed into a socialist economy.

社会主义革命 shèhuì zhǔyì gémìng
socialist revolution

A revolution, led by the proletarian class and its vanguard the Communist Party, which takes as its goals the overthrow of the capitalist system, the establishment of the socialist system, and the realization of communism. Also called 无产阶级革命 proletarian revolution.

社会主义建设总路线 shèhuì zhǔyì jiànshè zǒnglùxiàn
the general line for socialist construction

A commonly used term for the line first put forward by Mao Zedong and later debated and promulgated in the Second Session of the Eighth National Congress of the Chinese Communist Party in May 1958. It is stated as follows: "Go all out, aim high and achieve greater, faster, better, and more economical results in building socialism." This line spurred on the Great Leap Forward.

社会主义教育运动 shèhuì zhǔyì jiàoyù yùndòng
socialist education movement

Abbreviated as 社教运动 or 四清. (cf. 四清)

社会主义精神文明 shèhuì zhǔyì jīngshén wénmíng
socialist spiritual enlightenment

An important characteristic of socialism, and a manifestation of socialism's superiority. It is manifested primarily in the two areas of education and ideological development, i.e., the development of various cultural matters, the advance in the level of knowledge of the general populace, as well as advances in revolutionary ideology, morality, and discipline. The core of socialist spiritual enlightenment is communist ideology.

社会主义人道主义 shèhuì zhǔyì réndào zhǔyì
socialist humanitarianism

The ethical principles and moral standards that are founded on the ideological foundation of Marxism and historical materialism. It advocates eradicating the exploitative system and establishing a socialist system of public dictatorship. It takes collectivism as its core, views the individual as being inseparable from the group, advocates the unification of individual and collective interests, maintains that individuals must serve the group and that the group must serve individuals, that is, one for all, and all for one.

社会主义所有制 shèhuì zhǔyì suǒyǒuzhì
socialist system of ownership

A system of public ownership (by society) of production resources and labor products. This is the foundation of socialist production relationships. There are currently two forms of socialist ownership in China: ownership by all the people and ownership by the collective.

社会主义现实主义 shèhuì zhǔyì xiànshí zhǔyì

socialist realism

社会主义学院 shèhuì zhǔyì xuéyuàn

socialist institutes

The cadre institutes of the various democratic parties in China. Set up in 1956 there are two types: national socialist institutes and provincial socialist institutes. Their main task is to foster the study of Marxism-Leninism and Mao Zedong Thought, to upgrade the cadres' level of political ideology and their ability to serve socialism.

社会主义异化论 shèhuì zhǔyì yìhuàlùn

theory of socialist alienation

An erroneous theory which goes against the Marxism concept of labor alienation. Marx had analyzed labor alienation which arises from the capitalist system of ownership. Some people have carelessly misinterpreted labor alienation, thinking that alienation also exists in socialist societies, and construing bureaucratism, personality cults, and even the practical faults and mistakes in work as alienation. This kind of theory blurred the distinction between socialism and capitalism, and generated skeptical and negative attitudes toward socialism.

社交 shèjiāo

social interaction

Social intercourse occurring among people in society.

社教 shè-jiào

1) societal education; socialist thought education (particularly the thought education promoted in the countryside since 1990); 2) socialist education movement (cf. 社教运动)

社教运动 shè-jiào yùndòng

socialist education movement

Abbreviation for 社会主义教育运动. Also called the 四清 four cleanups movement. (cf. 四清)

社科 shè-kē

social science

Abbreviation for 社会科学.

E.g. 社科书籍 *social science books*

社科院 shè-kē-yuàn

academy of social sciences (particularly the Academy of Social Sciences of the PRC)

Abbreviation for 社会科学院.

社来社去 shèlái shèqù

coming from and returning to the commune

A method used during the Cultural Revolution by some agricultural and other institutions to train students in certain specialities. The students were selected by people's communes, a portion of them recruited from agricultural villages. After they had received training (long or short term) and graduated, they returned to their communes and brigades to work.

社情 shèqíng

societal conditions

E.g. 社情民意 *social conditions and the sentiments of the populace*

社庆 shèqìng

the day commemorating the founding of a newspaper, news agency, etc.

社区 shèqū

community

E.g. 社区文化 community culture / 社区服务 community service

社圈 shèquān

community activities circles

社群 shèqún

community groups

Abbreviation for 社会群体.

社务会 shèwùhuì

coop meetings

Abbreviated term for meetings held by a supply and marketing cooperative to discuss the internal affairs of the cooperative. The term can also be applied to meetings held by other units with the word "社 association" added.

社员 shèyuán

commune member

Normally, the term refers to members of rural people's communes, i.e., peasants. The term can also be applied to members of other organizations with the word "社 association" added.

社长 shèzhǎng

co-op chief

Normally, the term refers to the responsible person of an agricultural production cooperative. It can also be applied to the responsible person of some other organization with the word "社." added.

E.g. 他现在是人民日报社社长。 He is the head of the People's Daily newspaper office.

设籍 shèjí

to open a file for residential card

shen

申办 shēnbàn

to apply for and to go through the procedures; to apply for sponsorship

E.g. 申办奥运会 apply to be the sponsor of the Olympics

申领 shēnlǐng

to apply for and obtain

E.g. 申领营业执照 to apply for and receive a business license

伸手派 shēnshǒupài

those who hold out their hands (for favors)

A metaphor for those with a serious problem of individualism, who want things but don't want to work for them. They often hold out their hands to their units or other people, asking for positions, glory, or favorable treatment.

身份证 shēnfènzhèng

identification card (I.D. card)

深化 shēnhuà

to deepen; to develop to a higher level

E.g. 深化改革 to deepen the reform / 思想教育不断深化。 Thought education is continuously deepening.

深加工 shēnjiāgōng

to refine; to further process materials or semi-finished projects

深挖洞，广积粮，不称霸 shēn wādòng, guǎng jīliáng, bù chēngbà

to dig tunnels deep, store grain everywhere, and never seek hegemony

A summary of China's domestic and foreign policies formulated by Mao Zedong during the Cultural Revolution. It means to strengthen the armed forces and civilian defenses, to develop the economy, to emphasize agricultural production, to store up grains, to seek world peace, and to never seek hege-

深指 Shēn-zhǐ
Shenzhen index
The Shenzhen Stock Exchange stock price index.

神化 shénhuà
to deify (a person or thing in real life)
E.g. 不要宣传神化迷信思想。*Do not propagate a mentality of superstitious deification.* / 神化领导人 *to deify a leader*

神经兮兮 shénjīngxīxī
mentally off; psychologically abnormal or unbalanced
E.g. 他的汽车被盗，被弄得神经兮兮。*His car was stolen, so he became a bit unbalanced.*

神仙会 shénxiānhuì
a meeting of the divine
A discussion meeting of persons with experience and wisdom to resolve a major difficulty in work.

审干 shěn-gàn
to examine the personal record of cadres
To politically investigate cadres. Specifically, the comprehensive political investigation of all cadres in China in the 1950s. It was called 审干运动 cadre examination movement, or 审干 for short.

审计 shěnjì
fiscal investigation; audit
The investigation and supervision, conducted by the state's auditing organs, on the income and expenditure of government agencies at various levels, as well as those of the state's financial and monetary organs, enterprises, and institutions. The term also refers to the work, commissioned to accountants by those in charge, of checking the accounts, records, and accounting reports of relevant units.

审结 shěnjié
to investigate and to wrap up a case
E.g. 审结案件 *to investigate and wrap up a case*

审看 shěnkàn
to view and judge or assess a film, TV program, or drama; to scrutinize
E.g. 审看电影 *to view and assess a film* / 审看戏剧 *to view and assess a play* / 拿起报纸仔细审看 *to read a newspaper meticulously* / 他仔细审看那个新来的人。*He scrutinized the newly arrived person.*

审批 shěnpī
to examine and approve
The examination and approval of written plans, reports, etc.

审评 shěnpíng
to examine and appraise
To examine persons or products, evaluate them, and then determine which ones are advanced or of high quality.

审视 shěnshì
to scrutinize
To observe attentively.
E.g. 他审视着这张脸。*He scrutinized a face.*

审听 shěntīng
to listen and judge or assess a musical program
E.g. 审听演唱比赛录音 *to listen to and assess a recording of a singing contest.*

审验 shěnyàn

to investigate and verify
E.g. 对驾驶员进行审验 to examine drivers for the purpose of verification (driver's license)

审阅 shěnyuè
to read and scrutinize (writings, charts, etc.)
E.g. 审阅作战地图 to scrutinize battle maps / 审阅文章 to scrutinize articles

sheng

声控 shēngkòng
to use the human voice to control machines; voice control
E.g. 声控技术 sound-control technique / 声控喷泉 sound-control fountain / 声控飞机 sound-control airplanes / 声控电话 voice-control telephones

声情并茂 shēngqíng bìngmào
rich in voice and expression
Pertaining to excellent singing, in which the tone and language are full of musical sensibility, and the feelings expressed are penetrating and moving.

声讨会 shēngtǎohuì
denunciation meeting
A meeting to criticize people or events.

声讨书 shēngtǎoshū
denunciation paper (document, poster, etc., criticizing people or events)

声像 shēngxiàng
sounds and visual images (taped)

声讯 shēngxùn
voice mail
E.g. 电话自动声讯服务 automatic answering service

生搬硬套 shēngbān yìngtào
to mimic rigidly; to slavishly imitate
To mechanically and rigidly apply others' methods and experiences, disregarding one's own actual situation.

生产大队 shēngchǎn dàduì
production brigade
An administrative organ positioned between the people's commune and the production teams. It is composed of several production teams.

生产队 shēngchǎnduì
production team
Also called 生产小队. It is the basic accounting unit in rural people's communes, and is administered by the production team administrative committee. Under the leadership of the commune and the brigade, it carries out independent accounting, is responsible for its own gains and losses, and directly organizes the allocation of production and earnings. It has autonomous rights over the management and administration of the land, hills and forests, and pastures under its jurisdiction.

生产管理委员会 shēngchǎn guǎnlǐ wěiyuánhuì
production administrative committee
An organ responsible for making production arrangements in a rural people's commune or a production team.

生产建设兵团 shēngchǎn jiànshè bīngtuán
production-construction corps
(cf. 新疆生产建设兵团)

生产教养院 shēngchǎn jiàoyǎngyuàn
production education institutions

Institutions set up in the early 1950s to care for and educate urban old and young who have no livelihood.

生产经营型 shēngchǎn jīngyíngxíng
production management model
A progressive model of management and administration of industries and enterprises with the following characteristics: it is centered on economic efficiency, and production is organized according to the principles of "produce according to need" and "meet change with change". The effectiveness of the fully developed enterprise management is strong in each of these areas: investigation, forecasting, making policy decisions, purchasing, marketing, cooperation, publicity, and services. Enterprise administrative functions are coordinated with management functions, so that the ability of enterprises to adapt to market fluctuations is upgraded.

生产线 shēngchǎnxiàn
production line
In a factory, the path followed in the total production process, or a phase of it. The term also refers to the sequence of machinery required in this production.

生产型 shēngchǎnxíng
production model
A backward method of administering industries and enterprises. It is the opposite of the 生产经营型 production management model. This method of administration only deals with the internal administration of enterprises and is not concerned with management, and therefore does not bring into play the function of management.

生产要素 shēngchǎnyàosù
essentials of production
The basic operational requirements in a production process, including funds, labor, technology, information, real estate, property rights, etc.

生防 shēng-fáng
biological control
Contraction of 生物防治. It is a method that utilizes certain organisms to control plant diseases, insect pests, and soil erosion. In general, it refers to the use of certain insects fungi, germs, viruses, and protozoons which are parasitic to the insect pests to control or eradicate them, or it refers to the use of plants to treat water and prevent soil erosion.

生化 shēng-huà
biochemistry
Abbreviation for 生物化学.

生活补助 shēnghuó bǔzhù
living subsidies
The material assistance provided to employees in difficult circumstances. The subsidies usually come from the subsidy funds allocated by the state, welfare funds from various units, enterprise award funds, and union dues. The subsidies are divided into two types: long term and short term; for employee families whose per-capita income is lower than the local minimum living standard, a living subsidy is provided regularly; for employees temporarily in difficult circumstances that they themselves cannot overcome a temporary subsidy is provided.

生活福利 shēnghuó fúlì
welfare benefits

生活关 shēnghuóguān
life exigency
The various difficulties that individuals encounter in the areas of clothing, food, housing, and transportation due to changes in environment or conditions.
E.g. 过好生活关 *to weather a life exigency well*

生活作风 shēnghuó zuòfēng
life style; behavior
1) The attitudes and behavior that people manifest in life. 2) The term refers specifically to someone behaving in an immoral way or who is involved in an improper relationship with the opposite sex.
E.g. 这个人生活作风有问题。 *This person's life style is questionable.*

生拉硬扯 shēnglā yìngchě
metaphor for forcing the acceptance of a far-fetched interpretation or forcing unrelated matters together
Also called 生拉硬拽.

生猛 shēngměng
(Cantonese dialect) alive and jumping vigorously
E.g. 生猛海鲜 *live jumping seafood*

生命节律 shēngmìng jiélǜ
life cycle (biorhythm)

生态 shēngtài
the state of organisms; ecology

生态爆炸 shēngtài bàozhà
ecological explosion
In the development of a certain plant and animal communities and ecosystems, a loss of equilibrium in the ecology is brought about by certain causes, and results in a disastrous situation. For example, the cutting of mountain forests creates serious soil erosion and loss of water retention, or the elimination of natural enemies may cause certain insect pests to proliferate.

生态工程 shēngtài gōngchéng
ecological engineering

生态经济学 shēngtài jīngjìxué
eco-economics

生态农业 shēngtài nóngyè
eco-agriculture
To maintain a beneficial cycle within a greater agricultural system of farming, forestry, animal husbandry, fishery, and other sidelines, through full utilization of human and animal excrement, as well as plant and animal wastes. The goals are to protect agriculture by afforestation, to support animal husbandry by agriculture, to advance farming by animal husbandry, and to realize macroscopic eco-equilibrium.

生态平衡 shēngtài pínghéng
eco-equilibrium
Also called 自然平衡 natural equilibrium.

生态屏障 shēngtài píngzhàng
ecological protective screen
The conservation and protection of natural resources through the utilization of natural or artificial ecology. For example, planting grass and trees to prevent soil erosion and to prevent grasslands from becoming deserts.

生态系统 shēngtài xìtǒng
ecological system (ecosystem)

生态效益 shēngtài xiàoyì
ecological benefits
To construct a good eco-environment according to natural laws, so that the ecosystem can attain equilibrium and

thereby produce the best results and achieve the greatest benefits.

生态学 shēngtàixué
ecology

生物电 shēngwùdiàn
biological electricity (electricity in the bodies of animals)

生物防治 shēngwù fángzhì
to prevent and eliminate insect pests and weeds through biological means (cf. 生防)

生物工程 shēngwù gōngchéng
bio-engineering
Synonymous with 生物工程技术 bio-engineering technology.

生物节律 shēngwù jiélǜ
biorhythm
Synonymous with 生命节律.

生物能 shēngwùnéng
bio-energy

生物圈 shēngwùquān
biocenosis

生物物理学 shēngwù wùlǐxué
bio-physics

生物钟 shēngwùzhōng
biological clock

生育龄 shēngyùlíng
the entire period of giving birth to and nurturing children

生源 shēngyuán
source (origin) of students

牲畜肥 shēngchùféi
animal fertilizer
The excrement of domestic animals (pigs, sheep, horses, oxen, etc.). When fermented and applied to the fields, it increases soil fertility.

升级过渡 shēngjí guòdù
progressive transition

The progressive transition in ownership from the individual to the small collective, from the small collective to the large collective, and from the large collective to the entire people. This was a manifestation of erroneous leftist ideology on the issue of the ownership system. It went against the objective laws of economic development.

升级换代 shēngjí huàndài
replace with a higher level; to replace with a new generation
E.g. 产品升级换代 *to upgrade and replace with a new generation of products*

升温 shēngwēn
to heat up
A metaphor for speeding up or pressing development forward.
E.g. 农业要升温,工业要降温。
Agriculture needs to be speeded up; industry needs to be cooled down.

升溢 shēngyì
rising foam (head in beer)
Foaming in beverages such as beer after it is poured.

省报 shěngbào
newsletter of a provincial Party committee or a provincial government organ

省道 shěngdào
provincial highways

省府 shěngfǔ
provincial government; seat of the provincial government

省际 shěngjì
inter-provincial
E.g. 省际贸易 *inter-province commerce* / 打破省际界限 *to break through inter-provincial boundaries*

省委 shěngwěi
provincial Party committee

Abbreviation for a provincial level committee of the Chinese Communist Party. For example, the Hebei Provincial Committee of the Chinese Communist Party is abbreviated as 河北省委 Hebei Provincial Party Committee.

省优 shěngyōu
(of products) rated as superior at the provincial level

E.g. 省优产品 *products rated as superior at the provincial level*

省油灯 shěngyóudēng
oil-saving lamp

A metaphor for an honest, down to earth, law abiding person.

省直 shěngzhí
under the jurisdiction of the provincial government or the provincial Party committee

E.g. 省直单位 *units under provincial jurisdiction*

胜面 shèngmiàn
chance of winning a competition

E.g. 他胜面略大。 *He has a rather good chance of winning.*

胜券 shèngquàn
winning ticket

Metaphor for being assured of victory.

E.g. 稳操胜券 *to have a firm hold on the winning ticket*

胜券在握 shèngquàn zàiwò
winning ticket in hand

A metaphor for being absolutely assured of victory.

E.g. 实现收入过百亿的目标已是胜券在握。 *The goal of attaining an income exceeding 10 billion yuan is absolutely assured.*

圣火 shènghuǒ
sacred fire, such as the Olympic torch

E.g. 奥运圣火 *the Olympic torch*

shi

师德 shīdé
moral character or professional ethics befitting a teacher

师专 shī-zhuān
teachers' training school (a type of high school level vocational school)

Abbreviation for 师范专科学校.

师资 shīzī
qualified teachers

Persons with qualifications to be teachers.

E.g. 培养师资 *to train qualified teachers*

失衡 shīhéng
to lose balance

E.g. 失衡状态 *an unbalanced condition* / 经济调控失衡。 *Economic adjustments are unbalanced.* / 内心失衡 *psychologically unbalanced*

失控 shīkòng
out of control

失落感 shīluògǎn
feeling of being lost or neglected

失调 shītiáo
unbalanced

1) To lose equilibrium, to have the wrong proportions in a mixture.

E.g. 供求失调 *imbalance in supply and demand* / 雨水失调 *abnormal rainfall*

2) The term also refers to not receiving proper convalescent care.

E.g. 产后失调 *to lack proper postpartum care.*

失信于民 shīxìn yúmín
to lose the people's trust

失足青年 shīzú qīngnián
youths who have lost their footing
Young people who have committed serious errors, become degenerate, or gone astray.

尸检 shījiǎn
autopsy
Also called 病理尸体剖检 pathological dissection of a corpse.

十边地 shíbiāndì
ten kinds of side land
指农田以外可以种植的隙地。一般指田边、场边、路边、沟边、塘边、圩边、岩边、屋边、坟边、篱边的闲散土地。
The small spaces outside of agricultural fields that can be cultivated. These are the scattered pieces of land by the sides of fields, threshing grounds, roads, ditches, ponds, country markets, cliffs, houses, graves, and fences.

十大 Shí-Dà
the Tenth National Congress of the Chinese Communist Party (August 24-28, 1973, in Beijing)
Abbreviation for 中国共产党第十次全国代表大会.

十二大 Shí'èr-Dà
the Twelfth National Congress of the Chinese Communist Party (Sept.1-11, 1982, in Beijing)
Abbreviation for 中国共产党第十二次全国代表大会.

十佳 shíjiā
the ten best
E.g. 十佳运动员 *ten best athletes*

十六条 Shíliùtiáo
the sixteen articles
The "Resolutions on the Great Proletarian Cultural Revolution" promulgated by the Central Committee of the Chinese Communist Party on August 8, 1966. It contains sixteen articles, hence is called the "sixteen articles".

十年浩劫 shínián hàojié
the ten-year calamity
Refers to the Cultural Revolution (also called 十年动乱 and 十年内乱).

十年内乱 shínián nèiluàn
ten-year internal chaos
The ten years (1966 to 1976) of the Cultural Revolution. (cf. 文化大革命)

十七年 shíqīnián
the seventeen years
The seventeen years between the founding of the People's Republic of China in 1949 to the beginning of the Cultural Revolution in 1966. (cf. 黑线专政)

十三大 Shísān-Dà
the Thirteenth National Congress of the Chinese Communist Party (Oct. 25-Nov. 1, 1987, in Beijing)
Abbreviation for 中国共产党第十三次全国代表大会.

十一大 Shíyī-Dà
the Eleventh National Congress of the Chinese Communist Party (August 12-18, 1977, in Beijing)
Abbreviation for 中国共产党第十一次全国代表大会.

石化 shíhuà
petrochemistry
Contraction of 石油化学 petrochemistry.

石煤 shíméi
bone coal

A kind of grayish-black rock found along with coal in coal beds. It is relatively low in carbon content, and is harder than coal. Aside from serving as a fuel, it is used in extracting certain raw materials for chemical industries and for making building materials.

拾遗补缺 shíyí bǔquē

to pick up the neglected and to supply the deficient

To work in areas that are overlooked, neglected, or deficient.

E.g. 根据群众的需要扩大经营项目，拾遗补缺，方便群众。 *We should expand the range of goods and services on the basis of the people's needs, to pick up the neglected and to supply the deficient, in order to make things convenient for people.* / 为国营经济拾遗补缺 *to remedy the shortcomings of the state economy*

时弊 shíbì

curse of the times; societal malady of the period

E.g. 针砭时弊 *to identify and deal with societal maladies of the times* / 切中时弊 *to hit the curse of the times right on the mark*

时程 shíchéng

time table; schedule; program

E.g. 入会具体时程 *detailed schedule for joining a congress, conference or meeting* / 政治时程 *political time table*

时代感 shídàigǎn

sense of the time; Zeitgeist

The characteristic spirit of a period and people's feelings toward it.

E.g. 这部电影具有很强的时代感。 *This movie has a strong sense of the period.*

时代精神汇合论 shídài jīngshén huìhélùn

theory of merging the spirit of the times

A theory of artistic creation proposed by Zhou Gucheng in 1962. Its main thesis is: various kinds of philosophical consciousness arise during a period and they converge to become the spirit of that period. After this thesis was proposed, it was criticized as a bourgeois philosophy of literature and art. (cf. 黑八论)

食雕 shídiāo

culinary sculptures (foods carved into art objects)

E.g. 食雕工艺 *the art of culinary sculptures*

食街 shíjiē

food street

Abbreviation for 食品街.

食疗 shíliáo

food therapy

To treat certain ailments by ingesting food that contain specific elements and nutrients.

E.g. 推广食疗 *to popularize food therapy* / 征集食疗秘方 *to collect the secret formulas for therapeutic foods*

食品街 shípǐnjiē

a commercial street specializing in foods and beverages

Abbreviated as 食街.

食俗 shísú

eating habits

E.g. 年节食俗 *the food customs of New Year and holidays*

食宿 shísù

room and board

Food and lodging.

E.g. 食宿问题已得到解决。*The issue of room and board has been resolved.*

食协 shí-xié
food association
Abbreviation for 食品协会.

实诚 shíchéng
solid
1) Realistic and sincere. 2) Sturdy, not flimsy.

实干家 shígànjiā
workhorse
One who is responsible, steady, and puts his shoulder to the wheel.

实干精神 shígàn jīngshén
workhorse spirit
The spirit of putting in solid work, not seeking flashiness.

实绩 shíjì
actual achievement
The actual achievement attained in one's work.
E.g. 选拔干部要注意实绩。*In promoting cadres, we must pay attention to their actual achievements.*

实况转播 shíkuàng zhuǎnbō
live broadcast

实力政策 shílì zhèngcè
strong-arm policy
The method, used by certain nations, of relying on their superior military and economic strength to control and manipulate others.

实事 shíshì
real matters (in the practical sense); things that the people really need to have done
E.g. 为人民办实事 *to perform some real and practical service for the people*

实体 shítǐ
entity
1) Originally, a philosophical term referring to a substance that is perpetually in motion or development. 2) Now the term usually refers to an organization or enterprise of a certain scale and level of independence.
E.g. 政治实体 *political entity* / 经济实体 *economic entity*

识大体 shí dàtǐ
to discern the cardinal principles
To consider an issue or deal with a matter from the perspective of benefits to the entire situation.
E.g. 顾大局，识大体 *to consider the overall situation, discern the cardinal principles*

识字班 shízìbān
literacy class
A form of organized study set up in rural villages to eradicate illiteracy. The study times are in the evenings or during slack periods in farm work.

史无前例 shǐ wú qián lì
unprecedented
Specifically referring to the 1966-1976 Cultural Revolution.

使领馆 shǐ-lǐngguǎn
embassy and consulate
Composite for 大使馆 and 领事馆.

始发站 shǐfāzhàn
point of origin (of a public transport vehicle)

示范村 shìfàncūn
model village

示范户 shìfànhù
model household
Also called 科技示范户 technological model household. (cf. 科技示范户)

示范田 shìfàntián

model field

Fields cultivated by technological model households from which others can gain experience, learn from, and emulate.

世行 Shì–Háng

World Bank

Abbreviation for 世界银行.

E.g. 世行贷款扶贫项目资金已经到位。*The money for the aid the poor project which was loaned by the World Bank has arrived.*

世纪婴儿 shìjì yīng'ér

millennium infant (baby)

Infants born on January 1, 2000. Also called 千禧婴儿.

世界村 shìjiècūn

global village

世界环境日 shìjiè huánjìngrì

World Environmental Day

Also called Earth Day, designated as June 5.

世界贸易组织 Shìjiè Màoyì Zǔzhī

WTO (World Trade Organization)

世贸组织 Shìmào Zǔzhī

WTO (World Trade Organization)

Abbreviation for 世界贸易组织.

事典 shìdiǎn

topical reference book

A reference book that explains the history, current state, and developmental trend of a certain topic.

E.g. 经济事典 *reference book on economics*

事权 shìquán

jurisdiction or limits of authority over a matter

事务性工作 shìwùxìng gōngzuò

routine duties

The everyday duties aside from regular political work and normal business, such as sending children to nurseries, cleaning, resolving disputes, distributing bonuses, etc.

事务主义 shìwù zhǔyì

routinism

A work style exemplified by having no planning, not distinguishing the primary from the secondary, having no priorities, paying no attention to guiding principles, policies, and political thought, merely burying one's head in everyday trifling matters.

适体 shìtǐ

(re clothing) to fit (in terms of size and style)

适销 shìxiāo

suitable to the market

A commodity that is in demand on the market, and selling well.

E.g. 适销产品 *a product suitable to the market*

适销对路 shìxiāo duìlù

good concurrence in the market

Commodities on the market are liked by the masses; there is concurrence in supply and demand; and sales are good.

饰演 shìyǎn

to play a certain role in a drama

市场经济 shìchǎng jīngjì

market economy

由市场进行调节的国民经济。

A national economy regulated by the market.

市场调节 shìchǎng tiáojié

regulated by the market

To not have state planning over the production and circulation of some products and enterprises, but allow them to be regulated by the law of value on its own. That is, within a certain scope, stipulated by central state planning, relevant enterprises may arrange their own production and circulation, and adapt to changes in the market. At the same time, the state exerts control through relevant policies and laws, and through industrial and commercial administrative work.

市场信息 shìchǎng xìnxī

market information

Information concerning the supply and demand of commodities, their prices, variety, etc.

市场预测 shìchǎng yùcè

market forecast

市风 shìfēng

urban ambience, societal atmosphere of a city

市府 shìfǔ

municipal government

Abbreviation for 市政府.

市管人员 shì-guǎn rényuán

personnel supervising the market

市花 shìhuā

the designated flower of a city

市徽 shìhuī

emblem of a city

市况 shìkuàng

marketing situation

E.g. 新近的市况令人乐观。 *The present marketing shows good prospects.*

市容 shìróng

appearance of a city

The surface features of a city, including buildings, landscaping, window displays, etc.

E.g. 南京市容整洁美观, 给游人留下深刻的印象。 *Nanjing has a neat, clean, and beautiful appearance, which leaves a deep impression on visitors.*

市树 shìshù

the emblematic tree of a city

市委 shìwěi

municipal Party committee

A municipal level committee of the Chinese Communist Party. For example, the Beijing Municipal Committee of the Chinese Communist Party is abbreviated as 北京市委. Some municipalities are directly under the control of the central government. Their municipal Party committees rank at the same level as provincial Party committees. All other municipal Party committees are under the leadership of provincial Party committees.

市盈率 shìyínglǜ

dividend ratio

The ratio between the market value of a stock and its annual dividend.

市政工程 shìzhèng gōngchéng

municipal engineering

Various engineering projects involved in urban construction, including factories, stores, roads and transportation, hospitals, theaters, and schools.

视窗 shìchuāng

windows (computer)

视盘 shìpán

laser video disc

E.g. 视盘机 *video disc player*

视频 shìpín

video frequency (re television or radar)

视听 shìtīng

to view and listen; what one sees and hears

E.g. 混淆视听 *to mix up what one*

hears and sees / 视听教育 audio-visual education / 视听设备 audio-visual facilities / 视听中心 audio-visual center / 视听教材 audio-visual teaching materials / 视听教学 audio-visual teaching

视众 shìzhòng

television audience

Abbreviation for 电视观众.

试办 shìbàn

to set up on a trial basis

试播 shìbō

1) trial seed sowing

E.g. 试播草籽 *to sow grass seeds on a trial basis*

2) trial broadcast

E.g. 试播立体声节目 *to broadcast stereophonic programs on a trial basis*

试产 shìchǎn

trial production

E.g. 试产试销 *produce and market on a trial basis* / 试产成功。 *The trial production was successful.*

试点 shìdiǎn

experimental point

A certain unit or locale where small-scale experimentation is conducted to gain experience before formally proceeding with a certain task. The term also refers to the unit or locale where an experiment is formally conducted.

E.g. 他们工厂是这次整党的试点。 *Their factory is an experimental point for the Party rectification this time.*

试点班 shìdiǎnbān

experimental class

A class on which a teaching experiment is conducted.

E.g. 二年级五班为试点班。 *Class Five of the Second Grade is the experimental class.*

试读 shìdú

study on a probationary basis

A new student going through the observation stage. Whether the student will be admitted as a regular student is determined by his performance during the probationary period.

试飞 shìfēi

trial flight (trying out new flight equipment or new route)

E.g. 进行夜航试飞 *to carry out night flights on a trial basis* / 试飞成功。 *The trial flight was successful.*

试管婴儿 shìguǎn yīng'ér

test-tube baby

试刊 shìkān

trial publication

A publication published on a trial basis before it is formally issued.

试销 shìxiāo

trial marketing

E.g. 产品试销 *to market a product on a trial basis*

试验区 shìyànqū

experimental district

试验田 shìyàntián

experimental plot

A field in which scientific agricultural experimentation is conducted. The term is also a metaphor for experimental points in other areas of work.

试映 shìyìng

trial showing (of a movie); preview

To show a movie to a certain circle of people to solicit their opinions before it is formally released.

试种 shìzhòng

trial planting

E.g. 试种成功。 *Trial planting was successful.* / 试种新品种 *to plant a new variety on a trial basis*

收案 shōu'àn

to accept a case (for trial)

收存 shōucún

to collect and keep; to store away

收杆 shōugān

to put away the sticks or clubs; to conclude a sports event in ice hockey, golf, etc.

E.g. 高尔夫球友谊赛收杆。 *The friendly golf match concluded.* / 女子台球赛收杆。 *The women's ping-pong match concluded.*

收活 shōuhuó

take in work

Accepting parts and other materials to be processed and working on them.

E.g. 友谊服装店这个月收活太多, 一时做不完。 *The Friendship Tailor Shop has accepted too many jobs this month, and cannot finish them in a short time.*

收紧 shōujǐn

to tighten up (expenditure); to apply strict controls

E.g. 收紧银根 *to tighten up the money market* / 政治上收紧 *to tighten up on the political front*

收看 shōukàn

to watch (a TV program)

E.g. 收看现场实况转播 *to watch a live relayed broadcast*

收理 shōulǐ

to accept a case (for trial); to put in order

E.g. 收理案件 *to accept a case for trial* / 收理帐册 *to put the account book in order*

收录机 shōulùjī

radio recorder

A machine that can be used as a radio and as a tape recorder.

收拍 shōupāi

to put away the racquets; to conclude a sports competition in badminton, ping-pong, tennis, etc.

E.g. 国际羽球赛收拍 *to conclude the international badminton match*

收盘 shōupán

to put away the board; to conclude a competition in a board game such as chess

E.g. 中国象棋赛弈罢收盘。 *The Chinese chess match has concluded.*

收枰 shōupíng

to put away the chessboard; to conclude a competition in a board game such as chess

Same as 收盘.

E.g. 围棋赛收枰。 *The Go match has concluded.*

收审 shōushěn

detention

To detain for investigation, an administrative measure adopted by public security organs in dealing with people who have committed misdemeanors or who are suspects.

收视 shōushì

to watch a TV program

E.g. 收视范围 *the scope of television viewing* / 收视率 *viewing rate*

收托 shōutuō

(day care center or nursery school) to accept a child into its care

E.g. 收托孩子 *to accept a child (into a day-care facility)* / 收托量 *volume (number of children) of a day-*

care center / 收托能力 *capacity of a day-care center*

收尾工作 shōuwěi gōngzuò
round-off work
Synonymous with 扫尾工作. (cf. 扫尾工作)

收效 shōuxiào
attain results
To attain good results.
E.g. 他觉得听力课收效很大。*He feels that the aural comprehension class has yielded great results.*

收养人 shōuyǎngrén
adoptive parents
People who legally adopt other people's children.

收养子女 shōuyǎng zǐnǚ
adopted children
Children who have been legally adopted. Through the adoption process, a parent-child relationship is created between persons who have no direct blood ties.

收治 shōuzhì
to accept and treat (a patient)
A clinic or physician accepting a patient for treatment.
E.g. 收治疑难病症的患者 *to accept a patient with a difficult and complicated illness*

收贮 shōuzhù
to store up; to lay aside
E.g. 收贮野草 *the storage of hay* / 大白菜的收贮运销工作 *the shipping and storage of cabbage*

手读 shǒudú
to read Braille

手扶拖拉机 shǒufú tuōlājī
walking tractor
A small motorized farm machine. It is light and agile, and can pull various farm implements for tilling, sowing, harvesting, etc. It can also be used for transport.

手工业合作社 shǒugōngyè hézuòshè
handicraft cooperative
A high-level type of socialist collective economic organization formed by handicraft workers in China. There are various forms: handicraft supply, marketing, production cooperatives, handicraft production cooperatives, etc. Members maintain the principle of voluntary participation. They pay an initial fee to join, and share production materials. They must participate in the remuneration according to labor.

手机 shǒujī
cellular phone; mobile phone

手球 shǒuqiú
handball

手提电脑 shǒutí diànnǎo
portable computer; laptop computer

首创精神 shǒuchuàng jīngshén
pioneering spirit
The mentality of having the courage to break through impediments, to create, and to do what others have never done before.

首发 shǒufā
to be the first in publishing or issuing something
E.g. 举行首发仪式 *to put on an initial publication ceremony*

首发式 shǒufāshì
ceremony celebrating the first publication of a book, a magazine, an audio or videotape, etc.
E.g. 举行音像首发式 *to put on a*

ceremony celebration the issuing of a videotape

首钢 Shǒu – Gāng

Capital Iron and Steel Company (originally the Shijingshan Iron and Steel Plant)

Abbreviation for 首都钢铁公司.

首航 shǒuháng

maiden voyage (of an aircraft or ship)

E.g. 海军完成了首航南太平洋。 *The naval ship completed its maiden voyage through the South Pacific.*

首季 shǒujì

first season

首汽 Shǒu – Qì

Capital Automobile Company

Abbreviation for 首都汽车公司.

首日 shǒurì

first day

首日封 shǒurìfēng

first-day cover

A commemorative envelope bearing a new stamp issued on the same day as the stamp.

E.g. 首日封图案为总工会成立大会会场。 *The picture on the first-day cover is the meeting hall where the Federation of Trade Unions was founded.*

首演 shǒuyǎn

first performance (of a show); first showing

E.g. 美国艺术家在京首演。 *The American artists are putting on their premier performance in Beijing.*

首映 shǒuyìng

first public showing of a film

E.g. 电视连续剧在京首映。 *The television series is having its premier broadcast in Beijing.*

首映式 shǒuyìngshì

opening of a film (ceremony celebrating the first showing of a film)

E.g. 电影《火烧圆明园》昨天在京举行首映式。 *The film "The Burning of Yuanmingyuan" had its premier ceremony in Beijing yesterday.*

首战 shǒuzhàn

first-time combat; first competition

E.g. 中国女子排球队首战告捷。 *The Chinese women's volleyball team won the first match.* / 中国队首战美国队。 *The Chinese team is playing against the American team.*

守摊子 shǒutānzi

to keep a stall

A metaphor for lacking creativity, being conservative, being satisfied with the status quo.

售后服务 shòuhòu fúwù

after sales service (information, repair, return and exchange, etc.)

E.g. 加强售后服务 *to strengthen after sales service* / 搞好售后服务 *to manage after sales service well* / 售后服务工作 *after-sales service work*

售汇 shòuhuì

to sell foreign currency

E.g. 售汇工作 *the work of selling foreign currency* / 售汇制度 *the system for selling foreign currency*

售票员 shòupiàoyuán

ticket collector

售缺 shòuquē

(of commodities) sold out; out of stock

售武 shòu – wǔ

arms sale

E.g. 英国向伊拉克售武丑闻再起风波。 *There was another scandal about*

England selling arms to Iraq.

受冲击 shòu chōngjī
to suffer an assault or shock
A metaphor for being investigated or struggled against in a political movement.
E.g. 他在历次政治运动中多次受到冲击。*He was attacked many times in successive political movements.*

受惠 shòuhuì
to benefit
E.g. 改革开放,人民受惠。*Reforms and liberalization will benefit the people.*

受聘 shòupìn
to accept an appointment (to a job)
E.g. 受聘仪式 *appointment ceremony* / 他受聘担任学术委员会委员。*He was appointed to the Academic Committee.*

受阅 shòuyuè
to be reviewed (of troops, etc.)
E.g. 受阅部队 *troops being reviewed* / 参加受阅 (*of troops*) *to participate in being reviewed*

瘦肉型 shòuròuxíng
lean meat species
Species of pigs that produce a higher proportion of lean meat.

寿险 shòu-xiǎn
life insurance
Abbreviation for 人寿保险的简称.
E.g. 寿险代理人 *life insurance agent* / 寿险公司 *life insurance company*

shu

殊荣 shūróng
special honor

E.g. 获得殊荣 *to receive a special honor*

输家 shūjiā
loser
It refers to the party who loses at gambling or in a competition.

输面 shūmiàn
appearance of losing (at a game such as Go)
E.g. 他认为这个队的输面要大些。*He thinks that the chances of this team losing is greater.*

输血 shūxiě
to transfuse blood
A metaphor for relying on influx of external funds and materials to survive and develop.
E.g. 要使群众富裕起来,必须变"输血"为"造血"。*If the masses are to prosper, we must change the strategy of infusing the economy with external funds to that of creating funds.*

梳辫子 shūbiànzi
to braid the hair
原指女人用梳子梳理辫子。后来把对事物的归纳、整理、分类也比作梳辫子。
Originally, the term meant combing hair into braids. Later, it came to be used metaphorically to mean pulling together, arranging, and categorizing matters.

疏港 shūgǎng
to clear a harbor of too many ships and goods (being shipped); to dredge a harbor
E.g. 疏港工作 *the work of dredging a harbor*

疏解 shūjiě
decongest
To unjam and loosen up (congestion or

bottleneck in traffic or transportation).
E.g. 疏解积压的客流 *to clear a congestion in the flow of tourists*

疏离 shūlí
to drift apart; to become estranged
E.g. 疏离状态 *state of estrangement* / 文学不应与社会疏离。 *Literature should not drift away from society.*

疏理 shūlǐ
to unclog and readjust
E.g. 疏理商品的流通渠道 *to unclog and readjust channels for commodities*

疏运 shūyùn
to disperse and ship away
E.g. 保证外轮货物及时疏运 *to guarantee that the cargoes of foreign ships are shipped out on time*

书荒 shūhuāng
book famine
A shortage of good books being published and sold.

书市 shūshì
book fair (temporary book market)
E.g. 举办书市 *to hold a book fair* / 北京书市昨天开幕。 *The Beijing Book Fair opened yesterday.*

书展 shūzhǎn
book exhibition
E.g. 举办书展 *to hold a book exhibition* / 书展于昨天开幕。 *The book exhibition opened yesterday.*

赎买政策 shúmǎi zhèngcè
buy out policy
The policy of gradually nationalizing, with compensation, the production resources of the bourgeoisie after the proletarian class has attained political power and controls the economy. This is done in the following way: before the entire industry is put under public-private joint management, a method of allocation of profits is adopted; after public-private joint management is implemented, a fixed interest format is adopted. The buy out policy includes giving investors consideration in individual cases, attending to their living arrangements, and retaining a portion of the capitalists' high salaries.

暑运 shǔ-yùn
transport during summer vacation

数管齐下 shùguǎn qíxià
several pipes going down together
A metaphor for proceeding from several fronts simultaneously. Synonymous with 多管齐下.
E.g. 国库券发行将数管齐下。 *The distribution of state treasury bonds will proceed from several fronts simultaneously.*

数据库 shùjùkù
data bank

数控 shùkòng
digital control
Abbreviation for 数字控制.
E.g. 数控系统 *digital control system* / 数控机床 *digital-control machine tool* / 数控电话 *digital-control telephone* / 数控装置 *numerical control device*

数字地球 shùzì dìqiú
digital earth (globe)
The globe (earth) information mode. Information on politics, economics, culture, science and technology, and society is collected, and made into convenient and useful data by computers, and put on a globe information mode according to geographic location.

数字电视 shùzì diànshì
digital television
Refers to the complete process of making, transmitting, and receiving and adapting television programs to digital technology.

数字服装 shùzì fúzhuāng
digital clothing
Clothing equipped with digital information technology. Such clothes can receive and deliver (transmit) messages.

数字化 shùzìhuà
digitization
To turn information into digital signals for transmission.

数字激光视盘 shùzì jīguāng shìpán
digital laser video player
Laser video player made with digitized technology.

shua

耍态度 shuǎtàidù
to vent one's temper; to get into a huff

shuai

甩手掌柜 shuǎishǒu zhǎngguì
a laissez-faire supervisor or managing department

甩站 shuǎizhàn
(a bus or trolley) to throw off a stop (not stop at a stop)
E.g. 要克服甩站现象。 We must eradicate the phenomenon of public vehicles passing stops. / 有些电汽车故意甩站。 Some trolleys and buses pass stops deliberately.

帅气 shuàiqì
dashing
To be handsome in appearance and dapper in deportment.

shuang

双巴 shuāng-bā
double-decker bus

双百方针 shuāngbǎi fāngzhēn
double hundred guiding principle
即"百花齐放、百家争鸣"的方针。
The guiding principle of "let a hundred flowers bloom, and a hundred schools of thought contend". (cf. 百花齐放、百家争鸣)

双包 shuāngbāo
double contract
包产到户和包干到户的简称。
Abbreviation for both production contracted to the household and work contracted to the household. (cf. 包产到户 and 包干到户)

双包户 shuāngbāohù
double contract household
A household that contracts to manage a field or piece of land under the two systems of "production contracted to the household" and "work contracted to the household".

双保 shuāngbǎo
double guarantee
指企业保证上交国家税收和统配产品，国家保证企业主要的外部生产条件。
An enterprise guaranteeing to pay taxes and deliver stipulated products to the state, the state guaranteeing the main external production requirements (e.g.

supply of raw materials, energy, etc.)

双补 shuāngbǔ
double supplement

Abbreviation for the practice of providing supplemental classes in vocational skills to employees in their prime who joined the work force since the Cultural Revolution.

E.g. 双补学习班 *double supplement class*

双重国籍 shuāngchóng guójí
dual nationality

双重领导 shuāngchóng lǐngdǎo
under double leadership; dual leadership

A unit being under the leadership of two departments.

双反运动 shuāngfǎn yùndòng
double-opposition movement

指1958年全民整风运动后期开展的反浪费、反保守运动,简称"双反运动"。

Abbreviation for the campaign to oppose waste and to conserve that was launched in the latter part of the 1958 national rectification movement.

双扶 shuāngfú
double support

扶持贫困户、扶持优抚户的简称。

Supporting those in poverty, disabled servicemen and families of revolutionary martyrs.

E.g. 双扶对象 *persons to whom the double support is directed* / 双扶工作 *double support work*

双扶户 shuāngfúhù
those in poverty, and disabled servicemen and families of revolutionary martyrs, who receive special support

双轨制 shuāngguǐzhì
two-track system (metaphorical)

E.g. 价格实行双轨制。 *A two-track pricing system is applied.*

双铧犁 shuānghuálí
double plough

A farm implement with two ploughs attached. It is pulled by draft animals.

双基 shuāngjī
two basics: basic state of the nation and basic (political) line

E.g. 双基教育 *education about the two basics*

双佳活动 shuāngjiā huódòng
double-excellence movement

Abbreviation of the most excellent service personnel and most excellent team. Also called "create double excellence movement". Its goal was to rectify unhealthy tendencies and to develop the spirit of wholehearted service to the people.

双肩背 shuāngjiānbēi
backpack (a pack that hangs on the back)

双肩挑 shuāngjiāntiāo
carrying burdens on both shoulders

在教育、科研和其他技术部门中,有些人既担负具体的教学、科研或其他技术工作,又兼做行政管理工作,称为双肩挑。

The situation of some people in education, scientific research, and other technical fields, who shoulder both the responsibilities of teaching, scientific research, or other technical work, as well as administrative responsibilities.

E.g. 双肩挑干部 *a cadre carrying burdens on both shoulders*

双紧 shuāngjǐn
two tightenings: tightening up public

finance and credit

双卡 shuāngkǎ
double cassette
Double cassette tape recorder, which has two cassette tape decks and can be used to make duplicates.

双科学 shuāngkēxué
dual science

双料 shuāngliào
double material
The material for making a product is twice as much as would normally be used. It is a metaphor for the high quality of a product. It is also a metaphor for a person with two special skills(e.g. 双料大学生 a college student with double talents)or for a person being especially bad(e.g. 双料坏蛋 a double material scoundrel).

双面卡 shuāngmiànkǎ
double-faced khaki
A kind of cotton or woolen fabric with a distinctive twill on both sides. The woof and the warp are denser than that of serge.

双千田 shuāngqiāntián
double thousand fields
Agricultural fields that have a per *mu* yield of over a thousand catties of grain, valued at over a thousand yuan.

双抢 shuāngqiǎng
double rush
A rush to sow and a rush to harvest.

双声道 shuāngshēngdào
dual audio frequency line
E.g. 双声道立体声 *dual-track stereo sound* / 双声道声控 *dual-track phonic control* / 双声道传送 *dual-track transmission*

双突 shuāngtū

double crash
Abbreviation for the way of hurriedly admitting people into the Party and the hurried promotion of cadres in some locales during the Cultural Revolution.
E.g. 有些"双突"时入党的党员干部，在整党时更应该严格审查。*Some Party members and cadres who were admitted or promoted during the "double crash" period should be reviewed especially rigorously in the process of Party rectification.(cf.* 突击入党 *and* 突击提干)

双突干部 shuāngtū gànbù
double crash cadres
Cadres who were promoted to their positions in the "double crash" program.

双万户 shuāngwànhù
double ten thousand households
Rural households that have an annual grain yield of over ten thousand catties and an income of over ten thousand yuan.

双文明 shuāngwénmíng
material civilization and spiritual civilization
Abbreviation for 物质文明 material civilization and 精神文明 spiritual civilization.

双先 shuāngxiān
double advanced
Abbreviation for 先进个人 advanced individuals and 先进集体 advanced groups.

双向 shuāngxiàng
two-sided; bilateral; mutual; reciprocal
E.g. 双向选择 *mutual selection*

双休日 shuāngxiūrì
double rest day; two-day weekend

双学士 shuāngxuéshì
a bachelor's degree with a double major

双学位 shuāngxuéwèi
double degree
E.g. 双学位制 *double degree system* / 双学位专业 *double degree specialties*

双赢 shuāngyíng
be mutually satisfied; both achieve their purpose
E.g. 企业和银行出现双赢的局面。 *Both enterprises and banks are satisfied with the new conditions.*

双拥运动 shuāngyōng yùndòng
double support movement
Abbreviation for the movement to 拥军优属, 拥政爱民 support the army and give preferential treatment to their dependents, support the government and cherish the people. (cf. 拥军优属 and 拥政爱民)

双语 shuāngyǔ
bilingual
E.g. 双语教学 *bilingual education* / 双语日报 *bilingual newspaper* / 双语词典 *bilingual dictionary*

双证 shuāngzhèng
double certification: academic diploma and certificate of practical skills

双职工 shuāngzhígōng
two job employees
Husband and wife both employed.
E.g. 双职工家庭 *two job family*

shui

水电 shuǐdiàn
water and electricity
Abbreviation for 水力发电 hydroelectric generation; electricity generated by a hydroelectric plant.
E.g. 水电站 *hydroelectric station* / 发展水电 *to develop hydroelectric generation* / 水电成本低。 *The cost of hydroelectric generation is low.*

水电费 shuǐdiànfèi
composite term for water and electricity fees

水分 shuǐfèn
moisture content; exaggeration
Metaphor for component of exaggeration.
E.g. 产值中的水分相当大，浪费相当严重。 *There is quite a bit of exaggeration in the output value; the waste is actually quite serious.*

水荒 shuǐhuāng
serious water shortage
E.g. 闹水荒 *to be plagued by a shortage of water* / 水荒加剧。 *The water shortage is worse.*

水货 shuǐhuò
(originally) goods smuggled by waterways; (now) imported goods bought through improper channels

水浇地 shuǐjiāodì
irrigated fields
Agricultural fields that are irrigated mechanically.

水景 shuǐjǐng
scenery that includes a body of water

水警 shuǐjǐng
water patrol (on a lake, sea coast, river, etc.)

水利化 shuǐlìhuà
water conservancy
A way of benefiting mankind by building water engineering projects, in order to utilize water resources and to prevent

flood damage.
E.g. 水利化建设 *water conservancy construction*

水疗 shuǐliáo
hydro therapy
A kind of physiotherapy whereby the patient is bathed or immersed in water of various temperatures. Cold water can stimulate nerve centers, enhance the function of the heart and blood vessels, and reduce fever. Warm water can cure neuritis and arthritis. Hot water can promote circulation and induce perspiration.

水门事件 Shuǐmén Shìjiàn
the Watergate affair

水泥船 shuǐníchuán
concrete boat
A new type of boat made of inorganic non-metallic material. The main component is concrete, hence it is called "concrete boat".

水暖工 shuǐnuǎngōng
water (plumbing) and heating worker
A worker responsible for installing and maintaining water supply and heating facilities.

水文站 shuǐwénzhàn
hydrometric station
A station which monitors the water level, volume of flow, sand content, water temperature, etc., of a river, lake, canal, or reservoir.

水俣病 shuǐyǔbìng
mercury poisoning
A disease caused by environmental pollution and named after Shui-yu (in Kyushu, Japan), the town in Japan where it first occurred. The illness first arose from ingesting seafood contaminated by high levels of mercury discharged from a nearby chemical plant. The symptoms are slurred speech and stupor, followed by deafness, blindness, total paralysis, dementia, and death.

水源林 shuǐyuánlín
water resource woods
The trees and forests planted around water resources for protection.

水针疗法 shuǐzhēn liáofǎ
liquid acupuncture
Also called 穴位注射疗法 acupoint injection therapy, a method of acupuncture. It involves injecting into acupoints certain serums normally injected into muscles, and combining the impact of the acupoints and the medicine to bring about curative effect. It is often used for rheumatism, strain of soft tissues, and insomnia.

睡袋 shuìdài
sleeping bag

税负 shuìfù
tax burden
E.g. 纳税人的税负有所降低。 *The tax burden on tax payers has been reduced.*

税基 shuìjī
tax base
E.g. 扩大税基 *expand the tax base*

税款 shuìkuǎn
taxable income; tax money
E.g. 上交税款 *to remit taxes*

税利 shuì-lì
taxes and profits
Contraction of 税收 and 利润.

税政 shuìzhèng
tax administration

A nation's tax collection activities.

shun

顺产 shùnchǎn
natural labor
Normal childbirth, as distinguished from 难产 difficult labor.

顺价 shùnjià
favorable price
The price a merchant pays is less than it is sold for.
E.g. 粮食实行顺价销售政策。*A sale policy of a favorable price for grain is practiced.*

shuo

说服教育 shuōfú jiàoyù
persuasion education
Using the methods of presenting reality, reasoning, and patient guidance to lead those who have committed mistakes to recognize problems and to correct their mistakes.

硕导 shuò-dǎo
tutor of a graduate (master's degree) student

si

思想包袱 sīxiǎng bāofu
mental load
A burden on one's mind which impedes advancement in one's thoughts.
E.g. 背上了思想包袱 *to carry a mental load*

思想波动 sīxiǎng bōdòng
mental turmoil
Having doubts and feeling anxious because of some external factors.
E.g. 他近来思想波动很大。*He has been going through a great deal of mental turmoil recently.*

思想方法 sīxiǎng fāngfǎ
way of thinking
The style and method that people adopt in perceiving and transforming the world, or in considering and dealing with issues.

思想改造 sīxiǎng gǎizào
ideological reform
Through studying theory and participating in practical revolutionary work, to bring one's subjective consciousness in line with reality, get rid of non-proletarian ideology, establish a proletarian world view and an attitude of wholehearted service to the people.

思想疙瘩 sīxiǎng gēda
mental knot
A problem or contradiction that cannot be resolved in one's mind.
E.g. 解开了思想疙瘩 *to dispel a mental knot*

思想革命化 sīxiǎng gémìnghuà
revolutionizing one's ideology
Bringing one's ideology into line with the requirements of the revolution.

思想工作 sīxiǎng gōngzuò
ideological work
Using correct and advanced ideology to help and educate people to resolve difficulties that they encounter in life, work, and thought, so that their consciousness will be raised and they will be able to deal with issues appropriately.
E.g. 他很会做思想工作。*He is*

very good at doing ideological work.

思想过硬 sīxiǎng guòyìng
ideologically resilient
In unfavorable and complex circumstances or arduous and difficult conditions, to be able to stand up to the test, to remain unswerving and uncompromising, to place strict demands on oneself for the sake of revolutionary interests, and to accomplish the tasks that one has undertaken.

思想见面 sīxiǎng jiànmiàn
candid exchange of ideas
People openly and candidly exchanging their views on an issue, not holding back, not concealing, and being totally truthful, in order to achieve mutual understanding.
E.g. 同志之间只有经常思想见面，才能互相信任。*In order to achieve mutual trust, comrades must always exchange ideas candidly.*

思想建设 sīxiǎng jiànshè
ideological construction
The proletarian political party educating all Party members and the broad revolutionary masses on Marxist theory and the guiding principles and policies of the Party, raising their political consciousness and level of understanding, using proletarian ideology to triumph over anti-proletarian ideology, and attaining a high level of unity in ideology, so that people's ideology will be in line with the needs of the revolutionary mission.

思想僵化 sīxiǎng jiānghuà
ideological ossification
In the face of rapid developments in objective reality, the ideology of a person or a political party remaining static and unable to accept new phenomena, always maintaining the original view, and becoming conservative and passive.

思想交锋 sīxiǎng jiāofēng
confrontation (lit., crossing swords) of ideas
A metaphor for opening a fierce struggle between two opposing sets of ideas.
E.g. 开展批评一定要思想交锋。 *Launching criticisms must involve confrontation of ideas.*

思想禁区 sīxiǎng jìnqū
ideological forbidden zone
Certain issues in the ideological realm which could not be touched in discussion. This specifically refers to the period when Mao's personality cult held sway, every word of the leader was construed as absolute truth, and no one was allowed to raise any doubts or criticisms toward it.

思想境界 sīxiǎng jìngjiè
mental state (degree of awareness, etc.)

思想觉悟 sīxiǎng juéwù
ideological consciousness
The degree to which people understand objective reality, the extent of a person's sense of revolutionary responsibility, and the quality of a person's attitude toward work.
E.g. 思想觉悟高 *high ideological consciousness* / 思想觉悟低 *low ideological consciousness*

思想库 sīxiǎngkù
think tank

Also called 头脑公司 brain trust. A kind of research information organization composed of specialists and scholars who apply their collective skills to provide scientific basis for the organized management of society, economics, military affairs, science and technology, etc. They also provide the leadership sector with the most favorable theories, strategies, and plans from which to make choices.

思想懒汉 sīxiǎng lǎnhàn
mental sluggard

Someone who is unwilling to exercise his brains to think about issues or to create anything new, preferring to stick with conventions.

思想烙印 sīxiǎng làoyìn
ideological brand

The deeply rooted influences on one's ideology, which are as permanent as brand marks.
E.g. 资产阶级的思想烙印 *bourgeois ideological brand*

思想路线 sīxiǎng lùxiàn
ideological line

The basic path which one's ideological understanding follows. Also called 认识路线 *line of understanding*.

思想摸底 sīxiǎng mōdǐ
to touch the bottom of people's ideology

To investigate and clearly understand the real situation regarding people's ideology.
E.g. 进行思想摸底工作 *to get to the bottom of people's ideology*

思想体系 sīxiǎng tǐxì
ideological system

Systematic basic viewpoints and theories.
E.g. 马列主义思想体系 *the Marxist-Leninist ideological system*

思想问题 sīxiǎng wèntí
ideological problem

Contradictions or incorrect views in people's ideology.
E.g. 思想问题没有解决，工作就很难做好。*If ideological problems are not resolved, it will be very difficult to do the work well.*

思想武装 sīxiǎng wǔzhuāng
to arm with ideology

To fortify and elevate oneself with Marxist-Leninist theories, guiding principles, and policies, so that one will have the ability to resist the various anti-proletarian ideas.
E.g. 由于解除了思想武器，他终于成了香风臭气的俘虏、人民的罪人。*Because he removed his ideological armament, he finally became a slave to fragrant breezes and putrid airs and a criminal.*

思想性 sīxiǎngxìng
ideological character

Progressive political tendencies manifested in writing, literature and art.
E.g. 这是一篇思想性很强的作品。*This is a work with a strong ideological character.*

思想修养 sīxiǎng xiūyǎng
ideological cultivation

Through practical experience in society, the training and level attained by people in such areas as moral character and understanding.

思想意识 sīxiǎng yìshi
ideological consciousness

The reflection of objective reality in a

person's mind, which includes his way of looking at and handling a thing. In class society, ideological consciousness has class character.
E.g. 资产阶级思想意识 *bourgeois ideological consciousness*

思想政治工作 sīxiǎng zhèngzhì gōngzuò
ideological and political work
Solving the problems that people have in their thoughts, viewpoints, and political stances, mobilizing the masses of cadres and people to work diligently for the present practical situation and long-range revolutionary goals.
E.g. 要加强大学生的思想政治工作，使他们都能愉快地服从祖国的分配。 *We must strengthen ideological and political work on college graduates, so that they can all contentedly obey the motherland's job allocations.*

思想作风 sīxiǎng zuòfēng
ideological style
A person's attitudes and behavior manifested in his daily life, work, study, and the ways in which he treats people and deals with matters. These reflect the person's ideological consciousness and level of understanding.
E.g. 思想作风端正。 *The ideological style is correct.*

私倒 sīdǎo
private sector profiteering (through operating on the market); individuals or private groups engaged in this type of profiteering

私房 sīfáng
privately owned housing

私活 sīhuó
private business or affairs

私了 sīliǎo
to settle out of court

私企 sīqǐ
private enterprise
Abbreviation for 私人企业.
E.g. 审批私企的程序要简化。 *The procedure for approving private enterprises must be simplified.*

私售 sīshòu
to sell privately

私校 sī-xiào
private school

私养 sīyǎng
private animal husbandry
To raise domestic livestock privately.

私有化 sīyǒuhuà
privatization

私字当头 sīzì dāngtóu
the character "private" over one's head
The mentality and behavior of considering all matters only from the standpoint of one's own private interests, with no regard for others or for collective interests.

私枭 sīxiāo
head of a smuggling ring

司乘人员 sīchéng rényuán
driver and attendant (on a public vehicle)
Abbreviation for 司机 and 乘客.

司售人员 sī-shòu rényuán
drivers and ticket collectors
Abbreviation for 司机 and 售票员 on buses and trolleys.

丝绸之路 sīchóu zhīlù
the Silk Road

死不改悔 sǐbù gǎihuǐ
unrepentant even to death; absolute-

ly recalcitrant

死分活评 sǐfēn huópíng
fixed and variable assignment of work points
A method of work point allocation practiced by some rural production teams. 死分 fixed allocation means determining the basic work points for completing certain tasks on the basis of their difficulty. 活评 variable evaluation means making an evaluation according to the strength of each worker and his work attitude and quality. The number of work points a person gets in the end is based on these two factors.

死光武器 sǐguāng wǔqì
death ray weapon; laser weapon

死缓 sǐhuǎn
death penalty with reprieve
Abbreviated legal terminology for a death penalty with a two-year reprieve, during which the criminal undergoes labor reform and is put under observation (for a possible change in the sentence).

死教材 sǐjiàocái
fixed teaching material
Teaching material that cannot be changed at will; also teaching material that is divorced from reality. It is the opposite of 活教材 flexible teaching material.

死教条 sǐjiàotiáo
rigid doctrinairism
An especially stubborn brand of doctrinairism. (cf. 教条主义)

死老虎 sǐlǎohǔ
dead tiger
A metaphor for a powerful person who has been overthrown or has lost his prowess.

死面 sǐmiàn
dead side
A metaphor for an area unaffected by a trend or atmosphere.

死亡婚姻 sǐwáng hūnyīn
dead marriage
A marital relationship by which a couple stays together despite being totally and hopelessly estranged.

死硬派 sǐyìngpài
an individual or group with an unyielding attitude and who stubbornly sticks to its stance

四边地 sìbiāndì
four edge lands
The odd scattered pieces of land on the edges of houses, roads, rivers, and hills.

四不清干部 sìbùqīng gànbù
four types of impure cadres
指在"四清"运动中揭露出来的,在政治、经济、思想和组织四个方面有问题的干部。
Cadres shown during the Four Cleanups Movement to have problems in the four areas of politics, economics, ideology, and organization. (cf. 社会主义教育运动)

四大 sìdà
the four bigs
大鸣、大放、大字报、大辩论的简称。
Abbreviation for four things with the word "big" in them: expressing views in a big way, releasing ideas in a big way, big character posters, and big debate. These were four methods advocated in 1966 as a means of promoting the Cultural Revolution.

四大件 sìdàjiàn
four big items
Early on these were: washing machine, watch, sewing machine and transistor radio; later they became: electric fan, washing machine, refrigerator and television.

四大自由 sìdà zìyóu
four big freedoms
Freedom to buy and sell land, freedom to hire workers, freedom to borrow and lend, freedom to conduct trade. They were advocated by some people after China had entered the socialist revolutionary stage, and were criticized.

四当年工程 sìdāngnián gōngchéng
four-steps-in-a-year construction
Construction projects in which the survey, design, construction, and putting into operation all occur in the same year. This is an erroneous, overly ambitious method which goes against the basic laws of construction.

四二一综合症 sì'èryī zōnghé zhèng
the four-two-one syndrome
指独生子女特有的一种不良习惯。因这种不良习惯是由于祖辈四人（祖父、祖母、外祖父、外祖母）、父辈二人（父亲、母亲）共同宠爱和娇惯而形成的，故称。
The malady of being a spoiled only child of two parents and four grandparents.

四个窗口 sì gè chuāngkǒu
four windows
指技术的窗口、管理的窗口、知识的窗口、对外政策的窗口。指特区对外四个方面的作用。
Technology window, management window, knowledge window, foreign policy window (in reference to the four areas in which the special economic zones have brought about positive effects).

四个第一 sì gè dì-yī
four firsts
即"人的因素第一，政治工作第一，思想工作第一，活的思想第一"的简称。这是林彪于1960年提出的中国人民解放军进行思想政治工作所遵循的一条原则，是他"精神万能"思想的表现。
Abbreviated term for "top priority to the human factor, top priority to political work, top priority to ideological work, and top priority to flexible thinking". This was a principle which Lin Biao proposed in 1960 for the Chinese People's Liberation Army to follow when conducting ideological and political work. It was a manifestation of his concept of "spiritual omnipotence".

四个落实 sì gè luòshí
four practicalities
指在职工教育工作中要抓好"思想落实，计划落实，组织落实和措施落实"。
In the work of educating employees, practicality in four areas must be firmly adhered to: ideology, planning, organization, and measures.

四个伟大 sì gè wěidà
four greats
指林彪在"文化大革命"中大搞个人崇拜时加在毛泽东名字前边的四个修饰语。原话为"伟大的导师、伟大的领袖、伟大的统帅、伟大的舵手"。
The four attributives which Lin Biao added to Mao Zedong's name when he promoted Mao's personality cult during the Cultural Revolution. The original

wording was "great teacher, great leader, great commander, and great helmsman".

四个现代化 sì gè xiàndàihuà
four modernizations

指现代化的农业、现代化的工业、现代化的国防和现代化的科学技术。

Modernization in agriculture, industry, defense, and science and technology.

四个一样 sì gè yīyàng
four sames

The earnest, practical, and realistic work attitude of the Daqing Oilfield workers. The four sames are: day and night are the same, bad weather and good weather are the same, the leadership not present is the same as when the leadership is present, not to be investigated is the same as being investigated.

四害 sìhài
four pestilences

原指危害人民健康的四种动物，即老鼠、臭虫、苍蝇和蚊子。1976年后，人民也把"四人帮"称为"四害"。

Originally, the four animals that endanger people's health, i.e., rats, bedbugs, flies, and mosquitoes. After 1976, people also called the Gang of Four the four pestilences. (cf. 四人帮)

四好 sìhǎo
four goods

即"政治思想好、三八作风好、军事训练好、生活管理好"。这是六十、七十年代在中国人民解放军中开展的一项评选先进连队的运动，也称"四好连队运动"或"四好运动"。"文革"中一些地方单位也开展过这项运动，评选过"四好连队"。

To be good in political ideology, in the three-eight working style (cf. 三八作风), in military training, and in management of everyday life. The People's Liberation Army launched a movement during the 1960s and 1970s to evaluate and select advanced companies. The movement was called 四好连队运动 four-goods company movement or 四好运动 four-goods movement. During the Cultural Revolution, some local units also launched this movement, and selected four-goods companies.

四好家长 sìhǎo jiāzhǎng
four-good parents

指在"培养目标正确，教育思想好；教育子女德、智、体全面发展好；坚持正面教育，教育方法好；以身作则，言传身教好"，这四个方面做得都比较好的学生家长。Parents (of students) who have done well in these four areas: 1) correct goals in raising children, good educational philosophy; 2) good at educating the children in all aspects — morally, intellectually, and physically; 3) persevering in positive education, and good educational methods; 4) serving as a model, good at giving verbal instructions and acting as an example to follow.

四化 sìhuà
four-izations

1) Abbreviation for the 四个现代化 four modernizations. 2) In promoting cadres, the 四化 four-izations to be emphasized are 革命化 revolutionization, 年轻化 youth-ization, 知识化 knowledge-ization, and 专业化 specialization. Also called 干部四化 four-izations of cadres.

四环素 sìhuánsù
tetracycline

四荒 sìhuāng
four uncultivated areas
Uncultivated hills, beaches, water, and scattered pieces of land everywhere.

四旧 sìjiù
four olds
指"文化大革命"期间提出要破除的旧思想、旧文化、旧风俗、旧习惯。
The old ideology, old culture, old customs, and old habits that were targeted for destruction during the Cultural Revolution.

四类分子 sì lèi fènzǐ
four elements
指地主分子、富农分子、反革命分子和坏分子。他们是人民民主专政的对象。1979年以后,中央决定全部摘掉地主、富农分子的帽子。
Landlords, rich peasants, counter-revolutionaries, and bad elements. They were the targets for the people's democratic dictatorship. After 1979, the central government exonerated the landlords and rich peasants.

四马分肥 sìmǎ fēnféi
four horses dividing up the fat
The profit allocation system adopted before the 1956 implementation of public-private joint management in the entire industry. That is, the profits from an enterprise were divided approximately equally among four sectors: taxes paid to the state, the enterprise's public accumulation funds, employees' welfare and bonus funds, and the investors' dividends, and bonuses.

四旁 sìpáng
four sides
1) Areas to the front and back, right and left. 2) Specifically, the four areas to attend to in tree planting and afforestation, which are: by residential homes, villages, water, and roads.
E.g. 要实现四旁绿化。 *We must achieve the program of tree planting in the four side areas.*

四清 sìqīng
Four Cleanups
即社会主义教育运动,也叫四清运动。这是中国在1963年至1965年间先后在部分农村和少数城市工矿企业及学校开展的一次清政治、清经济、清组织、清思想运动。
Abbreviation for 社会主义教育运动 Socialist Education Movement, also called 四清运动 Four Cleanups Movement. It was a movement, launched between 1963 and 1965 in some of China's rural areas and a few urban industrial and mining enterprises and schools and was intended, to clean up politics, economics, organizations, and ideology.

四人帮 sìrénbāng
Gang of Four
指"文化大革命"中以江青(当时任中共中央政治局委员)为首,张春桥(曾任中共中央政治局常委、国务院副总理)、王洪文(当时任中共中央副主席)、姚文元(曾任中共中央政治局委员)为主要成员的反革命阴谋集团。
The counter-revolutionary conspiratorial clique during the Cultural Revolution, headed by Jiang Qing (at the time a member of the Political Bureau of the Chinese Communist Party Central Committee), with the leading members being Zhang Chunqiao (at one time a standing member of the Political Bureau of the Chinese Communist Party Central

Committee and Vice-Premier of State Council), Wang Hongwen (at the time Vice-Chairman of the Chinese Communist Party Central Committee), and Yao Wenyuan (at one time a member of the Political Bureau of the Chinese Communist Party Central Committee).

四属户 sìshǔhù
four categories of family dependents
The dependent families of revolutionary martyrs, military personnel, cadres, and workers.

四提倡、四反对 sìtíchàng sìfǎnduì
four things advocated and four things opposed
即提倡节俭,反对大办婚事;提倡男女平等、敬养老人,反对歧视、虐待妇女、老人;提倡相信科学,反对封建迷信;提倡健康的文化娱乐,反对赌博。这是1982年底在"五讲四美"活动中所开展的宣传教育运动。
Advocate frugality, oppose extravagant weddings; advocate equality of sexes, and respect and care for the elderly, oppose discrimination and maltreatment of women and the elderly; advocate belief in science, oppose feudal superstition; advocate healthy cultural entertainment, oppose gambling. This was the substance of the propaganda and education activities launched in the 五讲四美 five particulars and four beautifuls campaign at the end of 1982. (cf. 五讲四美)

四通一平 sìtōng yīpíng
four throughs and one level
指基本建设工程正式开工前应具备的条件。"四通"指水通、电通、道路通、通讯线路通;"一平"指施工场地平。有时由于所说的内容多少不一, 也称"三通一平"、"五通一平"等。
The conditions that must be in place before a basic construction project can be formally launched. The four throughs refer to water supply, electricity, roads, and postal service; the one level refers to leveling the construction site. Sometimes, in reference to a different number of conditions, terms such as 三通一平 three throughs and one level and 五通一平 five throughs and one level are also used.

四无限 sìwúxiàn
four infinites
指"文化大革命"中林彪、四人帮提出的政治口号,指对毛泽东、毛泽东思想、毛主席革命路线的所谓"无限热爱、无限信仰、无限崇拜、无限忠诚"。
(Political slogan promoted by Lin Biao and the Gang of Four during the Cultural Revolution) the four infinites: infinite love, trust, worship, and loyalty for Mao Zedong, his thoughts, and his revolutionary line.

四·五运动 Sì Wǔ Yùndòng
April Fifth Movement
The mass movement that erupted around the Qingming Festival (Tomb-Sweeping Day, April 4) in 1976 at Beijing's Tian'anmen Square and in many other cities. The movement was to commemorate Zhou Enlai, oppose the Gang of Four, and oppose the criticisms leveled at Deng Xiaoping. The demonstrations occurred on April fifth, hence it is called the April Fifth Movement.

四务缠身 sìwù chánshēn
burdened with four duties
指中年知识分子负担过重,业务、政

务、党务和家务(简称"四务")都要承担。The phenomenon among middle-aged intellectuals of having to shoulder heavy burdens in four areas: professional duties, political duties, Party duties, and domestic duties.

四项基本原则 sì xiàng jīběn yuánzé
four basic principles

邓小平于 1979 年 3 月明确提出"坚持社会主义道路；坚持无产阶级专政；坚持共产党的领导；坚持马列主义、毛泽东思想"。简称"四项基本原则"。这是中国共产党长期以来一贯坚持的原则，也是实现四个现代化的根本保证。

Abbreviation for the principles which Deng Xiaoping enunciated in March of 1979. They concern four things that must be upheld: the socialist path, proletarian dictatorship, leadership of the Communist Party, and Marxism-Leninism and Mao Zedong Thought. These are the principles that have always been upheld by the Chinese Communist Party, and are the basic things that guarantee the realization of the four modernizations.

四项政治保证 sì xiàng zhèngzhì bǎozhèng
four political guarantees

指中国进行社会主义现代化建设的四项政治保证。即"进行机构改革和经济体制改革，实现干部队伍的革命化、年轻化、知识化、专业化；建设社会主义精神文明；打击经济领域和其他领域内破坏社会主义的犯罪活动；整顿党的作风和组织。"这是邓小平在 1982 年 9 月中共十二大的开幕词中提出的。

The four political guarantees that go along with China's socialist modernization construction. They are: 1) implementation of reform in organizations and the economic system, realization of revolutionization, youth-ization, knowledge-ization, and specialization among the cadre ranks; 2) building socialist spiritual enlightenment; 3) striking at criminal activities, in economic and other realms, that damage socialism; and 4) rectification of the work style and organization of the Party. This was proposed by Deng Xiaoping in his opening speech to the Twelfth Congress of the Chinese Communist Party in September 1982.

四小龙 sìxiǎolóng
Four Little Dragons

The four Asian nations or areas of Taiwan, South Korea, Singapore, and Hong Kong where the economy has developed very rapidly.

四新 sìxīn
four news

指"文化大革命"期间提出的"新思想、新文化、新风俗、新习惯"。

New ideology, new culture, new customs, and new habits that were proposed during the Cultural Revolution.

四野 Sì-Yě
the Fourth Field Army of the Chinese People's Liberation Army

Abbreviation for 中国人民解放军第四野战军.

四有 sìyǒu
four haves

即有理想、有道德、有文化、有纪律。

To have ideals, morality, culture, and discipline.

E.g. 四有教育 *four-haves education* /

培养四有的一代新人 to cultivate a new generation of people with the four haves

四有三讲两不怕 sìyǒu sānjiǎng liǎngbùpà

four things to have, three things to attend to, and two things not to fear

中国人民解放军总政治部1981年2月向全军提出的口号。"四有"是：有理想、有道德、有知识、有体力；"三讲"是：讲军容、讲礼貌、讲纪律；"两不怕"是：不怕艰难困苦、不怕流血牺牲。1983年1月，总政治部又对"四有三讲两不怕"的内容进行了调整，调整后的内容是"有理想、有道德、有文化、有纪律；讲军容、讲礼貌、讲卫生；不怕艰难困苦、不怕流血牺牲。

A slogan that originated in the General Political Department of the Chinese People's Liberation Army and was presented to the entire army in February 1981. The four things to have are: ideals, morality, knowledge, and physical strength; the three things to attend to are: military decorum, courtesy, and discipline; the two things to not fear are: difficulties, and bloodshed and sacrifice. In January 1983, the General Political Department revised the content of the above to the following: have ideals, morality, culture, and discipline; attend to military decorum, courtesy, and hygiene; have no fear of difficulties, and bloodshed and sacrifice.

四专一包 sìzhuān yībāo

four specialities and one contract

农业生产责任制形式之一。即在生产队或生产大队统一经营的前提下，把林、牧、副、渔、工、商各业，分别组成专业队、专业组、专业户和专业工进行承包，实行联产计酬，超产奖励、减产受罚的制度。这种形式叫做多种经营和工副业"四专一包"责任制。

A form of the rural production responsibility system. Under the premise of unified management by the production team or brigade, the various enterprises of forestry, animal husbandry, sidelines, fishery, industry, and commerce are organized and contracted to speciality teams, speciality groups, speciality households, and individuals. Remuneration is based on production, rewards for exceeding quotas, and penalties for falling short of quotas. This form is called the "four specialities and one contract" responsibility system for diversified production and industrial sidelines.

四自精神 sìzì jīngshén

the four-self spirit

指妇女应具备的"自尊、自爱、自重和自强"的精神。1983年第五次全国妇女代表大会提出。

The spirit of self-respect, self-love, personal dignity, and self-strengthening which women should have. This was proposed at the Fifth National Congress of Women in 1983.

四自一联 sìzì yīlián

four things to do oneself and one unity

"自修门前路，自通门前水，自栽门前树，自搞门前卫生；统一规划，联合行动"的简称。这是在新时期的爱国卫生运动中创建的一种卫生责任制。

Abbreviated term for each household

maintaining the street, sewage, trees, and sanitation in front of its own house, to be done with unity in plan and action. This is a sanitation responsibility system established in the Patriotic Health Campaign of the new era.

饲养员 sìyǎngyuán
stockman

song

松绑 sōngbǎng
to unfetter
Metaphor' for removing unreasonable regulations and systems.
E.g. 为企业松绑 *to unfetter enterprises*

松脆 sōngcuì
(of foods) light and crisp, very refreshing to taste

松口鞋 sōngkǒuxié
shoes with an elastic opening
Shoe with an elastic band over the opening. Also called 懒汉鞋 loafer.

松垮 sōngkuǎ
loosely constructed, easy to fall apart

松松垮垮 sōngsōngkuǎkuǎ
a slack, relaxed work style

颂古非今 sònggǔ fēijīn
extol the ancient and negate the present
To sing the praise of ancient things, and to negate present-day things.

送审 sòngshěn
to send (a report or memo) to a supervisor for examination and comment

送养人 sòngyǎngrén
donors for adoption
People who legally give up their own natural-born children for others to raise as their own.

sou

馊主意 sōuzhǔyi
a lousy or rotten idea

su

苏区 sūqū
the Chinese Soviet Areas
Communist base during the Second Internal Revolutionary War, modeled after the Soviets.

俗众 súzhòng
popular; belonging to the masses
E.g. 俗众文化兴起。 *Mass culture is on the rise.*

素肉 sùròu
vegetarian meats
Various imitation meats made from plant food products such as beans.

速成材 sùchéngcái
fast growing wood
Wood from trees that can grow and mature relatively quickly.

速成识字法 sùchéng shízìfǎ
accelerated literacy method
A speedy method of acquiring literacy.

速递 sùdì
express delivery
Also called 快递.

速冻 sùdòng
quick frozen
E.g. 速冻器 *quick freezing device* / 速冻厂 *quick freezing plant* / 速冻蔬菜 *quick frozen vegetables*

速滑 sùhuá
speed skating
Abbreviation for 速度滑冰.

速溶 sùróng
fast dissolving; instant
Able to dissolve quickly in water under certain temperatures.
E.g. 速溶奶粉 *instant milk powder* / 速溶咖啡 *instant coffee*

速生丰产林 sùshēng fēngchǎnlín
fast-growing high-yield woods
Wood from tree species that were especially selected for fast growth. Their special characteristics are: fast growth, low investment, high return.

速效 sùxiào
quick acting
Able to produce results quickly.
E.g. 速效肥料 *quick acting fertilizer*

塑料 sùliào
plastic

塑料壁纸 sùliào bìzhǐ
plastic wallpaper

塑料袋 sùliàodài
plastic bags

塑料贴面 sùliào tiēmiàn
plastic facing
Thin sheets made of plastic which are stuck to the surfaces of furniture to enhance strength, durability, and appearance.

塑料鞋 sùliàoxié
plastic shoes

肃反 sù–fǎn
root out counter-revolutionaries
Abbreviation for 肃清反革命分子. The term refers specifically to the campaign launched in 1955 to root out hidden counter-revolutionaries.

肃反扩大化 sù–fǎn kuòdàhuà
expansion of the rooting out campaign
In the campaign to root out counter-revolutionaries, due to leftist interference, some people, who were not counter-revolutionaries were erroneously treated as counter-revolutionaries. The area of attack had thus expanded beyond what had been appropriate. (cf. 肃反)

肃贪 sù–tān
to eradicate graft and bribery

suan

酸豆乳 suāndòurǔ
soy yogurt (lit., sour soy milk)
A semi-solid food made by fermenting soy milk. It contains several aminoacids, and is similar to yogurt.

酸奶 suānnǎi
yogurt

酸雨 suānyǔ
acid rain
Rain which contains dissolved oxides of sulphur, nitrogen and carbon which have entered the atmosphere through industrial pollution. When the rain falls to the earth it can make the soil acidic and thus adversely affect the health of plants, animals and ultimately humans.

sui

随份子 suífènzi
to contribute a share toward a group gift

随军 suí–jūn
to follow the troops

Referring specifically to family dependents of military personnel.

随行就市 suí háng jiù shì
(re commodities) **prices fluctuating in response to market conditions**

随身听 suíshēntīng
Walkman

sun

损公肥私 sǔngōng féisī
damage the public and fatten the private
To seek private gains at the expense of the public.

SUO

缩微 suōwēi
microcopy
缩印 suōyìn
reduced reprint
E.g. 他最近买了一本缩印本的《汉英词典》。Recently, he bought a Chinese-English Dictionary in the reduced format reprint edition.

索贿 suǒhuì
to extort bribes
索赔 suǒpéi
to exact compensation or indemnity
索要 suǒyào
to exact; to demand

T

t

T恤 T-xù
T-shirt

ta

塔吊 tǎdiào
pagoda-shaped crane
It can be moved along on rails, used mainly in construction work.

塔楼 tǎlóu
tower-like building
E.g. 塔楼林立。 *There is a forest of tower-like buildings.*

塔式 tǎshì
pagoda-shaped
E.g. 塔式起重机 *pagoda-shaped cranes*

榻榻米 tàtàmǐ
tatami; floor mats

踏足 tàzú
to set foot on
E.g. 踏足月球 *to set foot on the moon*

tai

胎教 tāijiào
embryo teaching
To provide an expectant mother with a congenial environment and have her engage in activities conducive to the mental and physical development of the child.

苔肥 táiféi
peat fertilizer
An organic fertilizer found in swamps and beneath low-lying land. It is formed from the humus of vegetation such as moss.

抬轿子 táijiàozi
to carry a sedan chair
A metaphor for flattering and currying favor.

台胞 Tái-bāo
Taiwan compatriots
Contraction of 台湾同胞. The People's Republic of China recognizes Taiwan as a part of China, and therefore considers the people of Taiwan compatriots.

台笔 táibǐ
desk pen (with its cap fixed on a stand)

台独 Tái-dú
Taiwan independence
Abbreviation for 台湾独立. The activities of a small proportion of the Taiwanese people who support the idea of an independent nation and obstruct the unification of Taiwan with the mainland.

台港 Tái-Gǎng
Taiwan and Hong Kong

台件 táijiàn
A compound measure, used for expressing the number of devices and machines

E.g. 新组装的机器达 *48* 台件之多。 *There are as many forty-eight newly assembled machines.*

台阶 táijiē

steps; the various levels or ranks through which one moves up professionally; an "out" through which one can extricate oneself from an awkward situation

E.g. 干部要顺着台阶上。 *Cadres must advance through the ranks.* / 改革要再上一个新台阶。 *The reforms must move to a new level.*

台联 Tái-Lián

All-China Federation of Taiwan Compatriots

Abbreviation for 中华全国台湾同胞联谊会.

台盟 Tái-Méng

the Taiwan Democratic Self-Government League

Abbreviation for 台湾民主自治同盟, founded in November 1947.

台扇 táishàn

table fan

台商 Tái-shāng

Taiwanese businessmen

台属 Tái-shǔ

families of people in Taiwan

Family dependents on the mainland of people who have gone to Taiwan.

台资 Táizī

investment by Taiwanese businessmen or a financial institution

跆拳道 táiquándào

taekwondo; kickboxing

A Korean martial art form.

太空笔 tàikōngbǐ

outer space pen (for use in outer space)

太空病 tàikōngbìng

outer space sickness

A set of syndromes that plague astronauts in outer space.

太空城 tàikōngchéng

space city

Satellite in outer space created for human habitation.

太空服 tàikōngfú

space suit

太空垃圾 tàikōng lājī

waste materials (discarded flying objects, etc.) in outer space

Synonymous with 空间垃圾. (cf. 空间垃圾)

太空棉 tàikōngmián

outer space cotton

A super-thin, super-light, highly insulating fabric. Also called 宇航棉.

太空人 tàikōngrén

astronaut

太空食品 tàikōng shípǐn

space food (for astronauts' use)

太空站 tàikōngzhàn

space station

In outer space or on a celestial body. Also called 宇宙站.

太平官 tàipíngguān

a cadre leader who only seeks peace and stability and makes no attempt to accomplish anything

太阳房 tàiyángfáng

sun room (uses solar energy to maintain heat)

太阳镜 tàiyángjìng

sun glasses

Also called 墨镜 dark glasses.

太阳炉 tàiyánglú

solar energy stove

太阳帽 tàiyángmào
sun hat

太阳能 tàiyángnéng
solar energy

太阳能电池 tàiyángnéng diànchí
solar battery

太阳能热水器 tàiyángnéng rèshuǐqì
solar water heater
Also called 太阳热水器.

太阳灶 tàiyángzào
solar stove
Also called 太阳炉 solar furnace.

tan

摊车 tānchē
stall cart
E.g. 个体摊车 private stall carts / 饮食摊车 food and beverage stall carts

摊档 tāndàng
stall for selling things
E.g. 报刊摊档 newspaper and magazine stalls / 私人摊档 private stalls

摊点 tāndiǎn
location of stalls (for selling goods or providing services)
E.g. 流动摊点 floating (mobile) stalls / 个体摊点 private stalls

摊贩 tānfàn
stall vendors

摊棚 tānpéng
stall sheds

摊群 tānqún
cluster of stalls

摊商 tānshāng
stall vendors

摊市 tānshì
an open market made up of stalls

摊书 tānshū
bestsellers
Books that sell fast at little book stalls.
E.g.《中国知青部落》也是摊书。
The "Tribe of Chinese Educated Youths" is also a bestseller.

摊位 tānwèi
stall set up for business; position of a stall

摊主 tānzhǔ
stall manager; stall owner

贪大求全 tāndà qiúquán
greedy of the grandiose
In a constructive undertaking, to not take practical reality as the starting point, but solely seek to do things on a large scale complete with all facilities and departments.

贪大求洋 tāndà qiúyáng
greedy for the big and modern
In a constructive undertaking, to have no regard for the realistic situation and conditions, but blindly seek to do things on a large scale and incorporate advanced facilities.

贪占行为 tānzhàn xíngwéi
greedy behavior
Using the power of one's position to illegally appropriate things that belong to the state or to the collective.

弹拨乐 tánbōyuè
string music (played by plucking)

弹钢琴 tángāngqín
to play the piano
A metaphor for the work method of mapping out an overall scheme with due consideration for all the parts.

弹劾 tánhé
to impeach (a public official)

弹力衫 tánlìshān

stretch shirts
Athletic shirts, tops, etc., knitted from elastic fibers. They are quite elastic and crimpy.

坛坛罐罐 tántánguànguàn
jars and cans
Equivalent to pots and pans in English, the various household goods of daily life.

谈心活动 tánxīn huódòng
heart talk activity
Comrades speaking frankly and sincerely to each other from their hearts and exchanging thoughts.

谈资 tánzī
material for conversation or small talk

坦诚 tǎnchéng
frank and sincere
Contraction of 坦率诚恳.

探查 tànchá
to observe and investigate
E.g. 探查情况 *to observe and investigate the situation*

探察 tànchá
to probe and investigate

探风 tànfēng
to probe for information; to watch for developments

探家 tànjiā
(re persons working away from home) to go home and visit one's family

探空气球 tànkōng qìqiú
sounding balloon
A balloon for taking radio sound equipment up into the atmosphere.

探明 tànmíng
to explore, survey, and determine (mineral deposits, etc.)

探摸 tànmō
to grope for
E.g. 探摸东西 *to grope for things*

探亲假 tànqīnjià
home leaves
Leave periods for cadres, workers, and employees of the state, who live apart from their parents or spouses, to go home to visit or be reunited with their families, in accordance with the relevant national regulations.

探视 tànshì
to visit (a patient in a hospital or a convict in a penitentiary)
E.g. 探视病人 *to visit a patient*

tang

唐人街 tángrénjiē
Chinatown

糖弹 táng-dàn
sugar-coated bullet
Abbreviation for 糖衣炮弹. (cf. 糖衣炮弹)

糖衣炮弹 tángyī pàodàn
sugar-coated bullet
A metaphor for the tactics used to draw in and corrupt someone (revolutionaries during the Cultural Revolution). Abbreviated as 糖弹.

tao

逃单 táodān
(hotel) bill evasion; to slip away from a hotel without paying the bill
E.g. 逃单现象屡有发生。 *There are frequent cases of people slipping away from hotels without paying the bill.*

逃汇 táohuì
evasion of foreign exchange regulations
Using illegal tactics to circumvent the state's control over foreign exchange.

逃跑主义 táopǎo zhǔyì
flightism
Adopting an attitude of compromise and avoidance when faced with circumstances or matters that are not favorable to oneself.

逃票 táopiào
to sneak through without a ticket
E.g. 逃票者 ticket evader / 逃票现象严重。 *The phenomenon of ticket evading is serious.*

逃亡地主 táowáng dìzhǔ
fugitive landlords
Landlord elements who ran away when their home areas were liberated or about to be liberated during the Third Internal Revolutionary War period.

逃夜 táoyè
(mainly re juveniles) to sneak out overnight

陶雕 táodiāo
ceramic carving; sculpted ceramic art objects

陶艺 táoyì
ceramic art
E.g. 陶艺巨匠 *a great master of ceramics*

套裁 tàocái
to fit together and cut pieces for two or more garments to minimize waste of fabric
E.g. 为顾客套裁半成品裤料 *to pre-cut trouser fabric in sets to minimize waste for customers*

套餐 tàocān
set meal at a restaurant (vs. a la carte), includes several courses

套服 tàofú
coordinated outfit; suit
Also called 套装.

套改 tàogǎi
a systematic change in ranks and titles
E.g. 工资套改 *to make a systematic change in wages*

套购 tàogòu
fraudulent purchase
To purchase state controlled commodities or commodities in short supply through such improper tactics as deception or using connections.
E.g. 套购粮食 *to purchase grains fraudulently*

套红 tàohóng
(in printing) to add parts in red to a layout
E.g. 套红出版 *to add red to the layout and to publish*

套话 tàohuà
empty conventional talk
Speech or writing that is hollow, formulaic, and without substance.

套换 tàohuàn
to purchase or exchange (mainly currency) illegally
E.g. 套换外汇券 *to exchange foreign certificates illegally*

套汇 tàohuì
to profiteer by dealing in foreign currencies

套利 tàolì
to get profit by improper means in a business operation

套裙 tàoqún
matching skirt

A skirt that forms a set with a matching top.

套书 tàoshū
sets of book; book series

套用 tàoyòng
to indiscriminately and formulaically apply a method or model
E.g. 套用外国文艺作品的内容和形式 To adopt the content and form of foreign works of art and literature indiscriminately / 农业改革不能套用工业的办法 In agricultural reforms, we must not indiscriminately apply the methods used in industry.

套种 tàozhòng
intercropping
To sow a second crop between rows of a first crop during the first crop's latter stage of growth. This is a way of fully utilizing the land and growth period to increase productivity. Also called 套作.

套装 tàozhuāng
coordinated outfit
Synonymous with 套服.

te

特版 tèbǎn
special edition

特等劳模 tèděng láomó
special class model workers
Special class, most outstanding model workers. It is an honorary title that departments of the Chinese government bestow on workers who have made outstanding achievements in socialist construction.

特稿 tègǎo
special manuscript; especially commissioned manuscript
E.g. 发表特稿 to publish a special manuscript

特工 tègōng
secret service
Abbreviation for 特别工作. The term usually refers to the activities of spying and carrying out sabotage in the enemy's camp.
E.g. 特工部门 secret service department/ 特工人员 secret service agents

特供 tègòng
to provide especially; things provided especially
E.g. 取消领导特供 to rescind the system of providing goods especially to leaders

特护 tèhù
intensive care (for patients)
E.g. 特护病房 intensive care rooms (in a hospital)

特辑 tèjí
special issue (of a magazine, etc.)
A written work, newspaper, magazine, or movie that was based on a special topic.

特集 tèjí
anthology

特级教师 tèjí jiàoshī
special-class teacher
An honorary title which the relevant departments of the Chinese government bestow on people who have made outstanding achievements in the following categories: teachers in a nursery, elementary, and secondary schools, research personnel in teaching and research institutions, and leaders of professionals in educational organs.

特级战斗英雄 tèjí zhàndòu

yīngxióng
special-class combat heroes

Special-class, most outstanding combat heroes. An honorary title bestowed upon those officers and men of the Chinese People's Liberation Army and those militiamen who were especially meritorious in combat.

特教 tèjiào
special education

Abbreviation for 特殊教育.

E.g. 特教师资 / *special education teachers* / 特教学校 *special education school*

特警 tèjǐng
policemen assigned to special duties

特快 tèkuài
express (mail, transport, etc.); express bus or train

E.g. 特快列车 *express train* / 长途电话特快业务 *express long distance telephone service*

特困 tèkùn
especially difficult; special difficulties

特困户 tèkùnhù
households with special difficulties

特困生 tèkùnshēng
students whose family circumstances are especially difficult

E.g. 要解决特困生问题。 *We must solve the problem of students whose family circumstances are difficult.*

特批 tèpī
special approval

E.g. 经过特批这家公司成立了。 *After receiving special approval, this company was established.*

特区 tèqū
special zone

An area where special political, economic, or other specific policies apply.

E.g. 深圳经济特区 *the Shenzhen Special Economic Zone*

特权阶层 tèquán jiēcéng
privileged stratum

特首 tèshǒu
chief executive of a special administrative area (Hong Kong and Macao)

Abbreviation for (香港、澳门)特别行政区行政长官.

特殊化 tèshūhuà
to become special

The nature and situation of a certain matter differing from the ordinary.

E.g. 生活特殊化 *to become special (especially privileged) in everyday life*

特殊教育 tèshū jiàoyù
special education (for those with handicaps or learning disabilities)

特体 tètǐ
unusual physical build (re clothing, hats, shoes, etc.)

E.g. 特体柜台 *counters stocked with special-sized clothing* / 特体服装 *special-sized clothing*

特味 tèwèi
(re cuisine) special regional flavor

E.g. 特味加工 / *special-flavor processing* / 特味糕点 *special-flavor cake*

特嫌 tèxián
spy suspect

To be suspected of being a spy; someone suspected of being a spy.

特型演员 tèxíng yǎnyuán
performers with certain unusual appearances, such as an uncanny likeness to a high-level leader

特需 tèxū
to have a special need

E.g. 特需商品 *commodities in special*

特许经营 tèxǔ jīngyíng
specially permitted business

A method of sales and service. People who have been given special permission offer the rights of their trademark, brand, technology or management to merchants who run a business that requires special permission (e.g., arms sales). A certain proportion of the profits from the merchant's sales is remitted to the owner of the trademark, brand, etc.

特邀代表 tèyāo dàibiǎo
special representatives

Representatives who were especially invited.

特医 tèyī
special medical care

E.g. 对病人采取特医特护措施 *to provide patients with special medical and nursing care*

特艺 tèyì
special type of handicraft

Abbreviation for 特种工艺.

E.g. 特艺工厂 *factory for special handicrafts* / 特艺产品 *special handicraft products*

特异功能 tèyì gōngnéng
exceptional function

Special abilities of some people's physical faculties, such as special acuity in hearing or vision.

特优 tèyōu
exceedingly excellent or outstanding

E.g. 特优合格证书 *certificate of excellence*

特优生 tèyōushēng
outstanding student

Students who excel in academic studies and have an outstanding character.

E.g. 他当上了特优生。 *He was named outstanding student.*

特招 tèzhāo
to recruit especially

特诊 tèzhěn
special medical treatment

E.g. 特诊科 / *special medical treatment section* / 特诊中心 *special medical treatment center* / 挂特诊号 *to register for special medical treatment*

teng

腾出 téngchū
to clear out or vacate to make space for something else

E.g. 腾出住房 *to vacate rooms* / 腾出手 *to free someone from the task at hand* / 腾出时间 *to free up time* / 腾出资金 *to free up capital*

腾飞 téngfēi
to soar

A metaphor for radical changes or rapid development.

E.g. 要使中华民族腾飞不改革是不行的。 *Reforms are absolutely necessary if our nation is to soar.*

腾让 téngràng

Synonymous with 腾出 (cf. 腾出).

E.g. 腾让出码头 *to free up a docking space*

腾退 téngtuì
to vacate or withdraw from (housing, land, etc.)

E.g. 腾退私房 *to vacate a private room* / 腾退所占土地 *to vacate occupied land*

tī

梯次 tīcì
the various layers of an organized scheme
E.g. 合理布局，梯次推进。*Lay out plans rationally, push forward step by step, roll the development along.*

梯队 tīduì
(military) echelon; a level within an organization arranged in tier formation
E.g. 干部队伍要保持梯队结构。*The ranking of cadres must remain tiered.*

踢皮球 tī píqiú
kick the ball
1) A game in which a ball is kicked.
2) A metaphor for the work style of pushing jobs around, never really dealing with them.
E.g. 官僚主义者就是喜欢踢皮球。*Bureaucrats just love to kick the ball around.*

提纯复壮 tíchún fùzhuàng
purification and rejuvenation
Measures in propagating good strains of crops. With the objective of excluding inferior strains and maintaining purity, the best that are chosen; genealogical lines are separately compared, then they are crossbred to produce new strains.

提干 tígàn
promoting cadres
1) To promote cadres.
E.g. 提干工作 *the work of promoting cadres*
2) To be promoted to the rank of a cadre.
E.g. 他提干已经两年了。*It's been two years since he was promoted to the rank of a cadre.*

提级 tíjí
to upgrade or be upgraded in salary or rank

提价 tíjià
to raise the price
E.g. 提价幅度 *extent of price increase*

提留 tíliú
to deduct (from income)
To take out a portion of the total income for public accumulation funds, public welfare funds, and other expenses.

提速 tísù
to accelerate (of a train)
E.g. 提速实验 *speed acceleration test (experiment)* / 提速列车 *accelerating train* / 提速区段 *accelerating section*

提掖 tíyè
to promote and support
E.g. 提掖后进 *to promote and support the backward*

提职 tízhí
to upgrade or be upgraded in professional position or title

提租补贴 tízū bǔtiē
rent increase subsidy (subsidy provided to countervail against a rent increase so that the financial burden on renters does not increase)

题海战术 tíhǎi zhànshù
problem ocean tactic
The teaching method of giving students a massive number of problems to do for homework (abbreviated as 题海战).

题库 tíkù
question bank; a file containing a large pool of exam questions

题外话 tíwàihuà

a digression in a conversation

题写 tíxiě

to write an inscription or to autograph

E.g. 题写书名 *to inscribe the book title*

体改 tǐ-gǎi

organizational reform

Abbreviation for 体制改革.

E.g. 体改试点 *trial units for organizational reform* / 体改研究会 *research committee on organizational reform* / 体改工作 *organizational reform work*

体改委 Tǐ-Gǎi-Wěi

organizational reform committee

Abbreviation for 体制改革委员会.

体工队 tǐ-gōng-duì

physical education work team

Abbreviation for 体育工作大队.

体检 tǐ-jiǎn

physical exam; health checkup

E.g. 体检表 / *physical exam chart* / 体检材料 *physical exam material*

体力劳动 tǐlì láodòng

physical labor

It is the opposite of 脑力劳动 mental labor.

体疗 tǐ-liáo

physical therapy (for treating various ailments)

Abbreviation for 体育疗法.

体能 tǐnéng

physical ability (manifested in sports)

体坛 tǐtán

world of sports

体外受精 tǐwàishòujīng

in vitro fertilization

体外循环 tǐwài xúnhuán

external circulation

A metaphor for funds not circulating within the normal sphere.

体委 tǐ-wěi

physical culture and sports committee

Abbreviation for 体育运动委员会.

体校 tǐ-xiào

sports school

Contraction of 体育学校, middle schools that specialize in training athletes in various sports.

体院 tǐ-yuàn

institute of physical culture

Contraction of 体育学院.

替补 tìbǔ

to replace and replenish; replacement team members; reserves

替补队员 tìbǔ duìyuán

(in sports) replacement team members; second string players; reserves

替身演员 tìshēn yǎnyuán

stunt man

剃光头 tìguāngtóu

to shave the head

A metaphor for not getting a single point in a competition, or not having a single person within a unit pass an exam.

tian

天安门事件 Tiān'ānmén Shìjiàn

Tian'anmen Incident

Also called 四·五运动. (cf. 四·五运动)

天才论 tiāncáilùn

theory of geniuses

An a priori proposition that some people are born geniuses and that history is made by geniuses. Lin Biao at one time used this theory as the theoretical principle on which he usurped Party authority and state power.

天价 tiānjià
sky price
Refers to the peak price in stock quotations.

天量 tiānliàng
sky volume
Refers to an extremely large quantity.
E.g. 成交再创天量。 *The volume of transactions again reached sky volume.*

天南海北 tiānnán hǎiběi
south of heaven and north of the sea
1) Everywhere (in China or the world).
2) A facetious way of referring to the four major cities of Tianjin, Nanjing, Shanghai, and Beijing. The name of each of these cities contains a character found in the phrase 天南海北. It is a pun used by college graduates about to be assigned to jobs. Some of them say they are willing to be assigned to 天南海北 (ostensibly meaning anywhere in China, but actually meaning the four major cities), and not to 新西兰. Another pun ostensibly meaning New Zealand, but actually meaning the remote regions of China, i.e., Xinjiang, Tibet, and Lanzhou. Each of these three place names has a character in common with 新西兰. That is, they want to remain in major cities with better living conditions, and not go to remote areas where conditions are more difficult.

天然公园 tiānrán gōngyuán
natural park

天然气 tiānránqì
natural gas

Also called 天然煤气.

天天读 tiāntiāndú
study every day
The study system during the Cultural Revolution whereby the masses of people had to study Mao Zedong's works every day.

添加剂 tiānjiājì
additive

添砖加瓦 tiānzhuān jiāwǎ
to add a brick or a tile
A metaphor for making a small contribution to a large enterprise.
E.g. 为四化建设添砖加瓦 *to add building blocks for the four modernizations*

填平补齐 tiánpíng bǔqí
to fill the gaps
1) Measures, adopted in old liberated areas that had undergone relatively thorough land reform, to remedy the shortage of land and other production resources among some poor hired peasants; also the measures used to remedy other residual problems of land reform. On a relatively small scale, the concept of drawing from the fat to subsidize the lean and drawing from a surplus to supplement a shortage was adopted, and the distribution of land and other production resources was systematically adjusted. 2) Also filling in a gap in economic construction or other work, to create a balance.

填鸭式教学法 tiányāshì jiàoxuéfǎ
the spoon feeding (lit., stuffing ducks) method of teaching
Also called the "pouring into" teaching method. It is the opposite of heuristic teaching. Teachers only require students

to memorize facts and do not take into consideration their enthusiasm for learning, how effective they are, and whether the students can understand and digest the facts. This is like raising ducks by stuffing them, hence the terminology.

田联 tián–lián
track and field association
Abbreviation for 田径联合会.

田坛 tiántán
world of track and field

田协 tián–xié
athletics association
Abbreviation for 田径协会.

甜蜜事业 tiánmì shìyè
honey profession
planned-parenthood (i.e., birth control) work, also work related to helping people resolve problems concerning love and marriage.

tiao

挑食 tiāoshí
to be picky about food

条块 tiáo–kuài
Synonymous with 条条 and 块块. (cf. 条条 and 块块)

条块分割 tiáo–kuài fēngē
to divide up among government agencies
An economic system whereby each government office and field of jurisdiction is independent and sealed off from others. This is contrary to having a unified scheme for the whole nation and detrimental to the development of the national economy. (cf. 条条块块 and 全国一盘棋).

条码 tiáomǎ
Abbreviation for 条形码. (cf. 条形码)

条条 tiáotiáo
rules and regulations
1) The economic management system whereby enterprises are directly managed by various offices of the central government. (cf. 条条块块) 2) Regulations and provisions that impede people from carrying out normal creative activities.
E.g. 这么多条条，真让人没法干事了。*All these rules and regulations really make it impossible for people to do anything.* (cf. 条条框框)

条条块块 tiáotiáo kuàikuài
various levels of government jurisdiction
China's economic management system is divided into two levels. The one called 条条 is direct management of enterprises by the various responsible departments of the central government. The one called 块块 is management of enterprises by the various levels of local government. 条条块块 refers to these two systems of management.

条条框框 tiáotiáo kuàngkuàng
rules and regulations
All the unreasonable rules, regulations, and conventional ideas that dampened people's enthusiasm and creativity, and impeded work and production.
E.g. 敢于冲破条条框框 *dare to break unreasonable rules and regulations*

条条专政 tiáotiáo zhuānzhèng
dictatorship of the central government organs
An erroneous leftist concept of the Cul-

tural Revolution. In implementing the 条条块块 economic management system (whereby various levels of government had exclusive jurisdiction), in some cases there was a lopsided emphasis on the unified leadership of the central government; there was rigid control over those below, and enthusiasm at the local level was stifled. Using this pretext the Gang of Four fabricated accusations, attacked the central unified leadership – which the nation cannot do without – calling it "dictatorship of the central government". They also distorted the central-local relationship portraying it as dictatorship by one level, and raised the slogan "overthrow the dictatorship of the central government". (cf. 条条块块)

条形码 tiáoxíngmǎ

bar codes

Labels made up of black and white strips of varying width designed for computer-reading, used in merchandising.

条子工程 tiáozi gōngchéng

指不在统一计划安排之内，只凭某一个领导批的条子就上马兴建的工程。

A construction project that falls outside of an integrated plan, but is carried out solely on the basis of an approval note from one leader.

调房 tiáofáng

to adjust or exchange housing

E.g. 调房市场 *housing exchange market*

调峰措施 tiáofēng cuòshī

measures to regulate rush hour traffic

Measures by the transportation department to regulate the peak periods in public transportation.

调幅 tiáofú

to adjust amplitude (so that the carrier wave can transmit messages properly)

Abbreviation for 振幅调制.

E.g. 调幅转换 *change the amplitude adjustment* / 调幅收音机 *an amplitude modulation radio*

调改 tiáogǎi

to adjust and to reform

调高 tiáogāo

to adjust and raise

E.g. 调高利率 *to raise the interest rate*

调和主义 tiáohé zhǔyì

conciliationism

The mentality of not standing firm on principles when faced with important issues, but advocating compromise.

调级 tiáojí

adjust ranks

1) Abbreviation for 调整级别. In China, all people who receive their wages from the state have ranks; different ranks enjoy different political and material benefits. Rank adjustments usually mean upward adjustments in rank. 2) Another term for salary adjustment.

调价 tiáojià

to adjust commodity prices

调减 tiáojiǎn

to adjust and reduce

E.g. 调减建筑面积 *reduce the building area* / 调减调节税 *to reduce the adjustment tax*

调节器 tiáojiéqì

adjuster

调解委员会 tiáojiě wěiyuánhuì
mediation committees

Mass mediation organizations, which operate under the leadership of grass-roots people's committees and people's courts. Their duties, which are carried out according to the policies and laws of the people's government, are: to resolve civil disputes, to strengthen civilian education on the law and patriotism and to advance the people's internal solidarity, so that people's lives and national construction will be enhanced.

调解组织 tiáojiě zǔzhī
mediation organizations

Organizations such as mediation committees formed to resolve disputes among the masses.

调控 tiáokòng
to regulate and control

E.g. 宏观调控 *to regulate and control on a macro basis* / 用法律调控文化市场 *to regulate and control the market dealing in cultural articles (books, tapes, paintings, etc.) through laws*

调频 tiáopín
(re electricity) frequency modulation; to regulate radio frequency

调试 tiáoshì
debugging

The debugging of a computer or an instrument.

调休 tiáoxiū
to adjust and alternate work and rest time

E.g. 工厂因停电调休。*The factory is adjusting its work and rest times due to cuts in electricity.*

调资 tiáozī
to adjust salary

Abbreviation for 调整工资 adjusting salary. It means adjusting the salaries of workers (including workmen, employees, teachers, institutional personnel, military personnel, etc.) according to a wage system, so that their remuneration will continuously be in step with the level of development in the national economy, as well as with the changing nature of their work and contributions to society. Salary adjustments usually mean upward adjustments.

E.g. 调资工作 *salary adjustment work* / 调资指标 *salary adjustment norms*

挑大梁 tiǎodàliáng
to shoulder a big beam

To take responsibility for an important task.

E.g. 让年轻同志上来挑大梁。*Let young comrades rise and shoulder big beams.*

挑战书 tiǎozhànshū
letter of challenge

A letter sent by one person or unit to another proposing a competition with that person or unit.

跳槽 tiàocáo
to jump the stable (said of animals in rut or on heat); metaphor for being dissatisfied with one's position and attempting to transfer to another job

E.g. 雇员跳槽率下降。*The rate of employees transferring to other jobs has reduced.* / 他想跳槽到旅游局去。*He would like to get out of his present job and join the bureau of tourism.*

跳蚤市场 tiàozao shìchǎng
flea market

tie

贴标签 tiēbiāoqiān
to stick on a label or price tag; now a metaphor for giving something an irrelevant or unreal name

贴面 tiēmiàn
a covering put on furniture or a building

贴息贷款 tiēxī dàikuǎn
subsidized loans
Loans with no or low interest. To upgrade the economic efficiency of industries and enterprises, commercial banks at the behest of the state make loans at no or low interest to support the production of high quality brand name commodities. The banks are subsidized for the reduced interest by the Ministry of Finance, hence the term "subsidized loan".

铁板凳 tiěbǎndèng
Synonymous with 铁交椅. (cf. 铁交椅)

铁饭碗 tiěfànwǎn
iron rice bowl
A metaphor for a job that is stable, reliable, and guaranteed for life. That is, when a person becomes an employee of the state, as long as he doesn't commit any major errors, he will have a permanent job and income regardless of how well or poorly he works, and how much or how little he works. He cannot be demoted or dismissed. People call this the iron rice bowl. This system goes against the principle of "to each according to his work", and is tantamount to equalitarianism. It stifles the initiative of workers and impedes the development of productivity.

铁杆儿 tiěgǎnr
iron rod; diehard
The term is used to describe people who are incorrigibly obstinate and who absolutely refuse to budge from their reactionary stance.
E.g. 铁杆儿汉奸 *an iron rod traitor*

铁哥们 tiěgēmen
buddies; close friends
Refers mainly to young males.

铁画 tiěhuà
iron picture (an art form made from sheet metal)
An art of making iron pictures

铁交椅 tiějiāoyǐ
iron armchair
Also called 铁椅子 iron chair, a take-off on the term 铁饭碗 iron rice bowl. A metaphor for the system of lifelong cadre leadership. That is, cadre leaders retain their positions for life regardless of their actual performance. In the 1980s, China began to do away with "iron armchairs" and "iron rice bowls". (cf. 铁饭碗)

铁幕 tiěmù
iron curtain

铁娘子 tiěniángzǐ
iron lady
A sobriquet for Margaret Thatcher, one-time prime minister of Great Britain.

铁牛 tiěniú
iron ox; tractor

铁人 tiěrén
iron man
1) A metaphor for a staunch unyielding person. 2) Special reference to the outstanding Daqing Oilfield worker Wang

Jinxi. (cf. 铁人精神)

铁人精神 tiěrén jīngshén
spirit of the iron man
The spirit of not fearing difficulties, striving hard to break new ground, and giving oneself wholeheartedly to socialist construction. Iron man is the name given affectionately to Wang Jinxi by the Daqing Oilfield workers. He was originally an ordinary petroleum worker. In the struggle to open up the Daqing Oilfield in the 1960s, he showed the revolutionary spirit of not fearing hardship or death, opened up wells to obtain oil under the most arduous circumstances, fought night and day, and led workers in overcoming many difficulties. Later, this spirit of striving hard to break new ground was eulogized as spirit of the iron man.

ting

停产 tíngchǎn
to cease production
停机 tíngjī
to stop the movie camera; to finish a film project
停建 tíngjiàn
to stop a construction project in midstream
E.g. 停建缓建 *to abandon or to slow down a construction project* / 停建项目 *building projects which were stopped half way through*
停薪留职 tíngxīn liúzhí
Cf. 保职停薪
庭院经济 tíngyuàn jīngjì
courtyard economy
Small-scale economic enterprises carried out by peasants in their courtyards and areas around their houses.
挺升 tǐngshēng
(re currency value) rising strongly
E.g. 人民币挺升。*The RMB is rising robustly.*

tong

通关 tōngguān
to pass customs
通汇 tōnghuì
funds transfer
The business of transferring funds between various banking organs within the country. Also refers to the transfer of foreign currency between two countries or regions.
通膨 tōng-péng
(Taiwan usage) inflation
Abbreviation for 通货膨胀.
通气 tōngqì
to ventilate; to put gas lines into operation; to be in touch; to keep each other informed
通勤 tōngqín
to commute to work (from home) on a daily basis (i.e., not living at one's work place)
通勤车 tōngqínchē
commuter bus
Also called 通勤班车.
通天 tōngtiān
reach heaven; exceedingly high or great
1) To reach to heaven, descriptive of something exceedingly great or high.
E.g. 罪恶通天。*The crime is exceedingly great.*

2) To have ties with high level leaders.

E.g. 通天人物 *a person who has ties with those high up*

通透 tōngtòu

crystal clear

通信卫星 tōngxìn wèixīng

communication satellites

通用月票 tōngyòng yuèpiào

intra-city monthly ticket

A pass, purchased by the month, for all intra-city buses (excluding long-distance buses) and trolleys.

通胀 tōng-zhàng

inflation

E.g. 他对通胀问题发表了看法。*He expressed his views on inflation.*

同比 tóngbǐ

compared with the same period the previous year

E.g. 市场货值同比增加两成。*The market currency value increased 20% on the same period the previous year.*

同步 tóngbù

coordinated; synchronized

Two or more matters maintaining a coordinated relationship in their process of transformation, such as maintaining the same pace or moving in a coordinated unified manner.

E.g. 同步卫星 *synchronized satellites* / 同步建设 *synchronized construction* / 同步增长 *synchronized growth*

同步辐射 tóngbù fúshè

synchrotron radiation

Abbreviation for 同步加速器辐射.

同工同酬 tónggōng tóngchóu

equal pay for equal work

All workers who do the same kind of work and make an equal contribution to society receive equal remuneration regardless of differences in gender, age, ethnic nationality, or rank.

同龄 tónglíng

of comparable age

E.g. 同龄人 *peers* / 他和我同龄。*He is the same age as me.*

同声传译 tóngshēng chuányì

installation for simultaneous interpretation

Also called 译意风 interpretation phone.

同一性 tóngyīxìng

identity

1) In dialectics, the identity, unity, and unanimity of contradictions. It is a philosophical construct which states that, among the various contradictory aspects in all things, there is mutual penetration, mutual linkage, interdependence, interconnections, and mutual transformations. 2) Abstract absolute, and simple equivalence.

铜牌 tóngpái

bronze medal (third prize in athletic events)

童贩 tóngfàn

juvenile vendors

童商 tóngshāng

juvenile vendors

童星 tóngxīng

child star (in films or performances)

童装 tóngzhuāng

children's clothing

Abbreviation for 儿童服装.

捅马蜂窝 tǒng mǎfēngwō

to poke a hornet's nest

A metaphor for getting involved with a difficult person or a touchy situation.

筒裤 tǒngkù

tube trousers

Also called 筒子裤. Trousers with a short crotch and two legs shaped like tubes.

筒裙 tǒngqún
tube skirt; straight skirt

筒子楼 tǒngzilóu
tube buildings

Dormitory buildings in which each floor consists of a long hallway, lined on either side with rooms. The center of each floor resembles a long tube, hence the term "tube buildingsr". They are distinct from 单元楼 apartment buildings.

统包统配 tǒngbāo tǒngpèi
centralized allocation of labor

The system of labor allocation whereby labor employment in state enterprises is without exception centrally arranged by the labor department; the enterprises have no power to recruit or dismiss employees, and employees have no power to freely choose their jobs. As society has progressed, this system has caused serious problems and steps are being taken to reform it.

统保 tǒng-bǎo
(re insurance) several types of insurance in one policy

统编 tǒng-biān
centralized compilation

Abbreviation for 统一编写 centralized compilation and writing.
E.g. 统编教材 *centralized writing and compilation of teaching materials*

统筹安排 tǒngchóu ānpái
centralized planning and arrangements

To carry out centralized planning and preparation, to systematically settle mathers concerning personnel and other things.

统筹法 tǒngchóufǎ
method of overall planning

A scientific method of arranging work procedures in business management and basic constructions. On the basis of production demands, labor force, facilities and material resources, and the technological processes, an overall plan is mapped out to help people discover the main problems in work arrangements, so that adjustment scan be made in time, the quality of the project maintained and the project's progress ensured. This is also called 网络法 network method.

统筹兼顾 tǒngchóu jiāngù
overall planning and all-round consideration

Taking the overall situation as the starting point, making comprehensive plans, and considering all aspects and their interrelationships.

统筹学 tǒngchóuxué
study of centralized planning

A new field of study which takes centralized planning as the subject of research.

统筹医疗 tǒngchóu yīliáo
centralized medical care

A form of mutual aid medical care, and also a kind of medical insurance. Participants pay a fee at fixed intervals to build the centralized medical fund. When a participant falls ill, his medical expenses are paid fully or partly from this fund.

统存统贷 tǒngcún tǒngdài

centralized savings and loans

A system of credit based on centralized savings and loans.

统调统配 tǒngtiáo tǒngpèi
centralized transfer and allocation

A system of material management based on centralized allocating, transferring, and rationing.

统购包销 tǒnggòu bāoxiāo
centralized purchase and contracted marketing

1) An elementary form of national capitalism implemented with private industries during China's socialist reform period. Centralized purchase means: in accordance with the nation's legal regulations, state-managed commercial departments purchased commodities important to people's livelihoods from privately managed factories at stipulated prices. The private sector could not market the goods themselves. Contracted marketing means: in accordance with contracts signed between state-managed commercial departments and privately managed factories, the state purchased and marketed all of certain products that the factories produced according to stipulated specifications. 2) The state commercial and material departments purchase and market all products of enterprises.

统购统销 tǒnggòu tǒngxiāo
centralized purchase and marketing

Abbreviation for purchasing and supplying under a state plan. From 1951 on, China gradually and in a planned way implemented centralized purchasing and marketing of those consumer goods which are important to people's livelihoods (such as cotton, grain, and oil). Only enterprises commissioned by the state had the right to engage in the production of goods that came under the centralized purchasing and marketing plan. No other enterprises or individuals were permitted to engage in their production. The implementation of this policy served an important function in stabilizing prices, guaranteeing people's livelihoods, consolidating the alliance between workers and peasants, combating urban and rural capitalist forces, and ensuring the smooth progress of socialist revolution and construction. The disadvantages of the system have become apparent and the system underwent its first modification in 1985.

统观 tǒngguān
to take an overview

E.g. 统观这次演出 *to take an overview of this performance*

统管 tǒngguǎn
unified management; comprehensive management

E.g. 统管医药市场 *to comprehensively manage the pharmaceutical market* / 统管全校财务工作 *to manage the financial affairs of the entire school*

统建 tǒngjiàn
unified or integrated construction

E.g. 住宅实行集资统建 *the method of collective capital and unified construction is applied to residential housing* / 统建住房 *to build housing in a unified way*

统考 tǒng-kǎo
unified examination

Abbreviation for 统一考试, an examination that is set, proctored, and car-

ried out in an organized unified fashion.
E.g. 全国统考 *unified nationwide exam* / 英语统考 *unified English exam*

统揽 tǒnglǎn
to consider and plan in a integrated and comprehensive manner
E.g. 统揽全局 *to take every aspect of a situation into consideration and to make plans in an integrated and comprehensive manner*

统配 tǒngpèi
unified or centralized allocation (of goods and services, job assignments, etc.)
E.g. 统配工 *workers assigned to jobs by centralized allocation* / 统招统配办学体制 *a system of centralized recruitment and allocation in education*

统配煤 tǒngpèiméi
coal under the unified ration system
Coal that is rationed according to a unified state plan.

统配煤矿 tǒngpèi méikuàng
coal mine under the unified allocation system
A coal mine that turns over all the coal it produces to the state which allocates it according to a unified plan.

统配物资 tǒngpèi wùzī
goods under the unified ration plan
Goods which are subject to unified allocation by the State Planning Commission. (cf. 第一类物资)

统收统支 tǒngshōu tǒngzhī
centralized income and expenditure
A system of fiscal management practiced in China for a long period. It was characterized by a highly centralized fiscal authority. All incomes from state-managed enterprises were turned over to the central treasury department, and all necessary expenditure was disbursed from this department. This system had an adverse effect on the initiative of local areas and enterprises, and on economic efficiency. It is presently being reformed.

统算 tǒng-suàn
centralized accounting
Contraction of 统一核算.

统销 tǒngxiāo
centralized (government-controlled) marketing (of certain essential goods)
E.g. 过去吃粮靠统销。*In the past, people relied on centralized marketing for their grains.* / 统销粮 *grain under centralized marketing*

统一口径 tǒngyī kǒujìng
to adopt an identical or consistent story or attitude

统战 tǒng-zhàn
united front
Abbreviation for 统一战线.
E.g. 统战政策 *policy of a united front* / 统战工作 *united front work* / 统战对象 *target of a united front*

统战部 tǒng-zhàn-bù
United Front Work Department of the Chinese Communist Party Central Committee
Abbreviation for 中共中央统战部.

tou

偷渡 tōudù
to cross a border illegally
E.g. 偷渡去香港 *to cross the Hong Kong border illegally*

偷逃 tōutáo

to evade taxes

E.g. 目前偷逃税情况很普遍。 *At present, tax evasion is very common.*

投保 tóubǎo

to insure

To participate in an insurance plan.

E.g. 投保单位 *insured unit* / 投保户 *insured household* / 投保人 *insured individual*

投档 tóudàng

(in recruiting students) to sent the files of all applicants who passed the exam to relevant units for selection

E.g. 按以往办法投档。 *To send the files of all qualified applicants to relevant units in accordance with past practice.*

投递员 tóudìyuán

mail carrier

Also called 邮递员.

投工 tóugōng

to get going on a project; to put in manpower and proceed with the job

E.g. 每年投工 200 个劳动日 *to put in 200 work days annually*

投价 tóujià

(in negotiating a purchase) the buyer proposing a price to the seller

E.g. 投价 1000 元 *to put in a bid of 1,000 yuan*

投降主义 tóuxiáng zhǔyì

capitulationism

The mentality and behavior of compromising and yielding to the enemy and not persevering in the struggle. This is a manifestation of rightist opportunism.

投拍 tóupāi

to start filming (a film or television program)

E.g. 电视剧《红楼梦》在北京投拍。 *The filming of "A Dream of the Red Mansions" started in Beijing.*

投入产出 tóurù chǎnchū

to invest funds and manpower, and to produce

E.g. 投入产出指标 *Resource-input and product-output quotas* / 投入产出包干制 *the resource-input and product-output responsibility system*

投售 tóushòu

to put onto the market

E.g. 投售夏粮 *to put summer grains onto the market*

投诉 tóusù

to report someone's illegal activities to the relevant department

E.g. 投诉信件 *letters reporting on illegal activities to the relevant authorities* / 向法院投诉 *to report illegal activities to the court*

投向 tóuxiàng

the area toward which funds, manpower, resources, etc., are directed

E.g. 资金投向 *the direction of capital investments*

头道贩子 tóudào fànzi

front line middleman

One who purchases goods directly from producers and resells them to merchants.

头头儿 tóutour

head (of a unit, a group, a clique, etc.)

Also written as 头头.

头头脑脑 tóutóunǎonǎo

important officials; influential people

头针疗法 tóuzhēn liáofǎ

head acupuncture

A method of treating various illnesses by

using acupuncture needles on specific areas of the head. This method is suitable for treating illnesses that originate in the brain, such as brain thrombosis, brain hemorrhage, and paralysis.

透明度 tòumíngdù
transparency

The openness of an organization to the public. Specifically, political transparency, i.e., how much of the activities of the Party, and government organizations, and state affairs are made known to society.
E.g. 这次会议的透明度较高。 *This meeting has a higher transparency (made more open to public scrutiny).*

tu

突出政治 tūchū zhèngzhì
to give prominence to politics

To give politics priority over everything else. This was a pillar of the leftist ideological construct of the Cultural Revolution. This slogan is no longer used.

突发 tūfā
to occur or develop suddenly

E.g. 突发事件 *sudden incident* / 突发因素 *a factor suddenly playing an important role*

突发性 tūfāxìng
of an abrupt nature; occurring suddenly

E.g. 突发性事件 *a sudden incident*

突击队 tūjīduì
shock brigade

1) A small military company which leads in a fierce and sudden attack on the enemy's defenses. 2) A work group, staffed by young people and people in their prime, formed provisionally to speed up the progress of a certain task.
E.g. 青年突击队 *a young people's shock brigade* / 抢险突击队 *emergency shock squad*

突击入党 tūjī rùdǎng
to crash admission into the Party

Under the domination of the Lin Biao-Jiang Qing clique during the Cultural Revolution, some Party organizations forced the admission of certain people into the Chinese Communist Party for political purposes, and in the process disregarded organizational principles and standards for Party membership.

突击手 tūjīshǒu
shock worker

Someone who has achieved prominence by completing a certain task, or assuming a leadership role.
E.g. 新长征突击手 *a shock worker of the new Long March* / 青年突击手 *young shock worker*

突击提干 tūjī tígàn
to crash promotion of cadres

During the Cultural Revolution, for political purposes some organizations forced through the promotion of cadres to leadership ranks. In the process they violated regulations regarding the promotion of cadres.

突破口 tūpòkǒu
breakthrough point

1) Originally, a breach in the enemy's line of defense which the attacking army broke through. 2) Now the term is a metaphor for the crucial aspect of a matter which should be dealt with first.

E.g. 领导决定,把反对官僚主义作为整党的突破口。 *The leadership decided to take combating bureaucratism as the breakthrough point in rectifying the Party.*

突显 tūxiǎn

to make apparent; to stick out; suddenly appear

E.g. 美国近期突显进攻性战略动向。 *Suddenly the United States has appeared to be inclined to an offensive strategy.*

突增 tūzēng

growth spurt

(Re physical development) rapid growth.

E.g. 突增年龄提前。 *The age for growth spurts has become younger.*

图文并茂 túwén bìngmào

rich and exquisite in both pictures and words

土地入股 tǔdì rùgǔ

pooling of land as shares

When Chinese peasants joined elementary agricultural production cooperatives, they turned their private plots over to the cooperatives for centralized management. The plots were converted to shares according to their size and quality. The cooperatives calculated land remuneration on the basis of the land shares with which the members joined the cooperatives.

土地证 tǔdìzhèng

land certificates; title deed

Land and house ownership certificates. After China had undergone land reform, the People's Government issued a kind of real estate ownership certificate. The certificate lists the location, boundaries, and number of *mu* of the land, and the number of rooms, and names of all members of the family owning a house. Two kinds of certificates were issued on all the land in the suburbs of large cities that had undergone land reform: right of use certificates were issued for the state-owned land used by peasants, and ownership certificates were issued for land that originally belonged to peasants.

土法上马 tǔfǎ shàngmǎ

to get on the job with indigenous methods

A slogan raised during China's Great Leap Forward in 1958. It directed people to rely on the wisdom and strength of the masses, and use traditional facilities and technology to develop industry.

土风舞 tǔfēngwǔ

(Taiwan usage) folk dancing

土改 tǔ-gǎi

land reform

Short for 土地改革, the revolutionary movement led by the Chinese Communist Party to do away with the feudal exploitative land ownership system and to implement a system of land ownership by peasants. Land reform was conducted in the Soviet Area during the Second Internal Revolutionary War, and again in the liberated areas during the Third Internal Revolutionary War. After the founding of the People's Republic of China, the entire nation underwent land reform. By September 1952, land reform was basically completed.

土高炉 tǔgāolú

indigenous blast furnaces; backyard furnaces

Simple smelting furnaces used for smelting pig iron during the 1958 movement which call on the entire population to make iron and steel.

土建 tǔ-jiàn
building construction
Civil engineering construction projects, such as houses and roads.

土老帽 tǔlǎomào
clodhopper; (country) bumpkin
A colloquial term. Also written as 土老帽儿 or 土老冒.

土暖气 tǔnuǎnqì
rustic heating
Simple heating devices, most of which are homemade contraptions consisting of hot water or steam pipes and a heat disseminating apparatus.

土洋并举 tǔ-yáng bìngjǔ
to function in both old fashioned and modern ways
Abbreviation for using both old fashioned and modern methods for production. Under the premise of centralized leadership, overall planning, and division of labor with mutual cooperation, advanced technology and relatively backward technology are to be used together. Old fashioned and modern are relative terms.

土洋结合 tǔ-yáng jiéhé
to combine the old fashioned and the modern (cf. 土洋并举)

土政策 tǔzhèngcè
indigenous policy
Regulations made in certain local areas and units. Some indigenous policies can accord with practical situations and on the premise that they do not go against national policies; but some go against the relevant national policies.

吐故纳新 tǔgù nàxīn
to exhale the old and inhale the new
Originally, the term referred to breathing. Now it is a metaphor for relinquishing the old and absorbing the new. Specifically, in the ideological and organizational constructions within the Chinese Communist Party, there is a continuous need to undergo rectification: to insist on the proletarian Party spirit, to clean out the non-proletarian ideological style; to absorb those who conform to the standards of a Party member and clean out those who do not.

吐疏纳亲 tǔshū nàqīn
to rid the distant and absorb the intimate
A metaphor for attacking and ostracizing those who have relatively distant relationships with a person or who are in disagreement, and absorbing and putting in important positions those with relatively intimate relationships or who unscrupulously and blindly obey.

tuan

团场 tuán-chǎng
regiment farm
Abbreviation for 生产建设兵团农场 military regiment production construction farm. Because these farms are managed with the regiment as the unit, they are called "regiment farms."

团伙 tuánhuǒ
gangsters
Criminal elements who band together. They are a serious menace to people's life and property, as well as to security.

E.g. 流氓团伙 *gang of hooligans /* 帮派团伙 *group of faction lists*

团结－批评－团结 tuánjié – pīpíng – tuánjié
unite-criticize-unite

This is the correct method by which the Chinese Communist Party resolves the Party's and the people's internal contradictions. Hope for unity is the point of departure; the process of criticism or struggle is then used to resolve the contradictions, and from this, a new unity built on a new foundation.

团票 tuánpiào
(informal) qualification for membership in the Communist Youth League

E.g. 有的团员连团票都不要了。 *Some members of the Communist Youth League were even willing to relinquish their membership.*

团团转 tuántuánzhuàn
to be in a tizzy; very busy and hectic

E.g. 忙得团团转 *to be frantically busy /* 急得团团转 *to be frantic from anxiety or from being rushed*

团委会 tuán – wěi – huì
Communist Youth League Council

Abbreviation for 共青团委员会. The base-level council of the Chinese Communist Youth League. The council is elected at the Congress of League Members or Congress of League Representatives, and the term is two years. Under it are the League General Branches and the League Branches. Also called 团委.

团员 tuányuán
1) A member of a delegation or visiting group ; 2) A member of the Chinese Communist Youth League

团支部 tuánzhībù
League Branch

Abbreviation for 共青团支部委员会 Chinese Communist Youth League Branch Council, which is under the jurisdiction of the League Council or a League General Branch. The committee is elected at the Congress of League Members, and the term is one year.

团总支 tuánzǒngzhī
League General Branch

Abbreviation for 共青团总支部委员会 Chinese Communist Youth League General Branch Council. It is under the jurisdiction of the League Council, and has jurisdiction over League Branches. It is elected at the Congress of League Members, and the term is one year.

团组织 tuánzǔzhī
League organizations

The overall term for the organizations at various levels of the Chinese Communist Youth League.

tui

推陈出新 tuīchén chūxīn
to weed out the old and bring forth the new

To get rid of the dross from the old, extract the quintessence of what remains and allow it to develop in new directions (usually in reference to handing down cultural heritage).

推出 tuīchū
to push out; to come out with

To manufacture new products, perform new programs, or publish new works of literature and art.

E.g. 推出新成果 *to come out with*

new achievements / 糕点厂推出老年营养糕点。 *The bakery has come out with baked goods especially nutritious to the elderly.* / 北京人民艺术剧院推出两台表现老年人生活的话剧。 *The Beijing People's Art Theater has come out with two plays that portray the life of the elderly.*

推介 tuījiè

to promote and introduce to people

E.g. 澳门基本法推介活动 (*the activity of*) *promoting and introducing Macao's Basic Laws to the people.*

推拒 tuījù

to turn down; to decline; to reject

E.g. 没有一点推拒的意思 *to have no intention of declining or rejecting*

推理小说 tuīlǐ xiǎoshuō

analogy fiction; a work of fiction that unfolds its plot by analogy

推普 tuī-pǔ

to spread the use of the common spoken language (among dialect speakers)

Abbreviation of 推广普通话.

推入 tuīrù

to push in; to promote the sale (of certain commodities) in a particular market

推展 tuīzhǎn

to exhibit for the purpose of marketing or recommending

E.g. 中华国产精品推展活动 *the activity of exhibiting and marketing fine products made in China*

蜕化变质分子 tuìhuà biànzhì fēnzǐ

degenerate elements

People within the Communist Party or among the revolutionary ranks who have become dissolute and degenerate.

退场 tuìchǎng

to leave or withdraw from a meeting place or an arena

退党 tuìdǎng

to withdraw from a party

1) To leave (through dismissal or withdrawal) a certain political party. 2) Specifically, to leave the Chinese Communist Party.

退耕还林 tuìgēng huánlín

to quit cultivation and return to forest

To reafforest an area that had earlier been opened up for cultivation. This is a beneficial measure intended to preserve the natural ecological balance in mountain areas.

退居 tuìjū

to retreat

An old, weak, or sick cadre withdrawing from his original post to carry out work that is commensurate with his capacity.

E.g. 退居二、三线 *to retreat to the second and third lines (of work).*

退赔 tuìpéi

to return and compensate

1) To return and compensate for properties that have been seized or illegally obtained. 2) Specifically, to return and compensate for the property that had been equalized and transferred in the 1958 communization movement. (cf. 一平二调 and 共产风)

退生 tuìshēng

withdrawn graduates

Refers to graduates who had been assigned to jobs but were later turned back by their work units.

退团 tuìtuán
leave the League

1) To leave the Chinese Communist Youth League for a certain reason. 2) Specifically, to leave the Communist Youth League due to having passed the age limit, in accordance with regulations.

退休 tuìxiū
to retire

A metaphor for something being eliminated due to obsolescence.

E.g. 退休工人 *retired workers* / 干部退休制度 *cadres retirement system* / 那台机器应该退休了。 *That machine should be retired.*

退役 tuìyì
to retire from active military service; to retire from an athletic career

Metaphor for something being eliminated due to obsolescence.

E.g. 排球运动员周晓兰光荣退役。 *The volleyball player Zhou Xiaolan is retiring with honors from her athletic career.* / 空军有数千架飞机退役。 *Several thousand Air Force planes are being retired.* / 上海老车站宣告退役。 *The old Shanghai railway station has been declared obsolete and is being eliminated.*

退役军人 tuìyì jūnrén
veterans

Military personnel who have withdrawn from active service or who have left the service after serving the stipulated period.

退运 tuìyùn
to return a shipment

退赃 tuìzāng
to return spoils

To return and compensate for property that was obtained through such illegal tactics as bribery, embezzlement, and theft.

tuo

拖拉机手 tuōlājīshǒu
tractor driver

拖拉机站 tuōlājīzhàn
tractor station

Synonymous with 农机站 agricultural machinery station and 农业机器拖拉机站 agricultural machinery and tractor station. They are enterprises in socialist countries that serve agriculture with tractors and agricultural machines. Tractor stations are usually operated by the state. They do mechanized operations and other production services, in accordance with production contracts drawn up with collective economic organizations. Some are operated by peasant collectives. The term is also used to refer specifically to agricultural machinery management stations in China's rural communes.

托裱 tuōbiǎo
to mount a Chinese painting (usually onto a scroll)

E.g. 托裱书画 *to mount a calligraphy scroll*

托儿 tuōr
someone who abets a profiteer in enticing and swindling buyers

E.g. 倒爷儿们身边几乎都有托儿。 *Almost all profiteers are supported by a circle of abetters.*

托福 tuōfú
TOEFL (Test of English as a Foreign

托哥 tuōgē
men hired by stores to act as customers to entice others to make purchases

托姐 tuōjiě
women hired by stores to act as customers to entice others to make purchases

托老所 tuōlǎosuǒ
day care facility for the elderly

托卖 tuōmài
to consign to sell
E.g. 托卖手续费 *consignment fee*

托门子 tuōménzi
to seek a special favor through backdoor connections

托派 tuōpài
Trotskyite
A jocular term for those who take the TOEFL as part of the going abroad process. (cf. 托福)

托收 tuōshōu
to consign (to an agent) to collect (payments, etc.)
E.g. 托收款 *fees collected by an agent* / 票据托收 *the collection of bills by an agent*

托幼 tuōyòu
nursery and kindergarten
E.g. 托幼事业 *preschool vocation*

脱产 tuōchǎn
to release from regular work
To be released from directly productive work in order to specialize in administrative work, work of the Party, the Youth League, or a union, or to pursue studies.
E.g. 脱产干部 *a cadre who has been released from directly productive work* / 脱产学习 *to be released from work to pursue studies*

脱毒 tuōdú
to detoxify

脱岗 tuōgǎng
to leave one's post

脱钩 tuōgōu
to unhook
A metaphor for discontinuing the link between what was originally linked.
E.g. 可以允许他们同农业脱钩，专门从事林业生产。*They may be unhooked from agriculture to concentrate on forestry production.*

脱口秀 tuōkǒuxiù
talk show

脱困 tuōkùn
to shake off poverty; to get rid of poverty
E.g. 支持国有企业的改革和脱困 *to support the reform of state-owned enterprises and help them to shake off poverty*/ 脱困的目标完全能够实现。*The goal of getting rid of poverty can be realized.*

脱盲 tuōmáng
to cast off illiteracy
To become literate, thus to cast off the stigma of illiteracy.

脱帽加冕 tuōmào jiāmiǎn
to remove the hat (disgrace) and put on a crown
A metaphor for removing spiritual shackles from intellectuals, removing the political hat of bourgeois intellectuals that had been forced on their heads, proclaiming them to be the intellectuals of the laboring people and a constituency within the working class.

脱敏 tuōmǐn

to desensitize
To desensitize teeth so as to dispel the pain from heat or cold.
E.g. 脱敏牙膏 *desensitizing toothpaste*

脱贫 tuōpín
to shed poverty
To shake off the condition of poverty.
E.g. 脱贫致富 *to shed poverty and attain prosperity* / 帮助贫困户脱贫 *to help straitened households shed their poverty*

脱期 tuōqī
to miss a deadline
E.g. 部分工程脱期严重。 *A part of the project is running seriously behind schedule.*

脱销断档 tuōxiāo duàndàng
out of stock
A temporary interruption in the production or supply of a certain commodity.

脱氧核糖核酸
tuōyǎnghétánghésuān
DNA
Abbreviation for deoxyribonucleic acid.

脱脂 tuōzhī
to de-fat; to degrease
E.g. 脱脂棉 *absorbent cotton* / 脱脂奶粉 *nonfat dried milk*

脱瘾 tuōyǐn
to overcome an addiction (to drugs, etc.)

拓宽 tuòkuān
to widen
To expand in area or scope.
E.g. 拓宽道路 *to widen a road* / 拓宽销售门路 *to expand marketing channels*

拓展 tuòzhǎn
to open up or expand and to develop
E.g. 拓展业务 *to expand a business* / 拓展流通渠道 *to expand open channels* / 拓展技术交流领域 *to expand the sphere of technological exchange* / 向广度深度拓展 *to expand in breadth and depth*

W

wa

挖革改 wā-gé-gǎi
to tap, innovate, and reform
挖潜、革新、改造，指挖掘现有企业的生产能力，革新生产技术，改造生产工艺和老企业。
To tap the productivity of existing enterprises, to innovate technology of production, and to reform production techniques and old enterprises.

挖潜 wāqián
to tap potential
Contraction of 挖掘潜力.

挖墙角 wā qiáng jiǎo
to undermine the foundation (lit., to dig at the foot of the wall)
Synonymous with 拆台 to dismantle the support.
挖社会主义的墙角 *to undermine the foundation of socialism*

蛙人 wārén
frogman

wai

歪风 wāifēng
corrupt tendencies (lit., crooked wind)
Dishonest and corrupt ways, bad tendencies.
E.g. 坚决纠正党员干部在分房中的歪风。*We must steadfastly correct the corrupt tendencies in the housing allocation among Party members and cadres.*

歪嘴和尚 wāizuǐ héshang
monks with crooked mouths
A metaphor for cadres who are full of erroneous leftist ideas, who stick to conventions, who do not seek reforms, and who propagandize and carry out the Party's lines, guiding principles, and policies to the point of distortion.

外办 wài-bàn
foreign affairs office
Contraction of 外事办公室, departments set up in certain government organs and institutions to handle dealings with foreigners.

外调 wàidiào
1) to transfer out; to transfer material resources or personnel to another location or unit; 2) to investigate another unit or person
E.g. 科长出去外调了。*The section chief has gone to carry out investigations.*

外购 wàigòu
external purchase; to purchase from outside

外航 wàiháng
foreign airlines
Short for 外国航空公司.

外化 wàihuà
to externalize; to be or to make open

E.g. 外化形式 *external form* / 心理活动外化 *to externalize psychological activity*

外汇存底 wàihuì cúndǐ
foreign currency reserve
The amount of currency held by the central bank of a nation or region which can be exchanged for foreign currency. It is also the monetary assets placed in foreign countries, including accounts, stocks, bonds, and gold held in foreign banks.

外汇券 wàihuìquàn
foreign exchange currency(FEC)
Abbreviation for 外汇兑换券, issued by the Bank of China.

外货 wàihuò
foreign goods

外籍华人 wàijí huárén
Chinese of a foreign nationality
People of Chinese heritage who have become foreign nationals.

外挤内联 wàijǐ nèilián
to press externally and ally internally
Synonymous with 内联外挤. (cf. 内联外挤)

外借 wàijiè
to loan out
E.g. 此书不外借。 *This book may not be loaned out.* / 图书外借组 *library circulation department*

外经 wàijīng
foreign trade
E.g. 外经洽谈会 *Foreign Trade Fair*

外空 wàikōng
outer space
Short for 外层空间, also called 宇宙空间 *universe space*. The space beyond the earth's atmosphere.

外劳 wàiláo
foreign labor force

外流单干 wàiliú dāngàn
to go out to work independently
During the three years of economic hardship(1959-1961), some peasants were unwilling to join in the collective labor of production teams; they went elsewhere to pursue independent productive activities.
E.g. 家乡的生产发展了，那些外流单干的人也都陆续回来了。 *Production in the home area has developed; those who went out to work independently have also returned.*

外轮 wài–lún
foreign ships

外卖 wàimài
carry out; take aways
Convenient prepared foods sold to customers to take away.

外贸 wàimào
foreign trade

外派 wàipài
to send workers abroad (to work as employees of foreign companies)
E.g. 外派人数将有增加。 *The number of workers sent abroad will be increased.*

外片 wàipiān
foreign films
Including those made in Hong Kong, Macao, and Taiwan.

外企 wài–qǐ
foreign investment enterprises

外伤 wàishāng
external injury
A metaphor for visible damage to a nation or society's political life, ideology, economy, etc.

外商 wàishāng

foreign businessmen; foreign firms

外事 wàishì
foreign affairs
E.g. 外事工作 *foreign affairs work* / 外事部门 *foreign affairs department*

外事口 wàishìkǒu
foreign affairs departments
A term for various kinds of departments that deal with foreign affairs.

外事组 wàishìzǔ
foreign affairs section
Departments set up in such units as government offices, enterprises, and businesses that are responsible for foreign affairs.

外向型 wàixiàngxíng
(re production management) foreign-oriented or externally-oriented
E.g. 外向型经济 *foreign-oriented economy* / 外向型企业 *foreign-oriented enterprises*

外星人 wàixīngrén
extraterrestrial being

外需 wàixū
market demand abroad; overseas market demand (in foreign countries)

外烟 wàiyān
foreign cigarettes; imported cigarettes

外因论 wàiyīnlùn
theory of external causes
A philosophical view that things develop basically from external causes.

外引 wàiyǐn
to import
To bring in from other areas or from abroad.
E.g. 外引技术 *imported technology*

外引内联 wàiyǐn nèilián
import from abroad and linkage at home
This is a policy concerned with the development of China's open economy. To import funds, equipment and technology from abroad so that production, technology, management and the economic efficiency of enterprises in China will be improved. Also to forge links between enterprises so that they cooperate effectively in scientific research, production and marketing, etc.

外运 wàiyùn
ship out
To ship to other areas or abroad.
E.g. 外运物资 *to ship out material resources*

外战 wàizhàn
foreign war
As opposed to civil war.

外专局 wài-zhuān-jú
Bureau of Foreign Experts
Abbreviation for 外国专家局.

外资 wàizī
foreign capital
Foreign funds, capital invested from abroad.

wan

玩伴 wánbàn
playmate

玩车族 wánchēzú
people who are interested in and wish to own a luxury car

晚点 wǎndiǎn
delay
The time of departure, stage of progress, or arrival (of a bus, boat, plane, etc.) being later than the

scheduled time.

E.g. 飞机晚点一小时。*The plane is delayed by one hour.*

晚汇报 wǎnhuìbào
evening report

(during the Cultural Revolution) The evening ritual of reading Mao Zedong's quotations, paying tribute to Mao, etc.

晚婚 wǎnhūn
late marriage

晚恋 wǎnliàn
late romance

To engage in a romantic relationship at an older age.

晚生代 wǎnshēngdài
later generation

晚育 wǎnyù
late parenthood

To delay having children until several years after marriage.

万金油干部 wànjīnyóu gànbù
a cadre who is Jack of all trades but master of none

万金油 also called 清凉油, is a medicine known in the West as Tiger Balm Ointment. It has wide usage in relieving itching and pain, etc. 万金油干部 is a pejorative term for a cadre who is responsible for supervisory and political work but who has no special knowledge or skills.

万马奔腾 wànmǎ bēnténg
ten thousand horses galloping

A metaphor for constructive developments moving with great momentum and energy.

万元户 wànyuánhù
ten-thousand yuan household

A peasant household whose annual income from work exceeds ten thousand yuan.

腕 wàn
star

Referring to actors, singers, etc. Synonymous with 大腕, also written as 腕儿.

E.g. 歌坛巨腕 *big star singer* (*cf.* 大腕儿)

wang

王子 wángzǐ
prince

A metaphor for a person especially accomplished in a certain field.

E.g. 体操王子 "*gymnastics prince*", *an outstanding gymnast*

网吧 wǎngbā
Internet bar; web bar

A public service place which provides computer and Internet services to customers or consumers for the purpose of learning, gathering and exchanging information.

网虫 wǎngchóng
net worm; net fanatic; net fan

网大 wǎng-dà
college on the Internet; Internet college

Abbreviation for 网上大学的简称.

网点 wǎngdiǎn
network (lit. net and point)

"Net" is a net-like organization or system; "point" is a certain concrete unit or locale. A network is all the units of a certain trade (usually a service trade) at the various scattered locales. It is only a "point" when viewed from a certain concrete unit; but when viewed in its entirety, it is a "net" composed of innumerable points; hence the term "network".

E.g. 饮食网点 *food and drink network* / 缝纫网点 *sewing network* / 商业网点 *commercial network*

网路 wǎnglù
network (of communications, transportation, etc.)

E.g. 电话通讯网路 *telephone communication network* / 上海市交通正在形成平面、地铁、高架多层次的现代化立体交通网路。*The city traffic of Shanghai is becoming a modern three dimensional network of surface roads, subways, and overpasses.*

网络 wǎngluò
network; system

Now used most frequently as a metaphor for a system composed of many intersection components.

E.g. 交通网络 *communications network* / 经销网络 *marketing network* / 流通网络 *circulation network* / 信息网络 *information network*

网络电话 wǎngluò diànhuà
Internet phone

网络电视 wǎngluò diànshì
web TV

A television system for delivering net news or information through TV channels.

网络文学 wǎngluò wénxué
net literature

To put all kinds of literary works on the Internet.

网络银行 wǎngluò yínháng
Internet banking

网民 wǎngmín
netizen; net citizen; Internet user

网上大学 wǎngshàng dàxué
Internet college

A form of higher education spreading knowledge through the Internet.

网上购物 wǎngshàng gòuwù
net shopping

网坛 wǎngtán
the world of tennis

网校 wǎngxiào
Internet school; school on the Internet

A way of educating by spreading knowledge through the Internet system.

网页 wǎngyè
web page

网友 wǎngyǒu
web friend

网站 wǎngzhàn
web site

网址 wǎngzhǐ
web address

网主 wǎngzhǔ
web master

往返票 wǎngfǎnpiào
round trip ticket

Also called 来回票.

旺销 wàngxiāo
brisk sale

Commodities selling fast.

望子成龙 wàng zǐ chéng lóng
to hope that one's son becomes a "dragon", or a prominent successful person

忘本 wàngběn
to forget one's roots

When one's circumstances have turned for the better, to forget one's original circumstances.

E.g. 今天的生活好了, 可不能忘本哪! *Today our lives have improved, but*

we must not forget our roots!

wei

微波炉 wēibōlú
microwave oven

微波能 wēibōnéng
microwave energy

微车 wēichē
mini-vehicle

微电脑 wēidiànnǎo
microcomputer
Colloquial term for 微型电子计算机 microcomputer.

微电子技术 wēidiànzǐ jìshù
microelectronic technology

微雕 wēidiāo
microscopic carvings
The art form of carving (on miniature objects) characters, pictures, and other designs so small that they cannot be seen with the naked eye.
E.g. 他从事微雕已有三十多年了。 *He has been making microscopic carvings for over thirty years.*

微观经济 wēiguān jīngjì
microeconomics
It is the opposite of 宏观经济 macroeconomics.

微观世界 wēiguān shìjiè
microcosm
The world of extremely small material particles such as molecules, atoms, and electrons.

微货 wēihuò
mini-van; mini-lorry

微机 wēijī
microcomputer
Abbreviation for 微型电子计算机 miniature electronic computer. Also called 微型机 microcomputer.

微机病毒 wēijī bìngdú
computer virus (cf. 电脑病毒)

微轿 wēijiào
mini-car

微科学 wēikēxué
micro-science
The creation and application of microstructures (also called 微观建筑).

微客 wēikè
minibus

微刻 wēikè
miniature carving or engraving
Also called 微雕.

微脑 wēinǎo
mini laptop computer
A small and convenient portable computer. It has a large capacity for storing information and a high speed.

微软 wēiruǎn
Microsoft
E.g. 微软公司 *Microsoft Corporation*

微缩 wēisuō
microfilm
Also called 缩微.

微调 wēitiáo
micro-adjustment
The tuning device in certain types of electronic equipment.
E.g. 对书价作了微调 *to have made a slight adjustment in book prices*

微笑服务 wēixiào fúwù
service with a smile
Service personnel treating customers with warmth, courtesy, and a smile.

微型 wēixíng
miniature; mini; micro
E.g. 微型电脑 *microcomputers* / 微

型水电站 *miniature hydroelectric station* / 微型客房 *mini guest rooms* / 微型电影 *mini films*

微型机 wēixíngjī
microcomputer
Abbreviation for 微型电子计算机 microcomputer (also called 微机).

微型技术 wēixíng jìshù
the technology of creating mini-size machinery

微型小说 wēixíng xiǎoshuō
short short stories
Generally 1000 or so characters, also called 小小说.

危房 wēifáng
housing in danger of collapsing

危途 wēitú
hazardous road

危重 wēizhòng
(of illness) critical
E.g. 危重病人 *a critically ill patient*

违规 wéiguī
to violate regulations; illegal
E.g. 查出违规金额数亿元。*The investigation revealed several hundred million yuan's worth of illegal funds.*

违纪 wéijì
to violate discipline
E.g. 违纪案件 *a case of violation*

违价 wéijià
to sell at a price counter to that stipulated by the state
E.g. 违价案件 *a case of price control violation* / 违价所得金额要全部上交。*All income derived from price control violations must be turned over to the state.*

违控 wéikòng
to violate government control (in purchasing consumer goods)

违例 wéilì
to go against convention or usual practice
Specifically referring to violation of a regulation in an athletics competition.

违宪 wéixiàn
to violate a constitution or a charter
E.g. 违宪言论 *unconstitutional views and opinions* / 违宪行为 *unconstitutional acts*

违约 wéiyuē
to violate a treaty, a contract, or an agreement

违章 wéizhāng
unlawful; illicit
To go against ordinances and regulations.
E.g. 违章操作 *illicit operations* / 违章建筑 *illegal constructions*

围斗 wéidòu
to surround and assault

围堵 wéidǔ
to encircle and barricade
E.g. 四面围堵 *to be barricaded in on all sides*

围观 wéiguān
to encircle and watch
E.g. 围观外国人 *to encircle and watch foreigners* / 围观的群众 *a circle of staring people*

围垦 wéikěn
enclose and cultivate
To enclose an area of the seashore by building a dike and to cultivate that area.

唯成份论 wéichéngfènlùn
theory of the unique importance of class origin
An erroneous view concerning the training and appointment of cadres. It em-

phasizes only the family background and class origin of the cadre, and overlooks his actual abilities.

唯上 wéishàng
to act solely by one's superior's directives, without regard to the actual situation

唯生产力论 wéishēngchǎnlìlùn
doctrine of the unique importance of productivity
During the Cultural Revolution, Zhang Chunqiao denied the most basic practical experience of the masses, which is that productive activity plays a determinant role in the development of human history. Zhang vilified the efforts of the Party and the nation, which had been to organize the people to vigorously develop production and to diligently advance the four modernizations, calling them the "doctrine of the unique importance of productivity".

唯实 wéishí
pragmatism; to assess matters solely on the basis of practical reality

唯书 wéishū
to act solely by the book, i.e., unable to adapt to practical reality

唯条件论 wéitiáojiànlùn
theory of the unique importance of conditions
An erroneous viewpoint which emphasizes the function of objective conditions on production and work activities, and overlooks the function of people's subjective dynamics.

唯我独革 wéi wǒ dú gé
only I am revolutionary
A term from the Cultural Revolution. To believe oneself to be the most revolutionary

唯我独左 wéi wǒ dú zuǒ
only I am leftist
A term of the Cultural Revolution. To believe oneself to be the most steadfast leftist.

唯武器论 wéiwǔqìlùn
theory of the unique importance of weapons
The view that the only determinant of victory or defeat in a war is the superiority and quantity of weapons.

唯意志论 wéiyìzhìlùn
theory of the unique importance of will
Subjective idealism which believes that people's mentality and will can transform everything. This view greatly exaggerates the effect of mind over matter.

维和 wéi－hé
maintain peace
E.g. 维和部队 *peace-keeping forces*

维纶 wéilún
polyvinyl alcohol fiber
It is commonly called 维尼纶 or 维尼龙 winylon.

维棉 wéimián
vinylon and cotton blend
Also called 维棉布 vinylon-cotton cloth.

维尼纶 wéinílún
vinylon

维权 wéiquán
defend rights
E.g. 维权机构 *organizations concerned with defending rights*

维生素 wéishēngsù
vitamin
Formerly called 维他命. Transliteration of the English word "vitamin".

委培 wěi-péi
to consign the training of personnel to a certain school
E.g. 委培生 *personnel being trained at a certain school* / 委培单位 *unit (within a school) to which the training of personnel has been consigned*

伪劣 wěilüè
(of commodities) inferior imitations; counterfeits
E.g. 伪劣商品 *counterfeit commodities*

伪冒 wěimào
to counterfeit
E.g. 伪冒名牌产品 *to pass off counterfeits as name brand products*

伪证 wěizhèng
fake documents or certificates

伟哥 wěigē
viagra

尾巴 wěiba
tail
A metaphor for remnants of issues and problems; refers specifically to capitalist tail. (Metaphor for conceit and pomposity.) (cf. 资本主义尾巴)

尾巴工程 wěiba gōngchéng
tail constructions
In basic construction projects, some are put into operation before certain installations such as, storage, transport, and living facilities have been completed. The result is that much construction work remains to be done and the construction force is no longer integrated or productive. This is like dragging a very large tail, hence the term "tail constructions".

尾巴主义 wěiba zhǔyì
tailism
The mentality and behavior of relinquishing leadership and catering to the erroneous opinions of backward elements.

尾工 wěigōng
wrap up or clean up work; those engaged in wrap up or clean up work

尾牌 wěipái
rear plate (re vehicle license plates)

尾气 wěiqì
exhaust fumes

尾市 wěishì
the final stretch of a stock market trading session
E.g. 股价尾市略有回档。*There was a slight recovery in the stock market's final stretch.*

未来学 wèiláixué
futurology

未委会 wèi-wěi-huì
Juvenile Protection Commission
Abbreviation for 未成年人保护委员会.

位次 wèicì
seating order; ranking (of positions)

慰安妇 wèi'ānfù
comfort women
Women forced to serve as prostitutes for the Japanese military during World War Two.

卫冕 wèimiǎn
to retain the championship title (by winning a competition again)
E.g. 中国队卫冕成功。*The Chinese team succeeded in retaining the championship title*

卫生所 wèishēngsuǒ
health agency
A grass-roots organization for preventive

medicine and epidemic prevention.

卫生员 wèishēngyuán
paramedics
Elementary-level health workers who have received short-term training, and who have a basic knowledge of medicine, health and emergency care skills.

卫生院 wèishēngyuàn
health clinic
A grass-roots medical and disease prevention organization. Its main function is taking responsibility for medical and health work in a local area, organizing and leading mass health campaigns, and training paramedics.

卫生纸 wèishēngzhǐ
tissue paper; sanitary napkin

卫士 wèishì
guards
Such as the National Guards, private security guards, bodyguards, etc.

卫校 wèi-xiào
hygiene school
Abbreviation for 卫生学校.

卫星 wèixīng
satellites (natural and artificial)
E.g. 通讯卫星 *communications satellite* / 卫星资料 *satellite data* / 卫星通讯网 *satellite communications network*

卫星厂 wèixīngchǎng
satellite factory
A small factory which is subordinate to a large or central factory.

卫星城 wèixīngchéng
satellite town
A modern town built outside of a large city. In production and everyday life, it has connections with, but also a certain independence from, the city.

卫星国 wèixīng guó
satellite nation
A middle-sized or small nation that is an appendage to a superpower in political, military, foreign, and economic affairs. Moreover it acts in concert with the superpower.

卫星田 wèixīngtián
satellite fields
The agricultural fields that had record-breaking yields during the 1958 Great Leap Forward movement. (In this term, the word "satellite" is synonymous with the English word "sky-rocketed".

卫星云图 wèixīng yúntú
picture of cloud cover taken from a meteorological satellite

wen

瘟神 wēnshén
god of plague
Now the term refers mainly to highly contagious diseases.

温饱工程 wēnbǎo gōngchéng
bring-warmth fill-bellies project
To infuse agricultural technology and funds into a poor area so that it will attain self-sufficiency within a short period.

温室效应 wēnshì xiàoyìng
greenhouse effect
A result of the increase in carbon dioxide in the earth's atmosphere.

温馨 wēnxīn
warm and intimate
E.g. 温馨的家庭 *warm and intimate family life*

文保 wénbǎo
preservation of cultural artifacts
Abbreviation for 文物保护.

文代会 wén–dài–huì
Conference of Literary and Art Workers' Representatives
Abbreviation for 文学艺术工作者代表大会.

文电 wén–diàn
comprehensive term for documents, telegrams, and telephone calls

文斗 wéndòu
struggle by reasoning
To criticize and struggle in such ways as debating and writing big-character posters. It is the opposite of 武斗 struggle by coercion.

文牍主义 wéndú–zhǔyì
red-tapism
A kind of bureaucratism which is out of touch with reality, content with merely reading and dealing with documents in the office, and seeking to resolve issues by relying on documents and forms.

文改 wén–gǎi
script reform
Abbreviation for 文字改革.
E.g. 文改工作 *script reform work*

文革 wén–gé
Cultural Revolution
Abbreviation for 文化大革命. (cf. 文化大革命)

文攻武卫 wéngōng wǔwèi
to attack with civil tactics and defend with arms
A slogan raised during the Cultural Revolution when mass organizations were engaged in factional wars. "To attack with civil tactics" meant demolishing the opponent ideologically; "to defend with arms" meant responding to an opponent's armed attack with an armed counterattack. This slogan gave rise to all out civil war and intensified chaos within the nation.

文化产品 wénhuà chǎnpǐn
cultural products (i.e., books and newspapers, music, videotapes, paintings, etc.)

文化大革命 Wénhuà Dàgémìng
Cultural Revolution
A political movement initiated and led by Mao Zedong which lasted from May 1966 to October 1976. His main arguments were summarized as "the theory of continuing the revolution under the dictatorship of proletariate". This does not conform to Marxism-Leninism or to reality in China. The arguments were based on an inaccurate estimate of the class situation and political condition of the Party and China at that time. The movement was exploited by the two counter-revolutionary groups led by Lin Biao and Jiang Qing and resulted in serious calamities for the Party, the nation, and all the ethnic groups. The Cultural Revolution was not a revolution in any sense, but rather a period of internal chaos and calamity.

文化宫 wénhuàgōng
cultural palace
A large facility that provides cultural activities and entertainment for the masses.

文化馆 wénhuàguǎn
cultural center
A grass-roots-level facility that provides cultural activities for the masses.

文化户 wénhuàhù

cultural workers

Those who make their living by providing cultural entertainment to their community (also called 文化专业户 cultural professionals).

文化街 wénhuàjiē

cultural street

An elegant street with stores selling books, antiques, art objects, cultural equipment, musical instruments, etc.

文化垃圾 wénhuà lājī

trashy culture (i.e., base, obscene publications, audio and videotapes, etc.)

文化圈 wénhuàquān

cultural sphere

A realm that encompasses countries, regions, and peoples with a common cultural background.

文化衫 wénhuàshān

cultural shirts

Shirts with printed pictures or words.

文化市场 wénhuà shìchǎng

commercial establishments that provide various kinds of cultural entertainment, such as theaters, tea houses, dance halls, recreation rooms, etc.

文化站 wénhuàzhàn

cultural stations

Simple small-scale cultural entertainment centers (also called 文化室).

文化专制主义 wénhuà zhuānzhì zhǔyì

cultural tyranny

Dictatorial rule in the cultural realm. During the Cultural Revolution, the Lin Biao-Jiang Qing clique carried out "total dictatorship" in the cultural realm, rescinded the guiding principle of "let a hundred flowers bloom, and a hundred schools of thought contend", and rescinded the people's freedom to speak, publish, teach, research, create, and perform. What they enacted was feudal cultural tyranny.

文联 wén–lián

Federation of Literary and Art Circles

Abbreviation for 文学艺术界联合会.

文秘 wénmì

copy secretary

E.g. 文秘专业 *the specialty of being a copy secretary*

文明村 wénmíngcūn

civilized village

A rural residential area which has reached an advanced stage in building a spiritual and material socialist civilization.

文明公约 wénmíng gōngyuē

civilization pledge

Regulations drawn up by urban and rural residents concerning the building of a socialist spiritual civilization.

文山 wénshān

mountain of documents

文山会海 wénshān huìhǎi

mountain of documents and sea of meetings

Descriptive of a huge volume of documents and innumerable meetings.

文坛 wéntán

world of literature

文体活动 wén–tǐ huódòng

recreational and athletic activities

Contraction of 文娱体育活动.

文艺调演 wényì diàoyǎn

transfer and performance of the performing arts

A management department concerned with culture drawing together representative programs of performing art groups from various areas and arranging for them to give separate or combined performances, so that they may learn from each other, exchange experiences, and promote the development of their art.

文艺黑线专政论 wényì hēixiàn zhuānzhènglùn

theory of the dictatorship of the black line in literature and art

The ludicrous theory, advanced by the Lin Biao-Jiang Qing clique, concerning literature and works of art in the seventeen years after the founding of the People's Republic. This theory confounded right and wrong, and totally repudiated the achievements of the preceeding seventeen years. (cf. 黑线专政)

文艺会演 wényì huìyǎn

joint performance

To collect together the representative performing programs from various locales and units, and arrange for them to be performed separately or in combination. This allows the groups to learn from each other and benefit from each others' experiences. Also called 文艺汇演.

文艺轻骑队 wényì qīngqíduì

light performing art troop

A small-scale performing group which specializes in giving short cultural and propaganda programs to people in remote places such as mountain districts and grasslands.

文友 wényǒu

scholarly friends, friends in the cultural arena

文摘 wénzhāi

abstract (of a book or article); **excerpt**

A term often used in titles of publications.

E.g. 文摘报 *News Digest*

稳操胜券 wěncāo shèngquàn

to firmly grasp the winning ticket

A metaphor for being confident of victory.

稳产高产 wěnchǎn gāochǎn

stable and high yield

The per-unit crop yield is high and stable.

E.g. 这是稳产高产田。*This is a field with a stable high yield.*

稳拿 wěnná

to be totally confident of attaining

E:g. 稳拿冠军 *to win the championship with assurance*

稳准狠 wěn-zhǔn-hěn

sure, accurate, and relentless

The policy and tactics adopted by the Chinese Communist Party for struggling against an enemy. That is, one must be sure, accurate, and relentless in fighting the enemy. "Sure" means paying attention to tactics; "accurate" means not erring in killing; "relentless" means killing all those who should be killed (of course not killing those who should not be killed).

问鼎 wèndǐng

to seeking to seize political power; to win the championship in a competition

E.g. 参加比赛的各队都渴望问鼎桂冠。*Every team in the contest hopes to win the championship.* / 中国队实力强，问鼎不成问题。*The Chinese team* is strong, and should have no trouble winning the championship.

问卷 wènjuàn
survey questionnaire
E.g. 问卷调查 to investigate by using a survey questionnaire / 填写调查问卷 to fill out a survey questionnaire

问事处 wènshìchù
information office
Also called 询问处 information office.

问题小说 wèntí xiǎoshuō
problem novels (novels that raise social issues)

WO

窝边草 wōbiāncǎo
grass next to the rabbit's burrow
A metaphor for the property of one's neighbors or close associates.

窝电 wōdiàn
static electricity

窝工 wōgōng
work holdup
A situation where workers are idle because of poor planning or poor allocation.

窝里斗 wōlǐdòu
infighting

窝囊气 wōnángqì
bottle-up grievance or annoyance

窝气 wōqì
bottled-up grievance or annoyance

窝赃 wōzāng
to harbor criminals, stolen goods or money
E.g. 窝赃销赃罪 the crime of harboring and selling stolen goods

握手言和 wòshǒu yánhé
to shake hands and make peace; to settle for a tie (in a competition)

握手言欢 wòshǒu yánhuān
to shake hands and be merry (after a reconciliation)

WU

乌金 wūjīn
black gold; (colloquial term) coal

乌拉圭回合 Wūlāguī huíhé
the Uruguay round
Referring to the eighth round of the GATT negotiations, which took place in Uruguay.

乌兰牧骑 wūlán mùqí
an Inner Mongolian cultural troupe mounted on horseback
乌兰 and 牧骑 are two Mongolian words which literally mean "red" and "tender leaf". The combined term is a metaphor meaning "red cultural work team". It is a small troupe that uses short performances to propagandize the Party's guiding principles and policies, enliven the cultural and recreational life of pastoral peoples, and disseminate scientific and technological knowledge.

无笔画 wúbǐhuà
brushless paintings
A new painting technique based on the immiscibility of oil and water. Oil paint is dripped into water and after manipulation the paint falls onto a surface to form the work of art.

无产阶级国际主义 wúchǎn jiējí guójì zhǔyì
proletarian internationalism
The Marxist philosophy concerning international proletarian solidarity. In

their struggle for national liberation, and the overthrow of capitalism, the proletarian class in every nation should unite on the basis of Marxist-Leninist principles, rally together, and give mutual aid.

无党派人士 wúdǎngpài rénshì
nonpartisan figures
People of repute and influence in society who have not joined any political party.

无底洞 wúdǐdòng
bottomless hole
Metaphor for someone with insatiable demands.

无核 wúhé
seedless; nuclear free
E.g. 无核国家 *nuclear free nation*

无核化 wúhéhuà
to become nuclear free

无核区 wúhéqū
nuclear free zones
E.g. 非洲无核区 *African nuclear free zone* / 拉美无核区 *Latin American nuclear free zone* / 南亚无核区 *South Asian nuclear free zone*

无绳电话 wúshéng diànhuà
cordless telephone

无限上纲 wúxiàn shànggāng
to exaggerate matters to the level of principles
The erroneous way of elevating general issues of right or wrong or differences in opinion to the level of "class struggle" or "line struggle".
E.g. 他已习惯了"左"的那一套，动不动就给人家无限上纲。*He is already accustomed to the conventional leftist ways and exaggerates matters to the level of principles at the drop of a hat.*

无序 wúxù
without order
E.g. 社会从无序走向有序是一个漫长的过程。*For a society to go from one without order to one with order is a drawn out process.*

无烟工业 wúyān gōngyè
smokeless industry; tourist industry

武打片 wǔdǎpiān
kungfu movies

武斗 wǔdòu
struggle using force
1) Using violence to back up criticism and struggling against people. 2) The violent conflicts between mass organizations during the Cultural Revolution.

武检 wǔ-jiǎn
weapons inspection
E.g. 武检人员 *weapons inspection personnel*

武警 wǔ-jǐng
armed police
Contraction of 武装警察 armed police.

武林 wǔlín
martial arts circles
E.g. 武林人士 *martial artists* / 武林高手 *master of martial arts* / 武林名将 *famous martial arts expert*

武坛 wǔtán
world of martial arts

武卫 wǔwèi
(re Cultural Revolution) to protect oneself through violence

武校 wǔ-xiào
martial arts school
Abbreviation for 武术学校.

武星 wǔxīng
renowned martial artists or acrobatic fighting performers

武英 wǔyīng
martial arts hero
The highest rank of martial artists.
E.g. 20名武林名将取得武英称号。*Twenty martial arts stars have attained the title "martial arts hero".*

五爱 wǔ'ài
five loves
爱祖国、爱人民、爱劳动、爱科学、爱社会主义的简称。
Abbreviation for love of motherland, the people, labor, science, and socialism.
E.g. 五爱教育 *education concerning the five loves*

五保 wǔbǎo
five guarantees
农村集体经济组织对缺乏劳动力的农户给以物质保障,指保吃、保穿、保烧(燃料)、保教育(儿童和少年)、保葬。
Food, clothing, fuel, education, and burial (provided to families without manpower when the rural economy was collectivized).

五保户 wǔbǎohù
five-guarantee households
指农村中享受保吃、保穿、保烧、保教育、保葬(或保吃、保穿、保住、保医疗、保葬)等物质保障的老弱孤寡病残人员。
Peasants in rural villages with old, weak, orphaned, widowed, ill or handicapped folks who are beneficiaries of the five guarantees of food, clothing, fuel, education, and burial expenses. The five guarantees may include food, clothing, housing, medical care, and burial expenses.)

五定 wǔdìng
five items to be determined
指确定项目时,定建设规模、定投资总额、定建设工期、定投资效果、定外部协作条件。
In determining a construction project, there are five items to be determined. They are: the scale of construction, total amount of investment, period of construction, investment goals, and terms for outside assistance.

五定一奖 wǔdìng yījiǎng
five things to be determined and one reward
在实行农业生产责任制的过程中,生产队与社员共同制定的生产分配的管理办法。五定:定劳力、定地段、定产量、定投资、定报酬;一奖:超产奖励,减产赔偿。
The method of production and management jointly formulated by production teams and commune members in the process of implementing the agricultural production responsibility system. The five things to be determined are: manpower, area to be cultivated, target yield, investment, and remuneration. The "one reward" is the reward for exceeding the target and the penalty for falling short of it.

五毒 wǔdú
five vermins
1)指蝎、蛇、蜈蚣、壁虎、蟾蜍五种动物。2)指1952年"五反"运动中资本家行贿、偷税漏税、盗骗国家财产、偷工减料和盗窃经济情报五种违法行为。
1) The five animals: scorpions, vipers, centipedes, house lizards, and toads.
2) The five unlawful acts on the part of capitalists singled out in the 1952 "five-counter" movement. The five acts are: bribery, tax evasion, theft of state

property, cheating on government contracts, and theft of economic information.

五多 wǔduō
five excesses

指1953年前后,党政组织在农村工作中存在某些严重脱离群众,损害农民及其积极分子利益的问题,即所谓"五多"问题。"五多"就是任务多、会议集训多、公文报告表册多、组织多、积极分子兼职多。

Around 1953, Party and government organizations encountered in villages the problem of excesses in five areas. These problems led to alienation of the masses and damage to the interests of peasants and the active elements among them. The five excessive things were: assigned tasks, meetings and assemblies (for training), paper work (documents, written reports, and statistical forms), organizations, and concurrent jobs by active elements.

五反运动 wǔfǎn yùndòng
Five-Counter Movement

指1952年在全国资本主义工商业中开展的反行贿、反偷税漏税、反盗骗国家财产、反偷工减料和反盗窃国家经济情报的运动。

The movement launched in 1952 and directed at all capitalist industrial and commercial enterprises in the country. The five things to combat were: bribery, tax evasion, theft of state property, cheating on government contracts, and theft of economic information. Abbreviated as 五反 Five-Counter.

五分制 wǔfēnzhì
five-point system

The system of using five points for grading students on exams. That is, the numbers five, four, three, two, one or some other notations are used to represent the five levels of excellent, good, pass, below pass, and poor.

五风 wǔfēng
five tendencies

即共产风、浮夸风、瞎指挥风、命令风、干部特殊风。这是1958年人民公社化运动中曾一度出现的五种不良倾向。

The five unhealthy tendencies that surfaced for a time during the 1958 movement to form people's communes. These tendencies were: excessive communization, exaggeration, blind directives, commandism, and special (favorable) treatment of cadres.

五个一 wǔgèyī
Five One Project

指精神文明建设"五个一"工程,即每个省、市、自治区和有关部委党委宣传部,每年组织生产一部好电影、一部好电视、一台好戏、一本好书、一篇好文章。

Refers to the Five One Project for building spiritual civilization. It stipulates that the propaganda departments of every city, province and autonomous region gear themselves to produce one good movie, one good television program, one good play, one good book, and one good article every year.

五好家庭 wǔhǎo jiātíng
five-good family

80年代在社会主义精神文明建设中授予模范家庭的荣誉称号。五好标准一般是:遵纪守法,执行政策好;努力学习,参加社会活动好;计划生育,教育子女好;家庭和睦,邻里团结好；安全卫生，勤俭持家好。

The honorary title bestowed upon model families in the movement to build socialist spiritual civilization in the 1980s. The five areas to strive in were: 1. abiding by the law, carrying out policies; 2. studying diligently, joining societal activities; 3. birth control, educating one's children; 4. domestic harmony, uniting with neighbors; and 5. ensuring security and sanitary conditions in the household and being frugal.

五好竞赛 wǔhǎo jìngsài
five-good competitions
60年代初，中国各厂矿企业普遍开展的竞赛运动，包括五好企业和五好职工两个方面。参看"五好企业"和"五好职工"条。

The "five-good enterprises" and "five-good worker" competitions instituted in the various factories, mines, and enterprises in the early 1960s throughout China. (cf. 五好企业 and 五好职工)

五好企业 wǔhǎo qǐyè
five-good enterprises
在厂矿企业开展评比竞赛中授予先进企业的荣誉称号。五好标准是：政治工作好、执行政策完成计划好、经营管理好、生活管理好、干部作风好。

The honorary title bestowed upon advanced enterprises in the movement in the various factories, mines, and enterprises to evaluate and compete. The five areas to do well in are: political work, carrying out policies and completing plans, management of the enterprise, management in everyday life, and the work style of cadres.

五好文明家庭 wǔhǎo wénmíng jiātíng
five excellent and civilized family
即"首都五好文明家庭"，指的是遵纪守法、爱岗敬业、热心公益、计划生育、团结邻里的家庭。

Refers to Capital Five Excellent and Civilized Family. Family members should: observe public order and abide by the law; love their jobs and work hard; be interested in public welfare; practice birth control; and maintain a good relationship with neighbors.

五好战士 wǔhǎo zhànshì
five-good soldiers
60年代，人民解放军在开展五好运动中授予先进战士的荣誉称号。五好内容是：政治思想好、三八作风好、军事技术好、完成任务好、锻炼身体好。

The honorary title bestowed upon advanced soldiers in the Five-Good Movement launched in the 1960s by the People's Liberation Army. The five items were: political thought, the three-eight working style (cf. 三八作风), military skills, completion of tasks, and physical training.

五好职工 wǔhǎo zhígōng
five-good worker
指企业中政治思想好、完成任务好、遵守纪律好、经常学习好、团结互助好的职工。

A worker who excels in political ideology, completion of duties, discipline, continuing education, and rapport with colleagues.

五湖四海 wǔhú sìhǎi
all corners of the land (lit., five lakes and four seas)
1) All the areas of the nation. 2) A

metaphor for cadres from various areas of the nation. By extension, it refers to the correct policy regarding cadres, that is, to appoint the worthy (regardless of geographic origin) and to unite the great majority of cadres.

E.g. 要搞五湖四海。 *We must draw from all corners of the country.* / 五湖四海精神 *the spirit of drawing from the whole nation*

五荒 wǔhuāng

five uncultivated areas

即荒山、荒坡、荒滩、荒涂、荒水。

Uncultivated hills, slopes, seashores, shoals, and waters.

五荒一小 wǔhuāng yīxiǎo

five uncultivated areas and one small item

荒山、荒坡、荒滩、荒涂、荒水和水电的简称。

Uncultivated hills, slopes, seashores, shoals, and waters; and small hydroelectric stations.

五讲四美三热爱 wǔjiǎng sìměi sānrè'ài

five particulars, four beautifuls, and three loves

1983年3月全国开展"五讲四美三热爱"竞赛活动。"五讲": 讲文明、讲礼貌、讲卫生、讲秩序、讲道德。"四美": 心灵美、语言美、行为美、环境美。"三热爱": 热爱祖国、热爱社会主义、热爱共产党。

In March 1983, the whole nation launched competitive activities in the "five particulars, four beautifuls, and three loves". The five particulars to stress are: civility, courtesy, sanitation, orderliness, and morality. The four beautifuls are: beautiful soul, speech, behavior, and environment. The three loves are: love of motherland, socialism, and the Communist Party.

五匠 wǔjiàng

five kinds of craftsmen

泛指农村中的木匠、瓦匠(泥水匠)、铁匠、理发匠、豆腐匠等能工巧匠, 即有一技之长的手艺人。

Craftsmen with skills in particular areas. The skilled craftsmen in rural areas are carpenters, masons, blacksmiths, barbers, and bean curd makers. Five kinds of craftsmen also means: a carpenter, a brick-tile-cement worker, a blacksmith, a barber, and a bean curd maker.

五类分子 wǔlèi fènzǐ

five elements

Refers to landlords, rich peasants, counter-revolutionaries, bad elements, rightists (abbreviated as 地、富、反、坏、右).

五年计划 wǔnián jìhuà

five-year plan

A national plan for developing the national economy, using five years as a stage. The First Five-Year Plan of China began in 1953.

571工程纪要 Wǔqīyī Gōngchéng Jìyào

wu-qi-yi project summary

The code name for the military coup hatched by Lin Biao's counter-revolutionary group in March of 1971. "571 five-seven-one" is approximately homophonous with 武装起义 military insurrection. The scheme involved assassinating Mao Zedong, seizing political power, or creating a separatist regime. On September 8, Lin Biao sent out a personal order for Mao Zedong's assassination near Shanghai when Mao made an inspection tour of the south. The scheme was exposed and the plan fell through. On September 13, Lin Biao attempted to escape by air, and died in Mongolia.

五七道路 wǔ qī dàolù
May Seventh Path

The direction pointed out in Mao Zedong's May Seventh Directive during the Cultural Revolution. For example, going to a May Seventh Cadre School to labor and temper oneself and to receive re-education is called walking the May Seventh Path. (cf. 五七指示.)

五七干校 wǔ qī gànxiào
May Seventh Cadre School

Cadre schools founded in agricultural villages during the Cultural Revolution in accordance with Mao Zedong's May Seventh Directive. Their main activities were: political studies, physical labor, and thought reform. Intellectuals and the great majority of cadres in government organs were sent in groups at different times to May Seventh Cadre Schools to undergo tempering. (cf. 五七道路)

五七指示 wǔ qī zhǐshì
May Seventh Directive

The letter written on May 7, 1966 by Mao Zedong to Lin Biao after he had read a report from the Military Commission's General Logistic Department entitled "Report Concerning Improving the Agricultural Production of the Military". The letter said, "The People's Liberation Army should be a big school, where soldiers study politics, military affairs, and culture, and where they can carry out agricultural production and manage some middle- and small-sized industries to produce goods for their own needs and for bartering with the state. In this way, military studies, military farms, military industries, and military-civilian affairs can all be carried out concurrently". The letter also said, "Workers take industry to be primary, but they should concurrently study military affairs, politics, and culture, engage in socialist educational activities and criticize the bourgeoisie. Commune peasants take agriculture to be primary (including forestry, animal husbandry, sidelines, and fishery), but they also should concurrently study military affairs, politics, and culture. When conditions permit, they should collectively manage small factories and criticize the bourgeoisie. It's the same with students. They take studies as primary, but should concurrently study other things, not only books, but industry, agriculture, and military affairs. They should also criticize the bourgeoisie". The contents of this letter were later called the May Seventh Directive.

五七战士 wǔ-qī zhànshì
followers of the May Seventh Path
(cf. 五七道路)

五四三 wǔ-sì-sān
the five, four, and three

Abbreviation for 五讲四美三热爱 the five particulars, four beautifuls, and three loves. (cf. 五讲四美三热爱)

五通一平 wǔtōng yīpíng
five throughs and one level

五通是：通水、通电、通路、通讯、通

航；一平是平整土地。这是在开发经济特区时。为外商前来投资建设提供的基础设施。

The five throughs are: water supply, electricity, roads, postal service, and air transportation. The one level is level land. In developing special economic zones, these are the basic facilities to be provided to foreign businesses if they are to invest and construct.

五小 wǔxiǎo
five mini's

一般指小发明、小革新、小改造、小设计、小建议。

Mini-inventions, mini-innovations, mini-reforms, mini-designs, and mini-suggestions.

五小工业 wǔxiǎo gōngyè
five small industries

指60年代一些地方根据当地的资源和需要，自力更生兴办起来的小型工业，即小钢铁、小煤矿、小机械、小化肥、小水泥。

Small-scale industries built in some areas in the 1960s in accordance with local resources and needs, and intended to promote the principle of self reliance. They were small industries that produced iron and steel, coal, machinery, chemical fertilizers, and concrete.

五小竞赛 wǔxiǎo jìngsài
five-small competitions

指80年代青年职工为提高企业经济效益而开展的小发明、小革新、小改造、小设计、小建议的智慧杯竞赛活动。

Competitive activities, launched in the 1980s by young workers in enterprises, to upgrade economic efficiency. Wisdom Cups are awarded for inventions, innovations, reforms, designs, and suggestions.

五星红旗 wǔxīng hóngqí
five star red flag

National flag of the People's Republic of China. It is a rectangular flag with a red background, decorated on the upper left corner with five yellow five-pointed stars. One of the stars is larger, the other four smaller stars form an arc to the right of the larger star. The red of the flag symbolizes revolution. The five five-pointed stars and their relationship symbolize the unity of the revolutionary people under the leadership of the Chinese Communist Party.

五星级 wǔxīngjí
(re restaurants and hotels) five star level

五一六 wǔ-yāoliù
May Sixteenth

The May Sixteenth Regiment or its members. (cf. 五一六兵团)

五一六兵团 wǔ-yāoliù bīngtuán
May Sixteenth Regiment

A mass organization during the Cultural Revolution. At one time, it was considered a conspiratorial counter-revolutionary group, and a movement was launched throughout the nation to ferret out the group.

五一六通知 wǔ-yāoliù tōngzhī
the May Sixteenth Circular

Abbreviation for the "Chinese Communist Party Central Committee Circular" promulgated at the enlarged conference of the Political Bureau of the Chinese Communist Party Central Committee on May 16, 1966. This "Circular" was the programmatic document for the conduct of leading the Cultural Revolution. It demanded exposure and criticism of the bourgeois reactionary stance of the so-called "academic authority", seizure of leadership in the cultural realm, and a cleansing out of "bourgeois representatives that infiltrated the Party, the government, the military, and the cultural realm". This "leftist" policy, does not conform to Marxism-Leninism and, runs completely counter to the actual situation of China.

五种人 wǔzhǒngrén

five types of people (undesirables)

五种人是指追随林彪、江青反革命集团造反起家的人、帮派思想严重的人、打砸抢分子、反对党的十一届三中全会以后党中央路线的人、在经济领域和其他方面严重违法乱纪的人。

The five types are: those who made their way up by following the counter-revolutionary Lin Biao-Jiang Qing clique in creating disruption, those with a serious cliquish mentality, those elements who engage in beating, smashing, and looting, those who oppose the line adopted by the Party Central Committee after the Third Plenary Session of the Eleventh Party Central Committee, and those who have committed serious crimes.

捂盖子 wǔ – gàizi

to put a lid on; to conceal

Metaphor for covering up the truth and not letting others know. The term is often used in reference to certain people who make every effort to obstruct the discovery of mistakes and crimes by the masses and investigation by relevant departments.

舞迷 wǔmí

someone who is crazy about dancing

舞坛 wǔtán

world of dance

舞星 wǔxīng

renown dancers

物耗 wù – hào

consumption of material resources

物流 wù – liú

exchange or flow of material goods

E.g. 物流管理 *management of the flow of material goods*

物探 wù – tàn

geological survey

Abbreviation for 地球物理勘探.

E.g. 物探系 *department of geological survey*

物业 wùyè

A comprehensive term for residential, commercial, and office buildings.

E.g. 物业管理 *building management*

物质刺激 wùzhì cìjī

material incentive

The method of solely using material benefits to mobilize people to produce and work. The term has a derogatory connotation.

物质鼓励 wùzhì gǔlì

material encouragement

Giving material rewards (goods or money) to workers who have made certain achievements in the socialist revolution and construction.

务实 wùshí

to deal with concrete matters

1) To do or discuss concrete work. 2) Willing to do practical work. The opposite of 务虚 to deal with abstract matters.

务虚 wùxū

to deal with abstract matters

To study and discuss aspects of politics, ideology, policies, and theory as they relate to a certain task.

E.g. 务虚会 *a meeting on theoretical matters*. The opposite of 务实 *to deal with concrete matters*.

误班 wùbān

to be late for work; to waste work time (by doing other things)

E.g. 售票员误班 *The ticket seller missed his shift*.

误餐 wùcān

to miss a meal (due to working overtime, etc.)

E.g. 误餐补助 *subsidy for a missed meal* / 误餐费 *fee for a missed meal*

误导 wùdǎo

misguide

误工 wùgōng

to miss work

1) Failing to show up for work as in accordance with regulations. 2) Failing to end production work at the scheduled time (to quit early).

E.g. 第二小组今天又误工了。*The second squad again quit work early today*.

3) Failing to complete a production task on time.

误区 wùqū

pitfall

误诊 wùzhěn

to misdiagnose an illness or to not treat an illness in time

E.g. 一名患者因误诊致死。*A patient died from being misdiagnosed.* / 病例中有误诊死亡的。*There are some cases of deaths resulting from misdiagnosis.*

X

xī

嬉皮士 xīpíshì
hippie
Also called 嬉皮.

西北风 xīběifēng
folk songs and music from China's northwest which enjoyed popularity for a time

西部大开发 xībù dàkāifā
development of regions in the west

西单墙 Xīdānqiáng
Xidan Wall; Democracy Wall
A street corner in the Xidan district in Beijing where people aired their views by putting up big-character posters in 1979. Later, some people with ulterior motives took advantage of the situation; they disrupted order, and carried out unlawful activities. Permission to carry on such activities was rescinded in December 1979. It was popularly known as Democracy Wall in the West.

西风 xīfēng
west wind
A metaphor for the decadent influence and counter-revolutionary forces which are declining.
E.g. 国际形势是东风压倒西风。 *The international situation is one where the East will prevail over the West.*

西化 xīhuà
Westernization (in popular culture, etc.)
Synonymous with 西洋化.
E.g. "全盘西化"的主张是错误的。 *The proposition of total Westernization is erroneous.*

西兰花 xīlánhuā
broccoli

西欧共同体 Xī'ōu Gòngtóngtǐ
European Community
Synonymous with 欧洲共同体. (cf. 欧洲共同体)

西装鸡 xīzhuāngjī
western packed chicken
Chicken processed and wrapped in plastic for the market.

吸尘器 xīchénqì
vacuum cleaner

吸存 xīcún
the absorption of people's bank deposits by financial institutions
E.g. 这家银行吸存人民币总额居全国第一。 *The number of Renminbi deposits taken in by this bank is the highest in the nation.*

吸顶灯 xīdǐngdēng
ceiling light

吸毒 xīdú
to take drugs
To smoke opium, marijuana, etc.

吸纳 xīnà
to receive (funds, property, etc.)
E.g. 吸纳资金 *To receive investment capital* 吸纳货物 *to receive goods*

稀植 xīzhí
to plant sparsely; to enlarge the area per plant

息影 xīyǐng
(re movie stars) to retire from the screen
E.g. 息影近十年的一位老演员将重登银幕。 *An old movie star who has retired for almost ten years will soon re-emerge on screen.*

希望工程 xīwàng gōngchéng
Hope Project
The Aid Youth from Poverty Areas Deprived of Education Fund established in October 1989 by China's Youth Development Foundation to provide schooling for deserving children of poor families who had been deprived of education.

夕阳工程 xīyáng gōngchéng
Sunset Projects
Organizations and projects that provide services to the elderly.
E.g. 夕阳工程正在中国大奉兴建。 *Sunset Projects are flourishing in Dafeng, China.*

夕阳产业 xīyáng chǎnyè
sunset industries
Synonymous with 夕阳工业.

夕阳工业 xīyáng gōngyè
sunset industries
Traditional industries which are in decline due to decreasing demand, lack of technological innovation, reduced competitive edge, etc.

席梦思 xímèngsī
(English loan word) Simmons
General term for high-quality spring beds.

洗涤剂 xǐdíjì
detergent

洗发剂 xǐfàjì
shampoo

洗煤 xǐméi
to wash coal
Using a water spray to remove dust and grit from coal, and to divide the coal into different grades according to the degree of purity.

洗脑筋 xǐ nǎojīn
to brainwash
A pejorative term used by capitalists in referring to the thought reform of China's intellectuals

洗钱 xǐqián
money laundering
The various schemes for turning illegally acquired funds into funds from an apparently legitimate source.

洗手间 xǐshǒujiān
toilet; lavatory
Modern toilets equipped with hand washing facilities.

洗头膏 xǐtóugāo
shampoo paste

洗碗机 xǐwǎnjī
dishwashing machine

洗衣粉 xǐyīfěn
detergent; washing powder

洗衣机 xǐyījī
washing machine

系列 xìliè
a series
E.g. 系列化装品 *a set of cosmetics* / 系列组合 *combinations of related products or articles* / 系列服务 *a set of services* / 食品系列 *a series of food products*

系列化 xìlièhuà
seriation

A technical measure for selecting, finalizing and classifying industrial products of complicated standards and same functions.

E.g. 系列化食品 *seriated foods*

系列片 xìlièpiān
serialized movie
Also called 连续片 continuous movie.

系统工程 xìtǒng gōngchéng
systems engineering
It is a technology that organizes and manages the programming, research, design, creation, testing, and application of systems. It is guided by systems theory and it applies advanced scientific methods.

系统论 xìtǒnglùn
systems theory
A science of methodology that treats the object of research as a system. The extent of its applications is extremely broad, it ranges from biology to social sciences, from technology and science to culture and art.

戏说 xìshuō
to tell a story in a light or amusing way
Using techniques of deduction to portray (personages).

E.g. 戏说乾隆 *portraying (through techniques of deduction) the Emperor Qianlong (name of a television drama)*.

细菜 xìcài
fine vegetables
Vegetables grown with high capital input. They are of a high quality and are relatively costly, and include such vegetables as cucumbers, tomatoes, and garlic shoots sold in north China in the winter.

xia

瞎信 xiāxìn
blind letter
A letter with an address that is wrong, inaccurate, or unclear.

瞎指挥 xiāzhǐhuī
to blindly give orders
A subjective work method which does not take the actual situation as the point of departure and goes against the spirit of seeking truth from reality.

下拨 xiàbō
(a government agency or supervising unit) allocating materials or funds to units below

E.g. 市府下拨一批补助费。 *The municipal government is allocating a sum for income supplements*.

下放 xiàfàng
to transfer to a lower level
1) To transfer a certain unit's power to an organ at a lower level. 2) To send cadres to grass-roots organizations to work or to villages, factories, and mines for tempering.

E.g. 下放干部 *to send cadres down*

下岗 xiàgǎng
to withdraw from a professional post; to lay off

下馆子 xiàguǎnzi
to eat in a restaurant
Also called 上馆子.

下海 xiàhǎi
to go to sea
Originally refers to an amateur performer who becomes a professional entertainer; now it refers to people leaving their professions to go into business.

下连当兵 xiàlián dāngbīng
go to the companies as soldiers
Cadres at military offices and institutes go to the companies as contemporary common soldiers. It was once a measure for improving official style, training cadres and strengthening the establishment at low levels.

下马 xiàmǎ
abandon(a project)(lit., dismount)
A metaphor for stopping or giving up a certain important task, engineering project, or plan.
E.g. 下马工程 *an abandoned engineering project*

下马观花 xiàmǎ guānhuā
dismount to view flowers
Also called 下马看花。 A metaphor for cadres and intellectuals going to factories and villages over a long period of time to join in practical work in the three great revolutionary struggles. (cf. 三大革命实践)

下毛毛雨 xià máomáoyǔ
to drizzle
A metaphor for leaking information to certain people so that they will be prepared.

下三烂 xiàsānlàn
low-class people or things

下调 xiàtiáo
to adjust downward (re prices, targets, etc.)
E.g. 物价大幅度下调。 *Prices are being greatly reduced.*

下乡镀金论 xiàxiāng dùjīnlùn
doctrine of going down to the countryside to be gold-plated
During the Cultural Revolution, Lin Biao and the Gang of Four took Liu Shaoqi's words out of context, and distorted a speech he had made claiming that it lured country youths to follow a path to power and fortune (becoming cadres, being promoted, and getting rich). They called this doctrine of "going down to the countryside to be gold-plated". The speech actually exhorted country youths to keep their minds on agriculture and to diligently temper themselves.

下乡知识青年 xiàxiāng zhīshi qīngnián
rusticated educated youths
Urban high school graduates who went to rural villages to work in production teams to temper themselves or to settle there. Abbreviated as 下乡知青。

下游产品 xiàyóu chǎnpǐn
end product
The products produced at the final stage of a production process.
E.g. 下游产品成本上升。 *The production cost of end products has risen.*

下游企业 xiàyóu qǐyè
lower reaches enterprise; intensive (deeper) processing enterprise
An enterprise which intensively processes products after they are extensively processed by an upper reaches (extensively) processing enterprise.

下中农 xiàzhōngnóng
lower middle peasants
Middle peasants who own relatively few production resources, who must sell a small amount of their labor, and who have a relatively low standard of living.

夏播 xiàbō
summer sowing
Contraction of 夏季播种.

夏时制 xiàshízhì
summer time system; daylight saving time
The time system used in the summer season, also called 经济时制 economical time system.

夏收 xiàshōu
summer harvest
1) Crops harvested in summer. 2) Harvest of the summer season.

夏种 xiàzhòng
summer sowing
Contraction of 夏季播种 sowing in the summer season.

xian

先导市场 xiāndǎo shìchǎng
forerunner in the market

先锋派 xiānfēngpài
avant-garde

先进工作者 xiānjìn gōngzuòzhě
advanced workers
1) Persons in various lines of work, who make progress quickly, are efficient, have made outstanding achievements, and can be models for others. 2) Honorary title bestowed upon advanced workers.

先进集体 xiānjìn jítǐ
advanced group
1) A unit or group which makes progress quickly, is efficient, has made outstanding achievements, and can serve as a model. 2) Honorary title bestowed upon an advanced group.

鲜活 xiānhuó
fresh and lively
E.g. 注入鲜活的气息 *to imbue with a fresh and lively spirit* / 鲜活产品 *fresh or live products* / 鲜活商品 *fresh or live commodities*

纤维板 xiānwéibǎn
particle board; fiber board

贤内助 xiánnèizhù
virtuous inside assistant
A capable, virtuous, domestically oriented wife.

闲散资金 xiánsǎnzījīn
idle capital
Capital that is scattered among individuals or units and not being used (temporarily).

闲言碎语 xiányán suìyǔ
idle gossip
E.g. 不怕闲言碎语。 *Idle gossip is not to be feared.* / 闲言碎语没有市场。 *There is no market (i.e., audience) for idle gossip.*

显效 xiǎnxiào
obvious effects; to demonstrate efficacy

险段 xiǎnduàn
hazardous area

险工 xiǎngōng
dangerous constructions
Construction projects involving hazards, such as railroads through precipitous mountain areas.

险区 xiǎnqū
danger zone
A location or zone where a dangerous situation can easily arise.

险胜 xiǎnshèng
narrow victory
In an athletic competition, to win over an opponent by a very narrow margin.

现案 xiàn'àn

current cases (legal or criminal)
E.g. 要集中力量侦破重大现案。*We must concentrate our strength to break through the large current criminal cases.*

现场办公 xiànchǎng bàngōng
to handle matters on the spot; to study a task or deal with a problem directly on the spot

现场会议 xiànchǎng huìyì
on-site meeting
A meeting convened by the leadership at the location of an advanced unit or the site of an accident, so that those in attendance can examine the situation and learn from it.

现丑 xiànchǒu
to show one's ugly side; to embarrass oneself
E.g. 要使违法者现丑。*We must uncover illegal operators and expose their ugliness.*

现代迷信 xiàndài míxìn
modern superstition
The deification of the leader during the Cultural Revolution. In their attempt to usurp the Party and to seize power, Lin Biao and the Gang of Four greatly exaggerated the personal role of the leader, deified Mao Zedong with religious fervor and encouraged people to idolize him. This occurred not long ago, hence the term "modern superstition".

现代戏 xiàndàixì
modern drama
The various kinds of dramas that use modern societal life as their subject. They use techniques of expression from traditional operas, and retain the style and quality of the original operas, thus developing the original art form.

现反 xiàn-fǎn
active counter-revolutionaries
Abbreviation for 现行反革命分子.

现汇 xiànhuì
ready foreign exchange, cash reserve in foreign exchange

现市 xiànshì
current market
E.g. 现市交投活跃。*Trading on the current market is lively.*

现行反革命分子 xiànxíng fǎngémìng fènzǐ
active counter-revolutionaries
After the founding of the People's Republic of China, the criminal elements who aimed to overthrow the political power of the people's democratic dictatorship and the socialist system. Abbreviated as 现行反革命 or 现反. The term is used in opposition to 历史反革命分子 old line counter-revolutionaries.

现职 xiànzhí
current position

献血 xiànxiě
to donate blood
E.g. 无偿义务献血 *to donate blood free*

献演 xiànyǎn
to show one's artistry in a performance
E.g. 美国歌舞团首次来中国献演。*The American song and dance troupe gave a performance in China for the first time.* / 山东省京剧团向首都观众献演"武松打虎"。*The Shandong Opera Troupe gave a performance of "Wu Song Kills the Tiger" to an audience in the capital.*

献艺 xiànyì

to show one's artistry (to an audience)

E.g. 台湾和大陆表演艺术家今晚将同台献艺。 *The Taiwan and China's mainland performing artists are giving a performance on the same stage tonight.*

献映 xiànyìng

to show a movie or television program

E.g. 电影《红高粱》被送到上海献映。 *The film "Red Sorghum" has been sent to Shanghai for a showing.*

县委 xiànwěi

county committee

Abbreviation for a committee of the Chinese Communist Party at the county level.

限产产品 xiànchǎn chǎnpǐn

commodities under restricted production

Commodities that are produced in restricted quantities in accordance with a state plan.

限产压库 xiànchǎn yākù

to limit production and to reduce the stockpile in storage

限购 xiàngòu

to restrict purchase; to limit the quantity that can be purchased

E.g. 棉布不再限购。 *Cotton cloth is no longer rationed.* / 每人限购两张车票。 *Each person can only buy two tickets.*

限价 xiànjià

(re certain commodities) to stipulate prices; stipulated price

限收 xiànshōu

limited purchase

Contraction of 限制收购 limited purchase. The purchase of certain commodities by the state from producers is limited to a certain quantity.

线民 xiànmín

informer; an inner connection; spy

线报 xiànbào

report from an informer

E.g. 接到线报 *to receive a report from an informer*

xiang

香波 xiāngbō

(transliteration) shampoo

香风 xiāngfēng

fragrant air

Metaphor for the influence of bourgeois mentality and life style.

E.g. 青岛边防检查站被誉为"香风吹不进的边防关"。 *The Qingdao border check station has been eulogized as a "border defense pass impenetrable by fragrant air".*

香格里拉 xiānggélǐlā

(transliteration) Shangri-la (often used as the name of a hotel or company)

E.g. 香格里拉饭店 *Shangri-la Hotel* / 香格里拉汽车公司 *Shangri-la Auto Company*

乡规民约 xiāngguī mínyuē

folk regulations

Codes of behavior, formulated by peasants to promote the construction of socialist spiritual civilization.

乡企 xiāng-qǐ

enterprises in rural areas and small towns

Abbreviation for 乡镇企业.

E.g. 乡企效益居各行业之首。 *In terms of productivity, the enterprises in rural and small towns lead in every category.*

乡社合一 xiāng-shè héyī
combining township and commune

During the movement to form people's communes an effort was made to combine the organ of rural political authority – the township people's government – with the commune management organ to create a people's commune that combined the government with the commune. This could function as a political authority and be the basis of economic management. This movement was reversed in 1982. (cf. 政社分开)

乡土教材 xiāngtǔ jiàocái
local teaching materials

Supplementary teaching materials based on knowledge of the geography, history, literature, and biology of the local area.

乡土文学 xiāngtǔ wénxué
native soil literature

Literary works which are based on the life in the authors' hometowns, and which are rich in hometown flavor.

乡镇企业 xiāngzhèn qǐyè
town and township enterprises

The overall term for the various joint and independent enterprises in villages and towns. These were originally called 社队企业 commune- and team-managed enterprises; the name was changed in 1984. (cf. 社队企业)

详备 xiángbèi
thorough; exhaustive

Contraction of 详细 detailed and 完备 complete.

响当当 xiǎngdāngdāng
metaphor for being outstanding, masterful, or renowned

E.g. 响当当的人物 *renowned personage* / 响当当的成绩 *outstanding achievement*

橡皮图章 xiàngpí túzhāng
rubber stamp

An organization or bureaucrat who rubber-stamps (figuratively).

E.g. 不要把职代会当做橡皮图章。 *Don't take the Employees' Representatives Conference (labor union) to be a rubber stamp.*

向钱看 xiàngqiánkàn
money-grubbing

The bourgeois mentality and behavior of fixing one's eyes on money, doing everything for money, benefiting oneself at others' expense, and looking for every advantage.

向前看 xiàngqiánkàn
looking forward

Not to be tied down by old scores, to concentrate energy on studying new situations and solving new problems, to unite in mind and strength and strive together to realize the four modernizations.

向阳院 xiàngyángyuàn
sun facing compound

Synonymous with socialist compound. (cf. 社会主义大院)

象形食品 xiàngxíng shípǐn
food shaped into things

Foods that have been made in the shape of such things as animals, etc.

xiāo

销价 xiāojià

selling price

销量 xiāoliàng

sales volume (of a commodity)

E.g. 销量剧增。*The sales volume rose dramatically.* / 销量创记录。 *The sales volume broke previous records.*

销区 xiāoqū

sales region

销脏 xiāozāng

to sell stolen goods; to destroy stolen goods

E.g. 销赃罪 *crime of selling stolen goods*

消费合作社 xiāofèi hézuòshè

consumers' cooperative

A consumers' organization that buys commodities wholesale and retails them to coop members.

消费基金 xiāofèi jījīn

consumption fund; fund for buying consumer goods

The portion of gross national product in a socialist country which issued for non-productive consumption. It includes mainly individual consumption funds, education and health funds, social security funds, and state management funds.

消费税 xiāofèishuì

consumption tax

Tax levied on certain goods and services.

消化 xiāohuà

to digest (literal and figurative); to process grains into other products; (re enterprises) metaphor for overcoming certain obstacles in management through internal means

E.g. 发展畜牧业，农民剩余的粮食被消化了。 *After animal husbandry was developed, the peasants' surplus grain had an outlet.* / 消化文件精神 *to absorb the spirit of the documents* / 消化引进的先进技术 *to absorb imported advanced techniques* / 原材料提价后产品成本增加，主要靠企业内部消化。 *The increase in production cost as the result of a price increase for raw materials was largely absorbed by the enterprise through internal means.*

消极因素 xiāojí yīnsù

negative factor

It is the opposite of 积极因素 positive factor.

消纳 xiāonà

to dispose of and absorb (trash, waste materials, etc.)

E.g. 消纳垃圾 5 万吨 *to dispose of 50,000 tons of trash*

消纳场 xiāonàchǎng

waste dump

消纳站 xiāonàzhàn

waste dump

Synonymous with 消纳场.

消协 xiāo-xié

consumers' association

Abbreviation for 消费者协会.

消肿 xiāozhǒng

to reduce swelling; to trim

A metaphor for trimming organizations to remedy overstaffing and bureaucratic redundancy.

E.g. 机关消肿仍是个大问题。 *Reducing the swelling in organizations is a major issue.*

逍遥派 xiāoyáopài

the unfettered faction

Those people who "wandered" outside of all political movements during the Cultural Revolution. They did not join any mass organizations or factional struggles. They were not restricted by the regulations of mass organizations at that time, so they were unfettered and carefree in their actions.

小巴士 xiǎobāshì
minibus

Stops anywhere along a route for passengers, costs considerably more than regular buses. Also called 小巴.

小百货 xiǎobǎihuò
sundries

Small-scale light industrial and handicraft products used in everyday life, such as buttons, sewing needles, tooth brushes, etc.

小报告 xiǎobàogào
telling tales

To pass information to the leadership behind someone's back, the information is not necessarily objective or accurate. *E.g.* 打小报告 *to practice telling tales*

小辫子 xiǎobiànzi
small queue

A metaphor for a handle (by which one can be taken to task). (cf. 抓辫子)

小不拉子 xiǎobùlāzi
(colloquial) small child (under five or six years old)

小炒 xiǎochǎo
small stir-fried dish

Stir-fried dish cooked in a small wok, as distinguished from 大锅菜 big pot dish, or food mass-produced in a restaurant or institution. The term is often used for food made especially, and with special care, for a small group at an institution or restaurant.

小春耕 xiǎochūngēng
small spring planting

Also called 小春播 small spring sowing, the work of planting in scattered pieces of land and uncultivated hills by peasants in the spring planting season.

小春作物 xiǎochūn zuòwù
small spring crops

Crops such as wheat and peas sown in the tenth lunar month (because in some areas, the weather in the tenth lunar month is as warm as spring).

小打小闹 xiǎodǎ xiǎonào
(re jobs or production projects) small in scale and at a level low

E.g. 农民商业从小打小闹走向规模经营。 *Peasants' business enterprises went from small-scale operations to large scale.*

小道理 xiǎodàolǐ
petty principles

Principles that are disadvantageous in the long run and to the overall situation, but are advantageous only in the short run in a limited way.

小道消息 xiǎodào xiāoxi
hearsay

小段包工 xiǎoduàn bāogōng
contracting small sections

A form of the agricultural production responsibility system. Agricultural work is divided into sections; reasonable work quotas are then determined according to the size and difficulty of the jobs; time and quality requirements are set; the jobs then are contracted to teams or individuals. After the jobs are completed, they are checked and work points are recorded according to the quotas. Sometimes awards are given.

小而全 xiǎo ér quán
small but complete

An enterprise may be small, but it expects to be complete in technology, facilities, and the various departments. The risks in this are the dispersal of enterprise energy, low productivity, and the likelihood that it will hinder specialization and cooperation.

小儿科 xiǎo'érkē
kids stuff
1) Pediatrics.
2) A metaphor for professions disdained by people or matters not worthy of note. *E.g.* 有人说职业班是小儿科。*Some say that the vocational class is kids stuff.*

小费 xiǎofèi
tip
Also called 小帐 small bill.

小广播 xiǎoguǎngbō
petty broadcast; gossip
To privately spread unreliable information or information that should not be publicized.

小红书 xiǎohóngshū
little red book
Containing the sayings of Chairman Mao which was ubiquitous during the Cultural Revolution.

小呼隆 xiǎohūlóng
small-scale sound and fury
A name given by peasant masses to the system of contracting responsibility to the work team. Although productivity under this system has been raised one step above that of collective labor, it cannot totally avoid the problem of 大呼隆 making sound and fury en masse, hence it is called 小呼隆 small-scale sound and fury. (cf. 大呼隆)

小化肥 xiǎohuàféi
small-scale, relatively low-tech chemical fertilizer plants; the fertilizer produced in such plants

小皇帝 xiǎohuángdì
little emperors
The spoiled only children of contemporary China (also called 小太阳 little suns).

小集体 xiǎojítǐ
small group
A form of the socialist collective ownership system. It consists of collectively owned enterprises that carry out independent accounting, take responsibility for their own losses and gains, and are managed by their city or town neighborhoods. Some examples are factories and processing teams in neighborhoods and lanes. It is the opposite of 大集体.

小集团主义 xiǎojítuán zhǔyì
small groupism
Synonymous with 小团体主义. (cf. 小团体主义)

小家庭 xiǎojiātíng
little family
Young married couple with their own independent household.

小将 xiǎojiàng
little general
A metaphor for a young person with ability and a path-breaking spirit. *E.g.* 革命小将 *young revolutionary fighter*

小脚女人 xiǎojiǎo nǚrén
woman with bound feet (of the old society)
A metaphor for backward, slow moving persons.

小节无害论 xiǎojié wúhàilùn
the view that small matters can do no

harm

A fallacy about promoting cadres advocated by Lin Biao. It was that as long as a person was good in the political sense, even if he had faults and errors in the "small matter" of his personal life, these shortcomings should not be obstacles to him being promoted to an important position.

小金库 xiǎojīnkù
private gold storage

A metaphor for funds or materials that certain enterprise and business units retain privately for their own use, in violation of fiscal regulations. Also called 小钱柜 private money cupboard.

小康水平 xiǎokāng shuǐpíng
comfortably well-off standard

Also called 小康生活水平 comfortable living standard. The term refers specifically to the goal for the GNP by the end of the 20th century, which is approximately US $1,000 in annual per-capita income.

小款 xiǎokuǎn
little moneybag

A person of some wealth, but not as much as a big moneybag. (vs. 大款 big moneybag)

小流域 xiǎoliúyù
a defined area through which a water system flows

E.g. 小流域系统 ecological system of a defined drainage area / 小流域综合治理工作 general repair and control work of a drainage area

小米加步枪 xiǎomǐ jiā bùqiāng
millet plus rifles

A metaphor for the hard life and poor military equipment of the troops led by the Chinese Communist Party in the years of the revolutionary war. At that time, the main food was millet, and the main weapons were rifles.

小爬虫 xiǎopáchóng
small creepy animals

1) Vertebrates that have scales or shells on their bodies and are highly adaptable to external changes like chameleons.
2) A metaphor for those people during the Cultural Revolution who were politically opportunistic and good at camouflaging themselves.

小气候 xiǎoqìhòu
microclimate

1) The climate of a specific place within an area, contrasted with the climate of the area as a whole.
E.g. 植树可以改变小气候。 A microclimate can be changed through tree planting.
2) The conditions and situation of some areas.
E.g. 要为三资企业创造一个适宜的小气候 to create a favorable microclimate for the three kinds of ventures.

小钱柜 xiǎoqiánguì
private money cupboard

Synonymous with 小金库. (cf. 小金库)

小秋收 xiǎoqiūshōu
small autumn harvest

Collecting wild animals and plants carried out by peasants around autumn harvest time.

小区 xiǎoqū
a self-contained community within a city

E.g. 居民小区 residential community / 居住小区 residential community

小圈子 xiǎoquānzi
small circle
1) A narrow sphere of life.
E.g. 走出家庭的小圈子 *to walk beyond the small circle of the family*
2) A small group of people who draw in and use each other for private benefit.
E.g. 搞小圈子 *to engage in a small circle*

小人物 xiǎorénwù
the little people
Ordinary folk (as opposed to 大人物 the big shots).

小三线 xiǎosānxiàn
small third line
In the early 1960s China was divided into first, second, and third lines according to the area's strategic position. Areas of provinces and cities were also divided into first, second, and third lines. The large rear area of the whole nation was called the "big third line". The local strategic rear areas in provinces and cities were called "small third lines".

小山头 xiǎoshāntóu
small mountain stronghold
A metaphor for unhealthy tendencies of small circles and small groups. (cf. 山头主义)

小商品 xiǎoshāngpǐn
small commodities
Commodities that are scattered in their production, numerous in their variety, fast in turnover, low in cost, and difficult to incorporate into state planning. They include sundries such as small hardware items, certain items for everyday use and stationery items.

小商品经济 xiǎoshāngpǐn jīngjì
small commodity economy
The economy of peasants and handicrafters producing commodities through individual labor. The producers possess the production resources, rely on their own labor, and sell commodities only to meet their own needs.

小水电 xiǎoshuǐdiàn
small-scale hydroelectric plant (with installed capacity under 12 million watts, usually set up locally)

小水泥 xiǎoshuǐní
small-scale locally set up cement plants

小太阳 xiǎotàiyáng
little suns
Synonymous with 小皇帝 little emperors. (cf. 小皇帝)

小天地 xiǎotiāndì
small world
A metaphor for the relatively small sphere of activity of some people.

小土地出租者 xiǎotǔdì chūzūzhě
persons renting out small amounts of land
People in rural areas who rented out small amounts of land and were so classified during China's land reform period. These people included revolutionary soldiers, families of martyrs, white and blue collar workers, self-employed persons, pedlars, and people who rented out land because they were in other professions or because they lacked labor power. The class status of these people was sometimes determined by their profession; sometimes they were classified as persons renting out small amounts of land.

小土群 xiǎo-tǔ-qún

small old-fashioned flock

The small-scale iron and steel furnaces built by the masses using simple old-fashioned methods in the 1958 national movement to produce steel. Later, the term extended to all small-scale industries that used traditional technology and were established as a result of a mass movement.

小团体主义 xiǎotuāntǐ zhǔyì
small groupism

A manifestation of bourgeois individualism. It is a mentality within the proletarian ranks which is concerned with the interests of one's own small group, and not the whole. It may not seem on the surface to be for the individual, but in reality it is an extremely narrow kind of individualism.

小五金 xiǎowǔjīn
small hardware

An overall term for small tools and metal parts used in making buildings and furniture, such as nails, screws, wire, locks, and springs.

小媳妇 xiǎoxífù
young daughters-in-law

A metaphor for people in a lowly position who are bullied and controlled by others.

小鞋 xiǎoxié
tight shoes; small shoes

A metaphor for restrictive or tight situations covertly inflicted by someone with power.

E.g. 他不敢批评上级，怕打击报复，怕给小鞋穿。 *He does not dare criticize his superiors for fear that they will seek revenge and give him a hard time.*

小小说 xiǎoxiǎoshuō
short short stories; mini short stories

Synonymous with 微型小说. (cf. 微型小说)

小兄弟 xiǎoxiōngdì
little brothers

The younger members of a certain group or faction.

E.g. "四人帮"的小兄弟 *little brothers of the Gang of Four*.

小业主 xiǎoyèzhǔ
small entrepreneurs

Industrial and commercial entrepreneurs who possess small amounts of capital, engage in small-scale businesses, and employ a few or no workers. In general, they belong to the petty bourgeoisie.

小意思 xiǎoyìsi
a token of one's feelings (regard, appreciation, etc.); not worth mentioning

E.g. 这是我的一点小意思。 *This is just a small token of my feelings (gratitude, etc.).*

小资 xiǎozī
petty capitalist class

E.g. 小资情调 *petty capitalist sentiments*

小字报 xiǎozìbào
small-character posters

Posters with suggestions and requests written in small characters and posted for the public to see. They are the opposite of 大字报 big-character posters.

小字辈 xiǎozìbèi
younger generation

Young people in general.

校际 xiàojì
intercollegiate; inter-school

E.g. 校际关系 *inter-school relations* /

校际交流 inter-school exchange / 校际合作 inter-school cooperation

校纪 xiàojì
school discipline

校外辅导员 xiàowài fǔdǎoyuán
after school activities counselors
Personnel who volunteer to help or guide elementary and middle school young pioneers in organizing and engaging in activities outside of school. These people include workers, cadres, soldiers, and people who work with children.

笑星 xiàoxīng
comedian

效益工资 xiàoyì gōngzī
wages based on benefits
A wage system that directly links productivity with remuneration.

xie

歇班 xiēbān
off duty

歇菜 xiēcài
(Beijing patois) to stop and do nothing
E.g. 歇菜去,我不听那个。 *Quit it! I won't listen to that!*

协议离婚 xiéyì líhūn
consentual divorce
A divorce in which the two parties have reached an agreement and present it to the authorities for processing; the term also applies to a divorce in which the couple have reached agreement after the People's Court has heard and mediated the case.

协作区 xiézuòqū
coordinated regions
Synonymous with 经济协作区 economically coordinated regions and 经济区 economic region. (cf. 经济协作区)

写字楼 xiězìlóu
office building

xin

薪炭林 xīntànlín
fuel forests
Forests that produce mainly firewood. They are generally planted in a species of brushwood that sprouts easily, grows fast, and has high fuel value.

辛苦费 xīnkǔfèi
trouble fee
1) Money paid to someone for doing something that has been requested. 2) The work subsidy fee paid by responsible persons in some enterprise and service units.

新岸 xīn'àn
new shore
Metaphor for a new beginning for a former criminal.
E.g. 悔悟是走向新岸的起点。 *Remorse is the beginning of the path toward a "new shore".*

新产业革命 xīnchǎnyè gémìng
new industrial revolution
Also called the "fourth industrial revolution" and the "third wave". It is a popular concept in Western countries. As a result of the rapid development of a whole series of new and emerging industries based on computers various Western countries will transform from industrial societies into information societies. This development is called the "new industrial revolution". The abili-

ty to produce knowledge has already become a key factor in determining productivity, competitiveness, and economic success.

新长征 xīnchángzhēng
the New Long March

A metaphor for the new historical period from the downfall of the Gang of Four to the end of the 20th century, in which the chief mission of the Chinese people was to struggle to build their country into a strong modern socialist nation.

新长征突击手 xīnchángzhēng tūjīshǒu
shock workers of the New Long March

An honorary title bestowed upon the advanced young people who have surfaced in the various front lines in China's socialist modernization.

新潮 xīncháo
new trend

E.g. 具有新潮感的风雨衣 *a modish trench coat*

新高 xīngāo
new standard; new record; new level

E.g. 电脑销售将创新高。*The sales of computers will create a new record.*

新领工人 xīnlǐng gōngrén
new collar worker

Refers mainly to the American baby boomers born after World War Two, most of whom work in the service sector. Also called 新领阶层 new social class.

新苗 xīnmiáo
seedling

Newly risen, vital, promising person or thing.

E.g. 半工半读是教育的新苗. *Half-work, half-study is a new seedling in education.*

新贫族 xīnpínzú
new poverty class

White-collar people whose income does not match their high consumption complain that they live in poverty.

E.g. 新贫族被一些人称为败家子。*The new poverty class is called spendthrift by some people.*

新人口论 xīnrénkǒulùn
new population theory

A theory advanced by the well-known scholar Ma Yinchu in 1957. The theory advocates strenuously controlling the size of the population and upgrading its caliber. The theory includes the following main points: to incorporate population increases into the plans for societal and economic development of the nation; to control births and population growth; to implement planned parenthood.

新人类 xīnrénlèi
new generation

A generation that has grown up in cities. Their values and lifestyle are different from the previous generation, so they are called the new generation.

新生代 xīnshēngdài
The Cenozoic Era

This term originally referred to the fifth geological era. Now it also refers to the new generation of young people.

新生力量 xīnshēng lìliàng
newly emerging force

1) A force which has just appeared. 2) People full of vigor and promise (usually referring to young people).

新生事物 xīnshēng shìwù

newly emerging things

A cover term for all the new things that have just appeared, and are beneficial to society and rich in vitality.

新闻片 xīnwénpiān

documentary

A type of film or television news report. Also called 新闻纪录片.

新西兰 xīnxīlán

New Zealand; Xin-Xi-Lan

An facetious composite term for Xinjiang, Tibet, and Lanzhou, three distant rugged locales (contrasted with 天南海北 all over the territory, a pun acronym for Tianjin, Nanjing, Shanghai, and Beijing).

E.g. 他愿意去天南海北,不愿去新西兰。 *He is willing to go to Tianjin, Nanjing, Shanghai, and Beijing, but not to Xinjiang, Tibet, and Lanzhou.*

新新人类 xīnxīn rénlèi

new humankind

A term from Taiwan which refers to a generation of people born in a period between the mid or late 1970s and the 1980s. They are characteristically individualistic and like to show off.

新星 xīnxīng

new stars

Persons who have just made outstanding achievements in the realm of art, music, sports, etc.

新兴力量 xīnxīng lìliàng

new or rising force

A new or rising social force or nation. In the 1960s, the term referred specifically to the nations in the vast areas of Asia, Africa, and Latin America that had just attained independence.

新秀 xīnxiù

emerging persons of eminence

Young persons of outstanding achievements in the realm of literature, art, and athletics.

新医疗法 xīnyī liáofǎ

new medical treatment method

A new type of medical treatment method that combines Chinese and Western medical practices.

新意 xīnyì

new ideas

E.g. 作品要去陈规,出新意。 *Works (of literature) must break out of the old mode and come up with some new ideas.* / 这篇小说没有新意。 *This novel doesn't have any fresh ideas.*

新影厂 Xīn-Yǐng-Chǎng

Central Newsreel and Documentary Film Studio

Abbreviation for 中央新闻记录电影制片厂. Also called 新影.

新招 xīnzhāo

new scheme or tactic

E.g. 厂长又出新招。 *The factory manager came up with another new scheme.*

新殖民主义 xīn zhímínzhǔyì

new colonialism

新中农 xīnzhōngnóng

new middle peasants

After the various places in China implemented land reform, poor peasants who rose economically to middle peasants were called "new middle peasants". This category includes three subcategories: upper, middle, and lower middle peasants. The majority of them have a relatively high level of political consciousness and experience of poverty, and accept socialist reforms readily.

心态 xīntài

psychological state; psychological activity

心头肉 xīntóuròu

a piece of one's heart

Person or thing most near and dear to one's heart.

E.g. 儿女是父母的心头肉。 *Children are what's most near and dear to their parents' hearts.*

心有余悸 xīn yǒu yújì

to have lingering fear

To experience fear when thinking back on a past event, even though the danger is past.

心战 xīnzhàn

psychological warfare

信访 xìnfǎng

visitation by correspondence

Ordinary people writing to leadership organizations reporting on situations or requesting remedies to problems.

E.g. 信访案件 *a case brought through a letter (to the authorities)* / 信访工作 *work dealing with letters from the people* / 加强信访队伍建设 *to strengthen the building of a contingent dealing with letters from the people*

信访部门 xìnfǎng bùmén

correspondence and visitation departments

Departments set up by various levels of Party and government organs to handle letters and visits from the masses. The masses may send letters or visit to report on the ways in which the various guiding principles and policies are being carried out. They can criticize and make suggestions about the work of the Party and the government, expose misdeeds and wrong-doers, and to ask for solutions to difficulties and problems.

信息爆炸 xìnxī bàozhà

information explosion

信息处理 xìnxī chǔlǐ

information management

信息点 xìnxīdiǎn

information point

Places (organizations and personnel) set up in various urban and rural areas to collect and transmit information after China implemented the policy to enliven the economy in the post-Cultural Revolution era.

信息服务 xìnxī fúwù

information service

To provide relevant units or departments with accurate and timely information about production, supply, marketing, and developments in science and technology.

信息高速公路 xìnxī gāosù gōnglù

information super-highway

Also called 信息公路 information highway.

信息革命 xìnxī gémìng

information revolution (i.e., computer revolution)

信息工业 xìnxī gōngyè

information industry

An industry providing equipment and the means of producing, storing, processing and delivering of information. It includes: computers, microelectronic devices, long-distance communications, information techniques, software, etc.

信息工作者 xìnxī gōngzuòzhě

information workers

Personnel whose chief responsibility is to produce, manage, or relay information (such as administrators, managers, and secretaries), and personnel that build and maintain basic information facilities (such as installers of telephone networks, computer operators, and office machinery maintenance personnel).

信息经济 xìnxī jīngjì
information economy
An economy that relies on increasing knowledge and information to produce commodities which consume less materials and energy, and which are durable and of a high quality.

信息社会 xìnxī shèhuì
information society
Also called 知识社会 knowledge society.

信息网 xìnxīwǎng
information network

信息中心 xìnxī zhōngxīn
information center

信仰危机 xìnyǎng wēijī
crisis in moral convictions
The phenomenon of ideological chaos that especially affects young people at a time when society is undergoing abrupt changes and traditional mores and believes are challenged. The term refers specifically to the situation after the Cultural Revolution in China. As a result of the modern superstition and confusion of real and sham Marxism-Leninism instigated by Lin Biao and the Gang of Four, some young people for a time became disillusioned, depressed, directionless, and lost faith in Marxism-Leninism and Mao Zedong Thought.

信用卡 xìnyòngkǎ
credit card
It also serves as a certificate of the creditor-debtor relationship.

信用社 xìnyòngshè
credit cooperative
Synonymous with 信用合作社 credit cooperative, a collective economic organization of the working people which regulates funds, accepts savings, makes loans, and offers financial advice to its members. At present, rural credit cooperatives are the grass-roots organs of agricultural banking.

xing

星城 xīngchéng
satellite town
Abbreviation for 卫星城.

星火计划 xīnghuǒ jìhuà
spark plan
A technological development plan formulated by the Chinese Academy of Sciences. It was introduced in 1986 and is aimed at promoting the development of science and technology in the rural areas through the following activities: developing and disseminating practical technology and technical facilities; building forerunners of technological enterprises; training some peasants to become technological specialists. The name is derived from the saying "a single spark can start a prairie fire", meaning that the fire of science and technology will burn throughout the vast countryside.

星级 xīngjí
star rating (from one to five, for

星际 xīngjì
inter-stellar
E.g. 星际站 inter-stellar station / 星际航行 inter-stellar travel / 星际飞船 inter-stellar spaceship / 星际空间 inter-stellar space

星球大战计划 xīngqiú dàzhàn jìhuà
Star Wars plan
The Strategic Defense Initiative (SDI) proposed by American President Reagan on March 23, 1983. The proposal calls for the use of such weapons as lasers, particle beams, and microwaves beamed from the ground or from outer space, and installing an anti-ballistic missile system to attack satellites and intercept missiles.

星探 xīngtàn
talent scout
Someone who searches for movie and television performers.

星战 xīng-zhàn
Star Wars
Abbreviation for 星球大战 Star Wars. (cf. 星球大战计划)

兴无灭资 xīngwú mièzī
foster proletarianism and eradicate capitalism
Also called 灭资兴无. To strenuously promote, propagandize, and establish proletarian ideology, so that it will grow and strengthen; and to strenuously destroy bourgeois ideology, so that it will gradually wither away.

刑警 xíngjǐng
criminal police
Contraction of 刑事警察 criminal police. It includes detectives and professionals in the field of criminology.

形式主义 xíngshì zhǔyì
formalism
1) To one-sidedly emphasize form, paying no attention to the actual work style, or looking only at superficial phenomena, and not analyzing the actual way of thinking. 2) An anti-realist trend in art in the late nineteenth and early twentieth century. It is characterized by a departure from realism, lack of thought and works that are merely novel.

形象工程 xíngxiàng gōngchéng
image project
A decorative project such as a highrise building which some government departments favor to show off their achievements.

形象思维 xíngxiàng sīwéi
thinking in images
Synonymous with 艺术思维 artistic thinking. The mode of thinking of writers and artists – observing life, collecting material and eventually using it in creative work. The process follows general patterns of cognition. Concrete images are retained and that which is accidental, secondary or superficial is discarded. The creator's world view governs the process and this is related to the extent to which he is familiar with, and understands, life in society.

形"左"实右 xíngzuǒ shíyòu
leftist in form but rightist in reality
A kind of opportunist trend or stance that appears to be leftist but is rightist in reality.

行为科学 xíngwéi kēxué
behavioral science

行政公署 xíngzhèng gōngshǔ

administrative offices

1) Local organs of political authority set up in the various revolutionary bases before liberation and in some areas in the early days after liberation, such as the Yanbei administrative office. 2) The term also applies to local agencies set up in certain provinces. They are called 行署 for short.

行政拘留 xíngzhèng jūliú
administrative detention

A penalty meted out to those who violate public security regulations. The detention period ranges from half a day to ten days. Extended penalties cannot exceed fifteen days. The penalty is determined and executed by public security organs.

行政手段 xíngzhèng shǒuduàn
administrative measures

The methods adopted by the state in carrying out administrative control, such as promulgating decrees and orders, and making regulations, etc.

省思 xǐngsī
to reflect and contemplate

兴奋剂 xìngfènjì
stimulant (as a medication)

幸福院 xìngfúyuàn
happiness institute

Nursing home for elderly folks without families (also called 敬老院 respect the elderly institute and 养老院 care for the elderly institute).

幸运儿 xìngyùn'ér
lucky fellow

性别比 xìngbiébǐ
gender ratio

The male-female population ratio, using the female population as the percentage base and the male population as the percentage.

性感 xìnggǎn
sexy
E.g. 性感女明星 sexy movie actress

性解放 xìngjiěfàng
sexual liberation

性骚扰 xìngsāorǎo
sexual harassment

性状 xìngzhuàng
properties

Characteristics and form.
E.g. 土壤的理化性状 the physio-chemical properties of soil

性自由 xìngzìyóu
sexual freedom

姓公 xìnggōng
(re property) **public**; (re a person) **to be public spirited**

姓社 xìngshè
(re person or thing) **to have a socialist orientation**

姓私 xìngsī
(re property) **private**; (re a person) **self-interested; self-seeking**

姓资 xìngzī
(re person or organization) **to have a capitalist orientation**

xiong

兄弟单位 xiōngdì dānwèi
fraternal units

An affectionate term used among units with frequent contacts and close relationships.

兄弟党 xiōngdìdǎng
fraternal parties

An affectionate term used between the Marxist-Leninist political parties of various nations.

兄弟民族 xiōngdì mínzú
fraternal ethnic groups
An affectionate term used between the various ethnic groups in China. The term also refers to the various minority groups apart from the majority Han group.

兄弟院校 xiōngdì yuànxiào
fraternal institutions
An affectionate term used among various colleges and universities.

胸花 xiōnghuā
flower worn on the chest

胸卡 xiōngkǎ
card worn on the chest at certain gatherings identifying the individual and his organization.

胸章 xiōngzhāng
badge worn on the chest

胸针 xiōngzhēn
brooch

雄风 xióngfēng
majestic air
E.g. 中国女排重振雄风。 *The Chinese women's volleyball team staged a come-back after their defeat.*

雄踞 xióngjù
to sit or squat majestically; to solidly occupy a position
E.g. 高大的饭店雄踞江畔。 *A grandiose hotel stands majestically by the riverside.* / 北京代表团雄踞体坛盟主之位。 *The Beijing Delegation majestically occupies the leadership position in the world of sports.*

熊市 xióngshì
bear market
Refers to a falling stock market.
E.g. 西方股市再呈熊市。 *Stocks in the West are again having a bear market.*

xiu

休班 xiūbān
to be off duty
E.g. 今天他休班。 *He is off duty today.*

休市 xiūshì
off business; market closed; business suspended
A market (stock or foreign exchange) closed temporarily.

休养所 xiūyǎngsuǒ
sanitorium
An establishment set up for old, weak, or chronically ill staff members and cadres to rest and convalesce.

修旧利废 xiūjiù lìfèi
repair the old and utilize scraps
To recycle old materials and scraps with a certain utility value, and to use them to their full advantage through processing and repair.

修理地球 xiūlǐ dìqiú
to repair the globe
A jocular way of referring to farmers cultivating the land.
E.g. 我的工作是修理地球。 *My job is to repair the globe (i.e., engage in agriculture).*

修宪 xiū-xiàn
to amend the constitution

锈蚀 xiùshí
corrosion
The surface of metals such as copper and iron being corroded.

XU

虚拟网　xūnǐwǎng
virtual net

虚拟现实　xūnǐ xiànshí
virtual reality

虚拟银行　xūnǐ yínháng
virtual bank

蓄洪工程　xùhóng gōngchéng
flood storage project
A water conservancy project built to store floodwater and prevent disaster.

蓄洪区　xùhóngqū
flood storage areas
Areas such as lakes and low-lying land specifically designated as temporary storage areas for floodwaters. This is a method of preventing floods from becoming disasters.

蓄水保墒　xùshuǐ bǎoshāng
store water and retain soil moisture
To store and conserve moisture in the soil so that growing and sprouting crops will be resistant to drought. The commonly used methods are raking, tamping, and intertilling.

续建　xùjiàn
to resume construction
To continue a construction project that was for some reason interrupted.

续展　xùzhǎn
1) to extend the originally scheduled exhibition period, and to continue with the exhibition 2) to extend the effective date of a trademark registration
E.g. 注册商标从九月一日开始办理续展. *The processing of trademark registration extensions will begin on September 1.*

xuan

宣传车　xuānchuánchē
propaganda vehicle
A vehicle equipped with broadcasting equipment. Also called 广播车 broadcasting vehicle.

宣传队　xuānchuánduì
propaganda team
A small-scale organization formed by relevant personnel whose task is to persuade and mobilize the masses to participate actively in certain tasks.

宣传机器　xuānchuán jīqì
propaganda machinery
A cover term for all propaganda media such as newspapers, magazines, broadcasting and television.

宣教　xuān-jiào
propaganda and education
Contraction of 宣传教育.

悬疑　xuányí
mysterious; suspenseful
A plot (of a movie or novel) which is intriguing and unpredictable.

选编　xuǎnbiān
to compile a book by selecting from existing material

选点　xuǎndiǎn
to select a site

选调　xuǎndiào
select and transfer
Contraction of 选拔调动.

选读　xuǎndú
to select (certain chapters) for reading; anthology (a word often used in titles)

E.g. 《古典文学作品选读》 *An Anthology of Classical Literature*

选美 xuǎnměi
beauty contest
E.g. 世界小姐选美活动于1951年开始举办。 *The annual Miss Universe Beauty Contest was started in 1951.*

选民证 xuǎnmínzhèng
voter registration card

选配 xuǎnpèi
to select equipment
E.g. 选配干部 *to select and allocate cadres*

选聘 xuǎnpìn
to select and appoint or hire
E.g. 择优选聘 *to select the best in making appointments* / 选聘干部 *to select and appoint cadres*

选题 xuǎntí
to select a title; selected topics

选育 xuǎnyù
to select and cultivate
Contraction of 选种育种 to select and cultivate a breed.
E.g. 选育良种小麦 *to select and cultivate an improved strain of wheat*

xue

学部 xuébù
divisions of the Chinese Academy of Sciences, and the Chinese Academy of Engineering
Abbreviation for 中国科学院和中国工程院各学科的咨询机构.

学分 xuéfēn
academic credit

学分制 xuéfēnzhì
academic credit system
A system of course requirements for graduation.
E.g. 中国有些大学也开始采用学分制了。 *Some Chinese universities are beginning to adopt the academic credit system.*

学工 xuégōng
to learn industrial production
Going into factories to learn industrial production techniques and knowledge, and to emulate the fine qualities of the working class. (cf. 五七指示)

学军 xuéjūn
to learn military affairs
To go into the military ranks to learn military techniques and knowledge, to learn from the fine tradition of the People's Liberation Army, and to participate in military training. (cf. 五七指示)

学联 xué-lián
Students' Federation
Abbreviation for the All-China Students' Federation and its local organizations.

学农 xuénóng
to learn agricultural production
Going into agricultural villages to learn agricultural production and management knowledge, and to emulate the fine moral character of the peasant masses. (cf. 五七指示)

学前班 xuéqiánbān
pre-school

学前教育 xuéqián jiàoyù
pre-school education

学僧 xuésēng
Buddhist seminarian

学生官 xuéshēngguān
student officers
Military officers who have just graduated

from military academies. Their status is that of interns. They are distinguished from officers who rose through the ranks of ordinary soldiers.

学位制 xuéwèizhì
academic degree system

学习班 xuéxíbān
study class
Originally the abbreviation for 毛泽东思想学习班 Mao Zedong Thought study class. Now it is a term for all groups formed on a provisional basis to study certain things.

学运 xué-yùn
student movements

穴头 xuétóu
one who organizes performers to moonlight and profits from it (cf. 走穴)

雪雕 xuědiāo
to sculpt from snow; snow sculpture
E.g. 雪雕作品 snow sculptures / 雪雕比赛 snow sculpture contest

雪顿节 xuědùnjié
Xodoin Festival
The main activity is the performance of Tibetan drama. 雪顿 in Tibetan means "yogurt party".

雪柜 xuěguì
another name for refrigerator

雪坛 xuětán
world of skiing

血防 xuè-fáng
the prevention and treatment of schistosomiasis
E.g. 血防队伍 team of specialists for the prevention and treatment of schistosomiasis / 血防工作 prevention and treatment of schistosomiasis

血亲 xuèqīn
blood relationship
E.g. 直系血亲 directly related blood relatives / 旁系血亲 collateral blood relatives / 血亲鉴定 determination (through tests) of blood relationship

血统论 xuètǒnglùn
theory of blood lineage
An idealist view prevalent in society in the early period of the Cultural Revolution. It maintained that the mentality of a person was determined not by their practical experiences in society but by their family backgrounds.

血脂 xuèzhī
blood protein
E.g. 一些人血脂偏高。 Some people have a high blood protein level.

xun

询查 xúnchá
to inquire and seek out
E.g. 询查一个朋友的家庭住址 to inquire about the home address of a friend

询访 xúnfǎng
to inquire and investigate
E.g. 到处询访小说的作者 to inquire everywhere about the author of a novel

寻根 xúngēn
to search for roots
To search for one's ancestors and origins.

寻呼 xúnhū
to page (someone)
E.g. 很多城市建立了寻呼网。 Many cities have established public paging networks.

寻呼机 xúnhūjī

beeper

A communication device that receives radio signals. Also called BB 机 or BP 机.

寻呼台 xúnhūtái

paging station

A station for making contact and getting messages to people.

巡航导弹 xúnháng dǎodàn

cruise missiles

巡回学校 xúnhuí xuéxiào

circuit schools

A type of schooling whereby the teachers make the rounds of different places.

巡回演出 xúnhuí yǎnchū

performance tour

A performance troupe performing at various locations along a certain route.

巡回医疗 xúnhuí yīliáo

medical tour

Medical work done by medical personnel who go into factories, rural villages, and remote areas on a regular or irregular basis. When the medical personnel go on a medical tour, aside from treating illnesses, they actively propagandize, carry out disease prevention work, and help grass-roots traine medical personnel.

E.g. 巡回医疗队 *touring medical team*

巡展 xúnzhǎn

a touring exhibit

巡诊 xúnzhěn

to make the rounds in providing a medical service

E.g. 到农村去巡诊。*to make the rounds through villages to provide a medical service* / 为农民巡诊 *to make the rounds to provide a medical service to peasants*

殉葬品 xùnzàngpǐn

funerary object

A metaphor for someone who loses his life as a result of an outdated custom.

Y

ya

压逼 yābī
to coerce; to oppress
E.g. 压逼感 *oppressive feeling* 从上面压逼敌机 *to press the enemy plane from above*

压车 yāchē
vehicles being held up (due to delay in loading, road blocks, etc.)
E.g. 路口狭窄，压车20多辆。 *The intersection is narrow, so over 20 vehicles were held up.* / 压车造成重大经济损失。 *The holding up of vehicles has caused great economic loss.*

压船 yāchuán
cargo ships being held up
E.g. 港口压船现象严重。 *There is a serious holdup of cargo ships at the harbor.*

压港 yāgǎng
cargo or ships being held up at a harbor
E.g. 进口物资长期压港无人提取。 *Imported goods have been held up for a long time at the harbor, with no one coming to take them.*

压货 yāhuò
goods being held up at a train station or dock
E.g. 压货现象开始好转。 *The holdup of goods is beginning to ease up.*

压级 yājí
to force a reduction in rank

压级压价 yājí yājià
to hold down standards and prices
Government purchasing departments forcefully holding down standards, grades, and prices of commodities.

压库 yākù
to reduce warehoused stock

压力锅 yālìguō
pressure cooker
Synonymous with 高压锅. (cf. 高压锅)

压缩空气 yāsuō kōngqì
to reduce the atmosphere
A metaphor for slowing overheated momentum, reducing the scale of construction and expenditure, etc.

压轴戏 yāzhóuxì
the last, and especially good, number in a theatrical performance

押车 yāchē
escort vehicle (for transport vehicles)
E.g. 押车员 *escort vehicle personnel*

雅皮士 yǎpíshì
yuppies

雅钱 yǎqián
refined money
Money earned by writers and artists.
E.g. 对捞雅钱者也要规定个限度。 *There should be a limit on what writers and artists can earn.*

亚非拉 Yà-Fēi-Lā
Asia, Africa, Latin America
Abbreviation for 亚洲、非洲、拉丁美洲.

亚行 Yà-Háng
the Asian Development Bank
Abbreviation for 亚洲开发银行.

亚太 Yà-Tài
Asia and Pacific Ocean
Short for 亚洲 and 太平洋.
E.g. 亚太地区 *the Asia-Pacific region*

亚文化 yàwénhuà
subculture（within a society）

亚银 Yà-Yín
The Asian Development Bank
Abbreviation for 亚洲开发银行. Also called 亚行.

亚运村 yàyùncūn
Asian Games Village

亚运会 Yà-Yùn-Huì
Asian Games

yan

烟民 yānmín
smokers

严办 yánbàn
to severely punish
Abbreviation for 严厉惩办.

严处 yánchǔ
to treat a matter seriously
Abbreviation for 严肃查处.

严打 yándǎ
to seriously attack criminal activities
Abbreviation for 严厉打击严重违法犯罪活动.

严管 yánguǎn
to manage strictly
Abbreviation for 严格管理.

严控 yánkòng
to control strictly
Abbreviation for 严格控制.

严肃音乐 yánsù yīnyuè
serious music
As opposed to music for entertainment.

研读 yándú
to study intensively

研商 yánshāng
to consult and deliberate

研讨会 yántǎohuì
a conference to discuss specific issues

研习 yánxí
to study（at a high level）

研修 yánxiū
to engage in advanced studies
E.g. 业务研修 *professional advanced studies*/ 研修中心 *center for advanced studies*

研修生 yánxiūshēng
personnel engaged in research and study
Personnel in factories or enterprises who combine advanced studies with applied research in their practical productive work.

研议 yányì
to deliberate（i.e., to study and negotiate）

研制 yánzhì
to research and manufacture
Contraction of 研究 and 制造.

岩画 yánhuà
rock picture
A relief carving on the face of a large rock.

延安精神 Yán'ān jīngshén
the Yan'an spirit
Also called 延安作风 Yan'an style, the pioneering spirit manifested by the Party, government, and military in their revolutionary struggle under the leadership of the Chinese Communist Party in

Yan'an and the Shaanxi-Gansu-Ningxia Border Region. This spirit includes: solidarity and unanimity, striving with perseverance to strengthen the nation, self-reliance, and struggling under arduous conditions. (Yan'an was the headquarters of the Chinese Communist Party from 1936 to March of 1947.)

延安整风运动 Yán'ān zhěngfēng yùndòng

Yan'an rectification movement

The movement carried out by the Chinese Communist Party during the War of Resistance Against Japan to rectify the style of the Party. It included opposing subjectivism to rectify the style of learning, opposing factionalism to rectify the atmosphere within the Party, and opposing the Party eight-legged essay (cf. 党八股) in rectifying the style of literature. This was also a widespread Marxist-Leninist educational movement. Through this rectification, the entire Party attained a new unity founded on Marxism-Leninism and Mao Zedong Thought, and laid the ideological foundation to seize victory in the Chinese revolution.

延展 yánzhǎn

to expand; to spread; to extend

炎黄子孙 Yán–Huáng zǐsūn

descendants of the Emperors Yan and Huang; all the Chinese people

眼库 yǎnkù

facility for storing cornea transplant materials; organization for collecting, storing, and studying cornea materials

眼量 yǎnliàng

perceptivity

Ability to observe and analyze.

衍传 yǎnchuán

to propagate

Contraction of 繁衍 multiply and 传代 transmit to later generation.

演播 yǎnbō

to broadcast a performance

E.g. 演播设施 installation for broadcasting a performance / 演播大厅 broadcasting performance hall / 演播室 television broadcasting studio (also called 演播间)

演练 yǎnliàn

manoeuvres and training (military)

Military manoeuvres and training of troops.

演职人员 yǎnzhí rényuán

professionals in the performing arts

Performers and professionals engaged in audiotaping, videotaping, photography, cinematography, etc.

雁过拔毛 yànguò bámáo

to pull a feather from a flying wild goose

A metaphor for being extorted at every pass, or for taking every opportunity to extract some benefit.

验钞机 yànchāojī

a machine for checking paper money for counterfeits

Also called 验币机.

验收团 yànshōutuán

inspection and approval team (larger in scale than 验收组)

验收组 yànshōuzǔ

inspection and approval committee

验资 yànzī

to check the capital of a business or organization

yang

央行 yāng-háng
Central Bank
Abbreviation for 中央银行.

扬长避短 yáng cháng bì duǎn
play up strengths and avoid weaknesses
Taking objective reality of the local area or department as the starting point, suiting measures to the time and local conditions, bringing into play one's strengths and avoiding one's weaknesses, in order to promote the smooth development of the national economy and various tasks.

羊毛衫 yángmáoshān
knit woolen shirt

羊绒衫 yángróngshān
woolen shirt

洋八股 yángbāgǔ
modern eight-legged essay; foreign stereotyped writing
Cf. 党八股 Party eight-legged essay.

洋插队 yángchāduì
Metaphor for youths going abroad in droves to study or to seek work.

洋大全 yáng-dà-quán
foreign, big, and all-inclusive
An approach to running an enterprise in which the emphasis is on seeking advanced technology, and acquiring large scale, and complete facilities. The term also refers to such an enterprise unit.

洋倒 yángdǎo
foreign profiteers who buy up and resell goods

洋教条 yángjiàotiáo
foreign dogmas
1) Certain foreign tenets that do not permit skepticism. 2) The mentality of superstitiously believing in everything foreign, forgetting the reality of one's own country, and making fetishes of foreign theories and rules.

洋框框 yángkuàngkuang
restrictive foreign conventions
The conventional forms, traditional methods, and relevant rules and regulations used by foreigners in handling matters. Usually used in a derogatory sense.

洋冒进 yángmàojìn
modern leap forward
Synonymous with 洋跃进. (cf. 洋跃进)

洋奴思想 yángnú sīxiǎng
mentality of being slavish to things foreign
Synonymous with 洋奴哲学. (cf. 洋奴哲学)

洋奴哲学 yángnú zhéxué
foreign slave philosophy
Orginally, the slave mentality of worshipping and toadying to things foreign on the part of old China's comprador bourgeoisie. In their eyes, everything from foreign capitalist nations was good, and everything in China was bad. They were willing to be the slaves of foreigners. Later, this mentality of worshipping and toadying to things foreign in general came to be called 洋奴哲学 or 洋奴思想 foreign slave mentality.

洋啤 yángpí
foreign beer

洋为中用 yáng wèi zhōng yòng
to adapt foreign things to Chinese use
China's guiding principle in respect of

foreign culture, science, technology, etc. That is, with an analytical and critical approach, to absorb the good things from foreign countries, and use them to serve China's socialist revolution and construction.

洋跃进 yángyuèjìn
modern (foreign) leap forward

Foreign leap forward, the blanket importation of foreign facilities which occurred in the name of economic development in 1977-78, and caused a drastic foreign exchange outflow. Also called 洋冒进. It was a leftist error made in the 1978 movement to overhaul China's national economy. The mistake was in the overly ambitious scale of construction and speed of development. The mistake involved blindly using foreign capital and importing technology. It is distinguished from the 1958 Great Leap Forward characterized by getting on the job with indigenous methods, hence it is called 洋跃进 modern (foreign) leap forward.

阳刚 yánggāng
masculinity

E.g. 阳刚之美 *masculine beauty*
阳刚之气 *masculine spirit*

阳光产业 yángguāng chǎnyè
sunshine industry

An undertaking which has a bright future, such as building maintenance management.

阳光农业 yángguāng nóngyè
sunshine agriculture

To make full use of sunshine to develop agricultural production in a desert region.

阳谋 yángmóu
to do openly

Opposite of 阴谋 conspiratorial. To be open and aboveboard, not engaged in devious schemes.

养成教育 yǎngchéng jiàoyù
education in cultivation

Education about military decorum, disciplines, rules and regulations given to soldiers who have joined the Liberation Army, so they will develop a bearing befitting a revolutionary soldier.

养老金 yǎnglǎojīn
living allowance for the elderly provided by the government; funds earmarked for the care of the elderly

养殖 yǎngzhí
to breed

Contraction of 饲养 raise and 繁殖 propagate. (Usually used in reference to aquatic plants and animals.)

养殖业 yǎngzhíyè
aquaculture

The profession involved in breeding and propagating various kinds of animals and plants. Aside from aquatic life, it includes raising animals for meat, milk, eggs, fur and leather, labor, medicine, ornamentation, pest control, and animals with special characteristics.

氧吧 yǎngbā
oxygen bar

A shop that sells oxygen.
E.g. 氧吧是近年在北京出现的新事物。*An oxygen bar is a recent and new phenomenon in Beijing.*

样板 yàngbǎn
templet; model

1) A plate like tool used in industry or construction for contrasting and inspecting measurements, shapes, and smooth

finishes. 2) A standard specimen that meets all the specifications in machine processing. 3) A metaphor for a model for others to emulate.

样板田 yàngbǎntián
model fields
Agricultural fields that utilize new technology, are planted with improved seeds, and can serve as models for others to emulate.

样板戏 yàngbǎnxì
model theater
Also called 革命样板戏 revolutionary model theater. (cf. 革命样板戏)

样机 yàngjī
prototype machine

样片 yàngpiān
sample film shown on trial basis to censors
E.g. 审看样片 *(by censors) to review a film/* 样片试映 *to show a sample film on a trial basis*

样书 yàngshū
sample book
A sample copy of a newly published book, or a book sample displayed at an exhibition.

yao

腰牌 yāopái
a directory of the route shown in the middle of a bus or trolley car

摇摆乐 yáobǎiyuè
rock and roll music
Synonymous with 摇滚乐.

摇摆舞 yáobǎiwǔ
rock and roll (dance)

摇滚乐 yáogǔnyuè
rock and roll music

遥测 yáocè
telemetering

遥感 yáogǎn
remote sensing

遥控 yáokòng
remote control

遥想 yáoxiǎng
to reminisce
E.g. 遥想当年 *to reminisce about old times*

遥诊 yáozhěn
distant clinical diagnosis, i.e., to diagnose patients at distant locations through certain electronic facilities and imaging systems

药茶 yàochá
medicinal teas (teas with medicinal effects, or teas which contain medicinal herbs)

药点 yàodiǎn
snacks containing Chinese medicine

药工 yàogōng
processor or maker of Chinese medicine

药检 yàojiǎn
inspection of medicines; drug tests for athletes

药检所 yàojiǎnsuǒ
bureau for the inspection of medicines

药具 yàojù
medicines and devices
E.g. 避孕药具 *contraceptive devices*

药膳 yàoshàn
medicinal cuisine (i.e., cuisine containing medicinal ingredients)

药枕 yàozhěn
medicinal pillows (which contain

medicinal materials in the stuffing)

药政 yàozhèng
drug administration
Control and administration of drugs (by the government).
E.g. 药政法 *drug administration laws*/ 药政机构 *drug administration organs*

要案 yào'àn
important case
Contraction of 重要案件.

要害部门 yàohài bùmén
key department units in a party, government or military organization that are involved with important state secrets

要素市场 yàosù shìchǎng
markets for the essentials of production
The markets arising from the flow of essential elements in a production process, such as the money market, labor market, technology market, real estate market, property rights market, information market, etc.

ye

野人 yěrén
an uncouth person; savage
Now this term often refers to a yeti.

野战军 yězhànjūn
field army

业大 yè-dà
sparetime university
Contraction of 业余大学.

业务班子 yèwù bānzi
professional ranks
A cover term for departments and personnel that play a leadership role in the professional work of administrative organs and enterprise and business units.

业务第一 yèwù dìyī
professional work comes first
Also called 业务挂帅 professional work takes command. It means giving professional work priority over all other works. This unscientific term occurred after 政治挂帅 politics takes command. (cf. 政治挂帅)

业务挂帅 yèwù guàshuài
professional work takes command
Synonymous with 业务第一 professional work comes first. (cf. 业务第一)

业务尖子 yèwù jiānzi
outstanding professional person
A person who stands out from the crowd in his professional work.

业务专长 yèwù zhuāncháng
professional specialty

业余爱好 yèyú àihào
hobby
An activity outside of one's regular job in which one is deeply interested and actively involved.

业余华侨 yèyú huáqiáo
sparetime overseas Chinese
Youths who dress and make themselves up to be like overseas Chinese (pejorative).

业余教育 yèyú jiàoyù
sparetime education
Educational activities that take place after work to raise the political, cultural, scientific and technological level of workers, peasants, and cadres.

业余学校 yèyú xuéxiào
schools that carry out educational activities for employed cadres,

workers, or peasants during their spare time

夜大 yè-dà
evening college
Short for 夜大学.

夜生活 yèshēnghuó
night life (social and recreational activities)

夜市 yèshì
night market

液化气 yèhuàqì
liquefied petroleum gas (LPG)

液化气罐 yèhuàqìguàn
gas bottle (container for liquefied petroleum gas)

液压技术 yèyā jìshù
hydraulic pressure technique

yi

一把手 yībǎshǒu
first in command
Also called 第一把手. A metaphor for the most important persons in the Party, government, and military leadership ranks.

一班人 yībānrén
top group
General term for the leadership group in any unit.

一边倒 yībiāndǎo
to fall in one direction
1) A certain opinion or tendency being in an overwhelmingly dominant position. 2) To take a clear-cut stance in a situation with two opposing forces or opinions.

一不怕苦，二不怕死 yī bù pà kǔ, èr bù pà sǐ
not fearing hardship or death
The fine tradition cultivated by the People's Army in their protracted war. For the sake of liberating the people and for a bright future, they had no fear of difficulties, nor of bloodshed and sacrifice.

一次性 yīcìxìng
one time only; only once
E.g. 一次性削价处理 a one time price cut (on damaged, substandard, or overstocked goods)

一打三反 yīdǎ sānfǎn
one thing to attack and three things to oppose
即打击现行反革命分子的破坏活动，反对贪污盗窃、反对投机倒把、反对铺张浪费。这是1969年至1970年开展的运动。
To attack the destructive activities of contemporary counter-revolutionaries, corruption and thievery, renegadism, and extravagance and waste. This was a movement launched in 1969 to 1970.

一大二公 yīdà èrgōng
large and public
指人民公社的基本特点一是大，二是公。大，是说人民公社的规模大，人多地多，便于进行大规模的综合性生产建设。公，是说人民公社比高级社更加社会主义化和更加集体化。在人民公社化运动中片面强调一大二公，对农村的经济发展曾造成不良后果。
The basic characteristics of people's communes are that they are large and public. "Large" means that they are large in scale, have many people and much land, and are suitable for implementing large-scale comprehensive pro-

duction and construction. "Public" means that the communes are even more socialized and collectivized than advanced cooperatives. The lopsided emphasis on large and public during the communization movement led to some unfortunate consequences in the development of rural economies.

一刀切 yīdāoqiē

cut with one knife

A metaphor for adopting the same method in handling different situations, without making concrete analysis and without distinguishing different circumstances.

一点论 yīdiǎnlùn

the one aspect doctrine

Mao Zedong's clear but simple way of referring to metaphysical views, particularly lopsided views, which affirm only one aspect. It is the opposite of 两点论 the two aspects doctrine. (cf. 两点论)

一斗二批三改 yīdòu èrpī sāngǎi

one struggle, two criticisms, three reforms

Also called 斗批改. (cf. 斗批改)

一对红 yīduìhóng

a pair of reds

Two people who respect each other, help and learn from each other in political and professional work, and together raise their levels. In the 1960s, the Chinese People's Liberation Army conducted activities called 一帮一, 一对红 each helps one, a pair of reds.

一分为二 yīfēnwéièr

one divides into two

A figurative yet simple way of expressing the law of unity of opposites. That is, any matter contains two antithetical sides that are mutually opposing and yet interrelated.

一风吹 yīfēngchuī

to disappear with one gust of wind

A metaphor for writing off at one stroke.

一府两院 yīfǔ liǎngyuàn

people's government, people's court and people's procuratorate

一竿子插到底 yīgānzi chādàodǐ

one pole penetrating to the bottom

Metaphor for transmitting and implementing Party and government principles and policies to the lowest of the grass-roots in one go.

一个中心，两个基本点 yī gè zhōngxīn, liǎng gè jīběndiǎn

one central, two basics

中国共产党制定的社会主义初级阶段基本路线的主要内容。一个中心是，以经济建设为中心；两个基本点是，坚持四项基本原则，坚持改革开放。

The basic line of the Chinese Communist Party: economic construction is "central", adhering to the four basic principles (cf. 四项基本原则) and pursuing policies of reform and opening-up are the "two basics".

一贯制 yīguànzhì

consistent system

A metaphor for adhering to the same mode without change over the years.

E.g. 不能再搞几十年一贯制的老产品了。 *We cannot keep putting out the same decades-old products any more.*

一锅端 yīguōduān

to take in one pot

1) A metaphor for rounding up all enemies or criminals in one fell swoop. 2) To express one's views and opinions.

一锅煮 yīguōzhǔ
to cook in one pot
A metaphor for lumping everything together and treating them uniformly without making the appropriate distinctions.
E.g. 国营企业过去是吃大锅饭,盈亏一锅煮。 *State-run enterprises used to be "everyone eating out of the same big pot", regardless of whether something is profitable or not.*

一国两制 yīguó liǎngzhì
one nation, two systems
一个国家两种制度的简称。即在中华人民共和国内,大陆实行社会主义制度,香港、澳门和台湾实行资本主义制度。

The concept of having two systems within one nation in the People's Republic of China, i.e., the socialist system on China's mainland, and the capitalist system in Hong Kong, Macao, and Taiwan.

一哄而起 yīhōng érqǐ
to rise with one roar; to jump on the bandwagon; to rush headlong into mass action (also written as 一轰而起)
E.g. 冰箱生产要避免一哄而起,盲目发展。 *In producing refrigerators, we must avoid having everyone blindly jumping onto the bandwagon.*

一哄而散 yīhōng érsàn
to disperse with one roar; to suddenly jump off the bandwagon; to suddenly stop a project that had mass momentum (also written as 一轰而散)
E.g. 有些工程是一哄而起,然后又一哄而散,造成很大浪费。 *With some projects, everyone suddenly jumps on the bandwagon and then suddenly jump off, thus causing great losses.* 一帮人抢完东西后就一哄而散。 *After the gang finished looting, they dispersed with one roar.*

一哄而上 yīhōng érshàng
to jump on the bandwagon
Many people or units vying to do something without well thought out plans or arrangements.

一化三改 yīhuà sāngǎi
one transformation and three reforms
中国过渡时期总路线的基本内容。一化,指社会主义工业化;三改,指对农业、手工业和资本主义工商业的社会主义改造。

The overall path for China in the transitional period. One transformation is socialist industrialization. The three reforms are socialist reform in agriculture, handicrafts, and capitalist industry and commerce.

一看二帮 yīkàn èrbāng
to observe and help
The policy toward someone who has made a mistake, i.e., first observe his attitude toward his mistake, and second to help him correct his mistake. In other words, to adopt the guiding principle of unity and education toward comrades who have made mistakes.

一颗红心,两种准备 yī kē hóngxīn, liǎng zhǒng zhǔnbèi
one red heart and two kinds of preparation
五十年代党和政府对中小学毕业生提出的要求,即牢固树立一切服从祖国需要,听从祖国安排的"红心",做好继续升学或就业两种思想准备。

The request made by the Party and the government in the 1950s to elementary and high school graduates, that they firmly establish a red (i.e., patriotic and revolutionary) heart, obey the needs and assignments of the motherland, and mentally prepare for the two possibilities of continuing education or job assignment.

一课三会 yīkè sānhuì

one class and three meetings

Synonymous with 三会一课. (cf. 三会一课)

一拉平 yīlāpíng

egalitarianism (in allocation)

一揽子会议 yīlǎnzi huìyì

a package meeting

1) A meeting in which a complex problem is not dealt with in stages, and yet a total solution for it is expected. 2) A comprehensive meeting in which disparate agendas are collected together.

一揽子计划 yīlǎnzi jìhuà

package plan

An overall plan for handling matters and resolving problems.

一揽子交易 yīlǎnzi jiāoyì

package deal

A business dealt in which all the elements are settled at one time.

一揽子学校 yīlǎnzi xuéxiào

package school

A school which takes on the multiple functions of elementary education, spare-time education, and societal cultural work. This is one form of school in the rural areas of China.

一厘钱精神 yīlíqián jīngshén

penny pinching spirit

In socialist economic construction, the spirit of conserving the nation's material resources, making careful calculations, and being hardworking and frugal. (厘 is one tenth of a penny.)

一慢二看三通过 yīmàn èrkàn sāntōngguò

firstly slow down, secondly look, and thirdly go through

The required procedure for motor vehicle operators crossing an intersection. That is, to slow down, look for vehicles and pedestrians, then cross.

一盘棋 yīpánqí

the whole chess game

A metaphor for an entirety or an overall situation.

E.g. 树立一盘棋思想 *to establish a mentality of considering situations comprehensively (i.e., not just from one's own narrow perspective)* 全国经济一盘棋。*The economy of the nation is one inter-connected entity.*

一批二看 yīpī èrkàn

first criticize, then observe

A leftist policy implemented during the Cultural Revolution. That is, to criticize the mentality and academic views of the so-called "reactionary academic authority", then observe signs of their guilt and repentance.

一批二养 yīpī èryǎng

first criticize, then support

"文化大革命"期间,对年老、体弱、多病的专家、学者采取的一种"左"的政策,即批判其思想和学术观点,令其退休,由国家养起来。

A leftist policy adopted toward old, weak, and sick experts and scholars during the Cultural Revolution. That is, to criticize their mentality and academic views, order them to retire, and have the state support them.

一批二用 yīpī èryòng
first criticize, then put into service

"文化大革命"期间对许多专家、学者采取的一种"左"的政策。即批判其思想和学术观点,视其表现,分配一定的任务,给以重新工作的机会。

A leftist policy adopted toward many experts and scholars during the Cultural Revolution. That is, to criticize their mentality and academic views, observe them, then assign certain tasks to them and give them the opportunity to work again.

一批两打 yīpī liǎngdǎ
one criticism and two attacks

也说"一批双打"。即深入揭批"四人帮"罪行,打击阶级敌人的破坏活动,打击资本主义势力的进攻。这是打倒"四人帮"后提出的政治任务。

Also called 一批双打 one criticism and double attack。To expose and attack the crimes of the Gang of Four, to attack the destructive activities of class enemies, and to attack the infiltration of capitalist influence. This was the political mission proposed after the downfall of the Gang of Four.

一片红 yīpiànhóng
all painted red

A Cultural Revolution jargon, meaning that everything is involved in revolution.

E.g. 全国山河一片红。*Every corner of the nation has become revolutionary.*

一平二调 yīpíng èrdiào
equalitarianism and transfers

指平均主义和无偿调拨,简称平调,是1958年中国农村人民公社化运动初期出现的错误做法。具体内容是:否认公社内各单位在经济上的差别,否认按劳分配和等价交换原则,无偿调拨各集体经济组织的生产资料、产品、劳动力和资金,以及社员家庭的某些房屋、财产,分配上一律拉平,实行绝对平均主义。

Equalitarianism and gratuitous transfers, shorted for 平调. A form of equalitarianism that held sway in the 1958 movement to form people's rural communes. There was economic difference between the units of a commune; payment according to labor was denied; the products, manpower, funds and production resources were gratuitously transferred and absolute uniformity applied in all allocations.

一汽 Yī-Qì
the First Automobile Plant

Abbreviation for 第一汽车制造厂.

一穷二白 yīqióng èrbái
poor and blank

形容基础差、底子薄。穷,指经济落后,工农业生产不发达;白,指文化科学技术水平不高。这是指五十年代中国经济文化的实际状况。

Descriptive of having a poor foundation and a thin base. "Poor" means being economically backward and undeveloped in industrial and agricultural production; "blank" means the levels of culture, science, and technology are not high. This was descriptive of China's economy and culture in the 1950s.

一手硬,一手软 yīshǒuyìng, yīshǒuruǎn
one hand hard and one hand soft

The faulty tendency of keeping a firm

hand on building material civilization but being lax with building spiritual civilization.

一胎化 yītāihuà
transforming to one child per couple

一胎率 yītāilǜ
one child ratio
Within a certain time period, the percentage of women in the child-bearing age bracket who have given birth to only one child. The opposite of 多胎率 multiple children ratio.

一体化 yītǐhuà
consolidation (of several units or components into one)
E.g. 科技、生产一体化企业 *a consolidated enterprise melding technology with production*/ 欧洲经济一体化。 *The European economy has consolidated into one entity.*

一头沉 yītóuchén
heavy at one end
1) A form of construction for desks, with drawers or cabinets on one side and none on the other side. The term also refers to this type of desk. 2) A metaphor for leaning to one side when mediating.

一碗水端平 yīwǎnshuǐ duānpíng
to hold a bowl of water level
A metaphor for treating people and matters even handedly, not differentiating those who are near and dear from those who are not.

一五 Yī-Wǔ
the First Five-Year Plan
Abbreviation for 一五计划.

一五计划 Yī-Wǔ Jìhuà
the First Five-Year Plan
Abbreviation for 中华人民共和国国民经济和社会发展第一个五年计划 the First Five-Year Plan (1953-1957) for the National Economic and Social Development of the People's Republic of China.

一线 yīxiàn
the front line
The front line of the three levels of strategic military zones delineated in the early 1960s, front line (used figuratively in certain types of work).
E.g. 加强一线建设 *to strengthen front line construction*/ 生产一线工人 *workers at the front line of production*

一小撮 yīxiǎocuō
a small pinch, a tiny amount (pejorative)
E.g. 一小撮坏人 *a tiny group of bad people*

一言堂 yīyántáng
rule by the words of one
The style of a cadre leader who is undemocratic, and does not listen to the people's opinions. In all matters, only one man's words count. It is the opposite of 群言堂 rule by the voice of many. (cf. 群言堂)

一要吃饭，二要建设 yī yào chīfàn, èr yào jiànshè
it is necessary to eat and to construct
The dialectical relationship between improving the people's livelihood and national economic construction. That is, the nation must not only improve the livelihood of the masses, but must have surplus resources for economic construction. The two conditions, promote and limit each other.

一野 Yī-Yě
First Field Army

Abbreviation for 中国人民解放军第一野战军 First Field Army of the Chinese People's Liberation Army.

一用二批三改四创 yīyòng èrpī sāngǎi sìchuàng
to utilize, criticize, improve, and create
指对引进的外国技术设备采取使用、批判消化、改造、创新的原则。
The principle adopted toward imported foreign technology and devices, which is to utilize them, critically digest them, improve on them, and create anew.

一元化领导 yīyuánhuà lǐngdǎo
centralized leadership
Also called 党的一元化领导 centralized leadership of the Party. Of the seven sectors: industry, agriculture, commerce, education, military, government, and Party, the Party leads in everything; it is not on a par with the others, and certainly not antithetical to them. This terminology is from the period of the Cultural Revolution.

一月风暴 yīyuè fēngbào
January storm
The actions to seize power taken by the Shanghai rebel faction in January 1967, against the Shanghai Municipal Committee of the Chinese Communist Party and the Municipal Committee of the People's Congress.

一长制 yīzhǎngzhì
one head system
The leadership system whereby the management of production and professional activities of an enterprise or business unit are the personal responsibility of the head. That is, the leader has total power over all the work within his sphere of responsibility. It requires each worker to take responsibility for his assigned task, and to obey orders from the one leader.

一阵风 yīzhènfēng
a gust of wind
Metaphor for doing something perfunctorily, simply walking across the stage (cf. 走过场), and not following through.

一专多能 yīzhuān duōnéng
one specialty and many abilities
To be an expert in a certain professional field, and at the same time have knowledge and ability in other areas.

医德 yīdé
medical ethics; moral character befitting a doctor
E.g. 医德教育 *medical ethics education*/ 医德高尚。 *Medical ethics are high.*

医风 yīfēng
work style in the medical field

医改 yī-gǎi
medical reform
E.g. 医改方案已经确定。 *The plans for medical reform have been confirmed.*

医护 yī-hù
medical treatment and care
E.g. 医护人员 *medical professionals*/ 医护工作 *medical work*

医疗队 yīliáoduì
medical team
A group of medical personnel that works at preventing and treating illnesses.

医龄 yīlíng
years of service in the medical profession
E.g. 他有20多年医龄。 *He has worked in the medical field for over*

twenty years.

医务室 yīwùshì
medical office
A grass-roots health organization, that combines treatment with prevention. In general, they are small and their facilities are relatively unsophisticated.

医务所 yīwùsuǒ
medical clinic
A grass-roots health organization, set up in a government office, an enterprise, business unit, or a school, that combines treatment with prevention. It is larger in scale than the 医务室 medical office.

伊妹儿 yīmèir
e-mail
指电子邮件。英文 e-mail 的音译。
Transliteration of the English term "e-mail".

依循 yīxún
follow and abide by
Contraction of 依照 follow and 遵循 abide by.

遗传工程学 yíchuán gōng chéng xué
genetic engineering

遗传密码 yíchuán mìmǎ
genetic code

移动电话 yídòng diànhuà
cordless telephones

移动通讯 yídòng tōngxùn
mobile communications
A high-tech network system involving computer technology, electronic technology, radio technology, etc. It includes cellular phones, beepers, cordless phones, and group communication systems.

乙肝 yǐ-gān
type B hepatitis
Abbreviation for 乙型病毒性肝炎.

乙脑 yǐ-nǎo
type B meningitis
Abbreviation for 流行性乙型脑炎.

乙型肝炎 yǐxíng gānyán
hepatitis B

以党代政 yǐ dǎng dài zhèng
to substitute the Party for the government
The erroneous way of having certain Party organizations take over the leadership function of equivalent government or enterprise and business administrative organs. The problem when the Party is not separated from administrative organs is that it restricts the initiative, positivism, and creativity of the administrative departments and diminishes the Party's leadership function in the areas of ideology, politics, guiding principles, and policies.

以点带面 yǐ diǎn dài miàn
to lead the sphere with the point
The leadership goes to the grass-roots to investigate and research, to work arduously, to study and sum up the experience of advanced models, then to extend that experience to a large sphere, in order to promote the overall work. This is an important Marxist work method. (cf. 点面结合)

以丰补歉 yǐ fēng bǔ qiàn
to subsidize shortfall with a bumper harvest
To make up for a poor harvest or loss with a bumper harvest and surplus production.

以副养农 yǐ fù yǎng nóng
to support the agricultural sector by

developing sidelines

以干带学 yǐ gàn dài xué
to lead learning with doing
Using the actual activities of production, practical experience, and work to give impetus to the learning of theory, knowledge, and technology.

以钢为纲 yǐ gāng wéi gāng
to take steel as the key
A slogan raised in 1958. It took steel production to be the key for all industrial production. Experience has proven that this lopsided emphasis on developing the steel industry led to a serious imbalance.

以工补农 yǐ gōng bǔ nóng
to subsidize agriculture with industry
To take funds accumulated from village and town enterprises to subsidize the shortage of funds for agricultural production, as a way of promoting rapid development of agriculture.

以工代干 yǐ gōng dài gàn
to substitute a worker for a cadre
The situation where a worker has been promoted to a cadre to do a cadre's work, but the formal procedures for the transfer to cadre status have not been carried out, and that person's wages and benefits are still the same at those of a worker.

以古非今 yǐ gǔ fēi jīn
to negate the present with the ancient
To use ancient personages, events, and viewpoints to censure, attack, and deny present reality.

以假乱真 yǐ jiǎ luàn zhēn
to confuse the genuine with the fake
To pass off the fake as genuine, to make it difficult to distinguish the genuine from the fake.

以阶级斗争为纲 yǐ jiējí dòuzhēng wéi gāng
to take class struggle as the principle
The idea that, in the entire socialist historical period, all economic and societal work must serve the principle and core of the class struggle. This was an erroneous leftist slogan. At the Third Plenary Session of the Eleventh Party Central Committee, it was resolved to terminate the use of this slogan.

以进养出 yǐ jìn yǎng chū
to cultivate exports with imports
Through methods such as processing imported materials, assembling imported components, and exchanging goods, to increase the source and variety of goods for export.

以粮为纲 yǐ liáng wéi gāng
to take grain as the key
To make grain a top priority in agricultural production. This was a slogan raised under leftist influence. The problem with it was: grain production developed lopsidedly, diversification of the economy was neglected, and the development of the agricultural economy was impeded.

以论代史 yǐ lùn dài shǐ
to lead historical studies with theory
The proposition that Marxist-Leninist theory should guide historical research.

以农代干 yǐ nóng dài gàn
to substitute a peasant for a cadre
The situation where a peasant is doing the work of a cadre, but does not enjoy the material rewards of a cadre, and his material treatment is basically the same as ordinary peasants.

以派划线 yǐ pài huà xiàn
partisanship; to make judgments solely on the basis of factional lines

以偏概全 yǐ piān gài quán
to make a generalization
To make a generalization about an entirety on the basis of only apart of it.
E.g. 对一个人要具体分析，不能以偏概全。*We must analyze a person in a concrete way, and not make generalizations.*

以权谋私 yǐ quán móu sī
to seek private gain through power
To take advantage of the power of one's position to seek private gain.

以人划线 yǐ rén huà xiàn
to base judgment of a person on someone else's attitude toward them
To use someone else's attitude toward a certain key individual as the standard by which to evaluate whether his stance or path is correct.

以税代利 yǐ shuì dài lì
substituting tax for profit
Also called 利改税 profit changed to tax. That is, the profits from state-run enterprises, which were formerly turned over to the authorities, have been changed to taxes exacted according to tax types and rates stipulated by the state.

以太网 yǐtàiwǎng
Ethernet

以我为中心 yǐ wǒ wéi zhōngxīn
self-centered
A manifestation of bourgeois factionalism and individual heroism. A person with this mentality denies that the core is formed in the process of practical struggles, and often, on the basis of such factors as strength, subjectively proclaims himself or his unit, organization, or locale as the center or the core, and moreover forces others to acknowledge it.

以虚带实 yǐ xū dài shí
to lead practice with ideology
Metaphor for using correct ideology to lead people's practical activities.

以畜促农 yǐ xù cù nóng
to promote agriculture with animal husbandry
Developing animal husbandry to promote the development of agriculture.

艺德 yìdé
ethics of the artistic professions

艺术片 yìshùpiān
art film

艺坛 yìtán
the artistic fields; the world of arts
E.g. 艺坛新秀 *a new star in the arts world* 蜚声艺坛 *famous in the arts world*

艺校 yì-xiào
arts institute
Abbreviation for 艺术学校 (for creative and performing arts).

易拉罐 yìlāguàn
easy-to-open tin
E.g. 啤酒厂引进一条易拉罐生产线。*The brewery has imported a production line of easy-to-open tins.*

亦工亦农 yìgōng yìnóng
engaged in both industry and agriculture
After the system of combining industrial labor and agricultural labor was implemented, a peasant residing in a rural area may work in an enterprise during a contracted period, then go home and

work on the farm when the contract is up. He is both an industrial worker and a farmer.

意见簿 yìjiànbù

suggestion books

Booklets set up mainly by service trades for customers or visitors to write suggestions in.

意见箱 yìjiànxiāng

suggestion box

E.g. 设立意见箱 *to set up a suggestion box*

意气风发 yìqì fēngfā

high-spirited and vigorous

意识流 yìshíliú

stream of consciousness

意向书 yìxiàngshū

statement of intention

Business transaction documents in which the two parties express their wishes and intentions.

忆苦 yìkǔ

to reminisce about the bitter past

E.g. 忆苦报告 *a report on reminiscences of the bitter past*

忆苦饭 yìkǔfàn

meal for recalling past bitterness

Coarse food eaten in the course of class education to help people, especially the young, to understand the bitter life of the laboring masses in the old society.

忆苦会 yìkǔhuì

meetings to recall past bitterness

Meetings at which persons who suffered bitterly and nurse deep hatred are invited to tell others of the oppression and exploitation suffered by the laboring people in the old society. This is a way of educating the masses and arousing awareness and the revolutionary will to fight.

忆苦教育 yìkǔ jiàoyù

education to recall past bitterness

The various educational activities conducted to help the broad masses of soldiers and civilians to understand the bitter history of cruel exploitation and oppression suffered by the laboring people in the old society. These activities include meetings and meals for recalling bitterness. (cf. 忆苦饭 and 忆苦会)

忆苦思甜 yìkǔ sītián

recall past bitterness and think of present happiness

To recall the bitterness of the oppression and exploitation suffered by the laboring people in the old society, and to consider the sweet life of being the master of one's destiny in the new society. This contrasting of the new and old societies was a form of class education in the 1950s and 1960s in China.

义录 yìlù

to make sound recordings to raise funds for charity or public service projects

E.g. 参加义录活动 *to engage in voluntary recordings*

义卖 yìmài

benefit sale

E.g. 举办义卖 *to conduct a benefit sale* / 义卖活动 *benefit sale activity*

义赛 yìsài

benefit competition (sports)

E.g. 组织义赛表演 *to organize a benefit match (re sports)*

义演 yìyǎn

benefit performance

E.g. 进行义演 *to carry out a benefit performance* / 组织义演 *to organize a benefit performance*

义展 yìzhǎn

benefit exhibition (of books, paintings, etc.)

E.g. 举办义展 *to put on a benefit exhibition*

义诊 yìzhěn

to see patients on a volunteer basis

An unpaid doctor seeing patients in his own time for the sake of raising funds, or for public good.

E.g. 几位著名专家、教授将在诊所不定期义诊。 *Several well-known specialists and professors will see patients on a volunteer basis at the clinic on an irregular schedule.*

溢价 yìjià

(stocks) excessive price

An issue price that exceeds the face value.

E.g. 新上市的股票溢价发行，一般超过面值两倍多。 *The new stocks on the market were all sold at above face value; generally they sold for twice as much.*

议案 yì'àn

proposal submitted to a conference for deliberation

E.g. 通过议案 *to approve a proposal*

议购 yìgòu

to purchase according to the terms of a contract

议会道路 yìhuì dàolù

parliamentary road

The absurd proposition of old and new opportunists that, under capitalist conditions, the proletarian class only needs to obtain majority representation in a parliamentary body through election to legally attain political power, that is, there is a peaceful transition to socialism without a violent revolution or a proletarian dictatorship.

议会迷 yìhuìmí

believers in the parliamentary system

Opportunists who blindly believe in the bourgeois parliamentary system and favor the parliamentary road as a way of attaining political power. They take parliamentary struggle to be the primary and only form of struggle, oppose violent revolution and proletarian dictatorship, and advocate taking the parliamentary road for a peaceful transition to socialism. (cf. 议会道路)

议价 yìjià

negotiated price; free market price

As opposed to 平价 and 牌价 list price.

E.g. 议价市场 *free market (i.e., where prices are not set by the state)*

议价粮 yìjiàliáng

grain with a negotiated price

Commodity grain bought and sold at a price negotiated by the two parties concerned.

议价油 yìjiàyóu

oil with a negotiated price

Commodity edible oil bought and sold at a price negotiated by the two parties concerned.

议销 yìxiāo

negotiated sale

议政 yìzhèng

to negotiate political matters

译码 yìmǎ

to decode

译制 yìzhì

to translate and make; to dub

Contraction of 翻译 and 制作, the

process of converting a foreign film for a domestic audience, or vice versa.
E.g. 译制电视连续剧 *to translate and make over a television serial drama*

yin

因特网 yīntèwǎng
Internet
The largest open computer internet made up of many networks connected to each other.
E.g. 我国因特网用户逾百万。*Users of the internet in China exceed one million.*

音带 yīndài
audiotapes
Short for 录音带 audiotapes.

音碟 yīndié
laser CD

音箱 yīnxiāng
speaker (lit., sound box)
A domestic electrical appliance that contains a microphone.

音像带 yīnxiàngdài
audiotapes and videotapes
Composite term for 录音带 and 录像带.

音像制品 yīnxiàng zhìpǐn
taped products

音协 yīn-xié
musicians' association
Abbreviation for 音乐家协会.

音乐茶座 yīnyuè cházuò
music tea house
An establishment that offers musical entertainment along with beverages.

阴暗面 yīn'ànmiàn
the dark (seamy) side (of an organ-ization, society, etc.)

阴谋文艺 yīnmóu wényì
conspiratorial art and literature
During the Cultural Revolution, the Gang of Four tried to mold public opinion against revolution, and attacked revolutionary leading cadres by making use of works of literature and art to further their conspiracy to usurp the Party and seize power.

银弹 yíndàn
silver bullet
Financial weapon, economic strength deployed in attaining certain objectives.
E.g. 银弹攻势 *economic offensive*

银弹外交 yíndàn wàijiāo
silver bullet diplomacy
(re current Taiwan government) to carry out diplomatic activities using economic means.

银牌 yínpái
silver medal (for second place in athletic competitions)

银屏 yínpíng
(electronics) fluorescent plate in a cathode-ray tube; silver screen
The film and television world.
E.g. 先进工作者登上了银屏. *The advanced workers were shown on screen (i.e., television).*

银色浪潮 yínsè làngcháo
silver tide
A metaphor for the rapid increase in the proportion of the elderly within the population.

银坛 yíntán
the world of films
E.g. 她不满四岁就登上了银坛。*She got into the film world before she was four.*

银团 yíntuán
bank group
E.g. 银团贷款 *loan from a bank group*

饮品 yǐnpǐn
beverages that contain both liquids and suspended solids
E.g. 国际饮品及技术展览会 *international exhibition of the technology and products of liquid-solid beverages*

饮誉 yǐnyù
to drink renown to enjoy a good reputation
E.g. 中国女排饮誉全球。 *The Chinese women's volleyball team is world renowned.*

引产 yǐnchǎn
induced labor (child birth)

引发 yǐnfā
to ignite or detonate; to arouse (certain emotions)

引黄灌区 yǐn Huáng guànqū
areas irrigated by the Yellow River
Cover term for all areas that draw water from the Yellow River to irrigate agricultural fields.

引火烧身 yǐnhuǒ shāoshēn
to draw fire
1) A metaphor for asking for trouble and inviting destruction. 2) A metaphor for leading cadres voluntarily exposing problems to the masses to seek criticism and help.

引智 yǐnzhì
to import intellect; to recruit specialists and persons of talent from other parts or abroad

引种 yǐnzhǒng
to introduce a new biological breed or species from elsewhere

引种 yǐnzhòng
to plant a new breed or species introduced from elsewhere

瘾君子 yǐnjūnzǐ
drug addict; drug fanatic; narcotic addict

隐形 yǐnxíng
invisible; covert; indiscernible
E.g. 隐形亏损 *intangible loss* / 隐形收入 *covert income* (*bonuses, dividends, subsidies, etc.*)

隐形人 yǐnxíngrén
invisible person
A person who is unwilling to reveal his identity.

隐形眼镜 yǐnxíng yǎnjìng
contact lenses (lit., invisible glasses)
Also called 无形眼镜 or 隐形镜.

隐性 yǐnxìng
unopened or unexposed
E.g. 隐性采访是一种手段, 起码应该是不违法的。 *A secret interview is a method, which should be considered within the law.*

隐性就业 yǐnxìng jiùyè
invisible employment
指下岗职工没有与原企业终止劳动法律关系, 在外单位工作获取劳动收入的就业人员。
Refers to laid-off employees who still have a legal relationship with the original enterprise, but work for another company and receive payment.

印发 yìnfā
print and distribute; print and disseminate
E.g. 印发传单 *print and distribute fliers*

印件 yìnjiàn
printed matter

E.g. 一叠印件 *a stack of printed matter*

印售 yìn-shòu
to print and sell
E.g. 印售影星照片 *to print and sell photos of movie stars*

印制 yìnzhì
to print and produce
E.g. 印制地图 *to print and produce maps*

ying

英烈 yīngliè
heroic martyr
E.g. 中华女英烈纪念展览 *Heroic Chinese Women Martyrs Memorial Exhibition*

英模 yīng-mó
heroic model
Contraction of 英雄模范.

鹰派 yīngpài
hawks
A metaphor for persons in some countries and political groups that rely on strength to adopt a hard line policy.

营销 yíngxiāo
to manage sales
E.g. 营销人员 *sales management personnel* / 营销理论 *theory of sales management*

营销学 yíngxiāoxué
a field of study that examines sales management

营养钵 yíngyǎngbō
nutritional pots (peat pots)
Pots that contain nutritional materials for cultivating crop seedlings. They are used mostly for seedlings of such crops as cotton, eggplants and vegetables of the gourd family. The seedlings are transplanted with the pots in the fields.

营养食堂 yíngyǎng shítáng
nutrition dining hall
A dining hall that provides the old, weak, or chronically ill with foods that meet their nutritional requirements. Also called 营养灶 nutritional kitchen.

营养学 yíngyǎngxué
science of nutrition

营养灶 yíngyǎngzào
nutrition kitchen
Synonymous with 营养食堂 nutrition dining hall. (cf. 营养食堂)

营业员 yíngyèyuán
purchasing agents; sales clerks
Composite term for purchasing agents and sales clerks; sometimes refers only to salesclerks.

营员 yíngyuán
campers
E.g. 夏令营营员 *summer campers*

营运 yíngyùn
to engage in the transport business
Contraction of 经营运输 to be engaged in the business of transporting goods.

荧幕 yíngmù
fluorescent screen (of television); the tube
E.g. 诗人杜甫将搬上荧幕。 *The story of the poet Du Fu will soon be televised.*

荧屏 yíngpíng
fluorescent screen; the tube
Abbreviation for 荧光屏.
E.g. 荧屏艺术 *television art* / 今晚荧屏有服装表演。 *There is a fashion show on television tonight.*

赢面 yíngmiàn

the odds at winning
赢球 yíngqiú
to win a ball game
影城 yǐngchéng
video city
A multi-faceted entertainment center with the showing of videos as its main feature.
E.g. 影城拥有几个影视厅。 *The video city has several viewing halls.*

影带 yǐngdài
videotape (with recorded program)
影帝 yǐngdì
film king
Winner of the best lead male role movie actor award.
影调 yǐngdiào
the style and sentiment of a film
影碟 yǐngdié
video disc (with sound and image recordings)
影碟机 yǐngdiéjī
VCD
影后 yǐnghòu
film queen
Film actress who wins the best main role award.
影界 yǐngjiè
the world of films
E.g. 进入影界 *to enter the world of films*
影剧 yǐngjù
films and stage plays
E.g. 影剧界 *the film and theater world*
影剧院 yǐngjùyuàn
theater (for movies and plays)
影楼 yǐnglóu
An expensive photo studio

影票 yǐngpiào
movie ticket
影圈 yǐngquān
film circles; world of films
E.g. 影圈人士 *people in film circles*
影赛 yǐngsài
photography or film competition
影射史学 yǐngshè shǐxué
oblique historical studies
The so-called historical studies that used the past to disparage the present, which were made during the Cultural Revolution at the instigation of the Gang of Four. An example is using 评法批儒 evaluating Legalists and criticizing Confucius to point the spearhead at Premier Zhou Enlai.

影视 yǐngshì
cinema and television
Short for 电影 and 电视.
E.g. 影视节目 *movie and television program* / 影视配音 *sound dubbing for movies and television*

影坛 yǐngtán
world of film
E.g. 投入影坛 *to plunge into the world of films* / 影坛老将 *a veteran of the film world*

影协 yǐng-xié
association of workers in the film industry; photographers' association
Abbreviation for 电影工作者协会, or for 摄影协会 photographers' association.

影星 yǐngxīng
movie star
Contraction of 电影明星.
影业 yǐngyè
the film industry
影展 yǐng-zhǎn

photo exhibition; cinema exhibition
1) Contraction of 摄影展览 photo exhibition. Also called 摄影作品展览 exhibition of photographic creations. 2) Contraction of 电影展览 cinema exhibition.

影子股 yǐngzigǔ
shadow stocks

Literally "shadow stocks", also called 干股. Capital which nominally belongs to a certain party, but that party can only enjoy the dividends produced by the capital, and does not really own it. It is similar to endowed funds.

应标 yìngbiāo
to respond to a job opening

E.g. 应标承包 to tender a bid and contract a project

应聘 yìngpìn
to accept to a job appointment

E.g. 北京科技人员自愿应聘到边疆参加四化建设。 Sci-tech personnel in Beijing voluntarily accepted job assignments in the border regions to join in building the four modernizations. / 应聘者收入倍增。 The income of those who accepted job assignments doubled.

应市 yìngshì
to accommodate the market

To supply goods to meet market demands on a timely basis.

E.g. 应市商品 commodities that meet market demands / 新型电视机应市。 The new-style television sets are meeting market demands.

应试教育 yìngshì jiàoyù
exam-oriented education

应选 yìngxuǎn
to accept a position to which one has been elected; those who – according to certain regulations – should be elected

E.g. 候选人在本单位应选。 Candidates accepted positions within their own units. / 候选人要多于应选人。 The number of candidates should exceed the number of elected positions.

应用科学 yìngyòng kēxué
applied sciences

应战书 yìngzhànshū
letter accepting a challenge

A written document accepting the terms of a challenge from an opponent. It is a reply to 挑战书 letter of challenge.

硬笔 yìngbǐ
hard-tipped writing instruments; hard pen

Writing instruments with hard tips (as opposed to the traditional Chinese writing brush) such as pencils, fountain pens, and ballpoint pens.

E.g. 中国硬笔书法悠久。 Hard pen calligraphy has a long history in China.

硬赤字 yìngchìzì
hard deficit

The deficit shown in the difference between expenditure and revenue, including the income from debt collection.

硬功夫 yìnggōngfu
mastery

Having great proficiency and skill.

硬环境 yìnghuánjìng
hard environments

The material conditions including natural geography, houses and buildings, communications, life facilities, etc. It's the opposite of 软环境 soft environments. (cf. 软环境)

硬技术 yìngjìshù

hard technologies

Various concrete production technologies that primarily use machines, such as smelting technology, prospecting technology, and textile technology.

硬件 yìngjiàn
hardware

Synonymous with 硬设备 hardware. The opposite of 软件 software.

硬科学 yìngkēxué
the hard sciences (physics, chemistry, etc.)

As opposed to the 软科学 soft sciences.

硬任务 yìngrènwù
firm tasks

Tasks that must be completed on schedule and strictly in accordance with the requirements.

硬设备 yìngshèbèi
computer hardware

Alternative term for 计算机硬件 computer hardware. (cf. 硬件)

硬通货 yìngtōnghuò
hard currency

Also called 硬货币.
1) The currency of a certain country that can be converted freely to gold or the currencies of other countries. It can be used as an international currency. 2) A currency that is relatively stable in value on the international monetary market.

硬投入 yìngtóurù
hard investment

Material investment (in a project or enterprise), as opposed to 软投入 soft investment.

硬卧 yìngwò
hard sleepers

Relatively hard berths on trains where passengers may lie down and sleep. It is the opposite of 软卧 soft sleepers.

硬席 yìngxí
hard seats

Relatively spartan seats or berths on trains.

硬指标 yìngzhǐbiāo
firm objectives

Stipulated goals that must be realized in strict accordance with the requirements.

硬座 yìngzuò
hard seats

Relatively spartan seats on trains. The opposite of 软座 soft seats.

yong

拥军优属 yōngjūn yōushǔ
to support the army and give preferential treatment to their dependents

To support the People's Army, and to give preferential treatment to the families of revolutionary soldiers.

拥政爱民 yōngzhèng àimín
to support the government and love the people

The army supporting the government and cherishing the people.

泳坛 yǒngtán
the world of swimming

E.g. 泳坛名将 *a star in the world of swimming*/ 泳坛健儿 *an outstanding athlete in the world of swimming*

泳装 yǒngzhuāng
swim-wear

永久牌 yǒngjiǔpái
forever

(Originally) a brand of bicycle produced in Shanghai; (new metaphor) someone staying forever at a certain locale.

永久正常贸易关系 yǒngjiǔ zhèngcháng màoyì guānxì
PNTR (permanent normal trade relations)

用材林 yòngcáilín
timber forests
Forests cultivated mainly for wood and bamboo with economic value, the most common kind of forestry. Also called 经济用材林 economic timber forests.

you

优才生 yōucáishēng
an outstanding and talented student
Also written as 优材生.
E.g. 注重优才生的培养 to emphasize the nurturing of talented students

优等生 yōuděngshēng
a student who has an excellent character and excels academically; a student of outstanding character who shows wisdom and excels in the arts and labor

优抚 yōufǔ
preferential treatment and compensation
The preferential treatment and compensation given to dependents of revolutionary martyrs and soldiers, and to disabled veterans.
E.g. 优抚工作 preferential treatment and compensation work/ 优抚对象 beneficiaries of preferential treatment and compensation

优化 yōuhuà
to make superior
To adopt measures to make something even better.
E.g. 优化人种 to breed a superior species of humans/ 优化方案 to perfect the plan/ 优化措施 to perfect the measure

优化经济结构 yōuhuà jīngjì jiégòu
to optimize the economic structure

优价 yōujià
discounted price; a good price (good from the seller's point of view, therefore a high price)
E.g. 优价政策 discount policy/ 优价出售 to sell at a discount

优教 yōujiào
first-rate education
To educate children in a superior environment.

优生 yōushēng
eugenics
Giving birth to children with innately superior qualities.

优胜红旗 yōushèng hóngqí
red flag of victory
Flag obtained through the superior performance of the winner of a competition.

优胜劣汰 yōushèng liètài
triumph of the superior and elimination of the inferior; survival of the fittest

优先股 yōuxiāngǔ
preference stocks

优先认股权 yōuxiān rèngǔquán
stock options

优选 yōuxuǎn
the best choice; to select the best
E.g. 在各种方案中进行优选 to select the best plan/ 优选系列 top choice series

优选法 yōuxuǎnfǎ
optimal choice method
The method of speedily obtaining the best plan for a question raised in production or scientific experimentation. The method is based on mathematical principles and minimizes the number of experiments.

优养 yōuyǎng
superior raising (of children)
Using scientific and superior methods to rear children.
E.g. 优养方案 *a plan for superior child rearing*

优育 yōuyù
good upbringing (of children)
To provide children with good health care and education from early on.

优质高产 yōuzhì gāochǎn
superior quality and high output
A commodity that is produced in large numbers and is of a high quality.

优质名牌 yōuzhì míngpái
high quality brand name
The commodity is of high quality and has an established reputation.

优质优价 yōuzhì yōujià
high quality and high price
The commodity is of good quality and is sold at a high price.

忧思录 yōusīlù
to record questions of concern for contemplation
The term is used mostly in titles.

尤里卡 yóulǐkǎ
EURECA
Transliteration of the English acronym for the European Research Cooperation Agency, a large-scale research development plan proposed by the French President Mitterand in April 1985. It was set up to increase cooperation in the development of advanced technology and promote the economy of Western European nations.

邮编 yóubiān
zip code; postcode
Abbreviation for 邮政编码.

邮程 yóuchéng
postal route (through which mail passes)

邮发 yóufā
to distribute via the postal service

邮品 yóupǐn
postal items (stamps, postcards, etc., sold by the postal service)

邮商 yóushāng
philatelic dealers

邮市 yóushì
market for postal items

邮售 yóushòu
mail order marketing
To market goods through mail order.

邮坛 yóután
the world of philately

邮展 yóu-zhǎn
stamp show
Contraction of 邮票展览 stamp exhibition.

邮政编码 yóuzhèng biānmǎ
zip code; postcode

油耗 yóuhào
gasoline consumption
E.g. 降低油耗 *to reduce gasoline consumption*

油耗子 yóuhàozi
gasoline rats
Derogatory term for those who steal and sell public gasoline for personal gain.

油老虎 yóulǎohǔ
oil tigers
Devices or units that consume a large quantity of oil.

油票 yóupiào
oil tickets
Ration coupons for cooking oil, gasoline, etc.

油品 yóupǐn
oil products
Petroleum products such as gasoline, kerosene, and diesel oil.

游斗 yóudòu
to parade and to struggle against a culprit; to take a culprit on a circuit for public denouncement and struggle
A term used in Cultural Revolution.

游击习气 yóujī xíqì
guerrilla inveteracy
To habitually do things in an irregular way.

游乐场 yóulèchǎng
amusement park (large-scale)

游乐园 yóulèyuán
amusement park

游山玩水 yóushān wánshuǐ
to tour scenic spots and enjoy oneself

游戏机 yóuxìjī
recreational machines
Toys or devices for people's entertainment, specifically electrical or electronic recreational machines.

游资 yóuzī
floating capital; idle funds
E.g. 国际游资正在寻求新的投资场所。 *International floating capital is searching for new investment targets.*

有偿服务 yǒucháng fúwù
paid services

有偿新闻 yǒucháng xīnwén
paid news
News agencies or reporters extorting payment from interviewees.

有成分论 yǒuchéngfènlùn
theory of class background
The viewpoint that family background is a determining factor in people's stances, mentality, morality, and cultural attainment.

有破有立 yǒu pò yǒu lì
some to destroy and some to establish
To create something new it is sometimes necessary to criticize and negate the old.

有戏 yǒuxì
there is hope; there is possibility
As opposed to 没戏 no way; no hope.

有限战争 yǒuxiàn zhànzhēng
limited (in terms of area) warfare

有线电视 yǒuxiàn diànshì
cable television

有序 yǒuxù
sequential

友协 yǒu-xié
friendship association
Abbreviation for 友好协会.
E.g. 中日友协 *Sino-Japanese Friendship Association*

友谊第一，比赛第二 yǒuyì dì-yī, bǐsài dì-èr
friendship first and competition second
In athletic competitions, to take promoting friendship to be top priority. Through competition, people learn from each other, exchange experiences, develop their athletic skills, and cultivate sportsmanship and moral character.

右派分子 yòupài fènzǐ

rightist elements
Cf. 反右派斗争 struggle against rightists.

诱购 yòugòu
to lure customers by deceptive means

又红又专 yòuhóng yòuzhuān
both red and expert
"Red" refers to politics; "expert" refers to professional work. Both red and expert means having proletarian political consciousness as well as mastery of the knowledge and skills of one's professional specialty.

幼教 yòu–jiào
nursery school education
Contraction of 幼儿教育 education of young children.
E.g. 事实证明幼教工作是提高文化水平的重要环节。 *It has already been proven that the work of educating the very young is an important factor in raising their cultural level.*

幼师 yòu–shī
kindergarten education normal school; kindergarten teachers
1) Contraction of 幼儿师范学校 kindergarten education normal school.
2) Contraction of 幼儿园教师 kindergarten teachers.
E.g. 培训幼师 *to train kindergarten teachers*

yu

愚公精神 Yúgōng jīngshén
spirit of the Foolish Old Man
Originally, this term referred to the spirit of perseverance and fearless show by the Foolish Old Man in the ancient parable about moving a mountain. Now it is a metaphor for the heroic revolutionary spirit of fearing no difficulties, daring to struggle and being down to earth and quietly putting one's shoulder to the wheel.

愚人节 yúrénjié
April Fool's Day
Another name for April first in the West.

瑜珈 yújiā
yoga

余毒 yúdú
residual poison or curse

余粮 yúliáng
surplus grain
Grain that remains after food needs and other demands have been taken care of.

余权 yúquán
residual power
Specific reference to the influence of retired cadres.
E.g. 反对利用余权搞不正之风 *to oppose the use of residual power to create incorrect tendencies*

余热 yúrè
residual heat
1) Originally, the surplus heat in the process of industrial production.
E.g. 余热发电 *electricity generation from residual heat*
2) A metaphor for the energy and ability of retirees.
E.g. 为国为民献余热 *to contribute residual heat to the country and the people*

鱼品 yúpǐn
fish products

鱼水情 yúshuǐqíng
intimate congeniality
As the inseparability of fish and water,

generally used in respect to the relationship between soldiers and the people.
E.g. 军民鱼水情 *the intimate relationship between soldiers and the people*

渔工商联合企业 yú-gōng-shāng liánhé qǐyè
fishery-processing-sale joint enterprise
An integrated enterprise that combines fishery production, processing, and marketing.

渔区 yúqū
fishery district or region

渔政 yúzhèng
fishery (production, marketing, etc.)
E.g. 加强渔政管理 *to strengthen the management of fisheries*

娱乐片 yúlèpiān
film or TV program for entertainment

宇航服 yǔhángfú
space suit
Same as 宇宙服. (cf. 宇宙服)

宇航员 yǔhángyuán
spaceman; astronaut

宇宙飞船 yǔzhòu fēichuán
spaceships (launched by multi-staged rockets)

宇宙服 yǔzhòufú
space suit
Also called 航天服, 宇航服 and 太空服.

宇宙人 yǔzhòurén
extraterrestial being; creature from outer space

宇宙线 yǔzhòuxiàn
cosmic ray
Synonymous with 宇宙射线.

宇宙语 yǔzhòuyǔ
language of the universe
A system of mathematical codes designed by a Dutch scholar in the 1970s, which is based on universal mathematical laws and which can be used to communicate with intelligent beings from outer space.

宇宙站 yǔzhòuzhàn
space station
Also called 太空站. (cf. 太空站)

语感 yǔgǎn
a feel for the language
E.g. 对同一句话，不同的人可能有不同的语感。 *Different persons can derive different language feelings (i.e., nuances) from the same sentence.*

语境 yǔjìng
language environment
Contraction of 语言环境, the textual context or speech environment in which a speech fragment occurred. These include the social context, natural environment, time and location, the listener or reader, and the state of mind of the speaker or author.

语料 yǔliào
language material (for linguistic research)
E.g. 语料统计 *statistics on language materials*/ 现代汉语语料库 *modern Chinese language material data bank*

语流 yǔliú
flow of speech

语录 yǔlù
quotations (from a personage)
Specifically the quotations from Mao Zedong.

语录操 yǔlùcāo
calisthenics based on the quotations

of Mao Zedong
Calisthenics choreographed to the content of Mao Zedong's Quotations. The concept appeared in the Cultural Revolution.

语录歌 yǔlùgē
a song with lyrics from the quotations of Mao Zedong
Used in the Cultural Revolution.

语态 yǔtài
voice (grammatical)

语委 Yǔ-Wěi
State Language Work Committee
Abbreviation for 国家语言文字工作委员会 State Language Work Committee.

语音信箱 yǔyīn xìnxiāng
voice mail

语种 yǔzhǒng
varieties of language

羽球 yǔqiú
badminton

羽绒 yǔróng
feathers and down (used in clothing and bedding)
E.g. 羽绒厂 *down factory* / 羽绒博览会 *down products exhibition* / 羽绒制品 *down products*

羽绒服 yǔróngfú
down filled clothing
Clothing (coats, jackets, etc.) filled with processed down. They are very warm and light.

羽坛 yǔtán
world of badminton
E.g. 羽坛高手 *master of the badminton world* / 羽坛老将 *veteran of the badminton world* / 饮誉羽坛 *renowned in the badminton world*

玉雕 yùdiāo
jade carving

吁请 yùqǐng
to appeal to
E.g. 吁请各成员国反对这一决议草案 *to appeal to all member nations to oppose this draft resolution*

育龄 yùlíng
reproductive years
E.g. 育龄夫妇 *a couple in their reproductive years*

育秧 yùyāng
to cultivate seedlings
To cultivate seedlings of crops such as rice and yams in nurseries, greenhouses, or hot beds, in preparation for transplanting into fields.

浴帽 yùmào
shower cap

浴罩 yùzhào
bath canopy (circular plastic curtain used in bathing)

寓教于乐 yù jiào yú lè
to teach through lively activities

预备党员 yùbèi dǎngyuán
probationary Party member
Communist Party members in the probationary period, during which they are observed. Those found to have the necessary qualifications for Party membership are then made regular Party members. (cf. 预备期)

预备期 yùbèiqī
probationary period
Specifically, the probationary period for probationary members of the Chinese Communist Party. It is the period from when an application for admission to the Party has been approved by the branch general meeting to when the applicant formally becomes a Party member. The

Party constitution stipulates that the probationary period is one year. When the period is up, the Party branch should discuss whether he can be made a regular member. For those who need additional observation and education, the probationary period may be extended for up to another year.

预警 yùjǐng

to alert people in advance; early warning

E.g. 预警装置 *equipment for alerting the police*/ 预警飞机 *early warning plane*/ 预警制度 *system of alerting the police*

预考 yùkǎo

practice exam

In preparation for the real exam, it often refers to the college entrance exam.

E.g. 高考预考 *preliminary college entrance exam*

预售 yùshòu

advance sale

1) To sell in advance (train or bus tickets, theater tickets, etc.). 2) To collect payment in advance and to deliver the purchased article at a date.

E.g. 预售彩电 *to sell a color television by advanced payment*

预委会 Yù-Wěi-Huì

the Preliminary Working Committee

Abbreviation for 香港特别行政区筹备会预备工作委员会 the Preliminary Working Committee of the Preparatory Committee for the Hong Kong Special Administrative Region.

预选 yùxuǎn

primary election

预展 yùzhǎn

preliminary exhibition (in preparation for the real thing)

E.g. 举行预展 *to hold a preliminary exhibition*

预制板 yùzhìbǎn

prefabricated concrete sections used in construction

预制构件 yùzhì gòujiàn

prefabricated parts

Construction components made in advance in factories or on site from steel, wood, or concrete according to design specifications.

域名 yùmíng

internet connecting code

yuan

鸳鸯楼 yuānyānglóu

honeymoon apartment building

For short-term rental by newlyweds, also called 鸳鸯房 honeymoon housing.

冤假错案 yuān-jiǎ-cuò'àn

composite term for judicial cases involving false, fake, or mistaken charges

原声带 yuánshēngdài

original sound tape

原珠笔 yuánzhūbǐ

ballpoint pen

原装 yuánzhuāng

originally assembled (by the factory, as opposed to 改装 re-assembled or 组装 assembled from parts)

E.g. 日本原装佳能复印机 *Japanese Canon Xerox machine assembled at the original factory*

原子笔 yuánzǐbǐ

ballpoint pen

Also called 圆珠笔.

原子能发电站 yuánzǐnéng fādiànzhàn
nuclear power station
I.e. 核电站. (cf. 核电站)

援建 yuánjiàn
to aid construction
E.g. 援建工程 *to assist in a construction project*/ 援建人员 *personnel assisting in a construction project*/ 援建单位 *units assisting in a construction project*

援借 yuánjiè
to loan in the name of aid
E.g. 援借英国大熊猫 *to lend a panda to England (by way of aid)*

援藏 yuán-Zàng
to aid Tibet
E.g. 援藏人员 *personnel to aid Tibet*

园丁 yuándīng
gardener
1) Originally, caretakers of gardens.
2) Now, a metaphor for teachers.
E.g. 感谢培养祖国花朵的园丁们。*We thank all the gardeners who cultivate flowers in our motherland.*

园区 yuánqū
park
An area designated for the development of a certain type of enterprise.
E.g. 工业园区 *industrial park*/ 科学园区 *scientific park*

远程教育 yuǎnchéng jiàoyù
long-distance education
To spread knowledge by means of television, broadcasting and the internet.

远导 yuǎn-dǎo
long-range guided missiles
Abbreviation for **远程弹道导弹** long-range guided missiles.
E.g. 远导条约 *Agreement on Long-Range Guided Missiles*

远南 yuǎn-nán
the Far East and South Pacific region
E.g. 远东及南太平洋残疾人运动会 *the Far East and South Pacific Games for the Disabled*

远销 yuǎnxiāo
to sell on distant markets
E.g. 远销国外 *to sell abroad*/ 远销欧美 *to sell in Europe and America*

院部 yuànbù
institutes
The overall term for leadership organs such as the Chinese Academy of Sciences, the Design Institute, and academic institutions.

院风 yuànfēng
atmosphere of an institute
An overall term for the academic and work atmosphere of a scientific research or design institute.

院校 yuànxiào
educational institutions
Overall term for colleges, universities, and academic institutes.
E.g. 大专院校 *universities and technical institutes*/ 高等院校 *institutes of higher learning*

yue

约见 yuējiàn
appointment; to make an appointment

约请 yuēqǐng
to request (someone to do something) in advance

约谈 yuētán
to make an appointment to negotiate

跃居 yuèjū
to leap (to an advanced position)
E.g. 跃居全国第一 *to leap to number one position in the nation*/ 跃居国际先进水平 *to leap to an internationally advanced level*/ 跃居世界前列 *to leap to the forefront of the world*

月均 yuèjūn
monthly average
E.g. 月均收入 200 元。 *Average monthly income is 200 yuan.*

月月红 yuèyuèhóng
red every month
The situation where the workers, a workshop, or a team in an enterprise department meet or exceed production targets every month.

阅报栏 yuèbàolán
newspaper bulletin boards

阅卷 yuèjuàn
to go over exam papers
Contraction of 批阅试卷.
E.g. 他因熬夜阅卷而眼睛充满红丝。 *His eyes are all bloodshot because he went over exam papers the whole night.*

阅批 yuèpī
to read and comment on (a memorandum submitted by a subordinate)
E.g. 领导亲自阅批群众来信。 *The leader personally read and commented on the letters from the masses.*

乐迷 yuèmí
someone who is crazy about music

乐坛 yuètán
music circles

yun

云图 yúntú
(meteorological) cloud chart
E.g. 气象卫星云图 *cloud chart from a meteorological satellite*

运筹学 yùnchóuxué
operations research
Utilizing the achievements of modern mathematics particularly statistics – to study the application of and planning for manpower and material resources, so that they can be used to their maximum advantage. It is a science that emerged during World War Two.

运动员 yùndòngyuán
athlete
A metaphor for targets of political movements.
E.g. 他在历次政治运动中，经常当运动员，挨批挨斗。 *He was targeted for attack in successive political movements.*

运价 yùnjià
transport cost

运力 yùnlì
transport capacity
Contraction of 运输能力.

运量 yùnliàng
transport volume
The volume of goods or passengers transported within a certain period by a transport department.

运能 yùnnéng
transport capability
E.g. 增加运能 *to increase transport capacity*

运销 yùnxiāo
to ship and sell elsewhere

E.g. 运销全国 *to ship to and market everywhere in the nation/* 从事运销 *to be in the shipping and marketing profession*

运营 yùnyíng
(re transport vehicles) to move and do business
Also called 营运.
E.g. 新建铁路通车运营。 *The new railroad has been opened to the transport business./* 地铁运营准点。 *The subway opened to transport on time.*

运载火箭 yùnzài huǒjiàn
carrier rockets

运作 yùnzuò
to proceed and develop
E.g. 民主运作程序 *the process of democratization/* 经济运作 *economic procedures and development*

Z

zai

宰 zǎi
swindling money out
The term originally meant to kill. Now it means to swindle.
E.g. 他在咖啡馆被宰了500元。 *He was swindled out of 500 yuan at the coffee shop.*

宰客 zǎikè
to swindle money out of customers

仔猪 zǎizhū
piglet

载誉 zàiyù
to bear the honor that one has acquired; to be full of honor
E.g. 载誉回京 *to return to Beijing with honors* / 载誉归来 *to return with honors*

再教育 zàijiàoyù
re-education
The education proposed by Mao Zedong during the Cultural Revolution in which workers, peasants, and soldiers would educate intellectuals and help them to establish a proletarian world view.

在编人员 zàibiān rényuán
permanent staff
Personnel in the established authorized staff.

在岗 zàigǎng
to be at one's post; to be on duty

在建 zàijiàn
under construction
E.g. 在建项目 *items under construction* / 在建工程 *engineering projects under construction*

在野党 zàiyědǎng
(re capitalist nations) the political party not in office; opposition

在业 zàiyè
to be employed
E.g. 在业职工 *employed workers* / 在业人员 *employed personnel* / 在业人口 *employed population*

zan

赞助 zànzhù
to support (financially)
To give financial support to a public cause.
E.g. 修复长城受到很多单位的赞助。 *The renovation of the Great Wall has received financial support from many units.*

zang

脏话 zānghuà
vulgar words; words unfit for the ear

藏胞 Zàngbāo
Tibetan compatriots
Abbreviation for 藏族同胞.

藏学 Zàngxué

Tibetan studies; Tibetanology
E.g. 藏学研究专家 expert in Tibetan studies

藏医 Zàngyī
Tibetan medicine
Traditional Tibetan medical science. Also, physicians who use the theories and methods of Tibetan medicine.

zao

遭灾 zāozāi
to be hit by a natural disaster

早班车 zǎobānchē
early morning buses or trucks
A metaphor for jobs or things done early or ahead of schedule.

早市 zǎoshì
morning market

噪声监控 zàoshēng jiānkòng
noise monitoring

噪光 zàoguāng
light pollution
The excessive light in cities which is harmful to humans, such as the reflected light from glass and metal and excessive night time light.
E.g. 噪光是城市里的一种新污染源。 Light pollution is a new source of pollution in cities.

造反派 zàofǎnpài
rebel faction
People who during the Cultural Revolution advocated "kicking aside the Party committee and carrying out revolution". They rebelled against the so-called "capitalist roaders" and the "capitalist and reactionary line" and engaged in beatings, smashing things, looting, searches and confiscations, and arrests.

造神运动 zàoshén yùndòng
idol-making movement
The various activities used to incite religious fervor and deify the revolutionary leader during the Cultural Revolution. They were conducted by the Lin Biao-Jiang Qing clique in order to usurp the Party and seize power.

造势 zàoshì
to make a noise; build up momentum
E.g. 传媒群起造势。 All the media rose to make a noise at once.

造血 zàoxiě
to create blood
A metaphor for body's own function in sustaining and developing itself.
E.g. 必须健全教育事业自身的造血功能。 We must strengthen the educational sector's ability to sustain its own health and vitality.

ze

责编 zé-biān
the responsible editor
Abbreviation for 责任编辑 the responsible editor (the editor in charge of a publication).

责权利 zé-quán-lì
responsibility, power, and benefits
Cotraction of 责任、权力、利益. In the socialist economic responsibility system, linking responsibility, power, and benefits is a technique for realizing the integration and concerted growth in benefits for the state, collective, and the individual. It accords with the principle of integrating the benefits of these three sectors.

责任山 zérènshān
responsibility hill

After agricultural villages implemented the production responsibility system, uncultivated hills that production teams contracted out to production groups, households, or individuals to manage are called "responsibility hills". All the rights of these hills belong to the production team; commune members have only the right of use.

责任事故 zérèn shìgù
accidents due to negligence

Accidents caused by someone neglecting his responsibilities.

责任田 zérèntián
responsibility field

The land which a production team contracts out to a production group, household, or individual to cultivate after the rural production responsibility system was implemented. The rights of this land belong to the production team; the contractor has only the right of use.

责任制 zérènzhì
responsibility system

A management system in which responsibility for various tasks are assigned to specific persons and the responsibilities, awards and penalties are clearly defined.

责任状 zérènzhuàng
responsibility contract

Usually an economic responsibility contract, colloquially called 军令状 military command contract. It is a guarantee, submitted by a responsible person or the leadership of an enterprise unit, to the supervisory department. The supervisory unit proposes production targets and provides the necessary facilities; the enterprise will, according to the stipulated requirements, guarantee to complete the assignment and meet the quality and quantity specifications within a certain period. The two sides sign the responsibility contract. When the assignment is completed according to the contract, the contractor is rewarded or penalized.

择优 zéyōu
to select the best

E.g. 择优录取 *to enroll the best* / 择优选用 *to select and employ the best*

zeng

增产节约 zēngchǎn jiéyuē
to increase production and to economize on consumption (of raw materials, energy, etc.) **and expenditure**

增幅 zēngfú
the extent of an expansion

增亏 zēngkuī
to increase a loss or deficit

E.g. 去年企业增亏两倍。 *The enterprise's loss increased two-fold last year.*

增量 zēngliàng
increment

增容 zēngróng
1) to increase (enlarge, add) capacity; 2) to improve conditions in a city so that it can accommodate an increase in population and vehicles

E.g. 使电表增容 *to increase the capacity of the watt-hour meter*

增容费 zēngróngfèi
capacity increasing fee

A fee charged by the city government for the recent increase in population and vehicles.

增设 zēngshè

to increase facilities by installing additional units or by expanding on the original foundation

E.g. 增设机构 *to set up more organs* / 增设商业服务网点 *to increase commercial service networks* / 电台增设了经济专题节目。 *The radio station added a program specializing in economics.* / 学校增设了两个新专业。 *The school added two new specialties.*

增收 zēngshōu

1) to increase one's income 2) increased income 3) to increase the receipts (payment for services, etc.)

增收增支 zēngshōu zēngzhī

to increase income and economize on expenditure

增销 zēngxiāo

increase in sales

增选 zēngxuǎn

to select and add to the original membership

E.g. 增选了两个副主席 *to have elected and added two vice chairmen.* / 会上他被增选为协会主任委员。 *At the conference, he was elected chairman of the association's executive committee.*

增殖 zēngzhí

to proliferate; to propagate

1) Proliferate or reproduce. 2) Synonymous with 繁殖 propagate.

E.g. 增殖率 *rate of propagation* / 增殖耕牛 *to propagate from oxen*

增值 zēngzhí

to increase output value; increased output value

增值税 zēngzhíshuì

value added tax

The tax levied on the value added at the various links in the flow of goods and services.

增资 zēngzī

to increase wages

E.g. 增资指标 *the quota for a wage increase* / 增资 10% *to increase wages by 10%*

zha

扎堆 zhāduī

to hang out together (with nothing much to do); to cluster together

E.g. 上班时间不准扎堆聊天。 *Employees are not permitted to cluster together and chat during work hours.*

扎根串连 zhāgēn chuànlián

to take roots and visit

A work method to motivate the masses to join a certain struggle. It works as follows: A person responsible for a certain assignment goes to a new location. First he visits several reliable locales in order to gain a foothold. Then he helps these locales to gain awareness, and through them makes contact with more people and kindles their enthusiasm to join the struggle.

扎根农村 zhāgēn nóngcūn

to take roots in a rural area

To live and work permanently in a rural area. (Said of a person who originally came to the countryside from a city.)

扎啤 zhāpí

draft beer

扎 is transliterated from the English word "draft".

E.g. 扎啤机 *draft beer machine* / 扎啤设备 *draft beer facility*

zhai

摘播 zhāibō

to make extracts for broadcasting

摘除 zhāichú

to pluck; to remove (bad or excess parts from an organism)

E.g. 摘除树上长虫子的果子 *to remove bug infested fruit from the trees* / 摘除白内障 *to remove cataracts*

摘帽 zhāimào

to remove the hat

To take away a bad name that had been erroneously foisted on someone or something (also called 摘帽子).

E.g. 帮助穷队摘帽 *to help the poor teams overcome their stigma* / 给地、富、反、坏分子摘帽工作已经结束。*The work of taking away the bad names from landlords, rich peasants, counter-revolutionaries, and evildoers has already been completed.*

摘帽右派 zhāimào yòupài

rehabilitated rightist

Pejorative term for someone who has already had his bourgeois rightist hat removed.

摘取 zhāiqǔ

to attain; to quote an excerpt

E.g. 摘取博士头衔 *to attain the title of Ph.D.* / 摘取金牌 *to win the gold medal* / 摘取一些革命的词句当旗号 *to excerpt some revolutionary phrases to put on banners*

zhan

崭露头角 zhǎnlù tóujiǎo

(re a young person) to show one's potential ability in a striking way

E.g. 他十岁时就在钢琴比赛中崭露头角。*When he was ten, his potential was shown in a striking way at a piano competition.* / 一批青年作家崭露头角。*A group of young writers showed their potential in a striking way.*

展播 zhǎnbō

preceptive broadcasting

Television programs for people to watch and emulate.

展馆 zhǎnguǎn

exhibition hall; a hall that functions as a specific section within a large-scale exhibition

E.g. 中国展馆 *the China exhibition hall* / 手工艺品展馆 *handicrafts exhibition hall*

展柜 zhǎnguì

showcase (used in exhibitions)

E.g. 展柜中陈列着新出版的书。*Newly published books are exhibited in the showcase.*

展览业 zhǎnlǎnyè

the exhibition management profession

E.g. 展览业已成为深圳的窗口行业。*The profession of managing exhibitions has already become a service industry in Shenzhen.*

展卖 zhǎnmài

exhibition and sales (of some items being exhibited)

E.g. 展卖活动 *exhibition and sales activities* / 展卖会 *exhibition and sales fair*

展评 zhǎnpíng

to exhibit and evaluate

To exhibit, test the market, and evaluate new commodities.

展区 zhǎnqū

an area (for a specific group or type of products) within a large-scale exhibition

展台 zhǎntái

counters for exhibits or counter like set-ups

展厅 zhǎntīng

exhibition hall (a large room)

展团 zhǎntuán

delegations participating in an exhibition

展销 zhǎnxiāo

exhibition and sales

The exhibiting and marketing of new products.

E.g. 展销会 *trade fair (lit., exhibition and sales meeting, where products are exhibited and marketed)*

展延 zhǎnyán

to postpone; to expand; to extend

展映 zhǎnyìng

to show or broadcast a film or TV program as an exhibition

E.g. 举办各种影片展映 *to conduct showings of various films at an exhibition*

占线 zhànxiàn

busy (telephone)

To be unable to get through on a telephone line because the line is engaged.

占用 zhànyòng

to hold in one's possession and use; to grab and use

E.g. 占用耕地 *to grab and use agricultural land* / 占用时间 *to occupy time* / 占用资金 *to use capital*

战和 zhànhé

draw (in a chess game)

E.g. 他俩经过 5 个多小时的较量，首次战和。 *The two played over five hours in the contest and finally came to a draw.*

战区导弹防御系统 zhànqū dǎodàn fángyù xìtǒng

TMD

站风 zhànfēng

station atmosphere

The mentality and work style of personnel at a train or bus station.

zhang

长官意志 zhǎngguān yìzhì

commanding officer's will

The expectations and administrative orders of a leader which are not appropriate to the actual situation.

涨幅 zhǎngfú

scale of inflation

E.g. 物价涨幅逐步回落。 *The scale of inflation gradually subsided.*

zhao

朝阳工业 zhāoyáng gōngyè

rising sun industries

Cutting edge high-tech industries, such as microelectronic information management, bioengineering, new material science, etc.

招办 zhāo-bàn

office of student recruitment, admissions office

Abbreviation for 招生办公室 office of student recruitment, admissions office

招干 zhāogàn
to recruit cadres

To recruit cadres through an examination system.

E.g. 招干考试 *exam for cadre recruits* / 张榜招干 *to post announcements of cadre recruitment (by examination)*

招工 zhāogōng
to recruit workers

招股 zhāogǔ
to attract buyers for stocks

E.g. 招股说明书 *a prospectus that explains the stock*

招行 Zhāo–Háng
China Merchants Bank

Abbreviation of 招商银行.

招商 zhāoshāng
to attract business (re large-scale trade)

E.g. 组团到香港去招商 *to organize a delegation to go to Hong Kong to attract business*

招贤榜 zhāoxiánbǎng
bulletin for recruiting worthy persons; situation vacant notice

找米下锅 zhǎo mǐ xià guō
to find rice for the cooker

A production unit relying on itself, instead of its supervising unit, to obtain raw materials.

沼气池 zhǎoqìchí
methane-generation pit

照排 zhào–pái
(re printing) to photograph and compose; photocomposition

E.g. 激光照排系统 *laser photocomposition system*

照主 zhàozhǔ
person holding a business license

zhe

遮幅电影 zhēfú diànyǐng
covered-up movie

Also called 遮幅式宽银幕电影 covered-up wide-screen movie and 假宽银幕电影 pseudo wide-screen movie.

折叠床 zhédiéchuáng
folding bed

A kind of simple, foldable bed used in the home. It is opened up for use and folded up for storage.

折叠伞 zhédiésǎn
folding umbrella

折叠椅 zhédiéyǐ
folding chair

A chair with a seat that can be folded.

折返线 zhéfǎnxiàn
the route which one retraced

折股 zhégǔ
to convert into shares

E.g. 严禁将国有资产折股。 *It is strictly forbidden to convert state-owned capital into shares.*

zhen

珍稀 zhēnxī
rare and precious

E.g. 珍稀动植物 *rare and precious animals and plants* / 珍稀鸟类 *rare and precious birds*

针刺疗法 zhēncì liáofǎ
acupuncture treatment

A method of curing illness whereby specially made metal needles are pierced into acupoints on a patient's body, and techniques such as raising and twirling the needle are applied.

针刺麻醉 zhēncì mázuì
acupuncture anesthesia
Also called 针麻. A new technique of anesthesia unique to China. Acupuncture needles are applied to certain acupoints until an analgesic effect is attained, and a patient may undergo surgery in a conscious state.

针麻 zhēn-má
acupuncture anesthesia
Abbreviation for 针刺麻醉.

侦办 zhēnbàn
to investigate and handle (a case)
E.g. 把犯罪分子送法院侦办 *to send criminals to the court for investigation and punishment*

侦察卫星 zhēnchá wèixīng
reconnaissance satellites

侦破 zhēnpò
(re detectives) to investigate and solve a case
E.g. 侦破组 *the investigative team that solved a case* / 侦破一起特大经济犯罪案件 *to have solved a major case of economic crime*

枕头风 zhěntóufēng
pillow wind
A metaphor for the influence exerted by a wife's captious comments to her husband. Also called 枕边风.
E.g. 不要在炕上吹枕头风。 *Don't influence your spouse by captious comments in bed.*

震派 zhènpài
shakers
Persons during the Cultural Revolution who frequently instigated sudden political incidents. They are referred to colloquially as those who instigate "political earthquakes".

震情 zhènqíng
earthquake conditions

镇反运动 zhèn-fǎn yùndòng
movement to suppress counter-revolutionaries
Abbreviation for 镇压反革命运动. It was a political movement from 1950 to 1952 by the whole nation under the leadership of the Chinese Communist Party to investigate and suppress counter-revolutionaries.

zheng

蒸气浴 zhēngqìyù
steam bath, i.e., sauna (cf. 桑那浴)

蒸气熨斗 zhēngqì yùndǒu
steam iron

征订 zhēngdìng
to solicit subscriptions (to newspapers and magazines)
E.g. 征订广告 *to solicit advertisements* / 征订报刊 *to solicit newspaper and journal subscriptions*

征购 zhēnggòu
levied purchase
The state, in accordance with the law, purchases (agricultural products, land, etc.) from producers or owners.
E.g. 征购任务 *state purchase quotas* / 征购指标 *state purchase targets*

征管 zhēngguǎn
to levy and administer taxes
E.g. 征管力量不足。 *The capacity for levying and administering taxes is inadequate.* / 改进征管办法 *to improve the method of levying and administering taxes*

征婚 zhēnghūn

to solicit potential marriage partners
E.g. 征婚广告 ads soliciting marriage partners / 征婚信息 information concerning the solicitation of marriage partners

征迁 zhēngqiān
to be requisitioned and moved
An individual or a collective state enterprise or business moving to another location because the government has taken over (for another use) the person's or unit's residence, land, office, or place of business.

争分夺秒 zhēngfēn duómiǎo
to fight for every minute
To make the most of every minute or second of time (in work, production, or studies).

整党 zhěngdǎng
Party rectification
The rectification carried out by the Chinese Communist Party in respect to its existing problems in ideology, work style, and organization. This consists of unifying ideology, rectifying the work style, strengthening discipline, and purifying the organization.

整党建党 zhěngdǎng jiàndǎng
rectify and build the Party
Specifically, the Chinese Communist Party carrying out rectification in respect to problems in its ideology, work style, and organization, and strengthening the Party's ideological and organizational structures.

整风 zhěngfēng
to rectify style
To rectify ideological and work style.

整复 zhěngfù
to renovate
E.g. 整复手术 renovation surgery

整改 zhěnggǎi
to rectify and reform
While in the process of rectifying the Party, to concurrently carry out adjustments in the economic system and reforms in the government. Also called 边整边改 to rectify and reform concurrently. (cf. 整党)

整合 zhěnghé
(re philosophy) the process of systematically fitting knowledge into a cognitive structure, synthesis

整社 zhěngshè
to rectify cooperatives
The rectification, within the 1955 movement to cooperativize agriculture, in those agricultural production cooperatives which were not well run. This involved mainly ensuring quality and combating the tendency to concentrate on quantity at the expense of quality.

整团 zhěngtuán
to rectify the Youth League
To rectify the ideology, work style and organization of the Communist Youth League.

正餐 zhèngcān
proper meals (as distinguished from snacks and fast foods)

正儿八百 zhèng'erbābǎi
serious (as opposed to frivolous); in earnest
Also called 正经八百.

正面教育 zhèngmiàn jiàoyù
positive education
To educate with a positive perspective, such as publicizing virtuous persons and good deeds, and promoting lofty thoughts and sentiments, so that people

are inspired to advance.

正面经验 zhèngmiàn jīngyàn
positive experience
Experience of success, the opposite of 反面经验 negative experience.

正面人物 zhèngmiàn rénwù
positive characters
Characters in literary and artistic works who are advanced and highly regarded. They are the opposite of 反面人物 negative characters.

正研 zhèng–yán
fully fledged researcher (vs. assistant or technician)
E.g. 他已具备了正研的资格。 He already has the qualifications of a fully fledged researcher.

政策性亏损 zhèngcèxìng kuīsǔn
losses due to policy
Losses that occur within production management plans, which result from having the state enterprise implement certain erroneous Party and state guiding principles and policies.

政风 zhèngfēng
government style
The operational style of government administrative organs.

政工 zhèng–gōng
political work
Short for 政治工作 political work.
E.g. 政工部门 political work sector / 政工干部 political work cadre

政工组 zhènggōngzǔ
political work group
The department within a unit that has responsibility for political work within that unit.

政纪 zhèngjì
administrative regulations
Contraction of 行政纪律 administrative regulation.

政经 zhèng–jīng
government administrative and economic sector

政历 zhènglì
political history
The state of a person's political history.

政企合一 zhèng–qǐ héyī
merging government administration and enterprise management into one
To merge the grass-roots government organization and enterprise management organization into one, so that it is both an economic organization and a grass-roots government authority. This was the trend during the communization movement. It was reversed in the early 1980s.

政社分开 zhèng–shè fēnkāi
separation of government administration and commune management
To separate the function of a government authority from the people's commune which had hitherto been an organization that combined government with commune management. After the separation, the township people's government – the organ of government authority at the grass-roots level – is set up separately. The people's commune exists only as a collective economic organization.

政社合一 zhèng–shè héyī
merging government administration with commune management
The format of people's communes founded in 1958, which were organizations of both rural government authority

at the grass-roots level and collective economic management.

政审 zhèngshěn
political investigation

The investigation of an individual's political history.

政坛 zhèngtán
the world of politics

政委 zhèng-wěi
political commissar

Abbreviation of 政治委员 political commissar (of a PLA unit at or above the regimental level).

政务院 zhèngwùyuàn
Executive Council

Abbreviation for 中华人民共和国中央人民政府政务院 Executive Council of the Central People's Government of the PRC, the name of the highest executive organ of the nation before 1954. After September 1954, it was renamed State Council.

政协 zhèng-xié
Political Consultative Conference

Abbreviation of 政治协商会议 Political Consultative Conference. Under the leadership of the Chinese Communist Party, various democratic parties, non party members, people's organizations, minority figures, and patriots from various quarters participate in this conference. It comprises representatives of all socialist workers, patriots who support socialism or support the unification of the motherland, including the broadest patriotic united front of compatriots in Taiwan, Hong Kong, Macao, and foreign countries. The national organization is the Chinese People's Political Consultative Conference (CPPCC), various areas have political consultative conferences at various local levels.

政制 zhèngzhì
political system

政治部 zhèngzhìbù
political departments

Departments under the jurisdiction of Party committees which are responsible for political and Party work in units of the PLA at or above divisional level, in certain large government organs, and in enterprise and business units.

政治辅导员 zhèngzhì fǔdǎoyuán
political counselors

Persons invited by certain elementary and middle schools, urban neighborhood committees, and rural communes and teams to guide and assist with political ideology. They are mostly old retired cadres and PLA officers and men stationed at those places.

政治挂帅 zhèngzhì guàshuài
politics takes command

Metaphor for putting politics in the role of the leader and commander, letting it command everything else in a variety of work situations. Because this slogan is quite slanted and cannot embody the relationship between politics and professional work, it is no longer used.

政治局 zhèngzhìjú
the Political Bureau

Abbreviation for 中共中央政治局 the Political Bureau of the Central Committee of the Chinese Communist Party. It is the highest leadership organ in the central organization of the Chinese Communist Party. The Political Bureau and its Standing Committee are elected to office at the plenary session of the

Party Central Committee. They exercise the functions and authority of the Central Committee when the latter is not in session.

政治觉悟 zhèngzhì juéwù
political consciousness

Generally it refers to the proletariat class' knowledge of their position, historical mission, basic rights, etc., and their comportment.

E.g. 他政治觉悟不高。*He is not high on political consciousness.*

政治立场 zhèngzhì lìchǎng
political stand

The political stance and attitude one maintains in perceiving and handling important issues of principle.

政治路线 zhèngzhì lùxiàn
political line

The codes of action formulated and basic path followed by a political party to realize its political goals at a certain historical period. The term sometimes refers to the overall line, sometimes to the ideological, organizational, economic, or military line.

政治面目 zhèngzhì miànmù
political aspect

An individual's political stance, political attitude, and various social relationships that have a political bearing.

政治扒手 zhèngzhì páshǒu
political pickpockets

Metaphor for opportunists who curry favors in social life and scheme to take political advantage.

政治骗子 zhèngzhì piànzi
political swindlers

People engaged in political opportunism.

政治素质 zhèngzhì sùzhì
political caliber

The cultivation of an individual or a group in politics. It includes: a person's family background, political stand, political consciousness and the theoretical level attained.

政治台风 zhèngzhì táifēng
political typhoon

A metaphor for political incidents that have great effects on society.

政治委员 zhèngzhì wěiyuán
political commissars

Abbreviated as 政委. Political workers in units of the PLA at or above the regimental level (including independent battalions). They are usually those in charge of the routine work of the Party committee.

政治协商会议 Zhèngzhì Xiéshāng Huìyì
Political Consultative Conference

Abbreviated as 政协. (cf. 政协)

政治嗅觉 zhèngzhì xiùjué
political sense of smell

A metaphor for the degree of sensitivity to, and ability to perceive, the political nature of things, which an individual manifests in his work or struggle.

政治学习 zhèngzhì xuéxí
political studies

The activities or system of studying politics carried out by workers in various types of work. That is, at stipulated times, they study mainly the classical works of Marxism-Leninism, Mao Zedong's writings, Party documents, and current policies.

政治夜校 zhèngzhì yèxiào
political night schools

Sparetime schools operated in the evenings to teach political theory.

政治庸人 zhèngzhì yōngrén
politically mediocre person

A person who is not particularly politically aware, has few ambitions and tends to be politically passive.

政治帐 zhèngzhìzhàng
political account

To do political accounting, a frequently used phrase, is a metaphor for considering and weighing political advantages and disadvantages, gains and losses, when perceiving or handling something.

政治指导员 zhèngzhì zhǐdǎoyuán
political instructor

Abbreviated as 指导员 instructor. The political worker in a company of the PLA. He is one of the leaders of the company.

政治资本 zhèngzhì zīběn
political capital

Metaphor for factors one can make use of politically in seeking advantages. The term has a derogatory connotation.

证监会 zhèng-jiān-huì
the Securities Supervision and Management Commission

Abbreviation for 证券监督管理委员会.

证交所 zhèng-jiāo-suǒ
the Securities Exchange

Abbreviation for 证券交易所.

证券交易所 zhèngquàn jiāoyìsuǒ
the Securities Exchange

zhi

支边 zhī-biān
support the remote border regions

Abbreviation for 支援边远地区.

支部书记 zhībù shūjì
branch secretary

Specifically, the most responsible person of a branch committee of the Chinese Communist Party. Also called the 党支部书记 Party branch secretary. The most responsible person of a branch committee of the Chinese Communist Youth League is called 团支部书记 League branch secretary.

支持产业 zhīchí chǎnyè
supportive industries

Industries within a community of industries that serve a supportive function for the pillar industries. (cf. 支柱产业)

支工 zhī-gōng
to support industries

Specifically, the support given to industries by the PLA during the Cultural Revolution. (cf. 三支两军)

支教 zhī-jiào
to aid education

Abbreviation for 支援教育 to aid education.

E.g. 支教工作 *educational assistance work* / 支教人员 *personnel in educational assistance work*

支节产业 zhījié chǎnyè
link supporting industries

Certain industries within a community of industries that integrate the utilization of resources and products of pillar industries and supportive industries. (cf. 支柱产业)

支农 zhī-nóng
to support agriculture

Specifically, the support given to agriculture by the PLA during the Cultural Revolution. (cf. 三支两军)

支派 zhī-pài
to support factions

Specifically, the PLA's support for certain factions of local mass movements during the Cultural Revolution. After the PLA intervened in local movements, it supported certain mass organizations, engaged in factionalism, and suppressed certain other factions.

支前 zhī-qián
to aid the front line (or battle front)

Abbreviation for 支援前线.

支书 zhī-shū
branch secretary

Contraction of 支部书记.

E.g. 党支书 *Party branch secretary* / 团支书 *Youth League branch secretary*

支委 zhī-wěi
branch member

A member of a branch committee (grass-roots level organization) of the Chinese Communist Party or the Chinese Communist Youth League.

E.g. 他是这个党支部的支委。*He is a member of this Party branch committee.*

支柱产业 zhīzhù chǎnyè
pillar industries

When a city or region is in the process of selecting and determining the development of dominant industries, it needs to examine the organic relationships among the dominant industries, and build a group of organically related industries on the foundation of their dominance. Industries among the dominant industries which have a core or backbone function are called "pillar industries". Those industries that ensure the normal functioning of the "pillar industries" are called "supportive industries". Those industries which can best integrate the use of resources and products (including by-products) of the "pillar industries" and "supporting industries" are called "link supporting industries". These three kinds of industries form an organic "industrial community". They are interdependent and support each other.

支左 zhī-zuǒ
supporting the left

Specifically, during the Cultural Revolution, the PLA, acting under orders, supported those who were considered leftists at the time. Support of the left by the military had a beneficial effect, the stabilization of the situation. It also had a negative side, factionalization. Moreover, some leftist activities were very damaging to the prestige of the military. (cf. 三支两军)

知本 zhīběn
knowledge capital

知本家 zhīběnjiā
knowledge capitalist

Intellectuals who become rich by creating new knowledge.

知本主义 zhīběn zhǔyì
knowledge capitalism

知产阶级 zhīchǎn jiējí
intellectual property class

A group within developed capitalist societies who derive their income from their knowledge and intellectual ability.

知名度 zhīmíngdù
notoriety

E.g. 这个企业知名度很高。*This enterprise is widely known.*

知难而进 zhīnán érjìn

to advance knowing of the difficulties; to forge ahead in the face of difficulties

知青 zhī-qīng
educated youths
Contraction of 知识青年. (cf. 知识青年)

知青商店 zhī-qīng shāngdiàn
educated youth stores
Stores run by educated youths. A term was used during the Cultural Revolution.

知识产权 zhīshi chǎnquán
intellectual property rights
The right to legal protection of patents, trademarks, copyrighted publications, etc.

知识产业 zhīshi chǎnyè
knowledge estates
Enterprises that develop or provide knowledge, such as educational, research, and information service enterprises.

知识管理 zhīshi guǎnlǐ
information management

知识化 zhīshihuà
knowledge-ization
To make those who have little scientific and cultural knowledge gain more through their study.

知识经济 zhīshi jīngjì
knowledge economy
An economy in which intangible assets such as knowledge and intelligence play a decisive role.

知识库 zhīshikù
knowledge bank
A computer that stores specialized knowledge that has been encoded and made into a computer program. When using it, one can retrieve specialized knowledge from a computer terminal. This kind of computer is called "knowledge bank".

知识流动 zhīshi liúdòng
circulation of knowledge
Also called 人才流动 circulation of talent. That is, to break through the system of departmental ownership of talent, so that intellectuals with expertise in specialized fields may be employed wherever they are most needed and their abilities may be brought into full play.

知识青年 zhīshi qīngnián
educated youths
Youths who graduated from junior or senior high school, but could not continue with their education. During the Cultural Revolution, most of them were assigned to take part in the rustication movement (cf. 上山下乡). They are a large constituency of the urban population and present a challenge to society in areas such as employment.

肢残人 zhīcánrén
a handicapped person with one or more disabled limbs

肢障 zhīzhàng
handicapped; handicapped person

脂肪肝 zhīfánggān
fatty liver
Ailment caused by having a layer of fat surrounding the liver.

织补 zhībǔ
darning
To mend holes in clothing by weaving in yarn or thread.

职大 zhí-dà
workers' colleges

Abbreviation for 职工大学 or 职业大学. Institutes of higher learning run specifically for employees of enterprises and other work units. In general, classes are held after work hours.

职代会 zhí-dài-huì
employees' representatives conference
Contraction of 职工代表大会. (cf. 职工代表大会)

职等 zhíděng
professional ranks
The ranking system is determined by analyzing and comparing the types of work, levels of complexity and difficulty, degrees of responsibility, and the required qualifications.

职改 zhí-gǎi
reform of the system of professional titles
Abbreviation for 职称制度改革.
E.g. 职改工作 *the work of reforming the system of professional titles*

职改办 zhí-gǎi-bàn
office of professional titles system reforms
Abbreviation for 职称制度改革办公室.

职高 zhí-gāo
vocational high school
Abbreviation for 职业高中.

职工代表大会 zhígōng dàibiǎo dàhuì
employees' representatives conference
The basic form in which an enterprise implements democratic management under the leadership of the Party committee. It is the organ of authority through which workers participate in policy decisions, management, and supervision of cadres. Union meetings are held periodically. The representatives are chosen by democratic election. The union has the right to hear and discuss the reports of the enterprise's leadership, to examine major issues such as production plans, labor organization, the fiscal situation, welfare benefits, and labor protection, to criticize and to make suggestions, etc. When the union is not holding a meeting, the labor union of the enterprise is the standing body of the employees' representatives conference.

职级 zhíjí
professional rank

职介 zhíjiè
career consulting; employment service
E.g. 这些职介机构大都是个体办的。 *These employment service institutions are mostly private.* / 职介单位免费为下岗职工服务。 *Employment service units provide free services for laid-off employees.*

职介所 zhí-jiè-suǒ
employment service center (office)
Abbreviation for 职业介绍所.

职务工资 zhíwù gōngzī
professional wages
A wage system whereby the wages for different professionals – such as leaders, sci-tech personnel, teachers, and physicians – are determined by at hourly rate.

职校 zhí-xiào
vocational school
Abbreviation for 职业学校.

职业病 zhíyèbìng

occupational disease
1) Occupational disease, chronic ailments of certain occupations. 2) A metaphor for the occupational prejudices or ruts developed over a long period.

职业道德 zhíyè dàodé
professional ethics
The code of behavior and regulations that people should observe in their professional activities.

职业中学 zhíyè zhōngxué
vocational middle school

职中 zhí-zhōng
vocational middle school
Abbreviation for 职业中学 vocational middle school.

直播 zhíbō
live radio or television broadcast
E.g. 直播室 *live broadcast room* / 直播新闻 *to broadcast news live* / 现场直播 *to broadcast live from the site*

直挂 zhíguà
to form or build a direct link
E.g. 产销直挂 *to form a direct link between production and marketing*

直观教学 zhíguān jiàoxué
teaching by direct observation
A teaching method that uses audio-visual aids (including actual objects) in class. Students can observe the audio-visual aids or objects directly.

直航 zhíháng
direct flight or boat voyage
E.g. 由台北到大陆直航可以节省很多旅费。 *Flying direct between Taipei and the mainland can save much money.*

直落 zhíluò
to have a winning streak
E.g. 中国队直落三局战胜意大利队。 *The Chinese team beat the Italian team in a three-game winning streak.*

直面 zhímiàn
to face directly
E.g. 直面现实人生 *to face real life directly* / 直面改革 *to face reforms directly*

直销 zhíxiāo
direct sale
Producers selling directly to consumers.
E.g. 产品直销 *direct sale of products*

直选 zhíxuǎn
direct election
E.g. 有些农村家族宗派势力控制直选、影响直选。 *Clan factional forces in some rural areas have placed the direct election under their control and affected the outcome.*

植保 zhí-bǎo
plant protection
Contraction of 植物保护.

植被 zhíbèi
vegetation cover
All the plants that cover the surface of an area.

植物人 zhíwùrén
a person who has become a vegetable

执导 zhídǎo
to direct
To direct a movie or a play.
E.g. 电影《嫌疑犯》由韩小磊执导。 *"The Suspect" is directed by Han Xiaolei.*

执教 zhíjiào
to take up the teaching or (athletic) coaching profession
E.g. 他已执教40年。 *He has been teaching (or coaching) for 40 years already.*

执委会 zhí-wěi-huì

executive committee

Contraction of 执行委员会.

执政党 zhízhèngdǎng
the political party in power

值周生 zhízhōushēng
students on weekly duty

Students whose turn is to carry out duties for a week. They handle the routine matters in studies and everyday life. The weekly or daily duties system is a form of self governance in a school.
E.g. 今天轮到你作值周生了。 *It is your turn today to go on duty for a week.*

指导性计划 zhǐdǎoxìng jìhuà
plans in the nature of guidelines

State plans which are not strictly directive. In implementing these plans, units have the right to make adjustments based on the actual circumstances within the units and the market, and to formulate their own plans and report them to their supervisory departments. If the plans formulated by a unit are detrimental to the overall situation, the supervisory department has the right to intervene.

指导员 zhǐdǎoyuán
instructor (political)

Abbreviation for 政治指导员. (cf. 政治指导员)

指挥棒 zhǐhuībàng
baton

1) A thin metal baton used by a conductor in conducting an orchestra. 2) A wooden or metal stick made especially for use by a traffic policeman in directing traffic. 3) A metaphor for the will and commands of an individual or group (who demand that others obey).

指控 zhǐkòng
to accuse

Contraction of 指责 censure and 控诉 accuse.

指令性 zhǐlìngxìng
of a directive nature

In the nature of an order or directive which must be executed.

指令性计划 zhǐlìngxìng jìhuà
plans in the nature of directives

Important targets and projects in the realms of production, construction, and allocation which impinge upon the national economy and the people's livelihood, and which are state plans sent in the form of directive targets. The planning and administrative units at all levels must strictly follow and implement these plans and targets, and ensure their completion. For those plans and targets for which the state has stipulated limits, breaking the limits is strictly forbidden. For those that need adjustment due to changes in circumstances, reports must be sent to the supervisory departments for approval.

指令长 zhǐlìngzhǎng
commander

The responsible person in a space flight who receives instructions from earth and issues orders.

指认 zhǐrèn
to point out

To point out (a person or thing) on the spot.

指压疗法 zhǐyā liáofǎ
acupressure treatment

A method of treating certain illnesses by pressing acupoints with the fingers.

指战员 zhǐ-zhànyuán

commander and combatants

Contraction of 指挥员 and 战斗员.

纸老虎 zhǐlǎohǔ

paper tiger

Metaphor for a person or group that appears to be strong and ferocious but is not. Something that is outwardly strong and inwardly weak.

致富 zhìfù

to work hard for or to devote oneself to prosperity

E.g. 劳动致富 *to become rich through hard work* / 共同致富 *to become rich together* / 集体致富 *to become rich collectively*

致公党 Zhìgōngdǎng

Public Interest Party

Short for 中国致公党 China Zhi Gong Dang, one of China's patriotic democratic parties, founded in December 1925 in San Francisco.

致气 zhìqì

to have a tiff

制导系统 zhìdǎo xìtǒng

guidance system

A system that controls and guides flying devices by selecting their flight paths and carrying out maneuvers. There are various forms of guidance systems, such as autonomous guidance, remote guidance, target seeking guidance, and joint guidance.

制衡 zhìhéng

to regulate to achieve balance

制冷 zhìlěng

to refrigerate

E.g. 制冷设备 *refrigeration facility*

制式 zhìshì

standard model

Uniform specifications and style.

E.g. 制式标准 *specified standards* / 电视制式 *standard television model*

制售 zhìshòu

to manufacture and sell

制种 zhìzhǒng

to process seeds

To scientifically select seeds with the goal of upgrading the yield.

智残 zhìcán

mentally retarded

智产阶级 zhìchǎn jiējí

intellectual property class

Also called 知产阶级. (cf. 知产阶级)

智力测验 zhìlì cèyàn

intelligence test

智力工程 zhìlì gōngchéng

intelligence engineering

A plan to raise the intelligence quotient in the population by preventing and curing thyroid deficiency.

智力开发 zhìlì kāifā

to develop intellectual ability

To treat knowledge and human intelligence as resources in developing and capitalizing on them.

智力库 zhìlìkù

intelligence bank

Locations and units with a concentration of experts and scholars.

E.g. 政协要发挥智力库的优势。 *The Chinese People's Political Consultative Conference must make good use of the strength of its intelligence bank.*

智力投资 zhìlì tóuzī

intellectual investment

Also called 人才投资 *investment of talent*. To treat knowledge and human intellect as a resource to be developed and used. Intellectual investment involves employing economics, science, culture, management, and education in an integrated way to study ways of developing talents and making the best use of them.

智力引进 zhìlì yǐnjìn

import of intellect

To import from other areas or abroad people with management experience, professional talents or qualifications in science and technology.

智力支边 zhìlì zhībiān

to aid the border areas with intellect

To send scholars and experts in culture, science and technology to border minority regions, to lecture, teach, train teachers and develop economic advisory services.

智龄 zhìlíng

cognitive age

Abbreviation for 智力年龄, as a measure of a child's cognitive development.

智密区 zhìmìqū

high intelligence density district

An area with a concentration of universities and research facilities.

智囊团 zhìnángtuán

brains trust

智能 zhìnéng

wisdom and ability; (re animals and machines) a certain kind of intelligence and ability typical of humans

E.g. 儿童的智能要全面发展。 *The intelligence and ability of children must be developed in all spheres.* /人工智能 *artificial intelligence* / 智能机器人 *robots with intelligence*

智能服装 zhìnéng fúzhuāng

intellectualized clothing; clothing with special properties ability

Clothing made of high-tech synthetic fiber which possesses special properties such as the ability to change color according to external conditions. The clothing's temperature and moisture content can also be adjusted.

智能化产品 zhìnénghuà chǎnpǐn

intelligent products

Electronic machines, such as translating machines and robots, which have the ability to follow logic, store information, and calculate. They are characterized by being speedy, efficient, and reliable.

智能建筑 zhìnéng jiànzhù

intellectualized architecture (building)

Architecture (buildings) equipped with complete and perfect functional installations for management automation, office automation, and telecommunications automation.

智能卡 zhìnéngkǎ

intelligence card

A kind of credit card which uses a micro chip rather than the ordinary magnetic strip, so that its data-storage capacity is greatly increased. (cf. 信用卡)

智能型 zhìnéngxíng

intellectual type

Personnel with a certain level of scientific and cultural knowledge.

E.g. 智能型干部 *cadres of the intellectual type*

智商 zhìshāng

intelligence quotient; I.Q.

智育第一 zhìyù dì-yī

putting intellectual education in top position

In schools, the erroneous practice of

emphasizing intellectual education and neglecting social, moral and physical education.

智障 zhìzhàng
mentally handicapped

质检员 zhì-jiǎn-yuán
quality inspection personnel
Abbreviation for 质量检查员.

质量经济学 zhìliàng jīngjìxué
quality economics
A branch of economics concerned with raising economic efficiency by determining optimal quality.

质量月活动 zhìliàngyuè huódòng
quality month activities
Activities aimed at upgrading the quality of products. They involve a combination of widespread publicity and awards. Generally, they are carried out in a certain month each year, hence they are called "quality month activities". Since 1978, there have been quality month activities every September in China.

滞背 zhìbèi
(re merchandise) unsalable or slow selling
E.g. 滞背货 *merchandise with no or few buyers*

滞洪 zhìhóng
flood retention
A method of controlling floods, by using the lakes, low-lying land, and designated retention basins next to a river. Overflow is temporarily stored through the use of check gates until the flow in the riverbed is reduced to a certain level.

滞后 zhìhòu
to stagnate and fall behind
E.g. 法制建设滞后. *The construction of a legal system is stagnating.* / 农业发展滞后. *Agricultural development is stagnating.* / 滞后期 *period of stagnation*

滞缓 zhìhuǎn
stagnant
To be at a standstill or to move very slowly.
E.g. 农民收入滞缓。 *Increase in peasants' income is very slow.*

滞容 zhìróng
holding capacity
The capacity for accommodating in-transit people or goods at a certain place.
E.g. 新车站能滞容旅客二万人。 *The new railway station has a holding capacity for 20,000 travelers.*

滞压 zhìyā
(re material resources, etc.) being held up and lying idle
E.g. 滞压货车严重。 *There is a serious holdup of transport trucks.* / 将电报滞压不处理 *to hold up a telegram and not deal with it*

滞胀 zhìzhàng
stagnation and inflation; stagflation
Contraction of 停滞 stagnation and 膨胀 inflation. The dual situation of economic stagnation and inflation.

治保 zhì-bǎo
pubic security protection
Abbreviation for 治安保卫.
E.g. 治保工作 *public security work* / 治保队伍 *the ranks of public security workers* / 治保小组 *public security committee*

治厂 zhìchǎng
to run or to put a factory in order
E.g. 从严治厂 *to run a factory*

strictly

治国安邦 zhìguó ānbāng
to govern and bring peace to the nation
To govern the nation, and bring peace and security to society.

治贫 zhìpín
to bring poverty under control

治穷 zhìqióng
to bring poverty under control

治穷致富 zhìqióng zhìfù
to end poverty and bring about prosperity
E.g. 帮助贫困地区发展生产, 治穷致富 *to help the poor areas develop production, in order to cure poverty and bring about prosperity.*

zhong

中巴 zhōngbā
mid-size buses

中办 Zhōng – Bàn
General Office of the Central Committee of the Chinese Communist Party
Abbreviation for 中共中央办公室.

中层干部 zhōngcéng gànbù
middle ranking cadres

中产阶级 zhōngchǎn jiējí
middle class

中长纤维 zhōngcháng xiānwéi
medium-length fibers
Abbreviation for 中长型短纤维 medium-length short fibers.

中成药 zhōngchéngyào
prepared Chinese medicine
Pharmaceuticals that are prepared by a pharmacy for use in Chinese medicine. The term also applies to various mass produced Chinese medicines.

中程导弹 zhōngchéng dǎodàn
intermediate missiles

中档 zhōngdàng
(re merchandise) middle grade (vs. 高档 high grade and 低档 low grade)
E.g. 中档面食 *middle grade wheat products* / 中档炒菜 *middle grade stir-fried dishes* / 中档服装 *middle grade clothing*

中导 zhōng – dǎo
middle range guided missiles
Abbreviation for 中程弹道导弹.

中导条约 zhōng – dǎo tiáoyuē
Middle Range Guided Missile Treaty
A disarmament treaty signed by Reagan and Gorbachev on December 8, 1987 in Washington to destroy all mid and short range nuclear missiles. It stipulated the destruction of over 2,400 nuclear warheads by 1991.

中梗阻 zhōnggěngzǔ
midcourse obstructions
Obstructions encountered in the course of implementing Party or government guiding principles or policies.

中顾委 Zhōng – Gù – Wěi
Central Advisory Commission of the Chinese Communist Party
Abbreviation for 中国共产党中央顾问委员会.

中观 zhōngguān
intermediate perspective
Between microcosmic and macrocosmic pertaining to the intermediate or a link. *E.g.* 中观改革 *reforms at the intermediate level*

中国通 zhōngguótōng

China expert

Foreigners who are exceptionally knowledgeable about China.

E.g. 他这个外国人真是个中国通。 *This foreigner is truly an authority on China.*

中行 Zhōng-Háng

Bank of China

Abbreviation for 中国银行.

E.g. 中行全力开拓住房信贷业务。 *The Bank of China has opened a credit business for housing.*

中航 Zhōng-Háng

China Airline

Short for 中国航空公司.

中技术 zhōngjìshù

mid-tech (between high-tech and low-tech)

中纪委 Zhōng-Jì-Wěi

the Central Commission for Discipline Inspection of the Chinese Communist Party

Abbreviation for 中国共产党中央纪律检查委员会.

中间产品 zhōngjiān chǎnpǐn

intermediate product

A product manufactured by a certain industry for its own use in making its products.

中间地带 zhōngjiān dìdài

intermediate zone

The regions situated politically between the United States and the former Soviet Union after World War Two, i.e., the many capitalist nations, colonial and semi-colonial nations of Europe, Asia, and Africa.

中间人物 zhōngjiān rénwù

middle characters

Persons in society who are not heroic, advanced, nor backward, who are simply situated in the middle. The advanced and backward characters are in the minority, middle characters are the greater majority.

中考 zhōngkǎo

high school entrance exam (taken by junior high graduates)

中科院 Zhōng-Kē-Yuàn

Chinese Academy of Sciences

Abbreviation for 中国科学院.

中联部 Zhōng-Lián-Bù

International Liaison Department of the Central Committee of the Chinese Communist Party

Abbreviation for 中共中央对外联络部.

中农 zhōngnóng

middle peasants

During land reform, in assigning class status to people in the countryside, those peasants whose economic position was between rich and poor peasants were called "middle peasants". The majority of middle peasants owned land and some of the production tools. Their source of livelihood derived mainly from their own labor. In general, they did not exploit others and did not sell their own labor.

中生代 zhōngshēngdài

the generation of middle-aged people

中师 zhōng-shī

secondary normal school

A normal school at the secondary level, or education from such a school.

E.g. 中师教育 *secondary normal school education* / 他是中师毕业的。 *He is a graduate of a secondary normal school.*

中试 zhōngshì

intermediate testing (of a prototype before going into production)

中委 zhōng–wěi

the central committee; central committee member

Abbreviation for 中央委员会 the central committee or 中央委员 central committee member.

中西医结合 zhōng–xīyī jiéhé

integrating Chinese and Western medicines

To integrate Chinese and Western medical practices and medicines, to bring into full play the strengths of each.

中心小学 zhōngxīn xiǎoxué

core elementary school

The key elementary school in an area that covers first through to sixth grades. Its teachers, buildings, and facilities are better than average. Academically, it has certain links with surrounding elementary schools.

中宣部 Zhōng–Xuān–Bù

Propaganda Department of the Central Committee of the Chinese Communist Party

Abbreviation for 中共中央宣传部.

中央文革 Zhōngyāng Wén–Gé

Cultural Revolutionary Leading Group under the Party Central Committee

Abbreviation for 中央文化革命小组, the central government's organ for leading the nationwide Cultural Revolution. It was established in May 1966, under the jurisdiction of the Standing Committee of the Political Bureau of the Central Committee of the Chinese Communist Party.

中央政治局 Zhōngyāng Zhèngzhìjú

Political Bureau of the Central Committee of the Chinese Communist Party

Short of 中共中央政治局, the leading organ of the Party Central Committee, formed by the plenary session of the Central Committee (also called 政治局).

中游思想 zhōngyóu sīxiǎng

middling mentality

Metaphor for the mentality of not wishing to be advanced and yet unwilling to be backward.

中直 zhōng–zhí

(a unit or department) directly under the jurisdiction of the Central Committee of the Chinese Communist Party

E.g. 中直机关 *organs directly under the jurisdiction of the Central Committee of the Chinese Communist Party* / 中直单位 *units directly under the jurisdiction of the Central Committee of the Chinese Communist Party* / 中直党委 *Party Committee directly under the jurisdiction of the Central Committee of the Chinese Communist Party* / 中直招待所 *guest house directly under the jurisdiction of the Central Committee of the Chinese Communist Party.*

中指委 Zhōng–Zhǐ–Wěi

the Central Committee of the Chinese Communist Party for Party Rectification

Abbreviation for 中国共产党中央整党工作指导委员会.

中专 zhōng–zhuān

specialized or technical secondary school

Abbreviation for 中等专科学校.

中转 zhōngzhuǎn
to transfer (to another bus, etc.); to transmit or relay
E.g. 在北京中转换车 *to transfer at Beijing* / 减少旅客中转停留时间 *to reduce travelers' stopover time* / 长途电话中转。 *The long distance telephone connection was made by relay.* / 经人中转他才拿到那本书。 *It was through an intermediary that he received that book.*

中资 zhōngzī
(re business enterprises) undertaken with Chinese funding
E.g. 中资航运企业 *Air transport and shipping enterprises funded by Chinese sources*

中子弹 zhōngzǐdàn
neutron bomb

中组部 Zhōng-Zǔ-Bù
Organization Department of the Central Committee of the Chinese Communist Party
Abbreviation for 中共中央组织部.

忠字舞 zhōngzìwǔ
(popular during the Cultural Revolution) a group dance expressing loyalty toward the Great Helmsman

终端 zhōngduān
computer terminal
E.g. 终端设备 *computer terminal equipment* / 终端显示器 *computer terminal monitor*

终身教育 zhōngshēn jiàoyù
lifelong education (organized and otherwise)

终身制 zhōngshēnzhì
lifelong system
The method of allowing cadres to assume leadership functions for a lifetime. Under the socialist economic system, there is no law specifying that cadres have leadership functions for life, but in reality, this is prevalent.

终审 zhōngshěn
final trial
The last level of trial in a judicial system. (In China, there are two trial levels, so the second is the final trial. The first trial at the Supreme Court is also the final trial.)
E.g. 终审裁定 *ruling made at the final trial* / 终审判决 *verdict of the final trial*

种畜 zhǒngchù
breeding stock
Male domesticated animals used in breeding.

种蛋 zhǒngdàn
breeding eggs
Eggs used in propagating chickens.

种苗 zhǒngmiáo
breeding seedlings
Plant seedlings used in large-scale planting.

种禽 zhǒngqín
fowls used in breeding; improved breeding fowls

种猪 zhǒngzhū
boars used for breeding

种子队 zhǒngziduì
seed team
An athletic team that gets preferential treatment in an athletic tournament: it automatically bypasses the first round of the tournament, so that its first game in the tournament is against a team that has already won in the first round.

种子公司 zhǒngzi gōngsī

companies that research and market seeds

种子基金 zhǒngzi jījīn
seed money
Capital used in attracting more capitals.

种子球员 zhǒngzi qiúyuán
seed player
An athletic who gets preferential treatment in a tournament by by-passing the first round.

种子选手 zhǒngzi xuǎnshǒu
a top seeded athlete
Also called 种子.

种子站 zhǒngzizhàn
seed stations
Places that specialize in cultivating or disseminating and supplying superior seeds for crops.

重点户 zhòngdiǎnhù
key households
Rural households that focus their supplemental or main labor force on the production of certain commodities in their spare time. In general, these products account for about half of their family incomes.

重点学校 zhòngdiǎn xuéxiào
key schools
Full-time day schools (including elementary schools, secondary schools, and universities) recognized by various levels of government as being superior to most. This includes academic programs, caliber of the teachers and facilities such as libraries. These schools are given preferential treatment in allocation of educational funding, etc., so that they may serve as a model for other schools.

重奖 zhòngjiǎng
to bestow on someone a very high honor or a very substantial material award
E.g. 重奖作出重大贡献的科技人员 *to bestow substantial honors and rewards to the sci-tech personnel who made major contributions*

重头 zhòngtóu
"weighty" in the sense of being important or of high caliber
E.g. 重头中篇小说 *a "weighty" mid-length novel*

zhou

周边 zhōubiān
surroundings; outer boundaries
E.g. 周边国家 *surrounding countries* / 周边组织 *peripheral organizations*

周界 zhōujiè
boundaries

周转粮 zhōuzhuǎnliáng
turnover grain
The grain sold to the state by peasants after harvest, and bought back within a certain time period. This was a method adopted in the 1950s, after the nation implemented the system of unified purchase and marketing of grains, to satisfy the peasants' need to circulate grain and adjust the distribution of grain types.

洲际导弹 zhōujì dǎodàn
intercontinental missiles

zhu

珠峰 Zhū-Fēng
Mount Qomolangma (Everest)

Abbreviation for 珠穆朗玛峰, highest peak of the Himalayas.

珠影 Zhū-Yǐng
Pearl River Film Studio
Abbreviation for 珠江电影制片厂.

株式会社 zhūshì huìshè
joint-stock corporation
The Japanese word synonymous with the Chinese word 股份公司.
E.g. 富士通株式会社 *the Fujito Corporation*

诸葛亮会 zhūgéliànghuì
Zhuge Liang meeting
A meeting of people, who have expertise, experience, and skills, to discuss and solve difficult problems in production or work. Zhuge Liang is a historical figure portrayed in the *Romance of the Three Kingdoms*. He is popularly regarded as a wise and clever fellow, hence his name is used in this metaphor.

诸侯经济 zhūhóu jīngjì
"local principality economics"
An economic state where each region develops its economy autonomously.

竹雕 zhúdiāo
to carve on bamboo; bamboo carvings

竹幕 zhúmù
"bamboo curtain"
A name given by Western political circles in the 1950s-1960s for the barrier that separated China's mainland from Western capitalist society.

竹筒倒豆子 zhútǒng dào dòuzi
spilling beans out of the bamboo tube
A metaphor for candidly revealing all.

主刀 zhǔdāo
to wield the scalpel (to operate on a patient); the surgeon
E.g. 手术由有经验的医师主刀。
The surgery was done by an experienced physician. / 这次手术由他主刀 *This surgery was done by him.*

主干家庭 zhǔgàn jiātíng
main trunk family
A three-generation family composed of a married couple, their children, and one set of grandparents.

主观能动性 zhǔguān néngdòngxìng
subjective initiative
The ability and effectiveness of a person in perceiving the objective world through his practical experiences, and in self-consciously reforming the world and promoting developments in accordance with objective laws.

主教练 zhǔjiàoliàn
head coach

主流 zhǔliú
main current
Synonymous with 干流. A metaphor for the main aspect of a development or the basic nature of something.

主题词 zhǔtící
topical words (for use in indexing and searching for relevant library materials)
Also called 检索词.

主体错误 zhǔtǐ cuòwù
principle error
Error in the major aspect of a task or error of a comprehensive nature, such as the long-term leftist error in China's economic construction.

主体工程 zhǔtǐ gōngchéng
main project
The main component of a large con-

struction project.

主线 zhǔxiàn
main thread
Main line or issue that runs throughout, specifically the main thread in the plot of a literary work.

主页 zhǔyè
home page

主战场 zhǔzhànchǎng
the main battleground
Also used as a metaphor for the main arena of a struggle or activity.

主治医生 zhǔzhì yīshēng
physician in charge
A certain rank of physicians who have the credentials to diagnose and treat patients independently (without supervision).

著作权 zhùzuòquán
copyright

助编 zhù–biān
assistant editor
Short for 助理编辑.

助残 zhùcán
to aid handicapped people
E.g. 助残日 *Aid the Handicapped Day* / 助残单位 *unit advanced in aiding the handicapped*

助导 zhù–dǎo
assistant director
Short for 助理导演.

助耕包户 zhùgēng bāohù
aid with farming and take responsibility for households
After the system of contracting production to households was implemented in rural areas, young people voluntarily formed teams and took responsibility for families in the surrounding areas who had difficulties in production and everyday life to help them solve their difficulties.

助耕队 zhùgēngduì
aid farming teams
Temporary voluntary organizations made up of rural young people and formed to help households in hardship to farm their land.

助工 zhù–gōng
assistant engineer
Short for 助理工程师.

助学 zhùxué
to support and aid a scholar (usually referring to one engaged in independent study)

助研 zhù–yán
assistant researcher
Short for 助理研究员.

贮运 zhùyùn
storage and shipping
Contraction of 贮存 and 运输.

住读 zhùdú
to study at a boarding school
E.g. 住读生 *a student who lives at school* / 住读学校 *boarding school*

注资 zhùzī
to infuse with capital

zhua

抓辫子 zhuābiànzi
to grab by the queue
Also called 揪辫子. A metaphor for seizing on someone's faults or errors and using them to manipulate him.

抓捕 zhuābǔ
to arrest; to capture

抓点带面 zhuādiǎn dàimiàn
to grab hold of the points and bring

along the sphere

A work method of cadre leaders. Before a certain task is launched, one or two grass-roots units are selected. After listing the task through the experiences of these units, the work is extended to the overall situation. The experience attained at the points issued to help the extension of the task to the overall sphere. (cf. 点面结合.)

抓典型 zhuādiǎnxíng
to grab hold of typical cases

A work method of cadre leaders. To select representative departments, persons, or instances within the unit (good or bad, advanced or backward), and use them to educate the whole work force and to promote the development of a task.

抓纲治国 zhuāgāng zhìguó
to grab hold of the guiding principle in governing the nation

1976年10月粉碎"四人帮"反革命集团后,华国锋主持中共中央工作时提出的错误口号。按照当时的解释,所谓"抓纲治国""就是在两个阶级、两条路线的激烈斗争中,实现安定团结,巩固无产阶级专政,巩固和发展无产阶级文化大革命的胜利成果,达到天下大治。"这个口号仍以"阶级斗争为纲",肯定"文化大革命"和"左"的理论。直到1978年底党的十一届三中全会才停止使用。

An erroneous slogan used by Hua Guofeng in heading the work of the Central Committee of the Chinese Communist Party after the downfall of the Gang of Four counter-revolutionary group in 1976. According to the interpretation at the time, this slogan meant taking a firm stand on the fierce struggle between two classes and between two lines, realizing stability and solidarity, consolidating the proletarian dictatorship, consolidating and developing the victorious results of the proletarian Cultural Revolution, and thus attaining order across the land. This slogan still took class struggle as the guiding principle and affirmed the Cultural Revolution and the leftist doctrine. It was not until the Third Plenary Session of the Eleventh Central Committee of the Chinese Communist Party in 1978 that it was discarded.

抓革命,促生产 zhuā gémìng, cù shēngchǎn
to grab hold of revolution and promote production

A slogan of the Cultural Revolution which meant advocating class struggle and cultural revolution as a means of promoting the development of industrial and agricultural production. Practical experience proved that this approach created chaos and was unscientific, therefore it was discarded after the Third Plenary Session of the Eleventh Central Committee of the Chinese Communist Party.

抓根本 zhuā gēnběn
to grab hold of the roots

A metaphor for getting to the essentials and doing the most important tasks first when there are many to deal with. During the Cultural Revolution, "grabbing hold of the roots" was interpreted as grabbing hold of class struggle. This was an erroneous leftist approach.

抓获 zhuāhuò
to arrest; to catch (a criminal)

抓两头, 带中间 zhuā liǎngtóu dài zhōngjiān

to grab hold of the two ends and bring along the middle

A method of leadership advocated by Mao Zedong. There are always two elements in the masses, the advanced and the backward (conservative). Whether it is in thinking, working or studying the two ends are always the minority. In the middle is always the majority. Leaders should first grab hold of the two ends, and by working with them, make the advanced more advanced and turn the backward elements in the direction of the advanced. They will then carry along those in the middle, transform the overall situation, and push forward the development of the task.

抓苗头 zhuā miáotou

to grab hold of the bud

To act early in a development, as soon as certain trends begin to show.

抓拍 zhuāpāi

to catch the perfect moment to photograph

E.g. 抓拍到一个好镜头 *to have taken a good shot (in photography)* / 抓拍手法 *technique in catching perfect photographic moments*

抓生产 zhuā shēngchǎn

to grab hold of production

To take responsibility and lead the work in the sphere of production.

抓思想 zhuā sīxiǎng

to grab hold of ideology

To investigate, analyze, and study ideological problems that arise, and moreover to carry out the work of ideological education and persuasion.

zhuan

专案组 zhuān'ànzǔ

groups for handling special cases

Temporary organizations formed to handle special cases. During the Cultural Revolution, such special groups were formed indiscriminately, and as a result unjust cases were fabricated on a massive scale.

专访 zhuānfǎng

special interview; an article written in the form of a special interview

专柜 zhuānguì

a counter for a specific type of merchandise

E.g. 开办专柜 *to operate a counter for special merchandise* / 专柜销售 *to sell at a special counter*

专家路线 zhuānjiā lùxiàn

the experts line

The slanderous name intended to lower the esteem of expertise, talent and intellect. It also denigrated the employment of these qualities. It originated from people with an erroneous leftist mentality.

专家至上 zhuānjiā zhìshàng

experts are supreme

Placing experts in a position above everyone else. This was the erroneous interpretation, of those with an erroneous leftist mentality, of the esteem given to expertise and talent.

专控 zhuānkòng

to control the buying and selling of commodities rationed by the state

专控商品 zhuānkòng shāngpǐn

controlled commodities

Commodities for which production and marketing are under special control of the government.

专列 zhuānliè
special train
Contraction of 专用列车 train for special use.

专区 zhuānqū
subprovincial administrative regions
Administrative regions, including a number of counties and municipalities, set up by provinces and autonomous regions on the basis of need.

专署 zhuānshǔ
commissioner's office
Contraction of 专员公署. An agency set up by a province or autonomous region in China on the basis of need.

专属渔区 zhuānshǔ yúqū
exclusive fishing zone
An oceanic zone in which a nation has exclusive fishing rights. An area of the sea bordering a nation.

专业承包 zhuānyè chéngbāo
responsibility contracts on specialties
After the rural production responsibility system was implemented, the production team may divide the scope of a task into a number of specialties and contract them to individual commune members or groups. On the basis of the different specialties, duties, output, work points, investments, awards and penalties, etc., are determined, and contracts are signed. Among the various specialties within a production team, work point valuation and distribution are linked.

专业村 zhuānyècūn
specialty village
A village which engages mainly in specialized production, and derives its income primarily from the production of commodities. These villages surfaced in 1983. They allow agricultural production to evolve from being commercialized to being specialized, and from being scattered among various specialty households to being collective economic entities.

专业户 zhuānyèhù
specialty households
A type of rural households that surfaced after the rural production responsibility system was implemented. A specialty household engages in some kind of specialized production. The income from these commodity products comprises the main component of the family's total income.

专营 zhuānyíng
to specialize in marketing certain types of commodities; to sell through special organizations
E.g. 那个商店专营男女皮鞋。
That store specializes in men's and women's leather shoes.

专政对象 zhuānzhèng duìxiàng
target of dictatorship
Everything in a nation is essentially under the dictatorship of a certain class. The target of dictatorship consists of the classes, groups, or individuals within a nation who are antagonistic to the ruling class. Used specifically in the Chinese context, the term refers to the target of proletarian dictatorship, that is, the forces that resist socialist revolution and sabotage socialist construction.

专政工具 zhuānzhèng gōngjù

instruments of dictatorship
The military, police, courts, and prisons of a nation. Nations differ in their nature, hence the instruments of dictatorship that they use also differ.

专政机关 zhuānzhèng jīguān
organs of dictatorship
The organs of state, such as public security and judicial departments, that execute the duties of class dictatorship.

专著 zhuānzhù
special work (written)
A special work which studies or expounds on a certain topic.

转氨酶 zhuǎn'ānméi
transaminase (aminotransferase) enzymes
Abbreviation for 转胺基酶.

转包 zhuǎnbāo
to transfer contracted responsibilities
E.g. 把土地转包出去 *to transfer contracted land*

转产 zhuǎnchǎn
shift in production
A factory, for certain reasons, discontinues the production of its original commodities and shifts to producing another type of commodities.

转发 zhuǎnfā
to transmit
To send documents, memorandums, etc., to concerned departments after they have been read and commented upon.

转干 zhuǎngàn
to become a cadre
A worker becoming a regular cadre.

转岗 zhuǎngǎng
to transfer to another post
E.g. 企业改革后,有不少职工干部下岗、转岗乃至待业。 *After enterprises underwent reforms, quite a few cadre workers left or changed their posts, or even became unemployed.*

转轨 zhuǎnguǐ
to transfer to another system; to switch tracks
Used metaphorically in referring to ideological shift, etc.

转轨经济 zhuǎnguǐ jīngjì
transition economy

转基因 zhuǎnjīyīn
gene transfer
Technology for transferring genes from one plant or animal to another.
E.g. 转基因食品 *genetically engineered food*/ 转基因作物 *genetically altered crop*

转基因 zhuǎnjīyīn
the biotechnology of gene transfer

转口贸易 zhuǎnkǒu màoyì
transit trade
Trade between a producing nation or locale and a consuming nation or locale conducted through an intermediary.

转录 zhuǎnlù
to dub an audio or videotape
E.g. 他在转录音乐。 *He is dubbing some music.*

转销 zhuǎnxiāo
to ship merchandise elsewhere to sell
E.g. 中国商品经香港商人转销到西欧。 *Chinese commodities are sold to Western Europe through intermediary businessmen in Hong Kong.*

转型 zhuǎnxíng
to undergo a transformation; a matter undergoing a major, fundamental change

转业 zhuǎnyè

career shift

Change from one profession to another. Used specifically, it means the transfer of a cadre of the Chinese People's Liberation Army to civilian work in a local area.

转业军人 zhuǎnyè jūnrén

armyman transferred to civilian work

A cadre of the Chinese People's Liberation Army who has been demobilized and transferred to work in a local area.

转正 zhuǎnzhèng

to become a regular member

A temporary or probationary member of an organization becoming a regular member.

zhuang

庄家 zhuāngjia

large shareholder (in the stock market)

A large shareholder who can control the rise and fall of certain stocks in the market.

E.g. 庄家已经完全控盘。 *The large shareholders completely controlled the price of certain shares.*

装卸工人 zhuāngxiè gōngrén

workers who load and unload

Workers who load and unload goods from transport vehicles.

撞车 zhuàngchē

vehicular collision; clash

1) Originally, the collision of two vehicles. 2) A metaphor for two or more identical things sometimes carried out simultaneously, thereby creating a conflicting situation.

E.g. 有时电影、电视几家同时抢一个剧目, 造成撞车现象。 *Several movie or television studios vie for the same program, creating a clash in the process.*

壮行 zhuàngxíng

to encourage and raise the expectations of someone who is leaving at a farewell

E.g. 为考察南极的勇士们壮行 *to give a rousing farewell party to the courageous South Pole explorers* / 举行壮行大会 *to hold a rousing farewell party*

zhui

追肥 zhuīféi

topdressing with fertilizer; to fertilize a growing crop

E.g. 棉花打尖以后要追肥。 *Cotton should be fertilized after topping.*

追加 zhuījiā

to add to the original quota

E.g. 追加教育经费 *to increase educational funds (from the original allocation)*

追烈 zhuī-liè

to posthumously confer the status of martyr on someone

追授 zhuīshòu

to bestow an honorary title on someone posthumously

追星 zhuīxīng

to pursue movie stars, popular singers, etc.

追星族 zhuīxīngzú

the category of people who are hung up on stars

zhun

准工业化 zhǔngōngyèhuà
quasi-industrialize

准妈妈 zhǔnmāma
pregnant woman; mother to be

zhuo

着装 zhuózhuāng
attire
E.g. 有些人着装随随便便。 *Some people dress very casually.*

zi

资本主义尾巴 zīběn zhǔyì wěiba
capitalist tail (cf. 割资本主义尾巴)

资本主义自发势力 zīběn zhǔyì zìfā shìlì
spontaneous capitalist force
The individual economies of small producers who have the tendency to spontaneously follow the capitalist road.

资不抵债 zī bù dǐ zhài
all the assets are insufficient to cover the debt

资产重组 zīchǎn chóngzǔ
consolidation of industry

资产阶级法权 zīchǎn jiējí fǎquán
bourgeois right
An old term for 资产阶级权利. (cf. 资产阶级权利)

资产阶级反动路线 zīchǎn jiējí fǎndòng lùxiàn
bourgeois reactionary line
The slanderous name given by the Lin Biao-Jiang Qing clique during the Cultural Revolution to the policies advocated by Liu Shaoqi. At the time, this line was said to be in opposition to the proletarian revolutionary line advocated by Mao Zedong.

资产阶级反动学术权威 zīchǎn jiējí fǎndòng xuéshù quánwēi
bourgeois reactionary academic authority
Authoritative persons who hold bourgeois academic viewpoints and who oppose the proletarian revolutionary mission. During the Cultural Revolution, many accomplished scientists, professors, experts, writers, and artists were branded "reactionary academic authorities" because they persisted in their correct academic views or because they held variant views. They were violently criticized, struggled against, and were cruelly persecuted.

资产阶级权利 zīchǎn jiējí quánlì
bourgeois right
Translation of the German word "dad burgerliche recht", formerly translated as 资产阶级法权. It is a right that arises from the capitalist system of ownership of production resources. It is egalitarian in form but not in reality. It is distinguished from feudal prerogative, which is not egalitarian in both form and substance.

资产阶级司令部 zīchǎn jiējí sīlìngbù
bourgeois headquarters
During the Cultural Revolution, the Lin Biao-Jiang Qing counter-revolutionary group, in attempting to usurp the Party and seize power, spread the slander that, aside from the proletarian head-

quarters headed by Mao Zedong, the Party Central Committee harbored a "bourgeois headquarters" headed by Liu Shaoqi and Deng Xiaoping. This was a fabricated charge forced upon the Party and the national leaders Liu Shaoqi and Deng Xiaoping.

资产阶级右派 zīchǎn jiējí yòupài
bourgeois rightists
Also called 右派 rightists and 右派分子 rightist elements. (cf. 反右派斗争)

资产阶级自由化 zīchǎn jiējí zìyóuhuà
bourgeois liberalization
An unhealthy tendency to doubt the four basic principles (cf. 四项基本原则) which surfaced early in 1981. It advocated the following: to attempt to shake off the leadership of the Communist Party, to break away from the socialist track, and to advocate implementation of the Western bourgeois democratic system.

资敌罪 zīdízuì
crime of abetting the enemy
An act of aiding the enemy, which is a counter-revolutionary crime. Spying, stealing and supplying state secrets to the enemy, or supplying the enemy with weapons, ammunition, or other materials for military use, are construed and handled as crimes of abetting the enemy.

资费 zīfèi
expenses
E.g. 我国对部分电信业务资费进行了调整。 *China has readjusted the expenses of some telecommunication transactions.*

资深 zīshēn
very experienced and well qualified
资深院士 zīshēn yuànshì
senior academician
Academicians of the Chinese Academy of Sciences and Academy of Engineering who are in their 80s. They can enjoy the rights and obligations of consultation and assessment, and promote academic exchanges and popular science. They do not take leading posts in academies and academic departments, nor do they participate in nominating and electing candidates for academicians.

资信 zīxìn
capital and credit
E.g. 资信能力 *capital and credit power* / 资信调查 *investigation into capital and credit*

资讯 zīxùn
data and information

滋扰 zīrǎo
to stir up trouble and create a disturbance

姊妹城 zǐmèichéng
sister cities
Symbolic of international friendship.

子弹列车 zǐdàn lièchē
bullet train

子公司 zǐgōngsī
subsidiary company
Also called 分公司 branch company.

自办 zìbàn
an individual or unit initiating an undertaking
E.g. 自办企业 *self-initiated enterprise* / 自办乐队 *self-initiated orchestra*

自报公议 zìbào gōngyì
self-assessment and public discussion

To report on the state of one's labor, then have everybody evaluate it and pass judgment on it.

自筹 zìchóu

an individual or unit raising funds or materials

E.g. 自筹资金 (a unit) raising capital on its own / 自筹经费 (a unit) raising funds on its own

自动柜员机 zìdòng guìyuánjī

ATM (automatic teller machine)

自发户 zìfāhù

self-risen households

Families in rural areas who developed certain specialized products on their own and quickly became rich, without help from any organization.

自费生 zìfèishēng

self-funded students

As opposed to 公费生 publicly funded students.

自负盈亏 zìfù yíngkuī

to assume responsibility for one's own profits and losses

When enterprises implement independent management, they take responsibility for their own profits and losses.

自护 zì-hù

self-protection; self-defense

E.g. 孩子的自护能力必须经过一定的训练才能奏效。 Children must be trained so that they have the ability to defend themselves.

自画衫 zìhuàshān

self-painted shirt

Shirts (usually T-shirts) with pictures painted on by the owner.

自考 zì-kǎo

an examination for extra mural students

E.g. 考试的组织与管理是社会看自考的窗口。 The organization and administration of the examination for extra mural students are the window through which the society gives its evaluation of their studies.

自控 zì-kòng

automatic control

Contraction of 自动控制.

E.g. 自控系统 automatic control system / 自控装置 automatic control device

自来红 zìláihóng

automatically red

Also called 自然红 naturally red, meaning that one is born revolutionary. In the early 1960s, some young people from families of workers, poor, and lower middle peasants, and revolutionary cadres and soldiers thought that, since they were born in the new society and raised under the red flag, they could naturally become successors to the revolutionary cause without receiving Marxist-Leninist education. This was an erroneous view.

自留畜 zìliúchù

private livestock

After agriculture was collectivized, the small number of livestock that commune members in pastoral areas could retain and raise for their own use.

自留地 zìliúdì

private plots

After agricultural collectivization was implemented, the small amount of land that commune members were allowed to retain and till for their own use. The produce from these plots belonged to the individuals.

自留山 zìliúshān
private hills

After agriculture was collectivized, the small number of hills that production teams in mountainous areas allocated to commune members for their own use. Commune members raised mainly fruit, firewood, medicinal herbs, and other economic crops on these hills. Ownership of private hills belonged to the collective, the products harvested belonged to the commune members themselves.

自律 zìlǜ
self-restraint; self-control

E.g. 自律是他到达所希望的目标的途径。 *He reached the goal he aspired to through self-restraint.*

E.g. 帮助孩子自尊自律 *to help children develop self-respect and self-restraint* / 大学生自律委员会 *College Students Self-Restraint Committee* / 干部要廉洁自律。 *Cadres must be honest and self-restraint.*

自然保护区 zìrán bǎohùqū
protected natural region; nature reserve

Also called 禁伐禁猎区 region off limits to woodcutting and hunting.

自我设计 zìwǒ shèjì
to formulate one's own path in life; to follow one's ideals in planning for the future

自销 zìxiāo
to sell one's own products

E.g. 自产自销 *to produce and market something*

自选市场 zìxuǎn shìchǎng
self-selection markets

A kind of retail store that surfaced in China in 1980s.

自学考试 zìxué kǎoshì
independent study exams (administered to students who pursued independent study for the purpose of academic certification)

自营 zìyíng
a producer or production unit managing (marketing, etc.) its own products

自由化 zìyóuhuà
liberalization

Synonymous with 资产阶级自由化 bourgeois liberalization. (cf. 资产阶级自由化)

自由市场 zìyóu shìchǎng
free markets

Also called 农贸市场 farmers' markets.

自由王国 zìyóu wángguó
realm of freedom

A term in philosophy referring to the realm where people have recognized and grasped the laws of the objective world, and can self-consciously reform the world according to their own will.

自娱 zìyú
self-recreation

Recreational activities in which the masses themselves perform.

E.g. 这里经常举行自娱晚会. *Self-recreation evening parties are often held here.*

自助 zìzhù
to help oneself (in a restaurant, store, etc.)

E.g. 自助电脑储蓄 *self-help computer savings deposit (e.g., at an ATM)*

自助餐 zìzhùcān
self-help meal (e.g., a buffet)

自助银行 zìzhù yínháng
self-help bank
A bank equipped with ATM (automatic teller machine) and information machines. Clients (customers) do all the business of banking, withdrawing and account checking on the machines by themselves.

自助邮局 zìzhù yóujú
self-aid post office
All the postal business is done by people themselves on machines.

字根 zìgēn
character root
Basic units from which Chinese characters are composed, including radicals and non-radicals.

zong

宗派主义 zōngpài zhǔyì
sectarianism
A manifestation of subjectivism in organizational relationships. It is characterized by having a narrow mentality, caring only about the benefits of a small group, asserting one's independence, employing only those close to oneself, pulling in certain people, ostracizing certain other people, and unprincipled factional struggles.

综合大学 zōnghé dàxué
comprehensive university

综合劳动服务 zōnghé láodòng fúwù
comprehensive labor services
Domestic manual labor services. Certain departments have organized unemployed youths to form comprehensive labor service teams, which perform all kinds of domestic services for urban residents.

综合平衡 zōnghé pínghéng
overall balance
The overall balance in the national economy. It is the basic approach to implementing planned management of the entire national economy. The task is to ensure constant balance — according to the basic socialist economic laws — between the two major sectors of production (production resources and consumer resources). Essentially, it includes public finance, credit, total supply and demand of goods, and balance of international payments.

综合治理 zōnghé zhìlǐ
comprehensive administration
The comprehensive administration of public security work, that is, to organize various departments, and social sectors, and to adopt various ideological, political, economic, administrative, and legal measures and methods, to propagate security systems appropriate to the various situations.

综指 zōng-zhǐ
overall stock price index, such as the Dow
E.g. 综指昨日下滑。 *The overall stock price index slid yesterday.*

总参 Zǒngcān
the Headquarters of the General Staff (of the PLA)
Abbreviation for 中国人民解放军总参谋部. It's one of three Generals in the army.

总工 zǒnggōng
chief engineer
Abbreviation for 总工程师.

总工会 Zǒnggōnghuì

All-China Federation of Trade Unions
Abbreviation for 中华全国总工会. The leadership organization of all the trade unions of the entire nation, which is under the leadership of the Chinese Communist Party.

总后 Zǒng-Hòu
General Logistics Department (of the PLA)
Abbreviation for 中国人民解放军总后勤部. The leadership organization responsible for all service work of the entire army. Also abbreviated as 总后勤部.

总路线 zǒnglùxiàn
general line
The most basic guiding principles and norms for guiding the work in various areas in a certain historical period. The term is used specifically to refer to two things: 1) The general line proposed by Mao Zedong in 1952 for the transitional period from capitalism to socialism. 2) The general line for building socialism which was proposed by Mao Zedong and promulgated by the Second Session of the Eighth National Congress of the Chinese Communist Party in May 1958. That general line was "go all out, aim high, and achieve greater, faster, better, and more economical results in building socialism". (cf. 过渡时期总路线 and 社会主义建设总路线)

总体规划 zǒngtǐ guīhuà
overall plan
Comprehensive, long-term development plans.

总政 Zǒng-Zhèng
General Political Department (of the PLA)
Abbreviation for 中国人民解放军总政治部. It is the highest leadership organization and is responsible for the Party's work and political work within the army. Also abbreviated as 总政治部.
E.g. 总政军乐队 *Musical Troupe of the General Political Department of the People's Liberation Army*

总支 zǒngzhī
general branch committee
Abbreviation for 总支部委员会, specifically a Chinese Communist Party general branch committee at the grass-roots level.
E.g. 总支书记 *secretary of the general branch committee (of the CPC)* / 总支委员 *committee member of the general branch committee (of the CPC)*

纵向 zòngxiàng
vertical

ZOU

走村串户 zǒucūn chuànhù
to make the rounds in rural villages

走低 zǒudī
to go down; to decline

走跌 zǒudiē
to drop; to fall
E.g. 货币走跌。 *The value of the currency is dropping.*

走访 zǒufǎng
to visit and/or interview (relevant persons for specific purpose)
E.g. 登门走访 *to come for an interview* / 走访调查 *to make an investigative visit* / 走访了有关领导 *to have interviewed relevant leaders* / 进行个别走访 *to conduct individual visits*

走钢丝 zǒugāngsī
to walk the steel wire
Originally an acrobatic act, now often used in the figurative sense of "walking a tightrope" or maintaining a precarious balance.

走过场 zǒuguòchǎng
to walk across the stage
A character in an opera entering the stage from one end, quickly going across, then exiting at the other end, without staying on the stage. Metaphor for perfunctorily going through the formalities in handling a matter without resolving the actual issue.

走红 zǒuhóng
to have a streak of good luck

走后门 zǒuhòumén
go through the back door
A metaphor for deploying improper tactics and going through irregular channels to attain private benefits.

走街串巷 zǒujiē chuànxiàng
to make the rounds of the streets and alleys in a city or town

走俏 zǒuqiào
to sell well
A commodity high in market demand and selling very quickly.
E.g. "凤凰"自行车走俏. *"Phoenix" brand bicycles sell very well.*

走势 zǒushì
trend
Frequently referring to the market and economic development.
E.g. 这家报纸定期发出经济走势信息。 *This newspaper periodically publishes news about economic trends.*

走穴 zǒuxuè
moonlight
(Originally) performing artists getting together to put on a show for some remuneration; (now) performers in government troupes getting together to moonlight for extra earnings.

走资派 zǒu-zī-pài
capitalist roader
Abbreviation for 党内走资本主义的当权派 authoritative figures within the Party who walk the capitalist road. This was a term that appeared during the leadership of erroneous leftist ideology, which confused the distinction between the enemy and friends. The term was first raised by Mao Zedong in 1965. During the Cultural Revolution, and there was a movement to round up capitalist roaders. The so-called "capitalist roaders" were all cadre leaders in various Party and state organizations, and the backbone of the socialist cause.

ZU

足坛 zútán
world of soccer

足协 zú-xié
soccer association
Short for 足球协会.

组办 zǔbàn
to organize and undertake a project
E.g. 组办国际博览会 *to organize an international fair*

组编 zǔbiān
to organize and lay out (an article, material for printing, etc.)
E.g. 把材料组编成一个整体 *to organize the material into a coherent whole (for publication)*

组雕 zǔdiāo

a set of sculptures based on a theme

组稿 zǔgǎo

to solicit manuscripts

组歌 zǔgē

a series of songs with the same theme

组阁 zǔgé

to organize the cabinet

1) Contraction of 组织内阁. 2) A metaphor for organizing and building leadership ranks.

组合柜 zǔhéguì

assembled cabinet

A cabinet made by assembling several independent components.

组合机床 zǔhé jīchuáng

combined machine tool

A machine tool composed of commonly used driving components (such a drive head and slide), bearing components (such as lathe bed and vertical shaft), and a small number of specialized parts. It is flexible in its functions.

组合家具 zǔhé jiājù

a set of matching furniture

组建 zǔjiàn

to organize and establish

Contraction of 组织 and 建立.

组台 zǔtái

to organize a set of act into a show

E.g. 组台演出 *to organize acts and put on a show*

组团 zǔtuán

to organize a group (performing troupe, delegation, tour group, etc.)

E.g. 组团访问 *to organize a delegation for a visit (e.g., to a foreign country)*

组织关系 zǔzhī-guānxì

membership credentials

Membership credentials of a member of a political party or organization. A document showing membership in an organization.

E.g. 党的组织关系 *Party membership credentials*

组织建设 zǔzhī jiànshè

organizational construction

Construction in the organizational aspect of a political party or group, such as building strong leadership ranks and absorbing new members.

组织疗法 zǔzhī liáofǎ

tissue therapy

A method of medical treatment. To inject or plant in the human body certain plant or animal tissues, after they have gone through such processes as cold storage and germ extermination, to promote metabolism and strengthen resistance to organisms. This kind of therapy is effective to a certain degree in treating chronic ulcers, psoriasis, keratitis, etc.

组织生活 zǔzhī shēnghuó

organizational life

Activities such as exchanging ideas and discussing issues that members of political parties and other organizations engage in periodically.

组装 zǔzhuāng

to compose and assemble

E.g. 组装车间 *an assembly shop* / 组装自行车 *to assemble bicycles*

zuan

钻劲 zuānjìn

zest in probing into something

The enthusiasm with which one probes into a matter.

zui

嘴烟 zuǐyān
filter cigarette
Abbreviation for 过滤嘴香烟.

最高指示 zuìgāo zhǐshì
the highest directive
It meant that Mao Zedong was the supreme commander, and all his words were orders and directives to those below, and therefore must be carried out. This was a one way Lin Biao instigated Mao's personality cult.

最佳 zuìjiā
the best; top rate
E.g. 最佳年龄 *the best age* / 最佳民警 *the best people's police* / 最佳女演员 *the best actress* / 最佳选择 *the best choice*

最佳精神 zuìjiā jīngshén
the most excellent spirit
The persevering and dauntless spirit of courageously forging ahead even in the face of difficulties and setbacks. This is how the mentality and competitive style of Chinese athletes was depicted in the 1980s. This spirit includes the following: dedicating oneself to persevering and training assiduously for the revolutionary cause; exerting oneself to the utmost, being unwilling to fall behind, and daring to catch up and surpass; showing solidarity, cooperation, and coordination in fighting; resolving to achieve and to win honor for the motherland.

zun

尊师 zūnshī
to respect teachers

尊师爱生 zūnshī àishēng
to respect teachers and love students
Students must respect their teachers, and teachers must love their students.

尊师重教 zūnshī zhòngjiào
to respect teachers and to value education

遵纪守法 zūnjì shǒufǎ
to abide by regulations and laws

zuo

做爱 zuò'ài
to make love

做秀 zuòxiù
to show; to make a show
Often used in a derogatory sense.
E.g. 尽管贪官"做秀"有术, 但法网恢恢, 纸终包不住火。 *Corrupt officials are skillful at making a show, but justice has a long arm and a fire cannot be wrapped in paper.*

作协 Zuò-Xié
Writers Association
Abbreviation for 作家协会.

作业班 zuòyèbān
work squad
A form of labor organization in production activities. Workers are organized into work teams, work squads, and work groups, according to the magnitude and nature of the production tasks. This is a way of facilitating organization of production and establishing a system of responsibility.

作业面 zuòyèmiàn
work surface or scope
The work location in direct mining or quarrying, which moves as mining progresses. The term also refers to the work scope of various sectors in building construction.

坐班 zuòbān
to have office hours
The system in some schools, and research institutions whereby teachers and researchers are required to work in their offices during certain hours.
E.g. 大学的老师与中小学的老师不同，一般是不坐班的。*University teachers are different from elementary and secondary school teachers in that they do not have stipulated office hours.*

坐机关 zuòjīguān
to work in an office
The bureaucratic mode of leading a comfortable office life: attending meetings, shoveling papers, etc., while being insulated from practical reality.

坐喷气式 zuò pēnqìshì
to ride a jet
A kind of corporal punishment used during the Cultural Revolution, in which one is bent over, with head raised high, and both arms stretched toward the back, in the form of a jet.

坐直升飞机 zuò zhíshēng fēijī
to ride a helicopter
A metaphor for the meteoric rise of certain individuals of the rebel faction during the Cultural Revolution. Overnight they climbed from ordinary positions (cadres, workers, or peasants) to high leadership positions in the Party or the government.

座果率 zuòguǒlǜ
fruition rate; rate of bearing fruit
Also called 着果率.

音序索引
Alphabetical Index

	A			伴	13		壁	26
ā	阿	1		半	13		避	26
āi	挨	1		办	13	biān	鞭	27
ái	癌	1	bāng	邦	14		边	27
ài	艾	1		帮	14		编	27
	爱	2	bàng	棒	14	biǎn	贬	27
ān	鞍	3		傍	15	biàn	便	28
	安	3	bāo	胞	15		变	28
àn	按	5		包	15		辩	29
	暗	5		褒	18	biāo	标	29
	岸	5	bǎo	保	18		飙	29
	案	6		宝	21	biǎo	表	29
áng	昂	6	bào	抱	21	bīng	兵	29
áo	熬	6		报	21		冰	30
ào	奥	6		暴	22	bǐng	饼	30
	澳	6		爆	22	bìng	病	30
				曝	23		并	30
	B		bēi	杯	23	bō	玻	31
bā	吧	7		碑	23		播	31
	八	7		背	23		拨	31
	巴	8	běi	北	23	bó	薄	32
bá	拔	9	bèi	背	24		博	32
bǎ	把	9		钡	24		伯	32
bà	霸	9		倍	24		泊	32
	罢	9		备	24	bǔ	捕	32
bái	白	9		被	24		补	32
bǎi	百	11	běn	本	24	bù	不	33
	摆	11	bèn	笨	25		布	34
bài	败	12	bèng	蹦	25		步	35
bān	斑	12		泵	25		部	35
	班	12	bī	逼	25			
	搬	12	bǐ	比	25		C	
bǎn	板	12		笔	25	cā	擦	36
	版	12	bì	闭	26	cāi	猜	36
bàn	扮	13		弊	26	cái	财	36
				必	26			

cǎi		踩	37		沉	51		词	65
		采	37	chéng	城	51	cì	刺	65
		彩	37		成	51		次	65
cài		菜	38		乘	52	cóng	从	65
cān		餐	38		程	52	cū	粗	66
		参	38		惩	52	cù	促	66
cán		残	39		承	52	cuàn	篡	66
cāng		仓	39	chī	吃	53		窜	67
cáng		藏	40	chí	持	55	cuī	催	67
cāo		操	40	chì	赤	55	cūn	村	67
cǎo		草	40		斥	55	cún	存	67
cè		侧	40	chōng	充	55	cùn	寸	67
		测	40		冲	55	cuō	撮	67
céng		层	41	chóng	崇	55	cuò	错	68
chā		差	41		重	56			
		插	41	chǒng	宠	56	**D**		
chá		茶	42	chòng	冲	56			
		查	42	chōu	抽	56	dā	搭	69
chà		差	42	chóu	酬	57	dá	达	69
chāi		差	42		筹	57		答	70
		拆	43	chǒu	丑	57	dǎ	打	70
chái		柴	43	chòu	臭	57	dà	大	72
chān		搀	43	chū	初	58	dài	戴	79
		掺	43		出	58		带	79
chǎn		产	43	chú	厨	60		代	80
cháng		常	44		除	60		贷	81
		长	44	chǔ	储	60		袋	81
chǎng		厂	45		处	60		待	81
		场	46	chù	触	60	dān	单	81
		敞	46	chuān	穿	61		担	83
chàng		唱	46	chuán	传	61	dàn	淡	83
		倡	46		船	62		蛋	83
chāo		超	46	chuàn	串	62	dāng	当	83
		抄	49	chuāng	窗	63	dǎng	党	83
		钞	49	chuáng	床	63	dàng	档	86
cháo		潮	49	chuǎng	闯	63	dǎo	倒	86
chǎo		炒	49	chuàng	创	64		导	87
chē		车	50	chuī	吹	64	dào	到	87
chě		扯	50		炊	65		倒	87
chè		撤	50	chuí	垂	65		道	88
chén		尘	50	chūn	春	65		盗	88
		晨	51	cí	磁	65	dé	德	88

		得	88	duì	兑	107		飞	125
dēng		登	88		队	107	féi	肥	125
děng		等	88		对	107	fèi	沸	126
dèng		邓	88	dūn	吨	109	fēn	分	126
dī		低	89		蹲	109	fěn	粉	128
		滴	89	duō	多	109	fèn	奋	128
dí		迪	89	duó	夺	110		份	128
		的	89	duǒ	躲	110		氛	128
		敌	90				fēng	丰	128
		涤	90	**E**				封	128
dǐ		底	90	é	额	111		蜂	129
dì		地	90	è	恶	111		风	129
		第	92		厄	111	fū	肤	130
		递	95	ēn	恩	111	fú	扶	130
diǎn		点	95	ér	儿	111		辐	130
		典	95	ěr	耳	111		服	130
diàn		电	95	èr	二	112		浮	131
		店	98					福	131
		殿	98	**F**			fǔ	辅	131
diào		吊	99	fā	发	115		腐	131
		钓	99	fá	罚	115	fù	副	131
		调	99	fǎ	法	115		覆	132
diē		跌	100	fà	发	115		复	132
dīng		丁	100	fān	帆	116		父	133
		钉	100		翻	116		负	133
dǐng		顶	100	fán	繁	117		富	133
dìng		定	101		凡	117		附	133
dōng		东	103	fǎn	反	117		妇	134
		冬	103		返	120			
dòng		动	103	fàn	范	120	**G**		
		冻	103		贩	120	gǎi	改	135
dòu		斗	103		饭	120	gài	概	135
		豆	104		泛	121		盖	135
dū		督	104	fāng	方	121	gān	干	136
dú		毒	105	fáng	房	121		甘	136
		渎	105		防	121		肝	136
		独	105	fǎng	仿	122	gǎn	赶	136
		读	105		访	122		感	136
dǔ		赌	106	fàng	放	122		敢	136
dù		度	106	fēi	非	124	gàn	干	136
duǎn		短	106		绯	125	gāng	钢	137
duàn		断	106						

	纲	137	guān	关	157	hè	贺	175
gǎng	岗	137		官	158	hēi	黑	175
	港	137		观	159	héng	横	178
gàng	杠	138	guǎn	管	159	hōng	哄	179
gāo	高	138	guàn	罐	160	hóng	洪	179
gǎo	搞	141		惯	160		宏	179
gào	告	141		灌	160		弘	179
gē	歌	141					红	179
	鸽	141	guāng	光	161	hóu	猴	183
	割	141	guǎng	广	161	hòu	厚	183
gé	革	141	guī	规	162		候	183
	隔	144		硅	162		后	183
gè	个	144		归	162	hū	呼	184
gěi	给	145	guǐ	轨	162	hú	胡	184
gēn	根	145	guì	柜	162		湖	184
	跟	145	gǔn	滚	162	hù	护	184
gēng	耕	145	gùn	棍	163		互	185
	更	145	guó	国	163		户	185
gōng	工	146	guǒ	果	165	huā	花	185
	攻	149	guò	过	165	huá	华	185
	功	149					滑	186
	供	149	**H**			huà	画	186
	公	149	há	蛤	167		划	186
gòng	共	152	hǎ	哈	167		化	187
gǒu	狗	153	hǎi	海	167		话	187
gòu	构	153	hán	含	168	huài	坏	187
	购	153		涵	168	huān	欢	187
	购	153		函	168	huán	环	187
gū	估	153		旱	168	huǎn	缓	188
gǔ	鼓	154	hàn	汉	169	huàn	换	188
	古	154	háng	航	169	huāng	荒	189
	骨	154	háo	豪	170	huáng	黄	189
	谷	154	hǎo	好	170		皇	189
	股	154	hào	耗	170	huī	灰	189
gù	顾	155		号	170		徽	190
	固	155	hē	喝	170	huí	回	190
	雇	155	hé	荷	170	huì	会	190
guā	刮	155		核	171		汇	191
	瓜	155		和	172		绘	191
guà	挂	155		合	173	hūn	婚	191
guǎi	拐	157		盒	175	hùn	混	192
guài	怪	157		河	175	huó	活	192

huǒ	火	193		简	207		尽	222
huò	获	193		剪	208		劲	223
	和	193		减	208	jīng	晶	223
	货	194	jiàn	鉴	208		京	223
				见	208		精	223
	J			件	209		腈	225
jī	跻	195		毽	209		经	225
	击	195		健	209	jǐng	井	230
	基	195		溅	209		警	230
	机	196		建	209		景	230
	积	198	jiāng	将	210	jìng	静	230
	激	198	jiǎng	奖	210		境	230
	绩	198		讲	210		敬	230
	缉	198	jiàng	降	211		竞	231
jí	吉	198	jiāo	焦	211		净	231
	极	198		胶	211	jiū	揪	231
	集	199		交	211		纠	231
jǐ	挤	200		跤	212	jiǔ	九	231
jì	技	200		郊	212	jiù	旧	231
	季	201		浇	212	jū	居	232
	寄	201		角	212	jú	局	232
	计	201	jiǎo	绞	213	jǔ	举	232
	记	201		教	213	jù	巨	232
	继	201	jiào	叫	214		句	232
	纪	202	jiē	揭	214		剧	233
jiā	夹	202		接	215	juān	捐	233
	佳	202		街	215	juǎn	卷	233
	家	202		阶	215	jué	角	233
	加	204	jié	截	217		决	233
jiá	夹	205		劫	218		绝	234
jiǎ	贾	205		节	218	jūn	均	234
	甲	205		结	218		军	234
	假	205	jiě	解	219			
jià	假	205	jiè	戒	220		**K**	
	价	205		界	220	kā	咖	237
	架	206		借	220	kǎ	卡	237
	驾	206	jīn	金	221	kāi	开	237
jiān	监	206	jǐn	紧	221	kān	刊	239
	坚	206		锦	222	kǎn	侃	240
	尖	206	jìn	进	222		砍	240
jiǎn	检	207		晋	222	kàn	看	240
				禁	222			

kāng	康	240		拉	252		劣	274
kàng	抗	240	lǎ	喇	253		猎	274
	炕	241	lái	来	253	lín	林	275
kǎo	考	241	lán	蓝	253		临	275
	烤	242		拦	253	líng	零	275
kào	靠	242		篮	253	lǐng	领	275
kē	科	242	lǎn	揽	254	lìng	另	276
kě	可	243		览	254	liū	溜	276
kè	克	244		懒	254	liú	留	276
	刻	244	làn	烂	254		流	277
	客	244		滥	254	liù	六	277
	课	245	láng	狼	254		遛	279
kěn	肯	245	lāo	捞	254	lóng	龙	279
	垦	245	láo	劳	254		聋	279
	恳	245	lǎo	老	258		隆	279
kēng	坑	245	léi	雷	260	lǒng	陇	279
kōng	空	245		镭	261	lóu	楼	279
kǒng	孔	247	lěng	冷	261	lòu	漏	279
kòng	控	247	lí	离	261	lù	路	279
kōu	抠	247	lǐ	理	262		录	280
kǒu	口	247		礼	162	lǚ	旅	280
kòu	扣	247	lì	历	262	lǜ	滤	280
kǔ	苦	248		利	262		绿	280
kù	库	248		例	263	lüè	掠	282
	裤	248		立	263	lún	轮	282
	酷	248		力	264	lùn	论	282
kuā	夸	248	lián	联	264	luǒ	裸	282
kuà	跨	248		连	266	luò	落	282
kuài	快	249		廉	266			
	块	249	liàn	恋	266		**M**	
kuān	宽	249		练	266	mā	妈	284
kuǎn	款	250	liáng	粮	266	mǎ	马	284
kuāng	匡	250		良	267		蚂	284
kuàng	框	250	liǎng	两	267	mà	骂	284
	矿	250	liàng	量	273	mái	埋	285
kuī	亏	250		亮	273	mǎi	买	285
kūn	昆	250	liáo	疗	273	mài	麦	285
kùn	困	250		燎	274		卖	285
kuò	扩	250	liào	撂	274	mán	瞒	285
				料	274	mǎn	满	285
	L		liè	列	274	màn	慢	286
lā	垃	252		裂	274			

máng	盲	286	mǔ	亩	298	pá	扒	313
	忙	286		母	298		爬	313
māo	猫	286	mù	墓	298	pà	怕	313
máo	毛	287		幕	298	pāi	拍	313
	矛	287		木	298	pái	排	313
mào	冒	287		目	298		牌	314
	贸	288		牧	298	pài	派	314
méi	煤	288				pān	攀	315
	没	288		**N**		pán	盘	315
	媒	288	ná	拿	299	pàn	判	315
měi	美	288	nà	呐	299		叛	315
mèi	媚	289		那	299	pāo	抛	316
mén	门	289		纳	299	pǎo	跑	316
mèn	闷	289	nǎi	奶	299	pào	泡	316
méng	蒙	289	nán	南	299		炮	316
	朦	290		男	300	péi	培	317
měng	蒙	290		难	301		陪	317
	猛	290	nǎo	脑	301	pèi	配	318
mèng	孟	290	nào	闹	301	pēn	喷	318
mí	迷	290	nèi	内	301	pén	盆	319
	谜	290	néng	能	303	péng	棚	319
mǐ	米	290	ní	泥	304		膨	319
mì	密	290		尼	304	pěng	捧	319
mián	棉	291	nì	逆	304	pèng	碰	319
miàn	面	291		溺	304	pī	霹	320
miáo	苗	292	nián	年	304		批	321
miào	庙	292	niáng	娘	304	pí	啤	321
miè	灭	292	nìng	宁	305		皮	321
mín	民	292	niú	牛	305	pǐ	匹	321
míng	明	296	niǔ	扭	305		痞	321
	鸣	296	nóng	农	306	piān	偏	321
	名	296	nú	奴	310	piàn	片	322
	明	297	nǚ	女	310		骗	322
mìng	命	297	nuǎn	暖	311	piào	票	322
mō	摸	297	nuó	挪	311	pīn	拼	322
mó	蘑	297				pín	贫	323
	模	297		**O**		pǐn	品	323
	磨	297	ōu	欧	312	pìn	聘	324
	摩	297	ǒu	偶	312	pīng	乒	324
	魔	297				píng	平	324
mò	末	297		**P**			瓶	325
móu	谋	298	pā	趴	313		评	325

	屏	326	qīn	侵	336	róng	荣	356
pó	婆	326		亲	336		融	356
pò	破	326	qín	秦	336		容	357
	迫	327		勤	336	rǒng	冗	357
pōu	剖	327		禽	337	ròu	肉	357
pū	铺	327	qīng	青	337	rú	儒	357
pǔ	普	327		轻	337	rǔ	乳	357
	蹼	328		倾	338	rù	入	357
				清	338	ruǎn	软	358
	Q		qíng	情	339	ruò	弱	360
qī	期	329	qǐng	请	339			
	欺	329	qióng	穷	340		**S**	
	栖	329	qiū	秋	340	sài	赛	362
	妻	329	qiú	球	340	sān	三	362
	七	329		求	341	sǎn	散	378
qí	棋	330	qū	趋	341	sāng	桑	379
	奇	330		区	341	sǎo	扫	379
	齐	330		屈	342	sè	色	379
	旗	330		驱	342	sēn	森	379
	骑	330		曲	342	shā	砂	379
qǐ	起	330	qǔ	取	342		杀	379
	企	330	qù	去	342		刹	380
qì	气	331	quān	圈	343	shǎ	傻	380
qiǎ	卡	332	quán	权	343	shāi	筛	380
qià	洽	332		全	343	shǎi	色	380
qiān	牵	332		拳	345	shān	山	380
	千	332	quàn	劝	345		煽	380
	迁	332	quē	缺	346	shǎn	闪	380
	签	332	què	确	346	shàn	善	381
qián	前	333	qún	裙	346	shāng	伤	381
	潜	333		群	346		商	381
qiǎn	遣	333				shàng	上	382
qiàn	欠	333		**R**		shāo	烧	384
qiāng	枪	333	rán	燃	348	shǎo	少	384
qiáng	墙	333	ràng	让	348	shào	少	384
	强	333	rǎo	扰	348	shé	蛇	385
qiǎng	抢	334	rè	热	348	shè	摄	385
qiāo	敲	335	rén	人	350		射	385
qiáo	侨	335	rèn	韧	355		涉	385
qiào	翘	336		任	355		社	385
	俏	336		认	356		设	389
qiè	窃	336	rì	日	356	shēn	申	389

	伸	389		输	405	tà	榻	426
	身	389		梳	405		踏	426
	深	389		疏	405	tāi	胎	426
shén	神	390		书	406	tái	苔	426
shěn	审	390	shú	赎	406		抬	426
shēng	声	391	shǔ	暑	406		台	426
	生	391	shù	数	406		跆	427
	牲	394	shuǎ	耍	407	tài	太	427
	升	394	shuǎi	甩	407	tān	摊	428
shěng	省	394	shuài	帅	407		贪	428
shèng	胜	395	shuāng	双	407	tán	弹	428
	圣	395	shuǐ	水	410		坛	429
shī	师	395	shuì	睡	411		谈	429
	失	395		税	411	tǎn	坦	429
	尸	396	shùn	顺	412	tàn	探	429
shí	十	396	shuō	说	412	táng	唐	429
	石	396	shuò	硕	412		糖	429
	拾	397	sī	思	412	táo	逃	429
	时	397		私	415		陶	430
	食	397		司	415	tào	套	430
	实	398		丝	415	tè	特	431
	识	398	sǐ	死	415	téng	腾	433
shǐ	史	398	sì	四	416	tī	梯	434
	使	398		饲	423		踢	434
	始	398	sōng	松	423	tí	提	434
shì	示	398	sòng	颂	423		题	434
	世	399		送	423	tǐ	体	435
	事	399	sōu	馊	423	tì	替	435
	适	399	sū	苏	423		剃	435
	饰	399	sú	俗	423	tiān	天	435
	市	399	sù	素	423		添	436
	视	400		速	423	tián	填	436
	试	401		塑	424		田	437
shōu	收	402		肃	424		甜	437
shǒu	手	403	suān	酸	424	tiāo	挑	437
	首	403	suí	随	424	tiáo	条	437
	守	404	sǔn	损	425		调	438
shòu	售	404	suō	缩	425	tiǎo	挑	439
	受	405	suǒ	索	425	tiào	跳	439
	瘦	405				tiē	贴	440
	寿	405		**T**		tiě	铁	440
shū	殊	405	tǎ	塔	426	tíng	停	441

	庭	441		危	461		细	480
tǐng	挺	441	wéi	违	461	xiā	瞎	480
tōng	通	441		围	461	xià	下	480
tóng	同	442		唯	461		夏	481
	铜	442		维	462	xiān	先	482
	童	442	wěi	委	463		鲜	482
tǒng	捅	442		伪	463		纤	482
	筒	442		伟	463	xián	贤	482
	统	443		尾	463		闲	482
tōu	偷	445	wèi	未	463	xiǎn	显	482
tóu	投	446		位	463		险	482
	头	446		慰	463	xiàn	现	482
tòu	透	447		卫	463		献	483
tū	突	447	wēn	瘟	464		县	484
tú	图	448		温	464		限	484
tǔ	土	448	wén	文	465		线	484
	吐	449	wěn	稳	467	xiāng	香	484
tuán	团	449	wèn	问	467		乡	484
tuī	推	450	wō	窝	468	xiáng	详	485
tuì	蜕	451	wò	握	468	xiǎng	响	485
	退	451	wū	乌	468	xiàng	橡	485
tuō	拖	452	wú	无	468		向	485
	托	452	wǔ	武	469		象	485
	脱	453		五	470	xiāo	销	485
tuò	拓	454		捂	476		消	486
				舞	476		逍	486
W			wù	物	476	xiǎo	小	487
				务	476	xiào	校	491
wā	挖	455		误	477		笑	492
	蛙	455					效	492
wāi	歪	455	**X**			xiē	歇	492
wài	外	455	xī	嬉	478	xié	协	492
wán	玩	457		西	478	xiě	写	492
wǎn	晚	457		吸	478	xīn	薪	492
wàn	万	458		稀	479		辛	492
	腕	458		息	479		新	492
wáng	王	458		希	479		心	495
wǎng	网	458		夕	479	xìn	信	496
	往	459	xí	席	479	xīng	星	497
wàng	旺	459		洗	479		兴	497
	望	459	xǐ	系	479	xíng	刑	497
	忘	459	xì	戏	480		形	497
wēi	微	460						

	行	497	yàn	雁	506		瘾	524
xǐng	省	498		验	506		隐	524
xìng	兴	498	yāng	央	507	yìn	印	524
	幸	498	yáng	扬	507	yīng	英	525
	性	498		羊	507		鹰	525
	姓	498		洋	507	yíng	营	525
xiōng	兄	498		阳	508		荧	525
	胸	499	yǎng	养	508		赢	525
xióng	雄	499		氧	508	yǐng	影	526
	熊	499	yàng	样	508	yìng	应	527
xiū	休	499	yāo	腰	509		硬	527
	修	499	yáo	摇	509	yōng	拥	528
xiù	锈	499		遥	509	yǒng	泳	528
xū	虚	500	yào	药	509		永	528
xù	蓄	500		要	510	yòng	用	529
	续	500	yě	野	510	yōu	优	529
xuān	宣	500	yè	业	510		忧	530
xuán	悬	500		夜	511	yóu	尤	530
xuǎn	选	500		液	511		邮	530
xué	学	501	yī	一	511		油	530
	穴	502		医	511		游	531
xuě	雪	502		伊	518	yǒu	有	531
xuè	血	502		依	518		友	531
xún	询	502	yí	遗	518	yòu	右	531
	寻	502		移	518		诱	532
	巡	503	yǐ	乙	518		又	532
xùn	殉	503		以	518		幼	532
			yì	艺	520	yú	愚	532
Y				易	520		瑜	532
yā	压	504		亦	520		余	532
	押	504		意	521		鱼	532
yǎ	雅	504		忆	521		渔	533
yà	亚	504		义	521		娱	533
yān	烟	505		溢	522	yǔ	宇	533
yán	严	505		议	522		语	533
	研	505		译	522		羽	534
	岩	505	yīn	因	523	yù	玉	534
	延	505		音	523		吁	534
	炎	506		阴	523		育	534
yǎn	眼	506	yín	银	523		浴	534
	衍	506	yǐn	饮	524		寓	534
	演	506		引	524		预	534

	域	535	zhǎo	找	545	zhū	珠	564
yuān	鸳	535		沼	545		株	565
	冤	535	zhào	照	545		诸	565
yuán	原	535	zhē	遮	545	zhú	竹	565
	援	536	zhé	折	545	zhǔ	主	565
	园	536	zhēn	珍	545	zhù	著	566
yuǎn	远	536		针	545		助	566
yuàn	院	536		侦	546		贮	566
yuē	约	536	zhěn	枕	546		住	566
yuè	跃	537	zhèn	震	546		注	566
	月	537		镇	546	zhuā	抓	566
	阅	537	zhēng	蒸	546	zhuān	专	568
	乐	537		征	546	zhuǎn	转	570
yún	云	537		争	547	zhuāng	庄	571
yùn	运	537	zhěng	整	547		装	571
			zhèng	正	547	zhuàng	撞	571
Z				政	548		壮	571
zǎi	宰	539		证	551	zhuī	追	571
	仔	539	zhī	支	551	zhǔn	准	572
zài	载	539		知	552	zhuó	着	572
	再	539		肢	553	zī	资	572
	在	539		脂	553		滋	573
zàn	赞	539		织	553	zǐ	姊	573
zāng	脏	539	zhí	职	553		子	573
zàng	藏	539		直	555	zì	自	573
zāo	遭	540		植	555		字	576
zǎo	早	540		执	555	zōng	宗	576
zào	噪	540		值	556		综	576
	造	540	zhǐ	指	556	zǒng	总	576
zé	责	540		纸	557	zòng	纵	577
	择	541	zhì	致	557	zǒu	走	577
zēng	增	541		制	557	zú	足	578
zhā	扎	542		智	557	zǔ	组	578
zhāi	摘	543		质	559	zuān	钻	579
zhǎn	崭	543		滞	559	zuǐ	嘴	580
	展	543		治	559	zuì	最	580
zhàn	占	544	zhōng	中	560	zūn	尊	580
	战	544		忠	560		遵	580
	站	544		终	560	zuò	做	580
zhǎng	长	544		种	560		作	580
	涨	544	zhǒng	种	564		坐	581
zhāo	朝	544	zhòng	重	564		座	581
	招	544	zhōu	周	564			
				洲	564			

图书在版编目(CIP)数据

英文详解汉语新词语词典 / 李振杰,凌志韫编著
— 北京 新世界出版社,2000.9
ISBN 7-80005-566-3
I.英... II.①李... ②凌... III.①英语-词典
②汉语-新词语-词典-英、汉 IV.H 316

中国版本图书馆 CIP 数据核字(2000)第 44608 号

英文详解汉语新词语词典

编　　著：李振杰　凌志韫
责任编辑：李淑娟　任玲娟
特邀编辑：钱王驷
封面设计：贺玉婷
排　　版：倪真如　方·维
责任印制：黄厚清
出版发行：新世界出版社
社　　址：北京阜成门外百万庄大街 24 号
邮政编码：100037
电　　话：0086-10-68994118（出版发行部）
传　　真：0086-10-68326679
电子邮件：nwpcn@public.bta.net.cn
经　　销：新华书店　外文书店
印　　刷：北京外文印刷厂
开　　本：850 × 1168（毫米）1/32　字数：700 千字
印　　张：20.875
印　　数：1-5000
版　　次：2000 年 9 月第一版第一次印刷
书　　号：ISBN 7-80005-566-3 / H·023
定　　价：58.00 元

新世界版图书　如印装错误可随时退换